GLOBAL KEYNESIANISM
UNEQUAL EXCHANGE AND GLOBAL EXPLOITATION

GLOBAL KEYNESIANISM
UNEQUAL EXCHANGE AND GLOBAL EXPLOITATION

GERNOT KÖHLER AND ARNO TAUSCH

Nova Science Publishers, Inc.
New York

Senior Editors: Susan Boriotti and Donna Dennis
Coordinating Editor: Tatiana Shohov
Office Manager: Annette Hellinger
Graphics: Wanda Serrano
Book Production: Matthew Kozlowski, Jonathan Rose and Jennifer Vogt
Circulation: Cathy DeGregory, Ave Maria Gonzalez and Raheem Miller
Communications and Acquisitions: Serge P. Shohov

Library of Congress Cataloging-in-Publication Data

Kohler, Gernot.

Global keynesianism : critique of unequal exchange, global exploitation and global neoliberalism, theory of world income, productivity, growth and employment, critique of the social and economic development of Europe / Gernot Köhler and Arno Tausch.

p. cm.

Includes bibliographical references and index.

ISBN 1-59033-002-1

1. International economic relations. 2. Globalization – Economic aspects. 3. International trade. 4. Commercial policy. 5. Economic policy. 6. Economic development. 7. European union countries – Foreign economic relations. 8. European union countries – Commercial policy. 9. European union countries – Economic policy. 10. Keynesian economics. I. Tausch, Arno 1951- II. Title.

HF1359.K592 2000 CIP
338.94 – dc21 2001045290

227 Main Street, Suite 100
Huntington, New York 11743
Tele. 631-424-6682 Fax 631-425-5933
e-mail: Novascience@earthlink.net
Web Site: http://www.nexusworld.com/nova

Printed in the United States of America

In Memoriam

László Lantos

born October 24, 1910 in Nagyborosnyó, Hungary
national swimming champion
democratic socialist
political prisoner and murdered in prison August 3, 1951 in Budapest, Hungary

CONTENTS

ACKNOWLEDGEMENTS

We would like to thank Christopher Chase-Dunn for his encouragement and support for our research, even though his views may be different. The novelty of some of our ideas fits well into the vision of the publishing house Nova Science of Frank Columbus, president, whose interest in our work we appreciate.

Chapters 2 and 5 were previously published as articles in the *Journal of World Systems Research*. The "hands" picture on the cover was circulated on the internet by a contributor from Latin America.

Arno Tausch would like to mention his beloved wife Krystyna and his children - this is his first book written after a seven year absence from his family due to his official position abroad. Gernot Köhler dedicates his contribution to the memory of László Lantos, born October 24, 1910 in Nagyborosnyó, Hungary, democratic socialist, political prisoner and murdered in prison August 3, 1951 in Budapest, Hungary.

Gernot Köhler and Arno Tausch
Oakville (Canada) and Vienna (Austria), August 2001

INTRODUCTION

Global inequality and unfettered globalization are characterizing features of the world economy at the beginning of the millennium. We believe that a renewed debate about international exploitation is necessary for theoretical and practical reasons. The successive crises - or let's term them abysses - that shattered entire continents since the 1980s, spreading the burden of misery from Latin America to Africa, Asia and Russia, brought home to the world and to millions and millions of human beings, that their livelihoods are determined by the ups and downs of the world market and the forces of the international economy. Europe, having launched a common, single currency, is characterized by a process of non-convergence of wages and incomes which could, ultimately, accelerate centrifugal political tendencies, as long as the structures of unequal exchange are not overcome.

Unequal exchange is a determining mechanism of this world economy. The amount of unequal exchange (global exploitation, transfer value) can be calculated according to a new formula presented in this book, namely:

$$T = d*X - X$$

where "T" means transfer value (gain or loss of value as a result of unequal exchange); "X" means exports of a low-income country to the high-income countries in the world economy; and "d" means exchange rate deviation, also called ERDI (exchange rate deviation index)

The work of the Hungaro-Austrian Karl Polanyi provides already a clear vision of the problems facing the world economy and facing Europe at the beginning of the new millenium. More recent world system theories, which picture the capitalist world economy as a single, conflict-producing mechanism which evolved in cycles of economics and war since around 1450, and which is characterized by a relative stability of a division of the world into centers, semi-peripheries and peripheries, necessarily start from the assumption that there is an unequal exchange between the centers, and the peripheries which transfers, in some fashion or another, the surplus of the labor in the peripheries to the centers. So, the central questions of our study are: how does this unequal exchange come about? How is it measured? And what effects does it have, in comparison to other operationalizations of that vital concept of world system theories and dependency theory, especially on a cross-national level? And what consequences does this unequal exchange have for world wide and European development?

Compared to the mysticism that surrounds much of the earlier writing on unequal exchange, with the exception of the contributions of Amin and Raffer, our approach might appear overly empiricist to some. However, our joint study presents both theoretical and empirical material. Unequal exchange is a politically highly relevant and even explosive issue which is hardly recognized in its existence by many main-stream scholars, especially from the economics profession, while the few political economists, who take the issue of unequal exchange seriously, never arrived at a cross-nationally testable data series of unequal exchange. Needless to say that the centers draw the benefits from such an exploitation, while the peripheries and semi-peripheries stagnate, at least relatively and in relation to the fortunate few who could 'make it'.

It is essential to understand the polarizing nature of the world economy. Our study rediscovers insights of Raul Prebisch, whose contribution to the theory of periphery capitalism is described in the following quote from a recent contribution by the German economist, Steffen Flechsig, in another study recently edited by this publisher:

> *'Contrary to the equalizing and harmonious predictions of neo-classical international trade theory, the prevailing international division of labor and trade were not of mutual benefit for all participants. Peripheral countries were not able to realize the "comparative advantage" of its participation nor the benefits of an increased productivity in primary production could be enjoyed by them (...) Prebisch's explanation consistent - operated on two levels. First, the main argument dealt with the different income elasticity of demand for imports by the Center and periphery (Engel's law, technical progress et cetera) (...) Secondly, the different impact of the business cycle on prices, profits and wages in the industrial Center and primary producing periphery due to internal differences in the structure of productive factors and the nature of the Center-periphery relationship (viz. bargaining power of well organized entrepreneurs and trade unions in the Center which* ***defended profits and wages from falling****; segmented capital and unorganized and surplus labor in the periphery,* ***lagging international mobility of labor, protectionist trade policy in the centers*** *et cetera). Productivity gains in the centers are not appropriately transferred to the periphery by lower prices and vice versa, because there are no real conditions for a free competition and a market economy. Relying on "imperfect markets" or "oligopolistic competition" and power relationships within and between countries, Prebisch blames the centers and the international economy for the unfair operation, for "unfair prices" or for monopolistic pricing.' (Flechsig in Andreas Muller OFM et al., 2000)*

In Part A of our book, this Prebischean tradition is taken up and we propose to develop it by connecting it with theoretical concepts from world-systems theory and post-Keynesianism and with empirical evidence which was not available to Prebisch at his time. World-systems theory views the present world as a single socio-economic system, see, for example, the work of Amin, Bornschier, Chase-Dunn, Frank, and Wallerstein, to name some. Keynesian and Post-Keynesian economic theory is critical of mainstream economics with its emphasis on laissez-faire market mechanisms and on the supply side of economic growth, while neglecting the income and demand side. Economists of particular relevance for our Part A include Keynes and authors like Davidson, Pasinetti, and Shaikh, in addition to Prebisch. By combining theoretical notions from world-systems theory and post-Keynesian economics we arrive at something which we call global Keynesianism. Within this perspective we develop a theory of world income which is based on a disequilibrium view of the economic process. We postulate the possibility of a global full-employment equilibrium, combining notions from Keynes and Prebisch. Central concepts in this theorizing are global demand and unequal exchange. Global demand and global disequilibrium are also central in our theory of global economic growth and globalization, which leans heavily on Shaikh's work on isomorphism and Pasinetti's theory of structural dynamics.

Prebisch's critique of dependency and the deteriorating terms of trade for developing countries was further developed in Emmanuel's critique of "unequal exchange" between developed and developing countries, a concept which is the theme of an entire literature on unequal exchange and uneven development. In spite of the strong interest in the concept of unequal exchange in the 1970's and 1980's, the debate about it stayed mainly at the theoretical level. Raffer (1987) reviewed and synthesized the unequal exchange debate up to the mid-1980's and observed that the problem of measuring unequal exchange had not been resolved in a comprehensive manner at that time. Our book proposes a new way of quantifying unequal exchange and presents world tables of unequal exchange for the years 1965 and 1995. These tables are not only of descriptive value. Just like telescopes and other new scientific instruments in the history of science have facilitated observations which helped to advance theory, we believe that the measurement of unequal exchange on a comprehensive, worldwide scale gives new impulses to the theory of unequal exchange and to related theorizing about the world economy. The empirical and theoretical studies presented in Part A are thus connected through the concept of unequal exchange. We are well aware that numerous theoretical questions arise from that and remain to be clarified. That includes, for example, questions about the very concept of unequal exchange itself. The earlier theoretical formulations about unequal exchange tended to emphasize the commodity side of the exchange (trade of goods and services), whereas our approach places strong emphasis on the monetary side -- namely, on unequal exchange, in the sense of, unequal exchange rates.

Our method of quantifying unequal exchange is not very complicated, given certain cross-national and global data which have become available in recent years. Earlier suggestions by Amin for measuring unequal exchange were based on the concept of the double factoral terms of trade. Amin's criterion of "equal exchange" is the point where the double factoral terms of trade are equal to unity. Consequently, the amount of deviation from the criterion of "double factoral terms of trade = unity" is Amin's recommended measure of unequal exchange. It is fair to say that this approach to the measurement of unequal exchange had virtually no followers, so that the measurement of unequal exchange remained a relatively unresolved problem well into the 1980's. It appears that this may have been due to the difficulty of obtaining and collecting the data required for that kind of estimate. In contrast, our approach uses data which are readily available to date, namely, (nominal) exchange rates and cross-national purchasing power data. World Bank and other sources publish income and GDP data for all or most countries expressed in purchasing power values. We calculate unequal exchange by using the difference between purchasing power values and values at nominal exchange rates, which gives an "exchange rate deviation index". This index can be used by itself for certain analyses, or it can be applied to international trade data for estimating the amount of unequal exchange value gained by OECD countries and lost by non-OECD countries. This approach to estimating amounts of unequal exchange is not unproblematic, because it does not strictly correspond to earlier theoretical statements about unequal exchange. On the other hand, this approach brings to attention something that had not been articulated by earlier theories of unequal exchange -- namely, the apparent fact that a great deal of the inequality in the unequal exchanges between certain groups of countries is linked to biases in exchange rates, i.e., arises in the monetary domain. A practical advantage of this approach to measurement is its feasibility due to the availability of required data. The studies in this book suggest that our method of estimating unequal exchange leads to research results which are interesting from both an empirical and a theoretical point of view and, perhaps, even from a practical perspective.

Increased data availability is also facilitating new research about the historical development of international economic gaps. A series of articles is available from Williamson, who investigated the period of 1820 - 1940, covering the world regions of the Mediterranean Basin, Asia, and Latin America (e.g., Williamson 1998a, 1998b, 1998c). Williamson uses a new data base on real wages and relative factor prices which facilitates more refined observations about the existence, emergence and disappearance of global economic gaps than are possible with GNP-type data alone. For example, he observes that, by 1914, there were very large economic gaps between the European industrial core and countries around the Mediterranean Basin. In spite of a surge of globalization in the second half of the 19th century, the Mediterranean region fared poorly. "Globalization does not seem to have had any consistent positive impact on economic performance around the Basin between 1870 and World War I. There is no evidence of consistent catch up or of fall back. Yet, in the interwar period, the collapse of growth at the European industrial center *did* translate into an even poorer performance almost everywhere around the Basin except for Spain." (Williamson 1998a) While this research does not center on the concept of unequal exchange as such, it provides much needed information, and raises new questions, about the dynamic of international inequality over longer historical periods.

At the top of the international rank scale of unequal exchange according to the ERDI (exchange rate deviation) concept we find countries like Switzerland, Luxemburg, Scandinavian countries, and Japan, while nations like Nicaragua, China and Mozambique come at the bottom. It would be wrong to start from the assumption - as conventional economics is inclined to do, that the ERDI or 1/ERDI phenomenon - or call it unequal exchange - is an autonomous consequence of a relatively high price level in the non-tradable sector. If it were only so, there would be, among others, a high correlation between state sector expenditures (influencing the amount of non-tradables per total GDP) and the ERDI, which is not the case:

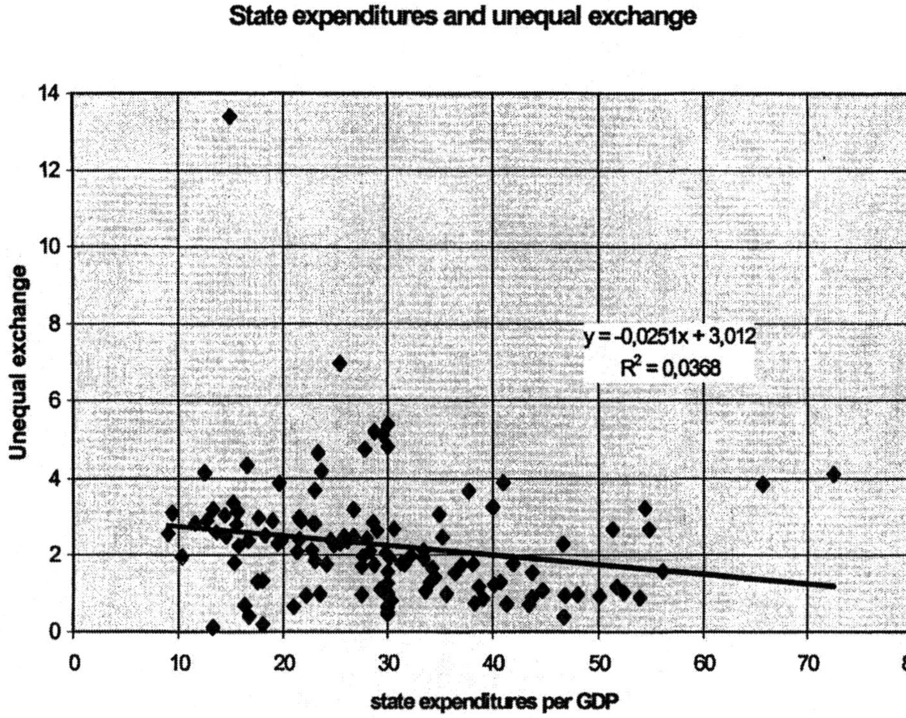

Legend: our own compilations from the data-base (Tausch, 1998)

However, market imperfections - especially in terms of land tenure, monopolistic conditions on the capital markets etc. certainly will influence ERDI and hence 1/ERDI. Monopolistic competition - and this is known ever since the early writings of Kurt Rothschild - are clearly interlinked with the structures of dependency. Unequal exchange is the constant feature of center-periphery relationships. Applied to the realities of European integration, it is the status quo, a Europe without enlargement of the European union and of the European Monetary Union. It increases over space and time, it blocs development in the periphery, and it creates unemployment in the center countries. Left to its design, it will ruin social stability in the world, and it will ruin European integration. The calculation of its losses indicate to European decision makers what price non-enlargement would have.

Most definitely, European capitalism is under profound transformations today, and underway towards astonishing rates of inequality (see, Figures 1, 2, 3, 4):

For further notes on the **Theil measure** of inequality:

http://www.worldbank.org/poverty/inequal/methods/measure.htm

http://www.economics.uni-linz.ac.at/Paper/papers/9614.htm

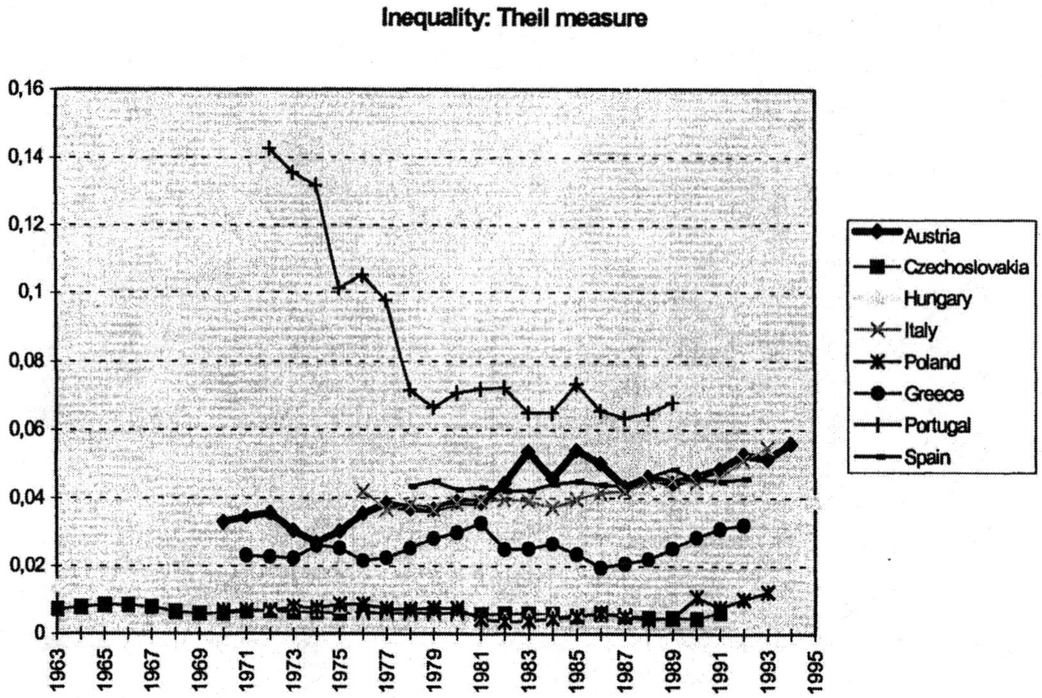

Source: our own compilation from University of Texas Inequality Project, University of Texas at Austin, http://utip.gov.utexas.edu/

Figure 1

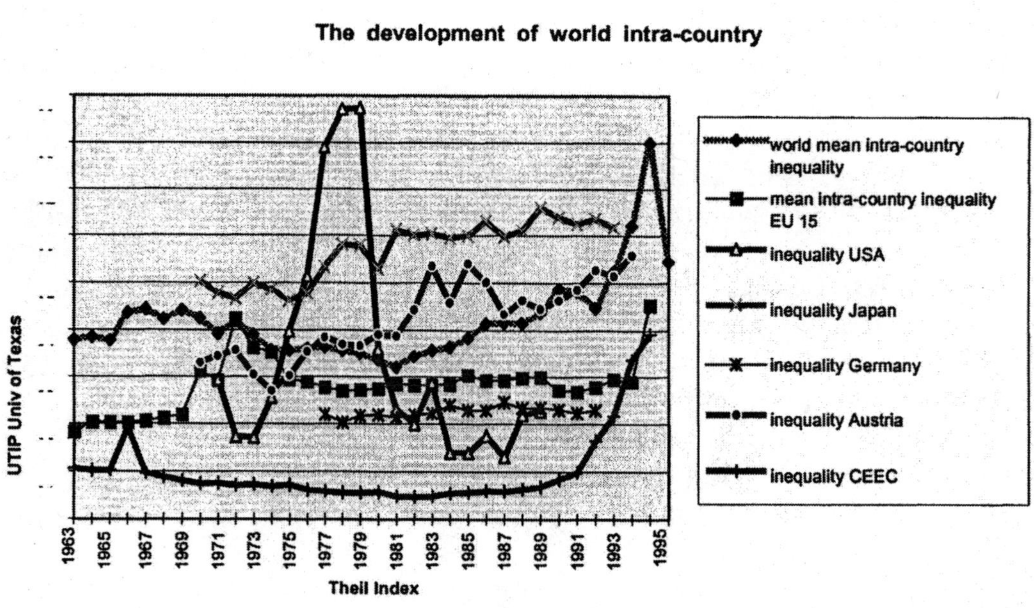

Figure 2

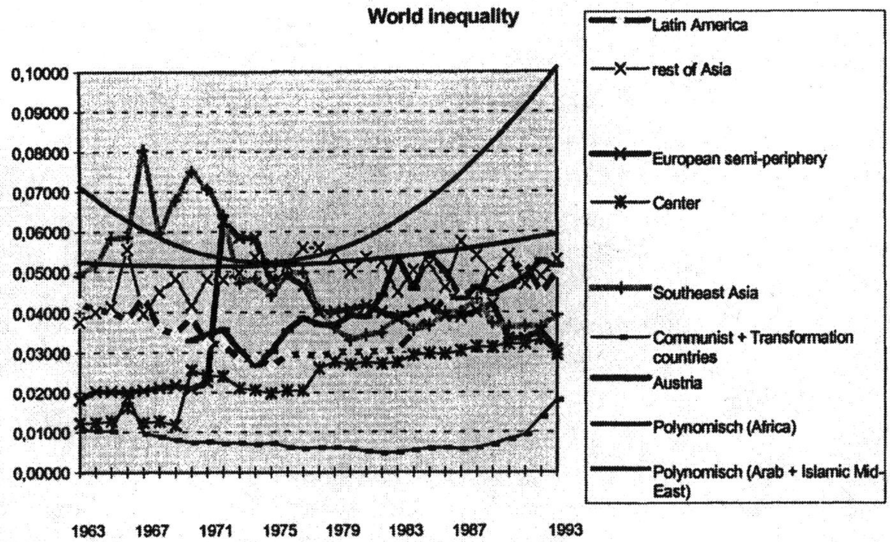

Figure 3

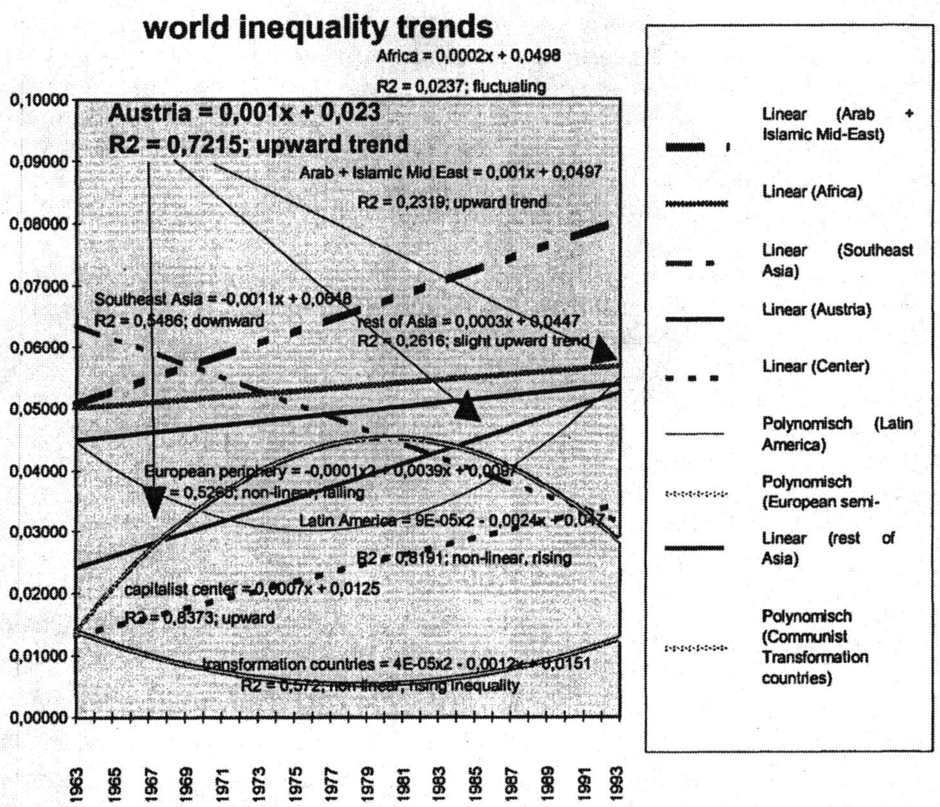

Sources: See above. European semi-periphery comprises Greece, the Irish Republic, Portugal, and Spain.

Figure 4

Kuwait, Ghana and Nigeria lead the scale, but also EU countries like Portugal and Austria have high inequality rates. Poland, the Czech Republic and other transformation countries would have the chance to avoid the errors of inegalitarian capitalism.

It has long been evident that theories of world capitalism/dependency explain cross-country variations in development/decay processes by - *inter alia* - measures of their integration into the one and single capitalist world economy. A lot has been written over the last decades about how, say, the penetration of a given country by transnational capital affects or does not affect economic growth, human development, life expectancy development, urbanization *et cetera.*

Part B of our study presents cross-national evidence and spells out some consequences for the process of EU enlargement. Let us again recall what Flechsig said about Prebisch's theory:

> *'Due to the fragmentation of the periphery, changing hegemony of the centers and changing patterns of international trade, the terms of trade analysis cannot be sustained in the same way as in Prebisch's times. New factors come in the picture such as the new role of the TNC and of financial capital, the debt burden, scientific and technological dependence, neo-protectionist policies of the centers, capital flight, selective migration and brain drain et cetera. But all of them contribute to deepen the periphery's external imbalance with the centers, their vulnerability and foreign exchange constraint. And - as the recent financial crisis shows - it will force them to counteract the foreign exchange problem beyond neo-monetarist cures and to substitute domestic production for imports from the centers (...) But the nucleus of Prebisch's terms of trade analysis which focuses on imperfect markets, monopoly power and its consequences retains validity: unequal distribution of the gains and incomes, polarization and uneven development in the world. The labor values, surplus or income "siphoned off" (in Prebisch's terms) from the periphery to the centers through different channels - according to calculations of the UNDP - amount to more than 500 billion dollars a year in the 1990s.*
>
> *Prevailing international trade is no positive-sum game, as neo-classical theory tells us. It rather produced such global asymmetries and imbalances which are challenging the world's stability and future. In today's globalized world the center's "triad" (European Union, NAFTA and Asian APEC), which makes for 20 percent of the world population, concentrates 85 - 90 percent of the world trade and the huge periphery - with 80 percent of human beings - makes only for 10 - 15 percent of the world trade.* ***There is a deep "structural break" in the world economy, a new Limes particularly between North and South which tends to marginalize or to make redundant the great majority of humanity in the periphery.*** *The time is ripe to put the economy in the service of the human beings worldwide (World Forum for Alternatives, 1997, 4).' (Flechsig, op. cit.)*

'Emerging markets' under such circumstances become an almost Orwellian misnomer; instead, we should speak of *'submerging markets'*, allowing for the fact, that more than five hundred million people in such 'emerging markets' around the globe suffer from the severest recession since the Great Depression in the 1930s. For Tausch, the world since 1960 - hardly ever studied in the totality of it's growth process - resembles a marathon race, where most of the participants stumble on their way or even race backward or wildly search for a direction which they lost underway. The old Greek mythology of the original tales telling the story of the race to Marathon come to one's mind, and certainly the (re)appearance of a God Pan - human capital oriented social

Keynesianism - would be a comfort to most of our thirsty runners, exhausted by a race which they can never finish, which resembles much more the tread mill of Sisyphos than a race.

Various key elements of development strategies from 1960 onwards are analyzed in this context to determine, why the unfortunate ones are so unfortunate, and the less unfortunate ones less unfortunate. Thus, the present publication also takes up an issue, that was touched upon by Jeffrey Kentor from Johns Hopkins University in a more recent publication (1998): the very long-run effects of MNC/TNC penetration. Transnational capital penetration has at best only a mixed result for the host countries concerned during the development marathon, with inequalities and social imbalances rising in the long run.

Only a very small number of countries - mainly the centers and a few exceptions in the periphery - followed the 'normal' path of having the lowest real per capita income in 1960, and the highest in 1995. There was an alarming trend of wide regions of our globe having their lowest historical income value over the last 4 decades in 1989 or even later. A very fortunate and small number of countries achieved their highest GNP per capita in 1995, while others have to realize that they were better off ten, fifteen, or even twenty years ago.

The issues dealt with in this study are of both theoretical and practical importance for the issues of continental integration and the extension and deepening of such entities as the European Union or NAFTA. In Europe, especially to continue the process of Eastern enlargement without tackling the fundamental consequences of unequal exchange would be paramount to risk the failure of the whole process. Wages in the East melt like the snow of winter in the spring sunshine under the impact of currency fluctuations:

	Latest	Year ago	absolute change in US$ over 1 year	Relative change (in %)	Today's wages relative to Portugal (777$=100)	number of years, in which at the current speed of change the level of Portugal today would be reached
Bulgaria	111	112	-1	-0.9	14.3	Never
Croatia	624	673	-49	-7.3	80.3	Never
Czech Republic	356	374	-18	-4.8	45.8	Never
Estonia	286.9	265.5	21.4	8.1	36.9	61 years
Hungary	324	322	2	0.6	41.7	755 years
Latvia	238	211.8	26.2	12.4	30.6	43 years
Lithuania	270.5	n.d.			34.8	
Poland	459	421	38	9	59.1	35 years
Romania	125	157	-32	-20.4	16.1	Never
Russia	67	71	-4	-5.6	8.6	Never
Slovakia	273	293	-20	-6.8	35.1	Never
Slovenia	953	1024	-71	-6.9	122.7	level of Portugal reached. but wages are falling again

Source: our own calculations from Business Central Europe, *http://www.bcemag.com/*

Wage earners from the non-export-oriented sectors in the West of the continent, confronted by increased social polarization, third-worldization become opposed to the European extension project, just as the export sector workers and farmers in the European Eastern semi-periphery, confronted by falling earnings for their labor, measured in current world market exchange rates. Exchange rates and internal buying power at purchasing power parity rates drift apart, and the differences increase, instead of decreasing.

Early on, the decade long strenuous fiscal efforts of the candidate countries to stabilize their economies should be honored to include them in the process of *European Monetary Union.* Eastward *European Monetary Union* extension would eliminate with a stroke the large, but unrealistic differences in wages as expressed in current world market exchange rates, and would provide the East with the stability needed to pursue its accession. Powerful motives for migration, especially daily migration in border regions, would be eliminated permanently. It would halt the polarizing effects of enlargement in both the old West and the new East in the Union. For the West, the process would be almost without risk, considering the economic power of such countries as Germany, France, Italy, or Spain, while for the East the benefits would be enormous, considering their present situation of instability of a small, stabilized, but vulnerable currency in the high seas of global capitalism. Short of the introduction of a global money on a world scale (at any rate the logical and final consequence of our study), thus further propelling the social forces of the world in the direction of global democratic government and a democratic world state, such a measure would greatly increase the success chances of the process of eastern enlargement of the European Union and would stop the polarizing tendencies of nationalism and provincialism, that prop up all over Europe in the wake of the enlargement process.

The study also shows the relevance of social-justice-based human capital centered development strategies and compares the relevance of these strategies for world development 1960-95 with strategies, based on mass migration. The result is that mass migration in global capitalism is not a viable strategy of world economic ascent. It is a *'second best'* strategy for the periphery to close the welfare gap to the centers. Various factors in the migration and wage and income conversion debate are being taken up in this study, from the new and global perspective of unequal exchange. Our findings are at least partially optimistic about the social tendencies in labor exporting countries among the EU applicants, caused by the long-run rise in the human development level, similar to Spain and Portugal in the 1980s, but there is also a pessimistic tendency, caused by the cyclical fluctuations of migration in the ups and downs of the world economy. Although it is particularly true that East European labor will not inundate Western European labor markets as a whole, some EU-15 member countries certainly will need transition phases to be able to manage the future EU-enlargement. Optimistic trends in the direction of a reduction of the migration potential from the accession countries would presuppose a thorough policy of human development on the part of these countries, and a neo-Keynesian policy of social nets, which, in the end, stabilize long-run economic and social development. By drawing out the negotiations with the EC on the migration issue,

Central and East European EU candidates would loose valuable time in terms of the benefits to be reaped from early EU integration in an unstable world economy.

Our analysis also shows the effects, that transnational migration has on the sending and on the receiving countries in the context of overall dependency mechanisms across long cycles. The hope of many semi-periphery and periphery nations to change their weak position in the world-wide structure of the division of labor by mass migration to the developed countries is not entirely realistic. These findings could have an implication not only for the social scientific, but also for the political debate in Europe. At present, 'green', 'alternative' and socialist-left-wing groups claim that Western Europe should allow more immigration from the South and the East. But migration increases inequality in the migration recipient countries, without really solving the long-run weak position of the sending countries in the international economy. If the 'migration industry' were right, then Jordan, Mexico, Jamaica, ex-Yugoslavia, Greece, Portugal and other highly migration-dependent countries would be 'economic miracles'. And Ireland could have foregone its heavy investments in human capital, and just 'let them go'.

Furthermore, we develop an accession model that is based on social justice and mass demand. A decent pension reform would be very necessary in this context. Traditional liberalism would have established social security altogether and have left people to determine for themselves. Our analysis not only shows the limits of the early generation of three-pillar pension system like in Chile, but it also establishes the central role of social security expenditures for global demand in the sense of the theory, presented here. It is shown that pension reforms must continue to contain a welfare society component, although a moderate three pillar model - like the one in Sweden – seems to be unadvoidable in view of the old age crisis in advanced societies.

East European EU accession and the future of the European model heavily will depend on the human capital effort; and in world political terms, Europe would we well advised to find its own role; a role which presupposes the creation of a European army and a European foreign policy.

Finally, we show the relevance of the theory of unequal exchange for the debate about unemployment, poverty and racism, and compare the cross-national relevance of the reformulation of dependency and world system approaches, undertaken in this study, and being based on the theory of unequal exchange, with earlier formulations, based on transnational capital penetration (based on the research traditions of Volker Bornschier), and presented in the main cross-national results, presented in the following table.

Dependency Theory by Comparison

	Model based on theory of:	R^2 for the 134 countries with fairly complete data	F for the entire equation	t-test for the dependency predictor and direction of the influence	Further positive. significant predictors	Further negative. significant predictors
Explanation of growth	Unequal exchange	57.20%	12.35	-1.33	mean years of mean years of education. population growth	labor force participation rate. military expenditures
	Bornschier	56%	11.86	-1.57	mean years of mean years of education. population growth	labor force participation rate. military expenditures
Explanation of infant mortality	Unequal exchange	91.30%	96.7	2.45		UN membership years. absolute GNP. years of Communism. military expenditures
	Bornschier	91.00%	95.04	2.08		UN membership years. absolute GNP. years of Communism. military expenditures
Explanation of early death	Unequal exchange	89.40%	93.14	2.87	agrarian share per GDP	years of Communism. human development index
	Bornschier	89.00%	93.12	2.84	agrarian share per GDP	years of Communism. human development index
Explanation of political repression	Unequal exchange	52.50%	10.2	0.68	educational level. labour force participation rate	military expenditures
	Bornschier	52.00%	9.9	0.45	educational level. labour force participation rate	military expenditures
Explanation of income concentration for the top 20%	Unequal exchange	41.00%	6.52	0.17	population growth	absolute GNP
	Bornschier	41.00%	6.5	0.16	population growth	absolute GNP
Explanation of life expectancy	Unequal exchange	95%	161.5	-1.14	state sector expenditures	population growth
	Bornschier	95%	161.3	-1.16	state sector expenditures. military expenditures	absolute GNP. agrarian share per GDP

Different theoretical points of emphasis and approaches should not be covered up in such a joint, transatlantic study. To formulate unequal exchange simply as the reciprocal value of the exchange rate deviation index (see Part B) presupposes to stronger take into consideration the overall market-distorting effects of relations of periphery and center, of tropical or export oriented agriculture in the world economy since 1450, irrespective of the size of the export sector in the total economy (and, in a way, also total size, since big countries are little export dependent), while to understand unequal exchange mainly as a percentage of the losses from unequal exchange per gross national product ties the theory of unequal exchange to an implicit theory of the size of nations (small nations have large export shares in total product). The present study should make such differences clearer, and invites scholars to take up for themselves different formulations for their own empirical work.

PART A: WORLD SYSTEM ECONOMICS

Gernot Köhler

Chapter 1

A THEORY OF WORLD INCOME

"Everyone has the right to a standard of living adequate for the health and well-being of himself and his family..."

Article 25, Universal Declaration of Human Rights, 1948

ABSTRACT

This chapter proposes a theory of world income and world employment. The presentation starts with the idea that the world-economy is a market economy. The study further proposes a conceptual model of global income determination; introduces the concept of a growth dialectic (disequilibrium); postulates the possibility of a global full-employment equilibrium (global Keynes-Prebisch equilibrium) as an alternative to a global unemployment equilibrium; discusses the income-generating and employment-generating implications of such an equilibrium; and, finally, examines various defects of global aggregate demand and states the need for public intervention in the world market.

1. WHY STUDY WORLD INCOME?

Citizens have *rights*. The people of the world have *inalienable* rights. Economic processes do *not* have inalienable rights. The present world economy does *not* conform to Article 25 of the Universal Declaration of Human Rights which states that: "Everyone has the right to a standard of living adequate for the health and well-being of himself and his family..." (We may amend this and say "of himself *or herself* and his *or her* family".) In my opinion, the world economy must be reformed so that it conforms to Article 25 of the human rights code. Theory of world income and employment can make a contribution to such a reformation.

2. Tasks of a Theory of World Income

When we study income and employment in the world-system, we cannot but have certain goals in mind. The goals which, in my opinion, should be supported by a theory of world income -- in addition to the obtaining of valid knowledge, are, as follows:

a. global full employment
b. improved global income distribution
c. global social security
d. global economic growth (of the sustainable kind)
e. ecological sustainability
f. democratic process

All of these goals are important. In practical situations, one may have to rank-order them. In view of these goals, we can, perhaps, say that a theory of world income must deal with the following topical areas:

1. growth of world income
2. sustainability of world income
3. distribution of world income
4. employment and world income
5. politics of world income

My study cannot deal with all of these issues. Instead, I will focus on some of them and leave others for another time. I have explained my general perspective on this elsewhere (Köhler 1999). The underlying paradigm does not have an agreed-upon name; it may be called perspective X or leftist global Keynesianism or something of that sort. As Shakespeare has Juliet say in *Romeo and Juliet*, a rose by any other name is still a rose.

3. Literature

I am not aware of another similar theory of world income and employment. However, great literature exists which is thinking in the same direction. "World system" and "world-systems" literature, publications from the World Order Models Project, the work of UNDP (United Nations Development Program), the literature concerning NIEO (New International Economic Order), and other like-minded literature -- I am referring to authors like Addo, Alexander, Amin, Arrighi, Bornschier, Boswell, Chase-Dunn, Dalby, Eckhardt, Elsenhans, Emmanuel, Falk, Frank, Galtung, Greider, Grimes, Kothari, Makhijani, Mazrui, Mendlovitz, Prebisch, Raffer, Rozov, Tandon, Tausch, Sakamoto, SEF (collective author), Shiva, Singh and Gatade, UNDP (collective author), Wagar, Wallace, Wallerstein, to name some -- have articulated the need for studying the modern world as a single unit, a single society, a single economy, a single polity, a single cultural system, a single normative system, or a single ecosystem, in short, as a single world-system. A global view of the world has been articulated in a large body of ecological literature and in the literature known as "global political economy". Among economists, a Keynesian scholar proposed to study what he calls "megaeconomics" (world-level economics), as opposed to macroeconomics or microeconomics (Mead 1989). Some recent neoclassical literature is also theorizing about the world economy using a globocentric perspective (Siebert 1997). Popularly, this view is known as a "one-world" view which emphasizes the fact that the world is a single system, as opposed to a nation-state view of the world which treats the world as a multitude of countries. This kind of theorizing received a major boost from space exploration which made the image of the "blue planet" a household item. Theory of world income and employment is theory of the economy of "spaceship earth".

World-systems theory of the world economy is important because there are numerous economic problems in the contemporary world which have not been sufficiently elucidated by existing state-centered theories (*statist* theories), including macroeconomics and the international economics of textbooks. Theory formation seems to lag behind reality. While a great deal of economic activity is being organized on a global scale by global corporations like Coca Cola or Toyota, by global banks like Chase-Manhattan and other global financial institutions, by global financial centers like the New York, Tokyo and London stock exchanges, and by global public organizations like IMF, World Bank, WTO and others, the theories we use most frequently have been framed with the use of statist (nation-centered) concepts which have their origins, for most part, in the 18th and 19th centuries.

4. Definition of World Income

World income is the aggregate income generated by the world economy; world product is the aggregate product generated by the world economy; both are commonly measured as world GDP (global GDP). This is the grand dependent variable of my theory. (Some ecologists have proposed alternatives to GDP measurement and Marxist economists have measured aggregate income as NMP, net material product; but I will leave this measurement problem aside for the time being.)

5. The World Economy as a Market

5.1 Concept

Qualified observers, including global investors, as well as Karl Marx and John Maynard Keynes, agree that the world economy is a market economy. What does that mean? There are four or more definitions of a "market", as follows: (1) the original concept of a market -- this kind of market can be found around the world and throughout history, in ancient China as well as in modern Canada -- namely, the market as a place in a village, town or city ("market place" or "market building") where shoppers go in order to buy something and vendors go in order to sell something. This is, of course, the market from which Adam Smith developed his abstract concept of a market. (2) The concept of a market in the sense of economic theory -- this is central to much of economic theory and refers to the notions of supply and demand and their interaction. This basic model has been applied in many different ways -- in microeconomics and macroeconomics; applied to product markets, labour markets, stock markets, and so on. (3) In political-economic analysis the emphasis is on the institutional dimension of "market" and we speak of a "market economy" (i.e., an economy organized around the concept of a market) or "market system", involving certain rules, laws, public organizations and policies. (4) Another important definiton of "market" is used in marketing, the art and science of designing and selling a company's products. In marketing, a company's "market" is defined as potential buyers with the ability, willingness, and purchasing power to buy the company's products. These could be individual buyers or organizational buyers (businesses or governments, etc.). In mass marketing, the "target market" is a mass of people (consumers). In global marketing, the target markets are potential buyers around the globe.

The world economy can be considered as a market in the sense of (2), (3) and (4) above. That is to say, the world economy can be conceptualized as (a) a market in the sense of economic theory (aggregate supply interacting with aggregate demand); (b) as a market in the sense of political economy (an institutional arrangement around the concept of a market); or (c) as a market in the sense of marketing (as in "Cocal Cola Company is selling to the world market"). The center of my theoretical discussion will be on the world economy as a market in the sense of economic theory.

5.2 Physical and Monetary (Real and Nominal)

The world economy has, at the same time, a physical and a monetary dimension. There are other sides like political, legal, military, cultural, and ecological; but I will focus on the physical and monetary sides which are also known as "real" and "nominal". In other words, the modern world economy is, for most part, not a barter economy in which goods or services are bartered for other goods or services, but rather a monetary economy in which economic value takes on the alternate forms of products (i.e., physical or "real" value) and money, broadly defined (i.e., monetary or "nominal" value). The relationship between the two sides -- physical and monetary, is complex, indeed, and has led theoreticians in different directions. Some treat money as a means of payment and not much else; others treat money as an autonomous element in the economic process which plays a role far beyond being a means of payment. Keynesians and Marxists subscribe to the second outlook and my discussion is placed in that broad camp as well. I do not see much sense in making the highly artificial assumption that the modern world economy is, in principle, a barter economy a la Robinson Crusoe. My general view of the relationship between "nominal" and "real", or "physical" and "monetary", is expressed by the Keynesian characterization of the (capitalist) (world) economy as a "monetary entrepreneurial economy" (see, e.g., Davidson 1994). While money is important for diagnostic purposes (namely, analysis and explanation of economic processes), I agree with the statement by Keynes that "consumption -- to repeat the obvious -- is the sole end of all economic activity" (Keynes 1964: 104). When we add an ecological perspective, we would have to say that the improvement of consumption must be within the bounds of what is ecologically sustainable. With this amendment, I am still agreeing with those who claim the *normative* supremacy of the real (physical) economy over the nominal (monetary) economy while acknowledging the *diagnostic* importance of money in the economic process.

6. GLOBAL INCOME DETERMINATION

6.1 Conceptual Model

I propose, as a conceptual model, that world income and world product (global GDP) are determined as a market outcome; that is to say, as the result of interactions ("feedback") between global aggregate supply and global aggregate demand, whereby global money has an active influence on the outcome as well -- an influence which goes beyond the role of money as a means of payment. These interactions take place in a political-institutional, an ecological, and an historical context.

6.2 Definition of Terms

Global aggregate supply is aggregate supply in the entire world economy. *Global aggregate demand* is aggregate (effective) demand in the entire world economy. The importance of these two concepts has been noted in the literature -- for example, by Wallerstein who stated:

> "there are 'expansions' and 'contractions' in the world economy ... I think they are linked to a basic contradiction of the system, which has to do with supply and demand,that is, *world-system* supply and world-system demand, not *firm* supply and demand, nor *state* supply and demand, but world-system supply and demand." (Wallerstein 1978: 232; emphasis original)

Global money is aggregate money in the entire world economy. Monetary theory is full of complexities and disagreements and the theory of global money, as opposed to money in the macroeconomy, is still underdeveloped.

Market interaction and feedback refers to a process of mutual causation. If A influences B, but B does not influence A (namely, if A B), then there is no feedback, since the influence is only in one direction. However, if A influences B and B also influences A (namely, if A ↔ B), then interactivity (feedback) exists. The concept of a market, in the sense of economic theory, implies that supply and demand are interactive (i.e., in a relationship of feedback), so that supply influences demand and demand influences supply. This is expressed in the standard supply-demand diagram with a supply curve and a demand curve. In this diagram the market outcome is represented as the point at which the supply curve and the demand curve intersect. This intersection represents the result of the interaction (feedback) between supply and demand.

6.3 Levels of Analysis

The conceptual model (above) implies that my theory is stated for the world-system level of analysis (global level), rather than for the state level of analysis (national level, macroeconomic level). As in the situation between micro and macro levels, causation between state and world levels may run in both directions. Certain large states (e.g., USA) or certain groups of states (e.g., the Asian economies) influence the world system and the world system influences individual states (countries, macroeconomies) -- for example, via the global technology transfer, global demand, global finance, and so on. No country is an island, so-to-speak. Robinson Crusoe is dead. All national economies are so-called "open economies" within one world.

6.4 History, Politics, Ecology

I should point out that the determination of world income and world product, as described above, does not occur in a political, historical or ecological vacuum. Concepts similar to the ones I mentioned have been used in globocentric *history* of the world economy. Furthermore, the abstract model of an economy never exists without a *political* context in which groups, classes, countries or empires push and fight for their interests by non-violent or violent means. Furthermore, the world economy (or, "world-economies" in the plural, as in historical sociology) never exist(s) without an *ecological* context.

6.5 Praxeology, Scientism, Theory

The term "theory" means many things to many people. It is important, therefore, to state at the outset what it means here. Theoreticians may pursue theory of various types and there is not necessarily any clear-cut proof that one is wrong and the other is right; all theories are limited in one way or another. I subscribe to the view that economic theory, in order to be of interest, must have a practical purpose. Keynes studied the great depression of the 1930's in order to end it. Marx studied economics, politics and society in order to change them. Business schools study the world economy in order to improve business. As historical reality unfolds, new knowledge must be found in order to deal with changing reality and changing practical problems. This theoretical outlook differs from a kind of scientism which treats the economy as some kind of Newtonian universe in which eternal, ahistorical laws can be discovered. I find this orientation less appealing since the world economy is an intelligent reality, as opposed to an inanimate reality as in Newtonian physics.

Rejecting pure scientism does not mean a rejection of scientific method, however. By "scientific method" I mean method in the sense of Popper, where analytic theories and hypotheses or historical interpretations are formulated and then confronted with factual evidence of various kinds and are exposed to rival theories, hypothes or interpretations. Philosophical essentialism, as in Marx or in medieval European scholasticism, does not appeal to my mind. These approaches may generate valuable ideas, but only in the sense of preliminary theories, hypotheses or interpretations which must be exposed to a reality test (confrontation with observables) and even a praxis test. Thus, if theory leads to policies which lead to disastrous practical results, then this theory did not pass a praxis test, and the praxis test may also reveal flaws in the analytic apparatus of the theory.

Given this general orientation, I distinguish between (1) a "paradigm", in the sense of Kuhn; (2) analytic theories or models, on the one hand, and (3) praxeological theory or thought, on the other hand. I have attempted to describe the paradigm underlying my present effort in a separate publication where the paradigm or perspective is called "global Keynesianism and beyond" (Köhler 1999). By paradigm I mean, along Kuhn's lines, a general pre-analytic perspective which contains general understandings about salient concepts, admissible evidence, modes of reasoning and preferred methods of inquiry, notions of causality and shared values. Within such a paradigm (which is like an umbrella, so-to-speak), more specific theories can be developed -- e.g., theories of economic growth, income distribution, entitlement, and so on. Moreover, one may also want to develop praxeological theory, policy thought, and practical advice. Neoclassical analytic theories are related to certain liberal, conservative or other policies; Keynesian analytic theory is related to certain Keynesian policies; Marxist analytic theory is related to certain Marxist praxeological ideas and prescriptions; and so on. These various endeavours can be looked at in terms of their analytic and factual strength and validity; in terms of their praxeological, practical and value dimensions; and in terms of ideology critique as mental systems which are used to advance the interests of various agents (individuals, groups, organizations, classes, nations, empires) in an open or disguised fashion.

The theory which I am proposing in this study is meant to support the greatest utility (well-being, welfare) of the greatest number of people around the globe and everybody's inalienable right to have an adequate standard of living, as stated in Article 25 of the Universal Declaration of Human Rights.

7. Accounting View of Global Aggregates (Ex-Post View)

The global aggregates mentioned in the conceptual statement of my theory -- namely, global income, global product, global supply, global demand, and global money, can be measured, given certain definitions and measurement procedures. This leads to a statistical picture of the world economy which is mostly descriptive. This descriptive statistical picture can be called the "accounting view" of the world economy. In Keynesian parlance, this is also known as an "ex post" view; that is to say, this is how the world economy looks at the end of an accounting period (usually, a year) when all the activity and turbulence of the economic process is "tuned out" and the accountants/statisticians total up all the variables.

Let's use symbolic notations, for example:

Z = world income or product
GAS = global aggregate supply
GAD = global aggregate demand
Mg = global money

In the ex-post view (accounting view) three of these magnitudes are identical, namely:

Z = global GDP
= (ex-post) GAS
= (ex-post) GAD

In words, the magnitude of global income for an accounting period is also the magnitude of the global product of the accounting period (both generally referred to as global GDP or world GDP). The actual (ex-post) global supply (namely, the amount actually supplied) and actual (ex-post) global demand (namely, the amount of demand actually satisfied) are identical to global GDP. It must be noted that these identities refer to the magnitudes of these variable *expressed in money terms* (e.g., in US dollars). For example, the magnitude of world income in the year 1995 was 28 trillion US dollars, based on standard currency conversion rates (World Bank 1997: 215). The magnitude of global aggregate money for the same year is more obscure and not readily available from published sources.

This accounting view of the global aggregates is a starting point for theory and analysis but reveals, by itself, relatively little about the dynamics, causes and determinants of world income and world product.

8. Dynamic View of Global Aggregates (Ex-Ante View)

Keynesian theory distinguishes between "ex-post" and "ex-ante" views. In dynamic (ex-ante) analysis, global supply and global demand are more than dead, descriptive, statistical aggregates; they are rather treated as dynamic "economic forces", "potentialities", "functions" or "market forces" which are ever-changing in their strength. Thus, the "market force" or "function" of aggregate supply interacts with the "market force" or "function" of aggregate demand in the abstract space called the "market". The relative strength of these variable "market forces" determines the aggregate outcome at the end of the accounting period.

In dynamic (ex-ante) analysis it is presumed that the two forces of aggregate supply and aggregate demand may be of different strengths, so that a tension, dialectic or dynamic disequilibrium between the two may exist. In fact, Keynesian and Marxist theories presume that such a tension or disequilibrium-in-process (dialectic) is the usual situation. Generated by this perpetually changing relation of forces between supply and demand, the aggregate result may be an economic growth rate of, let's say, three percent (+3%) in one year, or, alternatively, a decline of, let's say, one percent (-1%) in another year, and so on.

The interaction between the aggregate supply force and the aggregate demand force is further complicated by the role of money which, according to Keynesian presumptions, makes an autonomous additional contribution to the economic process (money is "non-neutral"; Davidson 1994); and which, according to the Marxist view, is an integral part of the accumulation process (as in the formula M - C - M').

These general theoretical notions have been applied at the macroeconomic level of analysis; they can also be applied at the world-system level.

9. The Global Growth Dialectic (Growth Disequilibrium)

9.1 General Statement

The preceding considerations lead to a concept of a global growth disequilibrium (dialectic), as follows.

Let's use the following symbolic notations (I am using the lower-case letters in order to signify that these are growth rates):

z = growth rate of global income or product
gas = growth rate of global aggregate supply
gad = growth rate of global aggregate demand
mg = growth rate of global monetary aggregate

Using these notations, the inherent disequilibrium (dialectic) of the global growth dynamic can be stated, in a first approximation, as:

z = minimum of (gas, gad, mg)

[where "gas, gad, mg" are to be understood as "potentials", "functions" or "market forces" (ex-ante view) and not as the observed (actual) accounting magnitudes (ex-post view)]

In words, global income growth (z) is a market outcome resulting from the interaction of three disequilibrated market forces, where the weakest market force sets the pace. Thus, actual global income growth (z) is equal to the *minimum* of either (a) the growth rate of the global aggregate supply potential (gas) or (2) the growth rate of the global aggregate demand potential (gad) or (3) the growth rate of the global monetary aggregate (mg). This is a first, approximate statement which ignores finer points of the interactivities.

Here is an example. If global income and product grew between time 1 and time 2 by x percent (say, +3.0 %) [as per ex-post observation], then it is implied that (actual) global aggregate supply and (actual) global aggregate demand grew at the same rate and that the global monetary aggregate may have grown at this rate as well (the last being less certain). In *ex-post* terms we can thus speak of a global growth *equilibrium* between the aggregates. In *ex-ante* analysis, however, we can presume that there was a *disequilibrium* at work during the accounting period. Thus, global aggregate supply (as a potential) may have grown at a rate of s percent (say, +5.0 %); global aggregate demand (as a potential) may have grown by d percent (say, +3.0 %); and the global monetary aggregate may have grown by m percent (say, +4.0 %). These disequilibrated market forces were interactive during the accounting period; that is to say, they influenced each other. As a general rule, it may be postulated that the weakest of the three forces tends to restrain the other two forces. In this example, global demand growth (+3%) most likely restrained overall growth of income and output to +3%. In other situations, the supply side may be the weakest force and may restrain aggregate income and output. In yet other situations, aggregate money growth may be so slow or negative that it constrains both aggregate supply and demand growth, with the effect of controlling the growth of global income and product.

9.2 Nation-State (Statist) View of Global Growth

A more conventional view of global growth of income and product is a statist view (nation-state view). Let's denote the economic growth rates of individual countries (in lower-case letters) as:

y1 = GDP growth rate of country 1
y2 = GDP growth rate of country 2
... etc.
y200 = GDP growth rate of country 200

Using these notations, the statist (traditional macroeconomic) view of global growth can be stated as:

z = function of (y1, y2, ..., y200)

In words, the growth rate of global income (z) is a function of the (national) GDP growth rates of the various countries around the world (y1, y2, etc.). Both the nation-state view and the world-system view are valid at the same time; they are two alternative ways of studying the same object.

9.3 Interactivity Between Global and National Income Growth

The relationships between the world-system level and the national (macro) level of analysis are complex. The question can be raised (a) which of the two levels (global, national) has the higher analytic status; and (b) which causes which? My answer to these questions is that the global and national levels relate to each other in a chicken-and-egg relationship. We cannot say whether the chicken was there before the egg or whether the egg was there before the chicken. Similarly, the world-system level and the national (macro) level have co-equal logical-analytic status. Both are categories of the mind which the mind superimposes on reality in order to make sense of reality (in Kant's philosophy, categories are superimposed on "the thing of itself", "das Ding an sich"). As a corollary of that, it makes sense to claim that causality between the two levels may run in either direction; that is to say, that the world-system level may influence the national level and, at the same time, the national level may influence the world-system level. Aggregate global economic growth may influence each and every individual national economic growth; and each national economic growth may make a contribution (positive or negative) to aggregate global economic growth. In the ex-post (accounting) view, global aggregate income (Z) is equal to the sum of all national aggregate incomes (Y1, Y2, ... Y200). This is a statistical identity. On the other hand, in ex-ante (dynamic) analysis, the growing (or declining) national and global aggregates may influence each other in either direction. We can thus postulate that:

y1, y2 ... y200 → z (i.e., national income growth influences global income growth);

and:

z → y1, y2 ... y200 (i.e., world income growth influences national income growth)

10. TAXONOMY OF THE DETERMINANTS OF WORLD INCOME

The main determinants of world income (as per my model) -- namely, global aggregate supply, global aggregate demand and the global monetary aggregate, are abstractions at a very high level of abstraction. There are various ways of classifying and describing these determinants.

10.1 The Components of Global Aggregate Supply

Global aggregate supply can be decomposed in several ways, as follows:

(a) By sector (1) -- agriculture, mining, industry, service
(b) By sector (2) -- private, public
(c) By end-use -- consumption, investment
(d) By national origin -- Mozambiquan, Canadian, etc.
(e) By class of productive agents -- land, labour, capital, information
(f) By ecological impact -- sustainable, non-sustainable
(g) By time -- year 1865, 1965, 2000 and so on
(h) other

When all these categories are put together, the components of global supply can be represented in a multidimensional matrix with a very large number of cells. Such a global matrix is impractical to work with, but it suggests, as a theoretical device, that global aggregate supply can be analyzed in many different ways, depending on how we simplify the matrix.

10.2 The Components of Global Aggregate Demand

Global aggregate demand can similarly be decomposed in several ways. We can also think of global aggregate demand as a matrix with a large number of dimensions and cells. A standard approach to demand analysis is captured in the macroeconomic formula of textbooks which reads:

$$Y = C + I + G + (EX - IM)$$

or, in words, national income (Y) can be decomposed into four demand streams -- namely, (private) consumption demand (C), fixed-investment demand demand (I), government demand (G) and net foreign demand (export demand (EX) less import demand (IM)). At the world- system level, there is one special feature -- namely, world exports and world imports are the same quantity. Therefore, the expression (EX - IM) equals zero (null) at the world-level, by definition. Statistical measurements of this show only very small deviations from null. As a consequence, total world demand (GAD) is:

GAD = global C + global I + global G

where global G is the aggregate of all public expenditures in the world. Note that (EX-IM) is null. This reflects the fact that the world economy is the only economic system which is truly a "closed system", i.e., has no external economic links.

10.3 Components of Global Money

10.3.1 Definition

Global money, as opposed to money in the macroeconomy, is a concept which is not widely used and its theory is not as well developed as that of money in a national (macroeconomic) context. When we speak of global money, we must first distinguish between the notions of "global currency" (e.g., is gold, is Stirling, is the U.S. dollar a "global currency"?) and global money as an aggregate of some value. In a first, simplistic definition, we can, perhaps, say that the volume of global money (Mg) is equal to the sum of all national monetary aggregates (Mn), expressed in a common numeraire, plus any other volumes of money which may be generated in the world-system in a "space" which is not strictly national ("transnational space"), e.g., so-called "Eurodollars" created by non-U.S. banks or SDRs issued by the IMF as transnational fiat money. Let's denote these kinds of "transnational money" as Mt. Using these concepts, we can, perhaps, define the global monetary aggregate (Mg) as the sum of all national monetary aggregates (Mn) plus all transnational monetary aggregates (Mt) -- or, in a very simple formula, Mg = Mn + Mt.

10.3.2 Components

Global money can be decomposed in various ways, as follows:

(a) by national currency -- dollars, yuan, pesos, etc.
(b) by degree of liquidity -- cash, credit, asset
(c) by legitimization: state-sanctioned ("legal tender"), informal
(d) by valuation -- nominal versus deflated (so-called "real" in statistical accounts)
(e) by functionality -- global money as means of payment; or global money as effective demand; or global money as capital
(f) other

The aggregate which may be called "global money" has various dimensions and components which are here only listed in a preliminary and incomplete manner. Most observers will probably agree with the general statement that "global money is important". This general statement may have various theoretical meanings. My general view on this is of a Keynesian or Marxist variety, namely, that global money is an integral part of the global accumulation process (Marxist view) or that money is a non-neutral force in the global "monetary entrepreneurial economy" (Keynesian view).

10.4 Growth Constraints and Growth Stimulants

The determinants of world income may function as constraints or stimulants of growth. The process of global economic growth may experience four broad types of aggregate constraints, namely: (1)inadequate global demand (global demand constraint); (2) inadequate global supply (global supply constraint); (3) inadequate global money supply (global monetary constraint); and (4) global ecological constraints. It is debatable, however, whether ecological constraints should be listed separately or treated as a type of supply constraint.

Similarly, the process of global economic growth may experience four broad types of stimulation, namely: (1) stimulation from the global demand side; (2) stimulation from the global supply side; (3) stimulation from the global monetary side; or (4) stimulation from the global ecological side. Certain kinds of ecologically motivated demand ("green" investment demand, "green" consumption demand) may be contained in demand-side stimulation and certain kinds of supply-side developments (e.g., alternative "green" technologies) may serve as supply-side stimulants of growth.

10.5 Interactivity and Relativity of the Determinants

These are broad conceptual categories of possible constraints or stimulants of global economic growth. In a market situation where feedback between these aggregates occurs, these determinants are *interactive* and act *relative* to each other. By "interactive" I mean that they influence each other in a pattern of mutual causation (feedback). By "relative to each other" I mean that *relative* magnitudes, as opposed to absolute magnitudes, are important. Thus, aggregate demand of, say, 10 billion dollars is relatively little in USA but relatively much in Canada or many other countries; and aggregate demand amounting to 10 billion dollars, if confronted with aggregate supply of 12 billion dollars is relatively weak; however, if confronted with aggregated supply of only 8 billion dollars, is relatively strong.

If supply is the weakest market force, it functions as the major constraint; as a consequence, positive changes on the supply side could be a major stimulant of growth. If, on the other hand, demand is the weakest market force, then this is the major constraint and, consequently, demand stimulation can spur growth, and similarly for the monetary side. However, if the supply is already the strongest market force, then further stimulation of supply does not spur growth but, rather, leads to overproduction. If money supply is already the strongest ex-ante force, then further stimulation of money growth does not spur economic growth, but rather inflation and similarly for demand.

11. Theories of Economic Growth

There are several broad families of theories of economic growth, including:

(a) *supply-side theories*: Here the presumption is that economic growth is critically dependent on the supply side and that the supply side must be strengthened.
(b) *ecological theories*: Here the presumption is that economic growth (i.e. both supply and demand growth) is critically dependent on the global ecosystem and that growth must be ecologically sustainable.
(c) *demand side theories*: Here the presumption is that global economic growth is critically dependent on the demand side and that the supply side is relatively less critical.
(d) *monetary theories*: Here the presumption is that economic growth (and the growth of both aggregate supply and demand) is critically dependent on the growth of monetary aggregates.
(e) *historical theories*: Here the presumption is that economic growth unfolds in long-term historical patterns, including "stages" (as in Rostow's "stages of economic growth" (Rostow 1978)), "long cycles" or "long waves" (e.g., Kondratieff cycles);
(f) *category by itself*: Marxist theories
(g) *other theories*.

It is unworkable to review all of these theories at this juncture. Disagreement between scholars of economic growth is high. No matter how much one might try to bring economists to agree with each other, there is an irreducible amount of disagreement resulting from differences in politics and values. Economic theories cannot but serve certain interests, be they public or private, business or labour, rich country or poor country interests, and so on. Agreement between the different economic schools of thought is not in sight because agreement on political and moral values is not in sight either. The ideal, cherished by some, of a value-free "economic physics" is unattainable.

12. Analysis of Global Aggregate Interactions and Feedback

12.1 Multiple Interactions

The interactions between the various dynamically changing global aggregates (global market forces) are complex and, indeed, more complex than interactions at the national level. In addition to the interactivity between global supply and global demand, the conceptual statement of my theory also mentions the influence of global money and other interactions (economic-political, economic-ecological, historical processes). Here is a small selection of existing theories which are relevant for the further development of my presentation.

Say's Law

In line with Keynesian and post-Keynesian literature, I do not believe in what is known as Say's Law -- namely, the view that supply creates its own demand and that, therefore, one need not worry about demand. The tendency for a market economy to generate a supply-demand gap has been recognized by Marx, Keynes, Samuelson, Pasinetti and others, albeit in different formulations. These formulations have been stated for the national level of analysis but can be applied at the world-system level as well.

12.2 Marx

Marx subdivides the aggregate income generated by the system into wages and surplus-value (i.e., "mass of surplus value", namely, that portion of aggregate income which is not paid to workers). Workers who, at his time, were living at subsistance levels, spent all their earnings, thus returning all wages to the system as aggregate demand. Surplus-value, on the other hand, was, partly, spent and, partly, accumulated by the bourgeois class (i.e., not spent). The system thus generates an aggregate gap -- namely, a situation where the capitalist class tries to produce more and more in order to increase profit (surplus value), but does not spend all of the surplus value. This creates a situation of (relative) overproduction. This disequilibrium is responsible for economic crises and the creation of a reserve army of the unemployed in Marxist theory.

12.3 Keynes

Keynes subdivides aggregate demand into consumption demand (D1 or C) and (fixed-)investment demand (D2 or I). He argues, in his *General Theory*, that both components of demand may be deficient relative to aggregate supply. In other words, recipients of wages and salaries may not spend all their earnings. Here he presents the consumption function which states that income distribution affects the re-spending of wages and salaries. Earners of low incomes tend to spend most of their earnings, while recipients of higher incomes may save a greater proportion of their incomes, thus effectively withdrawing certain amounts of income from potential consumption demand. At the side of (fixed-)investment another deficiency may develop. Entrepreneurs may anticipate falling consumption demand and may reduce their (fixed-)investment spending or, in a situation of depression or panic, lose their entrepreneurial "animal spirits" altogether for a while. In either case, the effect is that entrepreneurs have earned incomes from their business activity which they may not spend in full (or not at all) on (fixed-) investment or consumption. As a result of the possible D1 and D2 demand deficiencies, the system may generate a shortfall of aggregate demand relative to aggregate supply potential. This ex-ante disequilibrium may lead to an ex-post unemployment equilibrium of the system.

12.4 Pasinetti

In Pasinetti's theory technology is the driving force of economic growth ("primum movens", Pasinetti 1993:45). Pasinetti states that: "It is the acquisition of knowledge that eventually makes the wealth of nations." (Pasinetti 1993: 176). Technology drives both the supply and demand sides. "Technical change emerges as the crucial determinant in the dynamic process outlined by Pasinetti, since it contains both a demand and a supply aspect." (Halevi 1994:58). In this process technological change propels both labour productivity and per capita incomes simultaneously. However, there is no guarantee that there will be a proper match between changing magnitudes of productivity and changing magnitudes of income and demand. There is "no reliance on any automatic fulfillment of the macroeconomic condition that ensures the correct level of overall effective demand and hence full employment" (Pasinetti 1993: 116). Because of that, "(t)echnologcial progress can ... also cause net losses of wealth or social well-being in general" (Pasinetti 1993:57). Although aggregate supply-demand gaps are a quasi-normal occurrance in this process, there is, on the other hand, "no inherent impossibility of finding ways to counteract such tendencies" (Pasinetti 1993:116). The remedy for this unreliability of the system can be provided by the "institutions" of society or, as Halevi and Kriesler put it: "Without a visible hand, the invisible hand is likely to guide us on to the wrong path..." (Halevi/Kriesler 1992: 233).

12.5 Transferability to the World-System Level

The theories mentioned above are applicable at the world-system level as well. When Marx, Keynes or Pasinetti wrote about the economy (market system, capitalist economy), they had the *national* economy in mind (except for Marx who had a more global view). Their theories are stated in abstract terms which can easily be applied to a market economy (capitalist economy) at the *world-system* level, since the concepts of aggregate supply, aggregate demand and of an aggregate gap or mismatch between the two are similar at both the national and world-system levels of analysis.

13. The Inadequacy of Global Demand

Parallel to Marx, Keynes, Samuelson, Pasinetti and others (who were theorizing for the *national* level), I believe that aggregate demand tends to be inadequate at the *global* level of analysis as well. "Inadequate global demand" has three discernible meanings, namely:

(1) *social meaning (social-existential)* -- certain classes of people do not have enough purchasing power in order to have an adequate standard of living (which is their inalienable human right, as per Article 25 of the Universal Declaration of Human Rights);
(2) *economic meaning (circulatory-systemic)* -- the market force of global demand is weaker than the market force of global supply, creating an aggregate gap in the circulatory system of the world economy ("inadequate global demand", Keynesian; (relative) "global overproduction", Marxist);
(3) *ecological meaning* -- the composition of global demand is inadequate with respect to ecological sustainability.

14. Global Unemployment Equilibrium

I agree with the well-known Keynesian and Marxist view that inadequacy of effective demand (Keynesian) or (relative) overproduction (Marxist) will lead to unemployment. This mechanism can also be found at the world-system level, except that at this level we are speaking of a *global* unemployment equilibrium (world-system unemployment equilibrium) (see also, Köhler 1999).

15. Global Full-Employment Equilibrium

15.1 Concept

A global full-employment equilibrium can be defined as a state of the world economy in which global aggregate supply and global aggregate demand have a configuration in which all available labour is fully employed. This is a normative concept at first, namely, a concept describing a state of the world economy which is desirable, rather than one which is empirically extant. We can elaborate this concept by combining elements from Prebisch's and Keynes's theories.

15.2 Intellectual Origins

(a) From Keynes, Kalecki, and some post-Keynesians we may want to use the ideas that (1) aggregate demand may be deficient so that the system may be stuck in an unemployment equilibrium; (2) the unemployment equilibrium may be caused by inadequate aggregate demand (consumption demand or (fixed-)investment demand or both); (3) inadequacy of consumption demand may be caused by (i) a polarized income distribution and weakness of labour as a class, (ii) inadequate business activity, leading to inadequate (fixed-)investment demand, and (iii) other factors (e.g., of a monetary nature); (4) inadequacy of (fixed-)investment demand may be induced or autonomous -- namely,

it may be caused by low entrepreneurial expections of demand growth or by other factors leading to a low entrepreneurial appetite for innovation and capital investment; (5) the price and availability of money (credit) may influence all of the above in various ways; (6) full employment will result if the above adverse factors and mechanisms are reversed.

(b) From Prebisch we may want to use the idea that improved terms of trade for Third World countries could, conceivably, lead to a global equilibrium at a higher level, generating a positive-sum outcome for both center and periphery countries. Prebisch writes:

> "For the first time in the history of capitalist development the periphery, passive hitherto, might exert a dynamic influence on the centers, provided new forms of cooperation were devised. An increase in exports of goods requiring less advanced technology than that of the centers and their exchange for more highly developed goods would mean that both parties could obtain well-recognized advantages with the consequent increases in productivity ... We have reached a stage in our relations with the centers ... in which great possibilities of convergent interests arise." (Prebisch 1988: 40-41). However, in order for these non-zero-sum gains to materialize, "(n)ew formulas must be found that allow for the progressive participation of manufactures from the periphery in the growth of consumption in the centers. This would minimize the disruptive effects of competition through lower prices, which are harmful both to the centers and to the periphery, since the latter transfers part of its productivity through a lowering of prices." (Prebisch 1986: 4). The new formulas must include improved terms of trade for the periphery -- namely: "It cannot be doubted that the periphery has an enormous potential demand for those manufactures produced by the centers ... Nevertheless, to make this potential effective, the peripheral countries need to have the means to pay for such purchases through their own exports of manufactures." (Prebisch 1986: 4).

Let's put the two streams of theory together (Keynes, Prebisch) in the context of world-systems theory of world income. The result of such an exercise may read somewhat like the following.

15.3 Global Aggregates and Center/Periphery Aggregates (Ex-post View)

15.3.1 Terminology

I will use the term "center" as a short expression for "industrialized", "advanced", "high-income" or "OECD countries" and the term "periphery" as a short expression for "less developed", "less industrialized", "low- and middle-income" or "non-OECD countries". Furthermore, I will use the following symbols:

Z = world income (aggregate)
Zc = aggregate income of the center
Zp = aggregate income of the periphery
GAS = global aggregate supply
ASc = aggregate supply generated by the center
ASp = aggregate supply generated by the periphery

GAD = global aggregate demand
ADc = aggregate demand generated by the center
ADp = aggregate demand generated by the periphery

(These symbols are in upper case letters in order to indicate that these are ex-post accounting magnitudes.)

15.3.2 Ex-post Relationships

With the use of these symbols we can state the following:

(a) The *global* aggregates are the sum of the *regional* aggregates; and the regional aggregates are *components* of the global aggregates. For example:

Z = Zc + Zp

in words, world income equals center income plus periphery income; and center income and periphery income are components of world income; and:

GAS = ASc + ASp

in words, global aggregate supply equals center aggregate supply plus periphery aggregate supply; and center supply and periphery supply are components of global aggregate supply; and:

GAD = ADc + ADp

in words, global aggregate demand equals center aggregate demand plus periphery aggregate demand; and so on.

(b) In ex-post (accounting) analysis, (actual) global aggregate supply and (actual) global aggregate demand are identical magnitudes, which are also identical to world income, namely:

(ex-post) GAS = (ex-post) GAD = Z [which is the same as global GDP]

(c) Since global aggregate supply and global aggregate demand are composed of center and periphery aggregates, world income is (in ex-post accounting) also identical to the sums of (ex-post) center and periphery supply and (ex-post) center and periphery demand, namely:

Z = ASc + ASp
= ADc + ADp

(d) *Compositional theorem*: When *global* aggregate supply and *global* aggregate demand are balanced (identical) in *ex-post* accounting, it does not matter (for the accountant) whether aggregate supply and aggregate demand are also balanced within each region (*within-center* or *within-periphery*).

Example:

Z = 10 (i.e., let world income have the arbitrary magnitude of 10 units)

Since Z = (ex-post) GAS = (ex-post) GAD, we have an accounting identity between world income, (actual) global aggregate supply and (actual) global aggregate demand, as follows:

Z = 10
GAS = 10
GAD = 10

Since the global aggregate supply (ex-post) is composed of the center and periphery aggregates (namely, GAS = ASc+ASp) and since global aggregate demand (ex-post) is composed of the center and periphery aggregates (namely, GAD = ADc+ADp), the above global totals of 10 (arbitrary) units could have been the result of various alternative center-periphery constellations, for example:

Alternative 1 (balanced within the regions):

GAS = 10 = 5 + 5 [i.e., center and periphery contribute 5 each to (actual) global aggregate supply]

and

GAD = 10 = 5 + 5 [i.e., center and periphery contribute 5 each to (actual) global aggregate demand] ;or,

Alternative 2 (unbalanced within the regions):

GAS = 10 = 6 + 4

and

GAD = 10 = 4 + 6

In this alternative, the center contributed 6 units of aggregate supply and 4 units of aggregate demand (in ex-post accounting) and the periphery contributed 4 units of aggregate supply and 6 units of aggregate demand (in ex-post accounting). The global aggregates are the same as in Alternative (1) (namely, equal to 10), whereas the regional aggregates of supply and demand are now unbalanced within the regions. A *global* balance of global aggregate supply and global aggregate demand may thus coexist with regional imbalances of supply and demand.

15.3.3 Global Situation With Inadequate Global Demand (Relative Global Overproduction)

In a world situation of inadequate global demand, we can write:

(potential) GAD < (potential) GAS

or, in words, the market force of global aggregate demand is weaker than the market force of global aggregate supply.

[This is the Keynesian way of stating the supply-demand gap].

In a world situation of relative overproduction, we can write:

(potential) GAS > (potential) GAD

or, in words, the production power of society is stronger than the consumption power of society. [This is the Marxist way of stating the supply-demand gap.] (Both the Keynesian and Marxist formulations amount to the same.) The question arises what happens to world income (Z) if global aggregate supply and global aggregate demand are in a disequilibrium of this kind. This leads to a dynamic analysis.

15.4 Dynamic View with Center/Periphery

15.4.1 Terminology

In addition to the symbols used in the previous section, I will use growth rates of the various aggregates, denoted in lower case letters, as in an earlier section, namely:

z = growth rate of world income
gas = growth rate of global aggregate supply
gad = growth rate of global aggregate demand
mg = growth rate of the global monetary aggregate

15.4.2 Dynamic Effects of the Aggregate Gap

According to the notion of a growth disequilibrium (growth dialectic) introduced earlier in this study, three market forces are mainly responsible for global income growth, namely, the market forces of global supply, global demand and global money. In dynamic (ex-ante) analysis, we postulate that these market forces may not be of equal strength and that the weakest of them determines overall global income growth, namely:

z = minimum of (gas, gad, mg)

As per Keynesian and Marxist presupposition, global aggregate demand tends to be weaker than global aggregate supply and global aggregate demand is the major constraining factor. Let us ignore the growth rate of the global monetary aggregate for the time being and focus the analysis on global demand. With this cavalier trick, we can reduce our statement, namely to:

z = function of (gad) [simplified global-Keynesian view]

or, in words, the growth of world income is a function of the growth of global aggregate demand. This represents a popular leftist viewpoint (and is, of course, extremely simplified). However, it is not unreasonable to entertain this as a working hypothesis in view of the fact that ruling opinion makes another extremely simplified assumption, namely that:

z = function of (gas) [simplified global neoliberal view]

or, in words, the growth of world income is a function of the growth of global aggregate supply. I will ignore this global neoliberal view at this juncture.

15.4.3 Dynamic Center-Periphery Interaction With Inadequate Global Demand

My further discussion will (1) continue with an example, followed (2) by a generalized statement.

Example:

(a) Let's say that:
Z1 = 10 [world income at time 1 = 10 units], and
z = 20% [the ex-post growth rate of world income is 20%], so that
Z2 = 12 [world income at time 2 = 12 units]

(b) The market forces of global aggregate supply and global aggregate demand are dynamically disequilibrated and global aggregate demand is the weaker market force. The growth rate of world income of 20% may have been the result of various configurations between the market forces of global aggregate supply and global aggregate demand. However, per assumption, global aggregate demand was the determining force. Therefore, in our example:

GAD1 = 10 [actual global aggregate demand at time 1 = 10 units], and
gad = 20% [actual growth rate of global aggregate demand = 20%], and
GAD2 = 12 [actual global aggregate demand at time 2 = 12 units]

On the other hand, the market force of global aggregate supply was, *per assumption*, greater than the demand force. We don't know how much greater, but let us assume that the global aggregate supply potential may have grown by 40% and actual global aggregate supply would have grown by that much if global aggregate demand had been sufficient. We can state therefore that:

GAS1 = 10 [actual global aggregate supply at time 1 = 10 units], and
gas (potential) = 40% [potential global aggregate supply growth rate = 40%] however,
GAS2 = 12 [actual global aggregate supply at time 2 = 12 units, because of the global demand constraint] therefore,
gas (actual) = 20% [actual global aggregate supply growth rate = 20%]

The global demand constraint had the effect that global income at time 2 is only Z2 = 12 and that *actual* global supply growth was only 20%, whereas *potential* global supply growth *could have been* 40%. Without the global demand constraint, world income at time 2 *could, conceivably*, have been Z2 = 14, since there was enough global supply potential to accomplish that. The imbalance at time 2 can be stated as:

GAS2(potential) = 14 [supply side]

This is greater than:

GAD2(potential) = 12 [demand side]

Therefore:

Z2 = 12 [market result, Z2 = GAD2, since z = minimum of (gas, gad, mg)

(in words, the resulting world income Z2 is equal to the lower figure because of the demand constraint)

Example continued:
(c) Let's introduce a center-periphery view. I will use two alternatives.

Alternative 1 (even split):
The supply and demand potentials may have been split *evenly* between center and periphery. In this case, the imbalance at time 2 could have been thus:

GAS2(potential) = 14 = 7 + 7 [center and periphery contribute 7 units each to the global *supply* potential]

GAD2(potential) = 12 = 6 + 6 [center and periphery contribute 6 units each to the global *demand* potential]

Alternative 2 (uneven split):

The supply and demand potential may have been split *unevenly* between center and periphery. In this case, the imbalance at time 2 could have been thus:

GAS2(potential) = 14 = 8 + 6 [center contributes 8 units and periphery contributes 6 units to global *supply* potential]

GAD2(potential) = 12 = 5 + 7 [center contributes 5 units and periphery contributes 7 units to global *demand* potential]

In both Alternatives (1) and (2) there is a global supply-demand gap (inadequate demand, Keynesian; relative overproduction, Marxist). Based on the theorem of composition (see above), it does not matter (for the ex-post accountant) whether the global aggregate gap originates evenly or unevenly within the center and the periphery.

(d) Keynesian and Prebischian Aspects of the Dynamic Disequilibrium

The *Keynesian* aspect of this disequilibrium is that global aggregate demand in this example is inadequate (GAD < GAS) and that world income growth is constrained by this inadequacy of global demand. The amount of potential world income lost due to this dynamic is 12 - 14 = -2 units.

The *Prebischian* aspect of the disequilibrium is that a global center-periphery trade-off is thinkable. Prebisch has expressed this idea with reference to the center-periphery *terms of trade* -- namely, that, in his opinion, improvement of the terms of trade for the periphery could, under certain circumstances, lead to gains for both the center and the periphery (win-win situation; positive-sum situation, in terms of game theory). Prebisch's formulation is stating a specific case (related to terms of trade); however, the same idea can be generalized and expressed in terms of aggregate demand -- namely, if aggregate demand of the periphery could be increased (via terms of trade *or in other ways*), then the entire world-system, *including the center*, could be better off, in the sense of a positive-sum outcome. In my example above, this concept can be demonstrated, as follows (I am using the hypothetical figures from Alternative 2):

Step 1: The global imbalance is:

Z2(actual) - Z2(potential) = 12 - 14 = -2

in words, the difference between actual and potential world income at time 2 is two units.

This is the result of the following constellation of global market forces:

GAS2(potential) = 14 = 8 + 6 [center contributes 8 units and periphery contributes 6 units to global aggregate supply potential], and

GAD2(potential) = 12 = 5 + 7 [center contributes 5 units and periphery contributes 7 units to global aggregate demand potential]

Step 2: Augment periphery demand in a Keynes-Prebisch fashion:

Let us add 2 units of periphery demand (how to do that in practice is a different matter), leading to:

GAD2(potential) = 12 + 2 = 5 + (7 + 2)
= 14 = 5 + 9

Periphery demand is now 9 (up by 2 from the previous 7). As a result, *global* aggregate demand is now 14 (up by 2 from the previous 12). Since global supply potential in this example is GAS2 (potential) = 14, we now have a global supply-demand equilibrium at a higher level, which leads to higher world income, namely:

GAS2 (potential) = 14

GAD2 (potential) = 14 (this is up from 12)

This is a new equilibrium, therefore:

GAS2 (actual) = 14

GAD2 (actual) = 14

therefore:

Z2 (actual)(new and improved) = 14

The world-system is now in a Keynes-Prebisch full-employment equilibrium. The fact that *center* aggregate supply may not match center aggregate demand and that *periphery* aggregate supply may not match periphery aggregate demand is inconsequential (as per theorem of composition) for the fact that *global* aggregate supply and global aggregate demand balance at a higher level (Z2 = 14) than before (Z2 = 12).

(e) General Statement of the Global Keynes-Prebisch Equilibrium

The above examples can be restated in general terms. The dynamic global growth equilibrium (disequilibrium) is, as stated earlier: z = minimum of (gas, gad, mg) -- in words, the *actual* growth rate of global income is equal to the minimum of either *potential* global supply growth or *potential* global demand growth or *potential* global monetary growth. Let's ignore the global monetary aggregate for the time being. The global disequilibrium (growth dialectic) can be restated in center-periphery terms, namely:

Step 1: global growth disequilibrium (growth dialectic) *with center, periphery*:

z = minimum of [potential growth rate of (ASc+ASp), or potential growth rate of (ADc+ADp)]

where: potential growth rate of (ADc+ADp) < potential growth rate of (ASc+ASp) [this is the demand constraint]

***Step 2*:** global Keynes-Prebisch growth equilibrium:

If, in this situation, peripheral demand is augmented, leading to increased peripheral demand (ADp'= ADp + x), this will lead to a higher equilibrium growth rate of world income (z'), since now:

z' = minimum of [potential growth rate of (ASc+ASp), or potential growth rate of (ADc+ADp + x)]

where: (ADc+ADp+x) > (ADc+ADp) or, in words, x is a positive number

Since periphery demand has been increased, *unused* global supply potential is activated and real global income increases. As per the "compositional theorem" above, it does not matter whether supply and demand balance within each region (within-center, within-periphery). Increased periphery demand can be satisfied by either (1) increased (actual) *periphery* supply *or* (2) by increased (actual) *center* supply or (3) *both*. In other words, increased periphery demand can be beneficial for both the center and the periphery, as postulated by Prebisch.

(f) Summary of the Global Keynes-Prebisch Growth Equilibrium (in words)

The global Keynes-Prebisch equilibrium is a theoretically attainable global equilibrium between global aggregate supply and global aggregate demand in situations where global aggregate demand is inadequate relative to global aggregate supply. An increase in periphery demand will have the effect of increasing total global aggregate demand and, thereby, actualizing unused global supply potential. This leads to a global supply-demand equilibrium above the global equilibrium level before the increase in peripheral demand. The global Keynes-Prebisch equilibrium can be brought about through an improvement of the terms of trade for the periphery (as originally proposed by Prebisch) *or by other global-Keynesian methods of demand-building*. Other strategies from a global-Keynesian tool kit are, for example, (a) reducing the debt burden of the periphery, (b) issuing global (transnational) credit for the periphery, (c) global exchange rate reform, and others.

15.4.4 Ecological Aspects of the Global Keynes-Prebisch Equilibrium

The increase of global demand and output, as envisaged in connection with a global Keynes-Prebisch equilibrium, may alarm the ecologically aware. Is this not a recipe for unfettered industrial expansion of the world economy with disastrous consequences for the ecosystem and its sustainability? This criticism is legitimate and must be addressed. I do not have a satisfactory answer for this problem, but acknowledge its urgency. I would like to point out, however, that support for a global Keynes-Prebisch equilibrium leads one to support public intervention in the economy (of the world and/or the nation). This opens up possibilities for public stewardship which is ecologically aware. For example, added global demand can be additional *sustainable* demand (e.g., food, housing, social, health and education services). Public intervention can also be used to replace existing unsustainable demand streams by sustainable demand streams. Furthermore, to the extent that this approach leads to public support for fixed investment (capital expenditures) of some kind, this could be capital expenditure for technologies which are themselves sustainable and/or produce sustainable goods and services (e.g., energy production other than fossil and nuclear-based). Furthermore, the analytic device of the global Keynes-Prebisch equilibrium can, perhaps, also be used to find acceptable compromises between Northern ecological concerns, to the extent that they exist, and Southern material interest in more economic growth. These issues are too complex to permit a comprehensive treatment in this study.

16. Employment and Global Keynes-Prebisch Equilibrium

A global Keynes-Prebisch equilibrium will increase world income, as I have tried to show above; but will it also increase global employment and will it create global *full*-employment?

16.1 Trade-off Between Employment and Productivity

One way of examining the problem is in terms of a trade-off between employment and productivity. Let us use the following symbols:

Z	= world income
Ng	= global employment (volume)
Z/Ng	= average global labour productivity
z	= growth rate of world income
ng	= growth rate of global employment
q	= growth rate of average global labour productivity

Using these, we can write two statistical identities, as follows:

$$Z = Ng * (Z/Ng)$$

in words, world income equals global employment times average global labour productivity; and:

$$z = ng + q$$

in words, the growth rate of world income equals the growth rate of global employment plus the growth rate of average global labour productivity.

These identities reveal a trade-off situation. For example, a growth of world income of +3% could be the result of global employment growth of +3% with constant productivity (i.e., no productivity growth; namely: z = ng + q = +3 + 0). Alternatively, the same world income growth could come about through "jobless growth", where employment growth equals zero and productivity growth equals +3% (namely: z = ng + q = 0 + 3). Intermediate constellations are also possible -- for example, +2% employment growth with +1% productivity growth.

If we went along with Keynes's *General Theory*, we would hold technology and productivity constant. That means, when applied to our context, we would assume that Z/Ng = constant and that productivity growth (q) equals zero. Applied to the above identities, Keynes's approach would lead to a simplification, namely: Z = Ng * (a constant), and: z = ng + 0 = ng . Using this approach we would reach the conclusion that each increment in world income is accompanied by a proportional increment in world employment. We know for a fact, however, that productivity does not stand still.

An examination of some statistical data shows the following (Table 1):

Table 1 -- World-Level Growth Rates, 1980-1990

(a) growth rate of world income	z = 3.07 % per annum
(b) growth rate of world labour force	ng = 2.22 % per annum
(c) growth rate of average world labour force productivity	q = 0.84 % per annum

Source: Table 2 . *Note*: the income and productivity figures are based on constant 1987 U.S. dollar values

Table 1 shows that, between 1980 and 1990, world income grew by about 3% per year; the world labour force by about 2%; and average global labour force productivity by slightly less than one percent. This, admittedly limited, evidence suggests that the world economy seems to have generated employment growth at a rate higher than that of productivity growth. This suggests further that a global Keynes-Prebisch equilibrium might also lead to increased employment, not only to increased income.

On the critical side, we must be cautious about the above trends because they show data pertaining to the "labour force", which is not the same as "employment". "Labour force" includes the "unemployed" and "underemployed". The figures upon which Table 1 is based are shown in Table 2:

Table 2 -- Global Aggregates 1980, 1990

	1980	1990	
(a) world income (Z)	13,198	17,860	US dollars, billions (1987 = 100)
(b) world labour force (Ng)	2,037	2,536	million persons
(c) average global labour force productivity (Z/Ng) (c = a: b)	6,479	7,043	US dollars per person (1987 = 100)

Sources: (1) for labour force: World Bank. *World Development Report 1992* (p. 218-219) and *1997* (p. 220-221); (2) for world income: my calculation based on world population (same sources as for labour force) and gross national income per capita in constant U.S. dollars (1987=100) from World Bank. *World Tables 1995*, p. 8-9.

As a first correction for the difference between "labour force" and "employment", we may want to remove registered "unemployment". This figure is available for high-income countries and was 35 million persons in 1993 (UNDP 1997: 210). When we remove 35 million from Table 2 figures, we are changing 2,037 to 2,002 and 2,536 to 2,501. This does not change the overall trends in Table 1 significantly. A more difficult statistical problem is "underemployment", particularly, in the low- and middle-income countries. According to some estimates, about one third of the world's labour force (and their families) are destitute. The "world labour force" includes these underemployed/destitute persons. But the above trend figures (in Table 1) do not reveal whether their proportion has remained the same or changed during the decade of 1980-1990.

16.2 The Problem of "Full Employment"

A global Keynes-Prebisch equilibrium will not only lead to higher world income, but can also be expected to generate more world employment. Can we, consequently, claim that a global Keynes-Prebisch equilibrium is a "global full-employment equilibrium"?

16.2.1 Concept of Global Full Employment

Global full employment is a difficult concept. As a preliminary statement, we can define global full employment as a state of the world in which all persons who are capable of work and want to have employment are fully employed. Various questions can be raised about this concept of full employment, including the following:

a. Are there any *age* limits? How about child labour? How about old people?
b. How do we define "*capable* of work"? This seems to exclude the sick and disabled, but it is also possible that the sick and disabled are partially or fully employable.
c. How do we handle the difference between "*work*" and "*employment*"? There are various categories of persons who desire work, but not necessarily employment in the sense of factory employment or office employment -- for example, farmers

and business people who are their own bosses, so-to-speak, and do not wish to be other people's employees.

d. What is "*fully* employed"? Does this mean being employed for 16 hours a day, or 8 hours, or 4 hours per day? How does one treat, in the employment statistics, categories of working people like destitute slum dwellers, starving farm families, other "underemployed", "part-time employed", "seasonally employed", small businesses of one person who may have no work for periods of time, unpaid members of the family who work, and so on?
e. The concept of full employment implies some notion of *income*. Prisoners may be fully employed but do not receive a "full income" in the normal sense of the word. People may be working very hard but may hardly be able to survive. What amount of income received from employment is consistent with the notion of full employment?
f. How is *quality of work* related to "full employment"? Quality of work has many aspects, including working hours, working conditions, health and safety aspects, social security aspects, and other.

These problems are also important at the world-system level and are even more difficult at that level than at the national level because of societal and cultural differences between countries. In particular, wage levels differ so drastically around the globe that the definition of a "bad", "adequate", or "good" job in terms of income and job quality differs widely.

16.2.2 Definition of Global Full Employment in Terms of the Human Rights Code

One way of defining global full employment is in terms of the human rights code. Article 25 of the Universal Declaration of Human Rights states that "everybody has a right to an adequate standard of living for himself and his family...". With the help of this declaration, global full employment can, perhaps, be defined as a state of the world in which all persons who are capable of work and want to have income-generating work (in the form of employment by an employer or work without an employer; receiving money income or income "in kind", as on a farm) do, in fact, have income-generating work of acceptable quality (e.g., limited to eight hours per day) which provides an adequate standard of living for the working person and his or her family. (See also, other human rights provisions concerning work, leisure time, and social security.)

This definition is flexible in three ways -- namely, (1) it includes both work in an employer-employee relationship and self-directed work like farmers, small business owners, or independent professionals; (2) it includes remuneration "in cash or in kind" -- namely, in the form of either money or goods and services (the latter being important for farm populations); and (3) it provides flexibility with respect to the definition of "adequacy" of income from work between one country and another. For example, in 1999 an hourly wage of U.S. $ 4.00 is a low wage in USA but a high wage in many other countries. I will use the above definition of global full employment in terms of the human rights code as my guide in the subsequent discussion.

16.2.3 A Look at the Global Employment Situation

From an employment perspective, the world population can be subdivided, as follows:

(1) *not in the labour force* (i.e., not capable of work or not required to work like the sick, children, old people)
(2) *in the labour force*
(2a) in the labour force, working and *with* adequate income received from work ("adequately employed");
(2b) in the labour force, working but with *in*adequate income received from work ("underemployed");
(2c) in the labour force, but *without* income-generating work ("unemployed").

A statistical picture of the world labour situation, using some reported figures and some of my own estimates, may look somewhat like the following (Table 3):

Table 3 -- World Employment Situation, 1995

	High- Income Countries millions		Low- and Middle-income Countries millions	
1. population	902		4771	
2. labour force	432	100%	2263	100%
2a. adequately employed		84%?		60%?
2b. underemployed		8%?		35%?
2c. unemployed	35	8%		5%?

Sources: (a) World Bank. *World Development Report 1997*, p. 221 (for numbers without question marks).
(b) Numbers with question marks are author's estimates.

16.2.4 The Global Employment Gap (Estimate)

When we think of an "adequate job" as a "unit of employment", then an adequately employed person has *one* "unit of employment"; an "unemployed" person has *zero* units of employment. For the "underemployed", it is clear that they do not have an adequate job and, thus, do not have a full "unit of employment", but only a partial one, which may be anywhere between 0.0 and 1.0 "unit of employment". I will use this reasoning in order to estimate the size of the global employment gap -- namely, the number of units of employment missing in the world. "Unit of employment", as used in this exercise, can be interpreted as "adequate full-time job *or equivalent*". Thus, when two persons have half a job each, they *together* have the *equivalent* of one full unit of employment. Using the figures and estimates of Table 3, we can estimate a global employment gap for 1995, as follows (Table 4).

The estimates of the global employment gap shown in Table 4 are very rough but give an indication of the order of magnitude of the global unemployment problem --

namely, equivalent to 27% of the global labour force. During the great depression of the 1930s, the industrialized countries had unemployment rates of similar magnitude.

16.2.5 Political Barriers to Global Full Employment

The most powerful obstacles to global full employment are of a political nature. Here one can blame the ordinary people of the world just as much as the corporations and the elites. Workers who have a good job are most unwilling to share such a source of income and social security with others. Workers in rich countries are unwilling to share their standard of living with workers in less fortunate countries. Worker solidarity is an ideal talked about by some, rather than a reality. Politicians thus have little room for manouevre if they try to advance the cause of global full employment. In addition, the presently ruling elites of the world are not committed to global full employment to begin with.

Table 4 -- Global Employment Gap, 1995 (Estimate)

1. High-income countries				
	share	weight	base	**missing units of employment**
(a) fully employed	84%*	0.0*	432 mln	**= 0 millions**
(b) underemployed	8%*	0.5*	432	**= 17 mln**
(c) unemployed	8%*	1.0*	432	**= 35 mln**
2. Low- and middle- income countries				
(a) fully employed	60%*	0.0*	2263 mln	**= 0 mln**
(b) underemployed	35%*	0.7*	2263	**=554 mln**
(c) unemployed	5%*	1.0*	2263	**= 113 mln**
3. World Employment Gap (sums of items 1a to 2c)				**719 millions** (missing units of employment)
4. World Labour Force (432+2263=)				**2695 millions** (persons available for work)
5. World Employment Gap as percent of global labour force (line 5 = line 3: line 4)				**27 %**

Notes: (a) "share" and "base" and labour force data from Table 3; (b) "weight": my estimates, assuming that in high-wage countries the average "underemployed" person has one half of a full job; and that in low- and middle income countries the average "underemployed" person has three tenths of an adequate job, so that 0.7 of a "unit of work" is missing. The reader may want to recalculate the estimates with different assumptions.

A theoretically possible approach to global full employment would be via radical redistribution of available work around the world. With a world income of 28 trillion U.S. dollars (1995) and a world population of 6 billion persons, such a radical redistribution of work and income would leave every person with (28,000 billion U.S. dollars, divided by 6 billion people =) US $4,666 per capita per year, for every man, woman and child on earth. This shows how relatively rich the world really is. Of course, Swiss, Japanese, Canadian, and other rich-country workers would not want to go down from their present levels of income to US $4,666. There is also no worker solidarity to speak of *within* countries. Thus, employed workers in OECD countries would not want to work 10% less (and have 10% less income) so that the unemployed 10% of their fellow-countrymen could have a job.

Ironically, neoliberal labour market policies, as practiced in the United States, and *global* neoliberal policies have the effect of spreading availabale work more thinly among workers -- more part-time work, instead of straight unemployment, in the United States and, globally, redeployment of the jobs available from global corporations from high-wage countries to low-wage countries. Labour and labour unions in rich countries do not like these trends. Global full employment through radical redistribution of *available* work is thus not overly popular. The approach preferred by labour is rather another one, namely, national full employment and *global* full employment through economic growth which benefits the unemployed and underemployed, or, using an old formula, "economic growth with redistribution" (nationally and globally), so that the economically destitute, unemployed and underemployed members of the labour force are moved up without bringing the economically well-off members of the labour force down on the income scale. This is a major political constraint for the theory and praxis of global full employment.

16.2.6 Summary Regarding Global Full Employment

The question was posed above whether the global Keynes-Prebisch equilibrium can be called a genuine global full-employment equilibrium, taking into consideration that the pursuit of this equilibrium will lead to an increase in world income and world employment. My answer is "maybe" and "that depends" -- namely, whether or not genuine global full employment will be achieved, that depends on such variables as (a) the magnitude of global demand mobilized, (b) the duration of such efforts, and other factors.

17. Defects of Global Demand (Leakages and Losses)

17.1 Typology

Inadequacy of global aggregate demand may be due to a variety of defects which may be of two general types -- namely, (a) *structural* defects, and (b) *circulatory* defects. Circulatory defects are also known as "leakages" in Keynesian parlance; i.e., effective demand "leaks" from the circulatory flow of the economy. Both aspects may also be found together. Another typology is in terms of (a) short-term defects and (b) long-term defects. Here are a number of defects of global demand, out of a larger list, which I would like to comment on.

17.2 Recent Examples

Some recent examples of global demand defects are mentioned in the following passage: "...now as in the 1930s, it may be impolitic to ascribe the present crisis to a lack of effective demand relative to aggregate world supply capacity. Yet the fact remains that "over investment", "excess capacity" and "overproduction" are all relative to the level of effective demand. It is not rocket science to see that predatory capitalists were the chief beneficiaries of the Third World Debt bonanza of the 1970's, the U.S. S&L craze of the 1980s, and the Asia-Russia-Latin America credit bubble of the 1990s, while the clean-up costs in terms of bank "recapitalization" etc. have been shouldered by the average would-be consumer. Nor is it rocket science to see how this must deflate effective demand." (Tomasson and Daastol, 1998)

17.3 Global Wage Differential

A major structural defect of global demand results from the global wage differential. Having a low wage means having low purchasing power. Countries with comparatively low wages contribute comparatively small amounts of purchasing power (effective demand) to the world market.

An important theoretical question is whether the global wage differential is "natural" in some sense or "politically constructed" ("man-made"). Many people believe that the poor earn what they deserve (namely, little). At a more theoretical level, many economists, including many leftists, believe that wage differences between high-wage and low-wage countries reflect productivity differences and are natural in that sense. This point of view is questionable -- see, below on exchange rates and productivity.

17.4 Exchange Rate Differential (Undervaluation)

The majority of the world's people live in non-OECD countries like Brazil, China, India, Nigeria, Russia and so on. An important fact is emerging from the World Bank's data on purchasing power parities of currencies (PPP values). From these data it is apparent that the majority of the world's people live in countries whose currencies are under-valued. Tourists and traders know this exchange rate differential as "hard currencies" versus "soft currencies" -- e.g., U.S. dollar / Mexican peso; Swiss franc / Russian ruble; Japanese yen / Chinese yuan; and so on. The true purchasing power value (PPP value) of a currency can be measured and this reveals two facts -- namely: (a) within the "center" (OECD countries), exchange rates are, for the most part, relatively close to PPP rates; but (2) the exchange rates of the periphery countries tend to be significantly lower than their PPP rates. For example, in 1995 the undervaluation of periphery currencies (deviation from purchasing power parity) was, as follows: for low-income countries, undervaluation by a factor of 4.0 (on average); for middle-income countries, undervaluation by a factor of 2.4 (on average). The maximum distortion was recorded for Mozambique, which had an undervaluation of its currency by a factor of 10.1 (see, Penn World Tables; also, Köhler 1998: 151, Table 2). This exchange rate differential has profound implications for the low- and middle-income countries. See, on productivity and trade below.

17.5 Undervaluation of Productivity of the Low- and Middle-income Countries

The exchange rate differential between periphery and center of the world economy has the effect that productivity levels between periphery and center are measured incorrectly. Here is an example (USA, China) (Table 5):

Table 5 -- Productivity Differential (Nominal), USA and China, 1995

	USA	China
1. GNP (national currency)(a)		3,413 billion yuan
2. Labour force (b)	133	709 million persons
3. GNP at nominal exchange rate (c)	7,098	744 billion US $
4. Labour productivity(at actual exchange rate) (line 4 = line 3: line 2)	53,372	1,050 US $ per worker
5. Productivity ratio (nominal)	51: 1	

Sources: World Bank. *World Development Report 1997*: 214-215, Table 1; 220-221, Table 4, except note (a).

Notes (a): This is for 1993, from World Bank. *World Tables 1994*: 211); (b) this is "total labor force" in the source; (c) calculated from GNP per capita and population in the source

Table 5 shows the productivity differential between USA and China as being approximately 51: 1. This productivity differential is false (measured incorrectly). The mis-measurement is a consequence of the undervalued exchange rate. When we correct the measurement error, the corrected result is, as shown in Table 6.

Table 6-- Productivity Differential (Real), USA and China, 1995

	USA	China
1. GNP (national currency)(a)		3,413 billion yuan
2. Labour force (b)	133	709 million persons
3. GNP at PPP rate (c)	7,098	3,505 billion PPP $
4. Labour productivity (at PPP rate (line 4 = line 3: line 2))	53,372	4,943 PPP $ per worker
5. Productivity ratio (real)	11: 1	

Sources: World Bank. *World Development Report 1997*: 214-215, Table 1; 220-221, Table 4, except note (a).

Notes (a): This is for 1993, from World Bank. *World Tables 1994*: 211); (b) this is "total labor force" in the source; (c) calculated from GNP per capita (in PPP values) and population in the source

Table 6 shows that the real productivity differential between USA and China (using PPP rates) is 11: 1 (and not 51: 1 as incorrectly stated in Table 5). This is an example for one non-OECD country. The majority of the world's countries and people have undervalued currencies. Because of that, their real productivity is understated in the usual statistics based on actual exchange rates. The countries and people of the periphery (non-OECD countries) are much more productive in real terms than is shown by the standard statistics.

17.6 Undervaluation of Trading Demand of the Periphery

The undervaluation of non-OECD exchange rates has an additional valuation effect which is important for global aggregate demand -- namely, the effective trading demand of the periphery is distorted and undervalued. If the periphery was de-linked from the world market, this valuation effect could be ignored. However, the periphery is integrated into the global economy. For example, in 1995 the OECD countries (center) imported, from the non-OECD countries (periphery), goods and services in the amount of 940 billion U.S. dollars (at prevailing exchange rates). We saw that the exchange rates of the periphery are undervalued. The undervaluation factor implied in this trade flow is 2.86. If valued at PPP rates (purchasing power parity rates) the same imports to OECD (i.e., exports from non-OECD) would have been 940 * 2.86 = 2692 billion = 2.7 trillion dollars at PPP rates. Due to exchange rate undervaluation, the world economy lost 2692 - 940 = 1752 billion = 1.75 trillion dollars of global aggregate demand by virtue of the fact that the periphery could not spend dollars which it had not received, but should have received if the terms of trade had been fair; in other words, if there had been no "unequal exchange". This structural demand defect amounts to a loss of 6.6 % of global aggregate demand for a single year (1995). (See, Köhler 1998, Appendix, Table A-1 for detailed calculations.)

17.7 Globalization of Production

Global corporations are redeploying production from high-wage countries to low-wage countries. This has several effects -- namely: (a) low-wage countries gain jobs from global corporations, but may also lose traditional local jobs to the global competition. High-wage countries may lose jobs (or do not gain the newly created jobs) of global corporations. (b) *Global* aggregate demand is weakened (or grows relatively less vigorously) because jobs created for low-wage workers generate less *global* demand than jobs created for high-income workers. (However, these jobs generate more *local* demand and income in the low-wage country.) Globalization of production thus weakens the *global* demand side.

17.8 Defective Circulation of Global Money

There are various "leakages" (old Keynesian vocabulary) in the circulatory system of the world economy. "Leakages" are flows of money from the real side (physical side of goods and services) to the nominal side (financial side) of the economy. In other words, globally available money may be spent on goods and services -- i.e., become effective demand, or else, it may *not* be spent on goods and services -- i.e., become a *leakage* from effective demand. Leakages from effective global demand include:

(a) money hidden under the bed or in the chicken pen
(b) bank balances accumulating in domestic or foreign bank accounts (e.g., Swiss bank accounts for the world's dictators and lesser global investors)
(c) taxes collected by governments and not recycled into the economy through public spending but used to pay off public debts or to enrich certain politicians
(d) financial investments, instead of productive investment (capital expenditure)
(e) other

According to a recent estimate, the amount of money deposited in the world's private banks (category (b) above) amounted to US $10 trillion in 1997 (Gwynne 1998: 24). When other categories of leakages are added, the proportion of global leakages to global effective demand is enormous.

17.9 Ecological Defects of Global Demand

Ecological defects of global demand are both qualitative and quantitative in nature. Both the content of demand and the quantities of various components of demand matter with respect to ecological sustainability. Global demand may be demand for ecologically sound (sustainable) goods and services like bread, housing, health care and education, or ecologically unsound (not sustainable) goods and services like nuclear energy and nuclear war. Many categories of demand are ambivalent insofar as their sustainability rating depends on how the demand is satisfied. Thus, demand for fish may lead to overfishing of the seas. However, fish may also be grown in aquacultures. Quantities matter as well for a sustainability rating of demand. Thus, when one thousand people in the world want to own and operate automobiles, that is relatively sustainable. If, on the other hand, one billion people use automobiles, that is relatively unsustainable.

A related political-moral issue is: Who is more responsible for safeguarding the ecosystem -- the center or the periphery, the North or the South of the world? Another problem is the desirability of economic growth. Should the growth of world income be halted for ecological reasons? The answer depends on how we define "economic growth". Daly, for example, defines "growth" as ecologically damaging or wasteful "throughput" resulting from industrialization, Keynesianism, etc., and wants this to be halted. On the other hand, he concedes that "development" is desirable (Daly 1996). I prefer a terminology which distinguishes between (ecologically) "good growth" and (ecologically) "bad growth" (as, e.g., used by Douthwaite 1998). If growth is defined this way, then it makes sense to argue that bad growth must be halted, reversed and phased out and that good growth must be strenghtened. This implies a change in the content of global demand.

17.10 Political Defects of Global Demand

For regular, apolitical economists this is a non-issue. However, for political economists this is an issue of the highest importance. Global demand is defective (socially, economically, ecologically), partly or largely, because:

(a) the political and social institutions of the world-system support and create such defects;
(b) the ruling ideology supports and creates such defects; and
(c) the elites managing the world system support and create such defects of global demand through various deliberate policies of deregulation, neoliberal globalization, and so on.

One critic of global neoliberalism described the "essence of neoliberalism" as a "utopia of endless exploitation" (Bourdieu 1998).

18. Global Demand-Building Measures (Injections and Interventions)

Inadequacy of global demand is reversible. Available global demand-building measures are of two broad types -- (a) global anti-structural measures -- for example, improving the terms of trade for the low- and middle-income countries, as advocated by Prebisch; or commodity price stabilization schemes, or other; and (b) global "injections" (old Keynesian vocabulary) of purchasing power -- for example, increasing SDRs and global credit; cancelling debts of certain categories of countries; or other. There is a rich literature of such proposals.

Global demand-building requires public intervention. We have already global public intervention -- namely, on behalf of the interests of global business and global investors (global capital). But we need another kind of intervention in the global economy -- namely, pro-economic human rights; pro-periphery; pro-labour; pro-ecology. This political demand arises from Article 25 of the Universal Declaration of Human Rights.

19. Practical Conclusion

My theory suggests that billions, if not trillions, of dollars can be added to world income and millions, if not hundreds of millions, of jobs can be added to world employment through public intervention in the world market. The global wage differential can be significantly reduced through a reformation of the world-economy. Everyone has an inalienable right to an adequate standard of living. Economic reason and political legitimacy are thus on the side of the citizens of the world and their *hopes* for "life, liberty and the pursuit of happiness" (in the words of the American constitution); and their *striving* "to the sun, to freedom" (from the song of the Socialist International); and their *right* to an adequate standard of living (pursuant to Article 25 of the Universal Declaration of Human Rights).

Chapter 2

THE STRUCTURE OF GLOBAL MONEY

This chapter takes a global view of money. The term "global money" is appearing in recent discussions (Bellofiore 1997) and there is the occasional literature reference to "world money" (Marx 1992: 190). My thesis in this article is that money has a global structure. Stated more precisely, I am contending that (1) the value of money is non-homogeneous throughout the world system (even after exchange rates have been taken into account); that (2) the currencies of low-income countries tend to be undervalued, not overvalued as many economists claim; that (3) the exchange rate system is one of the mechanisms by which high-wage countries extract value from low-wage countries; and that (4) this situation contributes significantly to unequal exchange between periphery and center countries.

These theoretical considerations lead to a new method for quantifying unequal exchange. The Appendix of this study includes World Tables of Unequal Exchange for the year 1995 for 119 countries which are based on the theory and method developed in this article.

1. MONEY AS VALUE AND THE VALUE OF MONEY

It is common knowledge that: (1) money is a measure of value; and (2) money itself has a value. To elaborate the first point: When we buy goods or services, we pay with money (except in barter situations). For example, one pound of bananas is worth x dollars or y rupees in a specific place at a specific time. Or, the entire physical output of a country's goods and services of a year is measured, not in pounds, tons or number of pieces, but in terms of a single money figure (GDP). In these situations we use money as a measure of value.

To elaborate the second point: We know that money, our measure of value, does not have a constant value. The value of money may change over time ("inflation") or across space, from one currency zone to another ("exchange rate"). The value of money varies diachronically (longitudinally, over time) and synchronically (cross-nationally, from country to country). Of course, both aspects may be combined.

2. Longitudinal Valuation of Money

Longitudinal valuation of money is a well-known exercise. The measurement of inflation is in the public eye virtually all the time as, for example, when the media report the latest inflation rates. These inflation rates are based on scientifically established methods of inflation measurement. Typically, economists define a "basket of goods and services", measure its price at different points in time and calculate inflation rates from that. While there are disagreements about the finer points of inflation measurement, the longitudinal valuation of money (inflation measurement) is a well-established practice.

3. Cross-National Valuation of Money

In contrast, the cross-national valuation of money is, partly, well-known and, partly, more obscure. In order to determine the relative value of one currency in comparison with another, two conflicting concepts and measurement procedures exist, namely:

1. *currency exchange rates* between two countries (i.e., the rates at which units of one currency are exchanged for units of another currency; e.g., how many dollars do I get for 100 rupees; how many rupees do I get for 100 dollars? etc.); and
2. *purchasing power parity rates* (PPP rates) between two countries (i.e., the ratio of the purchasing power of money in countries A and B; e.g., how much money do I need in order to buy a pair of shoes in country A; and how much money do I need in order to buy an equivalent pair of shoes in country B?).

The two concepts differ significantly, even though they seem to be similar on the surface. The numbers which one obtains from either method are highly divergent in many situations.

My thesis concerning the global structure of money arises from the difference between these two methods of cross-national valuation of money -- namely, exchange rate versus purchasing power parity rate (PPP rate).

4. Examples

Here are some figures which exemplify the difference which I am talking about (Table 1):

Table 1 – Two Valuations of GNP Per Capita (GNP/Capita, 1992)

COUNTRY	METHOD 1: actual exchange rates US dollars	METHOD 2: PPP rates (purchasing power parity rates) "international dollars"	COMPARISON
Japan	28 190	20 160	col. 1 > col. 2
USA	23 120	23 240	similar values
Germany	23 030	20 610	similar values
UK	17 790	16 730	similar values
Australia	17 260	17 350	similar values
		PPP rate is greater by a factor of:	
Brazil	2 770	5 250	(factor 1.9)
Russia	2 510	6 220	(factor 2.5)
China	470	1 910	(factor 4.1)
India	310	1 210	(factor 3.9)
Bhutan	62	630	(factor 10.2)
Mozambique	60	570	(factor 9.5)

Source: World Bank. *World Development Report 1994*, p. 162, p. 220

As the examples in Table 1 show, the value of one country's money in relation to another country's money can be calculated with two different methods and expressed in two different rates -- exchange rates and PPP rates. For example, the actual exchange rate between Indian rupees and U.S. dollars "shows" that Indian GNP per capita was 310 dollars in 1992. In contrast, scientific measurement of purchasing power parity (PPP) "shows" that Indian GNP per capita was 1210 dollars, i.e. four times as much as shown in terms of exchange rates. In contrast, OECD countries like USA, Germany, UK and Australia have exchange rates to the U.S. dollar which are very similar to the relative purchasing power rates of the currencies.

Which of the two rates (exchange rate versus PPP rate) is the correct one? When we ask the question: "What is the value of rupees in relation to the value of U.S. dollars?", we obtain two sharply different answers (e.g., "310" and "1210" for GNP per capita in the above). That constitutes a puzzle -- not for practitioners, because they use exchange rates, but for scientists. It can be observed that exchange rates are real, in the sense that they are being used by money traders and traders of goods and services. The PPP rate, on the other hand, is scientifically arrived at. Does that mean that PPP rates are not real? Such a conclusion would be untenable. On the contrary, PPP rates are real as well -- they are based on carefully established methods of measurement.

The situation is one of a dual standard or a double standard -- namely, we have two standards for evaluating the same object. The object to be evaluated is the relationship between money A and money B (the evaluandum) and the two conflicting standards are exchange rate (standard 1) and PPP rate (standard 2). In order to deal with this discrepancy in a comprehensive manner, we require some theory.

5. Types of Theory Required

In order to address the problem as outlined, we require four broad types of theory, namely:

1. measurement theory -- what is it that we are measuring?
2. empirical theory and historical explanation -- how can we explain what we see? What causes it? How did it come about?
3. theory of value -- how can we evaluate what we see? Which standard is the correct one or the best?
4. theory of policy (praxis) -- what should be done, if anything?

In this study I will not attempt a comprehensive treatment of these issues. Instead, I will focus on two contentions, namely: (1) the discrepancies between the two measurement methods are systematic (non-random) and correlate with the global center-periphery structure (empirical claim); and (2) this situation constitutes a form of exploitation (normative claim).

6. How PPP Rates are Calculated

The measurement of PPP exchange rate (purchasing power parity rates) has some similarity with inflation measurement. The method consists of the following: (a) a "basket of goods and services" is defined (as in inflation measurement); (b) prices for this "basket" are collected in the countries around the world -- e.g., in country 1 in rubles, in country 2 in rupees, in country 3 in yuan, etc.; (c) the prices for the "basket" in the different countries are compared and permit the calculation of purchasing power parity rates (PPP rates). The World Bank developed and refined this methodology during the past decades to a point where it is as solid as inflation measurement.

The following is a more detailed description, with examples, of the method used for calculating PPP rates. The examples are taken from a handbook by the main authors who developed this method (Kravis, Heston, Summers 1978).

Step (a) -- Defining the "Basket"

The first step is to prepare a standardized list ("basket") of goods and services whose prices are to be compared across countries. The handbook lists 153 categories of goods and services, as follows (Kravis, Heston, Summers 1978: 224-231):

1. Rice
2. Meal, other cereals
3. Bread, rolls

4. Biscuits, cakes
5. Cereal preparations
6. Macaroni, spaghetti
7. Fresh beef, veal
8. Fresh lamb, mutton
9. Fresh poultry
10. Other fresh meat
11. Frozen, salted meat
12. Fresh, frozen fish
13. Canned fish
14. Fresh milk
15. Milk products
16. Eggs, egg products

    .....etc.

153. Government expenditures on commodities

These primary items are grouped in various ways, e.g., as follows (Kravis, Heston, Summers 1978: 222):

- Consumption
  - Food
  - Clothing and footwear
  - Gross rents and fuels
  - House furnishings and operations
  - Medical care
  - Transport and communications
  - Recreation and education
- Capital formation
  - Construction
  - Producers' durables
- Government
  - Compensation
  - Commodities

Step (b) -- Determine Prices in Local Currency

The handbook does not list the original local prices, but lists, e.g., how many French francs a Frenchman has to pay in order to buy the same amount of meat that an American gets for one dollar. Here are some examples for the Year 1970, for two countries -- France and Colombia (Kravis, Heston, Summers 1978: 175, Table 5.2 and 199, Table 5.18).

	FRANCE	COLOMBIA
When the American spends one dollar for...	the Frenchman pays for the same item...	the Colombian pays for the same item...
Bread and cereals	4.79 francs	14.1 pesos
Meat	5.15 francs	10.9 pesos
Fuel and Power	7.08 francs	7.0 pesos
etc.	etc.	etc.

Step (c) -- Calculate the PPP Rate

These items are further summarized in major groups and for the entire GDP, as follows (Kravis, Heston, Summers 1978: 176,200):

	FRANCE	COLOMBIA	
When the American spends one dollar for...	the Frenchman pays for the same item...	the Colombian pays for the same item...	
Aggregate Consumption (items 1-110)	4.38 francs	8.2 pesos	
Capital Formation (items 111-148)	4.09 francs	9.5 pesos	
Government (items 149-153)	4.21 francs	5.5 pesos	
GDP	**4.64 francs**	**8.1 pesos**	**= PPP rates**

(NOTE: the results for GDP are the purchasing power parity rates between the U.S. dollar and the French franc and between the U.S. dollar and the Colombian peso in 1970)

Step (d) -- Calculate the Exchange Rate Deviation

	FRANCE	COLOMBIA	Source
line 1: PPP rate (1970)	4.64 francs	8.1 pesos	step (c) above
line 2: official exchange rate (1970)	5.5289	18.352	Kravis,H,S (1978: 8)
line 3= line 2: line 1 exchange rate deviation	1.23	2.26	Kravis,H,S (1978: 219)

7. Practical Relevance of Investigation

This investigation may seem a bit abstract. It has great practical relevance, however. There is an entire chorus of economists who keep repeating that the exchange rates of poor countries are overvalued. The IMF, in particular, has, over the past two decades and as part of its "Structural Adjustment Programs" (SAPs), forced many countries to devalue their currencies, using the argument that the currency was "overvalued". This practice has important practical implications for the countries and people affected by SAPs and, furthermore, it reveals two things, namely: (1) the IMF (and the chorus of economists referred to) has a "theory of value" regarding exchange rates. This theory may be largely implicit, but it is there, or else they could not arrive at the evaluative judgment that "exchange rate of country X is overvalued". And: (2) value theory of exchange rates is of great practical relevance. Whereas most economists agree with the view that the currencies of low-income countries tend to be overvalued, if anything, I claim the opposite, namely, that the currencies of low-income countries tend to be undervalued.

8. Empirical Evidence: Correlation

A look at Table 1 above suggests several observations, namely:

1. for the countries of the core of the world system (OECD countries) exchange rates (method 1) and purchasing power rates (method 2) differ not at all or relatively little.
2. for the countries of the periphery and semi-periphery of the world system (non-OECD countries) exchange rates (method 1) and purchasing power rates (method 2) yield significantly different results. The difference can be stated in two ways -- namely, either: exchange rate values are lower than PPP values, or: the purchasing power value of the country's currency is greater than the exchange rate value.
3. overall, for all countries, it can be observed that the discrepancy tends to be greatest for the poorest countries and least for the richest countries. My Table 1 shows only eleven countries. However, when all countries are examined, the same correlation emerges. Statistical testing of these observations leads to the following results:
4. for all countries, there is a statistical correlation between the country's GNP per capita and the discrepancy between exchange rates and PPP rates. In other words, the poorer the country, the lower will be the exchange rate value of its currency in relation to the PPP value of its currency. Kravis and Lipsey examined this relationship for 34 countries for the year 1975 (including 12 OECD countries and 22 non-OECD countries) and found a very strong relationship between the discrepancy among the two rates and GDP per capita (Kravis and Lipsey 1983: 21). Subsequent studies confirmed the existence of this relationship. My own

calculations for 120 countries (based on World Bank data) yield the following observations for the year 1995 (Table 2):

Table 2 – Correlation between Currency Value Distortion and GNP per capita, 1995 (n=120 countries)

1. Correlation between the "distortion of currency value" and "income level" (GNP/capita)	r = - 0.63
2. Average distortion factor for 120 countries (standard deviation 1.5)	avg d = 2.65
3. Maximum distortion factor (Mozambique)	max d = 10.1
Minimum(Switzerland, Japan)	min d = 0.6
4. Classes: average distortion factor for:	
a. low-income (43 countries)	avg d = 4.0
b. middle-income (52 countries)	avg d = 2.4
c. high-income (25 countries)	avg d = 0.98
5. Average GNP/capita (at exchange rate) (standard deviation 9408)	US $ 6025
6. Minimum GNP/capita (at exchange rate)(Mozambique)	US $ 80
Maximum (at exchange rate)(Switzerland)	US $ 40630

Source: World Bank. *World Development Report 1997,* p. 214-215, Table 1

Note: "GNP per capita" in the correlation is in 1995 US dollars (exchange rate value). The distortion factor is the quotient of GNP per capita "in 1995 international dollars" (i.e. the PPP value), divided by GNP per capita in "1995 US dollars" (i.e. exchange rate value).

9. Interpretation of the Correlation

In the context of world system theory and related theories (structural theory, imperialism theory), the observed correlation means that a country's socio-economic status in the world system and the relative value of the country's money within the world system are related. Topdog countries tend to have "hard" or "strong" currencies (i.e. valuable currencies); underdog countries tend to have "soft" or "weak" currencies (i.e. less valuable currencies). The general power/wealth gradient in the world system can thus be found once more in the value structure of global money.

In terms of causality, it may be asked whether the global power/wealth structure determines the global money structure or vice versa. I assume that both causalities exist. The global power/wealth structure contributes to the global money structure and the global structure of money feeds back into the perpetuation of the global power/wealth structure.

10. Value Theory (Normative Discussion)

I will now shift from empirical observation to normative reasoning (theory of value). How can we evaluate this situation?

The discussion can be organized around two diametrically opposed evaluative (normative) propositions, namely:

Proposition (1): The exchange rates of low-income countries tend to be overvalued.
Proposition (2): The exchange rates of low-income countries tend to be undervalued.

Let's examine both propositions.

11. The Over-Valuation Argument

The over-valuation argument is common and is being used by the IMF, as mentioned earlier. In order to arrive at a verdict of "over-valuation" of a currency, the judging mind must have two things, namely, (a) certain kinds of factual information and (b) a normative standard by which to evaluate the facts; or an evaluation method which implies a normative standard. What normative standard or "yardstick" is being applied by experts who reach the verdict of "overvalued"?

In the practice the "Structural Adjustment Programs" of the IMF, conditions tend to be imposed on various countries -- conditions which tend to include stipulations about currency. "Typical conditionalities might be: the borrower's budget or balance of payments deficit must be reduced by x percent within one year; ... the currency must be devalued by x percent within six months, etc." (Brown 1993: 122). There is thus a great concern for balancing the government budget and balancing the balance of payments. The standard by which a currency is evaluated is the balancing of the balance of payments. The connection between this standard and the judgment of "overvaluation" is stated, for example, in the following:

> "The currencies of most developing countries are overvalued ... When exchange rates are fixed, a surplus demand for foreign currency tends to develop, which must be controlled ..." (Lachmann 1994: 196; my translation.)

The balancing of the balance of payments is thus a major "yardstick" with which poor countries' currencies are evaluated. (It should be noted that the same yardstick is being applied when the currencies of high-income countries are evaluated.) This may be a valid standard. However, I contend that the following is also a valid standard, even though that may seem paradoxical at first.

12. The Under-Valuation Argument

When a low-income country (with a structurally distorted currency value, see Table 1) trades with a high-income country, the high-income country gains a quantity of real value which does not show up in any account and the low-income country loses a quantity of real value which does not show up in any account. In colonial times, traders may have exchanged cheap glass beads for valuable ivory. Both sides agreed to the deal. Similarly, a low-income country may make a deal with a high-income country and the deal is balanced in monetary terms at the prevailing exchange rates. However, a quantity of real value has been extracted from the low-income country in this deal which does not show up in any account.

The normative standard in this argument is "real value". I measure "real value" in terms of purchasing power parity (PPP). On this basis it can be argued that the currencies of the low-income countries tend to be undervalued. Here is an example.

First, let's eliminate the theoretical possiblity of complete autarky of two countries. In this situation there is no trade and no international money exchange. PPP rates can be measured, but there are no exchange rates. This situation is of no practical interest.

Next, let us examine a situation of balanced trade between country LIC (low-income country) and country HIC (high-income country), with no financial investment across borders, just payments for traded goods and services. (Let's further assume that LIC has some features of India and HIC has some features of USA. I am using the distortion factor of 3.9 for India from Table 1; the rest in the following is "made up".)

Here is a 2-country scenario (hypothetical):
[LIC = low-income country HIC = high-income country]

1. LIC has a GDP of 1200 rupees
2. HIC has a GDP of 1010 dollars
3. The exchange rate of rupee: dollar is 20: 1
4. The two countries trade with each other. The volume of trade between the two countries is 200 rupees = 10 dollars in each direction. In other words, LIC exports goods and services valued as 200 rupees (or 10 dollars) and HIC exports goods and services valued as 10 dollars (or 200 rupees). The trade is balanced. The balance of payments is balanced.

Now let us examine the implication of the distortion factor. The distortion factor in cross-national currency valuation is 3.9 (from Table 1). This means that the purchasing power rate (PPP rate) between LIC's rupee and HIC's dollar is not 20: 1 but, rather, 20/3.9: 1 = 5.13: 1. I am rounding this off to 5: 1.

When we assume that the PPP rate reflects the true value of the currency, then it can be observed that:

(a) from LIC's point of view: LIC exported goods and services worth 200 rupees. In exchange, LIC imported goods and services worth 200 / 20 = 10 dollars at exchange rate. However, LIC would have imported 200 / 5 = 40 dollars worth at PPP rate. The monetary distortion factor had the effect that LIC lost 40 - 10 = 30 dollars worth of imports due to the distortion factor. This loss of 30 dollars, at PPP rate, corresponds to 150 rupees.

(b) from HIC's point of view: HIC exported goods and services worth 10 dollars. In exchange, HIC imported goods and services worth 10 * 20 = 200 rupees at exchange rate. However, HIC would have imported 10 * 5 = 50 rupees worth at PPP rate. The monetary distortion factor had the effect that HIC gained 200 - 50 = 150 rupees worth of imports due to the distortion factor. This gain of 150 rupees, at PPP rate, corresponds to 30 dollars.

(c) Summary: Due to the monetary distortion factor between the two currencies, LIC lost 150 rupees worth of import value; HIC gained 30 dollars worth of import value. These losses and gains of value do not show up in the accounts, because the value of money is itself structurally deformed. The trade is formally balanced.

As a percent of GDP, the gains and losses are, as follows: LIC has an "invisible loss" (unrecorded loss) of 150 rupees. With a GDP of 1200 rupees, the invisible loss of value is 150/1200 = 12.5% of GDP. HIC has an "invisible gain" (unrecorded gain) of 30 dollars. With a GDP of 1010 dollars, the invisible gain of value is 30/1010 = 3.0% of GDP.

Based on this reasoning, I conclude that the currency values of low-income countries tend to be undervalued. The effect is exploitative. The core countries appear to extract a large amount of value from the periphery countries through the clever monetary device called exchange rate system.

Babones (1997) has recently made a parallel observation with respect to global center-periphery relations, namely that: "Surplus value is not extracted solely through coercion, but also through the working of financial markets." (He is thinking of credit markets.)

13. Recent Literature on Undervaluation

Undervaluation of currencies has drawn some attention in the 1990's. A study which argues *for* currency undervaluation is by Havlik who argues, with reference to countries in Central and Eastern Europe, that "undervaluation is needed in order to overcome institutional, structural and quality deficiencies" (Havlik 1996). A study which argues *against* currency undervaluation is Yotopoulos (1996). This book combines theory, statistical-empirical research and case studies. Yotopoulos uses purchasing power parity (PPP) data from World Bank sources, compares them with nominal exchange rates (NER) and calculates an exchange rate deviation index (ERD) for all countries

(Yotopoulos 1996: 97-100). The study investigates the relationship between currency valuation and economic growth. His observations agree with mine in two important points -- namely, Yotopoulos writes: (1) "free currency markets ... have an inherent distortion" (Yotopoulos 1996: ii) and (2) with reference to low- and middle-income countries: There is "*under*valuation of the NER [sc. nominal exchange rate] ... Conventional wisdom, on the contrary, sees the problem as NER *over*valuation ..."(Yotopoulos 1996: 8. Emphasis original)

14. The Quantification Of Unequal Exchange

The availability of PPP data and the possibility of calculating an exchange rate deviation index (variable "d" in Table 2 above; or "ERD" in Yotopoulos 1996) opens up an intriguing new way of quantifying the degree of "unequal exchange" (losses and gains from unfair center-periphery trade).

In Emmanuel's theory the concept of "unequal exchange" is the grand dependent variable. Emmanuel defines:

> "...unequal exchange is the proportion between equilibrium prices that is established through the equalization of profits between regions in which the rate of surplus value is 'institutionally' different..." (Emmanuel 1972: 64).

This is a theoretical definition and not an operational definition. How unequal is the exchange? How much value is unfairly transferred from the periphery to the center? Emmanuel did not give any precise figures, and this measurement problem was still relatively unresolved in 1987, when Raffer reviewed the state of the art with respect to the measurement of unequal exchange (Raffer 1987: chapter 11). However, Emmanuel gave a sense of magnitudes involved when he wrote that the:

> "loss [sc. resulting from unequal exchange] ... is enormous in relation to the poverty of the underdeveloped countries while being far from negligible in relation to the wealth of the advanced countries." (Emmanuel 1972: 265)

Some authors provided estimates for individual countries. Gibson (1980) estimated a loss for Peru in 1969 in its trade with USA as 38% of its exports to the USA (see, Raffer 1987: 94). Webber and Foot (1984) estimated for the Philippines in 1961 that Philippine exports would have amounted to 5.269 billion pesos, if valued at Canadian wages and prices, instead of the actual 1.129 billion pesos (see, Raffer 1987: 95).

A worldwide estimate is available from Samir Amin. Amin estimated the loss incurred by developing countries for the year 1966 as being $22 billion. That corresponds to a loss of 15% of GDP for the developing countries and to a gain of 1.5% of GDP for the advanced countries. (Amin 1976: 143-144 and Raffer 1987: 93-94)

One expert on unequal exchange, Raffer, stated in 1987 that "precise statistical methods of measuring [sc. unequal exchange] are still lacking." (Raffer 1987: 194) That was the state of affairs in the late 1980's. In the meantime, a new type of data has become widely available, namely, the World Bank's PPP data which are now available for a majority of countries. In combination with a structural view of global money, these data can be used for estimating the degree of unequal exchange. The following calculations for 1993 are illustrative of such a possibility.

The proposed estimation method is, as follows: (a) calculate the distortion factor d (see above, Tables 1 and 2, or, as Yotopoulos calls it, the ERD -- exchange rate deviation index); and (b) apply it to the volume of trade, giving (c) the loss or gain due to unequal exchange, according to the formula:

$$T = d*X - X$$

where:

T = magnitude of unrecorded transfer (loss or gain) due to unequal exchange

X = volume of exports from a low-wage country to high-wage countries, and

d = the distortion factor (i.e. the deviation of the nominal exchange rate from the PPP rate, also known as ERD)

The formula means, in words, that the unrecorded transfer (T) resulting from unequal exchange is equal to the difference between the fair value of the export (d * X) and the unfair (actual) value of the export (X). For low-wage countries this magnitude T is a loss. For high-wage countries the same magnitude T is a gain.

Hypothetical example: A low-income country has exports to a high-wage country of X = $1000 and a distortion factor of d = 2.65 (which is average, see Table 2). Instead of earning $1000 from exports, the country could have earned 2.65 * $1000 = $2650. The difference 2650 (fair value) - 1000 (unfair value) = $1650 is the amount of unrecorded value lost by the low-wage country (and gained by the high-wage country) due to unequal exchange. When Emmanuel first presented his ideas (1962 and 1969/72), PPP data were not available, so that this kind of quantification of the effects of unequal exchange was not possible at the time.

15. Estimates of Unequal Exchange for 1993

This estimation method can be applied to export data for 1993. The export streams between center and periphery of the world are shown in Table 3:

Table 3 - World Export Flows, 1993

	U.S. dollars trillions (at exchange rates) TO: OECD	TO: non-OECD
FROM: OECD	1.84	0.70
FROM: non-OECD (a)	0.64	0.46
WORLD, total exports	= 3.70 US \$ trillions	

NOTE(a): non-OECD = "developing countries" + Eastern Europe and former USSR
Source: United Nations. *Yearbook of International Trade Statistics 1995*, Vol. 2, Special Table B, page S 22

The figure to watch in Table 3 is "0.64". This represents the exports from the periphery (all non-OECD countries) to the center of the world system (OECD countries) and shows periphery-to-center exports as US \$ 0.64 trillion (or, \$640 billion). When we value this volume of exports in terms of PPP rates, then the distortion factor of 2.65 (from above) can be applied as a first approximation. Given this preliminary assumption, the fair value of the export flow of US \$0.64 trillion can be valued as 0.64 * 2.65 = 1.7 trillions of PPP dollars. If this is the fair value of the exports from low- and middle-income countries to high-income countries, then the amount of income lost by low-and middle-income countries in 1993, due to unequal exchange, may be estimated as:

d*X -	X	= T
(fair value) less	(unfair value)	= (loss due to unequal exchange)

or,

1.7 -	0.64	= 1.06

In other words, in 1993 the loss incurred by low- and middle-income countries due to unequal exchange may have been 1.06 trillion of PPP dollars. At the same time, this is the estimated gain for OECD countries.

How does this figure compare with global GDP and the GDPs of low- and high-income countries? The GDP figures for the world in 1993 are given in Table 4:

Table 4-- World GDP, 1993

COUNTRY CLASS	(U.S. dollars trillions)
High-income	18.6
Low- and middle-income	5.0
WORLD	23.6

Source: World Bank, *World Tables 1995*, p. 29

Using Table 4 data we can calculate the unrecorded transfer (T) of $1.06 trillion, which results from unequal exchange, as a percent of GDP, namely:

(a) OECD countries: 1.06 / 18.6 = 5.7 % of GDP (of OECD)
(b) non-OECD countries: 1.06 / 5.0 = 21.2 % of GDP (of non-OECD)

16. Comparison of Estimates of Unequal Exchange

A comparison of Amin's and my estimates of the degree of unequal exchange leads to the following summary (Table 5):

Table 5 -- Comparison of Estimates of Unequal Exchange

	For Year	For Unit of analysis	Estimate In current US dollars	Estimate as a percent of GDP of	
				LIC(a)	HIC(a)
Amin	1966	developing countries	22 billion	-15%	+1.5%
Köhler	1993	non-OECD countries	1.06 trillion	-21%	+5.7%

NOTE (a): LIC = low- and middle-income countries; HIC = high-income countries
Sources: see text above

Table 5 shows similarities and discrepancies in the estimated percentages. Whether global exploitation increased between 1966 and 1993, as the table seems to suggest, is difficult to answer since Amin's and my estimates are based on two different methods. This problem requires further research. However, it can be observed that both methods lead to roughly comparable magnitudes. Furthermore, the figures are consistent with Emmanuel's non-quantitative statement -- namely, that the "loss [sc. resulting from unequal exchange]...is enormous in relation to the poverty of the underdeveloped countries while being far from negligible in relation to the wealth of the advanced countries." (Emmanuel 1972: 265)

17. Implications for the Theory of Unequal Exchange

In the history of science new instruments and new types of data have, on numerous occasions, led to innovations in theory--e.g., the invention of the telescope in astronomy; the invention of the microscope in biology; the development of computer-based time-series analysis in economics, etc. Similarly, the availability of PPP data, which were not available in the 1960's and 1970's and not fully available in the 1980's, are now adding new insights to the theory of unequal exchange. The subtitle of Emmanuel's book "Unequal Exchange" is "A Study of the Imperialism of Trade", where trade refers to commodity trade, not currency trade. With the help of now-available PPP data, it becomes increasingly apparent that the element of unfairness or exploitation in the notion of "unequal exchange" is not only a matter of unequal commodity exchange, but also a matter of unequal currency exchange, both being intricately linked.

Emmanuel's theory of unequal exchange includes the following views:

1. Trade between low-income and high-income countries (periphery and center of the world system) is unequal, meaning: unfair, biased against the low-income countries.
2. Wages in low-income countries are undervalued in relation to wages in high-income countries.
3. Export prices of exports from low-income countries are undervalued in relation to the export prices of high-income countries.
4. There is a relationship between the undervaluation of labour and the undervaluation of exports of low-income countries. Emmanuel stresses that: "... inequality of wages as such, all other things being equal, is alone the cause of the inequality of exchange." (Emmanuel 1972: 61) and: "wages, the independent variable of the system" (Emmanuel 1972: 64).

What causes the inequality of wages between high-wage and low-wage countries? Here Emmanuel discusses various possible influences -- physiological wage, historical wage, market wage, equilibrium wage, moral element, trade-union factor, wage zones and so on. (Emmanuel 1972: 109-122) Generally, the problem is seen as an "institutional" problem.

In terms of causal modelling, Emmanuel constructs a causal sequence from antecedent factors A1, A2, A3, etc. (called "determinants of wages"), which cause "inequality of wages" (X), which in turn is causing "unequal exchange of commodities" (Y), or:

A --> X --> Y

An alternative causal view, based on a structural view of global money, could be, as follows: The "undervaluation of a country's currency", due to the distorted structure of global money (M), has two simultaneous valuation effects, namely: (X) it leads to an undervaluation of labour in the low-income country relative to labour of high-income countries; and (Y) it leads to an undervaluation of the exports of the low-income country relative to the exports of high-income countries, or:

---> X

M

---> Y

Seen this way, the unfairness of commodity trade between low-wage and high-wage countries ("unequal exchange" in Emmanuel's sense) is, in part, caused by the structure of global money ("unequal exchange" in the sense of "unequal exchange rates"). The distortion of global money and of the exchange rate system is shaped by the historically grown structure of the world-system (center-periphery, imperialism, "global apartheid" (Köhler 1978, 1995)) and ideologically supported by neoclassical international economic theory (favouring free / unregulated currency markets).

18. Implications for Praxis

Unequal exchange theory supports an advocacy of labour struggle with the objective of raising the wages of workers in peripheral countries and/or an advocacy of global socialism, for example, along the lines of Amin's socialist polycentrism (Amin 1994). The structural view of global money suggests an additional strategy, which may be combined with the above strategies or pursued on its own, namely: a reform of the global exchange rate system in the direction of purchasing power parity (PPP) rates. Such a reform would raise the wages of low-income countries relative to high-income countries, as fought for by Emmanuel and others; it would improve the terms of trade for low-income countries, as fought for by Prebisch and others; and it would significantly reduce unequal exchange.

How much each low- or middle-income country could gain from such a global monetary reform -- and how much it is presently losing due to unequal exchange, can be seen from the World Tables of Unequal Exchange which are presented in Chapter 3. These tables are based on the theory and method developed in this article.

Chapter 3

UNEQUAL EXCHANGE: WORLD TABLES OF UNEQUAL EXCHANGE 1995

1. INTRODUCTION

The statistical tables below present quantitative estimates of unequal exchange for 119 countries. The tables are based on the theory and method developed in Chapter 2. The calculations are based on export/import data and the exchange rate deviation index. Losses or gains from unequal exchange are calculated as the difference between a "fair value" of exports/imports and the "actual (unfair) value" of exports/imports. The estimation formula is:

$$T = d^{*}X - X$$

where d = the exchange rate deviation index (also designated as "ERD" in the literature)
X = the volume of exports from a low- or middle-income country to high-income countries (valued at the actual exchange rate)
T = the unrecorded transfer of value (gain or loss) resulting from unequal exchange

In the tables (below) this formula is applied to the data for 119 countries for the year 1995.

2. HOW TO READ THE TABLES

Table 1 presents the step-by-step calculations. Countries are arranged in alphabetical order and in two groups -- first, non-OECD countries and, secondly, OECD countries. The losses or gains from unequal exchange are shown at the right-hand side (in terms of U.S. dollars and as a percent of the country's GNP).

Table 2 presents the losses and gains (same as in Table 1), sorted by dollar volume. Table 3 presents the losses and gains (same as in Table 1), sorted by percent of GNP. The tables are followed by a brief discussion and further methodological details.

3. THE WORLD TABLES

Table 1 - World Table of Unequal Exchange 1995

GROUP = NON-OECD 97 countries (mostly middle- and low-income)										
Country	GNP 1995 in US $ (millions) (A)	Population 1995 (millions) (B)	GNP per capita 1995 in US $ (C)	GNP per capita 1995 in PPP $ (D)	Exports to OECD (year) (E)	Exports to OECD in US $ (millions) (F)	Exchange Rate Deviation d =col.D / col.C (ratio) (G)	Fair value of exports (d/0.9)*col.F ($ millions) (H)	Unequal Exchange LOSS(-) J = F – H ($ millions) (J)	Unequal Exchange LOSS(-) K = J / A (% of GNP) (K)
Algeria	44,800	28.0	1,600	5,300	1994	7,807	3.31	28,712	-20,905	-47%
Angola	4,428	10.8	410	1,310	92	3,512	3.20	12,486	-8,974	-203%
Argentina	278,641	34.7	8,030	8,310	95	7,259	1.03	8,308	-1,049	0%
Armenia	2,774	3.8	730	2,260	92	4	3.10	14	-10	0%
Bahamas	3,295	0.3	11,940	14,710	91	120	1.23	164	-44	-1%
Bahrain	4,524	0.6	7,840	13,400	95	561	1.71	1,066	-505	-11%
Bangladesh	28,752	119.8	240	1,380	93	1,745	5.75	11,149	-9,404	-33%
Barbados	1,745	0.3	6,560	10,620	95	103	1.62	185	-82	-5%
Belize	568	0.2	2,630	5,400	95	151	2.05	343	-192	-34%
Benin	2,035	5.5	370	1,760	95	54	4.76	287	-233	-11%
Bhutan	292	0.7	420	1,260	92	0	3.00	0	0	0%
Bolivia	5,920	7.4	800	2,540	95	603	3.18	2,131	-1,528	-26%
Brazil	579,488	159.2	3,640	5,400	95	37,389	1.48	61,483	-24,095	-4%
Bulgaria	11,172	8.4	1,330	4,480	95	2,214	3.37	8,292	-6,077	-54%
Burkina Faso	2,392	10.4	230	780	91	62	3.39	233	-171	-7%
Cameroon	8,645	13.3	650	2,110	91	2,237	3.25	8,080	-5,842	-68%
Cape Verde	365	0.4	960	1,870	94	5	1.95	11	-6	-2%
Central African R	1,122	3.3	340	1,070	89	131	3.15	459	-328	-29%
Chile	59,072	14.2	4,160	9,520	95	10,067	2.29	25,614	-15,547	-26%
China	744,124	1200.2	620	2,920	95	83,105	4.71	434,917	-351,811	-47%

Colombia	70,288	36.8	1,910	6,130	95	6,685	3.21	23,845	-17,159	-24%
Comoros	235	0.5	470	1,320	94	9	2.81	29	-20	-8%
Congo	1,768	2.6	680	2,050	94	747	3.01	2,499	-1,752	-99%
Costa Rica	8,874	3.4	2,610	5,850	95	2,089	2.24	5,198	-3,110	-35%
Czech Republic	39,861	10.3	3,870	9,770	95	10,221	2.52	28,620	-18,399	-46%
Dominican Republic	11,388	7.8	1,460	3,870	94	1,927	2.65	5,673	-3,746	-33%
Ecuador	15,985	11.5	1,390	4,220	94	3,578	3.04	12,086	-8,508	-53%
Egypt	45,662	57.8	790	3,820	95	2,226	4.84	11,970	-9,744	-21%
El Salvador	9,016	5.6	1,610	2,610	94	406	1.62	731	-325	-4%
Estonia	4,290	1.5	2,860	4,220	95	1,081	1.48	1,777	-697	-16%
Ethiopia	5,640	56.4	100	450	93	144	4.50	718	-575	-10%
Fiji	1,891	0.8	2,440	5,780	95	450	2.37	1,184	-735	-39%
Gambia	352	1.1	320	930	91	15	2.91	49	-34	-10%
Ghana	6,669	17.1	390	1,990	92	432	5.10	2,446	-2,014	-30%
Greece	86,205	10.5	8,210	11,710	94	6,320	1.43	10,042	-3,722	-4%
Guatemala	14,204	10.6	1,340	3,340	95	994	2.49	2,751	-1,756	-12%
Honduras	3,540	5.9	600	1,900	95	554	3.17	1,951	-1,397	-39%
Hongkong	142,538	6.2	22,990	22,950	95	84,418	1.00	93,798	-9,380	-7%
Hungary	42,024	10.2	4,120	6,410	95	9,115	1.56	15,800	-6,684	-16%
India	315,996	929.4	340	1,400	94	15,717	4.12	71,947	-56,231	-18%
Indonesia	189,434	193.3	980	3,800	95	29,799	3.88	128,468	-98,668	-52%
Israel	87,560	5.5	15,920	16,490	94	12,051	1.04	13,926	-1,875	-2%
Jamaica	3,775	2.5	1,510	3,540	92	915	2.34	2,380	-1,464	-39%
Jordan	6,342	4.2	1,510	4,060	95	265	2.69	791	-526	-8%
Kasakstan	22,078	16.6	1,330	3,010	93	921	2.26	2,312	-1,391	-6%
Kenya	7,476	26.7	280	1,380	93	581	4.93	3,183	-2,602	-35%
Kuwait	29,563	1.7	17,390	23,790	95	7,194	1.37	10,951	-3,757	-13%
Kyrgystan	3,150	4.5	700	1,800	92	0	2.57	1	0	0%
Latvia	5,675	2.5	2,270	3,370	95	624	1.48	1,026	-402	-7%

Lithuania	7,030	3.7	1,900	4,120	95	1,095	2.17	2,641	-1,546	-22%
Madagascar	3,151	13.7	230	640	95	270	2.78	835	-565	-18%
Malawi	1,666	9.8	170	750	91	398	4.41	1,950	-1,552	-93%
Malaysia	78,189	20.1	3,890	9,020	95	39,275	2.32	101,242	-61,967	-79%
Maldives	250	0.3	990	3,080	93	16	3.11	56	-40	-16%
Mauritius	3,718	1.1	3,380	13,210	95	1,408	3.91	6,116	-4,708	-127%
Mexico	304,776	91.8	3,320	6,400	95	73,494	1.93	157,604	-84,110	-28%
Morocco	29,526	26.6	1,110	3,340	95	3,579	3.01	11,968	-8,390	-28%
Mozambique	1,296	16.2	80	810	94	95	10.13	1,068	-973	-75%
Nepal	4,300	21.5	200	1,170	95	282	5.85	1,832	-1,550	-36%
Nicaragua	1,672	4.4	380	2,000	95	386	5.26	2,257	-1,871	-112%
Niger	1,980	9.0	220	750	91	235	3.41	890	-655	-33%
Nigeria	28,938	111.3	260	1,220	91	11,806	4.69	61,523	-49,717	-172%
Oman	10,604	2.2	4,820	8,140	95	2,837	1.69	5,328	-2,491	-23%
Pakistan	59,754	129.9	460	2,230	95	3,630	4.85	19,563	-15,933	-27%
Panama	7,150	2.6	2,750	5,980	94	1,054	2.17	2,542	-1,488	-21%
Papua New Guinea	4,988	4.3	1,160	2,420	93	1,735	2.09	4,030	-2,294	-46%
Paraguay	8,112	4.8	1,690	3,650	95	218	2.16	524	-306	-4%
Peru	54,978	23.8	2,310	3,770	95	3,063	1.63	5,548	-2,485	-5%
Philippines	72,030	68.6	1,050	2,850	95	12,794	2.71	38,524	-25,730	-36%
Poland	107,694	38.6	2,790	5,400	95	17,208	1.94	37,093	-19,885	-18%
Qatar	7,447	0.6	11,600	17,690	94	461	1.53	784	-323	-4%
Romania	33,596	22.7	1,480	4,360	95	4,333	2.95	14,202	-9,869	-29%
Russian Federation	331,968	148.2	2,240	4,480	93	26,643	2.00	59,206	-32,563	-10%
Saint Kitts and N	212	0.0	5,170	9,410	91	21	1.82	43	-22	-10%
Senegal	5,100	8.5	600	1,780	93	275	2.97	908	-633	-12%
Singapore	80,190	3.0	26,730	22,770	95	54,755	0.85	51,713	+3,042	+4%
Slovakia	15,930	5.4	2,950	3,610	95	3,508	1.22	4,755	-1,247	-8%
Solomon I	341	0.4	910	2,190	94	235	2.41	630	-395	-116%

Southern Africa(CU)	131,140	41.5	3,160	5,030	95	13,426	1.59	23,719	-10,293	-8%
Sri Lanka	12,670	18.1	700	3,250	95	1,838	4.64	9,475	-7,637	-60%
Suriname	361	0.4	880	2,250	94	447	2.56	1,270	-824	-228%
Syrian Arab Republic	15,792	14.1	1,120	5,320	94	2,038	4.75	10,757	-8,718	-55%
Thailand	159,468	58.2	2,740	7,540	95	31,120	2.75	95,088	-63,968	-40%
Togo	1,271	4.1	310	1,130	94	74	3.65	302	-227	-18%
Trinidad and Tobago	4,901	1.3	3,770	8,610	95	1,355	2.28	3,432	-2,077	-42%
Tunisia	16,380	9.0	1,820	5,000	95	4,473	2.75	13,667	-9,194	-56%
Turkey	169,858	61.1	2,780	5,580	95	13,361	2.01	29,839	-16,478	-10%
Uganda	4,608	19.2	240	1,470	92	128	6.13	871	-743	-16%
Ukraine	84,108	51.6	1,630	2,400	93	1,373	1.47	2,243	-870	-1%
United Arab Emirates	43,500	2.5	17,400	16,470	93	752	0.95	794	-42	0%
United R of Tanzania	3,552	29.6	120	640	90	221	5.33	1,311	-1,090	-31%
Uruguay	16,544	3.2	5,170	6,630	95	628	1.28	893	-265	-2%
Uzbekistan	22,116	22.8	970	2,370	92	386	2.44	1,048	-661	-3%
Vanuatu	203	0.2	1,200	2,290	94	13	1.91	28	-15	-7%
Venezuela	65,534	21.7	3,020	7,900	95	11,863	2.62	34,535	-22,672	-35%
Zambia	3,600	9.0	400	930	90	384	2.33	994	-610	-17%
Zimbabwe	5,940	11.0	540	2,030	95	1,054	3.76	4,404	-3,350	-56%
GROUP NON-OECD										
Subtotals	4,993,765	4236.6				706,650		1,890,124	-1,183,474	
Subtotals w/o Ch, Ru	3,917,673	2,888				596,903		1,396,002	-799,099	
Averages (arithmetic)							2.88			-33%
Averages (weighted by exports to OECD)							2.41			-30%
Subtotal "Losses"/ Subtotal "GNP"										-24%
Subtotal "Losses"/ Subtotal "GNP" (w/o China, Russia)										-20%

GROUP = OECD 23 countries (high-income) (Belgium and Luxembourg combined)

Country	GNP 1995 in US $ (millions) (A)	Population 1995 (millions) (B)	GNP per capita 1995 in US $ (C)	GNP per capita 1995 in PPP $ (D)	Imports from OECD (year) (E)	Imports from OECD in US $ (millions) (F)	Exchange Rate Deviation d =col.D / col.C (ratio) (G)	Fair value of Imports (2.4/d)*col.F ($ millions) (H)	Unequal Exchange GAIN(+) J = F – H ($ millions) (J)	Unequal Exchange GAIN(+) K = J / A (% of GNP) (K)
Australia	338,832	18.1	18,720	18,940	95	14,493	1.01	34,438	+19,945	+6%
Austria	217,809	8.1	26,890	21,250	94	9,503	0.79	28,870	+19,367	+9%
Belgium-Luxembourg	249,571	10.1	24,710	21,660	95	20,572	0.88	56,105	+35,533	+14%
Canada	573,648	29.6	19,380	21,130	95	23,658	1.09	52,090	+28,433	+5%
Denmark	155,428	5.2	29,890	21,230	95	6,043	0.71	20,428	+14,384	+9%
Finland	104,958	5.1	20,580	17,760	94	5,230	0.86	14,596	+9,366	+9%
France incl Monaco	1,451,919	58.1	24,990	21,030	95	51,318	0.84	146,623	+95,305	+7%
Germany	2,253,069	81.9	27,510	20,070	95	105,345	0.73	346,339	+240,994	+11%
Iceland	6,687	0.3	24,950	20,460	95	200	0.82	584	+385	+6%
Ireland	52,956	3.6	14,710	15,680	95	5,536	1.07	12,417	+6,881	+13%
Italy	1,087,944	57.2	19,020	19,870	95	49,325	1.04	113,827	+64,502	+6%
Japan	4,962,928	125.2	39,640	22,110	95	158,686	0.56	680,081	+521,396	+11%
Korea, Republic of	435,530	44.9	9,700	11,450	95	42,927	1.18	87,308	+44,382	+10%
Netherlands	372,000	15.5	24,000	19,950	95	34,347	0.83	99,316	+64,970	+17%
New Zealand	51,624	3.6	14,340	16,360	95	2,627	1.14	5,531	+2,904	+6%
Norway, incl S & J	137,500	4.4	31,250	21,940	95	4,161	0.70	14,266	+10,105	+7%
Portugal	96,426	9.9	9,740	12,670	95	5,064	1.30	9,350	+4,285	+4%
Spain	532,336	39.2	13,580	14,520	95	23,671	1.07	53,095	+29,423	+6%
Sweden	209,000	8.8	23,750	18,540	94	7,442	0.78	22,898	+15,456	+7%
Switzerland incl L	284,410	7.0	40,630	25,860	95	7,365	0.64	27,619	+20,254	+7%
United Kingdom	1,093,950	58.5	18,700	19,260	95	46,286	1.03	107,851	+61,565	+6%
United States	7,098,438	263.1	26,980	26,980	95	315,889	1.00	758,133	+442,244	+6%

GROUP OECD							
Subtotals	21,766,963	857.4	939,687		2,691,765	+1,752,078	
Averages (arithmetic)				0.91			+8%
Averages (weighted by imports from non-OECD)				0.89			+8%
Subtotal "Gains"/Subtotal "GNP"							+8%

WORLD SUMMARY ON UNEQUAL EXCHANGE 1995 (N = 119 countries)

1. World GNP	26,760,727	US $ millions	= 26.8 US $ trillions			
2. Gains (OECD)	+1,752,078	$ millions	= 1.8	$ trillion	= 8% of GNP	of OECD
3. Losses (non-OECD)	-1,183,474	$ millions	= 1.2	$ trillion	= 24% of GNP	of NON-OECD
4. Error	-568,604	due to missing data for low- and middle-income countries				
5. Gains (OECD)	+6.55%	of world GNP				
6. Losses (non-OECD)	-4.42%	of world GNP				
7. Error	-2.12%	due to missing data for low- and middle-income countries				

SOURCES: for columns A, B, C, D (population, GNP per capita, PPP values, list of OECD countries): 1.World Bank. World Development Report 1997, p.214-215 (Table 1), p.248 (Table 1a), p.265 (Table 1). For columns E, F (year and volume of exports or imports): 2.United Nations. International Trade Statistics Yearbook 1995, Vol. 1. For each country, Table 3 ("Trade by Principal Countries of Production and last Consignment") was used.

"NON-OECD" = "World [from source:]"- "OECD".

"OECD" = "Northern America [from source:]" + "EEC" + "EFTA" + "other Europe" + "Oceania" + "Japan" + "Korea, Republic of"

CALCULATIONS

col. A = B * C

col. B, C, D, E: none

col. F: see "SOURCES #2"

col. G = D / C (= d, = exchange rate deviation)

col. H: two formula - Fair value: NON-OECD exports: (d/0.9)*exports = (colG/0.9)* col. F (0.9 is the average exchange rate deviation d for OECD countries, see above)

Fair value: OECD imports: (2.4/d)*imports = (2.4/G)* col. F (2.4 is the average exchange rate deviation d for NON-OECD countries, see above)

col. J -- for losses: J= F - H (actual value less fair value for losses) and -- for gains:J = H - F

col K = J / A as a percent

Table 2 -- World Table of Unequal Exchange 1995: Sorted by Volume

Country	GAIN(+) LOSS(-) (US $ millions)	
China	-351,811	
Indonesia	-98,668	
Mexico	-84,110	
Thailand	-63,968	
Malaysia	-61,967	
India	-56,231	
Nigeria	-49,717	
Russian Federation	-32,563	
Philippines	-25,730	
Brazil	-24,095	case #10
Venezuela	-22,672	
Algeria	-20,905	
Poland	-19,885	
Czech Republic	-18,399	
Colombia	-17,159	
Turkey	-16,478	
Pakistan	-15,933	
Chile	-15,547	
Southern Africa(CU)	10,293	
Romania	-9,869	case #20
Egypt	-9,744	
Bangladesh	-9,404	
Hongkong	-9,380	
Tunisia	-9,194	
Angola	-8,974	
Syrian Arab Republic	8,718	
Ecuador	-8,508	
Morocco	-8,390	
Sri Lanka	-7,637	
Hungary	-6,684	case #30
Bulgaria	-6,077	
Cameroon	-5,842	
Mauritius	-4,708	
Kuwait	-3,757	
Dominican Republic	-3,746	
Greece	-3,722	
Zimbabwe	-3,350	
Costa Rica	-3,110	
Kenya	-2,602	
Oman	-2,491	case #40

Peru	-2,485	
Papua New Guinea	-2,294	
Trinidad and Tobago	-2,077	
Ghana	-2,014	
Israel	-1,875	
Nicaragua	-1,871	
Guatemala	-1,756	
Congo	-1,752	
Malawi	-1,552	
Nepal	-1,550	case #50
Lithuania	-1,546	
Bolivia	-1,528	
Panama	-1,488	
Jamaica	-1,464	
Honduras	-1,397	
Kasakstan	-1,391	
Slovakia	-1,247	
United R of Tanzania	-1,090	
Argentina	-1,049	
Mozambique	-973	case #60
Ukraine	-870	
Suriname	-824	
Uganda	-743	
Fiji	-735	
Estonia	-697	
Uzbekistan	-661	
Niger	-655	
Senegal	-633	
Zambia	-610	
Ethiopia	-575	case #70
Madagascar	-565	
Jordan	-526	
Bahrain	-505	
Latvia	-402	
Solomon I	-395	
Central African R	-328	
El Salvador	-325	
Qatar	-323	
Paraguay	-306	
Uruguay	-265	case #80
Benin	-233	
Togo	-227	
Belize	-192	

Burkina Faso	-171	
Barbados	-82	
Bahamas	-44	
United Arab Emirates	-42	
Maldives	-40	
Gambia	-34	
Saint Kitts and N	-22	case #90
Comoros	-20	
Vanuatu	-15	
Armenia	-10	
Cape Verde	-6	
Kyrgystan	0	
Bhutan	0	
Iceland	+1,551	
New Zealand	+2,904	
Portugal	+4,285	
Ireland	+6,881	case #100
Finland	+9,366	
Norway	+10,105	
Denmark	+14,384	
Sweden	+15,456	
Austria	+19,367	
Australia	+19,945	
Switzerland	+20,254	
Canada	+28,433	
Spain	+29,423	
Belgium-Luxembourg	+35,533	case #110
Korea, Republic of	+44,382	
United Kingdom	+61,565	
Italy	+64,502	
Netherlands	+64,970	
France	+95,305	
Germany	+240,994	
United States	+442,244	
Japan	+521,396	

[Singapore omitted: no loss vis-a-vis OECD]

Table 3 -- World Table of Unequal Exchange 1995: Sorted by Percentage

Country	GAIN(+)LOSS(-)(% of GNP)	
Suriname	-228%	
Angola	-203%	
Nigeria	-172%	
Mauritius	-127%	
Solomon I	-116%	
Nicaragua	-112%	
Congo	-99%	
Malawi	-93%	
Malaysia	-79%	
Mozambique	-75%	case #10
Cameroon	-68%	
Sri Lanka	-60%	
Zimbabwe	-56%	
Tunisia	-56%	
Syrian Arab Republic	-55%	
Bulgaria	-54%	
Ecuador	-53%	
Indonesia	-52%	
China	-47%	
Algeria	-47%	case #20
Czech Republic	-46%	
Papua New Guinea	-46%	
Trinidad and Tobago	-42%	
Thailand	-40%	
Honduras	-39%	
Fiji	-39%	
Jamaica	-39%	
Nepal	-36%	
Philippines	-36%	
Costa Rica	-35%	case #30
Kenya	-35%	
Venezuela	-35%	
Belize	-34%	
Niger	-33%	
Dominican Republic	-33%	
Bangladesh	-33%	
United Rep Tanzania	-31%	
Ghana	-30%	
Romania	-29%	
Central African R	-29%	case #40

Morocco	-28%	
Mexico	-28%	
Pakistan	-27%	
Chile	-26%	
Bolivia	-26%	
Colombia	-24%	
Oman	-23%	
Lithuania	-22%	
Egypt	-21%	
Panama	-21%	case #50
Poland	-18%	
Madagascar	-18%	
Togo	-18%	
India	-18%	
Zambia	-17%	
Estonia	-16%	
Uganda	-16%	
Maldives	-16%	
Hungary	-16%	
Kuwait	-13%	case #60
Senegal	-12%	
Guatemala	-12%	
Benin	-11%	
Bahrain	-11%	
Saint Kitts and N	-10%	
Ethiopia	-10%	
Russian Federation	-10%	
Turkey	-10%	
Gambia	-10%	
Comoros	-8%	case #70
Jordan	-8%	
Southern Africa(CU)	-8%	
Slovakia	-8%	
Vanuatu	-7%	
Burkina Faso	-7%	
Latvia	-7%	
Hongkong	-7%	
Kasakstan	-6%	
Barbados	-5%	
Peru	-5%	case #80
Qatar	-4%	
Greece	-4%	
Brazil	-4%	

Paraguay	-4%	
El Salvador	-4%	
Uzbekistan	-3%	
Israel	-2%	
Uruguay	-2%	
Cape Verde	-2%	
Bahamas	-1%	case #90
Ukraine	-1%	
Argentina	0%	
Armenia	0%	
United Arab Emirates	0%	
Bhutan	0%	
Kyrgystan	0%	
Portugal	+4%	
Canada	+5%	
Spain	+6%	
New Zealand	+6%	case #100
United Kingdom	+6%	
Iceland	+6%	
Australia	+6%	
Italy	+6%	
United States	+6%	
France	+7%	
Switzerland	+7%	
Norway	+7%	
Sweden	+7%	
Austria	+9%	case #110
Finland	+9%	
Denmark	+9%	
Korea, Republic of	+10%	
Japan	+11%	
Germany	+11%	
Ireland	+13%	
Belgium-Luxembourg	+14%	
Netherlands	+17%	

[Singapore omitted: no loss vis-a-vis OECD]

4. Selected Findings for the Year 1995

(a) The average exchange rate deviation (from PPP = 1.0 = value of U.S. dollar) for the block of non-OECD countries is d = 2.4 and for the block of OECD countries d = 0.9.

(b) The aggregate gain by OECD countries due to unequal exchange is $1.75 trillion. The aggregate loss by non-OECD countries is the same as the gain by OECD countries. However, the table shows only an aggregate loss of $1.18 trillion for all non-OECD countries. The discrepancy is due to missing data for non-OECD countries.

(c) In percentage terms the gains and losses are, as follows: 6.6% of world GNP is transferred from low- and middle-income countries to high-income countries due to unequal exchange (unrecorded transfer of value). This is the equivalent of +8% of OECD GNP and -24% of non-OECD GNP (in the aggregate) or -33% on average of the GNPs of individual non-OECD countries.

(d) The three countries with the highest volume losses are: China (-0.35 trillion or 351 billion U.S. dollars), Indonesia (-0.1 trillion or 99 billion dollars), and Mexico (-0.08 trillion or 84 billion dollars). The three countries with the highest volume gains are Japan (+0.5 trillion of or 521 billion dollars), United States (+0.4 trillion or 442 billion dollars), and Germany (+0.24 trillion or 241 billion dollars).

(e) The three countries with the highest percentage losses are Suriname (-228% in relation to GNP), Angola (-203%), and Nigeria (-172%). The three countries with the highest percentage gains are Netherlands (+17% in relation to GNP), Belgium-Luxembourg (+14%), and Ireland (+13%).

5. DISCUSSION

5.1 Are the NumbersValid?

There are several reasons why these calculations may be valid, namely:

1. The numbers are based on data from reputable sources (United Nations and World Bank);
2. The numbers are broadly compatible with prior estimates of unequal exchange losses and gains -- e.g., Samir Amin estimated for 1966 an aggregate loss by developing countries of 22 billion U.S. dollars (1966 value), corresponding to 15% of the GNP of developing countries (Amin 1976: 143-144 and Raffer 1987: 93-94);
3. The numbers are consistent with notions of unequal exchange, unequal development and unequal terms of trade as discussed in a large body of theoretical literature;
4. The numbers give a statistical view of the world which corresponds to the experience of the people of low- and middle-income countries;
5. The numbers appear to have some explanatory power with respect to understanding the massive global polarization of incomes which has been observed and criticized by many observers.

5.2 Practical Value

These tables may be of practical value for low- and middle-income countries. The dollar losses from unequal exchange can be used as dollar claims against the world system and the high-income countries.

5.3 Do Low- and Middle-Income Countries Love to be Exploited?

Most existing trade theory argues that countries would not engage in international trade if they did not gain from that. Furthermore, earlier leftist calls for disengagement from the international capitalist trading system were more and more ignored by low- and middle-income countries. Even the relative isolation of present-day Cuba from world trade is involuntary. Can it be concluded from that that "no trade" is bad and "trade" is good for low- and middle-income countries?

Without going into a major theoretical argument at the conclusion of this study, I would like to offer the following observation, based on the statistical tables above. The amount of unequal exchange loss by a country is a function of two variables in the formula, namely, exchange rate deviation (d) and volume of trade with high-income countries (X). If a country has no trade with OECD, it cannot be exploited by OECD. On the down side, this country cannot "make money" by trading with OECD either. If a poor country engages in significant trade with the rich countries, it has a chance to "make money" (gains from trade). If its currency has a fair value, then this trade is fair and the gains are fair. If its currency does not have fair value, however, namely if it has a high exchange rate deviation (d), then this country experiences both (1) gains from trade and (2) exploitation through trade at the same time. The situation is comparable to that of a worker vis-a-vis an exploitative employer, as captured in the following table of options and outcomes (Table 4):

Table 4 - Options/Outcomes

OPTIONS			OUTCOMES
	worker-employer	poor country-rich country	
option 3	good job	fair trade	make good money, happy and satisfied
option 2	bad job, underpaid overworked	unequal exchange, undervalued unfair trade	make some money, have an income at exploitation rates
option 1	no job	no trade	make no money, starve

As Table 4 indicates, if the choice is between "no job" and a "bad job", the worker gains by taking the bad job. Similarly, if a country has a choice between "no trade" and "unfair trade", the country gains by engaging in unfair trade. However, a good job or fair trade are immensely preferable to a bad job or unfair trade. In this sense, it is possible to "gain from trade" and be "exploited through trade" at the same time. A country may have little choice between options 1 and 2 but may want to fight for option 3.

6. Further Methodological Details Concerning the World Tables

(a) Exclusion of Countries

Countries which are not shown in the tables are missing due to missing data. For these countries either export data or PPP data or both were missing in my sources.

Luxembourg is lumped together with Belgium because the export/import data were given that way in the source. (The GNP-related data are for Belgium.)

(b) Two Calculation Models:

There are two calculation models, one for non-OECD countries and one for OECD countries. Both use the same formula (see above) with two slight variations.

MODEL 1 for non-OECD Countries:

Here I measure the export flow from each individual non-OECD country to the block of OECD countries. Since the exchange rate deviation for the block of OECD countries is d = 0.9 (i.e. deviation from the U.S. dollar), the exchange rate deviation between the individual non-OECD country and the block of OECD countries is not d(to OECD) = d/1.0 since the d calculated from the source gives the deviation to the U.S. dollar. Instead, the deviation to the block of OECD is d(to OECD) = d/0.9.

MODEL 2 for OECD Countries:

Here I measure the import flow from the block of non-OECD countries to each individual OECD country. Since the exchange rate deviation for the block of non-OECD countries is d = 2.4 (i.e. deviation from the U.S. dollar), the exchange rate deviation between the individual OECD country and the block of non-OECD countries is not d(to non-OECD) = 1.0/d since the d calculated from source gives the deviation to the U.S. dollar. Instead, the deviation to the block of non-OECD is d(to non-OECD) = 2.4/d .

(c) Statistical Discrepancies and Errors:

There are three statistical discrepancies and errors which the reader should be aware of, namely:

1. The world GNP shown in the table is not exactly the same as the world GNP which may be shown elsewhere. This is due to the fact that numerous non-OECD countries are missing in the table, including major oil producers like Saudi Arabia, Iran and Iraq. However, I did not correct that in order to keep the numbers in the table consistent with each other. (The same applies to world population.)
2. The total of exports from non-OECD to OECD shown in the table is not the same as the total of imports by OECD from non-OECD. This is a result of a large number of missing non-OECD countries. As the data for the OECD countries are complete, the larger of the two totals (namely, total imports by OECD from non-OECD) is the correct figure and the total of exports from non-OECD to OECD is understated.
3. The total losses shown for non-OECD countries are not the same as the total gains by OECD countries. This is a consequence of missing data for non-OECD countries. As the data for OECD countries are complete, the total gains by OECD countries is the correct total for global exploitation due to unequal exchange. The total of losses by non-OECD countries is understated. However, the losses for individual non-OECD countries shown in the table are correct for each individual country.

Chapter 4

UNEQUAL EXCHANGE: WORLD TABLES 1965 AND WORLD TREND 1865 - 1965 - 1995

1. INTRODUCTION

This study continues my measurements of unequal exchange and includes data for the years 1965 and 1995. I am presenting (1) highlights and a summary of global trends of unequal exchange, 1965 - 1995; and (2) the statistical tables upon which this summary is based (in the Appendices). The calculations are based on trade data from U.N. trade statistics and on purchasing power parity data from the World Bank (and Penn World Tables). The underlying theory and method are explained in the previous study.

2. CORROBORATION OF AMIN'S ESTIMATE

Professor Amin published an estimate of the magnitude of unequal exchange between developing and advanced countries for the year 1966. According to Amin the global total of unequal exchange in 1966 was US $ 22 billion (22 thousand million) at exchange rates of 1966 (Amin 1976:144). My estimate for 1965 is US $ 19 billion (see, Appendix B). Amin's and my estimates are thus very similar even though they are based on two different methods of estimation. (More on Amin's numbers, see Appendix D)

3. NATIONAL TRENDS: SELECTED COUNTRIES

Table 1 shows trends of unequal exchange for selected countries; other countries are listed in Appendix A.

Table 1 - Unequal Exchange 1965-95, Selected Countries

	Unequal Exchange gain (+) loss (-) as a percent of GDP	
	1965 %	1995 %
AFRICA		
Mozambique	-8	-75
Nigeria	-1	-172
Egypt	-1	-21
ASIA		
Indonesia	-8	-52
India	-1	-18
China (mainland)	0	-47
AMERICA, Central and South		
Brazil	-5	-4
Mexico	-3	-28
Peru	-6	-5
EUROPE, Central and East		
USSR/Russia	0	-10
Czechosl./Czech R	+1	-46
Romania	+1	-29
OECD Countries		
USA	+1	+6
France	+2	+7
Germany-W/Germany	+2	+11
Japan	+1	+11
United Kingdom	+3	+6

Sources and notes: see, Appendix A

Table 1 shows significant increases in the magnitudes of unequal exchange between 1965 and 1995; that means increased *losses* for many non-OECD countries (e.g., Indonesia, from a loss of -8% of GDP in 1965 to a loss of -52% of GDP in 1995, due to unequal exchange) and increased *gains* for OECD countries.

4. Trends by Center/Periphery of the World-System

When the world is subdivided into but two groups of countries -- namely, center versus periphery, or, OECD versus non-OECD countries, the trends are, as shown in Table 2.

Table 2 - Unequal Exchange 1965 and 1995, by Center/Periphery

	Unequal Exchange Gain (+) Loss (-)	
	CENTER (% of OECD GDP)	PERIPHERY (% of NON-OECD GDP)
1965	+1.4%	- 1.8%
1995	+8 %	-24 %

(Number of countries: OECD N=19 (1965) and N=22 (1995); NON-OECD N=88 (1965) and N=97 (1995))

Sources and notes: see, Appendix A

Table 2 shows that OECD countries (center) increased their gains from unequal exchange from +1.4 % of their combined GDPs (1965) to +8 % (in 1995). The losses for non-OECD countries (periphery) increased from -1.8% of their combined GDPs (1965) to -24 % (in 1995). ("Non-OECD" in this table includes China and USSR, as well as (ex-)Warsaw Pact countries).

5. Trends by "Three Worlds"

The center-periphery view above can be refined by separating out the Socialist/Communist camp. In Cold War times, the West (First World, NATO, OECD) was rivalling the East (Second World, Warsaw Pact, COMECON), both competing for allies in the South (Third World, non-aligned countries, developing countries). The trends of unequal exchange for these groups of countries are presented in Tables 3 and 4.

Table 3 - Unequal Exchange and "Three Worlds"

YEAR	OECD countries	USSR/ Russia	China	NON-OECD excl. China, USSR/Russia	NON-OECD incl. China, USSR/Russia
	(A)	(B)	(C)	(D)	(E)
	percent of aggregate GDP gain(+) loss(-)				
1965	+1.4%	0 %	0 %	- 3.9%	- 1.8%
1995	+8%	-10 %	-47 %	-20%	-24%

Sources and notes: see, Appendices A,B and Kohler (1998: Appendix)

Table 3 shows that the two major Socialist/Communist states -- namely, (mainland) China and the USSR, had fairly equitable trade with the West in 1965 (unequal exchange

= 0% of GDP). By 1995 this favourable situation had deteriorated to -10% for Russia and - 47% for China. The "South" ("Third World" without China and USSR) had already a significant amount of unequal exchange losses in 1965 -- namely, -3.9 percent of the combined Third World GDPs. This deteriorated to -20 % in 1995.

The data for (ex-)Socialist/Communist states are incomplete. Here is the available information (Table 4):

Table 4 - (Ex-)Socialist/Communist Countries

	Unequal Exchange Gain (+)Loss (-)As % of GDP	
	1965 %	1995 %
Bulgaria	*	-54
China	0	-47
Czechoslov./Czech R	+1	-46
Estonia	**	-16
Hungary	*	-16
Kasakstan	**	- 6
Kyrgystan	**	0
Latvia	**	- 7
Lithuania	**	-22
Poland	*	-18
Romania	+1	-29
USSR/Russian Fed	0	-10
Slovakia	**	- 8
Ukraine	**	- 1
Uzbekistan	**	- 3
Yugoslavia	0	.
All above	+0.1%	-31% (percent of aggregated GDPs)

Sources and notes: Appendix A
* = data incomplete ** = did not exist as an independent country

Table 4 shows that the Socialist/Communist countries had fair trade with the OECD countries in 1965 (unequal exchange ranging between 0% or +1% per country). By 1995 this situation deteriorated to unequal exchange amounting to -31% of their aggregate GDP.

6. World Trend

The global trend of unequal exchange between OECD countries and non-OECD countries is summarized in Table 5.

Table 5 - World Trend of Unequal Exchange 1965 - 1995

	World Total of Unequal Exchange		
	in current U.S. dollars at current exchange rates (billions) (A)	in constant U.S. dollars (1995=100) (billions) (B)	as a percent of global GDP (C)
1965	19	84	0.9 %
1995	1752	1752	6.6 %

Sources: Appendices A, B and Kohler (1998:Appendix)
Note: price deflator of 0.2274 based on World Bank. World Tables, various years.

Table 5 shows the global trend, as follows:

1. Column (A) shows the amount of unequal exchange in current U.S. dollars of 1965 and 1995. The figure of 19 billion in 1965 is similar to Amin's estimate of 22 billion for 1966. By 1995 the total volume of unequal exchange had increased to 1752 billion (= 1.75 trillion) U.S. dollars. -- These two figures include the effect of inflation and cannot be compared directly.
2. In column (B) the values from column (A) have been converted into constant U.S. dollars at 1995 values (1995=100). The figure for 1995 remains unchanged (namely, 1752) and the figure for 1965 becomes 84 billion (in terms of 1995 dollar values). The total amount of unequal exchange between non-OECD and OECD increased 21-fold between 1965 and 1995. This reflects two developments -- namely, (a) more trading volume (6 times more) and (b) greater exchange rate deviations.
3. Column (C) shows the trend of unequal exchange relative to global GDP. Unequal exchange between non-OECD and OECD increased from 0.9% of global GDP (in 1965) to 6.6 % of global GDP (in 1995).

7. Impact of the Exchange Rate System

The data suggest that the neoliberal system of exchange rates prevailing in 1995 created significantly more unequal exchange than the exchange rate system prevailing in 1965 which had some Keynesian features. A major reason for this is that the neoliberal exchange rate system allows for greater exchange rate deviations from purchasing power parity.

8. Historical Trend of Unequal Exchange 1865-1995

Going back a century, what was the magnitude of unequal exchange in the 19th century? The following quotation provides a preliminary estimate:

> "Mandel, Amin, and Arghiri Emmanuel (1972) contend that the core/periphery relationship altered during the late nineteenth century due to the emergence in the 1880s of a wage differential between core workers and peripheral workers. Previous to that, workers in both the core and the periphery had received subsistence wages, but in the late nineteenth century, due to the diminishing reserve army of labor in England and because of partial success of labor struggles there, wages for English workers began to rise above subsistence. This brought about the "unequal exchange" analyzed by Emmanuel (1972)..."(Chase-Dunn 1989: 59)

Based on this observation, it may be estimated that unequal exchange prior to 1880 may have been equal to zero (null). When we use this observation as an estimate for unequal exchange in 1865, we can construct an historical trend, as follows (Table 6):

Table 6 - Historical Trend of Unequal Exchange 1865 - 1995

	Unequal Exchange as a		
	% of World GDP	% of Periphery GDP	% of Center GDP
1865	0%	0 %	0 %
1965	0.9 %	- 1.8%	+1.4%
1995	6.6 %	-24 %	+8 %

Sources: Chase-Dunn 1989:59 and Table 2 above.

Table 6 shows an historical "explosion" of unequal exchange over the last three decades from 0.9% of world GDP to 6.6% of world GDP.

9. Conclusion

The findings suggest that the absolute and relative magnitude of unequal exchange has increased significantly within the last thirty years, taking from the poor and giving to the rich.

For further details the reader is invited to examine the tables in the Appendices and to pursue some questions of his/her own.

10. APPENDIX

The appendices are organized, as follows:

Appendix A -- World Table of Unequal Exchange 1965-1995 (Comparison Table)
Appendix B -- World Table of Unequal Exchange 1965 (Base Table)
Appendix C -- Methodological Details Concerning Base Table 1965
Appendix D -- Amin's Estimate for 1966

APPENDIX A -- WORLD TABLE OF UNEQUAL EXCHANGE 1965 – 1995 (COMPARISON TABLE)

GROUP = NON-OECD (N=88 countries (1965) and 97 countries (1995))

Country	UNEQUAL EXCHANGE gain (+) loss (-) % of GDP 1965	1995
Algeria	*	-47%
Angola	-25%	-203%
Argentina	-1%	0%
Armenia	*	0%
Bahamas	*	-1%
Bahrain	*	-11%
Bangladesh	*	-33%
Barbados	-13%	-5%
Belize	*	-34%
Benin	*	-11%
Bhutan	*	0%
Bolivia	-23%	-26%
Brazil	-5%	-4%
Bulgaria	*	-54%
Burkina Faso	*	-7%
Cameroon	-7%	-68%
Cape Verde	*	-2%
Central Afr R	-11%	-29%
Chad	-7%	*
Chile	-1%	-26%
China	0%	-47%
Colombia	-3%	-24%
Comoros	*	-8%
Congo	-15%	-99%
Costa Rica	-8%	-35%
Cyprus	-1%	*
Czech R/Czechoslovakia	+1%	-46%
Dominican Republic	-3%	-33%
Ecuador	-10%	-53%
Egypt	-1%	-21%

El Salvador	-13%	-4%
Estonia	**	-16%
Ethiopia	-3%	-10%
Fiji	-17%	-39%
Gabon	-7%	*
Gambia	-25%	-10%
Ghana	+2%	-30%
Greece	0%	-4%
Guatemala	-6%	-12%
Guyana	-8%	*
Honduras	-7%	-39%
Hong Kong	-13%	-7%
Hungary	*	-16%
India	-1%	-18%
Indonesia	-8%	-52%
Iran	-19%	*
Iraq	-41%	*
Israel	+2%	-2%
Ivory Coast	-17%	*
Jamaica	0%	-39%
Jordan	0%	-8%
Kasakstan	**	-6%
Kenya	-6%	-35%
Korea (note a)	-7%	
Kuwait	*	-13%
Kyrgystan	**	0%
Latvia	**	-7%
Liberia	+2%	*
Lithuania	**	-22%
Madagascar	-11%	-18%
Malawi	-4%	-93%
Malaysia	-12%	-79%
Maldives	*	-16%
Mali	-1%	*
Malta	+1%	*
Mauritania	-1%	*
Mauritius	-40%	-127%
Mexico	-3%	-28%
Morocco	-4%	-28%
Mozambique	-8%	-75%
Myanmar	-1%	*
Nepal	*	-36%
Nicaragua	-53%	-112%
Niger	0%	-33%
Nigeria	-1%	-172%
Oman	*	-23%
Pakistan	-6%	-27%
Panama	-1%	-21%

Papua New Guinea	-27%	-46%
Paraguay	-3%	-4%
Peru	-6%	-5%
Philippines	-11%	-36%
Poland	*	-18%
Portugal (note a)	-5%	
Qatar	*	-4%
Reunion	+7%	.
Romania	+1%	-29%
Rwanda	-12%	*
Saint Kitts and N	*	-10%
Saudi Arabia	-1%	*
Senegal	-5%	-12%
Sierra Leone	-54%	*
Singapore	+1%	+4%
Slovakia	**	-8%
Solomon I	*	-116%
Somalia	-10%	*
Southern Africa	-2%	-8%
Spain (note a)	-2%	
Sri Lanka	-12%	-60%
Suriname	-13%	-228%
Syrian Arab Republic	-1%	-55%
Taiwan	-9%	*
United R of Tanzania	-4%	-31%
Thailand	-9%	-40%
Togo	-3%	-18%
Trinidad and Tobago	-39%	-42%
Tunisia	-2%	-56%
Turkey	-3%	-10%
Uganda	+2%	-16%
Ukraine	**	-1%
Russian Fed./USSR	0%	-10%
United Arab Emirates	*	0%
Uruguay	-22%	-2%
Uzbekistan	**	-3%
Vanuatu	*	-7%
Venezuela	*	-35%
Yugoslavia	0%	*
Zaire	+2%	*
Zambia	-6%	-17%
Zimbabwe	-3%	-56%
NON-OECD SUMMARY		
number of countries	88	97
average (arithmetic)	-8%	-33%
unequal exchange as % of NON-OECD GDP	-1.8%	-24%

GROUP = OECD (N=19 countries (1965) and 22 countries (1995))		
Country	UNEQUAL EXCHANGE % of GDP	
	1965	1995
Australia	+1%	+6%
Austria	+1%	+9%
Belgium-Lux	+4%	+14%
Canada	+1%	+5%
Denmark	+2%	+9%
Finland	+4%	+9%
France	+2%	+7%
Germany, Fed R	+2%	+11%
Iceland	+8%	+6%
Ireland	+2%	+13%
Italy	+1%	+6%
Japan	+1%	+11%
Korea, R (note a)		+10%
Netherlands	+2%	+17%
New Zealand	+1%	+6%
Norway	+3%	+7%
Portugal (note a)		+4%
Spain (note a)		+6%
Sweden	+3%	+7%
Switzerland	+1%	+7%
United Kingdom	+3%	+6%
United States	+1%	+6%
OECD SUMMARY (note a)		
number of countries	19	22
average (arithmetic)	+2%	+8%
unequal exchange as % of OECD GDP (a)	+1.38%	+8%

LEGEND

(*) insufficient data

(**) country did not exist as a sovereign state

SOURCES

for 1965: *World Table of Unequal Exchange 1965* (Base Table), see Appendix B

for 1995: *World Table of Unequal Exchange 1995* see, Kohler 1998: Appendix

NOTE (a) Three countries (Republic of Korea, Portugal and Spain) were "developing countries" in 1965 and are placed with the "NON-OECD" group for 1965. The group summaries for 1965 treat these three countries as NON-OECD for the year 1965. However, in 1995 these three countries were OECD countries and are placed in "OECD" for 1995 and are included in the group summaries for OECD for the year 1995.

APPENDIX B
WORLD TABLE OF UNEQUAL EXCHANGE 1965 (BASE TABLE)

1. Introduction

Losses or gains from unequal exchange are calculated as the difference between a "fair value" of exports/imports and the "actual (unfair) value" of exports/imports. The estimation formula is:

$$T = d^*X - X$$

where

> d = the exchange rate deviation index (also designated as "ERD" in the literature)
> X = the volume of exports from a low- or middle-income country to high-income countries (valued at the actual exchange rate)
> T = the unrecorded transfer of value (gain or loss) resulting from unequal exchange

In the table (below) this formula is applied to the data for 107 countries for the year 1965.

2. HOW TO READ THE TABLE

The table presents the step-by-step calculations. Countries are arranged in alphabetical order and in two groups -- first, non-OECD countries and, secondly, OECD countries. The losses or gains from unequal exchange are shown at the right-hand side (in terms of U.S. dollars and as a percent of the country's GDP).

World Table Of Unequal Exchange 1965 (Base Table)

GROUP = NON-OECD (N=88)(= all except "industrialized countries")

Country	GDP 1965 US $ (mln) (A)	Popul 1965 (mln) (B)	GDP per capita 1965 US $ (mln) (C)	GDP per capita 1965 PPP $ (mln) (D)	Exports to OECD year (E)	Exports to OECD US $ (mln) (F)	Exchange Rate Deviation G = D/C (ratio) (G)	Fair Value of exports (G/1.2)*F ($ mln) (H)	Unequal Exchange LOSS(-) GAIN(+) J=F-H ($mln) (J)	Unequal Exchange LOSS(-) GAIN(+) K=J/A %of GDP (K)
Angola	580	5.3	109	306	1965	106	2.82	249	-143	-25%
Argentina	21,454	22.3	963	1529	65	926	1.59	1225	-299	-1%
Barbados	118	0.2	500	988	65	23	1.97	38	-15	-13%
Bolivia	584	3.8	152	412	65	105	2.71	237	-132	-23%
Brazil	21,071	84.3	250	576	65	1197	2.30	2298	-1101	-5%
Cameroon	729	5.8	125	211	64	131	1.69	184	-53	-7%
C. Afr. Rep.	153	1.7	88	200	65	18	2.26	35	-16	-11%
Chad	286	3.3	85	217	65	17	2.54	37	-19	-7%
Chile	6,667	8.6	772	1029	65	612	1.33	680	-68	-1%
China	70,177	715.2	98	170	65	600	1.73	866	-266	0%
Colombia	5,914	18.5	320	548	65	437	1.71	623	-187	-3%
Congo	169	1.1	158	309	65	40	1.95	65	-25	-15%
Costa Rica	593	1.5	398	742	65	88	1.87	138	-49	-8%
Cyprus	363	0.6	623	811	65	49	1.30	53	-4	-1%
Czechoslov.	8,834	14.1	626	556	65	403	0.89	298	+105	+1%
Dominican R	965	3.8	252	382	64	108	1.52	137	-29	-3%
Ecuador	1,106	5.3	209	484	64	115	2.32	222	-107	-10%
Egypt	5,614	29.4	191	295	65	157	1.54	202	-45	-1%
El Salvador	796	3.0	264	550	65	138	2.08	239	-101	-13%

Country	GDP 1965 US $ (mln) (A)	Popul 1965 (mln) (B)	GDP per capita 1965 US $ (mln) (C)	GDP per capita 1965 PPP $ (mln) (D)	Exports to OECD year (E)	Exports to OECD US $ (mln) (F)	Exchange Rate Deviation G = D/C (ratio) (G)	Fair Value of exports (G/1.2)*F ($ mln) (H)	Unequal Exchange LOSS(-) GAIN(+) J=F-H ($mln) (J)	Unequal Exchange LOSS(-) GAIN(+) K=J/A %of GDP (K)
Ethiopia	1,371	25.4	54	89	65	92	1.65	127	-35	-3%
Fiji	153	0.5	329	639	65	41	1.94	66	-25	-17%
Gabon	203	0.5	422	592	65	84	1.40	98	-14	-7%
Gambia	44	0.4	106	244	65	12	2.31	23	-11	-25%
Ghana	2,067	7.8	265	263	65	212	0.99	176	+37	+2%
Greece	5,996	8.6	701	912	65	207	1.30	224	-17	0%
Guatemala	1,333	4.5	295	581	65	135	1.97	221	-87	-6%
Guyana	212	0.6	348	506	65	76	1.46	92	-16	-8%
Honduras	513	2.3	224	359	65	103	1.60	138	-35	-7%
Hong Kong	2,181	3.6	609	1009	65	754	1.66	1042	-287	-13%
India	53,740	487.3	110	225	65	962	2.04	1636	-674	-1%
Indonesia	5,978	106.0	56	167	62	341	2.96	841	-500	-8%
Iran	6,480	24.1	269	763	65	923	2.84	2180	-1257	-19%
Iraq	2,478	8.0	311	961	65	644	3.09	1660	-1016	-41%
Israel	3,650	2.6	1424	1340	65	292	0.94	229	+63	+2%
Ivory Coast	956	4.6	208	434	65	227	2.08	394	-167	-17%
Jamaica	930	1.7	534	634	65	195	1.19	193	+2	0%
Jordan	417	2.0	212	496	65	2	2.33	3	-1	0%
Kenya	1,037	9.6	108	205	65	99	1.90	156	-58	-6%
Korea, R	3,012	28.4	106	318	65	131	3.00	328	-197	-7%
Liberia	297	1.2	248	282	65	126	1.14	119	+6	+2%
Madagascar	819	6.0	136	358	65	77	2.63	169	-92	-11%

Country	GDP 1965	Popul 1965	GDP per capita 1965	1965	Exports to OECD		Exchange Rate Deviation	Fair Value of exports	Unequal Exchange LOSS(-) GAIN(+)	
	US $ (mln) (A)	(mln) (B)	US $ (mln) (C)	PPP $ (mln) (D)	year (E)	US $ (mln) (F)	G = D/C (ratio) (G)	(G/1.2)*F ($ mln) (H)	J=F-H ($mln) (J)	K=J/A %of GDP (K)
Malawi	231	3.9	59	124	65	12	2.11	21	-9	-4%
Malaysia	2,711	9.5	285	509	65	678	1.79	1011	-332	-12%
Mali	245	4.7	52	149	65	1	2.87	3	-2	-1%
Malta	148	0.3	463	525	65	15	1.13	14	+1	+1%
Mauritania	188	1.1	172	273	64	5	1.58	7	-2	-1%
Mauritius	230	0.7	311	950	65	59	3.05	151	-92	-40%
Mexico	21,739	44.9	485	1015	65	837	2.09	1460	-623	-3%
Morocco	3,019	13.6	222	376	65	314	1.70	444	-130	-4%
Mozambique	744	8.4	88	387	65	24	4.38	87	-63	-8%
Myanmar	2,000	24.3	82	119	64	59	1.44	71	-12	-1%
Nicaragua	384	1.8	213	679	65	122	3.19	325	-203	-53%
Niger	587	3.7	160	183	65	15	1.14	15	+1	0%
Nigeria	6,967	58.5	119	158	65	668	1.33	739	-70	-1%
Pakistan	5,486	52.6	104	285	65	243	2.73	553	-310	-6%
Panama	635	1.3	479	617	65	69	1.29	74	-5	-1%
Papua New G	345	2.1	161	508	65	58	3.15	152	-94	-27%
Paraguay	443	2.1	214	390	65	28	1.82	42	-15	-3%
Peru	4,800	11.5	416	753	65	562	1.81	848	-286	-6%
Philippines	5,582	32.4	172	378	65	722	2.19	1319	-597	-11%
Portugal	3,777	9.1	414	764	65	357	1.85	550	-192	-5%
Reunion	230	0.4	588	379	65	33	0.64	18	+15	+7%
Romania	3,605	19.2	188	188	65	253	1.00	212	+42	+1%

Country	GDP 1965	Popul 1965	GDP per capita 1965	1965	Exports to OECD		Exchange Rate Deviation	Fair Value of exports	Unequal Exchange LOSS(-) GAIN(+)	
	US $ (mln) (A)	(mln) (B)	US $ (mln) (C)	PPP $ (mln) (D)	year (E)	US $ (mln) (F)	G = D/C (ratio) (G)	(G/1.2)*F ($ mln) (H)	J=F-H ($mln) (J)	K=J/A %of GDP (K)
Rwanda	129	3.2	40	104	65	13	2.57	29	-15	-12%
Saudi Arabia	2,320	4.8	484	595	65	900	1.23	921	-22	-1%
Senegal	832	3.9	212	349	65	118	1.65	162	-44	-5%
Sierra Leone	340	2.5	137	337	65	174	2.46	357	-183	-54%
Singapore	1,266	2.5	511	570	65	265	1.11	246	+19	+1%
Somalia	274	3.0	90	290	65	17	3.21	45	-28	-10%
South Africa	10,774	20.1	535	767	65	1086	1.43	1297	-211	-2%
Spain	23,778	32.1	742	1393	65	704	1.88	1101	-398	-2%
Sri Lanka	1,731	11.1	156	350	65	229	2.25	430	-201	-12%
Suriname	166	0.3	499	885	64	45	1.77	66	-21	-13%
Syria	1,632	5.3	306	565	65	40	1.84	62	-22	-1%
Taiwan	2,794	12.6	221	501	65	293	2.26	552	-259	-9%
Tanzania	884	11.6	76	118	65	120	1.55	155	-35	-4%
Thailand	4,079	30.7	133	359	64	288	2.70	650	-361	-9%
Togo	170	1.7	97	144	65	25	1.48	31	-6	-3%
Trinidad & T	709	0.9	782	1897	65	273	2.42	552	-279	-39%
Tunisia	1,016	4.6	219	354	65	72	1.61	97	-25	-2%
Turkey	8,425	31.2	270	563	65	321	2.08	557	-236	-3%
Uganda	1,745	8.1	216	179	65	124	0.83	85	+38	+2%
U.S.S.R.	283,214	230.1	1231	892	65	1388	0.72	838	+550	0%
Uruguay	978	2.7	363	1158	65	130	3.19	345	-215	-22%
Yugoslavia	12,274	19.4	632	735	65	436	1.16	423	+13	0%

Country	GDP 1965	Popul 1965	GDP per capita 1965	1965	Exports to OECD		Exchange Rate Deviation	Fair Value of exports	Unequal Exchange LOSS(-) GAIN(+)	
	US $ (mln) (A)	(mln) (B)	US $ (mln) (C)	PPP $ (mln) (D)	year (E)	US $ (mln) (F)	G = D/C (ratio) (G)	(G/1.2)*F ($ mln) (H)	J=F-H ($mln) (J)	K=J/A %of GDP (K)
Zaire	4,521	17.6	257	161	65	178	0.63	93	+85	+2%
Zambia	1,054	3.6	292	403	65	452	1.38	520	-68	-6%
Zimbabwe	1,042	4.4	238	329	65	217	1.38	249	-33	-3%

NON-OECD SUMMARY N=88

1. sum (for N=88):	
a. GDP 1965 (US $, mln) (col. A)	670,279
b. Population 1965 (mln) (col. B)	2,437.8
c. Exports to OECD 1965 (US $, mln) (col. F)	24,047
d. Unequal Exchange 1965 ($, mln) (col. J)	-11,870
2. sum without China, USSR (for N=86):	
a. GDP 1965 (US $, mln) (col. A)	316,888
b. Population 1965 (mln) (col. B)	1,492.6
c. Exports to OECD 1965 (US $, mln) (col. F)	22,059
d. Unequal Exchange 1965 ($, mln) (col. J)	-12,153
3. average (arithmetic, for N=88) of:	
a. Exchange rate deviation 1965 (ratio) (col. G)	1.91
b. Unequal Exchange as % of GDP (col. K)	-8%
4. average (weighted by exports, for N=88) of exhange rate deviation 1965 (ratio) (col. G)	1.79
5. unequal exchange as % of NON-OECD GDP (col. K)	
a. for N=88	-1.77 %
b. for N=86, without China, USSR	-3.84%

GROUP = OECD (N=19) (="industrialized countries")

Country	GDP 1965	Popul 1965	GDP per capita 1965	1965	Imports from NON-OECD		Exchange Rate Deviation	Fair Value of exports	Unequal Exchange LOSS(-) GAIN(+)	
	US$		US $	PPP $		US $	G = D/C	(1.79/G)*F	J=F-H	K=J/A
	(mln)	(mln)	(mln)	(mln)	year	(mln)	(ratio)		($mln)	%of GDP
	(A)	(B)	(C)	(D)	(E)	(F)	(G)	(H)	(J)	(K)
Australia	24,142	11.4	2120	2733	65	618	1.29	858	+240	+1%
Austria	9,539	7.3	1315	1871	65	420	1.42	528	+108	+1%
Belgium-Lux	16,543	9.4	1751	2082	65	1274	1.19	1919	+644	+4%
Canada	51,801	19.7	2632	2560	65	878	0.97	1615	+738	+1%
Denmark	10,172	4.8	2138	2616	65	508	1.22	743	+235	+2%
Finland	8,295	4.6	1818	1981	65	526	1.09	865	+338	+4%
France	99,277	48.8	2036	2243	65	3620	1.10	5882	+2262	+2%
Germany-W	114,391	58.6	1951	2400	65	4717	1.23	6866	+2149	+2%
Iceland	496	0.2	2559	1905	65	27	0.74	66	+39	+8%
Ireland	2,695	2.9	937	1215	65	166	1.30	229	+63	+2%
Italy	67,843	52.0	1305	1740	65	2792	1.33	3748	+956	+1%
Japan	91,022	98.9	920	1399	65	4166	1.52	4906	+740	+1%
Netherlands	20,048	12.3	1631	2289	65	1493	1.40	1904	+411	+2%
New Zealand	5,461	2.6	2072	2855	65	94	1.38	122	+28	+1%
Norway	6,984	3.7	1876	2034	65	309	1.08	510	+201	+3%
Sweden	22,305	7.7	2884	2912	65	788	1.01	1397	+609	+3%
Switzerland	13,914	5.9	2376	3300	65	437	1.39	563	+126	+1%
UK	100,026	54.4	1839	2310	65	6294	1.26	8971	+2677	+3%
USA	695,821	194.3	3581	3581	65	7905	1.00	14151	+6245	+1%

OECD SUMMARY

1. sum (for N=19) of:	
a. GDP 1965 (US $, mln) (col. A)	1,360,776
b. Imports from NON-OECD 1965 (US $, mln) (col. F)	37,033
c. Unequal Exchange 1965 ($, mln) (col. J)	+18,810
2. average (arithmetic, for N=19)	
a. Exchange rate deviation 1965 (ratio) (col. G)	1.21
b. Unequal Exchange as % of GDP (col. K)	+2%
3. average (weighted by imports from NON-OECD) (ratio) (col. G)	1.21
4. unequal exchange as % of OECD GDP (N=19) (col. K)	+1.38%

World Summary of Unequal Exchange 1965 (N=107 Countries)

1. World GDP	2,031,050 U.S. $ millions =2.03 trillion (=sum of GDPs for N=107)
2. Gains (OECD)	+18,810 U.S. $ millions (N=19)
3. Losses (NON-OECD)	-11,870 U.S. $ millions (N=88)
4. Error	-6,940 U.S. $ millions due to missing data for NON-OECD countries
5. Gains (OECD)	+0.93 % of world GDP
6. Losses (NON-OECD)	-0.58 % of world GDP
7. Error	-0.35 % due to missing data for NON-OECD countries

Sources

Source 1= U.N., International Trade Statistics Yearbook 1965, Table A and country tables #4 or #5 "Trade by principal countries..."
Source 2= Penn World Tables (1998), from the internet at: http://datacentre.chass.utoronto.ca:5680/pwt
Source 3= for classification of countries as "industrialized" or not: World Bank. World Tables 1980, p. 471

Calculations

variable P [not shown in the table, but used in some of the calculations] = "price level" from Penn World Tables (variable P in source)
col. A = B * C
col. B = from source (Penn World Tables)
col. C = D * P / 100

col. D = from source (Penn World Tables, variable CGDP)
col. E = from source (U.N., International Trade Statistics Yearbook 1965)
col. F = from source 1 (U.N.),

using the following conversions from local currency data to U.S. dollars:

(1) for exports of NON-OECD country to OECD:

(a) sum in local currency and obtain % of total exports

(b) apply percent (from a) to total exports given in U.S dollars

(2) for imports by OECD country from NON-OECD:

(a) sum in local currency and obtain % of total imports in local currency

(b) calculate total imports in U.S. Dollars = total imports in local currency (from source 1), divided by exchange rate (from source 2, Penn World Tables)

col. G = 100 / P (from source 2)
col. H = two formulae:

(1) for NON-OECD country: H = (d/1.2)*exports = (G/1.2)*F

(1.2 is the average exchange rate deviation of OECD countries, see above)

(2) for OECD: H = (1.79/d)*imports =(1.79/G)*F

(1.79 is the average exchange rate deviation of NON-OECD countries, see above)

col. J = F - H (for NON-OECD) and J = H - F (for OECD)
col K = J/A as a percent

China Data

China (mainland) was not recognized by the U.N in 1965 and is not included in Source 1 (U.N.) like the other countries. However, the imports from China (mainland) to OECD countries are given under each OECD country in local currency (e.g. French francs). I converted these local values to U.S. Dollars, using the exchange rates from Source 2 (Penn World Tables).

The resulting total for exports from China (mainland) is US$592 million.

The total of US$592 million is composed of trade flows from China (mainland) to OECD countries, as follows, in US $ millions (1965), to: Australia 26; Austria 5; Belgium-Luxembourg 14; Canada 13; Denmark 10; Finland 6; France 44; Germany FR 72; Iceland 0; Ireland 0; Italy 38; Japan 224; Netherlands 25; New Zealand 1; Norway 5; Sweden 15; Switzerland 12; United Kingdom 81; USA nil.

**end of 1965 Base Table

APPENDIX C -- FURTHER METHODOLOGICAL DETAILS CONCERNING THE WORLD TABLE FOR 1965 (BASE TABLE)

(a) Exclusion of Countries:

Countries which are not shown in the tables are missing due to missing data. For these countries either trade data or PPP data or both were missing in my sources.

Luxembourg is lumped together with Belgium because the export/import data were given that way in the source. (The GNP-related data are for Belgium.)

(b) Two Calculation Models:

There are two calculation models, one for non-OECD countries and one for OECD countries. Both use the same formula (see above) with two slight variations.

MODEL 1 for non-OECD Countries:

Here I measure the export flow from each individual non-OECD country to the block of OECD countries. Since the exchange rate deviation for the block of OECD countries is d = 1.2 (i.e. deviation from the U.S. dollar), the exchange rate deviation between the individual non-OECD country and the block of OECD countries is not d(to OECD) = d/1.0 since the d calculated from the source gives the deviation to the U.S. dollar. Instead, the deviation to the block of OECD is d(to OECD) = d/1.2 .

MODEL 2 for OECD Countries:

Here I measure the import flow from the block of non-OECD countries to each individual OECD country. Since the exchange rate deviation for the block of non-OECD countries is d = 1.79 (i.e. deviation from the U.S. dollar), the exchange rate deviation between the individual OECD country and the block of non-OECD countries is not d(to non-OECD) = 1.0/d since the d calculated from source gives the deviation to the U.S. dollar. Instead, the deviation to the block of non-OECD is d(to non-OECD) = 1.79/d .

(c) Statistical Discrepancies and Errors:

There are three statistical discrepancies and errors which the reader should be aware of, namely:

1. The world GNP shown in the table is not exactly the same as the world GNP which may be shown elsewhere. This is due to the fact that numerous non-OECD countries are missing in the table. However, I did not correct that in order to keep

the numbers in the table consistent with each other. (The same applies to world population.)

2. The total of exports from non-OECD to OECD shown in the table is not the same as the total of imports by OECD from non-OECD. This is a result of a large number of missing non-OECD countries. As the data for the OECD countries are complete, the larger of the two totals (namely, total imports by OECD from non-OECD) is the correct figure and the total of exports from non-OECD to OECD is understated.
3. The total losses shown for non-OECD countries are not the same as the total gains by OECD countries. This is a consequence of missing data for non-OECD countries. As the data for OECD countries are complete, the total gains by OECD countries is the correct total for global exploitation due to unequal exchange. The total of losses by non-OECD countries is understated. However, the losses for individual non-OECD countries shown in the table are correct for each individual country.

APPENDIX D -- AMIN'S ESTIMATE FOR 1966

Amin writes with reference to the year 1966:

"The hidden transfer of value from the periphery to the center, due to the mechanism of unequal exchange, are of the order of $22 billion ...The imports that the advanced countries of the West receive from the Third World represent, it is true, only 2 or 3 percent of their gross national product, which is about $1.2 billion in 1966. But these exports from the underdeveloped countries represent 20 percent of *their* product, which was about $150 billion. The hidden transfer of value due to unequal exchange is thus of the order of 15 percent of this product ... The contribution that this transfer makes ... comes to about 1.5 percent of the center's product." (Amin, Unequal Development, 1976, p. 144)

Comments:

(a) Amin estimates the magnitude of total unequal exchange (1966) as $22 billion. My estimate for 1965 is $19 billion. Both estimates are very similar.

(b) Amin expresses the $22 billion as a percent of the center's combined GDP as 1.5% (1966). My corresponding estimate for 1965 is 1.4%. Both estimates are very similar.

(c) Amin expresses the $22 billion as a percent of the periphery's combined GDP as 15% (1966). My corresponding estimate for 1965 is 3.9% (if China and USSR are excluded from "non-OECD") or 1.8% (if China and USSR are included). This discrepancy results from a difference in the numbers used for the periphery's product (Third World aggregate GDP). Amin uses $150 billion as the product of "the underdeveloped countries" (see quotation above). In my base table for 1965 (see, Appendix B) the combined GDP for non-OECD is $670 billion (with China, USSR included) or $317 billion (with China, USSR excluded). It appears that Amin's figure of $150 billion refers to the group of countries which the World Bank classifies as "low-income", whereas my figure is more inclusive and refers to NON-OECD (which includes low and middle-income countries).

Chapter 5

GLOBAL KEYNESIANISM AND BEYOND

1. INTRODUCTION

Something like "global Keynesianism" or "transnational socialism" has been mentioned as a desirable alternative to global neoliberalism (Redmond 1997). However, a definition of this kind of global Keynesianism is hard to find. Many leftists tend to associate Keynesianism with corporate power. However, there are also numerous other leftists who view this differently. For example, a member of parliament for the Green Party (Germany) stated in a recent interview that "a reformist party today has to be a left-Keynesian party which contradicts the logic of capital" (Ebermann 1998). A number of scholars from several countries, including Canada, pursue post-Keynesianism, in the sense of left-Keynesian economics (e.g., Seccareccia 1991). However, available left-Keynesian literature, as I see it, is lacking a world-system perspective. I am trying in this article to synthesize the two perspectives -- namely, left-Keynesianism and world-system theory, leading to a perspective of global left-Keynesianism. This leftist global Keynesianism can, perhaps, be described as an approach to economics which emphasizes responsible public management of economic problems in a world-system context. Common themes in global Keynesianism include the importance of public management, democratic politics, the mixed economy, global income distribution, the management of global demand, investment and money, ecological sustainability and the importance of multiple levels of public management -- local, national, regional and global.

The intellectual history of the term "global Keynesianism" is short. The expression "global Keynesianism" (or, "international Keynesianism") appeared in the literature in the early 1980's and was, initially, used by critics to describe the so-called Brandt Report, which proposed a kind of Marshall Plan for the Third World (Brandt Commission 1980). Critics left and right rejected that approach at the time (e.g., Dauderstaedt/Pfaller 1983; Corden 1987), but the idea of global Keynesianism lingered on, partly, as a whipping boy, but also as an inspiration. I am aware of two authors who developed contributions to global Keynesianism with this explicit label -- one American, namely, the global Keynesianism of Mead (Mead 1989), and one European, namely, the global left-Keynesianism of Elsenhans (Elsenhans 1996). One post-Keynesian economist observed as recently as 1995 that global Keynesianism is "only some system -- a mechanism that has not yet been worked out" (Galbraith 1995).

This essay is exploratory and synthetic. I am attempting to pull together various ideas which together might describe a perspective of leftist global Keynesianism. These materials are of two types -- theoretical/analytic and praxeological/political. Keynesian economics are traditionally interested in aggregate demand and its management. That is why my presentation starts with the concept of demand.

2. The Importance of Demand

The importance of aggregate demand has been acknowledged by such diverse economic theoreticians as Sismondi, Marx, Keynes, Samuelson, and Mandel, to name some. The concept of a market, as used in economic theory, implies the presence of supply and demand. The market mechanism is generally conceptualized as a process of feedback and equilibration between supply and demand. Demand plays an essential role in this mechanism; indeed, demand is a logical prerequisite of a market. Without a demand side there is no market, by definition.

There is consensus and controversy about the role of demand. A fair amount of agreement exists on two points. First, demand is important at the micro-level. If a supplier (individual or firm) cannot find enough customers for his (her, its) products, he is forced out of business or compelled to supply other goods or services for which there is a market (i.e., for which there is demand). Secondly, concerning *aggregate* demand (macro-level) there is a fair amount of consensus that aggregate demand is important *in the short run*. Thus, consumer spending and business spending, as well as their *intentions*, are routinely monitored through public surveys; and theoreticians tend to agree that short-term movements of demand influence national product and income (compare, for example, the textbooks, Heilbroner/Thurow 1978 and Mankiw 1994).

Major controversy rages about the role of aggregate demand *in the long run*; that is to say, about the importance of aggregate demand for the long-term growth of GDP, productivity, income and employment. Keynesians and Marxists tend to assign an important role to aggregate demand in long-term economic growth (or, accumulation). Others assign primacy to the supply side. Global Keynesianism rejects a pure supply-side view, emphasizing the interactivity of supply and demand, instead.

3. Critique of the Supply-Side Paradigm of Economic Growth and Accumulation

Disagreements about paradigms cannot be resolved in a stringent procedure of proof or falsification as in mathematics, logic or hypothesis-testing. The discussion of paradigms involves an element of philosophy or even persuasion. (Keynes wrote about the importance of persuasion for a similar reason.) I will not attempt to "disprove" the supply-side paradigm, therefore. Instead, I will merely state three reasons why I believe that a pure supply-side paradigm of economic growth (accumulation) is inadequate. These reasons are: (1) practical disappointment; (2) logical fallacy; (3) ideological bias. By "paradigm" I mean paradigm, in the sense of Thomas Kuhn, as a set of shared concepts, shared views about causality, shared views about relevant evidence and pertinent research methodologies, as well as shared values.

3.1 Practical Disappointment

The supply-side paradigm of economic growth gained increasing prevalence around the globe, starting in the early 1970's with the successive introduction of floating exchange rates, dismantling of controls on international capital movements, policies of deregulation and privatization, and so on. While these policies are propagated with the claim that they are superior to Keynesian or Marxist policies, they have, by and large, not generated impressive economic growth rates and have, on the contrary, lead to a great deal of wage stagnation, high unemployment, only modest productivity growth in many countries, even to economic depression or collapse as in some of the so-called transition economies of Central and Eastern Europe (Tausch 1997). The fact that the (open) unemployment rate in the United States is currently low, as defenders of neoliberalism may point out, is welcome news but does not account for problems of quality of employment (including the proportion of part-time employment in total employment) and inadequate wage levels of the working poor.

3.2 Logical Fallacy

The supply-side paradigm of economic growth has been formalized in such formulae as Cobb-Douglas functions or the Solow model. The Solow model postulates that long-term economic growth is caused by the supply side -- and nothing but the supply side, namely, by the conversion of three major categories of inputs into aggregate output (Y). The factor inputs in this model are capital (K), labour (L), and level of technology (A) -- according to the function $Y = f(K,L,A)$ (see, e.g., Solow 1956).

A major logical flaw in this model and the supply-side paradigm of economic growth generally is with respect to causal inference. The paradigm assumes that an economy functions like a machine without any feedback between supply and demand. The causation implied in this view is strictly uni-directional -- namely, from capital, labour and technology (and their growth) to national product (and its growth). However, the uni-directional view of causality implied in the supply-side paradigm contradicts the very concept of a market itself. In a market, aggregate outcome is thought to be the result of an interaction between supply and demand. Causation in a market is a two-way causation from supply to demand and from demand to supply; or, in other words, a feedback loop between supply and demand. The uni-directional view of causality implied in a pure supply-side paradigm of growth ignores the feedback mechanism in the concept of a market. The pure supply-side paradigm of economic growth is a primitive machine model, not a market model, which purports to explain economic growth (accumulation) in a market economy, nevertheless. This is a theoretical inconsistency and a logical fallacy.

3.3 Political Bias

The pure supply-side paradigm of economic growth neglects the demand side, two thirds of which is made up of the consumption demand of the mass of consumers. By neglecting this, the paradigm neglects what matters to labour--namely, wages and salaries and their role in national growth. The pure supply-side paradigm of economic growth (accumulation) thus exhibits a strong pro-business, pro-capital bias which is also evident in policies derived from this paradigm, like deregulation, privatization and so on.

The three points of criticism above are very brief and are merely stated in order to indicate the position of global Keynesianism, as I see it, for orientation purposes. The literature on these issues is voluminous and there is no intention here to repeat at length what is presented elsewhere.

4. Levels of Analysis

Global Keynesianism is concerned with the analysis and management of global demand. Economic analysis distinguishes between micro- and macro-analysis. These levels of analysis can be further subdivided and augmented and we can speak of a variety of units and levels of analysis, as follows:

- individual person
- household
- firm
- industry
- sector (public-private; agriculture-industry-service)
- class

or, geographically:

- local
- sub-national region
- national
- region (multiple countries, world region, like Africa etc.)
- global (all countries)

In global Keynesianism all these levels are of interest, but it is important that a global level of analysis is also present. Whether action can or should be taken at the global level or, rather, at regional, national, or sub-national levels is an additional problem which must be addressed.

5. THE IMPORTANCE OF WORLD-SYSTEM DEMAND (GLOBAL DEMAND)

Global demand is aggregate (effective) demand in the entire world-system (world economy), as opposed to demand in the economy of a single country (state, national economy, macroeconomy).

Wallerstein observed about "world-system demand" that:

> "there are 'expansions' and 'contractions' in the world economy ... I think they are linked to a basic contradiction of the system, which has to do with supply and demand, that is, *world-system* supply and world-system demand, not *firm* supply and demand, nor *state* supply and demand, but world-system supply and demand." (Wallerstein 1978: 232; emphasis original)

The concept of global demand is important in light of past and present world developments; it has been part of the analyses of a number of scholars and is also appearing in contemporary journalistic literature. The observers who have been interested in world-system demand (global demand) tend to be of various persuasions. Their theoretical differences notwithstanding, they tend to share the view that global demand is, tends to be, or is in danger of being inadequate. Here are some samples of opinion from diverse backgrounds:

> An anonymous editorial writer, writing about the "overcapacity bomb", stated: "It may be time to begin focusing policy on inadequate global demand, especially in Asia. Just as Keynesian economics is about to be buried, John Maynard Keynes's attention to demand may be more salient than ever -- even if his solutions are not." (Anonymous 1997: 138) Allen and Vines report various results and conclusions based on econometric modelling of the global economy. The authors refer to a "global paradox of thrift", which is Keynesian vocabulary, and the authors raise this question: "(T)here is paradoxically the problem that the world is currently in Keynesian recession. What could be worse than a massive reduction in injections of expenditure into the global economy, particularly for the developing countries, whose export revenues might appear to be particularly vulnerable?" (Allen and Vines 1993: 134) Mead developed a comprehensive set of policy proposals for the global and national levels. He writes: "The new system proposed here can be best described as multilateral global Keynesianism" (Mead 1989: 427). Singh and Zammit analyze unemployment and underemployment in the North and South of the world and conclude that global unemployment and underemployment are caused by inadequate global demand. They speak of a global "demand constraint", which they describe as "deeply institutional in nature". The authors call for three types of institutional/structural reform, namely: (1) "a new institutional and behavioural framework within the North"; (2) "within the South, a major change in policy direction";

(3) "(o)n the global scale, a rather different system of international arrangements between the North and the South." Furthermore, the authors note that such reforms "will have to pay full attention to ecological concerns". (Singh and Zammit 1995: 109-110) Elsenhans developed a leftist theory of global Keynesianism in which a "global demand gap" is a central concept. Furthermore, Elsenhans observes: "Enterprises are virtually incapable of expanding the market. They also cannot sustain the regulatory policy framework in its entirety. For this, they require the intervention of other social forces, for instance the labour movements and the state..." (Elsenhans 1996: 26). Mandel discusses global demand, for example, in *The Second Slump (1978),* from which the following quotations are taken. Mandel states: "Whatever the deeper meanderings of the analysis, the first phenomenon that must be grasped is this sharp break in the unstable equilibrium between supply and demand of commodities..." and: "Nothing illustrates the capitalist character of the market economy and its unjust and inhuman consequences better than this spectacle of half of humanity afflicted by hunger not because of lack of food products, but because *money demand* cannot keep up with physical demand." (Mandel 1978: 169 and 146, emphasis added)

The above quotations show that authors from different traditions who studied global demand converged on two opinions, namely: (1) global demand matters (is important); and (2) global demand may be inadequate at times; or tends to be inadequate; or is usually inadequate.

6. Absolute and Relative Inadequacy of Global Demand

"Inadequacy of global demand" has two distinguishable meanings which are frequently mixed together, namely:

a. *Absolute Inadequacy of Global Demand (social-existential* meaning) -- The people (workers, labour, global masses) do not have enough purchasing power for a decent standard of living. This meaning of "inadequate global demand" is an observation and judgement about an existential reality experienced by people.
b. *Relative Inadequacy of Global Demand (circulatory-systemic* meaning) -- There is a gap between global supply (aggregate production power) and global demand (aggregate purchasing power). This *global demand gap* is important in the circulatory flow of the world economy and has been alternately described as a problem of "overproduction" or a problem of "inadequate demand", reflecting different analytic and political emphases. I concur with Mandel who argues (see above) that one should not exaggerate the difference between these two interpretations. In my opinion, "overproduction" should be, more properly, called "relative overproduction" which coexists with "absolute underproduction" of goods and services for the provision of basic needs of masses of people.

7. The Global Unemployment Equilibrium

The concept of an unemployment equilibrium has been developed by Marx and Keynes, where Marx was thinking more of the long term (permanent feature of the capitalist economy) and Keynes more of the short term (depression of the 1930's). Marx explained how the capitalist economy, as a system, generates a "reserve army of the unemployed". Keynes, who was aware of Marx's work, explained how a demand gap in the economic system can lead to a stable unemployment equilibrium -- as in the depression of the 1930's. In global Keynesianism the concept of a systemic unemployment equilibrium is applied at the global level of analysis, leading to the notion of a *global* unemployment equilibrium, or a *world-system* unemployment equilibrium.

7.1 Global Equilibrium and National Equilibria

The world can, alternatively, be viewed as a single world-system ("one world") or as two hundred countries (nation-states, national macro-economies). Correspondingly, we can speak, alternatively, of a single *global* unemployment equilibrium or of two hundred *national* unemployment equilibria. The two levels of analysis coexist. The one global equilibrium and the many national equilibria exist at the same time. The equilibrium of the entire world-system functions as the "environment", as one might say, within which the many national equilibria exist. While there are relationships between the global-level equilibrium and the national-level equilibria (i.e., between the state of the world and the state of the nation), one cannot simply deduce one from the other. Thus, the world-system in its entirety may be in a state of a *global* unemployment equilibrium, which may have a depressive effect on all national equilibria. However, it is possible that, at the same time, an individual country may escape the global depressive effect and may be relatively free of unemployment -- just like a *national* economy may be in an overall state of recession or depression, while some individual firms may do well (as, for example, the alcohol industry in the United States during the depression of the 1930's).

At the present time, the United States has a lower unemployment rate than the majority of OECD countries and, traditionally, the OECD countries (core of the world system) have had less unemployment and underemployment than the non-OECD countries (periphery of the world system). According to the world-system view implied in global Keynesianism, the national equilibria of the two hundred countries are not totally isolated from the overall global equilibrium.

The transmission mechanisms between the global equilibrium and the national equilibria require special investigation. Since virtually all national economies are so-called "open economies" at the present time, transmission of misery or well-being (contagion) between countries and between the global and national levels occurs through such mechanisms as global investment flows (monetary and real investment), global trade flows, the global exchange rate system, global technology transfers, global institutional arrangements (organizations, rules and laws), global labour migration and brain drain, global spread of environmental decay, and so on.

In line with these theoretical considerations, it cannot be said that *national* unemployment and underemployment is an exclusively national phenomenon. The *global* reserve army of unemployed and underemployed is shared between nations; and the unemployment and underemployment generated by the *global* unemployment equilibrium is shared by two hundred national economies. It is easier for a national economy to have full employment when the entire world-system is in a full-employment equilibrium than when the entire world economy is in a global unemployment equilibrium, producing massive world-wide unemployment and underemployment. In response to a miserable *global* underemployment situation, which generates pressures for massive international migration (economic migrants), USA, the European Union and others have tough laws and law enforcement for keeping economic migrants from entering their economies and, once entered illegally, for expelling them.

7.2 Static View of the Global Unemployment Equilibrium

The world market economy, as a market in the sense of economic theory, has two constituent forces which interact -- namely, aggregate supply and aggregate demand. Whichever force of the two is smaller, determines the volume of total economic output and total employment (with additional influences from other variables). Both Keynesian and Marxist economics call attention to the fact that all the time (Marxist), or many times (Keynesian), the system has a tendency to generate an excess of aggregate supply over aggregate demand ("overproduction", Marxist), or a shortage of aggregate demand relative to aggregate supply ("demand gap", Keynesian). The smaller of the two forces -- namely, aggregate demand, limits ("constrains") the magnitude of total economic activity and output (GDP). Given the production methods available at any time and in the aggregate, an aggregate relationship exists between total economic activity and total employment. As a result, aggregate demand, as the constraining factor, limits total employment. Global Keynesianism claims that this situation exists in the entire world-system at the present time and that this situation of a relatively stable *global* unemployment (underemployment) equilibrium can only be overcome through public intervention ("public management"), broadly defined. This is in contradiction to the neoclassical / neoliberal opinion that the critically constraining factor in the world market economy is the supply side and that the free play of "market forces" can solve the problem without public intervention.

7.3 Dynamic View of the Global Unemployment Equilibrium

In the dynamic view, more attention is paid to time, process and growth rates than in the static view. Marxist analysis is traditionally dynamic in this sense and Keynesian and post-Keynesian scholars have also developed dynamic views of the problem (e.g.,

Asimakopulos 1991). In global Keynesianism, "dynamic view" means that *growth rates* of global product (global GDP) and global employment are an outcome of the interaction between the *growth rates* of global aggregate supply and global aggregate demand. The global unemployment equilibrium is a *growth equilibrium* between growing (or declining) global aggregate supply and growing (or declining) aggregate demand. In the evolution of these growing (or declining) aggregates, the global demand gap is ever-changing in its magnitude, both in absolute and relative terms, and the world-system has a *tendency* to generate a demand gap (tendency toward relative overproduction) of varying magnitude at all times or most of the time. Detailed analysis of these dynamic processes is complex and a great variety of views and models exist to describe these processes at the national level, but less literature deals with the global level of analysis. In very general terms, the factors and processes invoked to describe this dynamic reality can be grouped under two headings -- (a) conjunctural factors and processes; and (b) structural factors and processes. This distinction is in use at the national level of analysis and can also be applied at the world-system level.

7.4 Conjunctural and Structural Determinants of the Global Equilibrium (Disequilibrium)

The factors and processes determining the global equilibrium (disequilibrium) can be loosely grouped under two headings, namely:

1. *conjunctural* determinants (including "cyclical", in the sense of the short business cycle, and other short-term factors); and
2. *structural* determinants (including distributional, institutional, secular trends, long cycles, etc.)

For example, consider Mandel's analysis (see above). Mandel mentions the following with respect to the world recession of the 1970's: (1) conjunctural demand factor -- namely, contraction of world trade due to recession in the imperialist countries (core of world-system); (2) conjunctural management -- namely, "neo-Keynesian recovery techniques" ("enormous injection of purchasing power") in the core countries, which lead to a short-term surge in demand for consumer goods, which "effectively halted the recession"; and (3) structural demand factors -- namely, (a) marginality of people -- the starving billion of the world does not have enough food money to buy existing global food stuffs; (b) marginality of countries -- the global periphery generates comparatively modest trade demand in the international trading system. These structural causes of inadequate world-system demand place a major limit on the expansion of global economic growth, in Mandel's opinion, and, we may add, perpetuate a dynamic global unemployment equilibrium.

8. Global Full Employment Equilibrium

When the world-system (world economy, world market) is analyzed in terms of a dynamic equilibrium (or disequilibrium), we may observe that a global unemployment equilibrium exists; we can also postulate the possibility of a global full employment equilibrium -- that is to say, a state of the world in which aggregate supply and aggregate demand have a configuration in which all globally available labour is fully employed. Since a state of global full employment is mostly a dream (a utopia), the door is wide open for disagreements about praxeology (i.e., about how to get there). The traditional disagreements with respect to full employment at the national level carry over to the global level of analysis and action -- namely, in the traditional Marxist view, global full employment can only be achieved through an abolition of the capitalist world-system (world revolution); in the global-Keynesian view, global full employment can be achieved through active public management of the system; in the global-neoliberal view, global full employment is either (a) not desirable, or (b) of no particular interest, or (c) is thought to come about through the free play of "market forces". The global-Keynesian presumption is that a key role in achieving global full employment is played by active management of global demand. This global demand management must not be confused with, or reduced to, the old-Keynesian concept of "pump priming" (indiscriminate pumping of money into the system). Rather, new, more appropriate techniques of anti-cyclical and anti-structural demand management must be devised. In this context, more and more authors mention a global "Tobin tax" (tax on international financial transactions), global ecological taxes, transnational capital controls, and other global, regional, transnational, national and local instruments. Much more work is required to develop a full set of institutional, political and economic instruments. The political feasibility of such measures depends, to a large extent, on the ability to organize countervailing pressure throughout the world-system against the dominating interests of business (global capital).

9. The Importance of Anti-Structural Global Demand Management

Keynesianism at the national level has traditionally operated with a concept of anti-cyclical demand management (with reference to the short business cycle). At the world level, *anti-structural* demand management appears to be as important as, or more important than, anti-cyclical demand management. This view can be supported by three observations -- namely, (1) due to the multitude of two hundred national economies in the world, the short-term cyclical developments in each national economy tend to neutralize each other to some extent in the global aggregate; (2) from a management point of view, it is relatively more difficult to "fine-tune" any global short-term cycles which may exist at the world level, than to "fine-tune" national business cycles, albeit this is also very difficult; (3) the major demand problems in the world economy as a whole (in terms of magnitudes) tend to be more structural than (short-term) cyclical in nature -- notably, demand problems caused by the global monetary and exchange rate system, demand problems generated by the global income distribution, demand problems caused by the globalization of production, and so on.

I will select and examine three problem areas in which the world-system (the present "global formation" -- Chase-Dunn, 1989) has major structurally induced demand problems -- namely, (1) globalization of production; (2) global money and finance; and (3) exchange rate system.

10. Globalization of Production and Global Demand

Capitalism has always operated simultaneously in a national and a worldwide context, including international and colonial trade and investment. In recent decades, the production and supply of goods and services has increasingly been globalized through multinational production and marketing techniques. Multinational (transnational, global) corporations have been, and are, moving more and more production to countries were wages and other costs are low and are trying to sell as much as possible in countries where incomes are high. This global "buy-and-produce low and sell high" principle makes supply-side sense and tends to increase the efficiency of global production. However, this practice increases, on a global basis, the disequilibrium and gap between global supply and global demand, since a shift from high-wage to low-wage production (globally) has the effect of generating relatively less global aggregate demand. This mechanism has been recognized and has been called a "race to the bottom" or a "downward spiral". For example, Brecher and Costello write:

> "The most direct symptom of globalization is the 'race to the bottom' itself -- the reduction in labor, social, and environmental conditions that result directly from global competition for jobs and investment." (Brecher/Costello 1994: 22) Furthermore: "As corporations move jobs that paid $10 per hour to countries where they pay $1 per hour, workers can buy less of what they produce." (Brecher/Costello 1994: 25) And: "Unemployment and falling real wages led to declining consumer demand for products worldwide..." (Brecher/Costello 1994: 55)

Closely related to the globalization of the supply-side (globalization of production) is the issue of technological progress. New technologies of a labour-saving kind render the supply-side more efficient through automation and other kinds of labour-saving. On the one hand, technological advances are desirable for the sake of long-term economic growth. On the other hand, if such supply-side improvements are not matched by compensating job-creation and/or wage increases, then the relation between supply and demand is disturbed (the disequilibrium is exacerbated), nationally and/or globally. Furthermore, technological advances are not neutral with respect to ecological sustainablity (Daly 1996; Douthwaite 1998).

11. Global Money and Global Demand

11.1 Global Circulation of Money

Global demand is composed of global consumption demand (private and public) and global (fixed-)investment demand (private and public, including foreign direct investment). Money which circulates in the world-system may appear in a "real" (physical) economic circuit as effective demand for goods and services or in a "nominal" (financial) circuit in search of financial investment. Keynesians have traditionally analyzed this in terms of the relationship between aggregate saving and aggregate investment; Marxists in terms of surplus value. In both traditions, the circulation of money is closely related to the disequilibrium between supply and demand in the system.

In 1993 the global GDP was valued as 23.6 trillion U.S. dollars (World Bank 1995: 29). For the same time, the World Bank estimated the total resources of international financial institutions at about 14 trillion U.S. dollars (Patterson 1997). Whether one takes a Keynesian or Marxist view of this, the amount of global money which is withdrawn from, and circulating independent of, the real economy of world-system supply and world-system demand is enormous. This global situation is similar to what Keynes described, with respect to the depressed national economies in the 1930's, as a situation of "poverty in the midst of plenty" (Keynes 1964: 30); the world is awash with money, yet much of this money is not used to create employment or real consumption value.

11.2 Volatility of Global Finance

A problem which has received widespread attention is the volatility and instability of global financial investments. The deregulation of global capital markets has lead to a situation in which large amounts of finance capital can easily be moved from one country or world region to another. This has lead to drastic swings in effective demand (fixed investment and consumption) for countries and regions thus affected, either positively or negatively.

11.3 Exchange Rates and Global Demand

The distribution of global demand between high-income and middle- to low-income countries is distorted as a consequence of the existing exchange rate system. The currencies of peripheral and semi-peripheral countries (low- and middle-income countries) tend to be *under*valued in relation to the currencies of high-income countries. The last point is contentious and has been argued by Yotopoulos (1996), Havlik (1996) and Kohler (1998), whereas a majority of contemporary economists tend to take the opposite point of view.

Undervalued exchange rates contribute to unequal exchange and a distorted distribution of global demand. Unequal exchange (Emmanuel 1972), refers to imperialism of trade and exploitation through international trade. World tables of unequal exchange have been published for the year 1995 which show the magnitudes of losses and gains due to unequal exchange, resulting from undervalued exchange rates, for 119 countries (Kohler 1998). Based on these world tables of unequal exchange for 1995, it can be observed that the equivalent of 6.6 percent of global GDP (in 1995) was transferred from low- and middle-income countries to high-income countries as an "unrecorded transfer of value" due to distorted currency values. This amount corresponds to 24 percent of the combined GDP's of non-OECD countries (as a loss) and to 8 percent of the combined GDP's of OECD countries (as a gain). In 1995 the three countries with the highest amounts of unequal-exchange losses were China, Indonesia and Mexico; the three countries with the highest amounts of unequal-exchange gains were Japan, USA and Germany.

12. Global Keynesianism as Policy, Management, Action (Praxeology)

In addition to theoretical literature, a wide range of literature exists on policy proposals which may be called global-Keynesian, broadly conceived. Many of these proposals have been criticized for being either interventionist and dirigistic (neoliberal critique) or pro-capitalist and unrealistic (Marxist critique). Nevertheless, many of these ideas are valuable; some are receiving increasing public attention and acceptance.

12.1 What Global Keynesianism is Not

Global Keynesianism may be a rather fuzzy project, but it is not any of the following, as some critics may be inclined to think. (1) Global Keynesianism does not advocate indiscriminate "pump priming" or "printing of money". (2) Global Keynesianism is not limited to a "global Marshall plan", as proposed in the Brandt Report of 1980; this is only one of several proposals made from a global-Keynesian perspective. (3) Global Keynesianism may engage in global-level analysis (world-system analysis); this does not mean that the proposed policies or management techniques are necessarily at the global level; they may also be at a regional or national levels of action. (4) Global Keynesianism is not necessarily anti-ecological. The very term "sustainable development" originates in a report using a global-Keynesian paradigm, namely, the Brundtland Report (Brundtland Commission 1987). (5) Global-Keynesianism is not in bed with global corporations; rather, it advocates controls and containment of global capitalism.

12.2 Levels of Action and Management

The expression "global Keynesianism" should not mislead one into believing that global Keynesianism has only one level of action (i.e., the global level). I have pointed out earlier that global-Keynesian diagnostics, analysis and theory operate with many levels of analysis. Similarly, global-Keynesian praxeology operates with multiple levels of action, policy and management. These include agents (actors, units of action) like individual, class and state and levels of action and policy from local to global. For example, global-level diagnostics may lead to the conclusion that the most effective response to a problem is at the sectoral level (e.g., transnational collective bargaining by labour unions) or, alternatively, at the regional level (e.g., organization of regional development banks). Of course, the diagnosis may also lead to recommended action at the national level or the global level. For policy-, management-, and action-purposes, the world-system must be seen as a multi-level system with multiple levels of actors and multiple levels of activity and management.

12.3 Goals of Global Keynesianism

Global Keynesianism is not a political party but a fuzzy point of view. The goals of global Keynesianism have not been neatly catalogued anywhere. However, it may be fair to say that the broad, overall, long-term goals of global Keynesianism include: (1) global full employment; (2) improvement of the global income distribution; (3) world-wide social security; (4) economic growth (of the sustainable kind); (5) ecological sustainability; (6) democratic process; where the numbering does not imply a rank ordering of goals; all of them are important.

13. Selected Action Proposals of Global Keynesianism

Individual proposals for policy and management which are of a global-Keynesian nature, may conflict with each other, and various experts who may have global-Keynesian points of view or inclinations may not agree on individual proposals. Global Keynesianism is a pluralistic, open project, in a state of collective learning, where theory and practice have certain vague shapes, but are by no means crystallized into a fixed system. This may be a disadvantage, but may also be an advantage, as open-mindedness in an uncertain world can be a virtue.

13.1 Improving the Global Income Distribution

Global Keynesianism is generally in favour of improving the income distribution between high- middle- and low-income countries. To this end literature with a global-

Keynesian perspective supports (1) debt relief or debt forgiveness for certain categories of countries; (2) commodity price stabilization schemes; (3) foreign aid from high-income countries; (4) improved terms of trade for low- and middle-income countries, and other policies familiar in the "development" literature.

13.2 Improving Global and Regional Organizations

From the perspective of low- and middle-income countries, regional organization of economic interests has been advocated in order to fight global income polarization, for example by Amin and his concept of a "polycentric world" (Amin 1997). From the perspective of labour in high-income countries the implementation of labour charters in existing regional organizations like European Union or NAFTA is important.

13.3 Strengthening National Management

It has been observed that the power of the (nation-)state vis-a-vis global investors and global corporations has declined (e.g., Cox 1994: 47-48). Global Keynesianism supports a re-assertion of national management within a global context, as opposed to outright abdication of national power to "global markets" (global capital).

13.4 Strengthening Collective Bargaining Globally

Wallerstein has pointed out that a major strategy for increasing effective demand in the world-system is through "renegotiation of historically given wages" (Wallerstein 1978: 233). Collective bargaining between labour and capital is thus important for global demand management. Global Keynesianism looks toward worldwide strengthening and protection of collective bargaining, including transnational collective bargaining, as a major institutional feature for a sound world-economy.

13.5 Controlling Global Financial Capital

As a protection against the excessive power of deregulated and unregulated global financial capital ("the markets", as they are called in the media), global Keynesianism favours controls on global capital movements. For this purpose, a frequently quoted proposal is the "Tobin tax", namely, a tax on international financial capital transactions, with the purpose of slowing down speculative developments. Another strategy is, for example, the strengthening of regional organization. Thus, some see the strengthening of the European Union as a method for asserting more political control over unregulated global financial forces (Misik 1997).

13.6 Managing Global Fixed Investment

The traditional Keynesian view, namely, that fixed investment may not be forthcoming in sufficient quantity from the private sector or may not be well-distributed, is also applicable at regional and global levels. Here are some sample proposals: (1) The Brandt Report sought to respond to this need by proposing a global Marshall plan, financed by the high-income countries (Brandt 1980). (2) According to another proposal, global demand is crucially dependent on global credit creation and, whatever global credit is created, must be apportioned equitably between rich and poor countries, rather than in a biased manner toward the rich countries (Moore, 1988: 382,388). (3) Amin called for the creation of a "reformed" World Bank which would manage global credit for fixed investment in a more satisfactory manner than the present World Bank (Amin, 1997:54).

13.7 Exchange Rate Reform

The present exchange rate system distorts the distribution of global demand and generates unequal exchange (see above). Various reforms of the exchange rate system have been proposed, including (1) the institution of national currency boards, (2) return to exchange rate controls (e.g., Kuttner 1998); (3) purchasing power parity rates, (4) regional currencies, or even (5) a single global currency (Keynes's "bancor" proposal, which was reiterated by Mead 1989:434).

13.8 Other Proposals

There are other proposals which can be grouped under a "global left-Keynesianism" label. My objective in this section was to give some examples of global-Keynesian praxeological thought, rather than to critically review all that has been written. As global reality unfolds, old proposals may become obsolete and new praxeological thought may become necessary.

13.9 Feasibility of Global Keynesianism

A key problem is feasibility. For example, the Brandt Report, which triggered the talk about global Keynesianism in the 1980's, was published precisely at a time when dominant elite opinion was moving in the opposite direction -- namely, in the direction of "Thatcherism" and the "Washington consensus" of global neoliberalism. Economic analyses may lead to a call for political-institutional change or to the despairing observation that "the political will" for proposed changes is missing. The feasibility of the ideas and proposals which may be called global-Keynesian depends, in part, on their intrinsic merits and persuasiveness and, in large measure, on the successes of the political movements, parties and other organizations which fight against the errors of global neoliberalism.

14. In Conclusion

I have attempted in this essay to describe a theoretical and praxeological perspective which is rather new so that it does not have an agreed-upon name yet. Call it global left-Keynesianism or transnational socialism or perspective X; here it is called global Keynesianism and beyond. This perspective combines left-Keynesian economics with world-systems theory (in the form of a preliminary outline). Hopefully, some others will find this useful and I also hope that this will, ultimately, have some practical value for presently living people (Çakmak 1998). "You don't see those who stand in the dark" (line from Brecht/Weill, "Three Penny Opera"), but those in the dark could use some effective help from the presently living intelligentsia.

Chapter 6

A SIMULATION OF GLOBAL EXPLOITATION

1. ABSTRACT

Global income polarization ("the widening global gap") has been explained in various ways. My simulation assumes that some portion of global income polarization is due to global center-periphery exploitation. The simulation shows that even a small rate of global center-periphery exploitation can lead to significant global income polarization in the longer run. The abolition of this kind of center-periphery exploitation would lead to a closing of the global income gap.

2. GLOBAL EXPLOITATION

The term "global exploitation" is not well-defined in the literature. Several broad meanings of "global exploitation" are thinkable -- namely, (a) children's rights activists may think of the exploitation of children around the world; (b) feminists may think of "worldwide exploitation of women by men"; (c) others may think of "worldwide exploitation of workers by employers"; (d) yet others may think of "exploitation of poor countries by rich countries" or of "exploitation of the global periphery by the global center"; (e) yet others may think of "worldwide exploitation of non-whites by the white man" (or of ethnic groups X by ethnic group Y); and other notions. In the different meanings of the term, the two sides of the exploitative relationship are identified as different agents -- namely, children/adults, women/men; workers/employers; countries; ethno-cultural groups. My simulation uses the fourth meaning, namely, global center-periphery exploitation. This is close to, but not necessarily identical with, the term "unequal exchange", as used in the literature. Various mechanisms have been identified in the literature which can be considered as facets of "global exploitation", in the sense of center-periphery exploitation. These include: (1) the fact that the rules of the world economy are made by the center countries; (2) the fact that the transnational organizations regulating certain aspects of the world economy are dominated by the center countries; (3) the fact that the most powerful global corporations are corporations of the center countries; (4) unfair trade between center and periphery; (5) biased exchange rates between center and periphery; and other. Without going into the details of the discussions surrounding these issues, my simulation makes the assumption that the center countries (OECD countries) do exploit the rest of the world (non-OECD countries) through mechanisms of the mentioned kind. As a result center countries extract a certain amount of economic value, which I call "transfer value" (T), from the rest of the world which is due to the exploitative mechanisms rather than due to the center countries' own hard work and technological brilliance. In some historical empires this transfer value (T) was more explicit and was called "tribute" or "slave labour" and was extracted from the subdued peoples by the imperial country (e.g., in the Hapsburg or Ottoman or Chinese empires).

3. Simulation Logic

Simulation is a calculation exercise which can be used for constructing alternative "scenarios" (e.g., alternative ways of declaring taxes); for projecting "alternative futures" (e.g., alternative ecological developments); or for constructing "alternative histories". Simulations have also been called "What-If?-analysis". My simulation constructs an "alternative history" and pursues the question: What would have happened to the world income distribution between 1961 and 1989, if there had been less global exploitation?

The logic underlying this simulation can be explained with an example. Imagine two brothers (or sisters) -- LITTLE BROTHER and BIG BROTHER. Each brother has 100 dollars to invest. Both brothers invest their money in the same bank in two separate bank accounts. The bank gives, say, 2% interest per year. At the end of year 1, each brother will have $102; at the end of year 2, $104; and so on. The relation between the two accounts will remain 1: 1 at the end of every year since the accounts accumulate in exactly the same manner and independently from each other. There is no income polarization.

Now introduce exploitation. Let us assume that BIG BROTHER is a bully and forces LITTLE BROTHER to hand over one half of the interest he earns every year. As a result, the situation at the end of year 1 is: BIG BROTHER has $103 [= 102 + 1 (exploitation)] and LITTLE BROTHER has $101 [= 102 - 1 (exploitation)]. The situation at the end of year 2 will be: BIG BROTHER has $106 [= 103 + 2 (interest) + 1 (exploitation)] and LITTLE BROTHER has $102 [= 101 + 2 (interest) - 1 (exploitation)]. At the end of year 3, BIG BROTHER will have $109 [= 106 + 2 (interest) + 1 (exploitation)] and LITTLE BROTHER will have $103 [= 102 + 2 (interest) - 1 (exploitation)]. The relation between the two accounts at the end of year 3 is 109: 103. In other words, income polarization is underway.

Next, apply this at the world level, with LITTLE BROTHER = periphery and BIG BROTHER = center, and assume that the center is the exploitative bully. Note that the historical data we have about GDP growth rates are "after-exploitation" -- namely, they include the effect of exploitation. Thus, the observed growth rate of OECD countries include *gains* from global exploitation; and the observed growth rates of non-OECD countries include *losses* from global exploitation. (The situation is similar to the difference between "gross income" and "net income" or "before tax income" and "after tax income".) Thus, if the center shows a historical growth rate of, say, 3% per annum and the exploitation rate was 1%, then we may claim that the center's historical growth rate of 3% was composed of 2% self-generated growth ("before-exploitation growth") plus 1% exploitation [3 = 2 + 1]. Similarly, if the periphery shows an historical growth rate of, say, 3% per annum and the exploitation rate was 1%, then we may claim that the periphery's historical growth rate of 3% was composed of 4% self-generated growth ("before-exploitation growth") minus 1% exploitation [3 = 4 -1]. The simulation thus operates with the two concepts of "before-exploitation growth rate" and "after-exploitation growth rate".

The simulation exercise proceeds in five broad steps -- namely,

1. *collect* historical data
2. *make an assumption* about the transfer value (T). Here I am assuming that the T value was 1.5% of the GDP of the OECD countries in every year (exploitation rate = 1.5%). Feel free to make other assumptions (it's a simulation!). The T value is the amount of gain (loss) due to global center-periphery exploitation. As empirical-historical support for a 1.5% rate, see Amin (1976: 144) and Köhler (1998: Table 2), who found a rate of "unequal exchange" for the years 1965 (1966) amounting to 1.5% of the GDP of the industrialized countries (OECD, center).
3. *calculate* alternative growth rates for center (OECD) and periphery (non-OECD) by removing the influence of exploitation (i.e., subtract the T value from OECD GDP and add the T value to non-OECD GDP). For the center, the resulting "before-exploitation growth rates" will be *smaller* than the historically observed (after-exploitation) growth rates; for the periphery the resulting "before exploitation growth rates" will be *greater* than the historically observed (after-exploitation) growth rates.
4. *recalculate* the growth trajectories for 1961 - 1989 for center (OECD) and periphery (non-OECD), using the postulated "before-exploitation growth rates"
5. *display* the results in graphical form

For further details of the calculations, see the Appendix, Table 6.
The calculations were done with a computer "spreadsheet" software.

4. Simulation Results

The results of the simulation are summarized in four diagrams -- namely:

1. *Figure 1* shows *actual* polarization of *per capita* incomes, 1961 - 1989 (historical data);

2. *Figure 2* shows *simulated per capita* incomes, 1961 - 1989 (assuming and removing a global exploitation rate of 1.5% per annum);
3. *Figure 3* shows the *actual* development of *GDPs* (aggregate incomes), 1961 - 1989 (historical data);
4. *Figure 4* shows the *simulated* development of *GDPs* (aggregate incomes), 1961 - 1989 (assuming and removing a global exploitation rate of 1.5% per annum).

Fig. 1 GDP per capita (historical)

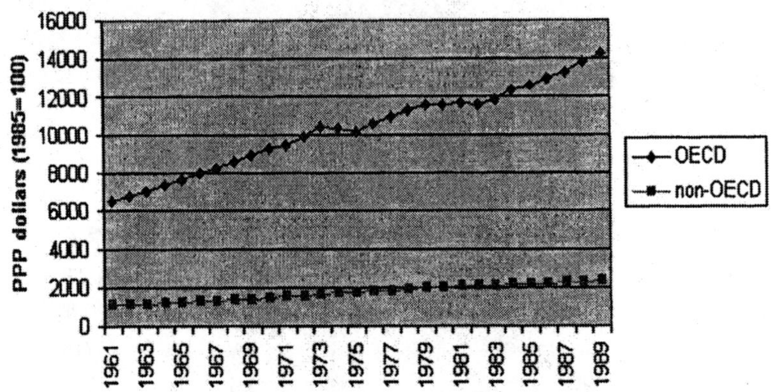

Figure 1 shows the actual polarization of world income which took place betwen 1961 and 1989. The values are expressed in constant "international prices" (PPP dollars, 1985=100). The data source is Penn World Table (1999). The exact values for this and the other diagrams can be found in the Appendix, Tables 1 - 6.

Fig. 2 GDP per capita (simulated)

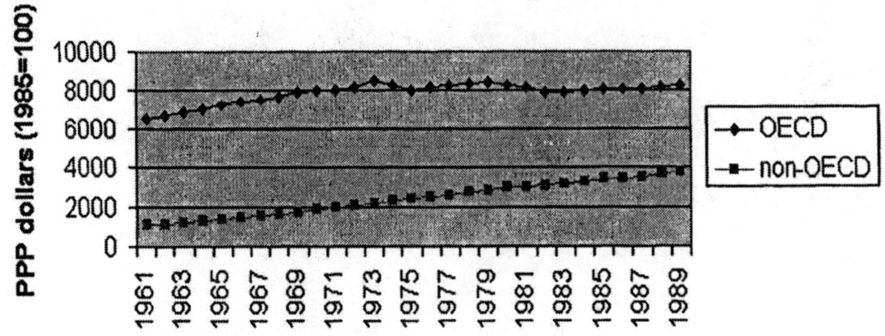

Figure 2 shows simulation results. After 1971-73 OECD income stays on a plateau around 8000 PPP dollars per capita. Non-OECD income increases to about 4000 PPP dollars per capita by 1989. The world income gap is closing.

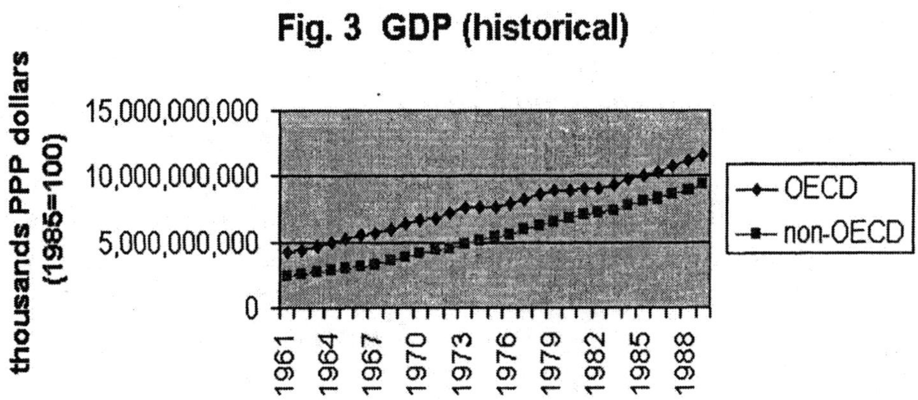

Figure 3 shows the historical development of GDPs which took place between 1961 and 1989. Throughout the period, the combined GDP of non-OECD (with about 80% of world population) stays below the combined GDP of OECD (with about 20% of world population).

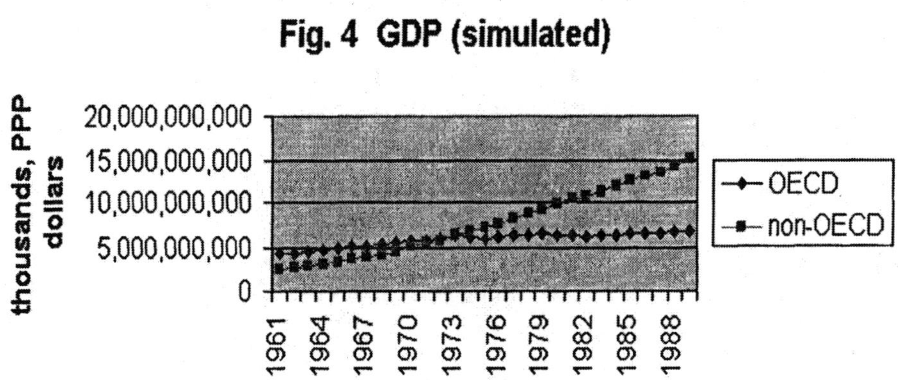

Figure 4 shows simulation results. Starting around 1972-73 the combined GDP of non-OECD moves ahead of the combined GDP of OECD.

5. Discussion

The results of the simulation are somewhat of a surprise to myself. I had been studying "unequal exchange" along Emmanuel's and Amin's lines. My own estimates of unequal exchange between periphery and center of the world showed the same result as Amin's -- namely, 1.5% of center GDP for 1966 (Amin 1976: 144; Köhler 1998). This gave me the idea of simulating the development of world income distribution by making the *assumption* that "unequal exchange" had *not* taken place. In other words: What would have happened, if there had been no global exploitation (unequal exchange)? I was expecting some consequences in the direction of the simulation results, but not as strong an impact as the simulation shows. The simulation thus poses two challenges -- (1) methodological; (2) substantive. I leave the methodological challenge to others who may want to develop their own simulations of global exploitation, using different definitions, assumptions, values and algorithms.

On the praxeological side, the simulation sends a hopeful message, namely: If political activists and/or socially responsible elites can raise enough consciousness and organize enough political pressure, so as to reduce global exploitation by 1.5% per annum, the global income gap will begin to close within a number of years (far less than eternity!) -- by virtue of the logic of compounding, as the simulation shows.

On the analytic-theoretical side, the simulation raises various difficult questions which I cannot answer right now. *Question 1*: Is it plausible to think that, as the simulation shows, OECD per capita income would have stayed at a plateau after 1971-73? The implication of this is that all per capita income growth of the OECD countries after 1971-73 was due to global exploitation. If that was so, then some more research and theory would be nice to have in order support such a view. *Question 2*: Can the fact that the simulation shows some special role for the years 1971-73 be used as an indictment of global neoliberalism which abolished the preceding Keynesian-influenced international economic regime around that time (USA going off the gold standard, dismantling of the preceding Bretton-Woods system, deregulation of the old system, enforcement of neoliberal regulations, IMF "Structural Adjustment Policies", and other)? *Question 3*: What would the First World do without global exploitation? Are all the people who see a technological superiority of the West wrong? *Question 4*: Is there truly such a thing as global exploitation (or, if you don't like this term, is there a transfer value (T))? "I don't know" is my answer to most these questions, except the last one -- I do believe that there is a transfer value T of some kind. It is the essence of a simulation to show something that is not real in an empirical sense. Potentialities are important for the understanding and evaluation of historical developments. If the Spanish Armada had not been destroyed in 1588, we might all be speaking Spanish today.

6. Appendix -- Tables

The simulation was done in a single computer spreadsheet with columns A - AC. The original spreadsheet is here broken up into 5 tables. The columns are numbered as in the original spreadsheet. Thus, you may load the material into your own spreadsheet and simulate something else. Notes to Tables 1-5 are given in Table 6, including method of calculation. Tables 1-3 (columns A - S) refer to the actual, historical situation, as captured in the statistical data available in the Penn World Table. Tables 4-5 (columns T - AC) contain the simulation exercise. The T value, which is central in this simulation, is in column (T). Abbreviations are explained in Table 6.

Table 1--Historical

TABLE 1 Cols. A - G

YEAR (A)	hist N=121 World GDP intlPr85 thousands (B)	hist N=24 OECD GDP intlPr85 thousands (C)	hist N=24 OECD GDP growth rate %pa (D)	hist N=97 non-OECD GDP intlPr85 thousands (E)	hist N=97 non-OECD GDP growth rate %pa (F)	hist N=97 non-OECD GDP as % of World GDP % (G)
1961	6,644,104,915	4,197,078,117		2,447,026,798		37
1962	6,958,334,783	4,425,741,925	5.4	2,532,592,858	3.5	36
1963	7,318,210,382	4,647,760,802	5.0	2,670,449,580	5.4	36
1964	7,821,126,619	4,945,690,202	6.4	2,875,436,417	7.7	37
1965	8,232,636,791	5,209,411,377	5.3	3,023,225,414	5.1	37
1966	8,658,136,099	5,488,116,456	5.4	3,170,019,643	4.9	37
1967	9,002,641,628	5,688,121,612	3.6	3,314,520,016	4.6	37
1968	9,510,313,561	6,008,199,875	5.6	3,502,113,686	5.7	37
1969	10,089,946,152	6,332,236,056	5.4	3,757,710,096	7.3	37
1970	10,704,718,432	6,596,442,496	4.2	4,108,275,936	9.3	38
1971	11,142,091,771	6,825,657,455	3.5	4,316,434,316	5.1	39
1972	11,676,755,998	7,171,841,543	5.1	4,504,914,455	4.4	39
1973	12,437,495,139	7,614,357,468	6.2	4,823,137,671	7.1	3
1974	12,758,961,281	7,648,802,862	0.5	5,110,158,419	6.0	40
1975	12,928,493,353	7,582,721,503	-0.9	5,345,771,850	4.6	41
1976	13,539,756,819	7,954,236,256	4.9	5,585,520,563	4.5	41
1977	14,146,256,616	8,255,775,960	3.8	5,890,480,656	5.5	42
1978	14,795,395,856	8,604,173,926	4.2	6,191,221,930	5.1	42

TABLE 1 Cols. A - G

YEAR (A)	hist N=121 World GDP intlPr85 thousands (B)	hist N=24 OECD GDP intlPr85 thousands (C)	hist N=24 OECD GDP growth rate %pa (D)	hist N=97 non-OECD GDP intlPr85 thousands (E)	hist N=97 non-OECD GDP growth rate %pa (F)	hist N=97 non-OECD GDP as % of World GDP % (G)
1979	15,357,073,622	8,903,480,174	3.5	6,453,593,448	4.2	42
1980	15,775,665,903	8,970,184,755	0.7	6,805,481,148	5.5	43
1981	16,138,431,535	9,109,550,613	1.6	7,028,880,922	3.3	44
1982	16,244,188,844	9,060,345,894	0.5	7,183,842,950	2.2	44
1983	16,709,104,924	9,318,985,537	2.9	7,390,119,387	2.9	44
1984	17,499,126,460	9,771,434,305	4.9	7,727,692,155	4.6	44
1985	18,172,039,417	10,087,409,006	3.2	8,084,630,411	4.6	44
1986	18,694,145,877	10,387,726,851	3.0	8,306,419,026	2.7	44
1987	19,315,927,688	10,743,245,634	3.4	8,572,682,054	3.2	44
1988	20,234,661,996	11,249,847,382	4.7	8,984,814,614	4.8	44
1989	20,941,943,905	11,650,765,699	3.6	9,291,178,206	3.4	44
			avg= 3.7		avg= 4.9	
			std= 1.9		std= 1.6	

Table 2--Historical

TABLE 2 Cols. H - P

YEAR	hist N=121 World POP	hist N=24 OECD POP	hist N=97 non-OECD POP	hist proportion OECD POP as %of World POP	hist N=121 World GDP/cap	hist N=24 OECD GDP/cap	hist N=97 non-OECD GDP/cap	hist ratio OECD GDP/capto non-OECD GDP/cap	hist difference OECD GDP/capless non-OECD GDP/cap
	persons thousands	persons thousands	persons thousands	%	intlPr85	intlPr85	intlPr85	ratio	intlPr85
(A)	(H)	(I)	(J)	(K)	(L)	(M)	N)	(O)	(P)
1961	2,858,189	645,972	2,212,217	23	2325	6497	1106	5.9	5391
1962	2,909,787	654,346	2,255,441	22	2391	6764	1123	6.0	5641
1963	2,972,467	662,313	2,310,154	22	2462	7017	1156	6.1	5862
1964	3,033,118	670,095	2,363,023	22	2579	7381	1217	6.1	6164
1965	3,095,949	677,836	2,418,113	22	2659	7685	1250	6.1	6435
1966	3,161,770	684,839	2,476,931	22	2738	8014	1280	6.3	6734
1967	3,226,711	691,232	2,535,479	21	2790	8229	1307	6.3	6922
1968	3,292,485	696,730	2,595,755	21	2888	8623	1349	6.4	7274
1969	3,363,212	704,386	2,658,826	21	3000	8990	1413	6.4	7576
1970	3,434,699	711,783	2,722,916	21	3117	9267	1509	6.1	7759
1971	3,492,117	719,319	2,772,798	21	3191	9489	1557	6.1	7932
1972	3,563,935	726,274	2,837,661	20	3276	9875	1588	6.2	8287
1973	3,634,780	732,356	2,902,424	20	3422	10397	1662	6.3	8735
1974	3,705,986	739,360	2,966,626	20	3443	10345	1723	6.0	8623
1975	3,775,319	745,870	3,029,449	20	3424	10166	1765	5.8	8402
1976	3,842,584	750,961	3,091,623	20	3524	10592	1807	5.9	8785

TABLE 2 Cols. H - P

YEAR	hist N=121 World POP	hist N=24 OECD POP	hist N=97 non-OECD POP	hist proportion OECD POP as %of World POP	hist N=121 World GDP/cap	hist N=24 OECD GDP/cap	hist N=97 non-OECD GDP/cap	hist ratio OECD GDP/capto non-OECD GDP/cap	hist difference OECD GDP/capless non-OECD GDP/cap
	persons thousands	persons thousands	persons thousands	%	intlPr85	intlPr85	intlPr85	ratio	intlPr85
(A)	(H)	(I)	(J)	(K)	(L)	(M)	N)	(O)	(P)
1977	3,909,379	756,458	3,152,921	19	3619	10914	1868	5.8	9045
1978	3,977,004	762,000	3,215,004	19	3720	11292	1926	5.9	9366
1979	4,046,192	767,659	3,278,533	19	3795	11598	1968	5.9	9630
1980	4,115,802	773,680	3,342,122	19	3833	11594	2036	5.7	9558
1981	4,186,282	779,383	3,406,899	19	3855	11688	2063	5.7	9625
1982	4,259,580	784,597	3,474,983	18	3814	11548	2067	5.6	9480
1983	4,333,177	789,442	3,543,735	18	3856	11805	2085	5.7	9719
1984	4,405,899	793,991	3,611,908	18	3972	12307	2140	5.8	10167
1985	4,480,046	798,728	3,681,318	18	4056	12629	2196	5.8	10433
1986	4,557,700	803,472	3,754,228	18	4102	12929	2213	5.8	10716
1987	4,637,452	808,305	3,829,147	17	4165	13291	2239	5.9	11052
1988	4,718,125	813,368	3,904,757	17	4289	13831	2301	6.0	11530
1989	4,797,981	817,538	3,980,443	17	4365	14251	2334	6.1	11917

Table 3 -- Historical

TABLE 3 Cols. Q - S			
YEAR	hist N=121 World GDP/cap growth ratebased on intlPr85 % pa	hist N=24 OECD GDP/cap growth ratebased on intlPr85 % pa	hist N=97 non-OECD GDP/cap growth ratebased on intlPr85 % pa
(A)	(Q)	(R)	(S)
1961			
1962	2.9	4.1	1.5
1963	3.0	3.8	2.9
1964	4.7	5.2	5.3
1965	3.1	4.1	2.7
1966	3.0	4.3	2.4
1967	1.9	2.7	2.1
1968	3.5	4.8	3.2
1969	3.9	4.2	4.8
1970	3.9	3.1	6.8
1971	2.4	2.4	3.2
1972	2.7	4.1	2.0
1973	4.4	5.3	4.7
1974	0.6	-0.5	3.7
1975	-0.5	-1.7	2.4
1976	2.9	4.2	2.4
1977	2.7	3.0	3.4
1978	2.8	3.5	3.1
1979	2.0	2.7	2.2
1980	1.0	-0.0	3.4
1981	0.6	0.8	1.3
1982	-1.1	-1.2	0.2
1983	1.1	2.2	0.9
1984	3.0	4.3	2.6
1985	2.1	2.6	2.6
1986	1.1	2.4	0.7
1987	1.5	2.8	1.2
1988	3.0	4.1	2.8
1989	1.8	3.0	1.4

Table 4 -- Simulation

TABLE 4 Cols. T - X

sim T transfer value 1.5% of OECD GDP intlPr85 thousands (T)	sim N=24 OECD hypoth. GDP using historical GDP growth rate less T value 1961 GDP=given) intlPr85 thousands (U)	sim N=97 non-OECD hypoth GDP using historical GDP growth rate plus T value (1961 GDP=given) intlPr85 thousands (V)	sim N=121 control difference hypGGDP/ histGGDP as % of hist GGDP % (W)	sim N=97 non-OECD hypoth GDP as % of hypoth GGDP % (X)	YEAR (A)
	4,197,078,117	2,447,026,798			1961
66,386,129	4,359,355,796	2,598,978,987	0.0	37	1962
69,716,412	4,508,327,978	2,810,165,720	-0.0	38	1963
74,185,353	4,723,134,143	3,100,062,684	-0.0	40	1964
78,141,171	4,896,846,694	3,337,537,983	-0.0	41	1965
82,321,747	5,076,507,722	3,581,915,563	-0.0	41	1966
85,321,824	5,176,190,667	3,830,513,390	-0.0	43	1967
90,122,998	5,377,338,888	4,137,434,012	-0.0	43	1968
94,983,541	5,572,367,729	4,534,381,845	-0.2	45	1969
98,946,637	5,705,922,759	5,056,351,904	-0.5	47	1970
102,384,862	5,801,808,837	5,414,932,318	-0.7	48	1971
107,577,623	5,988,487,688	5,758,956,767	-0.6	49	1972
114,215,362	6,243,773,124	6,279,979,797	-0.7	50	1973
114,732,043	6,157,286,304	6,768,428,002	-1.3	52	1974
113,740,823	5,990,349,987	7,194,239,883	-2.0	55	1975
119,313,544	6,164,533,098	7,636,202,765	-1.9	55	1976
123,836,639	6,274,389,730	8,176,963,321	-2.2	57	1977
129,062,609	6,410,109,575	8,723,504,657	-2.3	58	1978
133,552,203	6,499,540,527	9,226,741,420	-2.4	59	1979
134,552,771	6,413,682,100	9,864,390,155	-3.2	61	1980
136,643,259	6,376,685,429	10,324,846,306	-3.5	62	1981
135,905,188	6,206,336,937	10,688,377,932	-4.0	63	1982
139,784,783	6,243,720,310	11,135,068,160	-4.0	64	1983
146,571,515	6,400,289,470	11,790,277,707	-4.0	65	1984
151,311,135	6,455,941,764	12,486,175,903	-4.2	66	1985
155,815,903	6,492,329,282	12,984,529,624	-4.2	67	1986
161,148,685	6,553,379,837	13,561,898,60	-4.1	67	1987
168,747,711	6,693,659,192	14,382,635,966	-4.2	68	1988
174,761,485	6,757,444,105	15,047,815,585	-4.1	69	1989

Table 5--Simulation

Table 5 Cols. Y-AC

sim N=24 OECD GDP/cap intlPr85 (Y)	sim N=97 non-OECD GDP/cap intlPr85 (Z)	sim ratio OECD GDP/cap to non-OECD GDP/cap ratio (AA)	sim difference OECD GDP/cap less non-OECD GDP/cap intlPr85 (AB)	sim N=121 World GDP/cap intlPr85 (AC)	YEAR (A)
6497	1106	5.9	5391	2325	1961
6662	1152	5.8	5510	2391	1962
6807	1216	5.6	5591	2462	1963
7048	1312	5.4	5737	2579	1964
7224	1380	5.2	5844	2660	1965
7413	1446	5.1	5967	2738	1966
7488	1511	5.0	5978	2791	1967
7718	1594	4.8	6124	2890	1968
7911	1705	4.6	6206	3005	1969
8016	1857	4.3	6159	3133	1970
8066	1953	4.1	6113	3212	1971
8245	2029	4.1	6216	3296	1972
8526	2164	3.9	6362	3446	1973
8328	2282	3.7	6046	3488	1974
8031	2375	3.4	5657	3492	1975
8209	2470	3.3	5739	3592	1976
8294	2593	3.2	5701	3697	1977
8412	2713	3.1	5699	3805	1978
8467	2814	3.0	5652	3887	1979
8290	2952	2.8	5338	3955	1980
8182	3031	2.7	5151	3990	1981
7910	3076	2.6	4834	3966	1982
7909	3142	2.5	4767	4011	1983
8061	3264	2.5	4797	4129	1984
8083	3392	2.4	4691	4228	1985
8080	3459	2.3	4622	4273	1986
8108	3542	2.3	4566	4338	1987
8230	3683	2.2	4546	4467	1988
8266	3780	2.2	4485	4545	1989

TABLE 6 -- NOTES FOR TABLES 1 - 5

Abbreviations

%pa	percent per annum
avg	average
GDP	gross domestic product
GDP/cap	gross domestic product per capita
GGDP	global gross domestic product (world GDP)
hist	historical data, based on Penn World Tables (not simulated)
hypoth	hypothetical (=simulated)
intlPr85	international prices in constant 1985 values(i.e., purchasing power parity dollars,with US dollar 1985=100)
N	number of countries upon which the information is based
OECD	24 countries of the Organization for Economic Cooperation and Development
non-OECD	97 countries which are not OECD, including China, India, Indonesia, USSR
POP	population
PWT	Penn World Table (data source)
sim	simulated values
std	standard deviation
T	transfer value (aggregate)

Data Source

Penn World Table (Mark 5.6a)

(Col. B, C, E: GDP from Penn World Table, using variable RGDPCH from source, multiplied by variable POP from source)(Col. H, I,J: variable POP in source).

Calculations

Column	
A	none
B,C,E	from source: using RGDPCH * POP from PWT
D	growth rate for col. C
F	growth rate for col. E
G	= (E/B)*100
H,I,J	from source: using POP from PWT
K	=(I/H)*100
L	=B/H

M	=C/I
N	=E/J
O	=M/N
P	=M - N
Q	growth rate for col. L
R	growth rate for col. M
S	growth rate for col. N
T	=C * 0.015
U	U1961=given=C1961 U1962=U1961*(1+(D1962/100)) - T1962 and so on for the other years
V	V1961=given=E1961 V1962=V1961*(1+(F1962/100)) + T1962 and so on for the other years
W	=((B-U-V)/B)*100
X	=(V/(U+V))*100
Y	=U/I
Z	=V/J
AA	=Y/Z
AB	=Y - Z
AC	=(U+V)/H

Inclusion/Exclusion of Countries

The world has more than N=121 countries and more than N=97 non-OECD countries. I excluded countries on grounds of data availability. Only those countries are included which have complete data series for 1961-1989 in the source (Penn World Table). China, India, Indonesia and USSR are included. Some oil-producing countries and several countries of Eastern Europe are excluded, as are various other countries. The following countries are included in the study:

Ordered by continents as in Penn World Table:

Africa
America, North and Central
America, South
Asia, incl. "South-West Asia" = Arabian peninsula, incl. Israel and Syria
Europe, incl. USSR and Turkey
Oceania

N=121
Algeria
Angola
Benin
Botswana
Burkina Faso
Burundi
Cameroon
Cape Verde Is.
Central Afr. R.
Chad
Comoros
Congo
Egypt
Gabon
Gambia
Ghana
Guinea
Guinea-Biss
Ivory Coast
Kenya
Lesotho
Madagascar
Malawi
Mali
Mauritania
Mauritius
Morocco
Mozambique
Namibia
Niger
Nigeria
Reunion
Rwanda
Senegal
Seychelles
Sierra Leone
Somalia
South Africa
Swaziland
Togo
Tunisia
Uganda

Zaire
Zambia
Zimbabwe

Barbados
Canada
Costa Rica
Dominican Rep
El Salvador
Guatemala
Haiti
Honduras
Jamaica
Mexico
Nicaragua
Panama
Puerto Rico
Trinidad &Tobago
U.S.A.

Argentina
Bolivia
Brazil
Chile
Colombia
Ecuador
Guyana
Paraguay
Peru
Suriname
Uruguay
Venezuela

Bangladesh
China
Hong Kong
India
Indonesia
Iran
Israel
Japan
Jordan
Korea, Rep.

Malaysia
Myanmar
Pakistan
Philippines
Saudi Arabia
Singapore
Sri Lanka
Syria
Taiwan
Thailand

Austria
Belgium
Cyprus
Czechoslovakia
Denmark
Finland
France
Germany, West
Greece
Iceland
Ireland
Italy
Luxembourg
Malta
Netherlands
Norway
Portugal
Romania
Spain
Sweden
Switzerland
Turkey
U.K.
U.S.S.R.
Yugoslavia

Australia
Fiji
New Zealand
Papua N.Guinea

Chapter 7

THEORY OF ISOMORPHISM, PRODUCTIVITY AND GROWTH (GLOBALIZATION AS A SHAIKH-PASINETTI DYNAMIC)

1. SYNOPSIS

Neoclassical economists tend to be of the opinion that technological progress is the main engine of worldwide economic growth. In contrast, this study claims that technological progress is *only a necessary, not a sufficient condition* for global income and output growth; and that economic growth is *also* dependent on the growth of effective demand, both nationally and within the world-system. The article discusses Shaikh's isomorphism, explains it as a result of a Pasinetti-type growth process, and applies these notions at the world level. According to that view, long-term economic growth is driven by two "engines of growth", not just one -- namely, by technological innovation (similar to Schumpeter's notion) *and* by growth of effective demand (similar to Keynesian notions). Inadequate growth of global demand in an environment of global technological progress leads to economic growth rates below potential, to income polarization, unemployment and underemployment. In other words, whereas both supply constraints and demand constraints may exist in the circular flow of the world economy (or a national economy), the growth potential of the present world as a whole tends to be relatively more *demand-constrained* than supply-constrained. This is explained in terms of a Pasinetti dynamic. The institutions of world society must intervene in order to strengthen the growth of global demand and improve its distribution, while supporting technological innovation at the same time.

2. SCHUMPETER'S COLD DOUCHE

Heilbroner writes in *The Worldly Philosophers*: "When he lectured on the economy at Harvard in the midst of the depression, Joseph Schumpeter would stride into the lecture hall, and divesting himself of his European cloak, announce to the startled class in his Viennese accent, "Chentlemen, you are vorried about the depression. You should not be. For capitalism, a depression is a good cold *douche*." Having been one of those startled listeners, I can testify that the great majority of us did not know that a *douche* was a shower, but we did grasp that this was a very strange and certainly un-Keynesian message." (Heilbroner 1986: 291) Rather than rejecting either Schumpeter's or Keynes's theories, my strategy is to synthesize the two points of view. This can be accomplished by using more recent theoretical work by Shaikh, Felipe, McCombie, and Pasinetti. Given my interest in world-systems research, I will develop my argument for both the national and the world-system levels of analysis.

My presentation starts with a look at productivity growth. Two definitions of productivity will be considered -- namely, "aggregate labour productivity" (ALP, that is to say, GDP per worker; or, GDP per labour hour) and "total factor productivity" (TFP; i.e., GDP per a weighted mix of labour and capital inputs). Both concepts can be applied at the national and world-system levels. I will not deal with the microeconomic level. Ecological concerns must also be dealt with under the heading of "global growth", but that is beyond this article.

3. Productivity Growth and Standard of Living

Productivity growth is correlated with the growth of the standard of living of a community, but the relationship is neither automatic, nor is aggregate productivity growth necessarily benefiting all members of the community. In a polarized growth process, aggregate labour productivity may rise, but there are winners and losers. While the winners may increase their standard of living, the losers may have declining incomes at the same time. In particular, productivity growth may be associated with increasing unemployment. The productivity of the employed may increase, but at the price of throwing others out of work through rationalization and "downsizing", thus increasing unemployment.

4. Isomorphism and the Critique of "Total Factor Productivity"

An important critique of neoclassical views of productivity growth has been developed by heterodox economists under the heading "isomorphism". Isomorphism of economic growth is a discovery by Shaikh (1974) and was further developed by Felipe (1998) and Felipe/McCombie (1998) and others. The criticism of this argument is directed against neoclassical production functions. A description of the neoclassical approach to the analysis of economic growth is, as follows: "Following Solow's study, it has been generally assumed that the whole economy (or sectors such as the private business sector or manufacturing) can be adequately described by a simple mathematical function such as: Q = F (L, K, t) where Q is value added, L is the labour input, K is the capital stock (adjusted for capital utilization) as a proxy for the flow of capital services, and t is time which supposedly captures exogenous technical change....Assuming neutral technical progress, the production function may be expressed as

$$Q = A(t)\, f(K,L)$$

[end quote]" (Felipe/McCombie 1998: 7). [In this formula, A(t) represents the notion of "level of technology at time t".]

The heterodox critics have pointed out that this approach is isomorphic (tautological) with the national income side, as follows: "Following Shaikh, the accounting identity, which defines value added, is given by:

$$Q_t = w_t\, L_t + r_t\, K_t$$

where Q, w, L, r, and K denote output (value added), the real wage, employment, the average rate of profit and the capital stock." (Felipe/McCombie 1998: 11-12)

Shaikh demonstrated that the two formulae above are formally equivalent (isomorphic). Based on the discovery of this formal equivalence between the two approaches to the analysis of economic growth and productivity growth, the heterodox authors have developed several points of critique, as follows. The heterodox critics acknowledge that neoclassical aggregate production functions tend to fit statistical time series quite well (empirical fit), but that they are weak, false or misleading in various other ways (theoretical misfit). The main criticisms can, perhaps, be listed, as follows: (1) There is a level-of-analysis problem: "Fisher ... demonstrated that the aggregate production function is not just a logical extension of the microeconomic production function" (Felipe/McCombie 1998: 35-36). (2) Problem with the concept of technology: "there is no such thing as the aggregate technology of a country, and therefore such idea cannot be represented in the so-called aggregate production function." (Felipe 1998: 19). (3) Problem with the measurement of technological change: TFP [sc. total factor productivity; used in econometric studies of aggregate production functions] is not necessarily a measure of technical change, but an "artifact" (Shaikh 1987); "the measure of TFP growth ...is not necessarily a measure of technical change ... one can never be certain that the coefficients estimated are the "true" technological parameters ... the same is true for growth accounting" (Felipe/McCombie 1998: 35-36). (4) Problem with explanatory power: the neoclassical aggregate production functions are based on "a law of algebra, not a law of production" and are "humbug" (Shaikh 1987: 690-1). Along the same line, Felipe (1998: 19) writes: "production functions can be interpreted as approximations to the said identity. As such, no behavioral content can be attached to them ... isomorphism between the production function and the value added accounting identity ... do not permit any inference about the alleged aggregate technology ... there is no such thing as the aggregate technology of a country, and therefore such idea cannot be represented in the so-called aggregate production function."

The above contributions are of a critical/deconstructive variety. Thus, Felipe/McCombie (1998: 35-36) write: "We have neither provided new estimates of TFP

... nor a new theory of growth..." In my humble opinion, Luigi Pasinetti provides such an alternative theory of growth by making effective demand an integral part of the economic growth process, along with technological change.

5. Pasinetti on Growth, Technology and Effective Demand

While some heterodox economists were engaging in deconstruction of neoclassical growth models -- e.g., Shaikh (1974, 1980), Felipe (1998) and Felipe/McCombie (1998), Pasinetti engaged in construction of a post-Keynesian theory of economic growth. Pasinetti's work is influenced by Schumpeter who coined the phrase of capitalism as a process of "creative destruction". Both authors have in common a belief in the importance of innovation. Both authors share a broad, rather than narrow, concept of technological innovation, which they view as a process of learning how to do things in new ways. This concept of technological innovation goes beyond a narrow "hardware view" of technology which equates technological progress with new machinery and gadgets and nothing else. Thus, in the Schumpeter and Pasinetti view, a new operating procedure or a new form of organization is as much eligible to be called "technological innovation" as is a new type of computer hardware or a new type of nuclear missile. Pasinetti considers technological progress, in the sense of learning, as the major source of economic growth. Pasinetti writes: "It is the acquisition of knowledge that eventually makes the wealth of nations." (Pasinetti 1993: 176); and he describes technology as the "primum movens" of economic growth (Pasinetti 1993: 45; "primum movens" = primary moving force). This view of the importance of technological change is similar to what we find in neoclassical theory of economic growth, e.g., in Robert Solow's work (Solow 1956, 1994). Where Pasinetti's theory differs from the neoclassical one is regarding the role of effective demand. Neoclassicals tend to ignore or deny a role for effective demand in the process of economic growth or admit, at the most, that effective demand plays a minor, short-term role (e.g., Mankiw, 1994). In contrast, Pasinetti's theory assigns great importance to effective demand in long-term economic growth. The argument runs, as follows: "Technical change emerges as the crucial determinant in the dynamic process outlined by Pasinetti, since it contains both a demand and a supply aspect." (Halevi 1994: 58). In this process technological change propels both labour productivity and per capita income simultaneously. However, there is no guarantee that there will be a proper macroeconomic match between changing magnitudes of productivity and changing magnitudes of aggregate income and demand. There is "no reliance on any automatic fulfillment of the macroeconomic condition that ensures the correct level of overall effective demand and hence full employment " (Pasinetti 1993: 116). Technological progress and the growth of effective demand are thus both needed for overall economic growth; one without the other will not suffice. Thus, in the absence of sufficient effective demand, "(t)echnological progress can ... also cause net losses of wealth or social well-being in general" (Pasinetti 1993: 57). In Pasinetti's theory effective demand co-determines the benefits reaped from technological progress, and the institutions of society are seen as the guarantor who must assure that effective demand and technological change are properly matched for optimal social and economic results. Pasinetti's theory distinguishes between a "physical quantity system" and a "price system" in the economy; "(t)he *physical quantity* system is determined by the structural evolution of consumption *demand*", while "(t)he *price* system is determined by the structural evolution of *technology*" (Pasinetti 1993: 46; my emphasis). GDP (or, aggregate value added) is seen as the sum of the cross-products of physical quantities and their prices. Thus, demand determines one aspect of GDP and technology determines the other aspect.

6. Three Causal Views of Isomorphism

Isomorphism is not causation. The growth isomorphism described above can be interpreted in three different ways, depending on our postulates about causation, namely:

(1) *neoclassical* interpretation -- the supply side determines the income side, or,

A f(K,L) → Q → w L + r K [read as causal arrows]
(engine of growth) (passive)

(2) *Shaikh's* interpretation -- Q and incomes are determined by a "law of production"; the neoclassical side is "humbug", isomorphism is only a formal artifact; or,

A f(K,L) = Q = w L + r K
(humbug artifact) ↑ ↑ ↑ ↑
[read as causal arrows]
law of production

(3) *Pasinetti-style* interpretation -- the physical technology side and the effective demand side determine together, jointly and interactively, the value added (Q), or

A f(K,L) <---> Q <---> w L + r K
↑ [read as causal arrows]
technological innovation demand

Pasinetti, like Schumpeter, takes *innovation and technological change* seriously; and, like Kalecki, Keynes, Kaldor and Robinson, he takes *effective demand* seriously. I find the combination of both elements in a theory of economic growth (and productivity) very fruitful and will develop my further presentation from this vantage point.

7. CIRCULATION OF VALUE IN THE ECONOMY

In order to understand the relationship between technology and effective demand in the growth process, it is useful to examine the circular flow of value in the economy. See Figure 7.1. This figure is very simple and leaves out various important aspects of the circulation of value.)

Figure 7.1 Circular Flow (without Financial System, Public Sector, International Sector)

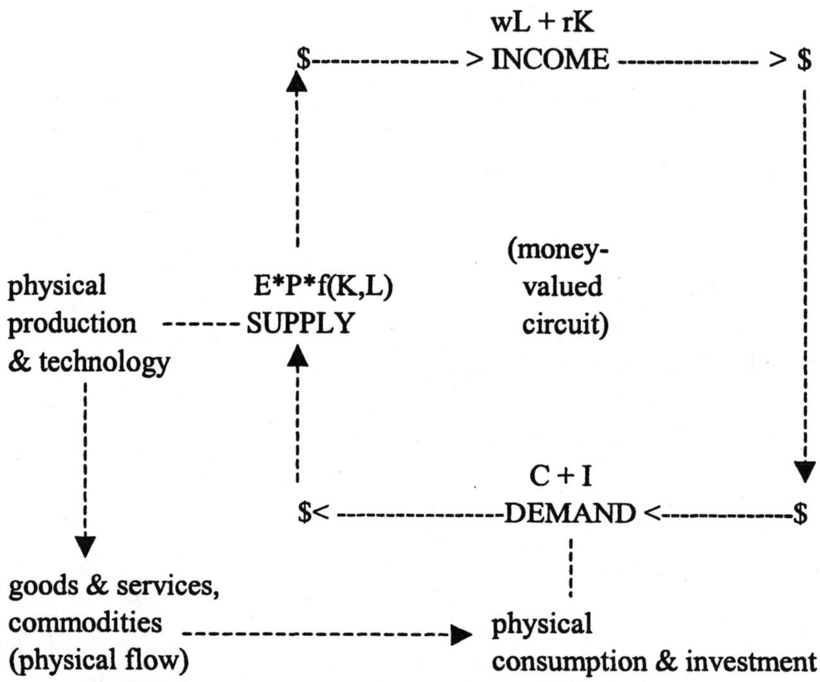

Note: for an explanation of the formulae, see the discussion in the text

Figure 7.1 shows a circular flow (sorry, folks, the circle looks like a square, but imagine a circle!). In this circular flow, money (here "$") flows between three accounts -- namely, "INCOME", "DEMAND", and "SUPPLY" accounts. Since this is a circular flow, one cannot be sure where the circular flow started (another "chicken-and-egg" problem!). In order to underline the perpetual flow character, we could write, as follows:

[*de infinito*]--income -- demand -- supply --income -- demand -- supply -- income --[*ad infinitum*]

Constraints in the circular flow may develop at any "transition stage", be it income, demand, supply or (here not elaborated:) additional money flows. Income dollars become demand dollars when the owner of the income decides to spend the income on purchases. Demand dollars become dollars in the producer/supplier's account when a purchase is made and paid for. The receipts from sales become payments to the factors of production, i.e., income of the factors "labour" and "capital". Note that this refers to the circulation of monetary value, not physical value. The physical objects and services (goods and services, commodities) which correspond to the circulation of monetary value, are physically produced on the supply side and and physically consumed on the demand side and circulate physically from the producer/supplier side to the purchaser/demand side.

8. Two Dimensions of Aggregate / Societal Value

There are two major dimensions of aggregate value in the circular flow of the economy: (1) physical, (2) monetary. (Each of these can be subdivided.)

1. *Physical value*: This is embodied in the physical objects and services which are physically produced, sold and used. The measurement of aggregate physical value leads to a listing of all physical goods and services. The unit of measurement varies between items -- e.g., "pieces", "tons", etc.
2. *Monetary value*: This is the money value attached to the physical values. The measurement of aggregate monetary value leads to a single figure of aggregate value, expressed as monetary value (e.g., as GDP) -- unit of measurement =monetary (e.g., US $).

Table 8.1 Example of Physical and Money-Valued Dimensions

Description	Matrix "Physical Quantities" (MOPh)	Matrix "Unit price" (MUP$)	Matrix "Group Value" (MGV$)
shoes	10 pieces	20 $	200 $
steel	50 tons	200 $	10,000$
dentist services	2 instances	70 $	140$
	etc.	etc.	etc.
GDP(aggregate value added)[sum of above]			10,340 $

In short:

Aggregate value (AV$) = Sum (MGV$) = Sum (MOPh * MUP$) = GDP$

The dual nature of aggregate value as physical value (things and actions) and monetary value (dollars, etc.) is important for understanding the relationship between technology and demand in the circular flow of the economy and in economic growth (or decline) processes, because technology (including machinery and know-how and organization) is physical ("real", as in a "thing"), whereas demand is monetary.

9. TECHNOLOGY AND PHYSICAL VALUE

When we think strictly in physical terms, an increase in technological knowledge has the effect that more physical value can be produced with the same amount of physical input. For example, if, in a situation A, we have 10 workers (L=10) and 10 simple machines (KPh=10), we may be able to produce 200 shoes per hour (OPh = 200). The physical labour productivity in this situation is ALPPh=200/10=20 shoes per worker per hour. If technological sophistication increases, leading to a situation B, we may have 10 workers with higher skills and 10 sophisticated machines and may be able to produce 400 shoes per hour (OPh=400). The physical labour productivity is now ALPPh=400/10=40 shoes per worker per hour. Thus the increased technological sophistication had the effect of increasing physical output per hour and physical labour productivity. This "physical labour productivity" can also be called "physical labour efficiency". In this example, the efficiency of production in situation B is twice the physical efficiency in situation A. If we think strictly in terms of production, irrespective of sales and prices, it can be stated that, in the example, the doubling of physical efficiency had the effect of doubling the physical output.

Note that something very important is missing in this description -- namely, there are no monetary values. There is no price information; and there is no information about the total monetary value of the physical output. We can describe an increase in aggregate *physical* value in matrix form, as follows (Table 9.1):

Table 9.1

	SITUATION A Matrix "Physical Quantities" (MOPh)		SITUATION B (with doubled physical efficiency) Matrix "Physical Quantities" (MOPh)
Description	Quantity	Description	Quantity
shoes	10 pieces	shoes	20 pieces
steel	50 tons	steel	100 tons
dentist services	40 instances	dentist services	20 instances
	etc.		etc.

In Table 9.1 physical output in Situation B is doubled in each category. Note that we cannot say anything about prices and GDP (total monetary value added), since we are strictly reasoning in physical terms. In this strictly physical view, the physical output in Situation B (which is double that in Situation A) cannot be summarized in a single number, because the units of physical measurement vary from one category to the other. We have no choice but to list the increased physical output by category (i.e., as a matrix).

10. TECHNOLOGY AND THE TWO VALUE FORMS OF OUTPUT

This point is very important in my theory -- namely, that (1) aggregate output can be described in two alternate forms -- namely, in *physical form,* as a matrix of categories and their quantities; or, alternatively, in *money-valued form,* as a single figure which summarizes all the monetary values of all the categories [as shown in Table 8.1]; and that (2) technological knowledge has a direct influence on the physical efficiency of production, but has only an indirect influence on the monetary value of the output, since the aggregate monetary value of the physical output is a compound of both the physical output and prices. If, as in Table 8.1, the physical value of the physical output can be represented as a matrix (MOPh), which contains no monetary information, then the monetary value of this physical matrix can be arrived at by multiplying the various physical quantities by their unit prices. We thus multiply a physical matrix (MOPh) by a price matrix (MUP$). When the resulting cross-products are summed, we arrive at the monetary value of the aggregate output (AV$). The relationship between physical and monetary value of aggregate output is thus:

AV$ = Sum (MOPh * MUP$) EQUATION 10.1

The differences between the two value forms of aggregate output can be described thus:

Table 10.1

	AGGREGATE / SOCIETAL OUTPUT	
	PHYSICAL FORM	MONEY-VALUED FORM
symbol in my examples	MOPh	AV$
full name of symbol	matrix of physical output	aggregate value in money terms
form of expression	matrix	single figure
content	physical(goods, services)	monetary
unit(s) of measurement	tons, pieces, instances, etc.	dollar, yuan, etc.
usual names for this	none	GDP, or (aggregate) value added, or (aggregate) output
symbol for this, as used in the literature	none	Y or Q or O

11. TWO DIMENSIONS OF AGGREGATE / SOCIETAL LABOUR PRODUCTIVITY

Parallel to the two value forms of aggregate output, there are two value forms of aggregate labour productivity -- namely, the *physical* and the *money-valued* form. The difference between physical and money-valued form of aggregate labour productivity results from the existence of the two forms of aggregate output (physical, monetary).

The *physical form* of aggregate labour productivity is in matrix notation (Equation 11.1):

MLPPh = MOPh / ML EQUATION 11.1

in words, the matrix of physical labour productivity (MLPPh) is equal to the matrix of physical output (MOPh) divided by the matrix of volume of labour (ML). If I understand Pasinetti correctly, the rate of change of the various physical productivities contained in this matrix is called "rho" by Pasinetti (he uses the Greek letter). From this, Pasinetti calculates a weighted average rate of change of physical labour productivity, which he calls "rho*" (Pasinetti 1993: 70).

The *money-valued form* of aggregate labour productivity is a single figure, rather than a matrix (Equation 11.2):

ALP = AV$/L = Sum (MOPh * MUP$) / L EQUATION 11.2

in words, aggregate labour productivity (ALP) is the quotient of aggregate output in monetary form (AV$) divided by volume of labour (L).

The differences between the two value forms of aggregate labour productivity are:

Table 11.1

	AGGREGATE / SOCIETAL LABOUR PRODUCTIVITY	
	PHYSICAL FORM	MONEY-VALUED FORM
symbol in my equations	MLPPh	ALP
full name of symbol	matrix of physical labour productivity	aggregate labour productivity in money terms
form of expression	matrix	single figure
content	physical (goods, services, jobs)	monetary (for output) and physical (for labour)
unit(s) of measurement	tons, pieces, instances, etc. and jobs (or labour hours)	dollar, yuan, etc. and jobs (or labour hours)
usual names for this	none	(aggregate) labour productivity
symbol for this, as used in the literature	none	Y/L or Q/L
other related terminology	rho and rho* (Pasinetti) for growth rates of "labour productivity" (physical)	q for "net output per worker" (Shaikh) and q' for "growth rate of net output per worker" (money-valued)

12. Does the Neoclassical Production Function Represent Physical or Monetary Values?

Using the above definitions, we can make the following observations.

- Observation 1: Equation 12.1 is true.

MOPh = MEPh * f (MKPh, MLPh) [true] EQUATION 12.1

or, in words, the matrix of physical output (MOPh) is equal to to the product of a matrix of physical efficiency indexes times a function of capital (K) and labour (L), understood as matrices of physical inputs. This corresponds to my example in Table 9.1, where the efficiency index for each category is assumed to be equal to 1.0 (in situation A) and 2.0 (in situation B).

- Observation 2: Equation 12.2 is false

AV$ = EPh * f (KPh, LPh) [false] EQUATION 12.2

or, in words, the monetary value of aggregate output (AV$) is equal to the product of physical efficiency (EPh) times a function of capital (K) and labour (L) inputs, understood as physical inputs. The reason why this equation is false is that the left hand side of the equation expresses *monetary* value, whereas all terms on the right hand side express *physical* values. If we wanted to correct this error, we would have to multiply the right hand side with a price term of some kind.

- Observation 3: The neoclassical production relation, as given by Solow (Equation 12.3), is problematic:

Q = A*f(K, L) [problematic] EQUATION 12.3

or, in words, aggregate output (Q) is equal to the product of level of technology (A) and a function of capital (K) and labour (L) inputs.

When we compare the three equations, the question arises whether Solow's neoclassical equation is equivalent to my equation 12.1 (which is true) or my equation 12.2 (which is false). My conclusion is that the neoclassical function *would be* true, if it was interpreted in strictly physical terms, as in my equation 12.1, where the letters symbolize matrices of physical items. However, in neoclassical research practice, Solow's equation is interpreted and operationally defined in *mixed* terms. In other words, GDP is placed on the left hand side (this being a *money-valued* term), while the terms on the right hand side are measured as (or, are intended to be measures of) *physical* terms. This leads to a gargantuan specification error in the research program of neoclassical growth research, because the theoretical definition of the concepts does not strictly correspond to the operational definitions of the concepts. I concur with Shaikh, Felipe and McCombie therefore when they state that the "Solow residual" (the "A" in Equation 12.3, or its growth form), as measured in empirical studies, is not a true (unobtrusive) measure of the (physical) level of technology but an "artifact" based on the isomorphism with the national income accounting identity.

13. Isomorphism Between Income and Demand

Shaikh and others described an isomorphism between the (neoclassical) aggregate production function and the (heterodox) national income accounting identity (namely, Q = wL + rK; see above). It is reasonable to posit an additional isomorphism -- namely, an isomorphism between aggregate income and effective demand. This is based on familiar notions like a Keynesian consumption function, etc. Let C be aggregate consumption demand and I be aggregate (fixed-)investment demand (i.e., demand generated by capital expenditures). If aggregate consumption demand is some function of wage income and aggregate investment demand some function of capital incomes, we can write: C = f1(wL) and I = f2 (rK). If aggregate (effective) demand in the economy is AD, we arrive at a demand equation which is not identical with, but isomorphic with, the national income accounting identity -- namely Equation 13.1:

$$AD = C + I = f1(wL) + f2(rK) \qquad \text{EQUATION 13.1}$$

where C is consumption demand and I is fixed-investment demand (also called CAPEX in the literature), both including public and private components. (This corresponds to the demand components D1 and D2 in Keynes's *General Theory*.)

(Effective demand (AD) is a concept in the realm of monetary value, rather than physical value. For example, effective demand in an economy may be measured as 10 billion dollars at a particular time.)

14. Difference Between Physical Output and Aggregate Supply

Aggregate supply (AS) is also a concept in the realm of monetary value, rather than physical value. For example, aggregate supply in an economy may be 10 billion dollars at a particular time. This figure does not reveal any information about physical quantities supplied. The missing link is price (more precisely, a matrix of unit prices). The relationship between physical output and aggregate supply can be stated as (Equation 14.1):

AS =Sum (MOPh * MUP$) EQUATION 14.1

where AS is aggregate supply; MOPh is the matrix of physical output; and MUP$ is the matrix of unit prices.

Note that aggregate supply is a money-valued concept.

15. Gains and Losses from Technological Progress

The thesis of my study is that technological progress is *only a necessary, not a sufficient* cause of economic growth. Economic growth is *also* dependent on the growth of effective demand. This is in line with Pasinetti's theory of economic growth. Pasinetti calls the growth process "structural economic dynamics" (Pasinetti 1993, see title of book). The approach is institutionalist, in the sense, that he calls his analysis "an inquiry into the evolution of industrial systems" (Pasinetti 1993: 39). In Pasinetti's theory "technological knowledge" and "learning" are seen as the ultimate engine of growth. Thus, he describes his theory also as "a theory of the economic consequences of learning" (Pasinetti 1993, see subtitle); he describes technological progress as the "primum movens" (Pasinetti 1993: 45); and: "the acquisition of technological knowledge as the primary source of the wealth of nations" (Pasinetti 1993: 174); and, again, in the last sentence of his major study: "It is the acquisition of knowledge that eventually makes the wealth of nations." (Pasinetti 1993: 176). We can see in this the influence of Schumpeter. However, in addition to a need for Schumpeterian innovation, Pasinetti diagnoses an equally important need for the growth of effective demand. Effective demand growth must match (physical) technological progress, or else a Marx/Keynes-type unemployment situation develops. There is "no reliance on any automatic fulfillment of the macroeconomic condition that ensures the correct level of overall effective demand and hence full employment" (Pasinetti 1993: 116). If this condition is not met, "(t)echnological progress can therefore -- through unemployment -- also cause net losses of wealth and of social well-being in general" (Pasinetti 1993: 57).

15.1 Losses from Technological Progress

Pasinetti's observation, namely, that a shortage of effective demand in an environment of technological progress may cause net losses of wealth and of social well-being, can be shown, as follows.

In ex-post analysis, the three magnitudes of GDP, aggregate supply and aggregate demand for a year are identical, namely:

GDP = AS = AD EQUATION 15.1 [in ex-post analysis]

It follows, using my preceding equations and definitions, that:

GDP = AS = Sum [MEPh * MUP$* f (MKPh, MLPh)] EQUATION 15.2
= AD = f1(wL) + f2(rK) [in ex-post analysis]

Let's simplify this by dropping the matrix notation, leading to:

GDP = Q
= AS = E * P * f(K, L) [supply side] EQUATION 15.3
= AD = f1(wL) + f2(rK) [demand side] [in ex-post analysis]

in words, aggregate output (GDP) equals, on the supply side, an average weighted physical efficiency index derived from a matrix (E) times an average weighted supplier's price derived from a matrix (P) times a function of capital and labour inputs (K,L). Aggregate output (GDP) equals, on the demand side, consumption demand, which is a function of aggregate labour income (wL), plus fixed-investment demand, which is a function of aggregate capital income (rK). All this is in ex-post, static analysis.

This Equation 15.3 allows us to discuss some possible growth processes in a preliminary manner. Three kinds of possible losses from technological progress are (1) job losses (less L, more unemployment); (2) loss of labour income (less wL); (3) increased income polarization (the ratio rK/wL increases). Such losses could come about in Scenario 15.1:

SCENARIO 15.1 (technological progress with demand constraint)

a. assume that physical technological efficiency increases (E increases)
b. assume that aggregate demand cannot change (AD = constant), this being a demand constraint
c. assume that suppliers' selling prices do not change (P = constant)

What are some of the implications of this scenario, using Equation 15.3 for discussion? If aggregate demand is held constant, then (ex-post) aggregate supply is constant as a result of the demand constraint (AS = AD). If, as a consequence, aggregate supply is constant and suppliers' selling prices are constant, then there are two expressions on the supply side which can change (E and f(K,L)). We assume technological progress (E increases); this forces the use of labour down (less L, more unemployment). What happens on the demand side? We assumed that total effective demand is constant (a demand constraint). Since there is a declining need for labour through rationalization and down-sizing, there are also fewer workers on the demand side. If wages are constant, there will be less effective demand from labour since wL is decreasing. However, we said that aggregate demand remained constant in this scenario. If total demand coming from labour declines (less wL), then total demand from capital (rK) increases, in this scenario, given the assumptions for this scenario. We thus have (1) technological progress, with (2) constrained effective demand (both per assumption), and, by implication, (3) more unemployment; (4) less total labour income; and (5) more income polarization between labour and capital and more income polarization between employed and unemployed labour. It is further noteworthy that, in this scenario, decreasing employment (L) is accompanied by increasing money-valued labour productivity (Q/L), since Q is constant and L is decreasing. However, this increasing labour productivity does not make all of society better off, since total output Q is constant in this scenario. For society as a whole there is no gain from technological progress in this scenario.

15.2 Gains from Technological Progress

Our Equation 15.3 allows us also to discuss possible *gains* from technological progress in a preliminary manner. Following Pasinetti, the thesis of my study is that technological progress can bring gains for society, but that these gains are conditional on parallel growth of effective demand. Such gains could come about as in Scenario 15.2:

SCENARIO 15.2 (technological progress with adequate demand growth)

a. assume that physical technological efficiency increases (E increases)
b. assume that aggregate demand can change (AD = increasing), there is no demand constraint
c. assume that suppliers' selling prices do not change (P = constant)

What are some of the implications of this scenario 2, using Equation 15.3 for discussion? If aggregate demand increases in response to technological progress, then all labour can remain employed (L = constant). With L and P (suppliers' selling prices) being constant and technological efficiency (E) increasing, total output (Q) increases. Since there is no demand constraint in this scenario, demand increases commensurately with increasing supply (as per assumption). Increasing demand implies that incomes for labour (wL) and capital (rK) are rising. There is less pressure toward income polarization than in Scenario 15.1 (with demand constraint). It is further noteworthy that, in this scenario, aggregate labour productivity (Q/L) is increasing, since Q is increasing and L is constant. Society as a whole gains from technological progress in this scenario.

15.3 Comparison of Gain and Loss Scenarios

A comparison of the two scenarios above shows the crucial role of effective demand in an environment of technological progress. Stagnant effective demand, coupled with technological progress, leads to losses from technological progress, including job losses, labour income losses and increasing income polarization. In contrast, increasing effective demand, coupled with technological progress, leads to gains from technological progress (growth with less pressure toward unequal distribution). In both scenarios aggregate labour productivity (Q/L) increases. However, the social effects are significantly different. In the situation with *stagnant* effective demand and with technological progress, increasing labour productivity is coupled with increasing unemployment and no increase in aggregate income. In contrast, in the situation with *expanding* effective demand and technological progress, labour productivity increases as well, but employment is steady and aggregate income increases.

16. TRANSFERABILITY TO THE WORLD-SYSTEM LEVEL

The concepts and inferences developed above in my theory section can also be applied at the world-system level. At the global level of analysis we treat the entire world economy as one organic whole (single system). My concepts and inferences were stated for "aggregates" and are equally applicable to "global aggregates". Thus we can re-write, for example, Equation 15.3 for the world-system level as Equation 16.1:

EQUATION 16.1 [in ex-post analysis]

World GDP

$= Z$

$= GAS = E * P * f(K, L)$ [supply side]

$= GAD = f1(wL) + f2(rK)$ [demand side]

where

Z = world product or world income
GAS = global aggregate supply
GAD = global aggregate demand
E = average weighted global physical technological efficiency
P = average weighted global suppliers' prices
K = volume of global capital
L = volume of global labour
w = global wage level
r = global rate of return on capital

In the same vain, the two definitions of (aggregate) labour productivity can be re-written from Equations 11.1 and 11.2 for the global level as Equations 16.2 and 16.3:

The *physical form* of global (aggregate) labour productivity is in matrix notation (Equation 16.2):

global MLPPh = global MOPh / global ML EQUATION 16.2

in words, the matrix of physical labour productivity (MLPPh) is equal to the matrix of physical output (MOPh) divided by the matrix of volume of labour (ML), all with a global scope.

The *money-valued form* of global aggregate labour productivity is a single figure, rather than a matrix (Equation 16.3):

global ALP = Z/L EQUATION 16.3
= global Sum (MOPh * MUP$) / L

in words, global aggregate labour productivity (ALP) is the quotient of global product (Z) divided by global volume of labour (L), which is also equal to the quotient of the global sum of all cross-products between physical quantities and their unit prices, divided by volume of global labour.

17. Global Isomorphism

The isomorphism described by Shaikh and others, and the critique of neoclassical growth theory derived from it, are also applicable at the world-system level, since at the world level we deal with aggregates just like at the national level. There is no difference in logic, if the world system is treated as a single system. The main criticisms of neoclassical aggregate production functions are also applicable at the world-system level, namely: (1) there is a level-of-analysis problem (macro is not micro): (2) there is a problem with the concept of technology; (3) there is a problem with TFP [sc. total factor productivity]; it is an "artifact" (Shaikh); (4) there is a problem with explanatory theory: neoclassical aggregate production functions are based on "a law of algebra, not a law of production" (Shaikh). (See also, section 4 above.)

18. Global Growth as a Pasinetti Process

I have argued above, along Pasinetti's lines, that technological progress may propel growth of aggregate product and income, but that this result is conditional on having sufficient growth of effective demand at the same time. This thesis is also applicable at the world-system level, except that at this level we speak of world income, global technological progress and global effective demand, which must grow together in a matching way, or else losses from global technological progress will ensue. These losses from global technological progress may include (1) job losses in the world-system; (2) stagnating world income; (3) increased global income polarization; (4) increased intra-national income polarization. In a *benign* scenario of global technological progress (i.e., with adequate growth of global effective demand), global technological progress propels global labour productivity and global aggregate income, without creating additional pressures for global income polarization (or even with a reduction of global income disparities). In a *malignant* scenario of global technological progress (i.e., with stagnating global effective demand), global aggregate labour productivity may also increase, but at the price of stagnating world income, increasing world unemployment and worldwide income polarization. (These statements are a transfer of corresponding statements from the national level, in my theory sections above, to the world-system level.).

19. World-System and National Productivity

19.1 In General

A number of interesting questions arise at the intersection between world-system and *national* system. How does the world-system affect national productivity? Is technological innovation a *global, national, or firm-level* process? How do world market conditions affect national productivity? and so on. My theory focuses on two concepts in particular, which affect aggregate output -- namely, technological innovation and effective demand. National economies are open to the world-system, especially to the flow of information within the world-system. Technological know-how is, on the one hand, guarded as company secrets and, on the other hand, much of it spreads freely around the globe. There are imitation, demonstration and catch-up effects, mingled with industrial espionage and theft of intellectual property. National and company technological learning is thus benefiting from a world-wide knowledge pool which influences national productivity. Similarly, it can be observed that *world* market conditions and *global* effective demand may have an impact on *national* productivity. Here is an interesting example.

19.2 The Example of Saudi Arabia

Saudi Arabia's productivity illustrates the influence of world market conditions on national productivity. The development of Saudi Arabian (aggregate) labour productivity is shown in Figure 1. (The data are from Penn World Tables -- see also, Appendix A below.)

Figure 1. Saudi Arabia, Aggregate Labour Productivity, 1960 - 1989

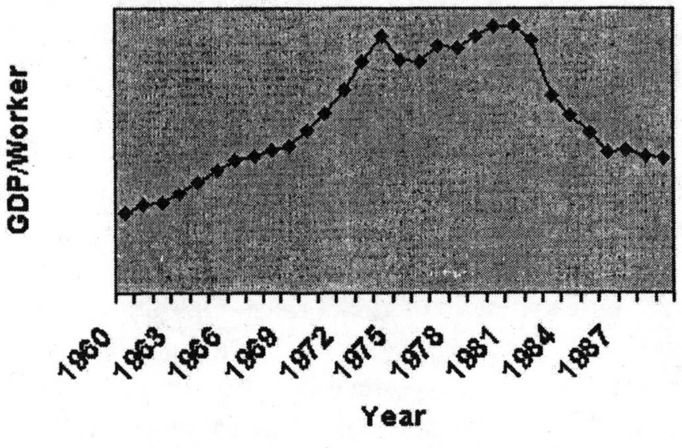

Notes: (1) Source: Penn World Tables; (2) For actual values, see Appendix A below; (3) GDP/worker is measured in constant 1985 "International Prices"

What explains the reversal of Saudi Arabia's (aggregate) labour productivity after 1982? According to a common view, productivity growth is propelled by technological progress (e.g., Solow) and/or improvement of "human capital" (e.g., Mankiw) and other *inputs*. In the Saudi case, these explanations appear inadequate for explaining the decline in aggregate productivity after 1982; another explanation appears more plausible -- please examine Figure 2.

Figure 2. Saudi Arabia -- GDP, Aggregate Labour Productivity and Labour Force, 1960 - 1989

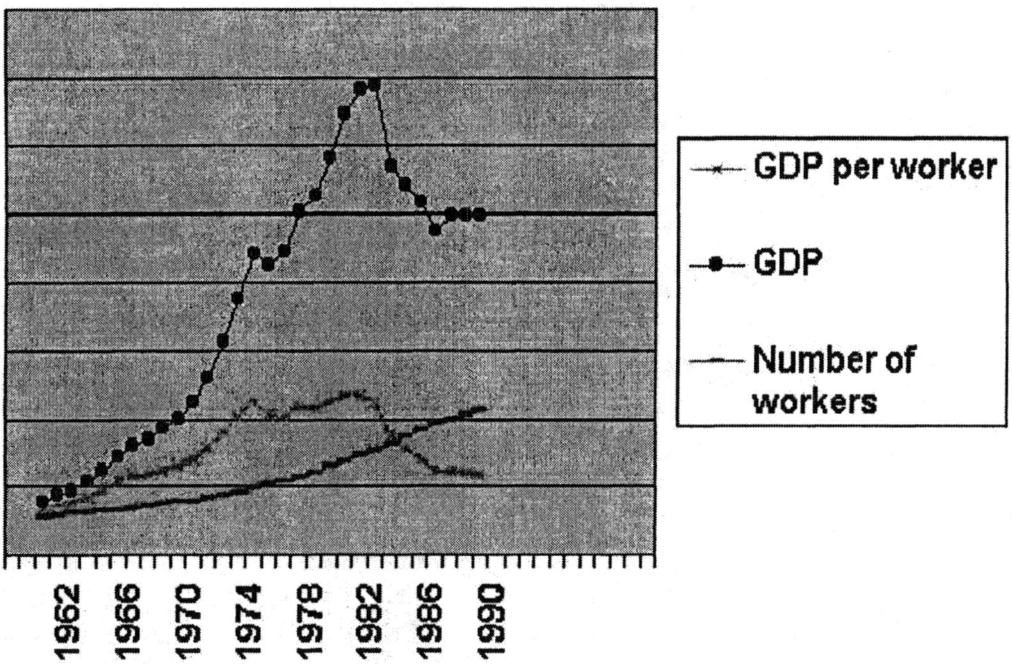

NOTES: (1) source: Penn World Tables; (2) for actual values, see the table in Appendix A below; (3) GDP and GDP per worker measured in constant 1985 "International Dollars" (PPP values)

Figure 2 shows that (1) the labour force (number of workers) increased steadily; (2) labour productivity (GDP per worker) first increased and then declined after 1982; and (3) GDP increased and, then, declined after 1982. There is a correlation between aggregate labour productivity (GDP per worker) and output (GDP).

The *correlation* between GDP and aggregate productivity is not surprising, but *causality* requires some examination. It is commonly assumed that variation in productivity (independent variable) causes variation in output (dependent variable) [or, productivity output]. This assumption is not fully plausible in this case. If Saudi enterprises and Saudi workers achieved a given level of technological sophistication up to 1982, it is not plausible to assume that such sophistication suddenly reversed itself after 1982. Another causal explanation is attractive -- namely, that the causation goes the other way, from GDP to productivity (or, value of output value of productivity); in other words: after 1982, GDP declined and, *therefore*, aggregate labour productivity declined. This view makes sense when we take world petroleum prices into consideration. Petroleum is the major export of Saudi Arabia; and petroleum revenue is a major component of Saudi GDP. When world oil prices and world oil consumption increased, Saudi GDP increased handsomely. When the world petroleum price declined in the 1980's, Saudi GDP slumped. Saudi Arabian aggregate labour productivity declined concomitantly with GDP.

The example of Saudi Arabia shows that the rise and fall of world prices and world effective demand may induce a rise or fall of national GDP, which may, in turn, induce a rise or fall in (national) aggregate (money-valued) labour productivity. National aggregate labour productivity, as commonly measured, may thus be a result of (a) world-system conditions, rather than being of purely national origin; and/or (b) a result of demand-side changes; there may thus ensue *demand-pull productivity growth* (or decline), as opposed to *supply-push productivity growth* (or decline) as in neoclassical theory.

20. Technological Progress, Effective Demand and the Institutions of the World-System

Pasinetti's theory of economic growth, with its dual emphasis on technological innovation and effective demand, argues that the capitalist economic system does not automatically bring about a proper match between growth of technological efficiency and growth of effective demand. "This is the point where the 'institutional problems' ... become relevant." (Pasinetti 1993: 116) The institutions of society must intervene in the market in order to bring about the proper level of effective demand. Pasinetti speaks of the "existence of a permanent task of pursuing ... effective demand and full employment" (Pasinetti 1993: 59). I have argued above that economic growth at the world-system level is a Pasinetti process of the same kind as that at the national (macroeconomic) level. It can be claimed, therefore, that the *institutions* of the world-system, as opposed to the *market* of the world-system, must assure that the growth of effective demand in the world system is keeping pace with technological progress. Under the heading of 'institutions of the world system' we find many categories, including global and transnational regulatory agencies like IMF, WTO, etc., corporate power structures, national governments, non-governmental organizations and movements, and so on. A recent topic of public debate has been "global financial architecture". This and other global institutions need to be reformed or, if we talk about labour and other citizens movements, then these movements need to assert themselves, in order to strengthen, and improve the distribution of, global effective demand and strengthen, and improve the distribution of, the gains from global technological progress. According to the Universal Declaration of Human Rights, everyone has an inalienable right to an adequate standard of living.

21. Appendix A -- Data for Saudi Arabia Case (see, Section 20.2)

Year	population	GDP per capita	GDP per worker	Number of workers POP*	GDP
YEAR	POP	RGDPL	RGDPW	RGDPL/RGDPW	POP* RGDPL
	from pwt	from pwt International prices 1985=100	from pwt International prices 1985=100	my calc	my calc
	1000's			1000's	Billions
1960	4075	3869	13798	1143	15.8
1961	4209	4238	15140	1178	17.8
1962	4348	4317	15459	1214	18.8
1963	4492	4851	17276	1261	21.8
1964	4640	5385	19315	1294	25.0
1965	4793	5981	21473	1335	28.7
1966	4970	6457	23200	1383	32.1
1967	5153	6612	23792	1432	34.1
1968	5343	6926	24949	1483	37.0
1969	5541	7151	25812	1535	39.6
1970	5745	7837	28345	1588	45.0
1971	5997	8755	31476	1668	52.5
1972	6275	9971	35625	1756	62.6
1973	6579	11445	40641	1853	75.3
1974	6905	12801	45195	1956	88.4
1975	7251	11714	41106	2066	84.9
1976	7617	11672	40730	2183	88.9
1977	8000	12549	43531	2306	100.4
1978	8410	12515	43131	2440	105.3
1979	8865	13130	45008	2586	116.4
1980	9372	13766	46849	2754	129.0
1981	9923	13779	46856	2918	136.7
1982	10510	13117	44608	3090	137.9
1983	11122	10214	34699	3274	113.6
1984	11750	9200	31216	3463	108.1
1985	12379	8313	28180	3652	102.9
1986	12991	7277	24716	3825	94.5
1987	13612	7300	24848	3999	99.4
1988	14016	7074	24128	4109	99.1
1989	14435	6876	23529	4218	99.3

Source: Penn World Tables

Notes:

1. "International Prices" = term from Penn World Tables = purchasing power parity dollars
2. "from pwt" = from Penn World Tables
3. "my calc" = my calculation from other data in the table
4. "RGDPL" etc. are the variable names used in the Penn World Tables

Chapter 8

SURPLUS VALUE AND TRANSFER VALUE

1. OBJECTIVE

This study attempts to clarify the conceptual relationship between "transfer value" (unequal exchange, superexploitation) and "surplus value".

2. CONTEXT

The global income gap is widening; the First World is dominating the world economy and shaping it so as to serve its own interests. "Unequal exchange" is taking place between periphery and center of the world, so that, in effect, the poor countries subsidize the rich and the labourers in the periphery countries are the most exploited in the world-system. Amin calls this the "superexploitation" of the labourers of the Third World. The process of "unequal exchange", "center-periphery exploitation", or "superexploitation" works through such channels as biased terms of trade and biased exchange rates, or, generally speaking, through the biased (global) "structure of prices". Thus, Amin writes: "...it follows that there is superexploitation of labor in the periphery which totals as much as $300 billion and which is largely hidden in the structure of prices" (Amin 1980: 19) The figure of US $300 billion is Amin's estimate of the annual outflow of value from the world's periphery to the center (around 1980, in current prices), due to "unequal exchange". Amin calls this value alternatively "unequal exchange" or *"transfer value"* and states: "It is this superexploitation that prevents the development of productive forces on the periphery." (Amin 1980: 25) I have argued separately that the same world-level mechanism is *also* responsible for massive unemployment in the *center* (First World, OECD). An interesting problem arises, namely: What is the conceptual relationship between "transfer value" and "surplus value"?

3. Surplus Value

The concept of "surplus value" is central to Marxist literature. Similar concepts appear under different names and symbols also in post-Keynesian and OECD literature. Conceptually, "surplus value" is the amount of value which the worker helps to produce but does not get. In the aggregate, the "mass of surplus value" in the economy is the difference between aggregate income and total wages. Thus, if a total of 10 billion dollars worth has been produced and earned by society and if the total amount of wages paid is 6 billion dollars, then the "mass of surplus value" (i.e., aggregate surplus value) is 4 billion dollars. Conceptually, this is clear. The heterodox "national accounting identity" uses a similar distinction, namely, $Q = w\,L + r\,K$ where wL is all wage income (namely, wage rate w times number of workers L) and rK is all other income (namely, rate of return on capital r times volume of capital K) (see, for example, Shaikh 1987). In Keynes's General Theory we find the expression "wage bill (W)" which corresponds to wL in the heterodox national income accounting identity (Keynes 1964). Finally, one finds a category of "operational surplus" in the statistical accounts of OECD (e.g., OECD 1995: 34.-- This "operational surplus" comes out to be about 25% of GDP, which is only about one half of "surplus value", but the concepts have some similarity.) At the measurement level (operational level) there are differences between authors. Some of these differences have to do with the fact that Marx wrote at a time long before modern GDP-type national accounting had been developed. A study which uses authentic Marx-based concepts and measurements of surplus value is Moseley (1991). Other Marxist authors calculate "surplus value" in a GDP-type context (see, the discussion in Moseley 1991). (As a result, measurements of surplus value differ between various authors.)

4. Global Transfer Value

The intellectual history of the concept of global transfer value starts, perhaps, with the Latin American school and Prebisch.

Prebisch criticized the *terms of trade* between center and periphery countries and argued that the terms of trade were deteriorating for the Third World. The notion of unfair terms of trade was then further developed by Arghiri Emmanuel who developed the theory, and coined the term, of "*unequal exchange*" (Emmanuel 1962, 1972). Emmanuel proposed a conceptual definition of unequal exchange, but did not have any operational definition nor quantitative estimates of the magnitude of unequal exchange. Emmanuel's theoretical definition of "unequal exchange" is, as follows:

> "...unequal exchange is the proportion between equilibrium prices that is established through the equalization of profits between regions in which the rate of surplus value is 'institutionally' different..." (Emmanuel 1972: 64).

This is a theoretical definition and not an operational definition. How unequal is the exchange? How much value is unfairly transferred from the periphery to the center?

Emmanuel did not give any precise figures. However, Emmanuel gave a sense of magnitudes involved when he wrote that: the "loss [sc. resulting from unequal exchange] ... is enormous in relation to the poverty of the underdeveloped countries while being far from negligible in relation to the wealth of the advanced countries." (Emmanuel 1972: 265) Some authors provided estimates for *individual countries*. Gibson (1980) estimated a loss for Peru in 1969 in its trade with USA as 38% of its exports to the USA (see, Raffer 1987: 94). Webber and Foot (1984) estimated for the Philippines in 1961 that Philippine exports would have amounted to 5.269 billion pesos, if valued at Canadian wages and prices, instead of the actual 1.129 billion pesos (see, Raffer 1987: 95). *Worldwide estimates of unequal exchange* are available from Amin and Köhler. Amin mentions global figures for unequal exchange in two separate publications -- an estimate of $22 billion for 1966 (Amin 1976: 143-144) and an estimate of $300 billion for around 1980 (Amin 1980: 19). Köhler presented estimates of global unequal exchange for 1965 and 1995 (Köhler 1998a, 1998b).

In the intellectual development from a purely theoretical definition of unequal exchange (Emmanuel) to some quantification of the concept (Amin) and more quantification (Köhler), the concept of a "transfer value" crept into the discussion (e.g., Amin 1980). The situation can, perhaps, be seen in such a way that the expressions of "unequal exchange" and "transfer value" are two sides of the same thing -- namely, "unequal exchange" describes the process or mechanism, whereas "transfer value" describes the quantity of value which moves from A to B in the process of unequal exchange. Some of the literature uses the term "unequal exchange" interchangeably for both the process and the quantity.

5. AMIN'S CONCEPT OF "SUPEREXPLOITATION"

In addition to the expressions "transfer value" and "unequal exchange", Amin also uses the term "superexploitation". While this expression can be understood in the sense of "*superlative* exploitation" or "extreme exploitation", there is more to it than that, namely, "superexploitation" has also the meaning of "exploitation *superimposed on* exploitation" or "double exploitation". In Amin's usage, superexploitation does not happen to labour in the center, no matter how exploited they may be. Superexploitation (double-exploitation) happens to labour in the periphery--namely, because the labourers in the periphery generate both surplus value (to the business owners, capitalist class) *and* global transfer value (to the rich countries, center countries). Who benefits from the "superexploitation" of the laborers of the periphery of the world-system? Here Amin lists three categories of beneficiaries, namely: "(1) the local classes exploiting them (landowners and local capitalists); (2) the capital that dominates the whole system -- that of the monopolies; and (3) the workers of the imperialist centers (or at least some of them)." (Amin 1980: 19) This can be interpreted in such a way that laborers anywhere (both in the periphery and the center) generate surplus value; but, in addition, the laborers of the periphery also generate global transfer value, part of which is benefiting labour in the center countries via the mechanism of unequal exchange

6. The Problematique

From an orthodox Marxist point of view, "unequal exchange" is not "exploitation", even though it is exploitation in the common sense of the word. That is probably one of the reasons why Emmanuel chose a name other than "exploitation" (namely, "unequal exchange") and why Amin coined yet another expression, namely "superexploitation", and why others use yet other special expressions like "world technological rent" (Çakmak 1998) and why the term "transfer value" comes in handy for purposes of communication. The exact relationship between "surplus value" and "transfer value" contains the following problematique: Whereas both concepts refer to value which is extracted from somebody by somebody, the "somebodies" on the giving and receiving end are different ontological entities and are overlapping (not mutually exclusive). When we speak of surplus value, the two entities are worker and capitalist (at the micro-level) or labour and capital (at the macro-level) -- i.e., *functionally* defined roles or classes. When we speak of transfer value, the two entities, which are referred to, are periphery country and center country, or, periphery and center -- i.e., *territorially* defined entities or entity classes. The categories "labour and capital" and "center and periphery" are overlapping. As a result, the value flows in the two types of relationships (surplus value, transfer value) are also overlapping categories. That requires some clarification.

7. Two Formulae

The problem can be discussed around two formulae. We can define aggregate surplus value, as follows:

$$SV = Y - W$$

in words, aggregate surplus value (SV) is the difference between aggregate income of a community (Y) less aggregate wages of a community (W). [Authors disagree about the measurement of Y and W, but let us ignore that for the time being.]

We can define "transfer value", as follows:

$$T = d*X - X$$

in words, aggregate transfer value (T) is the difference between the true value of exports from periphery to center (d*X) less the actually paid value for the same exports (X). [d is a distortion factor, measuring undervaluation. This is the formula which I proposed in

Köhler 1998a. Other components of transfer may have to be added in order to capture all value that is being transferred. But this formula is sufficient for the present exercise.]

8. A Two-Country Example

Let's assume that there is a world with only two countries -- namely, country N (for "North", rich) and country S (for "South", poor). Each country has 10 workers and one capitalist entrepreneur.

(a) the GDP of rich country N is 1000 francs
(b) the GDP of poor country S is 1000 yuan
(c) the wage bill W of rich country N is 600 francs (shared by 10 workers)
(d) the wage bill W of poor country S is 600 yuan (shared by 10 workers)

For this example we can calculate aggregate surplus values, as follows:

SV = Y - W, therefore:

(e) SV of country N = 1000 - 600 (francs) = 400 francs
(f) SV of country S = 1000 - 600 (yuan) = 400 yuan

What is the transfer value?

In order to answer that question, we must have additional information. Let's make the further assumptions that there is international trade between N and S;

(g) the exchange rate is 5: 1, namely, 5 yuan = 1 franc
(h) country S exports to N in the amount of 250 yuan
(i) country N exports to S in the amount of 50 francs
(i.e., the trade is balanced, since 250 yuan = 50 francs)

In order to calculate the transfer value, we must have still more information, namely, is this a fair exchange? If not, how unfair is it? Let us assume that it is an unequal exchange (unfair trade) and that it is unfair because the exchange rate is unfair. Let us assume that:

(j) the fair exchange rate would be 1: 1, namely, 1 yuan = 1 franc

We can now calculate the aggregate transfer value, as follows:

T = d*X - X, therefore:

(k) the distortion factor d is equal to the actual exchange rate divided by the fair exchange rate, or, (5/1): (1/1) = 5.0
(l) T (in terms of yuan) = 5*250 - 250 = 1000 yuan [expressed in undervalued yuan]
(m) T (in terms of francs) = 5*50 - 50 = 200 francs

The example shows that surplus value and transfer value are as different as apples and oranges. The surplus values (SV) for this situation are 400 francs and 400 yuan, while the transfer value (T) is either 1000 yuan or 200 francs. [See, lines (e), (f) and (l), (m)]

9. Conceptual Relationship

I stated above that surplus value (SV) refers to a value flow between *functionally* defined entities/classes (labour, capital), whereas transfer value refers to a value flow between *territorially* defined entities/classes (periphery, center). When we use the notation "c" for "capital" and (letter) "l" for "labour", then surplus value flows, as follows:

l ---[SV]-→ c [flow of surplus value, from labour to capital]

When we use the notation "P" for "periphery" and "C" for "center", then transfer value is a flow, as follows:

P ---[T]--→ C [flow of transfer value, from periphery to center]

The categories "capital/labour" and "center/periphery" overlap. We may want to use the following notations:

lP labour of periphery
cP capital of periphery
lC labour of center
cC capital of center

Given these notations, it can be stated that transfer value T flows, as follows:

from {lP and cP} ----[T]----→ to {lC and cC}

in words, transfer value is an aggregate value which is "sent" (lost) jointly by the inhabitants of territory P (i.e., peripheral labour and peripheral capital) and is "received" (gained) jointly by the inhabitants of territory C (i.e., central labour and central capital). Amin is talking about the fact that the global "labour aristocracy" is benefiting from Third World labour -- in my notation, that is the portion of T value which goes to lC. Amin points out that laborers of the Third World are "superexploited" -- in my notation, that is the idea that lP loses surplus value to cP and, *in addition*, loses a portion of T to the center countries.

Dual Status Classes

The above formal notation brings out an interesting aspect, namely, that there are, in the global pyramid, classes with dual status. In my simplified formal scheme, there are two classes with no contradictory status and two classes with contradictory status (dual status), namely:

1. capital of center (cC) -- *receives* surplus value SV *and* a portion of transfer value T -- homogenous status as exploiter
2. labour of periphery (lP)--*loses* surplus value SV *and* a portion of transfer value T -- homogenous status as exploited
3. capital of periphery (cP) -- *receives* surplus value SV and *loses* a portion of transfer value T -- dual status
4. labour of center (lC) -- *loses* surplus value SV and *receives* a portion of transfer value T -- dual status

Subdivision of Transfer Value

It follows from these notions that there is an important difference between surplus value and transfer value, as follows. Surplus value flows, in theory, from a single class (labour) to a single class (capital). In contrast, transfer value flows from two classes (lP and cP; labour and capital of the periphery) to two classes (lC and cC; labour and capital of the center). We can thus decompose the transfer value T in terms of either origin or destination, namely:

by origin:

$$T = T_{lP} + T_{cP}$$

by destination:

$$T = T_{lC} + T_{cC}$$

in words, the aggregate transfer value has two components in terms of origin, namely, T_{lP} (the portion of transfer value lost by peripheral labour) and T_{cP} (the portion of transfer value lost by peripheral capital); and there are two components in terms of destination, namely, T_{lC} (the portion of transfer value gained by central labour) and T_{cC} (the portion of transfer value gained by central capital).

Combined Gains and Losses by Class

The combined gains and losses for each of the four classes, factoring in both surplus value and transfer value, can now be stated as follows (SVC = surplus value of center and SVP = surplus value of periphery):

Table 1

Class	Payoffs (gets+/loses-)
1. capital of center (cC)	+ SVC + T_{cC}
2. labour of center (lC)	- SVC + T_{lC}
3. capital of periphery (cP)	+ SVP - T_{cP}
4. labour of periphery (lP)	- SVP - T_{lP}

10. EXAMPLE

The measurement of the various combinations of gains and losses due to SV and T (surplus value, transfer value) is difficult because the T value is based on the assumption that there is an actual (unfair) value and a postulated (fair) value, so that one must think in terms of two valuation systems, the unfair and the fair one. The example which I used above can be further developed to illustrate the various gains and losses, as follows.

Let's express the distribution in terms of the fair values (purchasing power parity values, PPP values) and work with the figures given in the example above. Note that we assumed that the (fair) PPP value of 1 yuan = 1 franc; the (unfair) exchange rate is 5 yuan = 1 franc. In PPP valuation, we have yuan=franc, therefore.

Let's call the two countries N and S together "the world-system" and use the following notations:

Z = world income = Y south + Y north
Wg = globally aggregated wages
SVg = globally aggregated surplus values

Calculations:

(n) global wages Wg = 600 + 600 = 1200 PPP francs (yuan) [from col. c,d]
(o) global surplus value SVg = 400 + 400 = 800 PPP francs (yuan) [from col. e,f]
(p) world income Z = 1000 + 1000 = 2000 PPP francs (yuan) [from col. a,b]
(q) global transfer value T = 200 PPP francs (yuan) [from col. m]

We do not have any firm information about the various components of the T value (namely, T_{lP}, T_{cP}, T_{lC}, and T_{cC}). Let us make a further assumption, namely, that these components are apportioned in the same way as wages and surplus values (in my example, a 60: 40 split in both countries and the world). That leads us to the following situation:

Table 2

Country	**Net Income (after transfer value is subtracted/added)**		
	Labour	Capital	Both Classes
South	480	320	800
	(600-120)	(400-80)	(1000-200)
North	720	480	1200
	(600+120)	(400+80)	(1000+200)
WORLD	1200	800	2000

Another breakdown of the same figures for each class is:

Table 3

	Gets	Gives	Give/Get Ratio	
Labour South	+480	-520	520/480	= 108% (superexploited)
Capital South	+320	- 80	80/320	= 25%
Labour North	+720	- 400	400/720	= 56%
Capital North	+480	0	0/480	= 0%
Total	+ 2000	-1000		

Note: The number –1000 in column 3 represents the total value moving upward in the system; it includes 800 for global surplus value (SVg) and 200 for transfer value (T).

11. Global Exploitation and Global Surplus Value

The above example uses hypothetical values. I selected a 60: 40 split for wages and surplus value in order to have some simple and recognizably different numbers to work with. Empirical values are to be determined separately. The same goes for transfer value. That notwithstanding, the example shows in an interesting way that, at the world-system level, surplus value (SVg, global surplus value) is an inadequate measure of total global exploitation (in the common sense of the word). In the example, the total value which moves upward in the global pyramid is 1000 (composed of 800 for global surplus value and 200 for global transfer value), which is more than global surplus value (800 in the example).

Chapter 9

UNEMPLOYMENT (CENTER) AND UNEQUAL EXCHANGE (CENTER-PERIPHERY)

1. ABSTRACT

The article examines the relationship between unemployment in the First World (center, OECD countries) and unequal exchange between global center and periphery and observes a correlation between unemployment in the First World and unequal exchange in the world-system. Some arguments are presented in support of the hypothesis that unequal exchange in the world causes unemployment in the First World.

2. TRENDS OF UNEMPLOYMENT AND UNEQUAL EXCHANGE 1965 - 1995

Here are some statistical data as reference material for the subsequent theoretical discussion. I am looking at a thirty-year period from the mid-1960s to the mid-1990s. *Unemployment* in the OECD countries was about 7 millions in 1964-65 and increased to 34 millions in 1993. *Unequal exchange* was 1.4% of OECD GDP in 1965 and increased to 8% of OECD GDP in 1995. Figure 1 shows this situation in the form of a diagram:

Figure 1 shows a simultaneous increase of unemployment in the core of the world-system (OECD countries) and unequal exchange (transfer value T) over a period of thirty years from the mid-1960s to the mid-1990s. The increases are of approximately the same proportion (factors 4.7 and 5.7, respectively). [For a comprehensive documentation of the unequal exchange data, see Köhler (1998a,b)]

Figure 1. Unemployment (OECD) and Unequal Exchange (T-value) 1965 - 1995

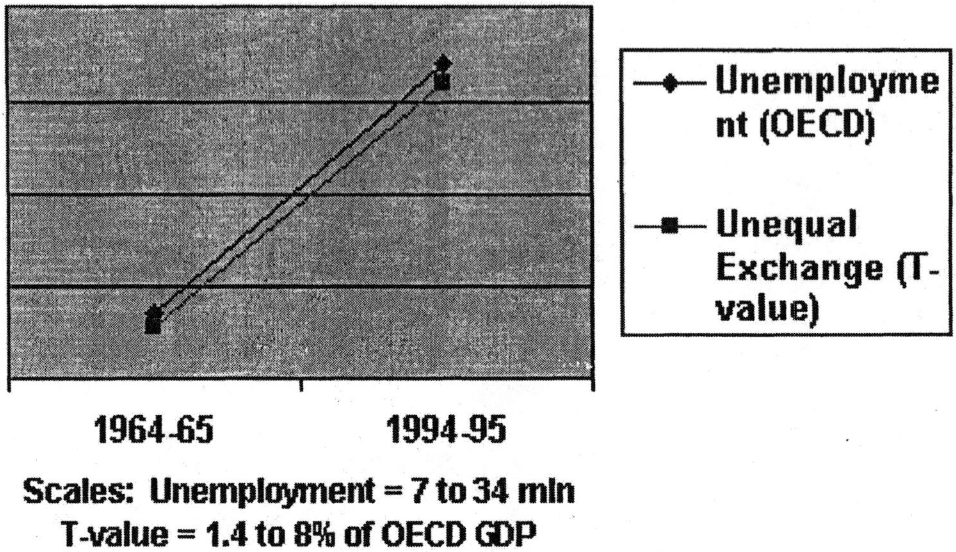

Sources: SEF(1996: 228) for "7 mln"; UNDP (1997: 210) for "34 mln"; Köhler (1998a,b) for T-values

What explains this simultaneous increase of unemployment in the First World and of unequal exchange in the whole world (Figure 1)? Is it a coincidence? Or is there a causal connection? A possible explanation could be in terms of inadequate global demand, namely, that: (1) unemployment in the First World (OECD) would not exist *if* there was sufficient *global* demand for OECD goods and services; (2) there would be more *global* demand *if* the Second and Third Worlds (non-OECD) had more purchasing power; (3) the Second and Third Worlds would have more purchasing power *if* they were less exploited by the First World (if there was less "unequal exchange", less "global transfer value T"); (4) in other words, the cause of unemployment in OECD countries is *world-systemic*, rather than *national* in nature; unequal exchange in the *world* leads to unemployment in the *First* World. I will try to support this hypothesis in two ways -- namely, (a) with expert opinion found in the literature, (b) empirically.

3. Literature

The relationship between unemployment and global demand has been discussed, for example, by *Singh and Zammit (1995)* who analyze unemployment and underemployment in the North and South of the world and conclude that these are caused by inadequate global demand. They describe the global "demand constraint" as "deeply institutional in nature" (Singh/Zammit 1995: 109-110). Numerous economists have been warning against *"beggar thy neighbour" policies* -- namely, economic policies which have the effect of weakening one's trading partners in an attempt to strengthen the own position; such policies may be counterproductive and may, ultimately, lead to a weakening of the own position as well. In 1931 *Keynes* was working with a MacMillan Committee (Britain) in order to develop a policy response to the "existing international slump". Keynes viewed *world* demand and *domestic* crisis as closely related. That is apparent from the following quotations. Keynes wrote (quoted from Moggridge 1981: 291-194; my emphasis):

> "It is not easy to see how we can expect a revival in our foreign trade ... by any other means than through revival of *world demand.* To meet the immediate problems, arising out of the *world slump*, a policy intended to direct *increased purchasing power* into the right channels, both at home *and abroad,* ... would ... be much wiser ... than a policy of trying to cut our costs faster than the rest of the world can cut theirs." (p. 291) Further, he speaks of "the efforts recommended in the Report of the Committee for *raising the international price level* by increasing, through investment and otherwise, *the effective volume of purchasing power throughout the world.*" (p. 292) Further: "We have ... postulated some *rise of international prices* as a necessary condition of the maintenance of the present level of British money incomes." (p. 293) Further: "Thus the problem ... is one of disequilibrium rather than of excessively high standards; and the task upon which we should concentrate is that of *remedying the disequilibrium* so as to bring our productive resources into full play, rather than of attempting to lower standards." (p. 293-4) He mentions that "nearly a quarter of our industrial resources" were "idle" at the time of writing. (p.293)

In the early 1990s some Western media discussed a so-called "locomotive theory". The question was debated which country (or countries) would be able to generate additional demand which could serve as a "locomotive" for the world economy. Some economists spoke of a "global paradox of thrift" (Allen / Vines 1993).

The theoretical notion that additional *world* demand may generate additional *national* employment is thus fairly well established.

4. Estimate of Demand Requirements

Next, is there any *empirical* support for my hypothesis? In my view, there is. I will consider three questions, namely: (1) How much additional global demand would be required in order to effectively combat unemployment in the First World (OECD) and (2) could the Second and Third Worlds possibly be the source of such additional global demand? and (3) how is that related to global center-periphery exploitation?

Let us examine the first problem: How much additional global demand would be required in order to effectively combat unemployment in the First World (OECD) via additional global demand?

In General

Let L stand for "number of employed workers" (="employed labour"), then it is true that:

$GDP_L = L * (GDP / L)$ Equation 1

in words, the GDP produced by a given number of employed workers (GDP_L) equals the number of employed workers (L) times average labour productivity (GDP/L) .

Next, let UL stand for "number of unemployed workers" (= volume of unemployment), then it is true that:

$GDP_{UL} = UL * (GDP / L)$ Equation 2

in words, the amount of GDP which *could* be produced by the unemployed workers (GDP_{UL}), *if they had work*, is equal to the number of unemployed workers (UL) times average labour productivity prevailing at that time in that country (GDP/L).

If there were customers who could buy this extra output in the amount of GDP_{UL}, all unemployed workers (UL) could be employed; UL would disappear (UL 0); and L would increase by the amount of UL to full employment.

Example

Here are some calculations for the year 1994. The data source is UNDP, *Human Development Report 1997*. [The page numbers in brackets refer to pages of the *Human Development Report 1997*]

(a) OECD population (1994) = 992 million persons [p.218]
(b) OECD labour force as percent of population (1990) = 48 % [p.209]
(c) OECD labour force (1994) [= (a) * (b)] = 476 million persons

The labour force is composed of L and UL, namely:

(d) OECD unemployed people (1993) [= my "UL"] = 34 million persons [p.210]
(e) OECD employed labour (1994), [=my "L"] [= (c) - (d)] = 442 million persons
(f) OECD gross national product GNP (1994) = 21 trillion US dollars [p.203]
(g) OECD aggregate labour productivity (1994) [=my (GDP/L)] = 47511 US dollars per worker per year [= (f) / (e)]

GDP_{UL} (potential GDP lost due to OECD unemployment) = *additional global demand required to achieve OECD full employment*

FORMULA: $GDP_{UL} = UL * (GDP / L)$

(h) OECD **GDP_{UL} (1994)** = 34 million persons * 47511 US dollars per worker = **1.6 trillion US dollars**

In words, the First World (OECD) could have produced an additional 1.6 trillion dollars worth of GDP in 1994 by using its reserve army of the unemployed *if* that output could have been sold to somebody. In other words, OECD countries were short by 1.6 trillion US dollars of global demand for their goods and services.

5. POTENTIAL SOURCE OF ADDITIONAL GLOBAL DEMAND

Let us examine the second problem -- namely, where could additional demand of sufficient magnitude come from?

OECD countries have not been able to generate this demand internally for some time. Worldwide there are many people who would like to buy this *potential* GDP_{UL} from the First World. However, they have a cash flow problem because the First World does not pay fair prices for Second and Third World goods and services. The rest of the world is thus short by some transfer value T. In a socially responsible world (the way I imagine it, anyway), the First World would pay the rest of the world at fair prices, so that the rest of the world would gain additional income in the amount of T. This T could then be used by the rest of the world to buy additional output from the First World. From the perspective of world-systems theory, a possibility is suggesting itself -- namely, the elimination of global center-periphery exploitation would lead to a surge in global effective demand of considerable magnitude.

A measure of the magnitude of global center-periphery exploitation is the "transfer value" which is an estimate of the amount of value lost by the Second and Third Worlds (non-OECD countries) due to unfair prices and exchange rates (unequal exchange). An estimate is available for the year 1995, namely:

Global Transfer Value T (1995) = 1.8 trillion US dollars

(For an extensive documentation of this estimate, see, Köhler 1998a; 162-163 in "World Table 1A") [The "1.8 trillion dollars of transfer value" are the same quantity as the "T-value of 8% of OECD GDP" mentioned in Figure 1 above.] This 1.8 trillion figure means that NON-OECD countries were effectively *underpaid* for their exports (in 1995) by 1.8 trillion US dollars due to biased exchange rates. Amin describes this kind of situation as "superexploitation of labor in the periphery ... which is largely hidden in the structure of prices" (Amin 1980: 19) As a consequence, international trading demand originating from the Second and Third worlds was reduced by 1.8 trillion US dollars from what it *could* have been in a world with *fair trade* and *fair exchange rates* (i.e., no unequal exchange, no center-periphery exploitation).

6. Comparison of Estimates

My two estimates of GDP_{UL} (1994) = 1.6 trillion US dollars and global "Transfer Value T" (1995) = 1.8 trillion US dollars are very similar. The 1.8 trillion US dollars of purchasing power which the Second and Third Worlds lost because of unfair trade and unfair exchange rates (unequal exchange) are approximately the same amount of global purchasing power (global demand) that the First World needed (namely, 1.6 trillion) in order to productively employ all its unemployed people, all 34 million of them. This evidence supports the claim that (a) the Second and Third Worlds lose purchasing power due to unequal exchange (global center-periphery exploitation); that (b) this situation creates a shortfall of global demand for OECD output; and that (c) this shortage of global demand causes substantial unemployment in the First World (OECD). Based on the above, it is not unreasonable to conclude that unemployment in the First World (OECD countries) is caused by unequal exchange in the world-system (unfair trade, unfair exchange rates, exploitation of the Second and Third Worlds by the First World).

7. Summary and Conclusion

The article examines the relationship between unemployment in the First World (OECD countries) and unequal exchange between global center and periphery and observes a correlation between unemployment in the First World and unequal exchange in the world-system. Some arguments are presented in support of the hypothesis that unequal exchange in the world causes unemployment in the First World. Assuming that this hypothesis is valid, it can be further observed that global center-periphery exploitation (unequal exchange) has two contradictory effects on labour in the center ("global labour aristocracy"), namely, (a) *gains* in consumption due to relatively low prices of imports from the rest of the world and (b) *losses* in employment due to the mentioned world-systemic causation of First World unemployment. These job losses are frequently perceived as "job exports" (from the West to the rest), but much of the disappearance of First World jobs may be due to the fact that neoliberal globalization leads to a comparative destruction of jobs on a world scale -- in the sense, that a world economy with unequal exchange generates fewer jobs than a world economy with fair exchange (fair trade, fair exchange rates). Rather than looking at non-OECD workers as "scabs" who "steal jobs" from OECD workers, First World labour should pay attention to the fact that they and labour in the Second and Third Worlds get hit by the same world-system in different ways (unemployment, superexploitation) -- some grounds for labour solidarity across continents. With respect to governments of the First World who are serious about fighting unemployment, my observations suggest that the governments of the First World (OECD) could reduce unemployment in their respective countries if they cooperated with other like-minded governments toward abolishing the global architecture of unequal exchange and organizing a system of fair exchange between center and periphery. The job-creation effect for First Worlders would come about through an expansion of global demand resulting from a transition to fair trade and fair exchange rates.

Chapter 10

GLOBAL UTOPIA, GREEN AND RED

ABSTRACT

This is an exercise in utopia design -- global utopia. As any utopia, it is incomplete but serves the purpose of guiding the imagination. The article is a package with two parts -- (1) green and (2) red (in the sense of political colours), both being elements of the same vision (utopia). Part 1 shows the possibility of a green mode of production (green as an engine of growth / accumulation). Part 2 shows the possibility of a red mode of remuneration (world wide wage parity, global pay equity).

PART 1: GREEN AS AN ENGINE OF GLOBAL GROWTH

1. Introduction

This part explores whether "green" (the goal of ecological sustainability) could be an engine of global economic growth (accumulation) in a "green mode of production and consumption". A scenario method is used. The "steady state" is defined as a physical, rather than a money-valued, state.

2. "Gray" and "Green"

One could think about concepts like "aggregate demand" and "technological innovation" in such a way that the concepts are split into "gray" and "green" components ("gray" = unsustainable; "green" = sustainable). Thus, one could say that:

aggregate demand = gray demand + green demand

and

technological advances = gray advances + green advances

At the present time, we have, say, 80% gray demand (non-sustainable) + 20% green demand (sustainable); correspondingly, we have, say, 80% gray technology (non-sustainable) and 20% green technology (sustainable). (The figures are probably wrong, but just for the sake of argument). "Green demand" includes health, education and social services demand and demand for software and computer-related services. And "green technology" includes technological support for those services, as well as the internet and computers as tools of work, commerce or entertainment, fish farms, windmills, and so on. Given these distinctions, it is quite imaginable that demand and technological output (and world income) could increase without being unsustainable -- namely, if the mix of gray and green is drastically shifted in the green direction -- say, from 80% gray and 20% green to 80% green and 20% gray. Seen this way, "green" could even be a driving force of (money-valued) "green growth" or "green accumulation" or "green development", or whatever you call it -- and could gain public acceptance. $10,000 worth of computer hardware and software is relatively "green", compared with $10,000 worth of automobile. $10,000 worth of solar collectors in the Sahara desert is relatively "green", compared with $10,000 worth of gasoline. $10,000 worth of hydrogen-powered busses is relatively "green", compared with $10,000 worth of gasoline-powered automobiles, and so on. By switching from the gray to the green variety, a Canadian consumer would not suffer a drop in (money-valued) consumption; and farmers in the Sudan don't care whether they get irrigation using solar-powered electrical pumps or gasoline-powered pumps, as long as they get them.

3. Physical and Money-Valued

The global ecosystem is under stress in more than one way -- from depletion of resources, to destruction of species of plants and animals, to pollution, and so on. The notions of sustainability and unsustainability imply that the global ecosystem has "limits to growth". Growing "ecostress" is thus developing against the "limits to growth". It is important to note that ecostress and limits to growth are *physical* concepts. Thus, air pollution is physical and is making people *physically* ill. The burning of gasoline is physical and is changing the atmosphere in *physical* ways. In contrast to these ecological concepts, which are physical, the wealth of a community is a *money-valued* concept which is commonly measured as GDP or GDP per capita. What is the relationship between these physical and monetary concepts? This question brings us to a very important point -- namely, that the same amount of monetary value can represent two radically different mixes of physical situations or processes. In my example above, $10,000 is the monetary value, but the physical situations corresponding to this monetary value differ radically from an ecological point of view, as follows:

monetary value	physical object or process(or portion of)	physical ecostress
$10,000	automobile	high
$10,000	gasoline consumption	high
$10,000	hydrogen-powered bus	low
$10,000	solar energy collectors	low

The ecostress associated with a given GDP is variable -- it depends on the gray/green mix on the physical side. For example:

gray/green mix of GDP				resulting ecostress
gray component		green component		
80%	+	20%	=	high ecostress
20%	+	80%	=	low ecosstress

How can ecodisaster(s) be prevented? One strategy is to stop economic growth (GDP growth) altogether. This strategy is predicated on the assumption that GDP growth is equal to the growth of "gray" (unsustainable) production and consumption and that the content of GDP is 100% "gray". An alternative strategy is to radically shift the content of GDP from "gray" to "green" (physically sustainable). By phasing out "gray growth" and phasing in "green growth", one could have a process in which ecostress is *decreasing* while GDP is *increasing* (for an illustration, see my scenario below, section 5).

4. Note on Terminology

Terminology in this field is not standardized so that misunderstandings may ensue due to differences in terminology. Here is a simple correspondence table for key concepts:

Author/Terminology			
general literature	Daly	Douthwaite	in this scenario
ecologically positive concept	sustainable development	good growth	low-ecostress growth
ecologically negative concept	economic growth	bad growth	high-ecostress growth

References: Daly (1997), Douthwaite (1998)

5. Scenario

For illustration of the relationship between "physical" and "money-valued", here is a scenario with some hypothetical numbers. The scenario works with three points in time -- namely, "now" (= year 0), 25 years into the future (=year 25), and 50 years into the future

(=year 50). The system which the scenario refers to could be the world-system or a national system. "Ecostress" and "limits to growth" are measured in physical units and GDP is measured in monetary units.

Assumptions:

(a) *Limits to growth* -- The limit to growth of the system is assumed to be constant over the 50 years. The limit is 1000 physical units. That is supposed to mean that the system cannot tolerate more than 1000 units of ecostress.

(b) *Ecostress* -- Measured in "stress units". Ecostress is multidimensional. Thus, using just one variable for ecostress is a gross oversimplification. But the purpose of this scenario is to clarify concepts rather than to provide a workable empirical model.

(c) *Alternative world processes* -- The scenario assumes two alternative world processes -- namely, a "gray" world process (high ecostress) and a "green" world process (low ecostress).

(d) *Gray world process* -- In the "gray" world process (high ecostress) the assumption is that the relationship between GDP and ecostress is 2: 1. In other words, for 1000 monetary units of GDP we have 500 physical units of ecostress; for 1500 monetary units of GDP we have 750 physical units of ecostress, and so on.

(e) *Green world process* -- In the "green" world process (low ecostress) the assumption is that the relationship between GDP and ecostress is 10: 1. In other words, for 1000 monetary units of GDP we have 100 physical units of ecostress; for 1500 monetary units of GDP we have 150 physical units of ecostress, and so on.

(f) *GDP growth* -- In order to keep the numbers simple and staying away from exponential figures, I assumed that GDP grows by 50% in the first 25 years (i.e., from 1000 to 1500) and another 50% in the second 25-year period (i.e., from 1500 to 2250).

These assumptions are summarized in Appendix 1. The scenario is shown in Figure 1.

Figure 1 shows four lines -- namely, a line for GDP (monetary values), increasing from 1000 monetary units to 2250 units; a line for limit to growth (constant at 1000 physical units); a line for the gray-world ecostress (from 500 to 1125 physical units); and a line for green-world ecostress (from 100 to 225 physical units). In the gray-world alternative, the ecosystem breaks down after about 40 years (i.e., at the point at which ecostress intersects with the limit to growth). In the green-world alternative, the ecosystem does not break down during the 50 years and ecostress stays well below the limit to growth of 1000 units. Note that the GDP is the same for both alternative world processes.

Figure 1. Scenario with GDP, Limit to Growth and Alternative Ecostresses

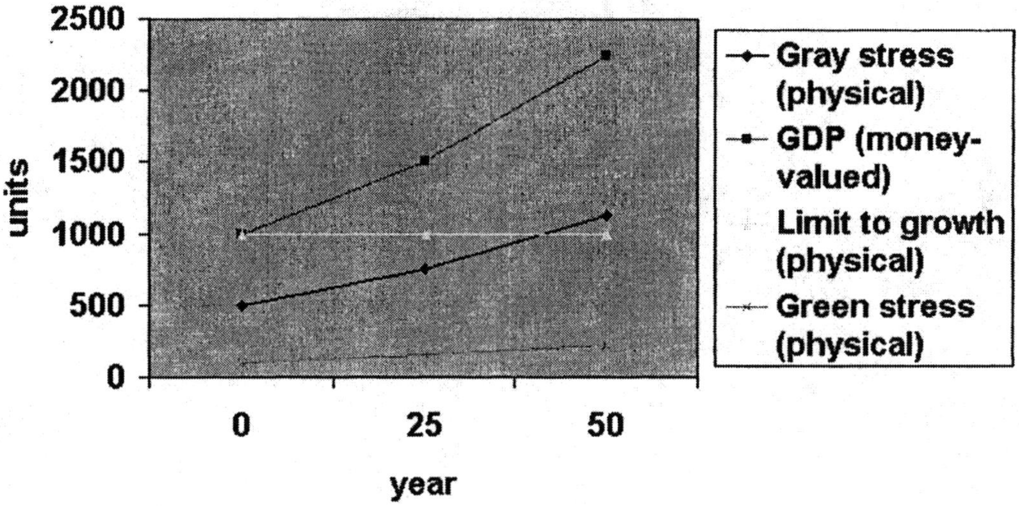

6. Scenario with Transition Path to Sustainability

The scenario can be enlarged for a thought experiment about transition to sustainability. Let us assume (a) that the present capital stock and consumption habits of the world-system are all "gray" (unsustainable, high ecostress); and (b) that the ecologically responsible managers and citizens of the world made a concerted effort to progressively abolish the "gray" capital stock and "gray" consumption patterns and replace them with "green" capital stock and "green" consumption patterns (sustainable, low ecostress); and (c) that this would be accomplished over 50 years. In our scenario that strategy leads to a transition process in which ecostress decreases from 500 (in year 0, i.e., the gray ecostress level) to 225 (in year 50, i.e., the green ecostress level). At the same time GDP growth (monetary units) is the same as in the other two world-processes. See, Figure 2.

Figure 2 illustrates how, during a transition process, ecostress *(physical)* may *de*crease while GDP *(money-valued)* may *in*crease at the same time -- namely, if there is a radical shift in the ecological composition of GDP during a transition to sustainability. The scenario serves to underline the claim that the relationship between GDP (money-valued) and ecostress (physical) is not necessarily a constant 1: 1 relationship, at least, not in theory. In other words, the ecological composition of GDP may change (i.e., the ecological composition of capital and the ecological composition of consumption).

Figure 2. Scenario with Transition Path to Sustainability

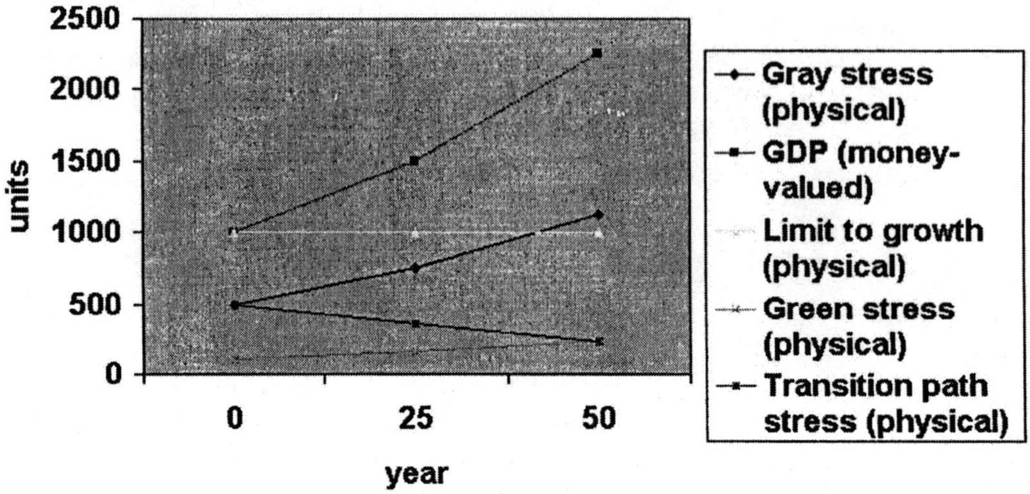

7. "Green" as an Engine of Growth

Progressively replacing the world's "gray" capital stock by "green" capital stock and "gray" consumption by "green" consumption is not only good for the ecosystem (lowering ecostress, increasing sustainability), but is also good for economic activity. Let's begin with a microlevel example. Think of a Canadian environmentalist family who had a house which was heated with an oil furnace. They replaced the oil furnace with alternative heating, including wood stoves, electrical heating, or solar heat (active and passive). The transition from the old engineering of the house to the new engineering meant phasing out "gray" capital stock and replacing it with "green" capital stock. In the process of re-engineering, money had to be spent for house restoration and new heating systems. This example shows that the "green re-engineering" at the microlevel generated money flows ("effective demand"). Similarly, a "green re-industrialization" of the world would generate large volumes of capital expenditures. For example, "green re-industrialization" in the transportation sector could mean the phasing in of hydrogen-powered vehicles and hydrogen-generating facilities. Such a "green re-industrialization" would involve both (a) a lowering of ecostress (physical, increase in sustainability) and (b) increases in GDP (money-valued). Seen this way, "green" (i.e., the active pursuit of sustainability) could actually be a prime engine of economic growth (in the sense of GDP growth). In this view, ecological concerns do not lead to an end of growth but, on the contrary, can be an engine (stimulus, motivator) of GDP growth. The very production of, and demand for, the new "green" output could be invigorating for the economy. If pursued on a global scale, "green" could be the basis for increased worldwide prosperity.

8. The 'Steady State'

The theoretical concept of a 'steady state' means, in the perspective of my scenario, a steady *physical* state of the economy -- i.e., a state in which the level of *physical* ecostress stays below the *physical* limit to growth of the system. As was shown above, that does not preclude the possibility of an expansion of aggregate wealth (GDP, global GDP), which is a *money-valued* concept.

9. Organizing the Transition to Sustainability

Keynesians of various stripes and market socialists accept market mechanisms in the economy, but they reject market situations in which the public interest is ignored and (global) corporations set the political, economic and social agenda. Public intervention in the economy is required, according those modes of thinking. Transition to sustainability requires a certain amount of public intervention in the economic process.

A recent proposal concerning one aspect of such a project is Kovel's proposed WPTO (World People's Trade Organization) which would introduce a form of planning into the international trade regime for the purpose of achieving ecological objectives. Kovel writes:

> "The core function of the WPTO would be the setting of a price structure according to which trade would be carried out. The key here would be to introduce--and enforce--an alternative calculus of pricing relative to that of the prevailing system. In place of the dominant calculus according to which goods are traded by their profitability to capitalists, we need an order wherein goods are traded according to their "ecological prices" (EP). The computation of such prices would go along with determining the differential between EP's and prices on the capitalist markets, and by the exacting of tariffs accordingly.
> In this scheme of things, production along ecological lines, for example, organic agriculture, would have minimal or no tariffing for purposes of trade. Furthermore, such production could also receive subsidies generated by tariffs exacted from those producers whose EP's exceed their price on the capitalist ("free") market. As an example of those commodities on which a high EP would be set, we could obviously turn first to an examination of the automobile industry in its current super-polluting and wantonly wasteful state." (Kovel 1999)

10. Opportunities for the Second and Third Worlds

The people of the Second and Third Worlds (the semi-periphery and periphery of the world economy) do not believe in austerity, neither in austerity for ecological reasons (on North-South differences regarding the environment, see, e.g., Bergesen/Parisi 1997: 364-5). The approach sketched above could, conceivably, satisfy their aspirations for growth of consumption while, simultaneously, actively protecting the global ecosystem.

11. Political Feasibility

The importance of public pressure for promoting ecological responsibility has been recognized by some -- see, for example, the campaigns by Greenpeace or a statement like the following:

> "The power for change lies with the general population world-wide. If they remain uninformed, their spontaneous revolts will simply accelerate the descent into anarchy. But if properly informed, the popular mobilization required to reorganize the social order--already implicit within the delegitimation of the current states--can be focused into a coherent global objective." (Grimes 1997)

The approach sketched in this article requires popular support. At the same time it is a concept which ecologically responsible leaders may want to promote. Advances are needed on several sides.

12. Green Mode of Production and Consumption

Producing wealth in the above manner could, perhaps, be called a "green mode of production and consumption". This view presupposes that a "mode of production" is not conceptualized as part of the essence of history but, rather, as an intellectual construct (tool) which may be useful for comprehending and *shaping* history (see also, Frank's critique of the concept of "mode of production" (Frank 1999)). Using the concept of a "mode of production" in this context may be controversial. However, it makes sense, based on the following considerations. The concept of "mode of production" has two sides and has been used in two ways. The two sides are (1) its factual-empirical-historical side and (2) its normative - utopian - futuristic side. The two uses are (1) in the analysis of history and (2) in the designing of an alternative future. Thus, if one talks about *capitalism* as a mode of production, he uses "mode of production" in the analysis of history and uses it as an historical - sociological - empirical concept. If, on the other hand, one talks about *socialism* as a mode of production, he may be referring to the mode of production in the Soviet Union and other socialist societies -- which is an empirical use, but he may also be referring to a *socialist counter-project*, in the sense of a socialist or communist utopia -- this is using "mode of production" in a futuristic - normative - utopian way. When I am postulating a "green mode of production", I am using the concept in a futuristic - normative - utopian way, namely, as a description of a counter-project, of something to be created rather than as something existing.

Chase-Dunn and Hall (1998) have analyzed world history using an approach which they call "institutional materialism", which contends "that there have been qualitatitively different logics of accumulation (kin-based, tributary and capitalist) and that these have transformed the nature of the social self and personality, as well as forms of calculation and rationality." (Chase-Dunn/Hall 1998: section 2). Whether the "green" logic of growth /production /accumulation discussed above would, if further developed and implemented, constitute a *sub-species* of the capitalist logic of accumulation or a *"qualitatively different logic"* remains to be debated. Tentatively speaking, a "green" logic of accumulation would be significantly different from an historically extant logic of capitalist accumulation and from a (traditional "red") socialist logic of accumulation. However, there would also be some overlap of a "green" logic of accumulation (economic growth) with either a capitalist or a socialist logic of accumulation. A study in which "green" overlaps with "capitalist" is, for example, a recent OECD study on the potential of a global boom resulting from new cyber-age technologies (OECD 1999). Moreover, "green" overlaps also with "socialist" or "communist"-- for example, in Schwartzmann's concept of "solar communism" (Schwartzmann 1996).

13. In Conclusion

This article explored, very briefly, the feasibility of "green" as an "engine of growth" in a "green mode of (global) production and consumption". Many observers have been complaining about a lack of vision in contemporary public life. My exploration suggests that "green" could, indeed, be an engine of global prosperity which respects the physical limits to growth and might even contribute to greater global justice.

14. Appendix

Table 1 -- Scenario Values

YEAR	GDP (monetary	gray world ecostress (physical)	green world ecostress (physical)	limit to growth (physical)
0	1000	500	100	1000
25	1500	750	150	1000
50	2250	1125	225	1000

PART 2: THE PRINCIPLE OF GLOBAL PAY EQUITY

Quotations

(1) "Everyone, without any discrimination, has the right to equal pay for equal work."
Universal Declaration of Human Rights (1948), Article 23 (2)
(2) "renegotiation of historically given wages"
Wallerstein 1978: 233

1. Introduction

This part examines wage disparities between countries and contends that a major portion of these global wage disparities can be described as "*un*equal pay for work of *equal value*". Furthermore, the article argues for international wage parity (global pay equity) as a general principle and long-term goal. Wages in the education sector are used as an example.

2. Wage Disparities in the Education Sector

Here are some statistical data as reference material for the subsequent theoretical discussion. Table 1 shows monthly incomes of educators in 22 countries. The table is based on data from ILO (International Labor Organization).

Table 1 shows monthly wages for teachers and other educators around the world at purchasing power parity values (PPP values). The wages range from 2959 PPP dollars in the Republic of Korea to 92 PPP dollars in Kyrgyzstan. The income gap for educators in this group of countries is 32: 1 in terms of purchasing power. [For wages in US dollars and in local currency, see Appendix A. The figures for Korea seem high, but this is what ILO reports.]

I would like to discuss two problems, namely: (a) On the one hand, the skills required for teaching reading, writing and arithmetic or many other subjects are the same whether one teaches this in Canada, Peru, or elsewhere. Providing education in schools, universities, and other institutions is a service which is very similar around the world. On the other hand, the incomes of educators are very different. What does that mean in terms of the *value of labour* ? (b) We are used to the fact that people have different wage rates in different countries and it is true that different countries have different abilities to pay. However, it is also true that the existing global wage structure violates the general principle of pay equity, which is the principle of "equal pay for work of equal value". What can we learn from the foregoing about the *principle of global pay equity*?

Table 1 - Wages 1995, Education Sector
All employees, Men and Women, per month, averages

Country	**"International dollars" (PPP values)** monthly
Korea, Rep	2959
United Kingdom	2880
Netherlands	2832
Finland	2279
Canada	2130
Isle of Man	1813
Netherlands Antilles	1497
Austria	1484
Israel	1303
Slovenia	1170
Czech Rep	705
Poland	496
Mexico	482
Peru	448
Hungary	434
Romania	363
China	255
Slovakia	255
Estonia	245
Lithuania	218
Latvia	182
Kyrgyzstan	92

Sources and notes: see, Appendix A

3. A Glance at the Labour Theory of Value

One might be inclined to think that the problem, as posed, can be solved by applying the labour theory of value. However, that does not seem to be the case. The labour theory of value theorizes about the value of *"commodities"* (goods and services). (Note that "value" is not the same as "price". The price of a good or service may deviate from its value in certain places or at certain times. However, in the long run the price will tend to reflect the value of the good or service, according to the labour theory of value in its Marxist form.) According to the labour theory of value, the value of a good or service ("commodity") is determined by the amount of labour which is embodied in the good or service -- or, more precisely, by the amount of "socially necessary simple labour" (Meek 1956: 164, 177).

When we apply these notions to the data shown in Table 1, the first question to be clarified is: Do the data in Table 1 show (a) the *price*of a service ("commodity"); (b) the *value* of a service ("commodity"); (c) the price of *labour* used for producing a service ("commodity"); or (d) the *value* of labour used for producing a service ("commodity")? The answer is (c) -- namely, the data in Table 1 show "wages", i.e., the *price of labour* used for producing a service ("commodity").

The next question is: Can the labour theory of value explain the difference of wage levels between different countries? My preliminary answer is "No", the reason being that the dependent variable of the labour theory of value (namely, that which is to be explained) is *commodity* value, and not *labour* value or labour *price* (wage level). In other words, in the labour theory of value the *dependent* variable is the value of *"commodities"*, while the value or price of *labour* is the *independent* variable (i.e., is given). Thus, the value of a good or service (commodity) is explained as the product of labour hours times labour value-per-hour. That leaves us with the problem of finding out what determines the different wage levels across countries? Without attempting to give a full answer to this problem, here is a correlation.

4. Wages and GDP/Capita

Table 2 - Correlation of Wages and GDP/Capita

Country	Monthly Wages Education Sector "International dollars" at PPP rate 1995	GDP per capita "International dollars" at PPP rate 1995
Canada	2130	21726
Austria	1484	21476
Netherlands	2832	19869
United Kingdom	2880	19498
Finland	2279	18515
Israel	1303	17752
Korea, Rep	2959	12275
Slovenia	1170	10942
Czech Rep	705	9945
Mexico	482	7658
Slovakia	255	6994
Hungary	434	6701
Poland	496	5735
Peru	448	4429
Estonia	245	4422
Romania	363	4384
Lithuania	218	3783
Latvia	182	3480
China	255	2661
Kyrgyzstan	92	1950

Correlation = 0.85

Source: Table 1 for wages. World Bank (1999) for GDP per capita

The wage level is correlated with the wealth of the country. Rich countries can afford to pay their educators better than poor countries (see, Table 2). The correlation between educators' wage levels and GDP per capita is high, but not perfect -- the correlation for the data in Table 2 is r = 0.85 (using PPP values, for N=20 countries).

Table 2 shows that the wage level of educators correlates strongly with the wealth of the country (GDP/capita) -- the correlation is r = 0.85. Does that mean that the work of the educators in a poor country is less *valuable* than the work of educators in rich countries? It is clear that the work of educators in those countries is less *money-valued,* but is it less *valuable*? This question leads us into a discussion of the problem of pay equity.

5. Concept of Global Pay Equity

The concept of pay equity is a *normative* concept or principle which states that workers *ought to* be paid the same wage for work of the same value, irrespective of other criteria ("equal pay for work of equal value"). The principle is an articulation of the value of fairness. An implication of the principle is that a deviation from the rule of "equal pay for work of equal value" constitutes discrimination. The women's movement developed this principle in order to gain wage parity of women's wages with men's wages. For example, if a person produces shoes or makes computer programs, it should not matter whether that person is male or female. What counts is the value generated. If person A generates the same value as person B, then the remuneration ought to be the same, according to this principle.

Parallel to "pay equity", *global* pay equity can be defined as a normative concept, rule, principle, or doctrine which states that workers ought to be paid the same wage for work of the same value, *irrespective of global location* (i.e., regardless in which country they work) -- in other words, "equal pay for work of equal value *globally*". Various questions arise from this concept and must be addressed.

6. Operationalization of "Work of Equal Value"

How can it be established whether work A and work B are of "equal value" or not? The problem can be subdivided. (a) If the work is the *same work,* then it is of equal value. For example, when a worker in a Canadian car factory assembles a certain number of doors per hour into cars and when a worker in a Mexican car factory assembles the same number of doors per hour into cars, then the work is the same. (b) If the work is not the same, it may still be of "equal value". The determination of equivalent value is not easy, but can be done. Labour unions and women's organizations have worked out certain practicable procedures to help with this kind of judgment.

How could we evaluate whether, in our example, the work of educators, say, in Canada is equivalent to, say, the work of educators in China or another country? It appears reasonable to assume that teaching arithmetic in Canada to, say, 30 children for one school year has the same value as teaching the same arithmetic to 30 children for one school year in China, provided the learning success is the same. If the learning success is greater in China, then it could be said that the value of that teaching service was greater in China (or, vice versa). This kind of reasoning is at the micro-level. In addition, we can make macro-level comparisons. The wage levels of educators in Table 1 are averages--i.e., they are based on the aggregate of all education services delivered in the country. These aggregates contain various "mixes" or "baskets" of education services. As a first approximation, one could look at the composition of all teaching services of a country in terms of "elementary level", "secondary level' and "tertiary level". Table 3 shows data for two of these levels.

Table 3 - School Enrollment, mid-1990s

Country	Primary Gross Enrollment %	Secondary Gross Enrollment %	Ratio Secondary / Primary Ratio
Netherlands	107	139	1.3
United Kingdom	115	134	1.2
Finland	100	116	1.2
Canada	102	106	1.0
Austria	101	104	1.0
Korea, Rep	101	101	1.0
Poland	98	96	1.0
Czech Republic	103	96	0.9
Slovak Republic	100	91	0.9
Israel	99	89	0.9
Slovenia	103	91	0.9
Lithuania	96	84	0.9
Hungary	97	81	0.8
Estonia	109	86	0.8
Romania	100	78	0.8
Kyrgyz Republic	107	81	0.8
China	120	69	0.6
Peru	123	70	0.6
Mexico	115	58	0.5
Latvia	89		nd
Isle of Man			nd
Netherlands Antilles			nd
	average= 104.3	average 93.2	nd=no data

Source: UNICEF (1999). Notes: see, Appendix B

Table 3 shows that school enrollment at the primary level was around 100% in virtually all countries shown (meaning, all children of the age group for primary education were enrolled. Numbers greater than 100 imply that some older children were also enrolled at the primary level.) In contrast, enrollment at the secondary level ranges from a high of 139% for Netherlands to a low of 58% for Mexico. That means that in Mexico only 58% of all pupils eligible for secondary education were actually enrolled. The over-enrollment in Netherlands means that many students were in secondary education who were older than the normal age range for secondary education. Table 3 suggests that the mix of educational services differs between countries. This would have to be noted in a careful assessment of equivalence of work between educational systems. An interesting case in Table 3 is the pair Poland and Canada (or other comparable pairs). Here the mix of primary and secondary education is nearly identical, whereas the average wages for educators of these countries differ greatly. The situation is one of unequal pay for work of equal value. Table 3 suggests further that differences in the value of educational services which may exist (e.g., Kyrgyz Republic versus Israel) are by no means as great as the wage disparities for the educators (compare Table 3 with Table 1).

7. Difference between the Principle of Pay Equity and the Labour Theory of Value

A theoretical issue to be discussed is the relationship between the principle of pay equity and the labour theory of value. The main difference between the labour theory of value and the principle of pay equity has to do with the difference between empirical and normative. The labour theory of value is an empirical theory which explains how the value of a product or service comes about -- namely, as a result of labour input. In formal notation, this can be written as: $Y = f(L)$ -- in words, Y (the value of output) is a function of L (the value of labour input). Such a theory can be used for supporting certain wage claims on behalf of labour (political use). Nevertheless, the theory is essentially an empirical theory. In contrast, the principle of pay equity is a normative principle to begin with -- namely, a doctrine about how labour ought to be evaluated. This doctrine is not about "IS" (i.e., not an empirical theory), but about "SHOULD" and "MUST"; it states that work efforts which generate output of equal value MUST be remunerated with the same wage. According to this doctrine, remuneration for work must be *fair* -- and fairness is operationally defined as equal pay for work of equal value. The empirical question "what determines the value of a certain product (commodity)?" is not raised and not answered by the principle of pay equity. Note that this principle does not specify absolute value levels, but its reasoning is in terms of comparative (relative) values, instead. Thus, if person L (low wage) receives a lower wage than person H (high wage) for the same work, fairness can, theoretically, be brought about by lowering the wage of H to the level of L. However, the practical and political intent of the principle is in the other direction -- namely, to support demands by L to raise his/her wage to the higher level of H. Labour unions use this reasoning when they want their group of workers to gain wage parity with another group; and the women's movement is using this principle in its demands for pay equity between women and men.

8. Could the World Economy Function with Global Pay Equity?

A call by workers of the global periphery for pay equity with workers of the global core would be a radical demand. The question arises: Is it at all possible to apply the principle of pay equity globally? Could the world economy function and prosper with global wage equity or would the world economy break down?

Argument against Global Pay Equity

Perhaps, the most important argument against global pay equity results from the lack of money. Most education is paid for by the state. States have spending limits. The state of China or Mexico could not pay its educators at Canadian or French rates. Or, when we talk about work in the business sector, a Peruvian or Hungarian business could not pay its employees at United States or Dutch rates. There may be other arguments against global pay equity, but this is probably to most important one.

Arguments for Global Pay Equity

(a) Historical Precedents

The present global wage gap is extremely large. One can point to various historical precedents which demonstrate that economic inequities can be reduced or abolished without damaging the prosperity of the system (national or world economy). These precedents include: (1) Global income inequality was less severe in 1965 than it was in 1995, yet the world economy flourished in 1965. It can even be claimed that the world economy flourished more in 1965, with less global inequality, than it did in 1995, with more inequality. (2) Pay equity for women has been promoted and partially implemented in various countries, yet the economies of those countries did not break down. (3) In the Europe of 1848 the call for an 8-hour work day and abolition of child labour were radical demands deemed detrimental to business, yet these demands were implemented in many countries without damaging the prosperity of those countries. (4) The United States economy survived the abolition of slavery in the 19th century.

(b) The Global Demand Argument

When wages rise, aggregate demand increases. If the wages of the mass of workers in the periphery (non-OECD countries) were raised in the direction of pay equity with wages in the core of the world-system (OECD countries), global demand would increase. According to global-Keynesian views, such an expansion of global demand would have beneficial, rather than detrimental, effects for aggregate global prosperity (world income).

(c) Fairness Argument

It is unfair to pay somebody less for work of equal value, just because they live in another country with a different culture.

9. Implementation Problems

Claiming that global pay equity is desirable and theoretically possible is not to say that implementation of global pay equity would be easy. How can global wage parity be brought about, in practical terms? Here we must pay attention to time frames and degrees of implementation. A "shock therapy" of implementing global wage parity from one day to the next is impossible and would create chaos and breakdown (more than there is already). On the other hand, global pay equity is a reasonable, desirable, and feasible goal for the long run. The powers that manage the world economy can take steps and implement policies and mechanisms which would move the world economy toward greater pay equity, and interested parties like labour organizations could fight for such a principle.

10. Summary and Conclusion

Wages are highly uneven between the countries of the world, even for work which is the same or which is of equivalent value. The present world situation is, to a large extent, a situation of *unequal* pay for work of *equal* value. Observers with a sense of fairness should be able to agree that global pay equity ("equal pay for work of equal value globally") is a desirable long-term goal. Implementation of such a goal is difficult in practice, but worthy of further research and action.

11. Appendix A for Part 2 (Table 1)

Table 1 is a segment of the more comprehensive Table 4.

Table 4 - Wages 1995, Education Sector

All employees, Men and Women's per month, averages

Country	"international dollars" at purchasing power parity rate monthly	US $ at exchang e rate monthly	Local currency	Local currency	Local currency monthly except:
Korea, Rep	2959	2507	1933900	Won	
United Kingdom	2880	2796	11.01	Pounds	per hour
Netherlands	2832	3412	5494	Guilders	
Finland	2279	2650	11582	Markka	
Canada	2130	1954	669.37	Dollars Cdn	per week
Isle of Man	1813	1760	277.23	Pounds	per week
Netherlands Antilles	1497	1804	3229	Guilders	
Austria	1484	1879	18937	Schillings	
Israel	1303	1252	3770	New Shekels	
Slovenia	1170	1004	118972	Tolars	
Czech Rep	705	280	7426	Koruny	
Poland	496	255	618.13	New Zlotys	
Mexico	482	250	1603.1	Nuevos Pesos	
Peru	448	275	30.9	Nuevos Soles	per day
Hungary	434	278	34975	Forint	
Romania	363	123	249911	Lei	
China	255	54	452.92	Yuan	
Slovakia	255	209	6205	Koruny	
Estonia	245	166	1900	Kroons	
Lithuania	218	100	401	Litas	
Latvia	182	123	65.28	Lats	
Kyrgyzstan	92	36	389.3	Soms	

Sources: ILO (1999) for wage rates in local currency. --World Bank (1999) for exchange rates to U.S. dollar. --Köhler (1998) for conversion factors from US $ to PPP rates.

Notes from the source database and notes on my estimates:

Canada: Monthly rate estimated as weekly rate * 4

China: "Incl. Cultural, art, radio and television activities"

Finland: "Full-time employees"

Isle of Man: Monthly rate estimated as weekly rate * 4 . Pound assumed to be equal to British pound.

Korea, Republic: "Incl. family allowances"

Netherlands Antilles: "Curacao"

Peru: "Wage earners", not "Employees". Monthly rate estimated as daily rate * 20

United Kingdom: "Excl. Northern Ireland". Monthly rate estimated as hourly rate * 160

PART B: SUBMERGING MARKETS

Arno Tausch

Chapter 11

The Development Marathon, 1960-2000

Introduction

> '**Marathon:** Long-distance race, a foot-race of 26 miles 385 yards, that is contested on an open course (...) According to tradition, in 490 BC a soldier ran from the battlefield of Marathon to Athens, a distance of about 25 miles, to bring news of a great victory of the Athenian army over the invading Persians. Having delivered his message, he immediately died. This story, however, cannot be traced further back than to a dubious (...) account in a work written almost 700 years after the battle (...) The Greek historian Herodotus (...) tells a remarkable story of a long-distance runner sent to Sparta to seek help when the Persians approached. This messenger ran 140 miles across the country, arrived in Sparta the day after leaving Athens, had his plea rejected by the Spartans, and ran back - meeting the God Pan, whom made an encouraging prediction, on the way'
>
> '**Mythology:** the myths dealing with the gods, demigods, and legendary heroes of a particular people and usually involving supernatural elements'
>
> Longman Dictionary of the English Language, London, 1995

This is one of the first systematic studies of TNC penetration, unequal exchange and long-run economic growth in the world economy over the entire period of the 1960s, 1970s, 1980s and 1990s. It is also one of the first cross-national studies of world development that already integrates the newly integrated countries of East and Central Europe into the sample of analysis. We are thus definitely leaving behind in macro-quantitative research the old divisions of the world that existed before the Fall of the Berlin Wall in 1989. To understand the dynamics of globalization, not only the short-run analysis is necessary. As we have tried to show elsewhere (Tausch, 1988, for a survey of the major theories and methodological concepts, of importance also in this empirical follow-up study), the period of the 1960s, 1970s, 1980s, and 1980s, for many states of the world their entire history as independent nations, can be distinguished analytically into three different phases of world capitalism: first, the full swing of the A phase of the 'fordist' Kondratieff cycle of world capitalism (1932 - 1982), based on mass demand and mass production, social partnership and Keynesianism, that ended around 1967/68 and gave way to the B phase of 'Fordism' with its two major recessions, 1973/75 and

1981/82. This second phase of our 'long duré' - study of the entire capitalist world system, the lost decades especially in the non-oil-exporting developing countries, gave way, according to our reasoning, to a third phase, which is a new Kondratieff cycle upswing, characterized by

- electronics and bio-technology
- neo-liberalism
- the opening up of global financial markets
- the renewed attempt by the United States to provide global leadership, this time as the last remaining superpower, and the drastic re-organization of the international system, with the end of the Soviet Union and the final and full re-integration of China into world capitalism
- the re-integration of the East European semi-periphery into world capitalism
- instability, war-lordism, in many parts of Africa and Central Asia and the increasing power of transnational crime in such countries as Colombia or Nigeria
- the rise and at least temporary, severe fall of the Southeast-Asian newly industrializing countries

We have maintained elsewhere, that the choice of the time period greatly determines the outcome of cross-national development research, because each Kondratieff cycle A and B phase has its own particular logic of rise and decline (Tausch and Prager, 1993; Tausch, 1997, 1998). There is a strong reason to believe that the very last phase in the history of world capitalism, roughly lasting from 1980 to the present, characterized by the dominance of neoliberalism, open financial markets, and renewed US hegemony, largely determines the outcome of the entire *long duré* of the period 1960 - 1995 (for which UN data are now available). For one, never before in history, globalization (the increasing cross-border trade of goods, services, capital, and labor) characterized so intensively the world economy (Boxberger and Klimenta, 1998). As the Asian and Russian crisis, and before that the agony of much of Latin America, the Arab world, Eastern Europe and Africa during the 1980s and the early 1990s clearly showed, the development progress of entire generations was practically wiped out in a few months of financial instability, followed by the familiar packages of *'adjustment'* and stabilization, dictated by the IMF. And secondly, never after 1917, the year of the Russian Revolution, we have had such a clear integration of the entire globe, including even the former socialist countries, into the mechanisms of the world economy.

Our analysis is a focus on the problem of the *'emerging markets'*. The term *'emerging markets'* was coined to lump together these countries with much of Asia and Latin America. And economic growth in most of these *'emerging markets'* is in a deep crisis (much of Africa submerged long ago, but that is another matter). A look at the *Economist* GDP growth figures for 1999 (unweighted by population growth) for the main 'emerging' markets of the world makes this clear at one glance, and suggests, that half a thousand million people in such 'emerging' markets are faced - in reality - with the **submerging** of their societies in the turbulent seas of world capitalism.

Submerging Markets	Growth in 1999	Population in millions
Russia	-7	146.6
Kazachstan	-2.5	16.6
Indonesia	-2.3	208.2
South Korea	-2.3	46.8
Hong Kong	-2.2	6.8
Malaysia	-2.1	22.7
Ukraine	-1	50.6
Thailand	-0.1	61.7
Total/average	***-2.4***	***560***
other former emerging markets		
Iran	0.6	63.4
Slovakia	0.8	5.4
Saudi Arabia	1	20.9
Pakistan	1.2	151.6
Singapore	1.4	3.2
Kenya	1.9	30.6
Jordan	1.9	6
Czech Republic	2	10.2
South Africa	2	40.2
Colombia	2.6	41.6
Venezuela	2.7	24.1
Brazil	2.8	163.8
Bulgaria	3	8.2
Romania	3	22.5
Argentina	3.4	36.2
Lebanon	3.6	4.2
Algeria	4	30.9
Turkey	4.1	65.7
Chile	4.1	15
Mexico	4.2	99.2
Nigeria	4.4	110.6
Hungary	***4.5***	***10.1***
Taiwan	***4.8***	***21.9***
Vietnam	***5***	***79.5***
Egypt	***5.1***	***64.5***
Poland	***5.6***	***38.7***
India	***5.7***	***986.2***
China	***7***	***1250***
Total/average	***3.3***	***3404.4***

Although capitalism in general will dive out also from these turbulences, the human toll - in terms of instability, raped religious or social minorities, will be enormous, marking perhaps the beginning of the phase of de-legitimatization of the global order (Goldstein, 1988; Tausch, 1998).

Perhaps the situation of the social scientist is like that of a doctor: the illness is more desperate than ever before, but much better data now exist for cancer research. Indeed, economic and social data about long-run performance of societies in the world economy now exist for more than one hundred countries since the early 1960s. More and more data also emerge about the re-capitalized countries of Eastern Europe and the former USSR (a term which the current author now prefers over the term 'transformation countries'), which makes the cross-national analysis of the preconditions of success and failure in the world economy a truly breathtaking enterprise.

Is economic growth and social cohesion and development in the time of globalization a question of endurance, of strategy, or of power? Does collapse and death await the successful runner, or enlightenment on the way back, after a futile first distance of 140 kilometers, as in the story above? What are the predictions of success to be encountered on the long run? Is migration any help? What is the effect of the human capital effort on long-run development? And what about social justice and the social security effort of a nation? **Many of the strategies of the day might turn out to be monsters in the end.**

As Immanuel Wallerstein so correctly remarked in his website *Commentary 3* available from the world systems archive on Japan, the **advantages in contemporary capitalism are rather passing,** and it is the long run, and not the short run, which is decisive (Wallerstein, 1998). Years ago - when Asia was 'in' - we all heard what we have to learn from the *Pacific Age of capitalism*. Now we hear that *crony capitalism* is no good, and that we should have known it all before. Sorry - where were the analysts of 'crony capitalism', when Latin America was told to follow the path of the Pacific Age of capitalism? Following the radical political economy tradition of social scientists like Ted Wheelwright, some Pacific Gods turned out to be monsters long ago, and as some of the re-converted capitalist countries set out on their way on the marathon race to Brussels, a **God Pan, an updated - human capital centered social 'Keynesianism',** that looked after flocks and shepherds, might be helpful to them in the end, although his first appearance is characterized by horns and legs of a goat, just as in the ancient Greek story (Longman, *op. cit.).* Such a **God Pan,** that gently leads the way for the exhausted marathon runner, in the end might be - the horrible horns and legs notwithstanding - the **human capital effort and a policy of social justice.** It might be that the following words are those of a malicious European, taking a critical look at the *'market economy superstar America'* literature, that is poured on us daily after the passing of the *Pacific Age of capitalism* exhortations, now substituted *by the crony capitalism* tradition. But it is entirely possible, that in a few years, if not months, after a thorough crash at Wall Street, we all of a sudden will hear the flutes of Pan, inviting America to change course, or - more realistically - preceded by an isolationist, right-wing, liberal Republican backlash against 8 years of Clinton in power.

The *long duré* investigation for example tells us, that 'superstar' America was only 61st in the list of economic growth in the world from 1960 to 1995, and that there are powerful forces that this is not going to change. The *long dure* also tells us that this is the time of the European semi-periphery, South and East, that will find excellent chances in the medium term. Our long-run investigation started with such simple analyses: who has been developing most efficiently over the last decade and over the last three decades, and why? For the EU-accession countries, the macro-quantitative analysis of the question which society in the world was more successful than the others in terms of growth, social development and stability, is of vital importance for the future debate about their accession strategy. Broadly speaking, we arrive at a distinction between a *'Greek'* or *'Philippine'*, aid and migration-driven model, and a knowledge-based, human-capital oriented model that even at times of world economic turbulence and globalization seems to offer a decisive 'comparative edge' over other strategies.

Theoretically, we arrive here at a vision of world development, which was structured mainly by the **French debate** on world capitalism, developed by authors like **Samir Amin. Development stability, above all, is a function of power; and in the long run, those prevail that wield power or are allied with power.** For that reason alone, the extension of the European Union (and, as we shall develop, a European-centered security concept in the longer run) is an absolute necessity for the East of the European continent. Our results partially re-vindicate the Amin hypotheses, and also point into the direction of the re-birth of the European periphery. But this re-birth has conditions, and it is up to the transition countries to seize the chance. This is the more hopeful aspect of our study; provided that the countries of East-Central Europe follow up their **accession strategy with massive investments in education** (a further assumption must be mentioned here: The values for economic growth in Germany and in Rwanda, 1960-95 had to be estimated from UNDP data about their performance during the late 1980s and the 1990s, since data for the entire period are not contained in the UNDP HDR data set. For 132 countries, the *estimation relationship* between short-term per capita economic growth 1980-94 (for which we *have* complete UNDP-data for our 134 nation sample (UNDP, HDR, 1997) and long-term GDP economic growth 1960-95 (for which the data from Germany and Rwanda are lacking) is the following: (1) y (long-term growth) = 0.7455 + 0.7242 * short-term growth. Long-term growth for Germany is thus estimated to be 2.3% p.a.; while the value for Rwanda is -0.1% p.a.).

THE GEOGRAPHY OF UNEQUAL DEVELOPMENT

One of the most persistent and robust findings of a serious analysis of world development 1960 - 96 is the fact, that the zones of development instability in the world economy have shifted and extended. In terms of a marathon race, there are those, who had a very poor start or were relegated back to the starting line all along the race, and there are those, who stumbled while approaching the finish, and finally, there are those unfortunate ones who even - during the race - missed the direction and raced back to the starting line, instead of running towards the finish. Their encounter with God Pan might, we hope, still come, but their experience rather recalls the experience of

> *'Sisyphus: a king of Corinth condemned in Hades to roll a heavy stone uphill but never to succeed in getting it to the top' (Longman Dictionary of the English Language, 1995)*

The danger of the present-day world constellation is that global capitalism is about to smash its own most spectacular success stories over recent years. Two of the most dynamic zones in recent years, East Asia and Latin America, are further threatened by financial instability, while growth in the centers was sluggish. At the time of preparing this essay, the *Economist* newsmagazines pictured a small vessel, with a Chinese flag, at the margin of a huge abyss. And Russia's treadmill of unsuccessful capitalism continues. In Western Europe, the center of dynamic shifted from the European Center to the former European Periphery. Norway, Ireland, Poland and Slovenia are the only high-growth zones of the first half of the 1990s, while wide regions of the former USSR and Africa have become zones of almost inescapable stagnation:

Map 11.1a: Growth in the World System, 1990-96

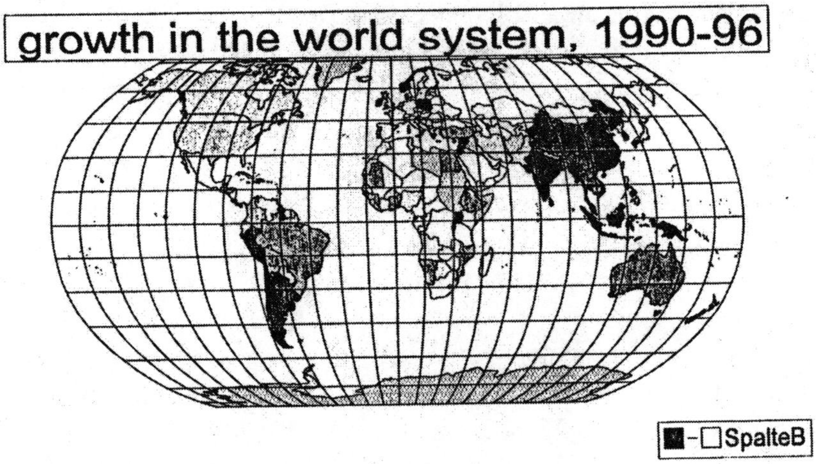

Legend: Economic growth (real GNP per capita per year).
Source: Fischer Weltalmanach, 1999. The darker, the higher the growth rate.

Map 11.1b: Unemployment in Europe

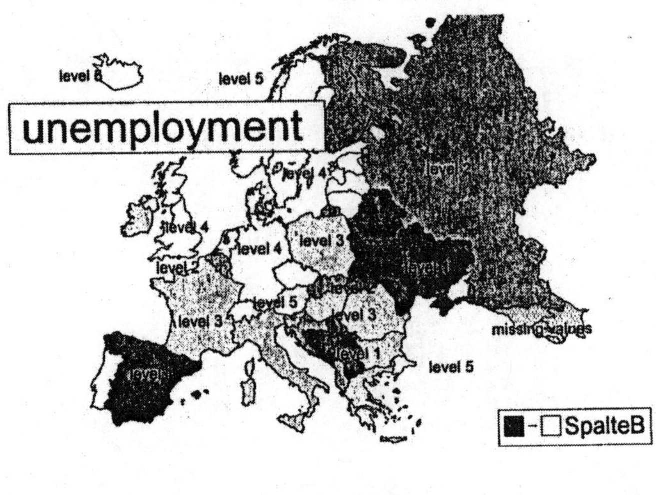

Legend: Our own compilations from Business Central Europe, March 1999, and Fischer Weltalmanach, 1999

The future will tell, whether or not capitalism becomes a

Moloch: *(..) God of fire to whom children were offered in sacrifice (Longman Dictionary of the English language, 1995)*

The further study of the long period, 1960-1995, on the basis of the UNDP data set (1998), provides a still more alarming picture about the stability and instability of world economic growth. The UNDP calculated, in which year a nation had its lowest and its highest per real per capita income during that period. **Only a very small number of countries - mainly the centers and a few exceptions in the periphery - followed the 'normal' path of having the lowest real per capita income in 1960, and the highest in 1995.** There was an **alarming trend of wide regions of our globe having their lowest historical income value over the last 4 decades in 1989 or even later.** In terms of a marathon race, there are countries, which - at least once during the race - were relegated back to the starting line, often running for 10 or 20 kilometers already in vain. The UNDP data series also permits the analysis of the question, in which year a country achieved its highest per capita income in real terms. **A very fortunate and small number of countries achieved their highest GNP per capita in 1995, while others have to realize that they were better off ten, fifteen, or even twenty years from now.** Their racing along the last 10, 15, or even 20 last kilometers was totally in vain, and they have to start again by kilometer 10 or 20. Will they ever mile number 26? In terms of the marathon race, they stumbled on their way while approaching the finish, or they even took a wrong direction. It is no wonder, that serious questions arise about the nature of the international system that permits such a periodic crushing of the economic progress of large sections of the earth's surface. After the Asian crisis, which stable and dynamic zones remain in the world periphery and semi-periphery? The East and the far North in the world system are under the threat of marginalization, too. Canada, Iceland, Sweden, Finland, Russia, and the three Baltic States are all confronted by the fact that their real income in 1995 was lower than that achieved earlier on in their development history. Interestingly enough, also Switzerland does not benefit from its isolated position in Europe.

We now try to answer a third question. Which countries had an overall 35 years positive development experience for the period 1960-95, and which countries had a negative, reverse record? To achieve a measurement scale, we simply subtracted the year with the lowest real per capita income from the year with the highest real per capita income. Ideally, this will lead to 35 as the maximum value. The worst performers will have their lowest value in 1995, and their highest value somewhere in the 1980s or even earlier on. **Libya, Mauritania, and Chad achieved their highest income back in 1970, and 82 countries out of a total of 159 classified nations were richer before 1990 than today. 55 countries followed the 'ideal path' of having their highest income in 1995, while 104 runners out of a total of 159 classified competitors stumbled on their way to the development marathon finish.** Even more dramatically, a **lamentable 13 nations - in Africa and the former USSR - were from 1960 to 1995 never as poor as in 1995; an astonishing number of 34 nations were throughout the period never as poor as in the 1990s, and 58 nations out of 159 classified competitors reached their poverty**

climax in 1980 or after, while only 88 nations can look back at the 1960s as the period of their worst well-being, measured in real per capita income.

These 'tectonic' shifts in world economic growth 1960-95 are now exacerbated by the dramatic consequences of the Asian and Latin American crashes, which threaten to ruin the little stable growth portions of the world economy, left from the debacles of the oil crisis, and the recession of the early 1980s and 1990s.

Political and/or military power seems to be one of the major pillars of the stability of growth in the long run. Apart from 'special cases' like Colombia or Thailand, whose very long-term economic stability again must be questioned, or might be explained by narco-capitalism, most of the 'dark zones' of thoroughly stable capitalist development throughout the period 1960-95 showed one or more of the following characteristics

(i) membership in a world political alliance with the US as the hegemonic power (NATO, ANZUS *et cetera)*
(ii) membership in the European Union or
(iii) a program of nuclear armaments of their own, like China, India and Pakistan

The overall results of the ranking process for industrialized nations are also surprising:

Country	Rank according to growth marathon	Rank according to avoidance of early death
Austria	35	21
France	40	25
Ireland	***19***	***9***
Poland	110	35
Spain	***22***	***10***
UK	**59**	**5**
USA	**61**	**24**

The United States rank only 61st among the nations of the world in terms of long-term economic growth.

The five pillars of international inequality - Giovanni Arrighi's and Samir Amin's view of world development in the framework of development theory.

Dependency and world system theory hold that poverty and backwardness in poor countries are caused by the peripheral position that these nations have in the international division of labor. Ever since the capitalist world system evolved, there is a stark distinction between the nations of the center and the nations of the periphery. Fernando Henrique Cardoso, when he was still a social scientist, summarized the quantifiable essence of dependency theories as follows:

(i) there is a financial and technological penetration by the developed capitalist centers of the countries of the periphery and semi-periphery

(ii) this produces an unbalanced economic structure both within the peripheral societies and between them and the centers
(iii) this leads to limitations on self-sustained growth in the periphery
(iv) this favors the appearance of specific patterns of class relations
(v) these require modifications in the role of the state to guarantee both the functioning of the economy and the political articulation of a society, which contains, within itself, foci of inarticulateness and structural imbalance (Cardoso, 1979)

Of lately, there has been a growing concern about mass demand as the motor of capitalist development in the centers. Already in his famous macro-economic model, Nicholas Kaldor explained the conditions of growth of a capitalist economy in the postwar-period by this mass demand. If mass demand is seriously undermined by the process of globalization, we are back to the long-term stagnation traps of 19th Century capitalism. Let total product Y be the sum of wages, W, and profits, P, let there be the identity between savings and investments, I = S, and let us divide the savings rate S into savings out of workers' incomes and out of profits, and let savings of workers S*w* be proportional to wages and savings of profit income recipients S*p* be proportional to profits, we arrive at the final, but still tautological formulation, that profits are a function of investments:

(1) $Y = W + P$

(2) $I = S$

(3) $S = Sw + S$

(4) $Sw = sw * W$

(5) $Sp = sp * P$

(6) $P/Y = f\,(I/Y)$

At given propensities to save out of profits and wages, the profit rate is a function of investments. On the way to a model of the real economy in the postwar period, Kaldor now says, that real wages have to be above subsistence wages, the profit rate must not fall below a certain minimum, the share of profits is institutionally determined at least at a certain minimum, and the capital output ratio must not be influenced by the profit rate. Only these conditions, Kaldor thinks, assure that the clear causal relationship between investment and profits holds. Else, especially, when wages fall down to the subsistence level, the Keynesian mechanism to guarantee full employment will not be in force anymore, output will be limited by available capital, and not by labor, and finally, the classic and not the Keynesian adjustment mechanism will be in operation: the surplus, available for investment, determines investments, and not investments savings.

Data limitations from the transformation countries severely limit the applicability of the structural equations, mentioned in Tausch, 1998, on the long-run development process. The following scheme should be applied to express the main theoretical expectations:

Scheme 11.1: The Expectations of the Three Main Competing "Development Theories:

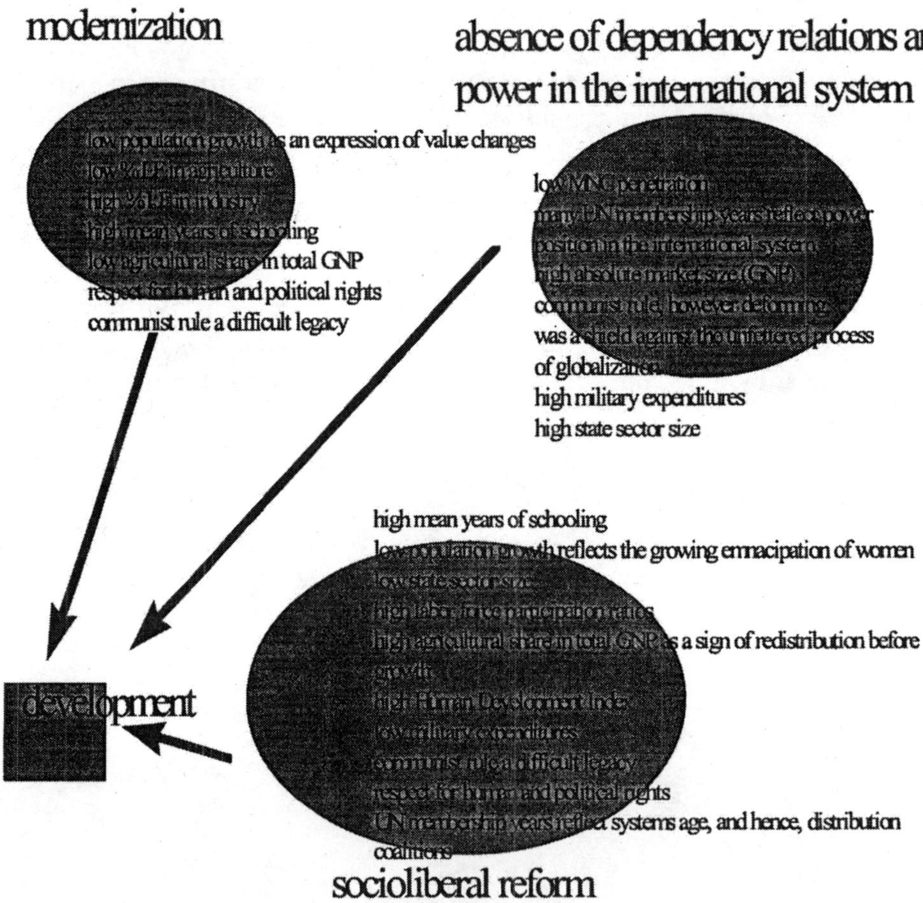

Source: Our own compilations from the theoretical literature

It is no wonder, that in an age of globalization, 'critical' theories of world capitalist development are gaining ground as a means of interpretation of these contradictory realities. The international system in the 1990s is characterized, as Arrighi correctly remarks, by two tendencies

(i) the growing international competition between the three power blocs, US, Japan and the European Union
(ii) the relative stability in the international hierarchies

For Arrighi, the GNP per capita at current exchange rates is the best available measurement of the goods and services that the residents of different countries command on the world markets (Arrighi *et al.*, 1996a). Personally, I have no doubt about Arrighi's results, although the implementation of his research program into empirical tests, based on polynomial regressions, might be surprising to some observers (see below). The international system is characterized by the relative stability of the long-run distribution between peripheries, semi-peripheries and centers: that is Arrighi's main research result. To control Arrighi's results, we use a slightly different methodology than his own (see equation (2), below). For us, the international hierarchy of the 123 countries of the world with fairly complete UNDP data about the social and economic system (listed in descending order of their UNDP Human Development Index) is also a stable hierarchy of real purchasing power parity rates (PPP $) in relation to the USA, the country with the highest PPP $ value in both 1960 and 1990 (USA = 100). The exponential regression lines for 1960 and 1990 show, that the 'band spread' of international distribution has widened, and that a considerable number of states even experienced a relative downward-mobility, while less than half of the states in the world system experienced an upward mobility, as evidenced by the two exponential trend lines and their cutting point:

Graph 11.1: Aspects of International Income Distribution, 1960-1990

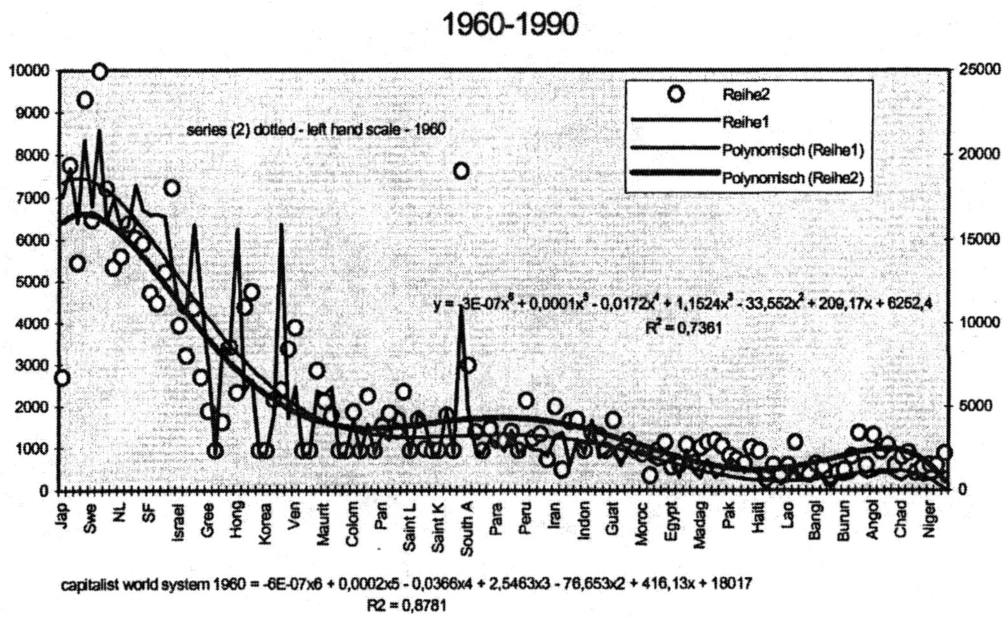

Legend: Real income per capita in purchasing power parity rates and constant US $, 1960 (left hand scale) and 1990 (right hand scale), ranging from the highly developed nations to the poorest countries. Put in simple terms: there is a trend, that the poorest countries lose in relative terms.

Arrighi's method, by contrast, is based on the following regression analysis of UNDP data about world development from 1960 onwards

% of world population = $a_0 + b_1 * (\ln(\text{GNP per cap/World GNP per capita})) +\!- b_2 * (...)^{\wedge 2} +\!- b_3 * (...)^{\wedge 3}$ ....

Graph 11.2: Arrighi's Hypothesis of the Constancy of International Inequality

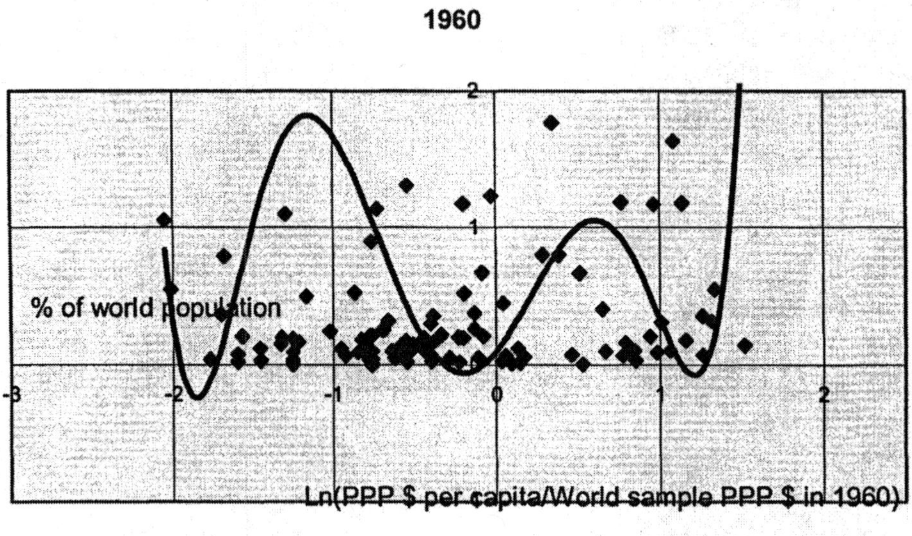

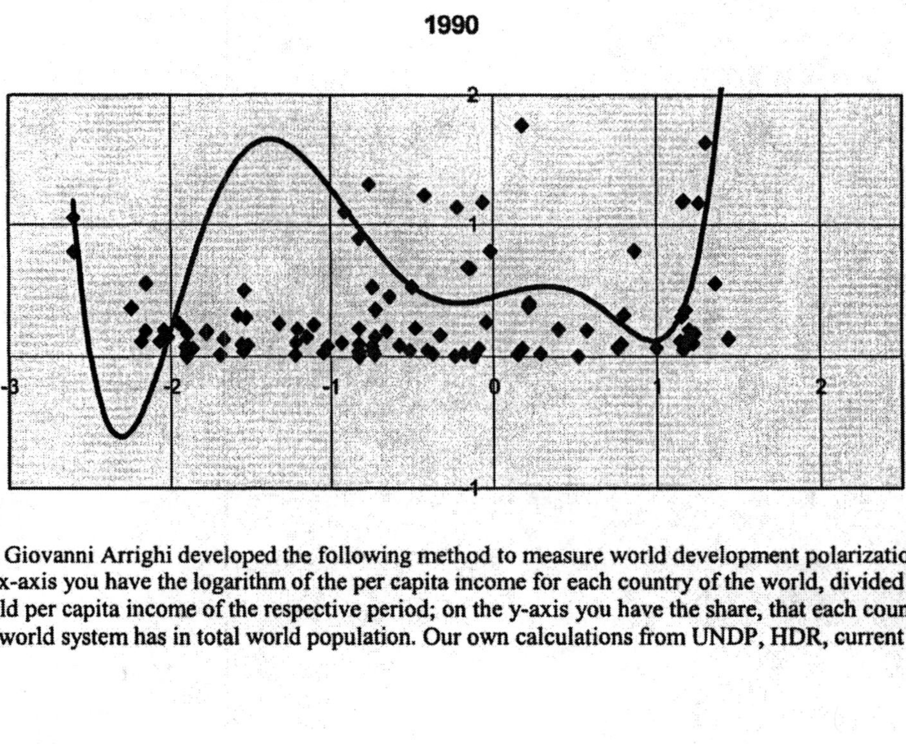

Legend: Giovanni Arrighi developed the following method to measure world development polarization: on the x-axis you have the logarithm of the per capita income for each country of the world, divided by the world per capita income of the respective period; on the y-axis you have the share, that each country of the world system has in total world population. Our own calculations from UNDP, HDR, current issues.

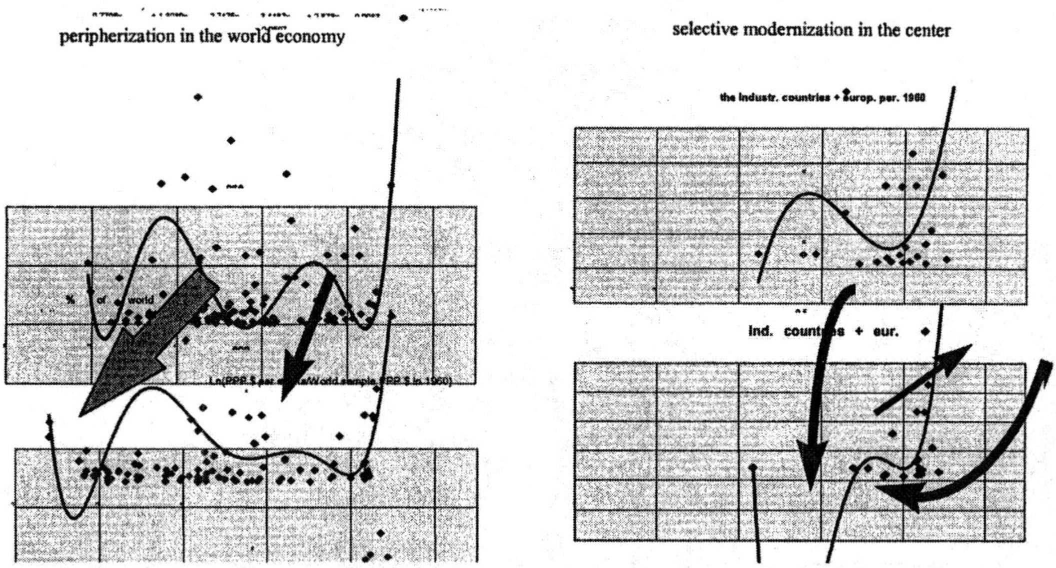

Legend: Results according to our methodology as compared to the results, based on Arrighi's method, based on the following regression analysis:

Alternatively, Arrighi's own peculiar methodology can also be applied:

$$\% \text{ of world population} = a_0 + b_1 * (\ln (\text{GNP per cap/World GNP per capita})) +\!- b_2 * (...)^{\wedge 2} +\!- b_3 * (...)^{\wedge 3} ...$$

We used here, like Arrighi (1996a), a polynomial regression of the 6th degree (Arrighi, 1996a; pages 11 and Figure 7).

Whatever methodological preference we have, our analysis confirms the shape of distribution, expected for the dependency model of global polarization, and certainly not the modernization hypothesis, which clearly would expect a closing of the gaps. Our results also show, that the W-shaped distribution with strong semi-peripheries, expected by the world system approach (Arrighi, 1996a), has become weaker over time, resembling more and more the distribution, expected by classic dependency theory. And this is also the link-up between Köhlers theory, presented in this volume, our own empirical results and many other contributions on periphery capitalism.

Thus, international mobility in the age of globalization is a myth. Asian, Russian or Brazilian crashes (who knows: Polish, or Chinese crashes in the future) are not accidents, but part and parcel of the very structure of the system, that crushes in periodical regularity the material progress of working generations in the semi-periphery countries and wipes out their dreams of ever catching-up one day with the center. This is the essence of the international system, and this destructive tendency will continue in the 21st Century.

Also, the emergence of dozens of nations after 1989 makes cross-national development research in the world of today an especially difficult task. Yet in the name of intellectual honesty and political foresight, such an attempt must be made, integrating the development lessons and experiences of Eastern Europe and the former USSR in a now truly globalized economy. Unfortunately, the lack of appropriate data severely limited the analytical possibilities of this investigation. Nevertheless, some important conclusions can be drawn in the light of our earlier debate. How 'general' is the 'particular', and how 'particular' is the 'general' path of world development from the 1980s onwards? Arrighi wrote in 1995:

> *'Partial as the current revival of a self-regulating world market has actually been, it has already issued unbearable verdicts. Entire communities, countries, even continents, as in the case of sub-Saharan Africa, have been declared 'redundant', superfluous to the changing economy of capital accumulation on a world scale. Combined with the collapse of the world power and territorial empire of the USSR, the unplugging of these 'redundant' communities and locales from the world supply system has triggered innumerable, mostly violent feuds over 'who is more superfluous than whom', or, more simply, over the appropriation of resources that were made absolutely scarce by the unplugging' (Arrighi, 1995: 330)*

On the other hand, it is clear that

Antigua, Botswana, China, Cyprus, Dominica, Hong Kong, Maldives, Mauritius, Saint Kitts, Saint Vincent, Singapore, South Korea, Thailand

had a GNP per capita growth rate of 4.5% or more per annum during 1980-93. The prediction of most world system theories for the future long-term prospects of the capitalist system are gloomy. Chase-Dunn and Hall cite especially population growth with its consequence on natural resources and pressures for migration as the elements that will ultimately cause systemic decline (Chase-Dunn and Hall, 1997: 199). Our reading of the post-1980s tendencies of world development is now in at least some accordance with hypotheses, put forward by Amin. For Samir Amin (1997), ascent and decline is largely being determined in our age by the following *'five monopolies'*

(i) the monopoly of technology, supported by military expenditures of the dominant nations
(ii) the monopoly of control over global finances and a strong position in the hierarchy of current account balances
(iii) the monopoly of access to natural resources
(iv) the monopoly over international communication and the media
(v) the monopoly of the military means of mass destruction

Performance over the last decades teaches us an important lesson about the evolving mechanisms of the future Kondratieff cycle, that began - our reasoning went - in the mid-1980s (Tausch, 1998). Let us recall, that for dependency and world system theory in the tradition of Samir Amin (1975), there are four main characteristics of the peripheral societal formation

(i) the predominance of agrarian capitalism in the 'national' sector
(ii) the formation of a local bourgeoisie, which is dependent from foreign capital, especially in the trading sector
(iii) the tendency of bureaucratization
(iv) specific and incomplete forms of proletarization of the labor force

In partial accordance with liberal thought, (i) and (iii) explain the tendency towards low savings; thus there will be

(a) huge state sector deficits and, in addition, their 'twin'
(b) chronic current account balance deficits

in the peripheral countries. High imports of the periphery, and hence, in the long run, capital imports, are the consequence of the already existing structural deformations of the role of peripheries in the world system, namely by

(i) rapid urbanization, combined with an insufficient local production of food (in the developing countries, urban population growth in the period 1995 - 2015 will be 2.9% per year; UNDP, 1998)
(ii) excessive expenditures of the local bureaucracies
(iii) changes in income distribution to the benefit of the local elites (demonstration effects)
(iv) insufficient growth of and structural imbalances in the industrial sector
(v) and the following reliance on foreign assistance

The history of periphery capitalism, Amin argues, is full of short-term 'miracles' and long-term blocks, stagnation and even regression. Our graph shows the dramatic decline, measured in real GDP per capita in 1987 $ for Eastern Europe during the world economic crisis of the 1980s (a crisis, which it shared with the Arab nations, Latin America and Sub-Saharan Africa); Latin America recovered more rapidly, however, while East Asia, South Asia and South-East Asia forged ahead from 1960 to 1994, with East and South-East Asia and Latin America thrown into a crisis in 1997:

Graph 11.3: Income Polarization in World Capitalism - 1960 - 1994

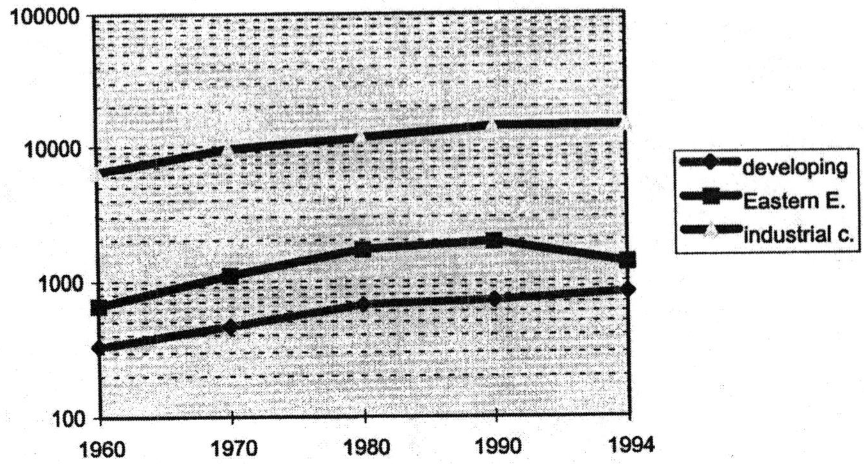

Legend: Real income, measured in real GDP per capita in 1987 during the world economic crisis of the 1980s and beyond (semi-log-scale). Our own compilations from UNDP, 1997. The data are:

Table 11.1: Income Polarization in the Capitalist World System, 1960 - 1994

	Sub S Africa	Eastern E.	Arab States	East Asia	Latin America	South Asia	SE Asia and Pacific
1960	495	658	989		1122	193	282
1970	598	1108	1893		1435	229	370
1980	634	1701	2757	2379	1965	363	575
1990	514	1954	1740	4674	1793	462	756
1994	507	1370	1595	5759	1931	514	935

Dependency has, according to Amin, a commercial, financial and technological aspect. *'Rent seeking'* - originally a neo-liberal concept, interpreted here from the viewpoint of dependency theory, - has its basis in big landholding, which throughout the periphery was introduced, supported and upheld by colonial and post-colonial structures. **Profitable investments in many periphery countries are - in part - constrained by the (emerging) unequal income distribution, which again determines, that the local 'surplus' is being squandered by luxurious consumption, transferred abroad in the form of capital flight, or being used for speculation.** Just to illustrate Amin's point: in the newly capitalist countries of Eastern Europe, only the Czech Republic, Hungary, and Poland attracted $bn 7.0 or more foreign direct investment. Foreign direct investment in Russia is just $bn 6.5, while recent poverty data on Russia are just alarming. Russia concentrates within its borders around half the income poor of the entire region, numbering in all 60 million poor Russians (poverty is defined here as $4 or less a day). Another 60 million Russians work in the shadow economy or live from crime, that now controls 45% of Russian GNP: and these are statements by the government, and not by Radio Liberty... (former Interior Minister Kulikov, quoted in *Agence France Press, 2nd July 1997).*

In the entire region of Eastern Europe, income poverty increased at an alarming speed between 1988 and 1994 - from 4% to 32% of the total population. 62% of all Russian children and 34% of the aged are poor; the suicide rate increased by more than 50% and the homicide rate more than doubled against 1989. 9.6% of all people are not expected to survive to age 40, 38% of Russians are living below the World Bank absolute world poverty line of a dollar a day, and the Human Development Index has fallen, compared to 1993 (UNDP, 1997). The poorest 20% have an income of 881 $ per capita and year in terms of real purchasing power, while the richest 20% have 12804 $ per capita and year (UNDP, 1997). Under these circumstances, the implementation of the Acquis Communautaire in the social field will become a very urgent necessity:

Map 11.2: Screening the *Acquis Communautaire* at One Glance

Socio-Economic Maturity

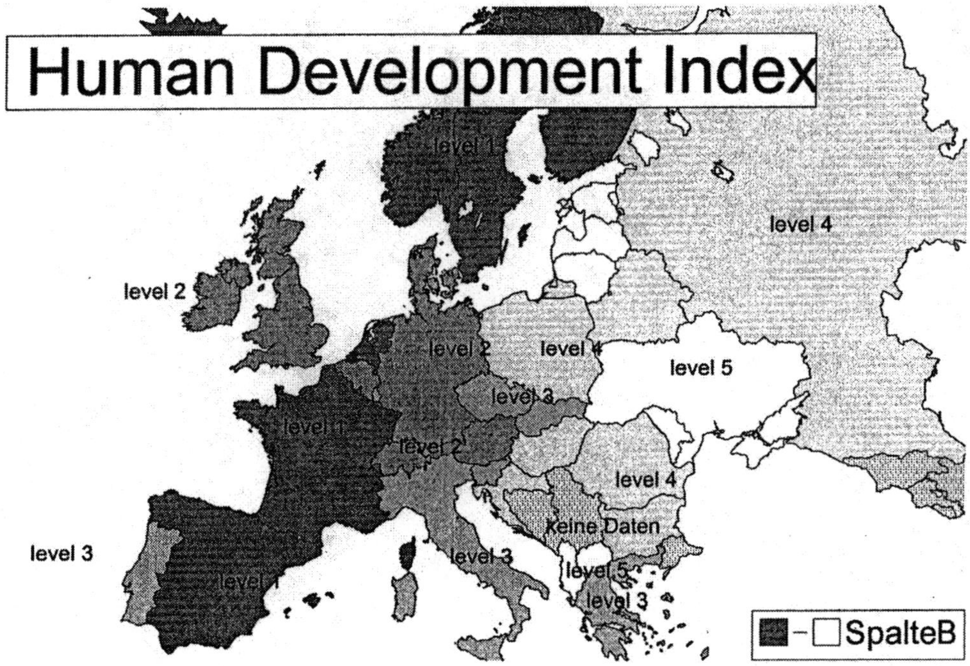

Politics of Gender Equality

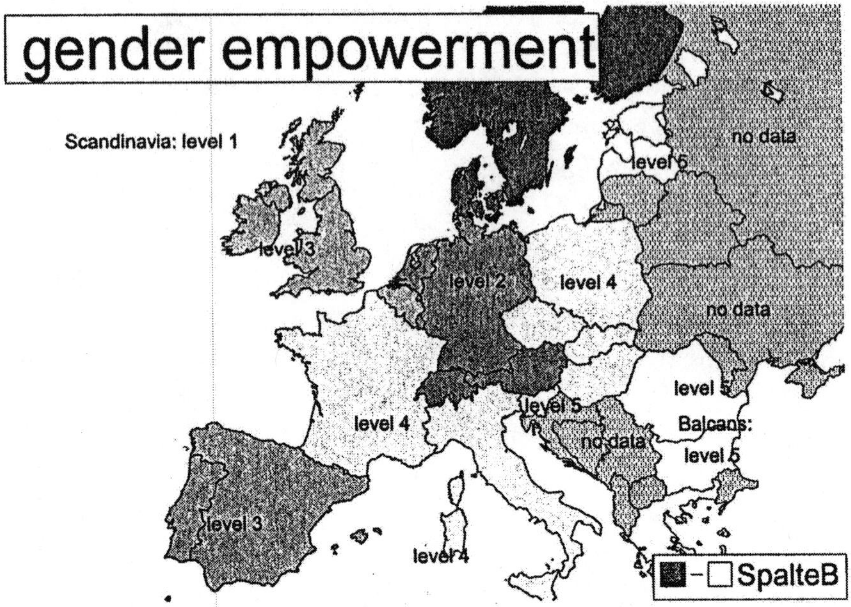

Insecurity

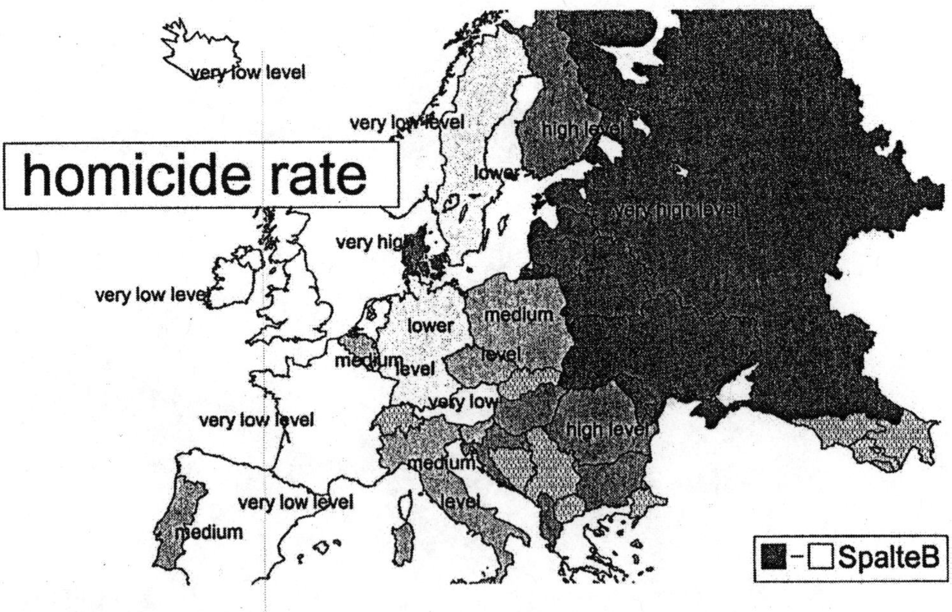

Note: Data for Slovakia, Switzerland, three states in former Yugoslavia, and in Transcaucasia were not available for this analysis. The map neatly shows, apart from the devastating effects of drinking habits on the crime rate, the effects of the expansion of transnational crime - very endangered countries, the ex-USSR and Denmark, as level 1 countries, the Balkans and Finland at level 2, Portugal, Belgium, Italy, Slovenia, the Czech Republic and Poland at level 3, Germany and Sweden as the next main target countries of transnational crime at level 4, and the rest of Europe still at level 5. For an in-depth analysis of these tendencies, see also Committee for a Safe Society at *http://www.alternatives.com/crime/menu.html* and the US State Department, based on the FBI *http://www.state.gov/www/global/narcotics_law/narc_re ports_mainhp.html*

Past and present foreign domination and colonialism cause long term **structural imbalances.** Countries as far apart as large parts of Africa and Asia, just as Poland from 1795 - 1918, were not constituting a national state during the important era of the Industrial Revolution. Their economies were geared to the needs of others, i.e. their colonizers. **The structural heterogeneity between the different economic sectors on the one hand and the 'modern', export oriented sector, the medium sector and the 'traditional sector' in agriculture, industry and services, became the main reason for the unequal income distribution in the countries of the periphery. Colonial trade, foreign investment in the 19th Century, import substitution in the first half of the 20th Century, and the new international division of labor that we observe from the middle of the 1960s onwards did not really change the structures of inequality in the world system.** While mass demand and agricultural structures (Elsenhans, 1983) were responsible for the transition from the tributary mode of production in Western Europe to capitalism from the Long 16th Century onwards, periphery capitalism was and is characterized by the following main tendencies (Amin, 1973 - 1997):

(i) regression in both agriculture and small scale industry characterizes the period after the onslaught of foreign domination and colonialism

(ii) unequal international specialization of the periphery leads to the concentration of activities in export oriented agriculture and or mining. Some industrialization of the periphery is possible under the condition of low wages, which, together with rising productivity, determine that unequal exchange sets in (double factorial terms of trade < 1.0; see Raffer, 1987)

(iii) these structures determine in the long run a rapidly growing tertiary sector with hidden unemployment and the rising importance of rent in the overall social and economic system

(iv) the development blocks of peripheral capitalism (chronic current account balance deficits, re-exported profits of foreign investments, deficient business cycles of the periphery, that provide important markets for the centers during world economic upswings)

(v) structural imbalances in the political and social relationships, *inter alia* a strong *'compradore'* element and the rising importance of state capitalism and an indebted state class

CAPITALISM AND CYCLES

Methodologically, this essay is again in the tradition of cross-national development research (see for surveys of the vast literature, Tausch/Prager, 1993, Tausch, 1997; and Tausch, 1998, for further methodological concepts, also used in this study).

The analysis of the marathon is complicated by the fact that capitalism develops not smoothly, but with very strong and self-repeating ups and downs, called cycles. Our analysis starts from well-known empirical research results of Joshua Goldstein, Volker

Bornschier, and Luigi Scandella; and we just re-analyzed and enlarged their perspective on cycles in some ways (Tausch, 1997, 1998). Cyclical fluctuations have also a profound effect on cross-national comparisons of economic growth and societal development in the medium and long run. What could have been spectacular long-run growth, in the end might turn out to be just a short run cyclical spurt after a long recession.

Our leading indicator of the process of dependence and globalization is the refined UNCTAD version for the old MNC (multinational corporation) penetration indicator of a country in the present Kondratieff-cycle. The UNCTAD MNC penetration indicator is based on the concept of the share of FDI stock in terms of total host-country GDP.

The more dependent a country is in the system of the world-wide market economy, the greater will be the penetration of its economy by transnational capital. Dependency theories (Cardoso/Faletto, 1971) hold, that the countries of the periphery were integrated into the world-economy in the following sequence of events

i *desarrollo hacia exterior* (development to the outside)
ii *desarrollo hacia adentro* (inward-looking development)
iii *transnacionalizacion de los mercados internos* (internationalization of the internal markets)

Starting from the late 1950s, the transnational system increasingly dominates the industrialization process of the periphery and the semi-periphery (phase iii). The penetration of the host countries by transnational investment becomes the most important scientific yardstick of dependency (Bornschier/Chase-Dunn, 1985).

To these phases in the evolution of the international division of labor, one would have to add

iv *financial capitalism and globalization*

as the latest stage of center-periphery relationships during the 1980s and 1990s.

Cycle time plays, as we already stated, an important role in our approach. Arrighi's thought is especially worthwhile mentioning here: that the logic of accumulation on a world scale shifts along time, and that we again witness during the 1980s and beyond a deregulated phase of world capitalism with a logic, characterized - in contrast to earlier regulatory cycles - by the dominance of financial capital. Arrighi further teaches us that even a century can be a 'short run' in the evolution of world capitalism. For Arrighi, there are ***signal crises*** of world capitalism (the usual Kondratieff depressions), and there are ***terminal crises*** of the world system, like the great crash of the early 1340s, which marked the beginning of the Genoese age, the 1560s, which marked the beginning of the Dutch era, the 1750s and 1760s, which marked the beginning of the British era, and the 1930s, which were the terminal crisis of British **world capitalist dominance**. Regulation can be successful, like after 1560, and 1930, and deregulation can be successful, like after 1340, 1760, and - most probably - the 1980s (compiled from Arrighi, 1995).

We think it fairly safe to assume, that the present recession is not a forthcoming terminal crisis of the capitalist system. The risk for such a crisis would be rather larger in the second half of the 21st Century, even allowing for the shortening of the crisis-mechanism of the world capitalist system. Even at the risk of gross oversimplification, the following scheme could be drawn:

Scheme 11.2: Terminal Crises of Capitalism

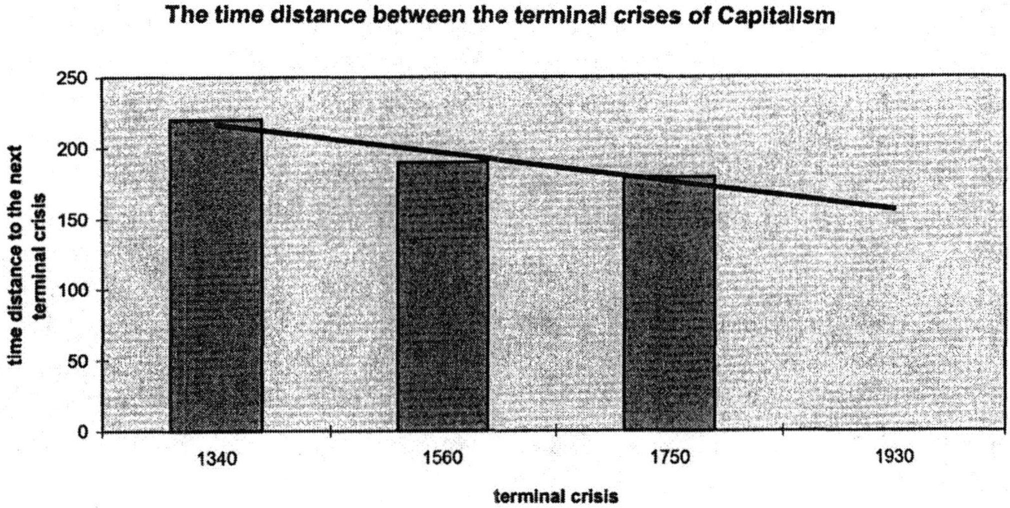

Source: Our own compilation from Arrighi, 1995, and Tausch, 1998. The above graph can be interpreted only as a very rough simplification.

The long cycle literature, largely overlooked by macroquantitative development studies, tells us why there is a recurrent pattern of instability in the social orders both at the level of national society as well as at the level of the international system. It also explains the often puzzling aspect, how **different studies, using different time perspectives, reach different results. There is no single 'correct' theory of economic growth and development, but only theories that explain correctly growth and development at a given, cyclical time period.**

Long cycles, themselves to be explained by at least 13 different types of theories, by themselves are quite a strong argument in the debate about the long-run viability of the world-wide market economy: the recurrence of cycles, depressions and wars was thematically portrayed, amongst others, by Scandella (1998), Goldstein (1988), Bornschier and Suter (1992), Bornschier (1988, expanded and updated English version 1996), Tausch (1998) and Arrighi (1995). The intense controversy about cycles should only be mentioned briefly here; for the policy-maker perhaps more important is the fact, that after the economic crisis of 1825, the stock exchange collapse of 1873, the Black Friday of 1929 and the world recession starting in 1973/75, world capitalism has experienced quite severe downswing-phases, that hit with elementary weight especially the countries of the periphery and the semi-periphery. The *Kondratieff cycles* of approximately *40-60 years duration* and the Kuznets cycles, 18-22 years long, are especially relevant for our understanding of the ups and downs of world economics and politics: our data series, constructed from Goldstein's original data, is explained quite markedly by the application of the Kondratieff and Kuznets-cycle hypotheses, even when there are no data filtering or smoothening operations being performed. And thus, we have to disagree in one fundamental aspect with Chase-Dunn and Grimes, 1995: Kondratieffs exist, especially when you filter out the very short-term Kitchin cycle. And add to this the lagged movement of world prices and interest rates, which are part and parcel of the cycle structure (Scandella, 1998; Bornschier and Suter, 1992; Tausch, 1998). The detailed empirical evidence on cycles is to be found, amongst others, in Tausch, 1997, and 1998.

One of the most alarming features of today's globalized casino capitalism is that cycles tend to become shorter again. Above we stated that the world economy will certainly enter a Juglar cycle B-phase and then a Juglar cycle trough in the not too distant future. In addition, yet another swing from the 18-22 year Kuznets cycle, that had its last trough internationally by around 1975, might combine with the next local Juglar cycle trough to produce quite a strong recession. However, it is entirely conceivable that Kuznets cycles will last in future 15 years or less, and Kondratieff cycles 30 years or less. This will mean an enormous growth of instability in the world capitalist system, with an ever shorter sequence of ups and downs, ins and outs, past and future 'models' and growth and decay regions, that will change like fashions. The savings and labor of entire generations will be thrown overboard and down the river in a few days of speculative storms. The length of the cycles is the following:

Table 11.2: The Length of Kuznets and Kondratieff Cycles in the History of World Capitalism

	Kuznets cycles	Kondratieff cycles
1756	18	**76**
1774	19	
1793	19	
1812	20	
1832	30	**53**
1862	23	
1885	23	**47**
1908	24	
1932	26	**43**
1958	17	
1975	17	
1992		

The following scheme now shows the continuation of what we interpret to be Arrighi's thought, above:

Scheme 11.3a: Kondratieff and Kuznets Cycles - Their Length Since 1740

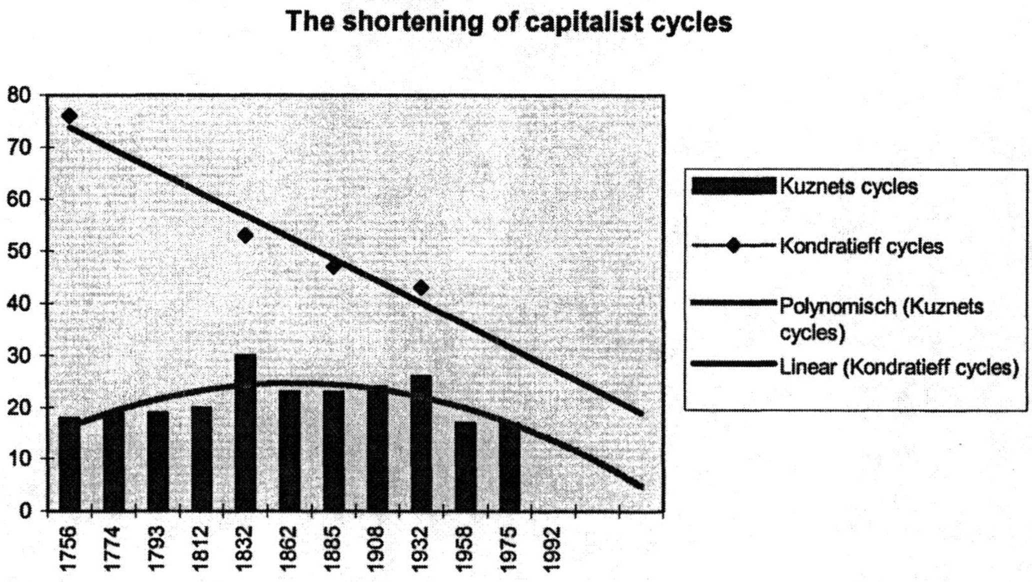

Legend: Kuznets and Kondratieff cycle length in years

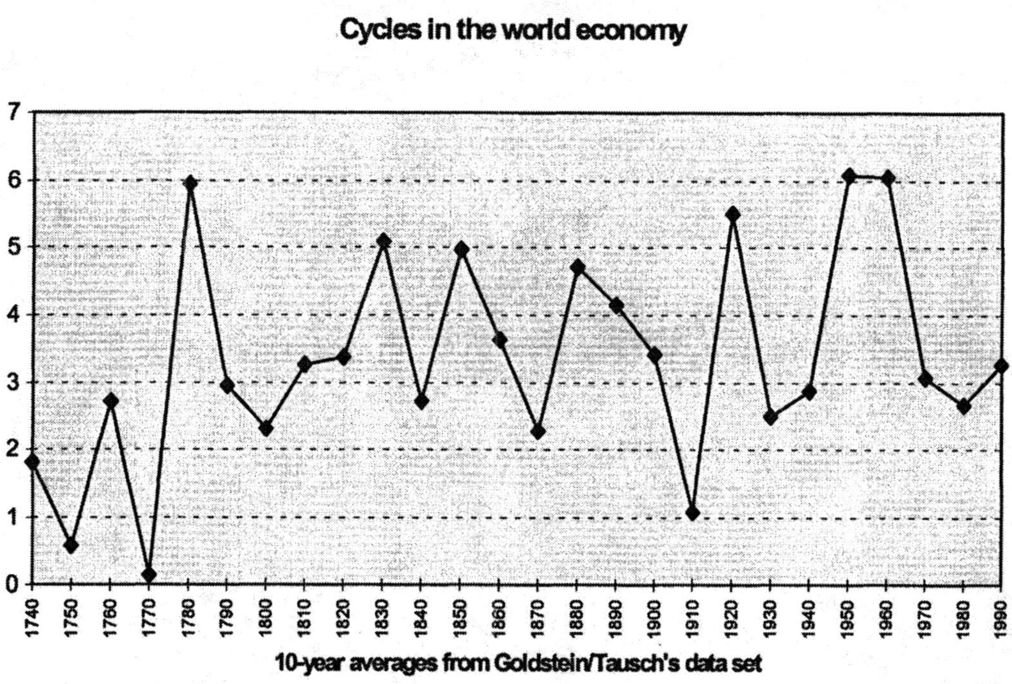

Legend: Average, decade-long growth rates 1740 - 1990

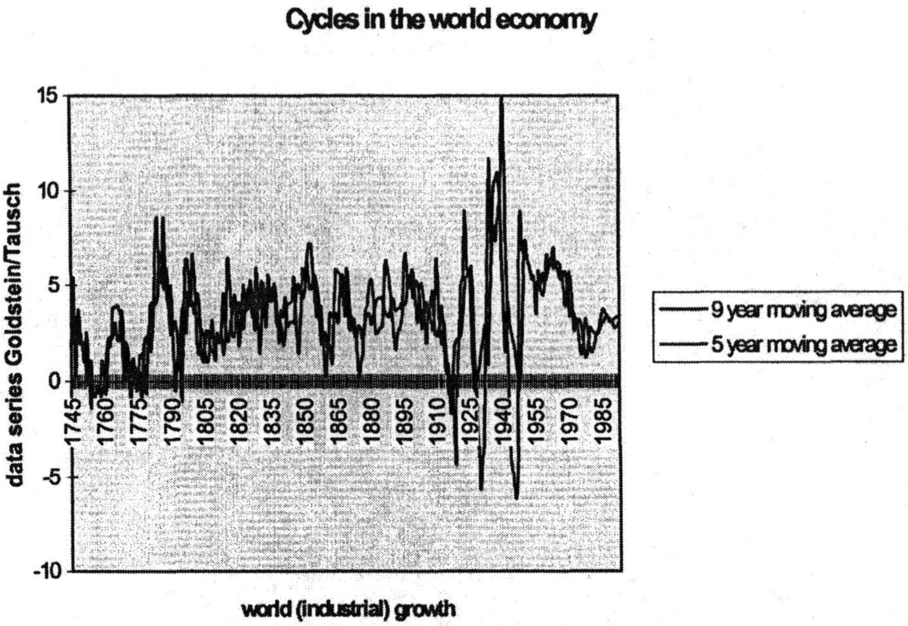

Scheme 11.3b: The Length of Kondratieff and Kuznets Cycles and Growth Rates Since 1740. Cycle Length in World Capitalism

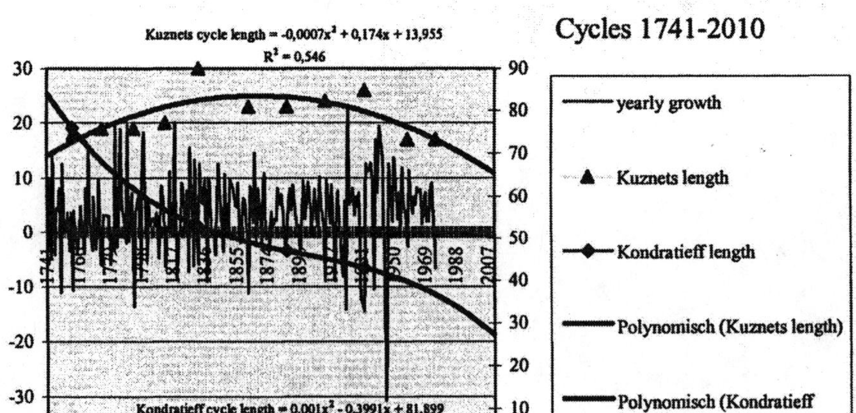

Legend: Yearly economic growth rate in %, left-hand scale. Length of the Kuznets cycle in years (left hand scale). Length of the Kondratieff cycle in years (right hand scale). Our own re-interpretation of the length of Kuznets and Kondratieff cycles in world capitalism, based on Goldstein's data on world growth, 1988. **1756, 1832, 1885, 1932** and **1975-82** are the beginnings of new **Kondratieff** cycles, while 1756, 1774, 1793, 1812, 1832, 1862, 1885, 1908, 1932, 1958, 1975, and 1992 are the turning points of Kuznets cycles. For further empirical evidence, see Tausch, 1998

In his new overview of Kondratieff cycle theories, Luigi Scandella re-interprets economic theories, like the Phillips curve and the Fisher equation, in the light of the long-cycle literature and arrives at the conclusion, that **price levels** and **interest rates** fluctuate as well in the above described way, with a time-lag of 5 to 10 years between production and price levels and again between price levels and interest rates. Thus the way is open for important further empirical research, since historic price level data are far more complete than historic production data.

Even in times of globalized capitalism, the social factor is important for long-run development: Casino capitalism, 1980-93

Modernization theories (So, 1990), dependency and world system theories (Amin, 1975), and socio-liberal reform theories (Tausch and Prager, 1993), were used here for the basic patterns of explanation of the shirt and long-run tendencies of economic and social development (Kentor, 1998; Tausch, 1998).

In order to determine, why some nations developed so differently from the others, we used the following data-set in accordance with the basic explanatory patterns of modernization, dependency and socio-liberal reform:

The data set, based on 134 countries

*% **labor force participation** ratio (UNDP, 1996)*
*% of the **labor force in agriculture** (UNDP, 1996; Fischer Weltalmanach, 1996)*
*% of the **labor force in industry** (see: labor force agriculture)*
***absolute GNP** (UNDP, 1996)*
***absolute income growth** (growth in the sense of Arrighi's and Amin's theory) 1960-1990.*
***Agricultural share** in GDP (UNDP, 1996; Fischer Weltalmanach, 1996)*
***average population growth** (UNDP, 1996)*
***economic growth 80 - 93**, pc. And year (UNDP, 1996)*
***economic growth 1960 - 95**, per capita and year (UNDP, 1998)*
***EU membership years** (Fischer Weltalmanach, 1995, 1996)*
***FDI per GDP** (UNCTAD, 1996; Business Central Europe, 1996)*
***human development index** (UNDP)*
***income distribution**: share of top 20% in total incomes (World Bank WDR 1996; UNDP 1996; Moaddel 1994; the few missing cases were substituted with the means from linear trendline estimates, based on the countries with complete data, using mean years of schooling and population growth as predictor variables)*
***infant mortality rates**, 1993 (UNDP, 1996)*
***inflation 93** (UNDP, 1996)*
***main telephone lines** per 100 population (UNDP, 1996)*
*mean **years of schooling**, population aged >25y*
***military expenditures per GDP** (UNDP, 1996)*
***state sector size** (gov. Expenditures per GDP; UNDP 1996; Weltalmanach, 1995, 1996; World Resources Institute)*
***structural heterogeneity** (labor force share in agriculture divided by product share of agriculture; see labor force data)*

***total fertility rate** (UNDP, 1996)*
***UN membership years** (Weltalmanach, 1996, 1995)*
***violation of political rights** (1, democracy, to 7, dictatorship) (Stiftung Entwicklung und Frieden, 1996, based on Freedom House)*
***violations of civil rights** (see political rights)*
***war years** (from D. Smith, 1997)*
***years of Communist Rule** (Autorenkollektiv; Weltalmanach)*

What tendencies, then, do emerge from the multivariate analysis of international development for the decade of Casino-capitalism in 134 countries with fairly consistent and complete data? Is Arrighi's hypothesis about the *'deregulatory logic'* of post-1980 capitalism confirmed by the data? And what about the other hypotheses of 'world system research'?

The results are fairly consistent with earlier research findings. First of all, **MNC penetration** (UNCTAD measure, 1985) significantly **lowers the human development index,** and **increases** - *ceteris paribus* - **infant mortality, and - as we show below, is also related to early death (percentage of people dying before age 40).** Under inclusion of the world of former 'real' socialism, the curve-linear effect of the development level on subsequent **economic growth** is partially taken over by variables, pertaining to the **employment structure**. Both the saturation effects of 'mature capitalism' with a high labor force participation rate as well as periphery capitalism's blocked rural transformation are responsible for slow economic growth. Again, only the statistically significant effects, that cannot be explained by simple random, are being taken into account. Countries with a large labor force participation ratio (the saturation effect of mature capitalism), and hence, a relatively smaller industrial de-facto **reserve army** of employment, grow **slower** than countries at the middle income level with a still larger industrial reserve army. Neoclassical theory would mention here wage flexibility in the urban sector as one of the main underlying processes. But on the other hand, **predominantly rural societies** at the present stage of globalization are being negatively affected by the ongoing **urban bias in world development** (M. Lipton). Seen from the perspective of Third World development, it is amazing to see how some European center countries repeat the experience of what Armando Cordova and Samir Amin once called **'structural heterogeneity'** and what development sociologists today call structural disarticulation. Especially those countries, that were once or still are characterized by big landholding and or extensive agriculture, implanted in the world system during the Long 16th Century, like most of the nations of the world's East and South, are still doomed to slow economic growth, slow human development, and relatively higher infant mortality rates. In terms of measurement, it boils down to the same effect: disarticulation, urban bias, structural heterogeneity - they all happen, whenever agriculture has a much larger share in national labor than in national product, reflecting the relative discrimination of the rural sector in society.

Some of the most surprising data from this comparison about the urban bias on a world level are:

Austria	4.0
Brazil	2.09
Germany	4.0
India	2.06
Israel	1.33
Japan	3.5
NL	1.25
New Zealand	1.11
Poland	4.5
UK	1.0
USA	2.14

Legend: employment share of agriculture, divided by product share of agriculture. For the ongoing debate about this 'urban bias', 'structural heterogeneity' or 'disarticulation' see Huang, 1995; Rothgeb, 1995, Wickrama and Mulford, 1996, as well as the earlier theoretical advances by Amin, 1976; Cordova, 1973, and Lipton, 1977. Our data analysis is based on EXCEL 7 and UNDP, 1996

Hence also the negative effect of agricultural employment on growth. **Redistribution** of incomes is significantly affected by the 'Kuznets curve', by the **labor supply** rate, and hence, population growth, and by the **power status** of a **nation** in the world economy (market size). **Katzenstein's small state theory is only partially vindicated here**. The process of **bourgeoisie nation formation** (Amin does not use the term 'nation building') before the First World War is a crucial determinant of today's growth and development chances in the world system. Those nations, that were founding members of the UN in 1945 - and hence have a high UN membership age - **disproportionately reap the benefits of economic growth today**. The **international system** indeed seems to work like a single, huge, **distribution coalition - or to put in Samir Amin's words - the international system favors at least some of the five monopolies**. Economic **growth disproportionately favors** countries with a **long-established record of UN-membership**. Participation in the 'distribution coalition' of world power allows for a better access to the distributed goods, while the predominantly rural or semi-rural societies of the 'Fourth' and 'Fifth' World, but also of the 'East' are being excluded from the benefits. Those, that have access in the established networks of distribution coalitions, accumulate even more economic power. And Deutsch's pessimistic stability theory is again vindicated; mainly because a strong state sector role in the economy and low initial *exposure* to 'modernization' (high population growth) still dampen war intensity, while *modernization under way* (high mean years of schooling) increase conflict intensity.

State sector size affects growth in a way, as predicted by both conventional and radical economic theory. But - contrary to Amin's expectations - **the economic burden of the military sector** today also significantly and **negative affects** economic growth at the level of the 134 nations under analysis. Amin's own wider theory would allow for such a hypothesis: the state class, and bureaucracies all block against development; militarization, first and foremost, is bureaucratization; while only a handful of nations might reap (if at all?) the benefits of militarily controlling the globe. **The effect of**

militarism must be further qualified: **growth is hampered by high military expenditures, and employment is hampered by state sector expenditures.** Thus Amin's hypotheses, derived from his theory, must be qualified: there is a negative employment, and a negative growth effect of monopoly number five in the world system, state capitalism and militarism. Further research should also look into the current account balance effects of militarism and world power political status. High military expenditures are closely linked to the conflict zones of this world, as measured by the indicator War Years from 1990 to 1995.

But some results from earlier research are partially contradicted here. Small states do not tend, in Katzenstein's sense, towards redistribution but towards a higher income inequality; but the economic burden of international power is seen in the negative correlation between absolute GNP and economic growth; or to put it in reverse, **small markets have a partially optimistic growth perspective**. Their growth will tend to be fast, but not egalitarian. Thus Katzenstein's old hypotheses are updated in a way. **Former communist countries could grow rapidly,** but often stagnate, not because they are former communist nations, but because their peripheral state is too bureaucratic and too big, because their reserve army is too small, because their military burden rate is too high, and because their **rural populations are being discriminated against.** But *per se,* the tendencies of world society after 1980 during the new cyclical set-up seem to suggest, that a world political experience as a **former communist** nation **does not block against** subsequent economic **growth.** Again: absolute market size is not a precondition of subsequent economic growth anymore, as successful island nations like Mauritius show impressively. Our equation determines **46.6% of economic growth** from 1980 onwards; the F-statistic for the whole equation is 8.05, with 120 degrees of freedom. What flexible specialization has to offer to the *megalomania* of current European center thinking, would be open for a debate.

Human development, on the other hand, is positively determined by a **high agricultural share,** and hence the absence of what Michael Lipton once called the 'urban bias of world development'. It is being negatively determined by a high ratio of **foreign direct investment penetration.** Thus, findings of earlier cross-national development research, most notably Huang (1995) are being confirmed anew. Our two statements are very well compatible with the essence of dependency theories. A development, that is dependent to a large extent on foreign capital, is socially polarizing and regionally exclusive. The rural regions stagnate relatively, while the rich urban centers are receiving disproportionate shares of the newly created wealth. But *ceteris paribus*, it also emerges, that a concerted effort in only one area of human capital formation - education - without the proper health policy effort can also be negatively affecting human development. Poland comes to my mind here: education data for Poland are still better than health data, where the need for reform is especially dramatic. Highly repressive totalitarian communist regimes - in the past - had a relatively good quantitative record in the education sector, that was connected with **severe deficits in other areas of social policy**. This same effect also holds for the determination of **infant mortality rates.** A policy of high labor force participation ratios, and hence, **full employment, less urban bias** and chances for rural employment all **reduce infant mortality** rates significantly, while

communist power experience, **foreign capital penetration** and a **one-sided human capital policy**, concentrated on schooling, and neglecting health, all **contributed significantly to higher infant mortality** rates. **Employment** - here labor force participation, is being determined by a **Kuznets-type non-linear process**. And employment is the one instance, where neo-liberal theories are vindicated in an important way. Foreign direct investment penetration pushes up the labor force participation rate, while human rights violations, state sector expenditures and past communist experience all determine the labor force participation rate - and hence employment - downward. The effect is of course significant, with an F-value of 8.13 and 42.3% of total variance explained.

The **war experience of a nation** is only weakly determined in our model (14.9%); yet, the most significant results are achieved by the state sector and low social mobilization (high population growth), working against a prolonged war experience, while military expenditures and mean years of schooling enhance the conflict potential: the **state neutralizes violence potential, while modernization and social mobilization increase it.** Finally, **income inequality** is being determined - in an almost brutal Wallersteinean sense - (41.3%) - by the **Kuznets curve, population growth, and by the absence of a position of power in the international system** (absolute GNP).

The multivariate results are in detail in Table 11.3.

ON THE WAY TO SPARTA AND BACK: THE MARATHON, 1960 - 95

As was mentioned elsewhere (Tausch, 1997, 1998), the logic of world development 1932 - 1982 was determined by what could be termed the *'fordist cycle'* of production, based on corporatist inter-mediation between capital, wage labor and the state, strong and encompassing trade unions, mass demand, and a thorough *'etatist'* regulation of the process of capitalist production. The new order, that seems to emerge out of the crisis of the 1980s, that destroyed the *'fordist'* authoritarian model of state capitalism in the East, based on mass production, heavy industry, the arms sector, the 'transmission belt' between state capital and dominated wage labor, and all-pervasive state control, is based, above all, on the electronic communication revolution, tele-working, new forms of production, and a thorough de-regulation of financial markets. Now, why are the front runners the **front runners during the growth marathon**, 1960 - 1995? The empirical results are in table 11.4

Table 11.3: The Multivariate Model of World Development for 134 Countries

a) Growth in the Period 1980 - 94

UN memb. y	mean y scho	absolute GNP	FDI per GDP	Years of Comm	population gr	state sector	% labor force	% lf agric.	% lf industry	agr. share GP	MILEX	HDI	constant
10.213	0.27658	-0.0449	-0.0038	0.04683	0.04623	-0.0412	-0.9458	-0.0299	-0.0034	1E-04	-0.372	-0.0035	-4.1729
2.44484	0.09678	0.02556	0.03757	0.02002	0.03517	0.01661	0.25246	0.01213	0.01112	0.0003	0.13	0.01406	3.1815
0.466													
8.04862	120												
4.177	**2.858**	**-1.755**	-0.1006	**2.339**	1.31457	**-2.481**	**-3.746**	**-2.463**	-0.308	0.33523	**-2.861**	-0.2517	t-test

b) The Human Development Index

UN memb.y	mean y scho	absolute GNP	FDI per GDP	Years of Comm	population gr	state sector	% labor force	% lf agric.	% lf industry	agr. share GP	MILEX	constant
-0.0017	-0.0042	-6E-05	-0.003	-0.0018	-0.0002	-0.0134	0.00027	0.00053	-7E-06	0.02086	-0.0001	0.86611
0.0036	0.00087	0.0014	0.00069	0.0013	0.00062	0.00931	0.00045	0.00041	1.1E-05	0.00445	0.00052	0.08829
0.88												
74.1983	121											
-0.4828	**-4.78**	-0.0435	**-4.383**	-1.3488	-0.3169	-1.4343	0.59058	1.29988	-0.6638	**4.691**	-0.2103	t-test

c) Employment

mean y school	absolute GNP	FDI per GDP	Years of Comm	population growth	state sector	viol hum rites	ln PPP	ln PPP^2	agr. share GP	MILEX	constant
-0.1821	-0.0119	3.2941	-55.631	-0.0743	-0.0998	-1.8049	0.108	0.0249	-5E-05	0.1234	281.05
0.2493	0.0652	0.5025	8.4382	0.4299	0.0415	0.6148	0.0275	0.0256	0.0008	0.3029	36.372
0.423											
8.1294	122										
-0.7305	-0.183	**6.555**	**-6.593**	-0.1728	**-2.402**	**-2.936**	**3.922**	0.9727	-0.0601	0.4073	

(d) Infant Mortality

UN memb. y	mean y school	absolute GNP	FDI per GDP	Years of Comm	population growth	state sector	% labor force	% lf agric.	% lf industry	agr. share GP	MILEX	constant
0.02855	0.32736	-0.2226	0.5792	0.53384	0.11911	2.52969	-0.2306	-0.1964	0.00208	-4.1766	0.0939	13.9921
0.83446	0.20233	0.32428	0.16052	0.30125	0.14331	2.16057	0.10451	0.0953	0.00256	1.03204	0.12131	20.4932
0.811												
43.3413	121											
0.03421	**1.618**	-0.6864	**3.608**	**1.772**	0.83112	1.17084	**-2.206**	**-2.061**	0.81363	**-4.047**	0.77406	t-test

(e) War Years. 1990-1995

viol pol rites	mean y school	absolute GNP	FDI per GDP	Years of Comm	population growth	state sector	% labor force	% lf agric.	% lf industry	agr. share GP	MILEX	HDI	constant
-13.4614	0.83461	0.04328	0.15409	0.11675	-0.33473	-0.17015	-0.16198	-0.09705	-0.01932	-0.00094	1.7409	0.66349	12.9576
12.1148	0.48782	0.12636	0.18622	0.09847	0.17369	0.08252	1.27292	0.0601	0.05313	0.00147	0.65095	0.63394	15.742
0.149													
1.61588	120												
-1.11115	**1.7109**	0.34251	0.82748	1.18565	**-1.927**	**-2.062**	-0.12725	-1.61495	-0.3636	-0.63412	**2.6744**	1.0466	

(f) income inequality

ln PPP	(ln PPP)^2	mean y school	absolute GNP	FDI per GDP	Years of Comm	population growth	state sector	% labor force	% lf agric.	% lf industry	agr. share GP	MILEX	constant
-0.2335	-0.1353	-0.0849	-0.1051	0.01724	-0.0049	3.23042	-0.0236	0.00432	-6E-05	-0.3733	-0.5457	6.41566	36.2921
0.25144	0.06956	0.09698	0.05241	0.10312	0.04445	0.64893	0.03575	0.02768	0.00079	0.3202	0.61236	10.3385	47.0594
0.413													
6.50195	120												
-0.9286	**-1.946**	-0.8756	**-2.004**	0.16716	-0.111	**4.978**	-0.6614	0.15599	-0.0814	-1.1657	-0.8911	0.62056	0.7712

(g) Life Expectancy

e-function	pi-function	mean y scho	viol pol rites	FDI per GDP	Years of Comm	population gr	state sector	constant
-0.0002	-0.0079	0.0007	0.0002	0.0004	0.0165	-5E-06	0.6557	-1.303
0.0004	0.0053	0.0002	0.0002	0.0028	0.0028	4E-07	0.028	0.078
0.955								
328.65	125							
-0.6104	-1.4894	**2.741**	0.6657	0.1386	**5.997**	**-13.04**	**23.46**	-16.71

Legend: War years (as of December, 1995) are calculated from D. Smith, 1997. Income inequality data are estimated from World Bank, WDR 1996, UNDP HDR 1996 and Moaddel, 1994. The existing data were augmented by averages of non-linear, second-order polynomial trend-line estimates of existing income inequality data projected onto the countries with missing data, with labor force participation rates and mean years of schooling serving as the two predictors. The choice of the predictors was made by calculating the highest linear correlation coefficients of income inequality data with the main variables of the model. The original war data were coded by subtracting the year, in which a war began, from the final year of a war (if unfinished, then 1995). Wars, which lasted less than a year, are coded as '1'. Source: Our EXCEL 5.0 and 7.0 calculations from UNDP and other data sources, quoted above. As in all EXCEL 5.0 outprints in this work, first row: unstandardized regression coefficients, second row: standard errors, last row: t-Test. The values immediately below the standard errors are R^2 (third row, left side entry), *F,* and degrees of freedom (fourth row). The figures reported here for employment should correct results, reported in Tausch, 1998, that were due to a printing error

Table 11.4: The Growth Marathon, 1960-1995

UN memb. y	**mean y scho**	absolute GNP	FDI per GDP	Years of Comm	**population gr**	state sector	**% labor force**	**ln PPP**	ln PPP^2	agr. share GP	MILEX	HDI	constant
3.3671	0.2137	-0.0099	-0.4256	7.4375	0.0868	-0.0076	-0.5488	-0.0945	0.0009	2E-05	-0.2166	0.0122	-34.301
3.7049	0.0993	0.027	0.2716	4.8161	0.0382	0.0177	0.2546	0.0129	0.0111	0.0003	0.138	0.0145	21.034
0.562													
11.863	120												
0.9088	**2.152**	-0.3651	-1.5669	1.5443	**2.271**	-0.4296	**-2.155**	**-7.315**	0.0767	0.0538	-1.569	0.8406	

Legend: Our own calculations with EXCEL 4.0 and 5.0. As in all EXCEL 5.0 outprints in this work, first row: unstandardized regression coefficients, second row: standard errors, last row: t-Test. The values immediately below the standard errors are R^2 (third row, left side entry), *F*, and degrees of freedom (fourth row).

Thus, which determinants survive the possible change of cycle growth logic, and are relevant for 'Fordism' and for post-'Fordism' alike? The following variables have a significant effect on victory or defeat in the development marathon: **% labor force participation** ratio (UNDP, 1996) (-); **average population growth** (UNDP, 1996) (+); mean **years of schooling, population aged >25y** (+); and the trade-off described in equation (3) above. The verdict of empirical investigation holds some surprising statements in store as well: **TNC penetration impedes long-term growth** at the 10%-significance level (significant almost at the 5% level), while the **communist legacy** - per se - is not necessarily connected with a bad growth performance (this effect is also significant at the 10% level). Our answer now is - if you like - very much patterned around the Irish experience after the 1960s: abundant labor reserves - per se - do not impede economic growth, especially in highly developed countries (thus repeating an almost common-sense wisdom of economic theory), but only under the additional condition of a **proper human capital policy**. The answer to the question of who will win and who will be lagging behind in the marathon thus corresponds to the **basic wisdom of both neo-classical and neo-Marxist theories of accumulation: capitalism 'transplants' its dynamism** to the **regions**, which are characterized by a still lower per-capita income, to regions which have **ample supplies of labor**, and whose reserve army is not yet dried up, but which **invested heavily in education**. For a country like Poland on its marathon, neither neo-liberalism nor a **classic** form of 'social Keynesianism' are the **model to achieve growth.** Also note, that **MNC penetration - contrary to most assumptions - is negatively related to long-run growth, and that the effect is significant at the 10% level** (but not at the 5% level). The mobilization of internal savings for growth is much more important than the inflows of transnational capital, which, in the long run and by their very oligopolistic structure, block against growth.

Secondly, why do the populations of the different countries of the world system **suffer** under such a divergent degree of **early death, poverty, and low human development**? The results are the following:

Table 11.5a: Structural Violence, Poverty and Human Development in 134 Countries

EARLY DEATH

FDI per GDP	Years of Comm	population gr	state sector	% labor force	ln PPP	ln PPP^2	agr. share GP	MILEX	UN memb. y	viol pol rites	constant
0.9822	0.0096	-0.0147	-0.0163	1.881	-40.01	0.2619	0.0917	1.064	-0.152	0.0166	195.77
0.2956	0.0331	0.2365	0.0632	0.548	9.347	0.089	0.041	0.584	0.0272	0.0257	42.495
0.832											
55.034	122										
3.322	0.2914	-0.0622	-0.2578	**3.432**	**-4.281**	**2.942**	**2.235**	**1.822**	**-5.585**	0.6464	

CPM POVERTY

FDI per GDP	Years of Comm	population gr	state sector	% labor force	ln PPP	ln PPP^2	agr. share GP	MILEX	UN memb. y	viol pol rites	constant
1.2866	-0.0245	0.4483	0.1375	1.4639	-36.716	0.0541	-0.0073	0.4917	-0.1826	-0.0249	219.44
0.5533	0.0619	0.4427	0.1183	1.0259	17.495	0.1666	0.0768	1.093	0.0509	0.0481	79.54
0.771											
37.281	122										
2.325	-0.3957	1.0128	1.1625	1.4269	**-2.099**	0.3249	-0.0955	0.4498	**-3.584**	-0.5166	

Human Development Index

FDI per GDP	Years of Comm	population gr	state sector	%labor force	ln PPP	ln PPP^2	agr. share GP	MILEX	UN memb. y	viol pol rites	constant
-0,0057	-1E-06	-0,002	-0,0007	-0,0256	0,6026	-0,0016	-0,0004	-0,0195	0,0014	-0,0002	-2,3833
0,0033	0,0004	0,0027	0,0007	0,0062	0,1059	0,001	0,0005	0,0066	0,0003	0,0003	0,4815
0,935											
159,28	122										
-1,7	-0,0025	-0,7625	-0,924	**-4,125**	**5,69**	**-1,631**	-0,9382	**-2,943**	**4,629**	-0,5438	

Legend: Our own calculations with EXCEL 4.0 and 5.0. As in all EXCEL 5.0 outprints in this work, first row: unstandardized regression coefficients, second row: standard errors, last row: t-Test. The values immediately below the standard errors are R^{2} (third row, left side entry), *F*, and degrees of freedom (fourth row). The specification for the Human Development Index equation is slightly different from Table 1.3

The following significant influences hold, in comparison to the other dependent variables:

Table 11.5b: The Analytical Conclusions Drawn from the Statistically Significant Effects, Reported Above

	reduction of structural violence	reduction of poverty	human development
dependency	-	-	-
labor force participation rate	-		-
agrarian share military	-		
expenditures years of UN	-		-
membership	+	+	+

Source: Our own compilation from Table 11.5a

Thus, the capitalist world economy assigns, more than 500 years after its initialization, the length of life of the poorest sectors of the population according to an easily discernible process: The long-run members of the UN afford longer life, the newer nations shorter ones, irrespective of the level of the logarithm of income per capita and its square. Long-established nationhood and the position of a country as a world investor rather than a world investment recipient country are nothing but a reflection of what Francois Perroux once called the 'dominant economy' as opposed to the dominated ones (Perroux, 1961). Apart from that, the transformation of the rural sector achieves overriding importance. The potential of economic growth originally is enhanced by *'unlimited supplies of labor'*, but - as Sir William Arthur Lewis has shown so clearly half a century ago - the backward rural sector urgently needs reform, combined with a policy of population quality rather than quantity alone, in order not to socially overburden the growth process. Fort that reason, our proposed strategy of development does not differ from the one, envisaged by Aghion and Williamson - investing in human capital, and trying to avoid excessive inequalities. Especially when capital markets are imperfect - as they are - inequality is bad for economic growth. Redistribution to the poor, i.e. to individuals who exhibit higher marginal returns to investments, will be growth-enhancing (Aghion and Williamson, 1998: 18). A large share of the rural sector enables economic growth, but is a burden on social development, as measured by the variable 'early death'. The way out from this abyss, dependent militarization, or dependent industrialization (high labor force participation ratios), provide no long-term solution to the problem of social transformation, because they both impede a long life of the poorest sectors of the population.

Chapter 12

MIGRATION AND UNEQUAL EXCHANGE

NAVIGATING BETWEEN SCYLLA AND CHARYBDIS. TENTATIVE GENERALIZATIONS ON THE GLOBAL SCALE

Under the conditions of unequal exchange in the world economy, analyzed in Part A of this study, it is no wonder that the peripheries and semi-peripheries somehow try to redress the unfavorable balances. For the periphery, migration is the second-best solution under the circumstances of unequal exchange. The best solution would be to overcome the conditions of unequal exchange, as analyzed in part A of this study. After meeting so many Gods and monsters on our way, the difficult homecoming of Eastern Europe back to the center stage of the continent is, like Ulysses' homecoming, confronted with yet another difficult trial. For Greek mythology, *Scylla* is a female sea monster, with the heads of dogs growing from her waist, who stood opposite *Charybdis,* a whirlpool in the straits between Italy and Sicily, that Ulysses had to cross. The sirens lured mariners to one of these two monsters by their singing. To be between *Scylla* and *Charybdis* is to be between two equally hazardous alternatives. The sirens lure the mariners in either one of the two dangerous directions: confronted with the *siren calls* of *'fortress Europe'* and *'Schengen means the re-erection of an Iron Curtain',* we should look anew at the process of mass migration and its relationship with the development marathon. **Ulysses survived the straits of Messina - by putting wax into his ears not to listen the sirens and thus to be able to follow his long-term strategy. *Scylla* today means: fortress Europe, while *Charybdis* is unlimited mass migration.**

Our research question deals with the long-run effects of migration on socio-economic development in the context of the five pillars of inequality, described below. The message of the present Chapter, that expands the presentation in Tausch, 1998, is fairly simple: building up and maintaining a viable social safety net is an option for both the recipient and the sending countries of international migration, an option which - in the long run and completely in agreement with a Myrdalian and Keynesian world view - is conducive to long-run economic growth. It is the long-term strategy to be followed, and neither of the siren calls, coming from two directions, should be heeded.

The movements of international migration since 1945 are clearly related to the large economic cycles, present in the world economy:

Graph 12.1a: World-Wide Migration and the Long Economic Cycles

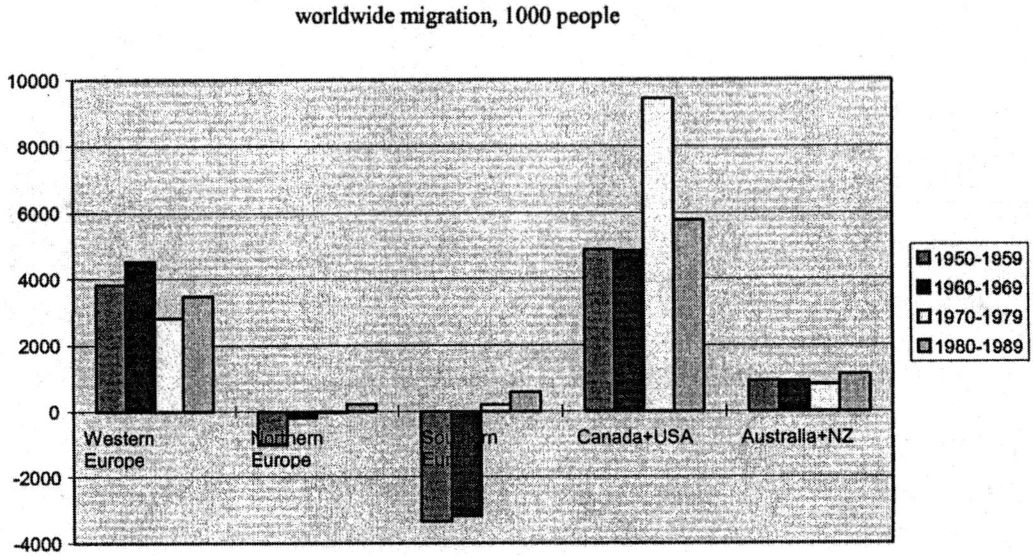

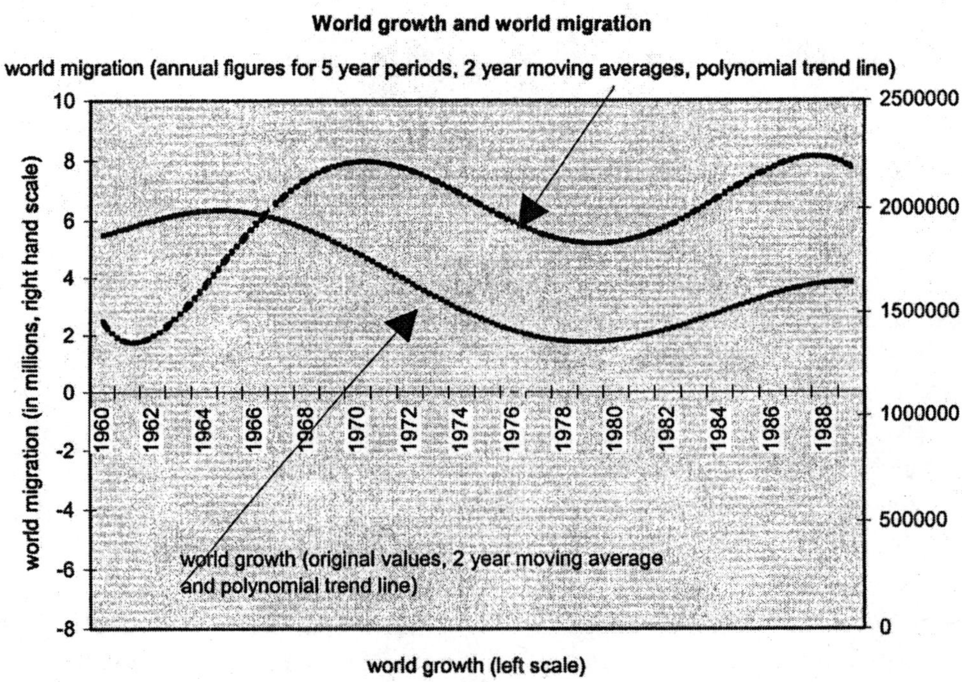

Source: Our own compilations from UN ECE, 1994; UN Population Division, as well as Tausch (1998), based on data by IMF, World Bank, and Goldstein (1988), also our own compilations from UN Population Information Network, *http://www.undp.org/popin/* and http://www.undp.org/popin/wdtrends/replamigration.htm United Nations publication, (ST/ESA/SER.A/176), Sales No. E.99.XIII.6, United Nations 1999)

We will be studying both macro-quantitative models on a global scale and some regional explorations for Poland, whose regional development and migration patterns are fairly typical for East Central Europe and are well-documented, thanks to the research efforts of the UNDP Warsaw Office over the years. Also, the political relevance of the analysis of the Polish migration potential is considerable, since Poland by far has the biggest present and future labor force among all candidate countries in East Central Europe.

Our Polish case studies are thought to be an invitation for further research in the other regions of East Central Europe as well and should explain in detail, how the structures of unequal exchange characterize the migration process. There is a bias in current migration research to overlook the regional factor and the wealth of regional data available especially from East Central Europe. Thus our input for the debate about future research strategies on migration is simple - we must take the social and regional dimensions of the determinants of migration more into account.

Above, we analyzed the trade-off between the **'unlimited supplies of labor'** and long-term economic growth. **Mass migration**, as Amin (1997) reminded us, is part and parcel of this process of transnational capitalism. Starting in the 1970s, Amin and the dependency research tradition developed a viewpoint on migration, which focuses on the effects of migration on the world periphery. There is a considerable brain drain and human capital export from the periphery, which blocs long-term development; worker remittances are being used mainly for luxury consumption and imports, and migration has a long-term devastating effect on the gender equilibrium in peripheral and semi-peripheral societies (Braun and Topan, 1998, for a survey of the literature). 3% of the scientists and 10% of the doctors in the United States are, in fact, imported from the pool of cheap, mostly free University education in the world periphery. If there are free riders in the world economy, certainly there are the customers, the big Universities, the hospitals and the communes in the United States, which employ the free human capital from Third and Second World countries. **The world periphery lost between 1960 and 1980 human capital to the tune of 16 billion $ to the center** (Braun and Topan, 1998: 35 - 37). **Critical, skilled and opposition elements leave the periphery, with the benefits of such a human capital import reaped by the center in the long run. Thus, selective migration is another pillar of the system of unequal exchange, and contributes to the perpetuation of the unequal structure of the world system.**

The market economies of western Europe first imported labor; now, with the transfer of production away from the European central zones, second generation foreigners become increasingly marginalized. In the inner cities of countries like France, Germany, and Britain, real *'ghettos'* develop, a process that began in the United States of America three or two decades ago. Women also have to suffer from these tendencies, as their jobs are being exported away to the still much-lower paid labor power of the periphery and the semi-periphery (Stiftung Entwicklung und Frieden, 1993). Migration, we recall, is even part of the *five pillars of international inequality* (Amin, 1997):

(i) unequal exchange: the gaps in wages are much greater than the gaps in productivities (see especially Köhler's contributions to this volume)
(ii) capital flight from the peripheries to the centers
(iii) selective migration from the peripheries into the centers
(iv) the monopoly position of the centers in the international division of labor
(v) the control of the centers over the earth's natural resources

The impact of migration on the sending countries under such conditions will be increasing the patterns of unequal exchange and the peripheral role in the world economy. It might be, that income distribution will become perhaps less unequal under the impact of the absence of millions of unskilled laborers from their home countries, but many other phenomena of peripheral development will be intensified; such as the deficient structures of agriculture, the environmental crisis (due to the intensification of traffic), and - in the end - the dependent character of accumulation, leading to slower economic growth and increased capital imports. World system oriented empirical research on migration confirmed, by and large, such a somber perspective (Amankwaa, 1995; Arrighi/Silver, 1984; Boehning and Schloeter-Paredes, 1994; Elsenhans, 1978; Parnreiter, 1994; Stalker, 1994; Stark and Taylor, 1991; Tausch, 1997, and Tausch 1998).

The Migration Potential from East Central Europe

Semi-peripheral and peripheral decision makers, largely representing the import-dependent, urban elites, - and here there is no basic difference between the Philippines and Poland - demand semi-peripheral or peripheral access to the labor markets of the centers, but they overlook the dire sociological implications of mass migration on their own sending peripheries and the disastrous effects of unequal exchange on their economies (Tausch, 1997, with a detailed debate about mainly ILO research). These tendencies could even increase after EU-accession + continued Eastern exclusion from membership in EMU (European Monetary Union), **basically because the problem of millions of small-scale peasants in East-Central Europe is unresolved. Unimpeded competition by high-tech and high-subvention Western agriculture will ruin millions of jobs in the peripheral rural structures of the East in the run-up towads accession, when agricultural customs are still a barrier for the East European agricultural exporters towards the Union. Belated, and not early membership of the East in the Union poses the real threat of mass migration from the East** (Tausch, 1997, 1998).

The application of the famous Barro/Sala-i-Martin-studies (1991/1995/98), which were basically studies on economic convergence in the United States, Japan and in Europe, to European migration potential projections based solely on an **income difference model** for the determination of future migration trends is highly problematic. The two mentioned authors want to explain economic convergence; migration only plays a minor part in that convergence.

They add multivariate pooled regression models for the US, Japan and Europe, taking into considerations such additional migration determining factors as heating (i.e. Sunbelt-motivated migration over the last Century) and population density. Barro and Sala-i-Martin explicitly warn against building migration determining models based on income alone (Barro/Sala-i-Martin, 1991: 129; 1995/98: 474 - 475; *ibid.,* 476).

Peter Huber (1999) from the *Austrian Institute for Economic Research* shattered further the foundations of such model building by demonstrating that regional net migration rates in Germany, Italy, Spain, Hungary and Poland are **only weakly determined** by the **wage rate**, but much more by regional **unemployment rates**. The variance of **net migration rates** explained for the regions of these 5 countries plus the Czech Republic is above 50% only in Germany, Italy, and Hungary, while in Spain, the Czech Republic and Poland explained variances are 16% or even below. Thus, even by including unemployment rates, **wage rates do tell us little about migration behavior in Europe.** Only in the Czech Republic, migration behavior is significantly dependent on the wage variable, thus corresponding to a vulgarized *'Barro/Sala-i-Martin-model'*, while in all other countries, except Spain, the unemployment rate is the driving force behind migration. And more optimistic still for the future of the European integration process, the constants in the equations for the Czech Republic and Hungary are even negative, i.e. the 'natural' tendency would be towards net immigration, and not net emigration. In Spain, neither unemployment nor the wage rate explain migration behavior to any significant degree. One might almost cynically say, it would be wise to include the heating variable in further studies on Spanish migration behavior.

Still, the original Barro and Sala-i-Martin unstandardized multiple regression coefficients form the backbone of current econometric research to estimate migration potentials in Europe, and thus also the current European migration policy debate at the level of the European Union. Some politicians have entered the scene and proclaimed the necessity of transition phases of up to 20 years for the East, or worse - until they reach the average wage level of the European Union - thus trying to prolong the division of Europe. The Barro/Sala-i-Martin US-coefficients, taken from a multiple and not bivariate regression, and ranging from 0.0177 to 0.0439 (logarithms of initial personal incomes, $y_{i,t-T}$), hardly were meant to be a generalized rule of migration determination across nations and across time, based on a single variable - income difference to the richer nations. To complicate issues further, the coefficients are obviously dependent over time on the Kondratieff and Kuznets cycle for their magnitude, with periods of high economic growth pushing the values upwards. Thus, future economic growth would have been a plausible predictor to be included in the equations.

Graph 12.1b: Income Difference Elasticity of Migration and the Economic Cycle - the Example of the United States

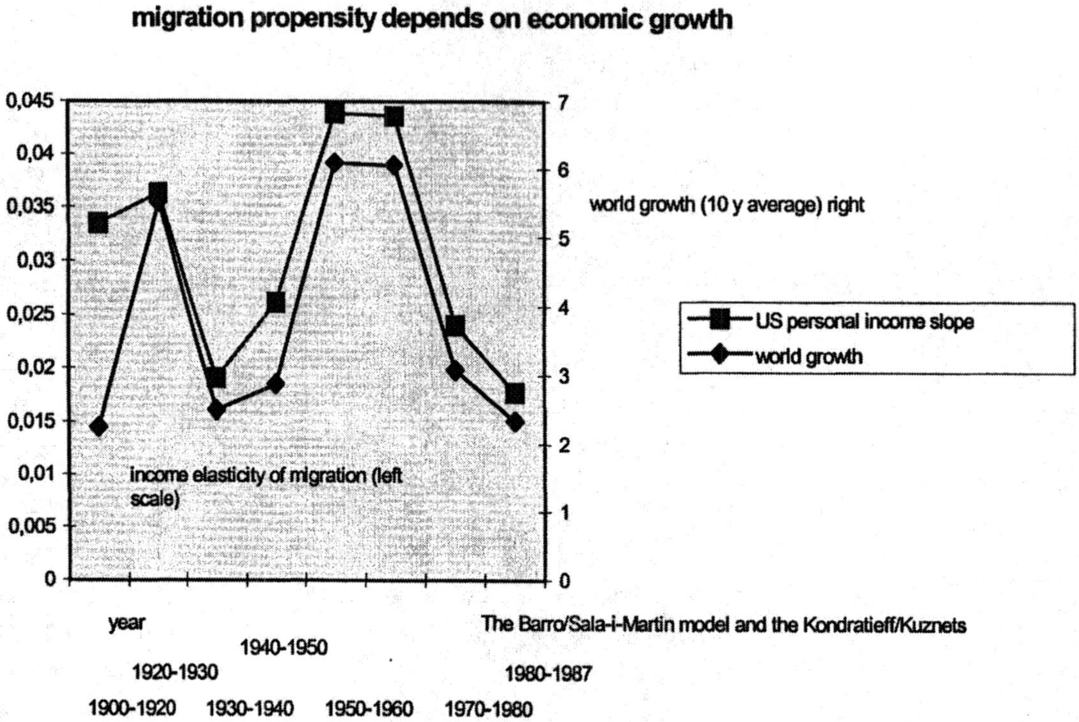

Legend: Our own compilations from Barro/Sala-i-Martin (1991) and Tausch (1998). The correlation as a first approximation towards the close connection between the two phenomena is very high: y (the Barro/Sala-i-Martin coefficients) = 0,0052x (world economic growth for the period in question) + 0,0107; R^2 = 0,7434

Also, migration in Europe is far less flexible for income incentives than in Japan or the United States of America:

Graph 12.1c: Income Difference Elasticity of Migration in the USA, Japan, and Europe

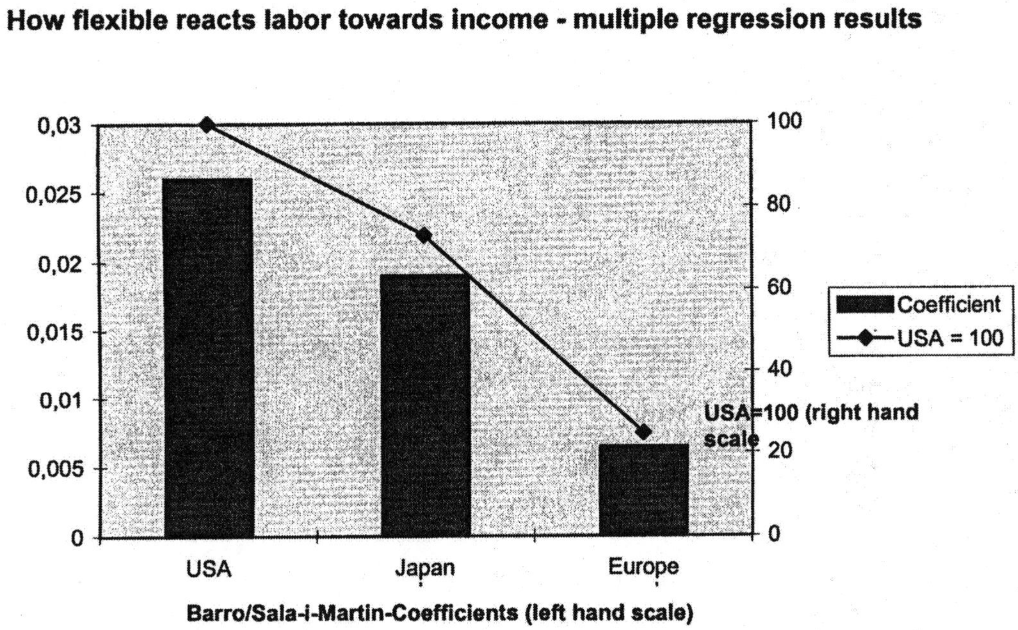

Source and legend: Multiple regression slopes for the prediction of migration rates in the USA, Japan and Europe by comparison - predictor variable: income. Our own compilation from Barro and Sala-i-Martin, 1995/1998

Also, **historic time series** data support our assertion, that income differences per se do not cause excessive migration flows, at least in Europe. Spain had pretty much the same position 1870 as it has today, i.e. 73% to 74% of the purchasing power of the European average; migration flows were low (-1.16 per 1000) in 1870, and they are negligible today. Portugal improved its position in terms of real purchasing power, less so in wages, but it is still miles away from the purchasing power of the European centers, and still, there is no large scale migration today, and in 1870 to 1910, migration rates were negligible. Spanish and Portuguese migration rates were high in the 1950s and 1960s, but this was during an extreme shortage of labor in Western Europe and much the result of deliberate government policy. Even in terms of relative real purchasing power development over time, not the entire European periphery caught up as rapidly as one would think with the centers over the last 125 years:

	real GDP per head **1870**	real GDP per head (average = 100)	real GDP per head, **1995** value	average = 100	gain/loss in relative position, 125 years of development
POR	793	**44**	12674	**64**	**20**
SF	1095	60	18547	93	33
N	1229	67	22427	113	46
SP	1338	**73**	14789	**74**	**1**
ITA	1568	86	20174	101	15
SW	1596	88	19297	97	9
GER	1619	89	20370	102	13
A	1847	101	21322	107	6
DK	1836	101	21983	111	10
F	1935	106	21176	107	1
CH	2476	136	24881	125	-11
NL	2490	137	19876	100	-37
BEL	2572	141	21548	108	-33
GB	3115	171	19302	97	-74

Source: Our own compilations and Aghion and Williamson, 1998

Migration **only marginally contributed** to the inner-**European convergence process,** but of course it did contribute to the **Atlantic** convergence process. The European hierarchy, 1870-1995 was changed only to the degree of 17% by migration in the 19th and early 20th Century:

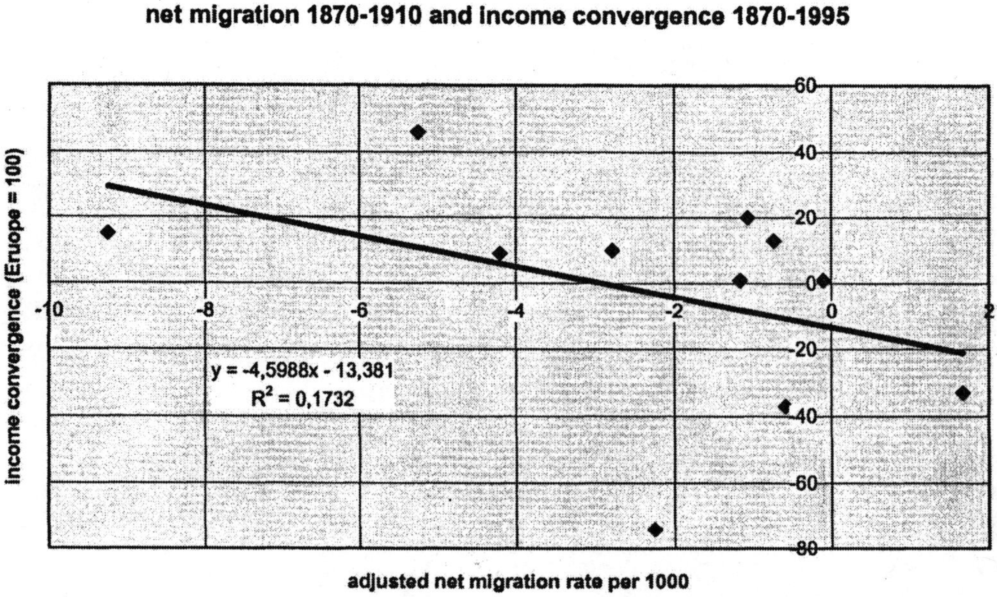

Source: Our own compilations from the above Table and Aghion and Williamson, 1998

Income differentials in Europe in 1870 only marginally explain the subsequent migration behavior in the long run, leading up to the days of the First World War. The explanatory power of income differences over migration in Europe is just 9%:

	adjusted migration rate 1870-1910	income level 1870 (Europe = 100)
POR	-1,06	44
GB	-2,25	171
N	-5,25	67
SP	-1,16	73
ITA	-9,25	86
SW	-4,2	88
GER	-0,73	89
BEL	1,67	141
DK	-2,78	101
F	-0,1	106
NL	-0,59	137

Source: Our own compilations from Aghion and Williamson, 1998

Income differentials and migration rates

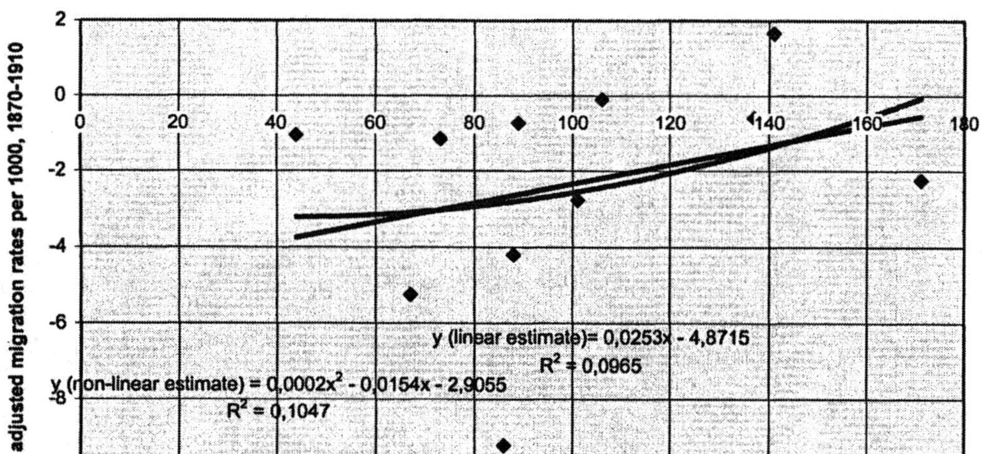

Source: Our own compilations from Aghion and Williamson, 1998

On a **world level,** income or wage difference models better live up to the reality of capitalist development 1870 - 1910. Looking at the following data and graph, again developed from Aghion and Williamson, we arrive at the conclusion, that approximately 38% of migration can be explained by income differentials. But this hypothesis includes Australia, Canada, Brazil, Argentina, and the United States during the heyday of worldwide labor migration:

	dispersion measure of wages, 1870 (variance divided by the square of the mean, 1870 = 100)	adjusted labor force migration rate per 1000, 1870-1910
Argentina	61	15,5
Australia	127	8,73
Belgium	60	2,2
Brazil	39	0,98
Canada	99	9,14
Denmark	36	-3,67
France	50	-0,13
Germany	58	-0,96
GB	67	-2,97
Ireland	49	-14,84
Italy	26	-12,21
NL	57	-0,78
Norway	32	-6,93
Portugal	18	-1,4
Spain	30	-1,53
Sweden	28	-5,55
USA	115	5,31

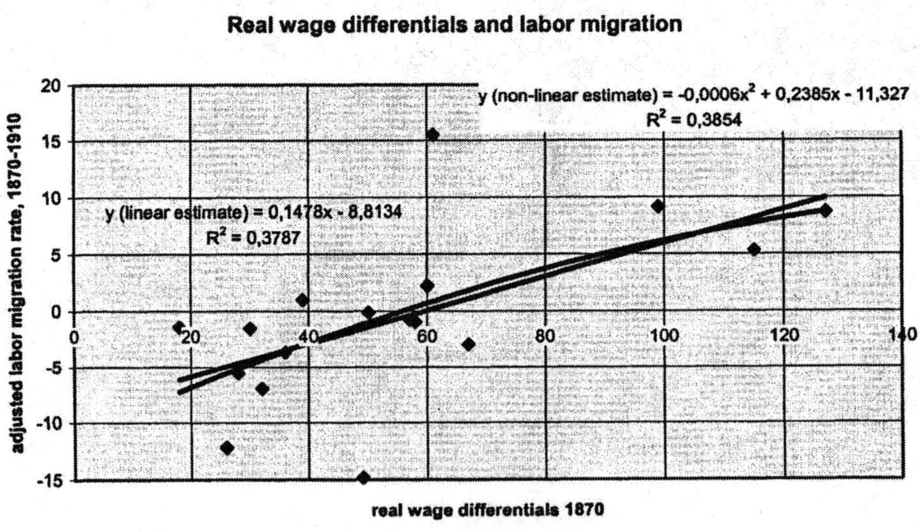

Source: Our own compilations from Aghion and Williamson, 1998

To be formulating tenable results at the European level, econometricians would have had to include at least heating and population densities into the estimates of future migration potentials for East Central Europe, and most plausibly also, projected future growth rates or a *'Kuznets/Kondratieff cycle dummy'*. To interpret regression slopes of multivariate regression models (as in Barró/Sala-i-Martin) in a bi-variate way, further would entail sources of error. An overview of current migration porjections would have to start from the following results:

assumption: Austria receives 2.61% of CEEC permanent migration (according to IOM/Wallace)

Author	Year	migration potential **CEEC 5**	study financed by	status	method
Layard/Blanchard	*1994*	**permanent:** WE **4 millions**	MIT Cambridge	published	econometric
Standardized value for Austria 10 years after CEEC EU accession: **69600 migrants**					
further notes:	authors project a decreasing migration potential 1994 - 2009				
Franzmeyer/Brücker	*1997*	labor influx Western Europe from PL, H, SLK, SLO, CS **340.000 to 680.000** migrants p.a.	DIW	published	econometric
Standardized value for Austria 10 years after CEEC EU accession: **88.740 until 177.480 migrants**					
further notes:	study has to be revised in the light of new DIW results				
Faßmann/Hintermann	*1997*	**permanent** migration-potential:in 9 EU-Staaten **512.292 migrants**	Austrian Academy-	published CEEC n = 1000, error prob = 2-3%	GALLUP
Standardized value for Austria 10 years after CEEC EU accession: **132.409 migrants**					
further notes:	3 CEECs (CS, H, PL)				

Walterskirchen/Dietz *1998* **migration potential** CEEC Western Europe **2,5 Millionen** — Austrian Chamber of Labor — published — econometric

Standardized value for Austria 10 years after CEEC EU accession:
200.000 to 250.000 migrants, >50% of them daily commuters

IOM/Claire Wallace *1998* **permanent:** — IOM — published — see Faßmann et al.
from **3 CEEC** to Western Europe **1.400.657 migrants**

Standardized value for Austria 10 years after CEEC EU accession:
from **7 CEEC (SLO, BUL, SLK, H, CS, ROM, PL)**
140.404 migrants
in addition **1.121.060 sesonal workers** (short-term migration)
from 3 CEEC (CS, U, PL)

DIW *1999* **permanent:** A **20668** p.a. — EC/Chamber of Labour Vienna — DIW website — econometric
Standardized value for Austria 12 years after CEEC EU accession:
248.013 migrants

further notes: study takes business cycles into account; calculates values for 12 candidate countries. For further details: http://www.diw-berlin.de/deutsch/publikationen/wochenberichte/docs/00-21-1.html

---

Salt *1999* **permanent:** WE 55.369 until 278.146 — MRU, London — published
west European
normal migration

1.445 until 7.268 migrants
further notes: study proposes transition phases

Study	Year	Estimate	Basis	Publication	Method
Bauer/Zimmermann	*1999*	permanent: WE 2-3% of the CEEC population of Employment	Ministry simulations, based on Southern enlargement	not published	econometric

Standardized value for Austria 10 years after CEEC EU accession: **69719 migrants**

PREDICTIONS FOR MIGRATION AND EU ENLARGEMENT

Our predictions for the effects of migration are based on a cross-national global model. In the centers, inequality will increase under the impact of mass migration, while at the same time, mass demand and technical progress, the 'twin engines' of auto-centered development, will suffer under the impact of the evolution of a '2/3-society' in the center countries.

Our prediction, based on the systematic study of 'hard' data about world development in the 1990s, is - as we have shown above - that there is hardly any 'mobility' in the international system; and that in particular, mass migration is not a generalizable strategy of ascent for the semi-periphery and periphery.

Western Europe could be tempted, in order not to fall behind China, to overexploit Latin America and Africa, and to try to shift the present East European current account balances further in its favor, while North America's negative balance with Asia is also an expression of the dramatic shifts in the production of multination US corporations.

Outward foreign direct investment stock of western European countries increased dramatically its share in West European gross domestic product, as one of the most visible signs of the process of globalization.

It is to be expected, that world capitalism is on its way towards an anti-egalitarian, and de-regulatory phase which will do away with many of the social advances that characterized the corporatist economic cycle of the post-World-War-II period. South Asia's and Latin America's inequality will decline, while in Sub-Saharan Africa, in the industrialized countries, and in Eastern Europe inequalities will increase considerably, and in the Middle East and North Africa there will be only a slight reduction of inequality rates. **The growth of inequality in Eastern Europe, in Sub-Saharan Africa and in the industrial countries might herald the advent of a 'Latin-American'-style capitalism of the 1960s and 1970s, that goes hand in hand with mass migration, the growth of transnational corporations penetration, short-term spurts of growth and long-term stagnation, and protected markets and economic distortions**. The imperative of *'balanced budgets', 'financial markets'* and *'de-regulation'* might, in the end, undermine the very logic of economic growth that the anti-Keynesianism of the 1990s maintains to uphold. Comparative data for the 1980s, 1990s and the first years of the new millenium show, that inequality - as in the past - has no positive relationship to economic growth, and that, rather, the opposite is true (Tausch, 1993, 1997; Aghion and Williamson, 1998).

Our analysis in Tausch (1998) showed the effects, that **transnational migration has on the sending and on the receiving countries in the context of overall dependency mechanisms across long cycles**. On the one hand, income differentials seem to play no part in explaining migration behavior in world society. **The hope of many semi-periphery and periphery nations to change their weak position in the world-wide structure of the division of labor by mass migration to the developed countries is also not realistic**. These findings could have an implication not only for the social scientific, but also for the political debate in Europe. At present, 'green', 'alternative' and socialist-left-wing groups claim, more often than not, that Western Europe should allow more immigration from the South and the East. **But migration greatly increases inequality in the migration recipient countries, without really solving the long-run weak position of the sending countries in the international economy. If the 'migration industry' were right, then Jordan, Mexico, Jamaica, ex-Yugoslavia, Greece, Portugal and other highly migration-dependent countries would be 'economic miracles'.** And Ireland could have foregone its heavy investments in human capital in the 1970s and 1980s, and just 'let them go'. The rank scale of dependency on the remittances of foreign labor per GNP in world society is the following:

Lesotho	47
Albania	17.5
Jordan	12.7
Egypt	11.9
Morocco	8.4
El Salvador	6
Dominican Republic	5.4
Tunesia	5.1
Sri Lanka	5
Pakistan	4.6
Benin	4.1
Mozambique	3.7
Turkey	3.5
Greece	3.47
Portugal	3.46
Bangladesh	3.4
Syria	3
Mali	3
Burkina Faso	2.8
Haiti	2
Papua New Guinea	1.5
Colombia	1.2
Mexico	0.9
Guatemala	0.8
India	0.7
Pilippines	0.6
Algeria	0.6
Niger	0.5
Armenia	0.44
Spain	0.4
New Zealand	0.34
Slovenia	0.32

Togo	0.3
Indonesia	0.2
Trinidad and Tobago	0.1
Thailand	0.1
Ghana	0.1
Sweden	0.05
South Korea	0.04
Argentina	0.04
China	0.04
Bolivia	0.04
Kenya	0.04
Cameroon	0.04
Tanzania	0.04
Nigeria	0.04
Bhutan	0.04
Mauretania	0.04
Chad	0.04
Sierra Leone	0.04
Poland	0.03
Austria	0.01
Italy	0.01
Lithuania	0.01
Romania	0.01
Denmark	0
Israel	0
Bulgaria	0
Czech Republic	0
Slovakia	0
Estonia	-0.02
Hungary	-0.03
France	-0.09
Netherlands	-0.11
Belgium	-0.16
Norway	-0.17
USA	-0.17
Germany	-0.24
Madagascar	-0.4
Rwanda	-0.6
Zambia	-0.7
Switzerland	-0.88
Venezuela	-1.2
Botswana	-1.6

Congo	-1.8
Gabon	-3.9
Cote d'Ivoire	-6.1

Legend: Our own calculations from UNDP *Human Development Reports,* various years

In the migration recipient countries, environmental decay, as measured by the UNDP greenhouse index, increases as one of the main consequences of the process of international migration, due to mass traffic and the consumption model that mass migration induces. For us, migration is - above all - an expression of a peripheral position in the world economy. At first sight, migration has practically no positive or negative effect on economic growth, but slightly increases sexist patterns of development and leads to slightly higher inequality in the migration recipient countries, as is to be shown in the following graph:

Graph 12.1d: Migration, Economic Growth, Inequality, the Greenhouse-Index and Human Development

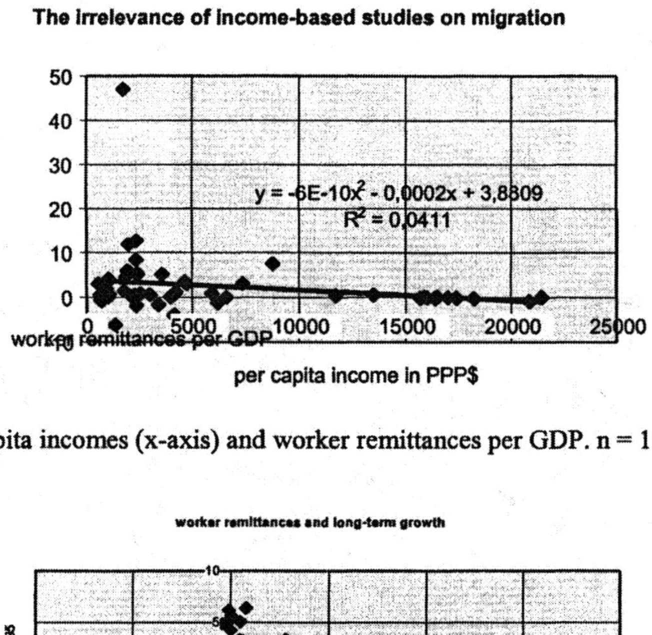

Legend: Per capita incomes (x-axis) and worker remittances per GDP. n = 123

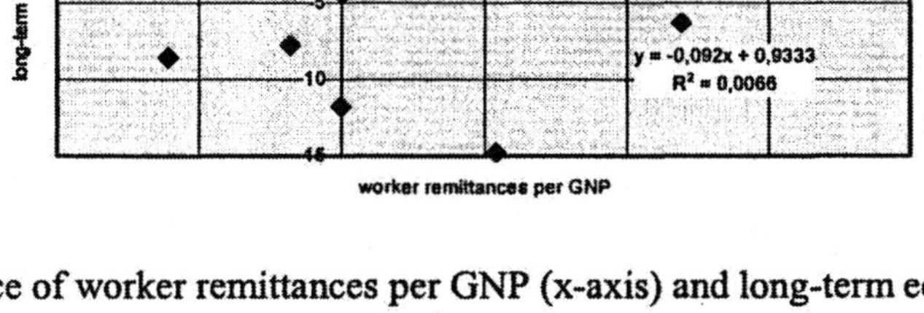

Legend: Balance of worker remittances per GNP (x-axis) and long-term economic growth (y-axis); n = 134

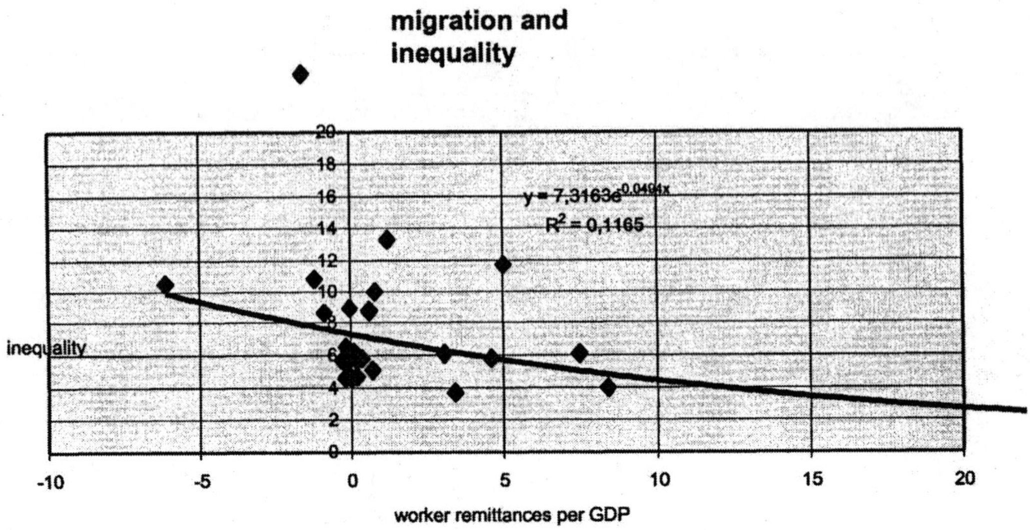

Legend: Balance of worker remittances per GDP (x-axis) and economic inequality (ratio of the income of the top 20% to the income of the bottom 20%)(y-axis); n = 123

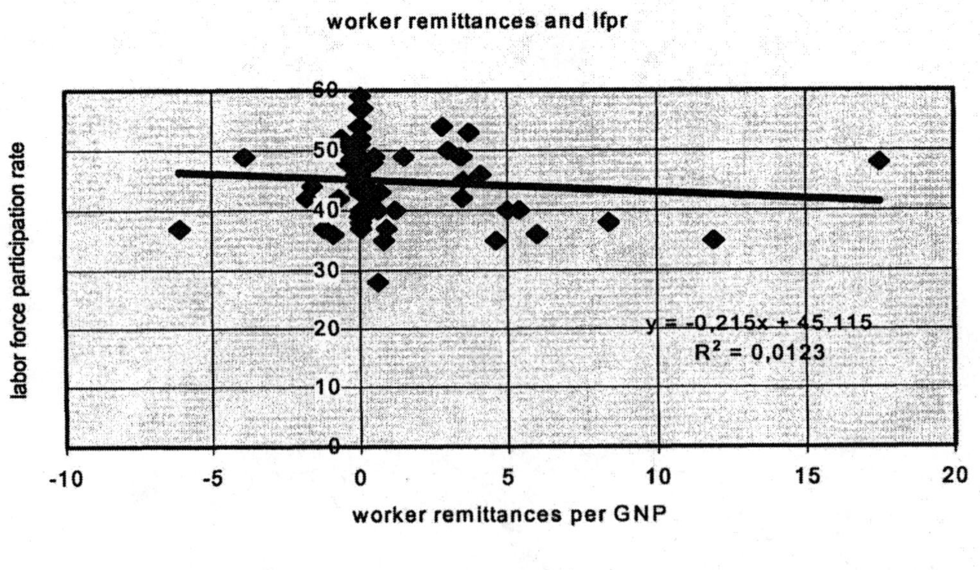

Legend: Worker remittances per GNP and labor force participation rates. n = 134 countries

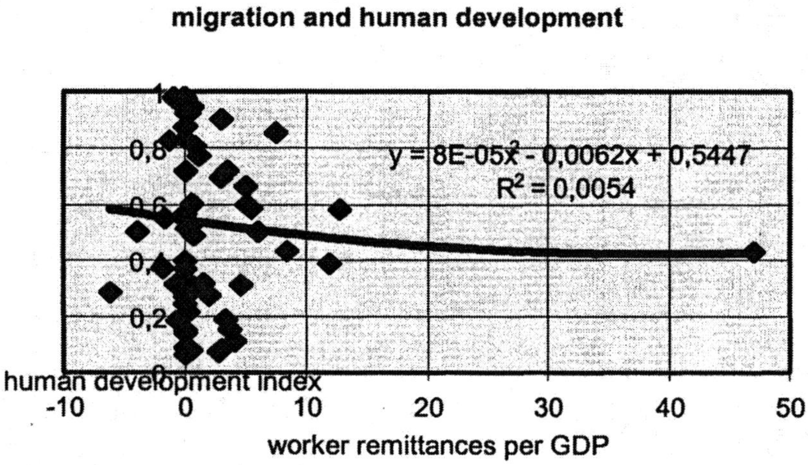

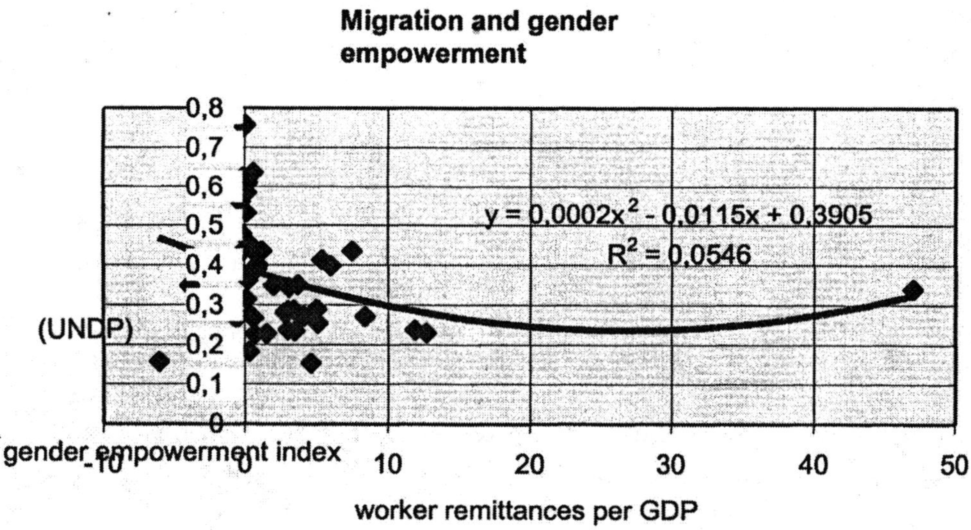

Legend: Balance of worker remittances per GDP (x-axis) and the human development index /gender empowerment index (y-axis). Sources: our own compilations from UNDP data. n = 123 countries

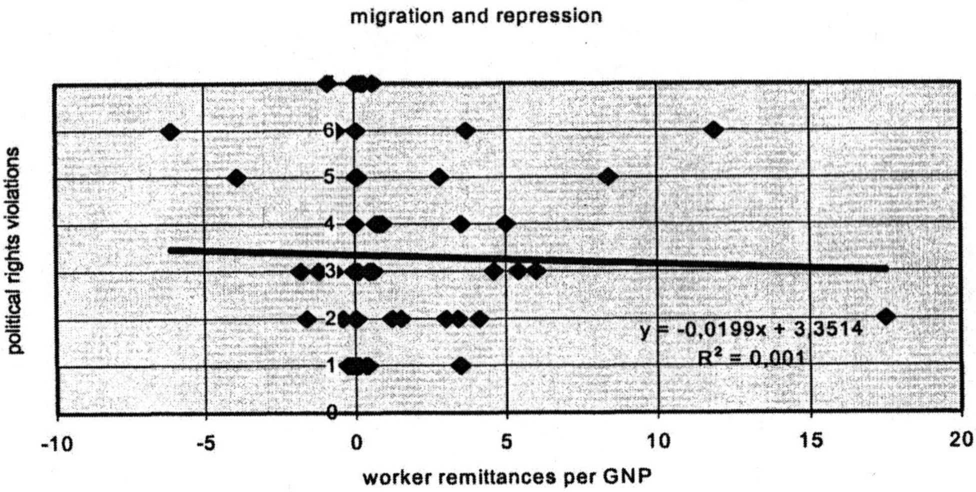

Legend: Worker remittances per GNP (x-axis) and political rights violations (y-axis). n = 134

The dominant countries, like Japan or the United States, send their managers abroad, but never their workforce. It is a sign of world economic weakness to be a net exporter of labor force. Poor and peripheral countries always send their workers abroad, and import their managers, and never the other way around. In the old colonial days, priests and soldiers were imported in most peripheries, timber, ivory, wheat, copper, slaves and bananas were exported.

Still, the structure exists, but at a much higher level, with a lot of *'soft body'* components as well. Interestingly enough, the effect of government size on growth in multtiple regressions becomes significantly and highly negative, once we consider the effect of migration on development. Introducing the variable: *'worker remittances per total GNP'* into the above equations, we achieve for the countries with complete data on worker remittances the following results (Table 12.2). Migration indeed is connected with state capitalism, with aid dependency; and world political instability, war, and refugee crises enhance the migration potential. Thus, a politometrically more viable migration potential prediction would take such factors, and not income differences (alone) into account. But economic dependence from migration is also characterized typically by the **absence of what characterizes the leading social welfare states in Europe: feminism (gender empowerment, years of female voting), high social security expenditures *et cetera.*** The multivariate results now show the interaction of the migration process with long-run development.

Table 12.1: The Pearson-Bravais-Correlations of Worker Remittances per GDP with Variables of Economic Growth

	correlation with migration remittances
Govex (government expenditures)	0.26
war/internal war	0.24
government consumption	0.19
aid per capita	0.18
public investment	0.17
refugees per population	0.15
violation of political Rights	0.14
MPR (military personnel ratio)	0.14
violation of civil rights	0.09
deforestation	0.05
LEX 1990 (life expectancy)	-0.03
SIPE-Index (Social Insurance Programme Experience Index)	-0.07
HDI (Human Development Index)	-0.07
GNP growth 80-92	-0.07
mean years of schooling	-0.09
gender empowerment	-0.11
reserves per GDP	-0.13
social security expenditures	-0.14
years of female voting	-0.17

inflation 93	FDI per GDP	UN member	UN memb. y	mean y scho	absolute GNP	FDI per GDP	Years of Comm	population gr	state sector	%labor force
-0.0563	-0.1282	-0.1461	0.1461	-0.1013	-0.0915	-0.1282	0.0453	0.0102	0.0986	-0.1107

ln PPP	ln PPP^2	agr.shareGP	MILEX	HDI	viol pol rites	viol hum rites
0.0635	0.0653	0.1292	0.2063	-0.0777	-0.031	0.1158

Source: Our own calculations from worker remittances and other UNDP structural data for n = 123 countries and n = 134 countries of the world system, bivariate correlations according to EXCEL 5.0

Table 12.2: International Dependency and its Effects on Growth and Adjustment, Allowing for the Influence of the Migration Process (n=64 Countries with Complete Data on Worker Remittances)

	MNC PEN73	Govex	Trade Dep	social sec	UN-membery	Women Parl	Women %LF	ln PCI	ln PCI^2	ln(MPR +1)	Fertility Rate	migration	constant
Adjustment	-0.143	-1.13	0.525	0.589	-11.5	-0.018	-0.033	-0.05	0.115	-0.02	-0.02	-0.004	60.89
	0.049	0.207	1.195	0.404	6.05	0.026	0.05	0.027	0.081	0.017	0.036	0.003	22.69
	0.56												
	5.402	51											
t-Test	**-2.897**	**-5.452**	0.439	1.456	**-1.901**	-0.671	-0.667	-1.852	1.426	-1.191	-0.552	-1.278	
	MNC PEN73	**Govex**	**Trade Dep**	social sec	UN-membery	Women Parl	Women %LF	ln PCI	ln PCI^2	ln(MPR+1)	Fertility Rate	migration	constant
growth	-0.119	-1.42	1.832	0.42	-9.152	-0.01	-0.008	-0.041	0.063	-0.019	-0.017	-3E-04	53.4
	0.046	0.194	1.12	0.379	5.671	0.025	0.047	0.025	0.076	0.016	0.034	0.003	21.27
	0.614												
t-Test	**-2.569**	**-7.307**	**1.636**	1.108	**-1.614**	-0.407	-0.179	**-1.637**	0.827	**-1.166**	-0.51	-0.113	

Legend: As in all EXCEL 5.0 outprints in this work, first row: unstandardized regression coefficients, second row: standard errors, last row: t-Test. The values immediately below the standard errors are R^{2} (third row, left side entry), *F*, and degrees of freedom (fourth row). The above results were achieved by inserting international migration remittances data (remittances per GDP) into our cross-national growth and development equations. Only countries with complete data from the original n=123 sample of OECD and underdeveloped countries were used.

Migration does not positively bring about today growth or adjustment; but is part and parcel of the state-class dominated structures that rely on state expenditures, militarization, and the influx of foreign capital. Our findings are in partial contradiction here with Jeffrey Williamson's studies on the long-run effects of migration in the world system before 1940, who thought that migration contributes - just like studies on economic convergence in the United States - to a narrowing of the gap between the rich and the poor regions in the world. For one thing, unequal exchange, analyzed in this volume, so greatly increasing in power over the decades in our contemporary world system, might explain this different trajectory. But also, the greatest proponents of mass migration from the semi-periphery and periphery today are in reality those very social strata, **that represent the powerful urban power monopolies at home, allied with the power of the transnational corporations: instead of bringing their monopolies under the discipline of the market and allowing their agricultural regions to prosper under a system of export-led growth and mass-demand at home, they are inclined to send a considerable part of their talented work-force abroad so that it does not constitute any threat to the elites' privileged social position at home.** State sector expenditures and a reliance on foreign aid will be part and parcel of a such a migration-driven development model. The migration-state sector effect described above is significant at the

12.5% level and narrowly misses the 10% mark. **61.4% of economic growth are explained by our migration-centered equation.**

MIGRATION AND THE EARLIER ENLARGEMENTS OF THE EU

There is a strong possibility of a long-run interrelation between human development and migration propensity. Such a strategy would presuppose a very thorough human capital effort on the part of the accession countries, similar to the one to be observed in Spain under Felipe Gonzales. As already predicted by Rostow and others, migration is also closely connected to the tendencies of the Kondratieff cycle, as is to be seen from the following Graph:

Graph 12.2: Migration Balances and the Kondratieff Cycle

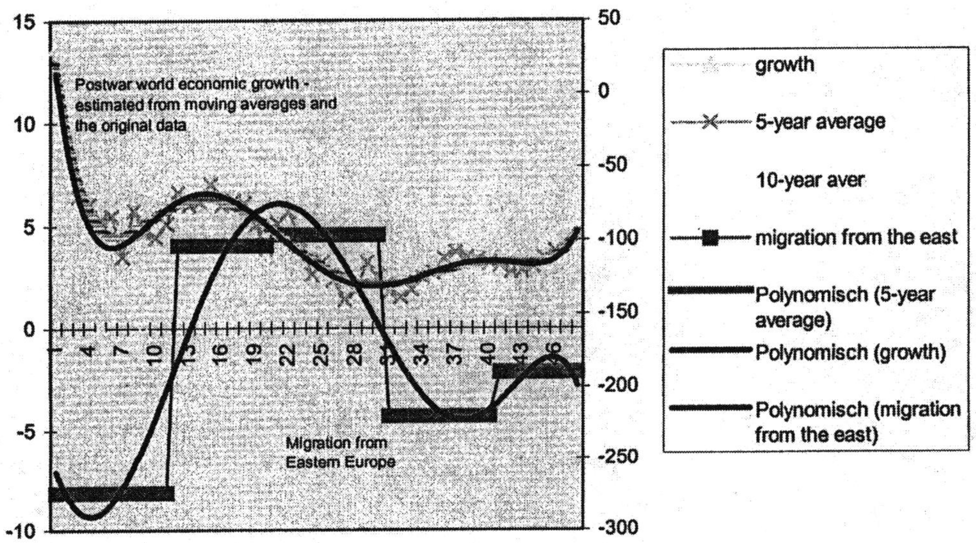

Legend: economic growth (left hand scale) and migration balances from Eastern Europe (right hand scale) during the Kondratieff cycle from 1950 onwards.

Under such a Gonzales scenario, slowly, Eastern Europe's outward migration potential will recede, as the countries could become immigration regions themselves, like Southern Europe before:

Graph 12.3: Eastern and Southern European Migration

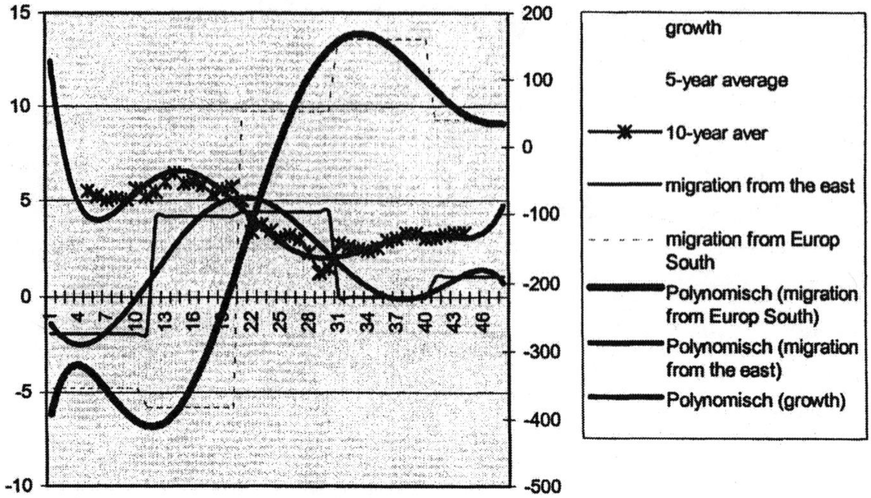

Legend: This graph compares the results from the above graph (economic growth, left-hand scale) with the migration balances in Eastern and Southern Europe (right hand scale).

Southern Europe became an immigration region long ago, and tightened its borders, as East Central Europe will probably tighten its own borders for some time to come as the future Schengen outer border of Europe:

Graph 12.4a: Human Development Migration Thresholds

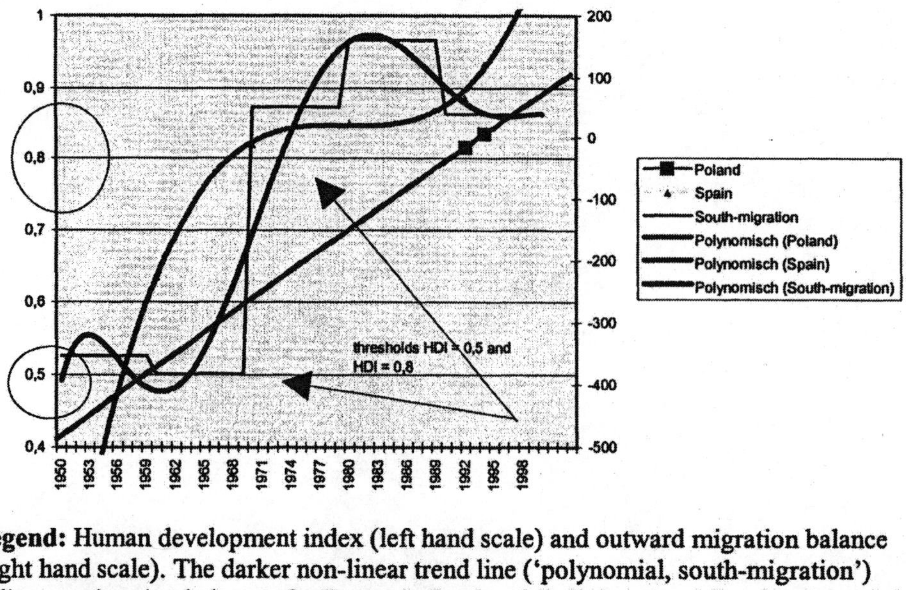

Legend: Human development index (left hand scale) and outward migration balance (right hand scale). The darker non-linear trend line ('polynomial, south-migration') indicates migration balances for Europe's South, while lighter trend line ('polynomial, Spain) indicates the human development experience of Spain since 1960 (left-hand

scale). The straight trend line is the probable course of Polish human development. It reaches the 0.900-human-development-threshold for migration by 2000 (last UNDP HDR Poland 1998 published measurement 0.883); the European South became a net importer of labor after reaching these human development levels. The graph, as before, combines data from this study and data about the globalization of migration from IFRI (1998). The economic cycle in Eastern Europe is time-lagged in comparison to the world economic cycle. Southern Europe becomes a major immigration region; whose importance grows with the future upswing of the world economic cycle. The data series again starts with 1950. The last graph compares the migration balance in the European South with the evolution of Spain's UNDP Human Development Index since 1960. The graph shows the two migration policy thresholds of HDI = 0.500 and HDI = 0.800 and compares the Spanish HDI performance over time with the UNDP figures for Poland. Not before long - or even today -, Poland could become - according to a Gonzales scenario - a net immigration country, reaching a human development index of 0.900. It should be emphasized that, due to regional inequalities, 12 regions (former voivodships) in Poland are still below the 0.8 threshold. They will still provide a reservoir of migration for some years to come (see below)

To try to predict migration behavior from income data, is practically impossible for most of the European regions. We show this for the Spanish case, which is typical for contemporary Europe. With total migration regime liberalization at the inner-EU-level, high rates of unemployment and still high income differentials to the European Union average in the European *mezzogiorno*, there is practically no outward migration from the Mediterranean regions to Northern Europe taking place today. Migration balances in richer regions of Spain are almost the same as in poorer regions, as the following empirical materials from the EC regional data base show. Both the regional per capita income (log) as well as the log of the unemployment rate only slightly positively affect the regional migration balances in Spain:

Graph 12.4b: Regional Incomes in Spain and Migration Balances

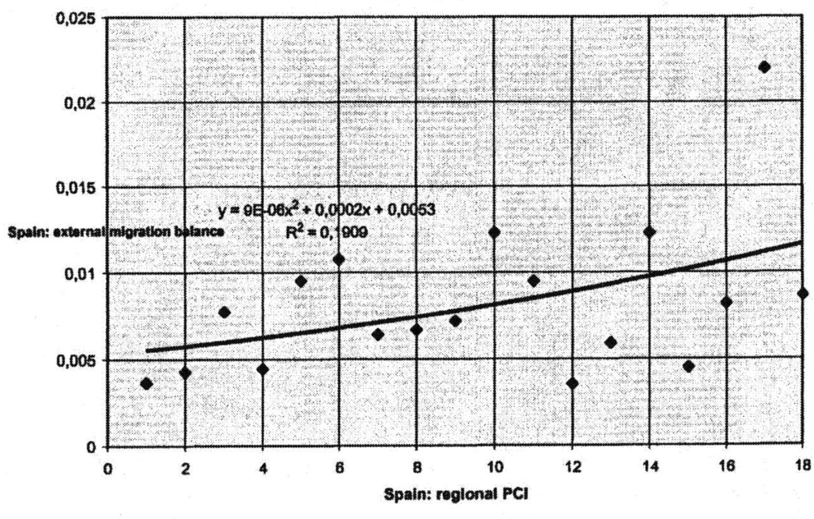

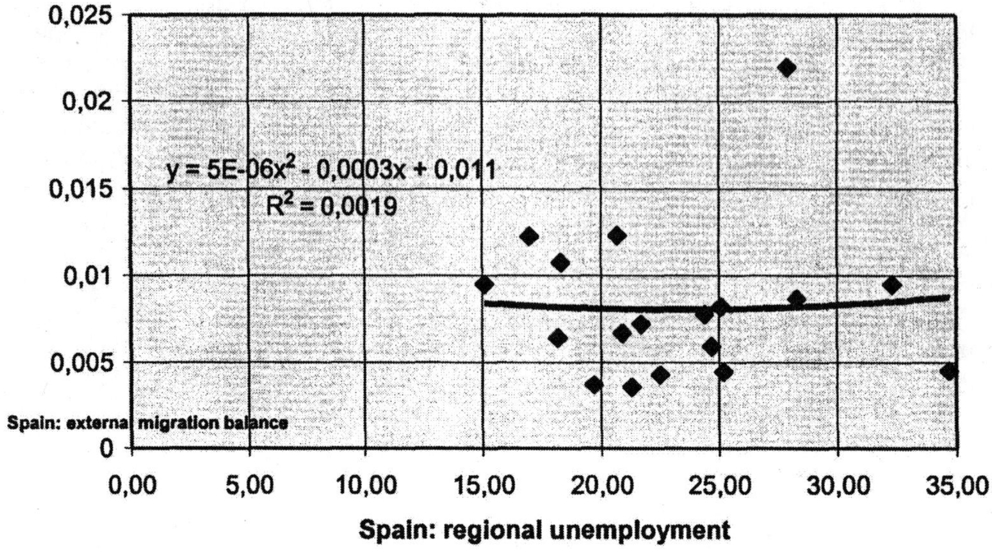

Spanish migration balance =

ln GNP cap	ln unemployment rate	constant
0,004660504	0,002578003	-0,02708485
0,0038269	0,004706467	0,053143779
0,1381059		
1,201764927	15	
1,217827544	0,547757549	T-Test

Note: As in all EXCEL 5.0 outprints, first rows are unstandardized regression coefficients, second rows are standard errors of the estimate, the third row shows the value for R^2 of the whole equation and the standard deviation of the estimate for y; the fourth row are the F-value and the degrees of freedom of the whole equation. Our own calculations from WIFO/EC Regional data bank; our thanks are expressed here to the Austrian Institute for Economic Research

PERIPHERAL WAGES, UNEQUAL EXCHANGE, MIGRATION AND EU-ENLARGEMENT PHOBIA

Unequal exchange could lead towards a race to the bottom in incomes and wages. The existing data series for European

- wages of production workers in manufacturing (BLS, United States Department of Labour)
- industrial wages (Statistisches Bundesamt, Wiesbaden, Germany)

- labor costs in industry (Bundeskammer der Gewerblichen Wirtschaft, Vienna, Austria)
- Nominal renumeration of workers and employees (**EC DG II**, AMECO DG II 5/10/1999)
- GNP per capita (World Bank Social Indicators)
- GDP in real purchasing power (OECD)

all indicate that there has been no convergence of incomes in Europe over time, and that the Arrighean three-layer structure of the world economy, discussed above, remained largely intact. The non-convergence in Europe notwithstanding, there have been no significant migration flows within the Union in the 1970s, 1980s and 1990s. Recently, there were sharp political controversies on the question of wages in East Central Europe. The 80% views (see below) were reflected in large segments of the Austrian public, including the Austrian Federation of Trade Unions (OeGB):

> *'Hungarian Prime Minister Viktor Orban blasted a statement by Austria's far-right Freedom Party head Joerg Haider* ***that EU enlargement should not happen until applicant countries reach EU wage levels (i.e. 80% of the EU-average).***
>
> *"I have to express my great concern about that position of the Austrian government," Orban said on Monday. "The statement was clearly against Hungarian citizens...and it is very much against the policy of the EU."*
>
> *Orban was referring to a Haider interview in the Hungarian daily Nepszabadsag on February 12. Haider is not a Cabinet minister himself but he continues to head the Freedom Party*
>
> *Hungary has tried to judge the new Austrian government by its concrete actions and decisions, but the statement was objectionable, nonetheless, Orban said.*
>
> *"It's obvious that none of the countries trying to get into the European Union can reach that level," he told reporters.*
>
> *"The Austrian government should understand that Hungary and Austria during the last 40 years were on different sides of history," Orban added.*
>
> *"If there is an anti-accession policy, it would harm Austria because it has four neighbors that want to join the European Union."'*

(Reuters, Budapest, Feb 22, 2000, Central Europe Online, http://www.centraleurope.com/)

The convergence of incomes and the determination of migration by income differentials are a myth:

Graph 12.4.c: The Mythology of Income Convergence in Europe

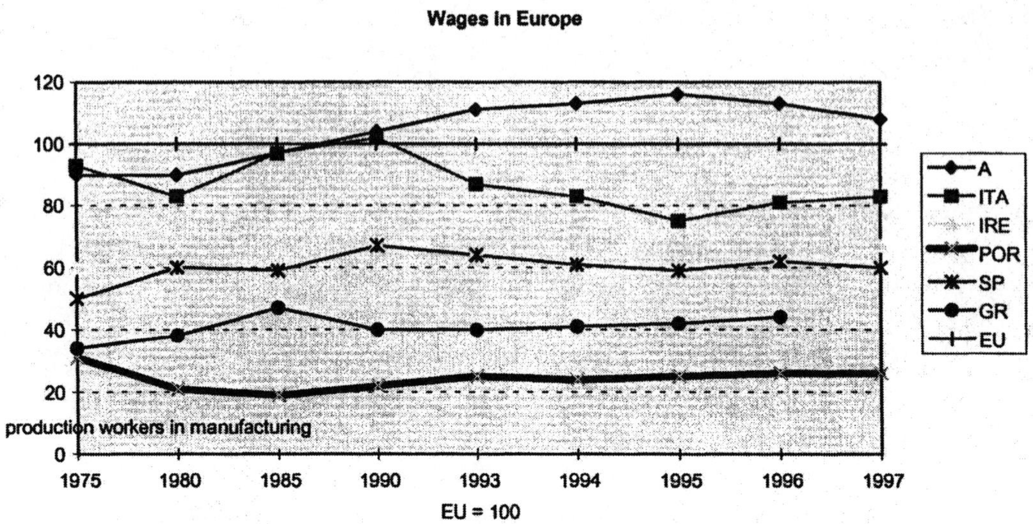

Source: Our own calculations from United States Department of Labor

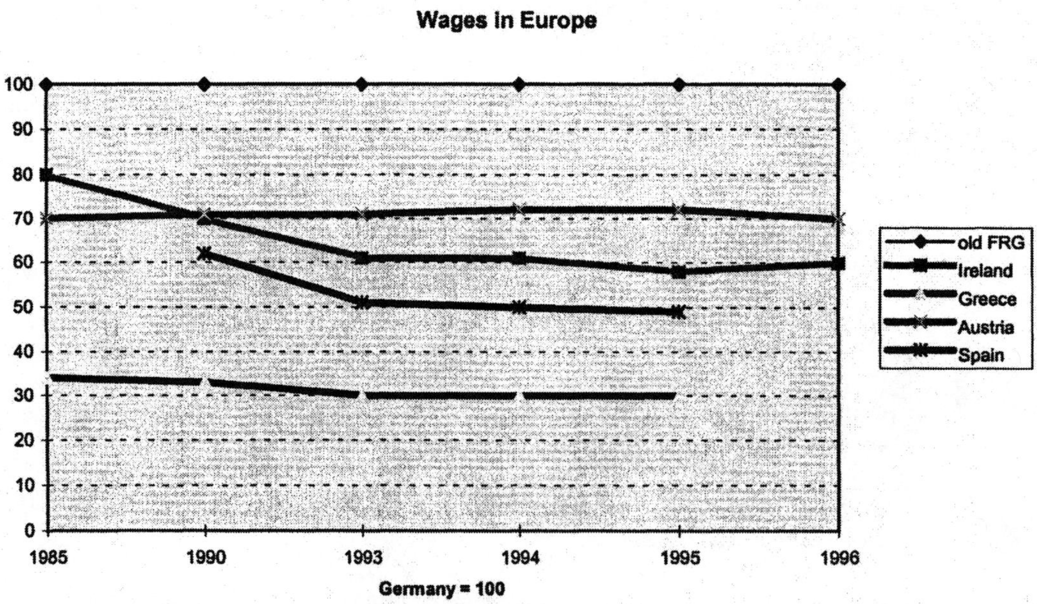

Source: Industrial wages; our own compilations from Statistisches Bundesamt

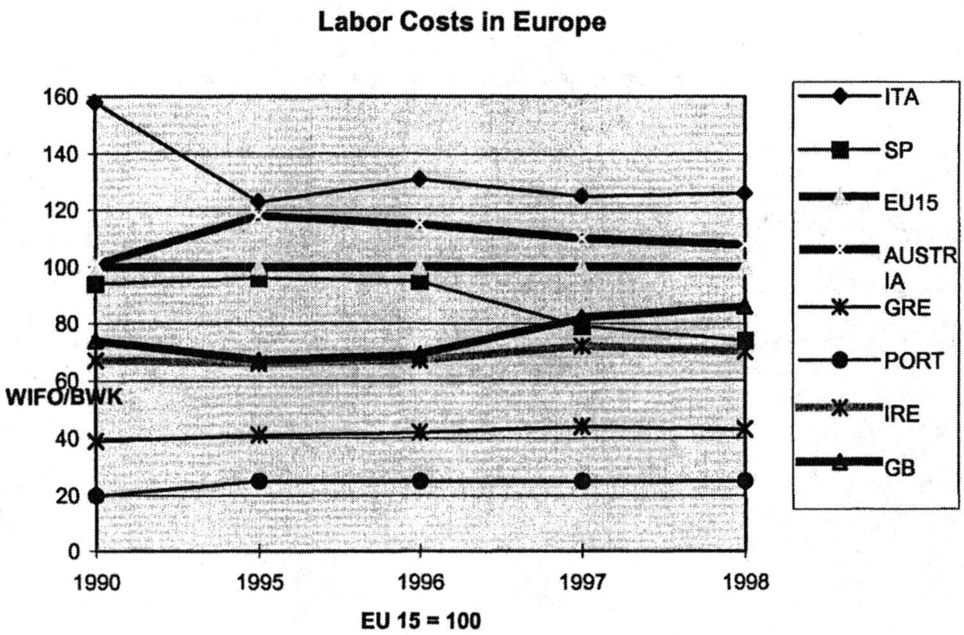

Source: Our own compilations from Federal Chamber of Economics, Vienna

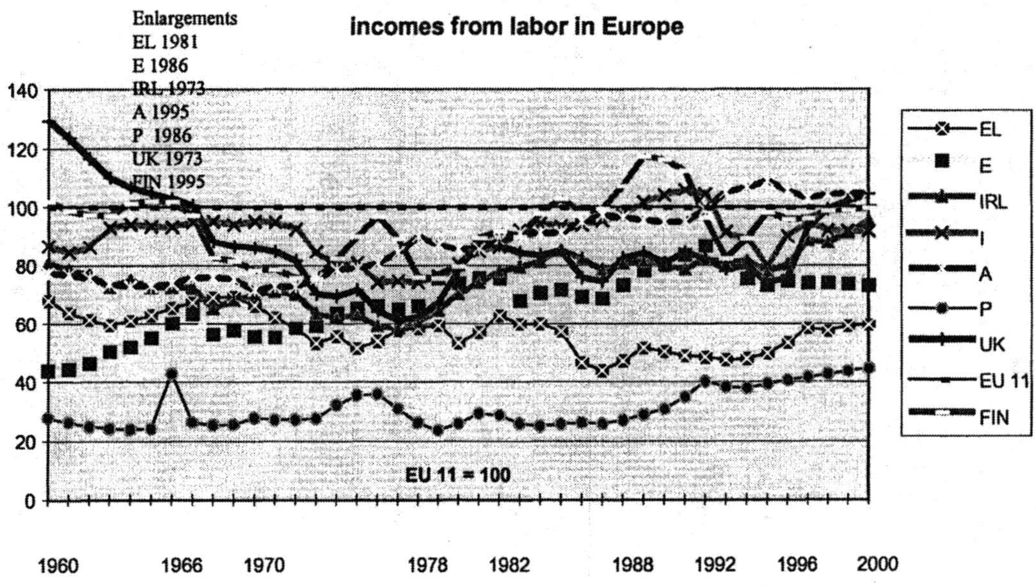

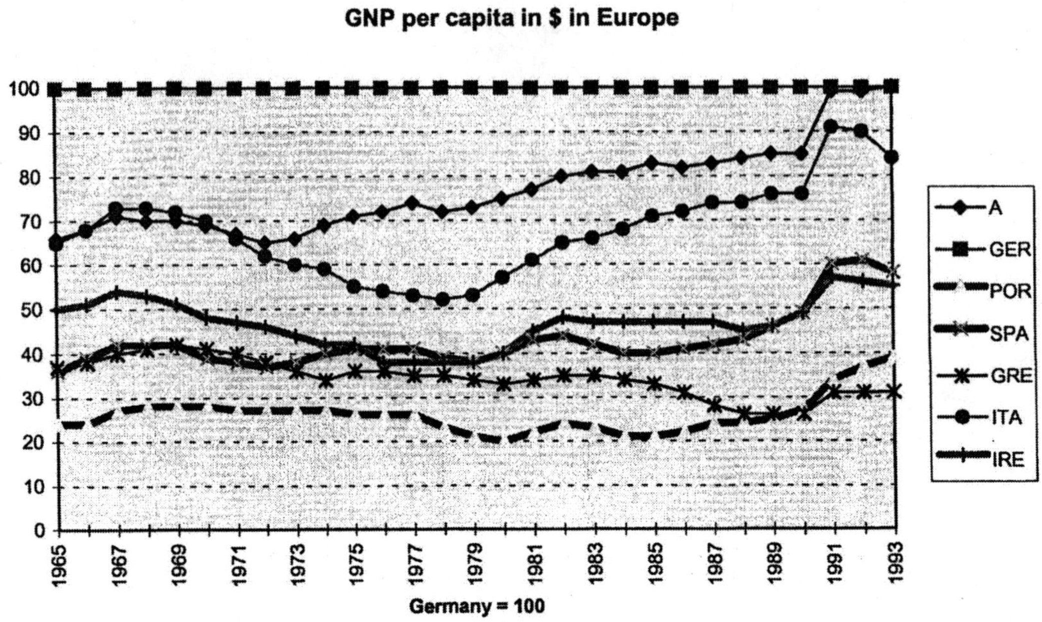

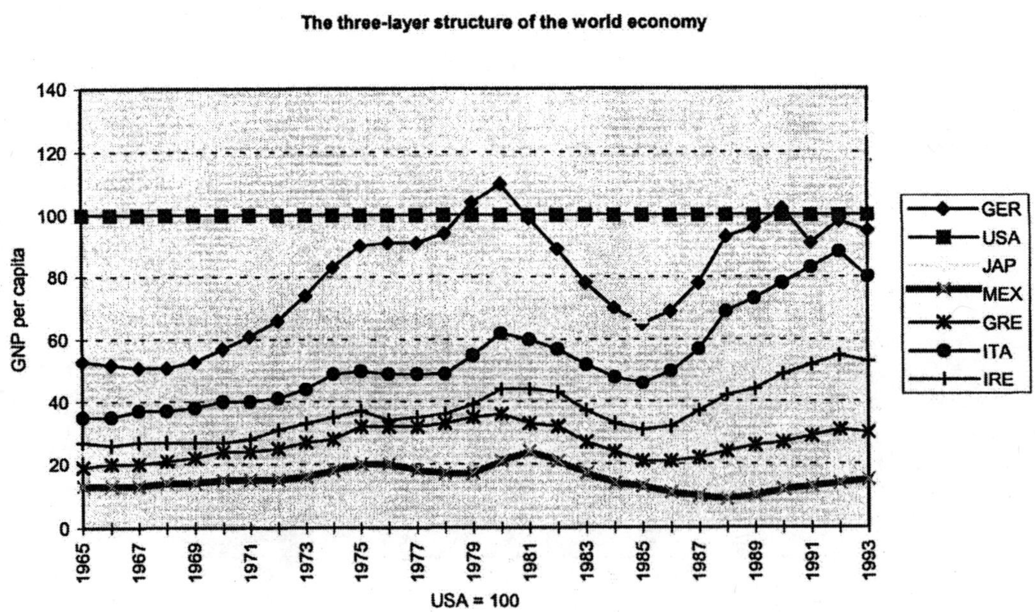

Source: Our own calculations from http://www.ciesin.org/prod/charlotte

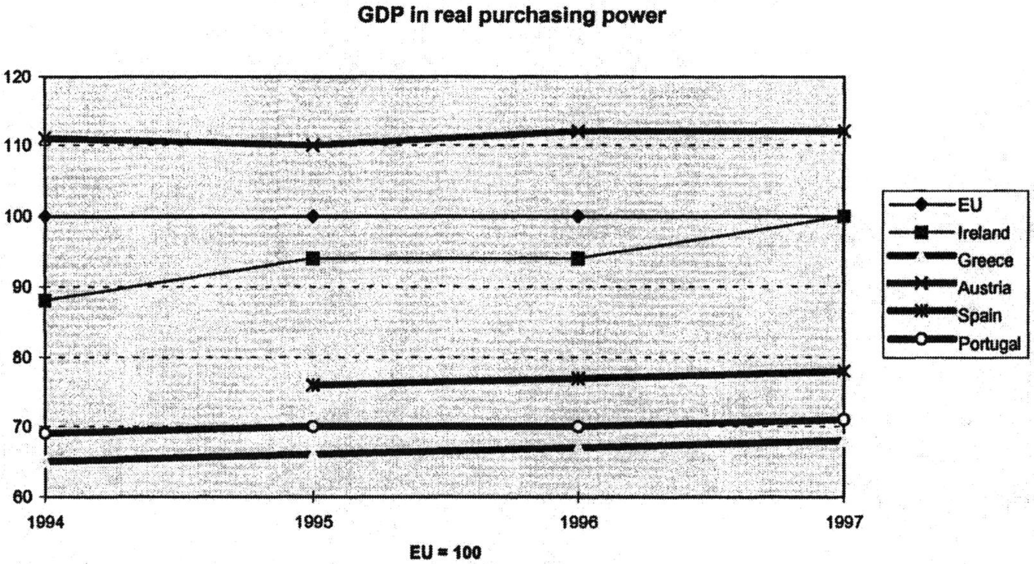

Graph 12.4.d: Regional Convergence

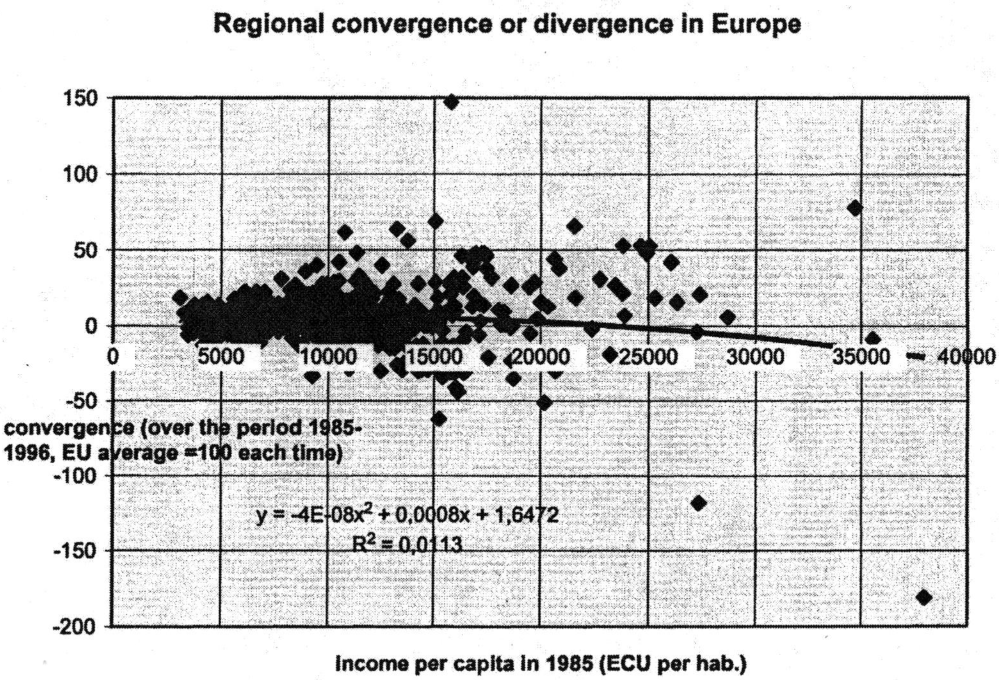

Legend: our own calculations from WIFO/EU data bank, per capita incomes in ECU per year. Regions with a high or low extent of poverty in 1985 were growing rapidly or slowly, irrespective of their original income level in 1985. In order to be convergent, regions in Europe would have to present a strong negative relationship between income level in 1985 and relative income growth

The synopsis of these data is:

	GDP PPP (OECD)	nominal compensation of workers and employees (EC DG II)	labor costs in industry (German Federal Office of Statistics)	hourly wages in manufacturing (US Dep of Labor)
EU	**100**	**100**	**100**	**100**
Ireland	100,4	95,5	70	67
Greece	67,7	59,6	43	44
Spain	77,8	73,2	74	60
Portugal	70,9	44,4	25	26

Also the European regions experienced no convergence over the last decades, without any major migration flows between the European regions.

The phobia about migration, leading to unemployment, is simply without justification. Our data analysis shows, that the contrary is the case:

Graph 12.4.e: Immigration and Unemployment

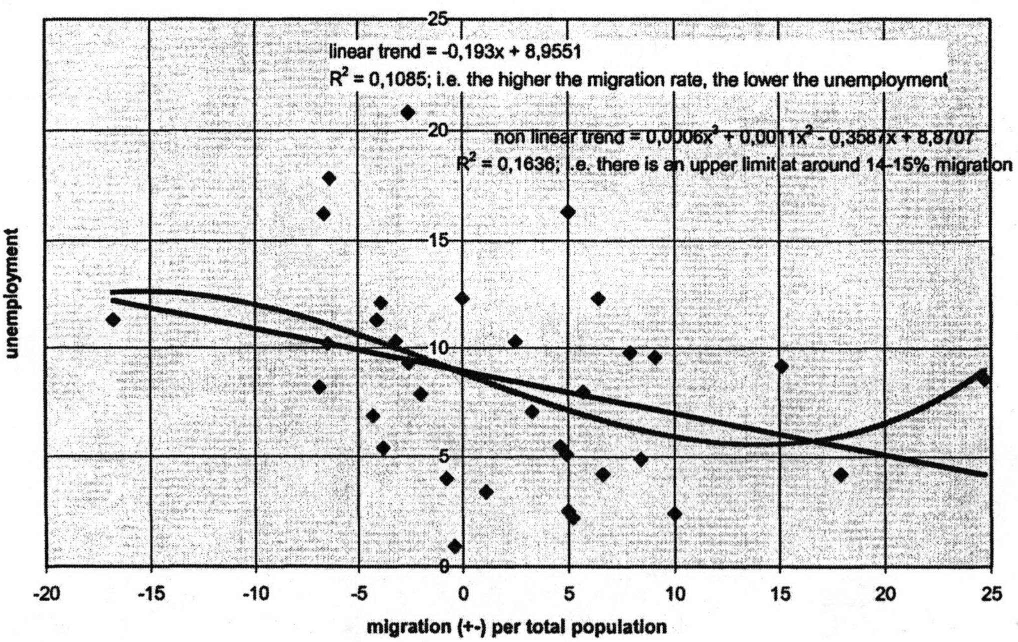

Source: Our own compilation from the above Tables, as well as P. Stalker (1994)

Also in a historical perspective, there is no ground for the hypothesis, that migration depresses the relative position of the centers in the world economy, as the following data show:

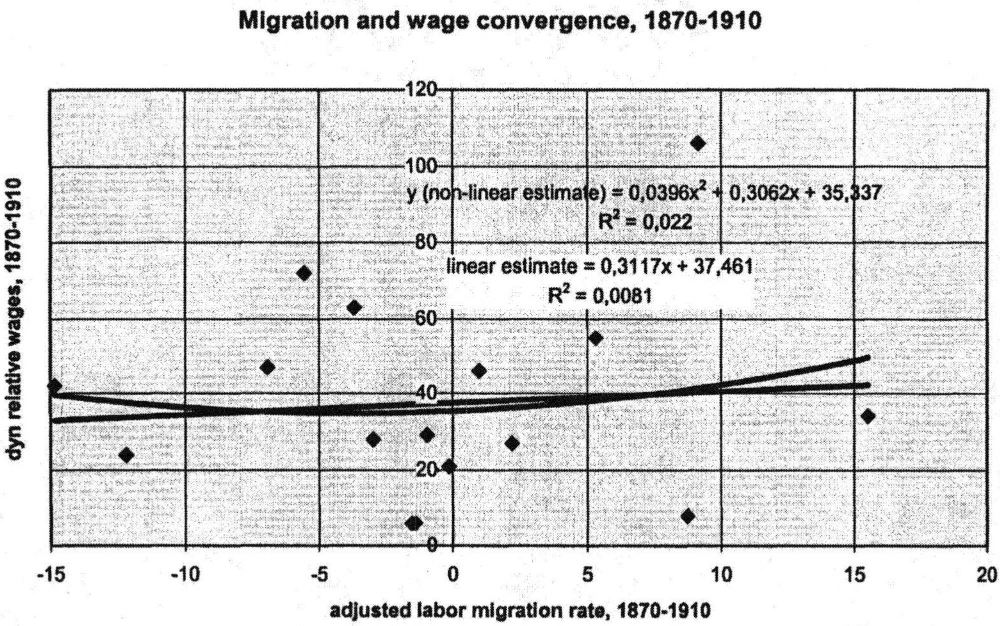

Legend: Our own compilations from Aghion and Williamson, 1998, see also Appendix

MIGRATION POLICY THRESHOLDS AND FOREIGN AID

In the following, we will deal with the issues of Polish migration as a case study for the effects of migration on a periphery country. Together with Italy and Greece, Poland was one of the main sources of international migration from Europe over centuries. Between 1950 and 1990, more than 1.1 million Poles were registered officially as emigrants (UN ECE, 1999). In Graph 12.5 we show the trade-off between the Human Development Index and migration propensity in 49 Polish voivodships (provinces). For many reasons, Poland can be regarded here as the key to the understanding of the problems of the entire region of East Central Europe. For one, Poland's population size of 38.7 million inhabitants accounts for a large part of the entire region. In addition, Poland's case can be regarded as the most well-documented case of the region.

By neglecting the poor and backward regions, Polish and East European post-1989 elites did not really address the issues, leading towards mass migration. A recent UN study on Polish migration says:

> 'Assuming no significant or dramatic departure from the present course of political and economic reforms in Poland, three important trends in international migration might be predicted for the near future: 1) continuing strong pressure to emigrate to overseas countries, 2) rising numbers of workers seeking short-term employment in Germany and other countries of Western Europe, and 3) increasing pressure to immigrate to Poland from the states of the former USSR' (UN ECE, 1998)

Graph 12.5: The Trade-Off Between Migration and Human Development in 49 Polish Voivodships

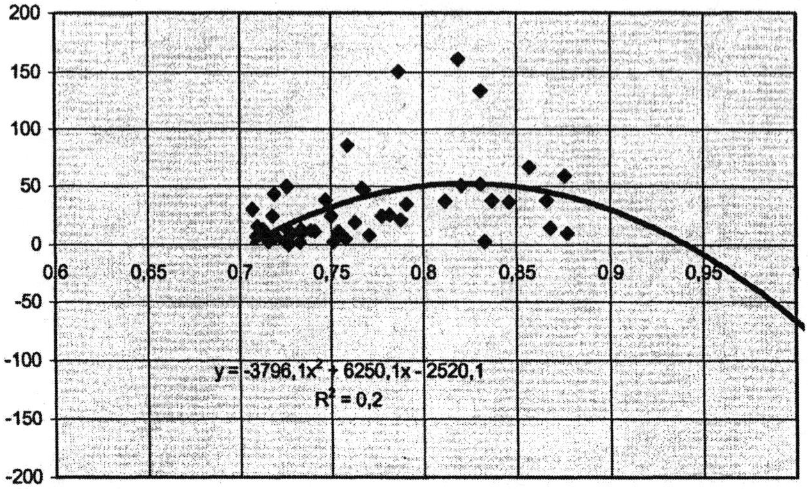

Legend: Polish voivodship migration propensity (y-axis) is being explained by the human development index of a voivodship (x-axis). Migration propensity of a province is measured by the migration balance of a province * 100 divided by the number of inhabitants of the province (thousands). Migration balance data: Polish Central Statistical Office; Human Development Index: UNDP Poland (1996). As a note of caution, it should be emphasized, though, that in 1996, only Warsaw surpassed the 0.9 threshold (UNDP, HDR Poland, 1998 figures).

But with a further rise of the Polish Human Development Index, dependent upon a thorough human development policy, migration propensity would decrease, and the country would become a net importer of labor. But as it is to be seen from the above graph, a number of regions (indeed the majority) will be first faced by a rising tendency towards outward migration. In other words: successful regional development will be the key to shortening the EU migration transition phases for Poland.

The application of GDP or GDP PPP data alone could be very misleading in determining *'migration policy thresholds'*, viz. the negotiations between the (East) Central European accession countries and the European Union. **The Human Development Index by far better reflects the overall social situation of a country than the mere application of real purchasing power parity rate GDP data.** We look therefore at the historic trajectory of human development in the world's main sending countries:

Graph 12.6: Human Development in Migration Societies

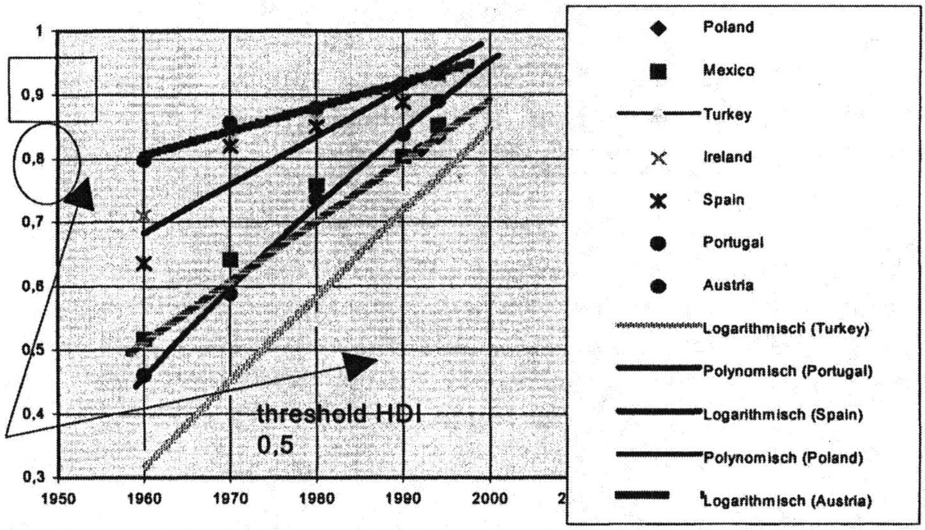

Legend: Data analysis and projections about the human development trajectory of migration societies in the world system since 1990. Y-axis: the Human Development Index. **Source:** Our own compilations from UNDP HDR, 1997 and IFRI, 1998. The number of people who emigrated from these countries were (millions of people)

Mexico	7.1
Bangladesh	5.0
Philippines	4.5
Afghanistan	4.2
Pakistan	2.9
Vietnam	2.2
Algeria	1.8
Egypt	1.5
Poland	1.4

Without doubt, migration propensity is highest at a human development level that corresponds to the value 0.6 to 0.5 of the HDI (Human Development Index); i.e. countries like the Ukraine, the Philippines, Indonesia, Mongolia, Albania, Armenia, China, Egypt, El Salvador, Morocco, Vietnam. Countries in the vicinity of HDI = 0.900 or more, like Portugal, Chile, Singapore, Italy, or Greece, cease to be the source of mass migration.

The three-layer structure corresponds also to careful interpretation of different migration 'waves': the migration of rural laborers, the migration of industrial workers, the migration of service-personnel, and the migration of intellectuals at all three levels.

It can be shown, that a large number of today's accession candidates already fulfill the conditions of the West European countries by 1980, while today's Croatia, Latvia, Lithuania, Moldova, Romania and Ukraine are at the level of Portugal 1980, Bulgaria,

Poland, and Turkey reach the level of Greek and Spanish human development in 1980, while Hungary and Slovakia are already at the level of Austria, Belgium, Finland, Ireland and Italy in 1980. Slovenia and the Czech Republic reach already a level of human development that is equal to that of Denmark, Germany, and the Netherlands in 1980. (**Source:** Our own compilations from UNDP Human Development Report, 1997. The contemporary human development differences in Europe range from France = 0.946 to Albania = 0.655. Thus, they are as large as those between, say, USA (0.942) and Peru (0.717)).

At any rate, it would be naive to assume that aid can be a substitute for structural policy to overcome the migration propensity of a society, which, in the end, is nothing but the reaction of a semi-periphery or a periphery to the ups and downs of three-layer structure of the international system in the Arrighian sense. In fact, aid recipients tend to be migratory labor exporters; and aid seems to be unable to reduce long-term migration propensity; on the contrary. The weak trade-off (R^2 = only 4.4%) between aid and migration propensity is the following:

Graph 12.7: Aid per Capita Received and Migration Propensity

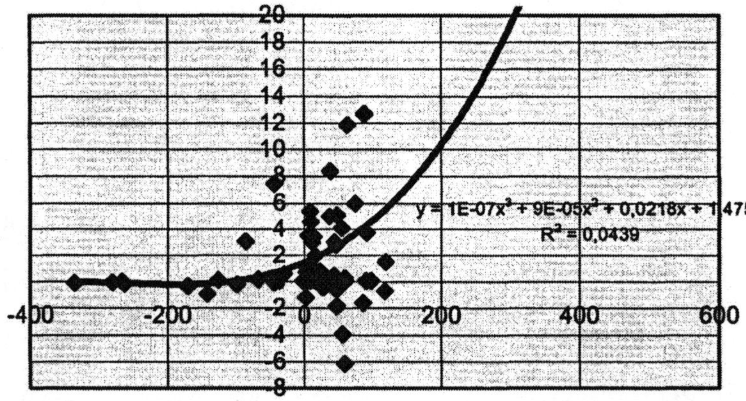

Legend: Aid per capita (x-axis) and balance of worker remittances per GDP (y-axis) in the countries of the world system. A negative figure for aid per capita means, that a country is a net donor country. **Source:** Our own compilations from UNDP HDR, various years. The graphical presentation excludes the out-layer Lesotho. Aid does not prevent migration.

The Thorny Issue of Transition Phases: A Polish Case Study

Both in demographic as well as in sociological terms, much of West European fears about Central East European migration tend to conceal the real, bigger issues of the future migration processes to Europe. An analysis of world population growth trends shows that **Africa, West Asia and Southeast-Asia** become the real future sending countries, while the demographic structure of East Central Europe more and more resembles the countries of Western Europe. Schengen, in a way, is likely to control these migration flows for some years. But after?

It is entirely possible, that outward migration pressure from Sub-Saharan Africa and West, Central and Southeast Asia in turn will have long-lasting effects on the countries of Eastern Europe, Turkey, and the Noerth African countries. For that reason, East Central Europe already by now should be integrated in a pan-European system of migration reception from third countries, that could be modeled for all practical purposes around the present-day Canadian immigration system. The East Central European accession countries must be early on brought into this system of selective immigration and border management.

However, the above mentioned tendencies of positive human development in the region of East Central Europe must not be misunderstood as an argument against transition phases for European Union accession of these countries. On the contrary: our evidence shows, that **the long-term positive developments, mainly caused by a rise in the Human Development Index, are compounded by the short-and medium term fluctuations of the business cycle and the restructuring problem of heavy industry.**

Some further generalizations can be risked, at least tentatively, from the Polish case. Our evidence at least suggests, that the neo-liberal growth strategy and unequal exchange, prevalent in Poland and elsewhere in the region after 1989, created such pressures, that the tendency for outward **migration** shows **only a very slow linear downward trend.** Data series from the Polish Central Statistical Office also show, that mass dismissals in industry might be on the rise again, due to industrial restructuring:

Graph 12.8: Industrial Restructuring in Poland

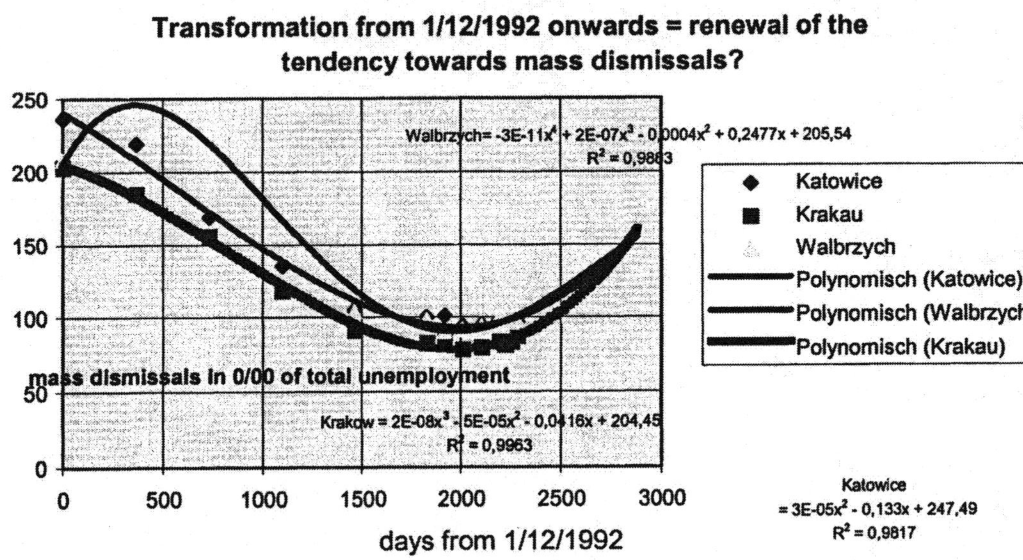

Source: Our own compilations from Polish Central Statistical Office, *Registered Unemployment in Poland*

Polish migration data seem to confirm the hypothesis, that migration is a cyclical as well as a structural phenomenon, as the data series from the Central Statistical Office data clearly show (IBnGR Gdansk, *Regionalne rynki pracy w procesie integracji Unia Europejska,* 16/1998)

Graph 12.9 Confirms the Cyclical Hypothesis:

Graph 12.9: Polish Migration Cycles

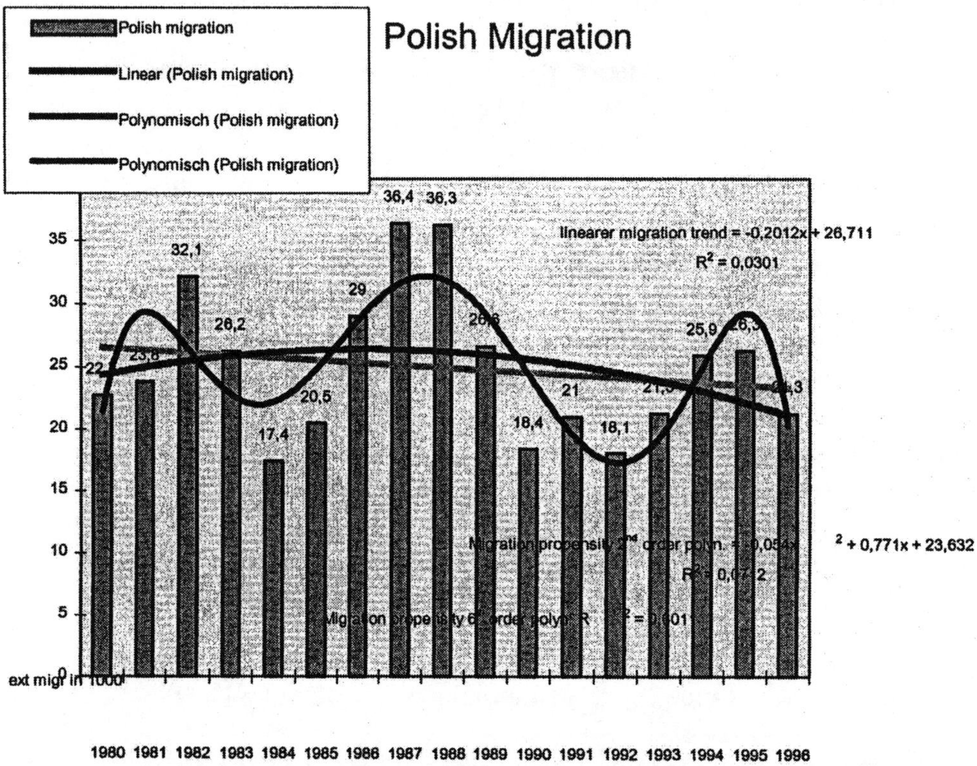

Source: Our own compilations from IBGR, above. *Id est:* Optimists must assume, that Polish migration has a downward trend, compared to the 1980s. One optimistic interpretation (implicit linear downward trend) has only 3% explanatory potential; another one - the most favorable possible interpretation - a 2nd order polynomial expression, yields only 7%, while a cyclical hypothesis, yields up to 60% in terms of $R^{\wedge 2}$

Graph 12.10 shows the cycles of the world economy and those of Polish migration:

Graph 12.10: Cycles of the World Economy and Cycles of Polish Migration

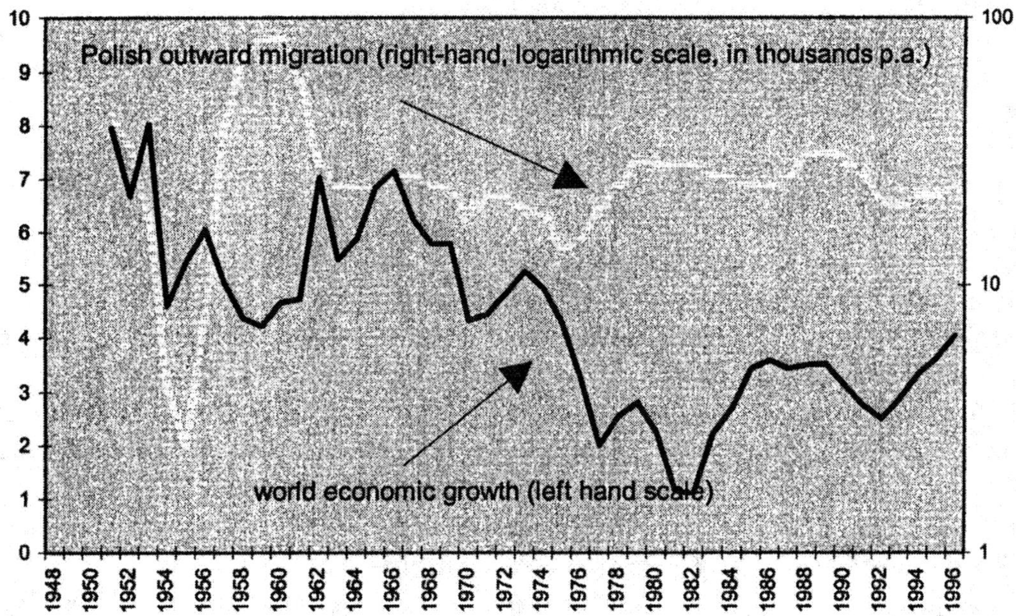

Legend: Our own compilations from IFRI (1998); Goldstein (1989) and UN ECE and UN Population Fund, 1998

Migration will fluctuate on and on in the course of development, until finally, the negative trends in the age-structure in Western Europe will provide the answer to the problem.

The Geography of Unequal Development in Poland, 1992 - 95 and the Issue of Regional Policy in an Enlarged European Union.

The theory of unequal exchange, presented in this study, can be also applied to understand the basic mechanisms of regional unequal development in a semi-periphery country. The *Human Development Report Poland,* 1998, published by the Warsaw UNDP office in late winter 1999, provides a wealth of information on the logic of regional development in Poland, bordering on mighty Germany and Russia and always being a periphery of the world capitalist system since the Long 16th Century. Unfortunately, social science data are calculated and published with a great time-lag, but the now available data again confirm the picture of regional inequality in the 1990s, already established above. A successful regional development, as we have shown, will be the cornerstone of any successful reduction of the tendency towards migration in the early 21st Century; and - even more important - it could bring a final turnaround for Poland to overcome its semi-peripheral status. What, then, is the brief empirical verdict that can be tentatively established on the basis of the recently made-available data?

Rapid development in Poland increased the per capita income of the different regions, but in a very unequal fashion. Although growth positively affected, say, both Zamosc and Warsaw, the real income increase for Warsaw was more than $2000 above the expected trend, while Zamosc and the other poor, mainly Eastern provinces were largely much slower in their income increases. In the short run, such a development might be viewed by some as positive; but development theory suggests that in the long run such instabilities are quite counter-productive. The relative differences between the richest and the poorest parts of Poland widened, contributing towards a feeling of 'exclusion' from the fruits of development. If there already was a *'Polska A'* and a *'Polska B'* in 1992, there was even more so such a division of the country in 1995 (and most probably, still further on in 2000).

Disturbing pictures emerge from such comparisons. Regional centers grow in power, but their hinterland stagnates. The axis Poznan - Wroclaw had a very remarkable growth, but Zielona Gora, on its western backdoor, was exceptionally slow in catching the benefits of growth. The same thing happens with Piotrkow Tribunalski, half way between Katowice/Opole/Czestochowa and Warsaw. And a similar picture emerges from Chelm, the hinterland of the growth center Lublin. Tourism (and perhaps also cross-border trade) explain the relative success of Suwalki, which managed to get away from its very poor position in 1992. Suwalki - with its Mazurian lakes will most probably make it - but Biala Podlaska, Chelm and Zamosc will become the new focus of stagnation in a changing Poland. Other regions, like Walbrzych and Jelenia Gora, will have to struggle hard to create a regional profile. The problem of the recently introduced regional reform is of course, that it still increases the power of mighty 'regional centers', thus creating a structure, where - in the end - Poland will have the following growth poles and stagnating *'hinterlands':*

Szczecin - *Western Pommerania*
Gdansk - *Central Pommerania and Warmia/Mazuria* (with the exception of the touristic 'enclaves')
Poznan/Wroclaw - *the outer western, southern and eastern ring of this growth pole*
Upper Silesia - Krakow - *the northern and eastern outer ring*
Lublin - *the eastern hinterland*
Warsaw - *the eastern and northern perimeter*

These developments can be highlighted by further statistical analyses of the development distances between the richest and the poorest provinces. While Warsaw, for example, was 2.37 times richer than the poorest region in 1992, the difference widened in just two years to 3.04, and will certainly have gone up further in the last 6 years.

Increases in life expectancy and decreases in infant mortality however, were concentrated in the *'catholic'* Southeast of the country, while in terms of life expectancy, the West and North, the main victim of the pauperization process in the Long 16th Century, did rather badly.

Assuming the continuation of the growth trends of the mid 1990s, there ***could*** be just 4 regions, which by the most probable date of entry into the European Union, January the

1st 2004, will not have reached the migration political 'safe' level of HDI = 0.900. **But this scenario depends on a great deal of good luck and a wise policy of human development in the Polish regions, and, above all, on the continuation of rapid economic growth.** The multivariate analysis of the UNDP Polish data again shows the relevance of the 'concentric' rings of development that have developed in post-transformation Poland. The typical characteristics of a region as a periphery, high external migration, and the legacy of post-feudal landholding before 1939, along with environmental strains, explain why regions were lagging behind in life expectancy increases, while the urbanized and capital-penetrated regions more than reaped away the benefits of social and health development in the country. Our equation explains 48.7% of life expectancy growth over time. Our determination of the growth privilege indicator (a region is above the predicted growth rates) shows again the concentric character of the 1992 - 1995 growth process, and in addition also - again - hints at the question of identity of a region in world society: paradoxically, perhaps, only at first sight, is thus the positive trade-off between religious practice and above than standard regional growth. Under the particular Polish circumstances, the functioning of a relatively well-defined civil society (in Poland a Catholic one) is an important precondition for economic growth, while the regions with only a traditionalist and decaying identification with the Catholic Church (as more often than not, in the East of the country), suffered the severest identity crises in the transformation process. And finally, the residuals from the non-linear function of the increase/decrease of the Human Development Index over time can be well explained by the

- concentric character of regional development in Poland
- by the long-term negative effects of foreign capital and mixed foreign capital penetration over time

Table 12.3: The Efficiency of Social and Health Policy (Above or Below average Life Expectancy Increase Over Time)

0,1347	0,1936	-0,027	-0,013	2E-07	-0,007	-0,034	0,0034	1E-06	0,0034	0,013	-3E-06	2,4388
0,1415	0,2784	0,0099	0,009	0,0002	0,0084	0,0135	0,0045	3E-06	0,0016	0,0079	5E-05	1,0733
0,4865												
2,8424	36											
real gdp pc	religious pra	**ext migr/pop**	**industr waste**	private land	peasants	**big estates**	fem exc inf m	ind. employm	**urbanisation**	**for cap pen**	mixed cap pen	
0,9523	0,6953	**-2,751**	**-1,458**	0,0009	-0,86	**-2,504**	0,7418	0,4958	**2,1478**	**1,6377**	-0,058	Constant

the **concentric character of regional development in Poland** (over time growth or decline of the development differential of the voivodship in comparison to Poland's poorest voivodship, 1992-95)

0,1328	0,202	0,0035	-1E-03	3E-05	-0,001	0,0039	0,0015	1E-06	0,0001	-0,006	-3E-05	-0,255
0,0846	0,1665	0,0059	0,0054	0,0001	0,005	0,0081	0,0027	2E-06	0,0009	0,0047	3E-05	0,6418
0,2608												
1,0583	36											
real gdp pc	***religious practice***	ext migr/pop	industrial waste	private land	peasants	big estates	fem exc inf m	ind. employm	urbanisation	for cap pen	mixed cap pen	
1,5691	1,213	0,5907	-0,18	0,2297	-0,209	0,4826	0,5673	0,684	0,1506	-1,165	-1,097	

the concentric character of the increase in the Human Development Index over time, 1992-1995

0,0188	0,0023	0,0005	0,0006	3E-06	6E-05	0,0003	0,0001	-2E-07	-7E-05	-8E-04	-5E-06	-0,04
0,0109	0,0214	0,0008	0,0007	2E-05	0,0006	0,001	0,0003	2E-07	0,0001	0,0006	4E-06	0,0826
0,2526	0,0225											
1,0138	36											
0,0062	0,0182											
real gdp pc	religious pra	ext migr/pop	industr waste	private land	peasants	big estates	fem exc inf m	ind. employm	urbanisation	for cap pen	***mixed cap pen***	constant
1,7314	0,1051	0,6727	0,8671	0,204	0,0935	0,2532	0,3736	-0,852	-0,577	-1,289	***-1,527***	

Legend: As in all EXCEL 5.0 outprints in this work, first row: unstandardized regression coefficients, second row: standard errors, last row: t-Test. The values immediately below the standard errors are R^2 (third row, left side entry), *F*, and degrees of freedom (fourth row).

Time will tell, whether or not Poland will be able to transform the more backward regions according the *'Terza Italia'* model (like in Tuscany and Venice), so aptly described by Michael Piore. **One of the keys to such a process will be the success of Poland's regional reform.**

Chapter 13

TOWARDS A SUSTAINABLE EU-ACCESSION POLICY. SOCIAL SECURITY, MASS DEMAND AND DEVELOPMENT

TOWARDS A SUSTAINABLE EU-ACCESSION POLICY: INTERNAL AND EXTERNAL CONDITIONS FOR A SUCCESSFUL ENLARGEMENT POLICY

What development strategy, then, is recommended to the transformation countries in this publication? After having stated, that migration is not the best strategy, what alternatives remain for the periphery and the semi-periphery? And why, in the end, the early extension of European Monetary Union to the East would be such a necessity? To be followed, say, in the second or third decade of the next Century, by global money and global government by a reformed United Nations?

Here again, the relevance of the theory of global Keynesianism becomes relevant. The 'external' package for such measures (see Part A of this study) would consist, amongst others, in reducing the debt burden of the periphery, issuing global credit for the periphery, and a global exchange rate reform. Improving the global income distribution, regional and global organizations, such as the United Nations, the implementation of social charters in existing regional organizations, the strengthening of national management and global collective bargaining, and controlling global financial capital all would contribute to a global Keynesian project. Most important, perhaps, would be a 'reformed World Bank' and global exchange rate reform. Only small shifts in the structure of unequal exchange already would have long-term beneficial effects on the periphery (see Part A, Chapter 5). Technological progress is only a necessary, not a sufficient cause of economic growth. Economic growth is also dependent on the growth of effective demand.

Generally, we at least partially share the optimism regarding the chances of European development, recently expressed by Wallerstein (1998). Already Coleman (1965) and Lipset (1994) started from the assumption of *'equality as the ethos of modernity'* (see also, So, 1990).

On the level of European social policy, it is the concentration on the reduction of poverty and on the formation of human capital, which, in the end, will yield the most long-lasting and thorough results, and that would transform the East Central European applicant countries into really successful new EU member countries. Such a success, however, would pre-suppose a true re-orientation towards European, and not 'Atlantic' social policy ideals, especially on the part of accession country decision-makers. East Central Europe has by far better social data than suggested by comparisons of incomes, wages, or even purchasing power parity rates, and thus would benefit from a quick accession to the European Union:

Graph 13.1: GNP Per Capita in Europe

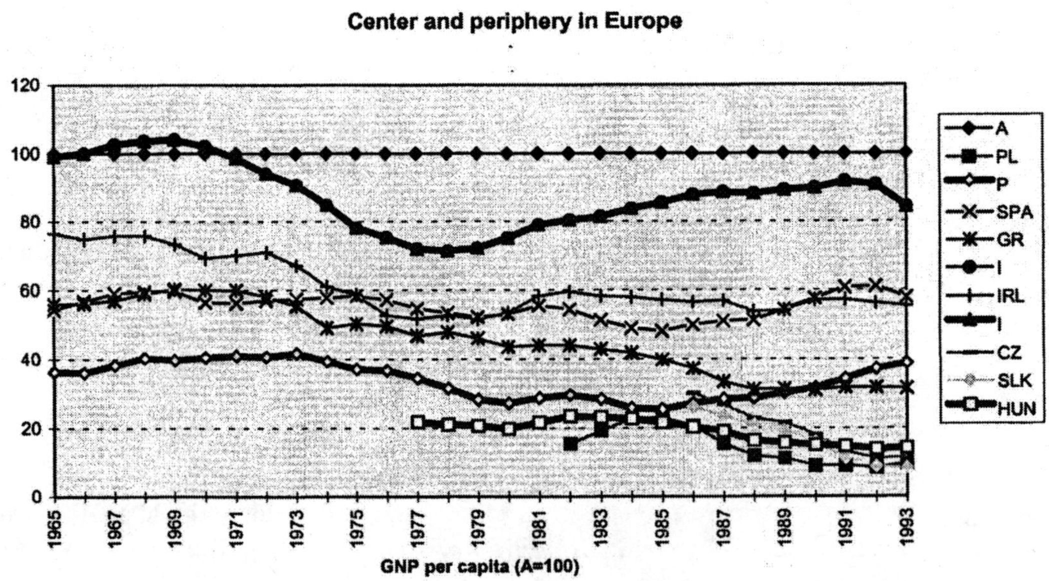

Source: *World Bank Social Indicators of Development,* our own compilations from the original tables

Table 13.1: Poverty Indicators for Industrial Countries

	UNDP HPI 2	death age 60	functional illiteracy	long-term unemployment	EU/OECD poverty line	UNDP 14.40$	Real GDP poorest 20%	maternal mortality	infant mortality	UNDP HDI	
CND	12	9	16,6	1,3	11,7	6	5971	6	6	0,96	CND
F	11,8	11	16,8	4,9	7,5	12	5359	15	5	0,946	F
N	11,3	9	16,8	1,3	6,6	3	6315	6	5	0,943	N
USA	16,5	13	20,7	0,5	19,1	14	5800		5	0,943	USA
Ice		8						11	4	0,942	Ice
SF	11,8	11	16,8	6,1	6,2	4	5141	12	8	0,942	SF
NL	8,2	9	10,5	3,2	6,7	14	7109	12	5	0,941	NL
JAP	12	8	16,8	0,6	11,8	4	8987	18	4	0,94	JAP
NZ	12,6	10	18,4	1,3	9,2		4264	25	7	0,939	NZ
SW	6,8	8	7,5	1,5	6,7	5	7160	7	4	0,936	SW
SP	13,1	10	16,8	13	10,4	21	5669	7	5	0,935	SP
BE	12,4	10	18,4	6,2	5,5	12	7718	10	6	0,933	BE
AUS		11		1,1	11			10	5	0,933	AUS
UK	15	9	21,8	3,8	13,5	13	3963	9	6	0,932	UK
AUSL	12,5	9	17	2,6	12,9	8	4077	9	6	0,932	AUSL
CH		9	18,9	1,1			5907	10	6	0,93	CH
IRE	15,2	9	22,6	7,6	11,1	37		6	5	0,93	IRE
DK	12	12	16,8	2	7,5	8	5454	9	6	0,928	DK
GER	10,5	11	14,4	4	5,9	12	6594	22	5	0,925	GER
GRE		9						10	8	0,924	GRE
ITA	11,6	9	16,8	7,6	6,5	2	6174	12	6	0,922	ITA
ISR		9					4539	7	8	0,913	ISR
LUX		11		0,7	5,4	4			7	0,9	LUX
POR		12		3,7				15	7	0,892	POR
PL		20	42,6		11,6	13	2186	19	12	0,851	PL

Sources: UNDP Human Development Report, 1998, BMAGS, Bericht über die soziale Lage 1996

Table 13.2a: Relative Poverty (Best Country = 100) in the OECD Countries

	UNDP HPI 2	death age 60	functional illiteracy	long-term unemployment	EU/OECD poverty line	UNDP 14.40$	low income poorest 20%	maternal mortality	infant mortality	low human development		overall index
CND	176	113	221	260	217	300	151	**100**	150	100	CND	1,79
F	174	138	224	980	139	600	168	250	125	101	F	2,9
N	166	113	224	260	122	150	142	**100**	125	102	N	1,5
USA	243	163	276	**100**	354	700	155		125	102	USA	2,46
Ice		**100**						183	**100**	102	Ice	1,21
SF	174	138	224	1220	115	200	175	200	200	102	SF	2,75
NL	121	113	140	640	124	700	126	200	125	102	NL	2,39
JAP	176	**100**	224	120	219	200	**100**	300	**100**	102	JAP	1,64
NZ	185	125	245	260	170		211	417	175	102	NZ	2,1
SW	**100**	**100**	**100**	300	124	250	126	117	**100**	103	SW	1,42
SP	***193***	***125***	***224***	***2600***	***193***	***1050***	***159***	***117***	***125***	***103***	***SP***	***4,89***
BE	***182***	***125***	***245***	***1240***	***102***	***600***	***116***	***167***	***150***	***103***	***BE***	***3,03***
AUS		138		220	204			167	125	103	AUS	1,6
UK	221	113	291	760	250	650	227	150	150	103	UK	2,92
AUSL	184	113	227	520	239	400	220	150	150	103	AUSL	2,31
CH		113	252	220			152	167	150	103	CH	1,65
IRE	***224***	***113***	***301***	***1520***	***206***	***1850***		***100***	***125***	***103***	***IRE***	***5,05***
DK	176	150	224	400	139	400	165	150	150	103	DK	2,06
GER	154	138	192	800	109	600	136	367	125	104	GER	2,73
GRE		113						167	200	104	GRE	1,46
ITA	171	113	224	1520	120	**100**	146	200	150	104	ITA	2,85
ISR		113					198	117	200	105	ISR	1,47
LUX		138		140	**100**	200			175	107	LUX	1,43

	UNDP HPI 2	death age 60	functional illiteracy	long-term unemployment	EU/OECD poverty line	UNDP 14.40$	low income poorest 20%	maternal mortality	infant mortality	low human development		overall index
POR		150		740				250	175	108	POR	2,85
PL		***250***	***568***		***215***	***650***	***411***	***317***	***300***	***113***	PL	3,53

Indicators:

UNDP HPI 2 = UNDP Human Poverty Index 2 (UNDP, 1998). Includes EU/OECD measure, functional illiteracy, long-term unemployment, and age 60 survival data

death age 60 = percent of people not surviving age 60.

long term unemployment = percentage of unemployed (>12 months) per total active population

EU/OECD poverty line = percentage of population with an income below 50% of the national average

UNDP 14.40 $ = percentage of population with an income below 14.40 $ PPP

real GDP poorest 20%

maternal mortality rate per 100000 life births

infant mortality rate per 100000 life births

UNDP HDI Index = *human development index*

Table 13.2b: An Index of Misery (Based on the Averages (A = 100) of all the 58 UNDP Social Development Indicators Existing for the Industrialized and Transformation Countries)

10 Sweden	96
3 Norway	99
13 Austria	100
18 Denmark	101
8 Japan	103
22 Israel	104
9 New Zealand	105
16 Switzerland	105
37 Slovenia	105
5 Iceland	107
1 Canada	108
19 Germany	108
15 Australia	115
26 Luxembourg	120
6 Finland	121
27 Malta	121
42 Slovakia	122
52 Poland	124
76 Croatia	124
20 Greece	126
12 Belgium	128
39 Czech Republic	134
77 Estonia	136
108 Georgia	136
67 Bulgaria	137
92 Latvia	138
33 Portugal	140
4 USA	143
47 Hungary	144
7 Netherlands	148
68 Belarus	148
79 Lithuania	150
21 Italy	151
2 France	158
105 Albania	158
14 United Kingdom	171
17 Ireland	176
99 Armenia	176
110 Azerbaijan	178

11 Spain	187
102 Ukraine	188
74 Romania	194
80 Macedonia, FYR	194
113 Moldova, Rep, of	196
109 Kyrgyzstan	205
104 Uzbekistan	208
72 Russian Federation	210
103 Turkmenistan	241
118 Tajikistan	260
93 Kazakhstan	261

Legend: Country ranking correspnds to the Human Development Index. Our misery index comprises the entries for: Human poverty profile and index; Women's access to education; Women's participation in economic and political life; Health profile; Education profile; Profile of people in work; Unemployment; Social stress and social change. The index thus comprises all available data on women, access to education, health, employment, social stress and social change, social cohesion from the UNDP statistics website *http://www.undp.org/hdro/indicators.html#industrial*

Our two combined measures, introduced above, fairly highly correlate with each other:

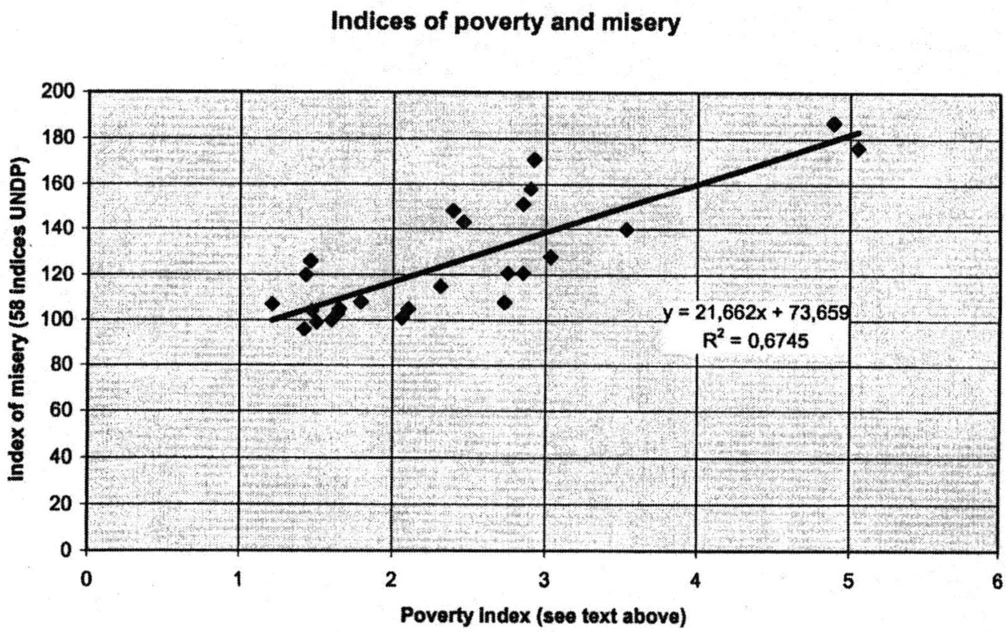

Legend: Our own compilation from the above mentioned research materials

The research materials, reported in Tausch, 1998, already strongly supported dependency theory on the basis of a 123 nation sample with fairly complete data. There were 19 variables and processes of development measured there. MNC penetration **significantly** and negatively affected 15 of the 19 dimensions reported, the rest - life expectancy increases, the greenhouse index, ethno-warfare, and the existence of war and political destabilization in a country, were still affected in a fashion, as predicted by the theory, but not significantly.

MNC penetration also increased significantly poverty, as measured by the UNDP 1996 CPM poverty measure. International system participation age - or early statehood - was an important control variable in the whole process of the explanation of post-1982 growth and development/stagnation. It significantly enhanced the increase of life expectancy over time, gender empowerment, and the educational and employment record of a given country (the strong points of long established nations), while it significantly failed to block the deforestation process, especially due to the divergence between professed ideals and dire realities in the long-established nations in Latin America and in Eastern Europe. Terms of trade had a significant effect in the expected direction on the process of maternal mortality, and life expectancy.

One of the basic tenets of social Keynesianism is, that social security expenditures are an important part of social expenditures, and that they enhance long-term economic growth. Table 13.3 and 13.4 now shows the Pearson-Bravais correlations of social security benefits expenditures with poverty indicators in the world's industrial nations and on a world level. Social (security) expenditures are of enormous importance in combating mass poverty, early death, and underdevelopment, thus supporting the general neo-Keynesian argument, proposed in this study:

Table 13.3: Poverty Indicators and Social Security - The Correlation Evidence on the Level of the Industrialized Countries

UNDP HPI2	-0,66
EU/OECD poverty	-0,61
illiteracy	-0,53
infant mortality	-0,39
early death	-0,17
maternal mortality	-0,15
UNDP 14.40$	-0,09
long-term unemployment	0,02
UNDP HDI	0,32
real GDP poorest	0,35

Table 13.4: The Correlation Evidence on the World Level

	income difference t20%/b20%	social security expenditures	education expenditures	health expenditures	top 20%	
capability poverty	-0,248	-0,6043	-0,1596	0,0029	-0,3399	capability poverty
growth 60-95	-0,1436	0,0319	-0,2195	-0,0965	-0,0255	growth 60-95
early death	0,2685	-0,6001	-0,3291	-0,3996	0,2829	early death
share of top 20%	0,8261	-0,5772	-0,1468	-0,33	1	share of top 20%
infant mortality	0,2583	-0,6528	-0,3522	-0,4355	0,3137	infant mortality
human development	-0,2117	0,6424	0,2928	0,4501	-0,2653	human development
income difference t20%/b20%	1	-0,4149	-0,0774	-0,1861	0,8261	income difference t20%/b20%
labor force participation rate	-0,2442	0,3899	-0,0258	0,1839	-0,31	labor force participation rate

Legend: Our data base is documented in the Appendix. The **income difference t20%/b20%** measure was designed by the UNDP (1996) and is an indicator for the absolute income difference between the richest 20% and the poorest 20%. **Social security:** social security benefits expenditures per GDP, 1993, UNDP 1996-98; **education expenditures:** public expenditure on education as % of GNP, 1992, UNDP 1996-98; **health expenditures:** as percentage of GDP, 1990, UNDP 1996-98, Fischer Weltalmanach and UN data on state sector expenditures per total GDP. **Capability poverty:** our estimates of the capability poverty measure, according to UNDP; **growth 1960-95**: real growth per capita and year in the long run (UNDP, 1998); **early death** (death at age 40, UNDP, 1998); **top 20%** - our measure of the share of the richest 20% in total incomes; **infant mortality** (UNDP, 1996 infant mortality rate); **human development** (UNDP 1996 Human Development Index); **labor force participation rate**: labor force participation ratio, UNDP, 1996

Some important effects, studied by the wealth of literature in the tradition of Bornschier and Chase-Dunn, up to Kentor's recent long-term study of world capitalism since 1940, are again shown to be valid in this research design, while other effects are relatively new and link up with the socio-liberal theory tradition, presented in Tausch and Prager, 1993. And in addition, as time progresses, the old-age crisis of especially the Eastern and Western European economies with its negative effects on growth is manifesting itself already. Thus, those visions of dependency research that stress the role of accumulation, population resources, and growth, will receive an enhanced importance in future research (Singer, 1971; So, 1990; Ross and Trachte, 1990; Tausch 1991b):

Scheme 13.1: The Long-Run Success of Development Strategies

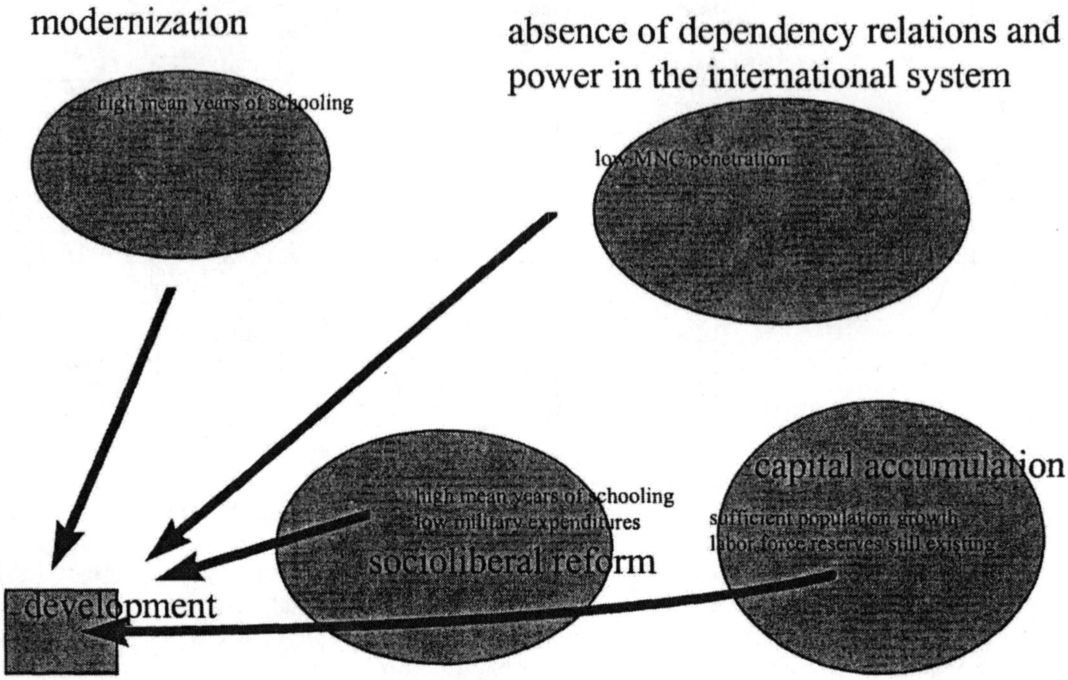

R^2 = 56.2%; real economic growth p.c.p.a. 1960-95

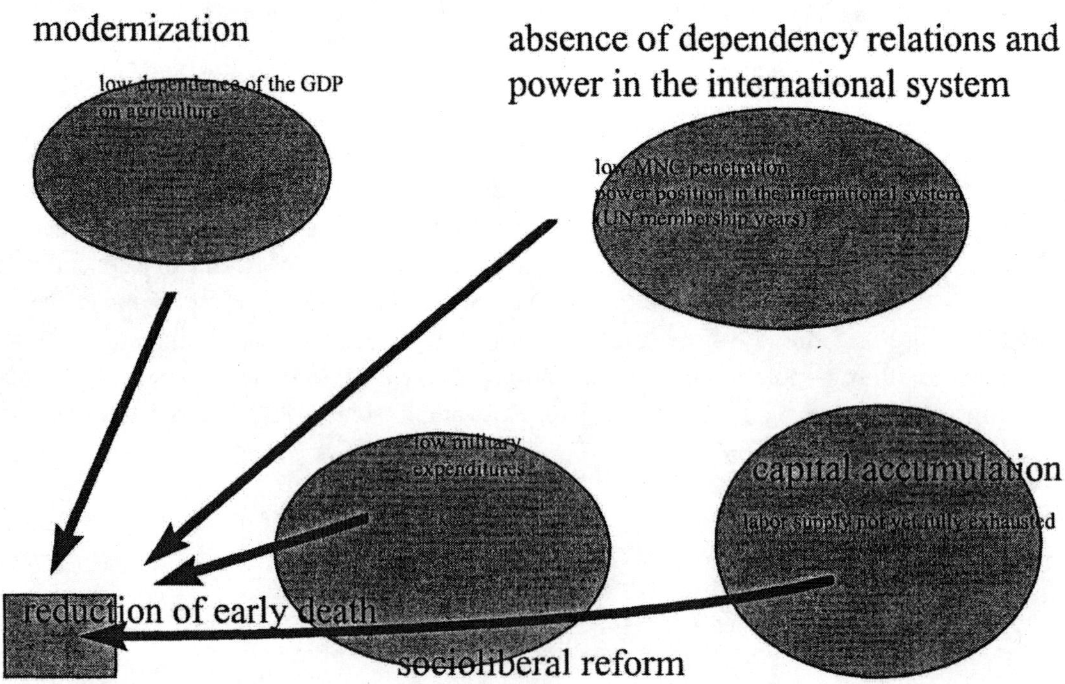

R^2 = 83.2% death at age 40 in % of total population

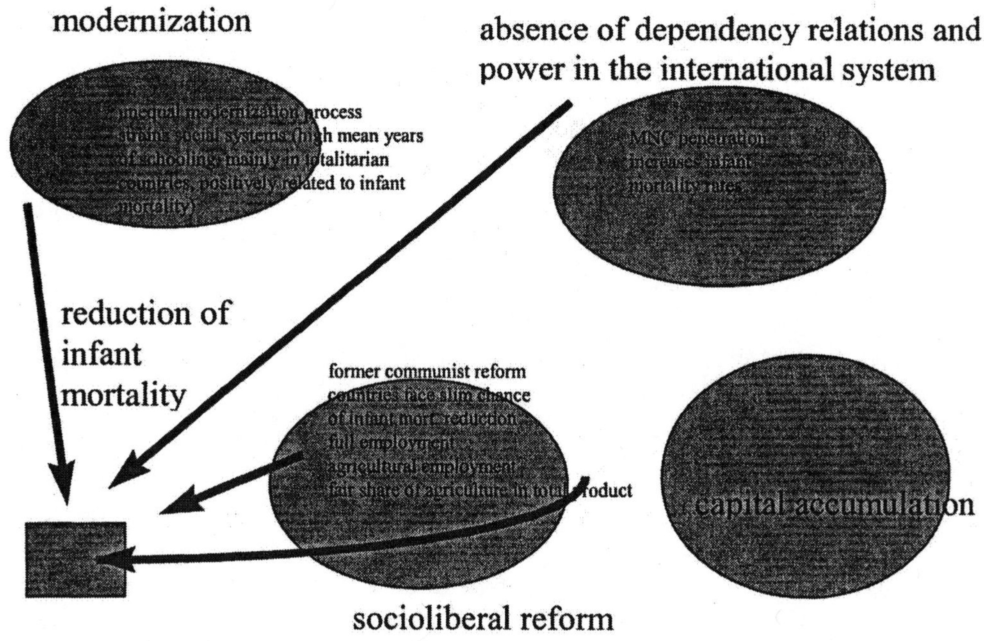

R^2 = 81.1% of infant mortality rates

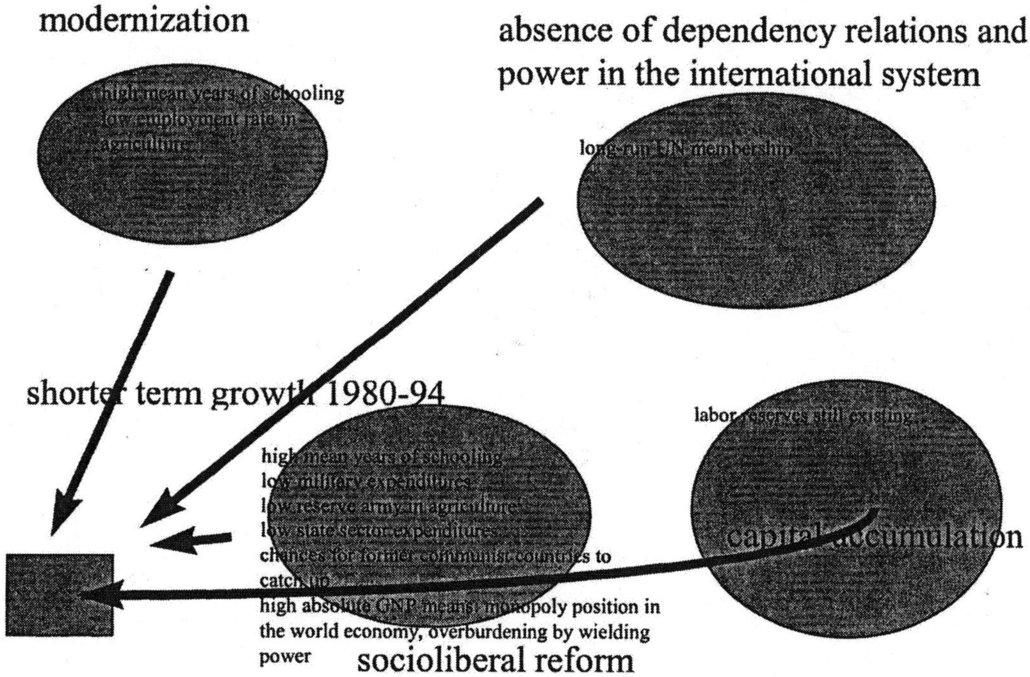

R^2 = 46.6% of real economic p.c.p.a. growth 1980-94

We have already shown on the basis of our multivariate analysis in Part B, Chapter 1 of this work, that - high FDIs per GDP (UNCTAD, 1997), hence, a high foreign capital penetration, are *ceteris paribus* significantly related to:

- the still existing prevalence of early death at age 40 (UNDP, 1998)

- the still existing existence of poverty, measured by the capability poverty measure of the UN (UNDP, 1996)
- the lack of a satisfactory human development performance, measured by the Human Development Index (UNDP, 1998)

This still does not preclude that foreign direct investments contribute to (unequal) growth. But it is the (sole or almost exclusive) reliance on them, that makes the difference, and that produces socially polarizing results. In the case of the industrialized countries, dependence on foreign capital and hence, a high FDI per GDP score, is today complicated by the effects of 'run-away' capital, so that the non-linear negative growth-effects are fairly clear (R^{2} = 53.9%). Countries with relatively low MNC penetration grow fast, because dependence does not bloc development. Center countries with a very high MNC penetration grow rapidly, because their MNCs earn enough profits in the periphery that fuel growth back home. Middle range penetrated center countries, however, grow slowly, because their MNC capital tends to flow abroad towards run-away-industries. By contrast, the trade-off between FDI penetration and growth in the periphery and semi-periphery is shaped like an inverted 'U'. The countries with a high coefficient of penetration grow slowly, because dependency blocs their development. And only the medium range penetrated countries still reap the benefits of the first dynamic years of MNC penetration, while the countries with a low penetration score are the 'marginal' countries of the majority of Africa, Asia, and Latin America. Also, the bivariate analysis of economic growth leads to important conclusions. To attempt the realization of socio-liberal human-capital-oriented development strategies is never wrong, even in the age of globalization:

Graph 13.2: Dependency's Consequences by Comparison: The Determinants of Economic Growth, 1960-95

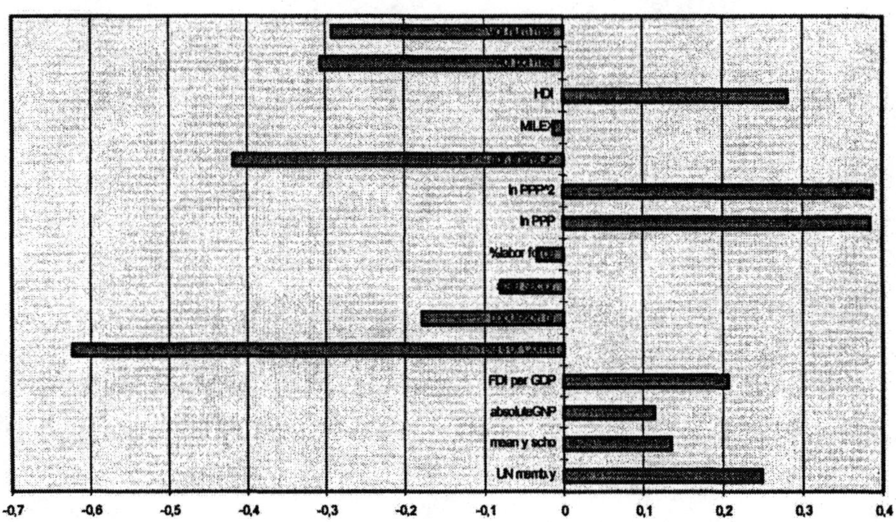

Graph 13.3: The Determinants of Income Concentration at the Level of the Top 20% of the Population

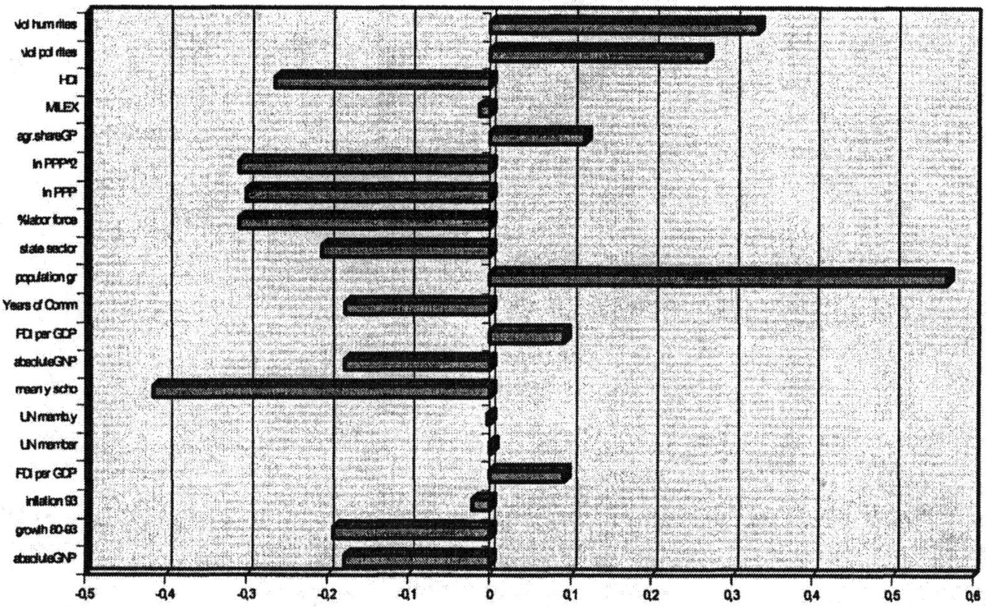

Graph 13.4: The Determinants of Poverty (CPM-Poverty)

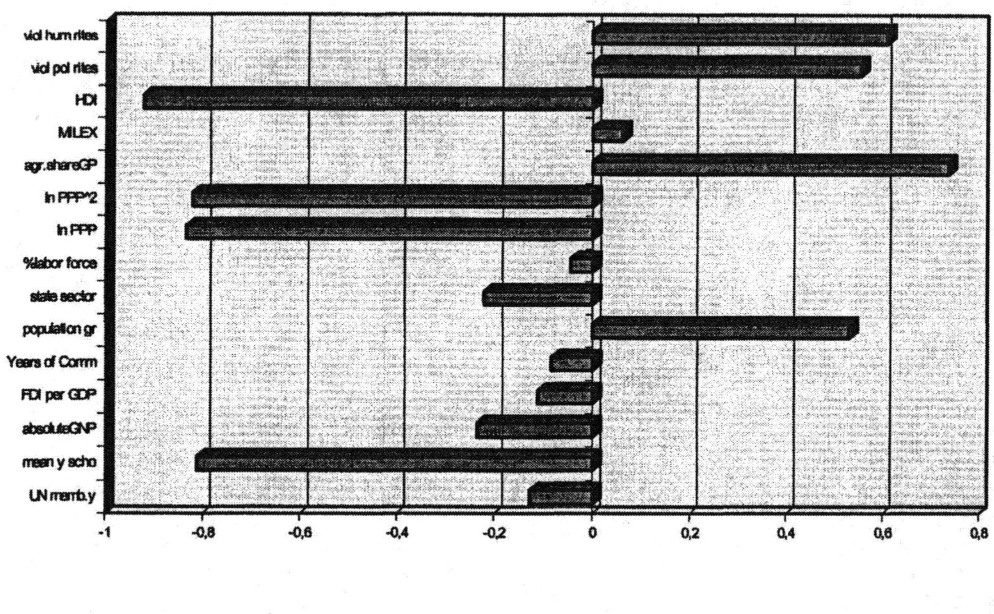

Graph 13.5: The Determinants of Human Development

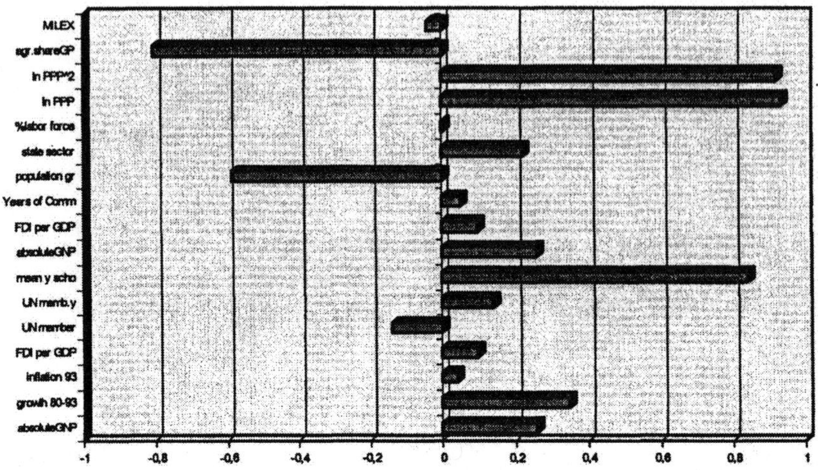

Thus it has been established that a human-capital, re-distribution, and human rights oriented approach will benefit economic growth, human development, and poverty reduction. Some important trade-offs between the variables above with inequality and growth are also shown in the non-linear functions below. State sector expenditures re-distribute incomes only up to a certain limit, as would be expected anyway by the socio-liberal development paradigm (Tausch and Prager, 1993). The 'Matlthusian' population trap seems to apply only to today's periphery and the transformation countries, but not to the countries of the Center. Income concentration and population growth are clearly linked to each other:

Graph 13.6: The Determinants of Inequality and Growth

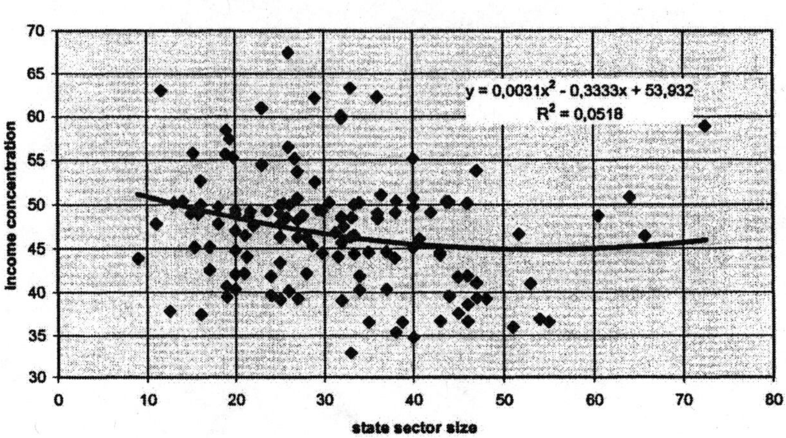

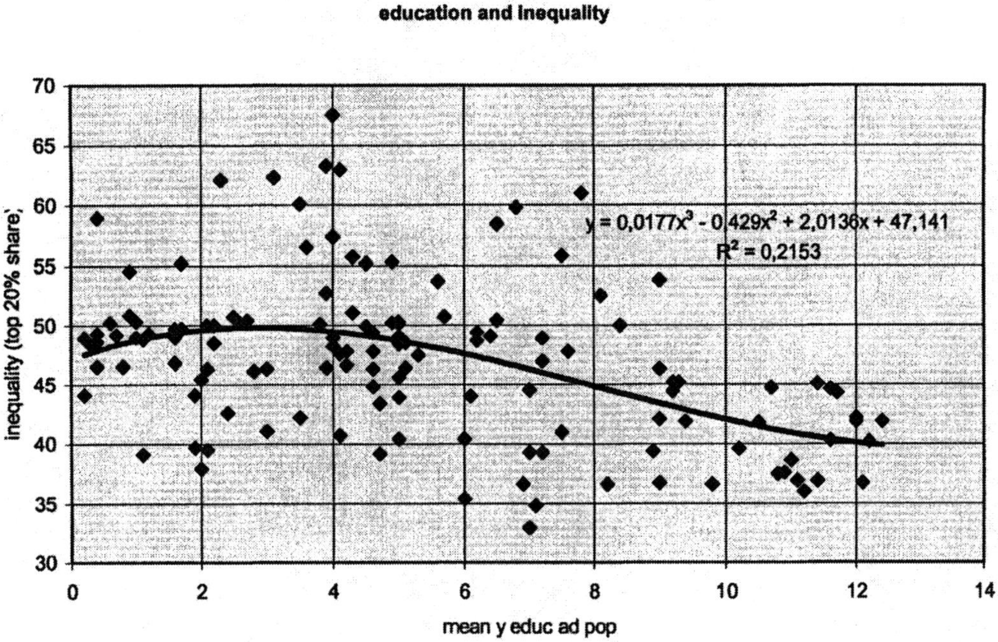
education and inequality
y = 0,0177x³ - 0,429x² + 2,0136x + 47,141
R² = 0,2153
inequality (top 20% share)
mean y educ ad pop
70
65
60
55
50
45
40
35
30
0
2
4
6
8
10
12
14

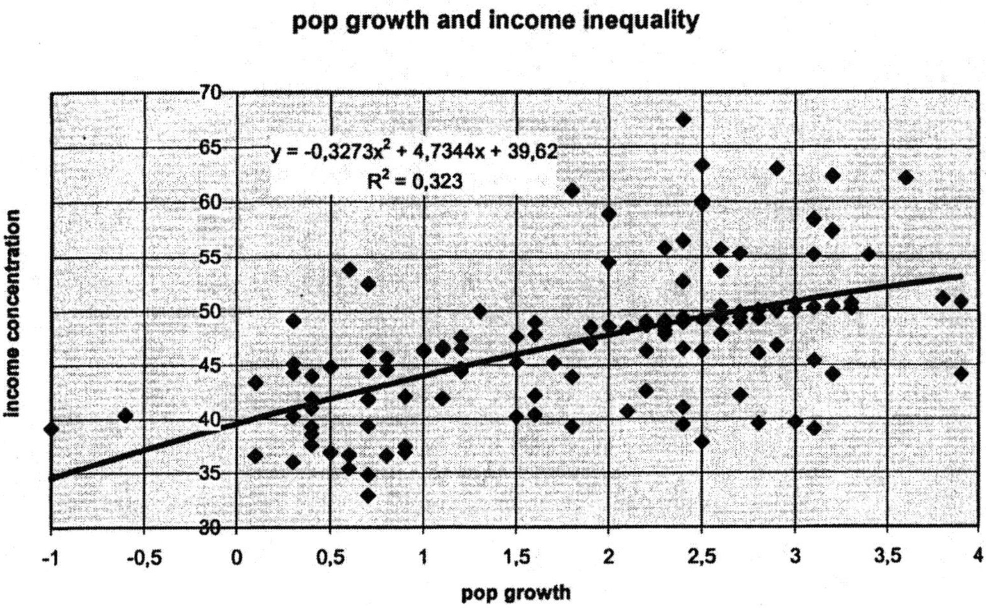
pop growth and income inequality
y = -0,3273x² + 4,7344x + 39,62
R² = 0,323
income concentration
pop growth
70
65
60
55
50
45
40
35
30
-1
-0,5
0
0,5
1
1,5
2
2,5
3
3,5
4

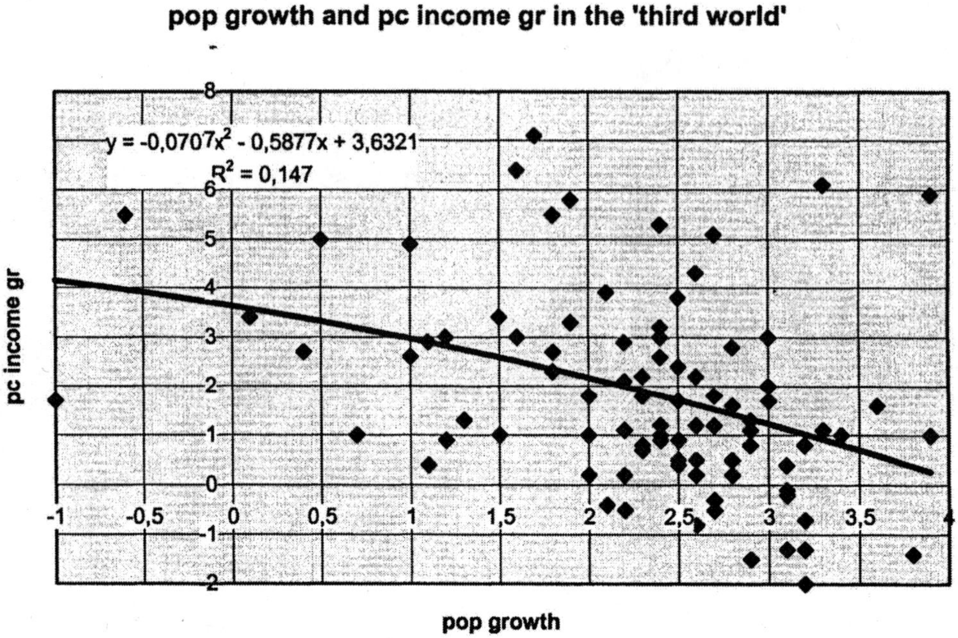

The data set, based on 134 countries

average population growth *(UNDP, 1996)*

economic growth 1960 - 95*, per capita and year (UNDP, 1998)*

share of top 20% *in total incomes (World Bank WDR 1996; UNDP 1996; Moaddel 1994; the few missing cases were substituted with the means from linear trendline estimates, based on the countries with complete data, using mean years of schooling and population growth as predictor variables)*

mean years of schooling*, population aged >25y*

state sector size *(gov. Expenditures per GDP; UNDP 1996; Weltalmanach, 1995, 1996; World Resources Institute)*

In the long run, public education expenditures re-distribute incomes towards the poorer sectors of the population. The peripheries' and semi-peripheries' - by international standards - still highly educated workforce would suggest, that there is a way out - the continuation of a path of human capital oriented growth. **Re-directing EU finances towards a more human-capital-oriented development strategy will become one of the prime tasks of future integration policy in Europe:**

Map 3.1: Mean Years of Education in the World System

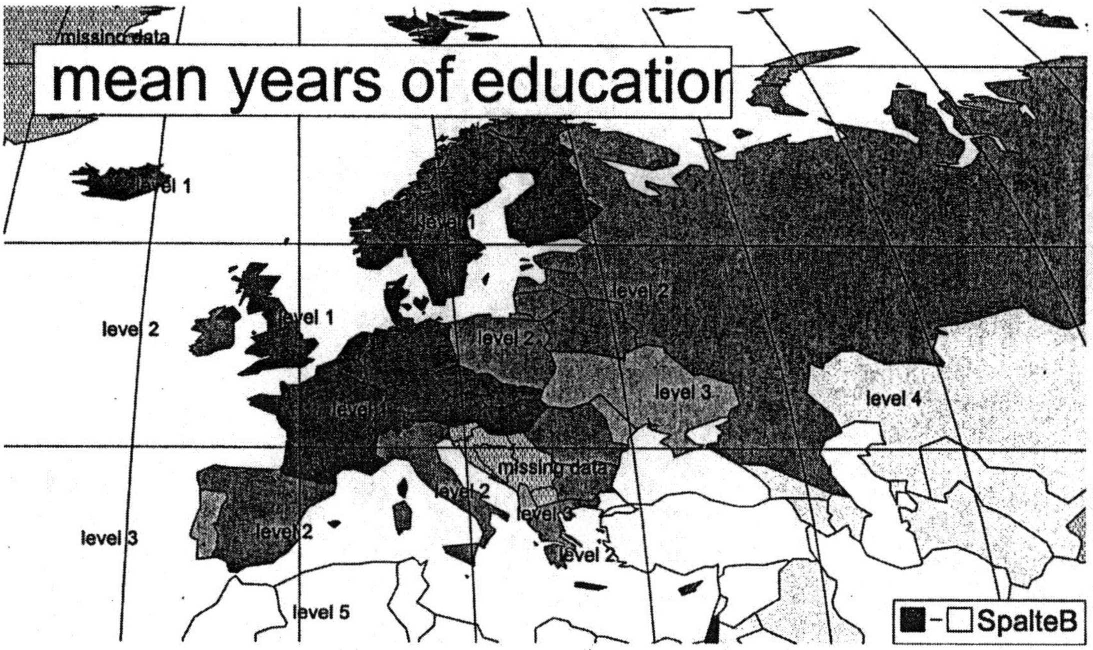

Legend: The EXCEL 5.0 program provides for a 5-level classification of the countries of the world, ranging from best level (darkest) to lowest level (lightest color). The political implications of our data are far-reaching indeed:

level 1: *center countries:* **EU members in Northern Europe**, NATO members in Northern Europe, USA, Australia, Japan, NZ, Israel, South Korea, Argentina
level 2: *semi-periphery 1:* **EU members Ireland, Spain, Italy, Greece**; EU candidates Poland, Cyprus, Baltic States, Bulgaria, Romania, in addition Russia, Belarus, Colombia, Chile, Uruguay, Panama, Cuba, Philippines
level 3: *semi-periphery 2:* **EU member Portugal**, in addition Moldova, Ukraine, Albania, Costa Rica, Jamaica, Colombia, Ecuador, Venezuela, Peru, Guyana, Malaysia, Brunei, North Korea
level 4: *periphery 1:* Transcaucasia, former Soviet Central Asia, Jordan, Lebanon, Iraq, Mexico, Honduras, Paraguay, Dominican Republic, China, Vietnam
level 5: *periphery 2:* EU candidate Turkey, Syria, North Africa, Iran, Brazil, Bolivia, Indonesia, Thailand, Myanmar, Kampuchea, Laos, Papua-NG

The picture is even more optimistic, when we compare East European human capital stocks with other European countries, leaving aside the nations on the Southern and Eastern rim of the Mediterranean:

Map 3.2: European Center and European Periphery

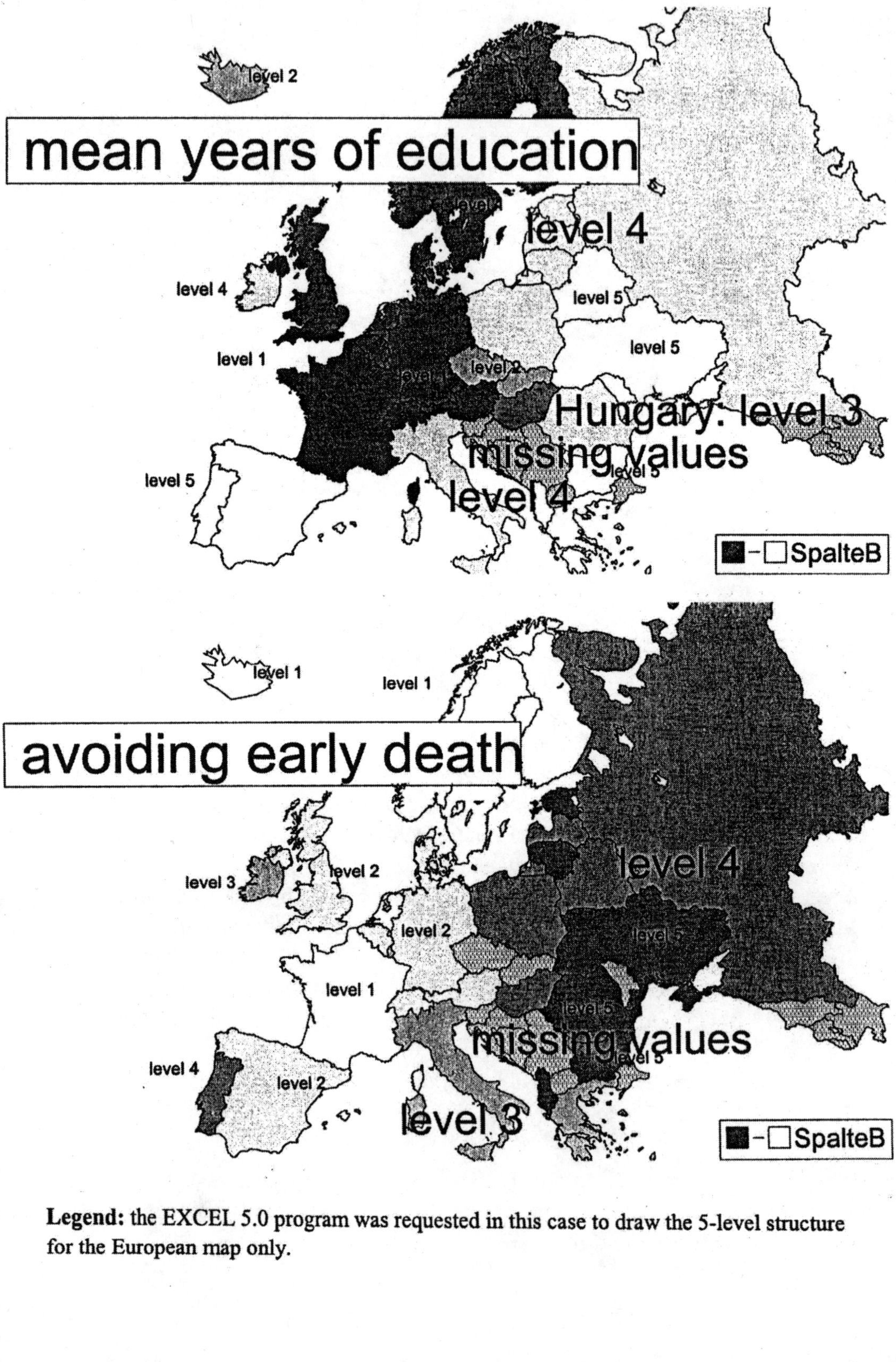

Legend: the EXCEL 5.0 program was requested in this case to draw the 5-level structure for the European map only.

Again, Poland's performance at least would warrant some longer-term optimism, as the following map shows. The real sinners against human capital formation in the EU are the UK, Belgium, Luxembourg, Germany, Italy, Spain, Portugal and Greece:

Map 3.3: Public Education Expenditure in Europe

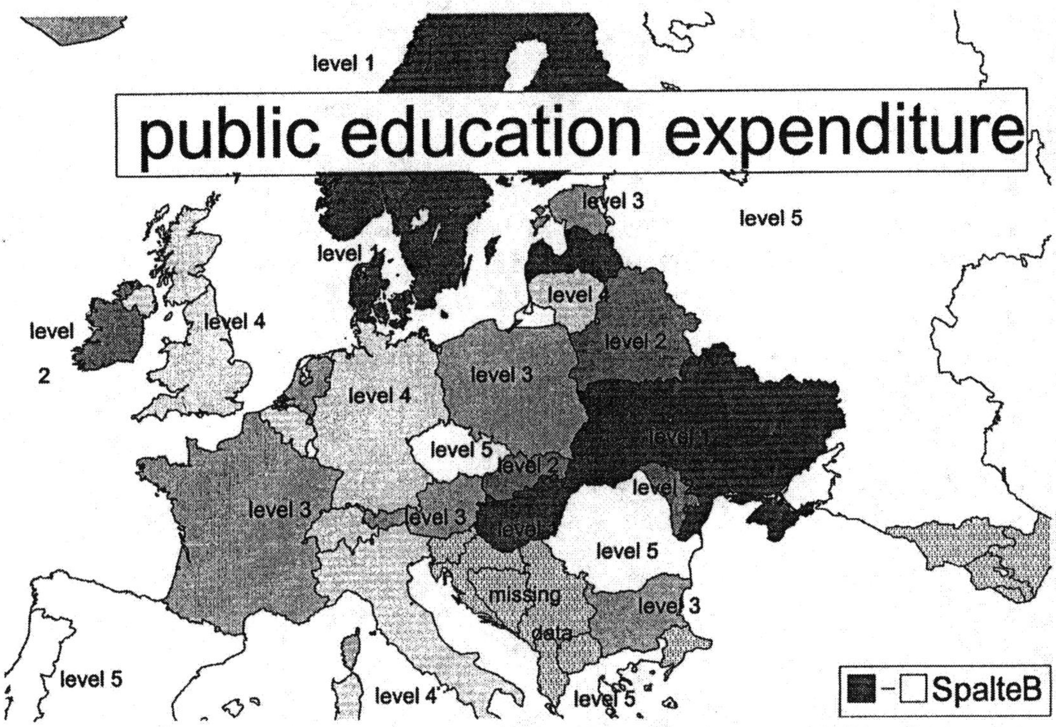

Legend: 5-layer classification of European education expenditures per GNP, EXCEL 5.0 with UNDP 1996 data.

Our analysis furthermore shows

- the close interrelationship between the UNDP capability poverty measure 1996, which combines lack of access to health personnel during birth, underweight children, female illiteracy, and real per capita income in purchasing power parity rates
- the UNDP Human Development Index 1998, which combines life expectancy, adult literacy, educational enrollment, and real per capita income in purchasing power parity rates
- the UNDP 1998 measure of early death at age 40 in % of total population
- mean years of schooling of the adult population (UNDP, 1994)
- and the respect for human and political rights as a precondition for successful development.

More traditional concerns of development theory, like FDI per GDP (dependency theory), state sector size (neo-liberal theory) and military expenditures (peace research) have no real direct and strong influences on the avoidance of early death. However,

- early nationhood has a positive influence on the development perspectives of a nation, while the newcomers and states with a long state socialist tradition after 1970 find it harder and harder to find their place in world society

The graph below also summarizes the properties of the three measures of poverty and development, used in Table 13.3 and Table 13.4, above:

Graph 13.7: Measures of Poverty and Measures of Development. The UNDP Human Development Report Measures and their Relationships to Some of the Main Variables of this Analysis

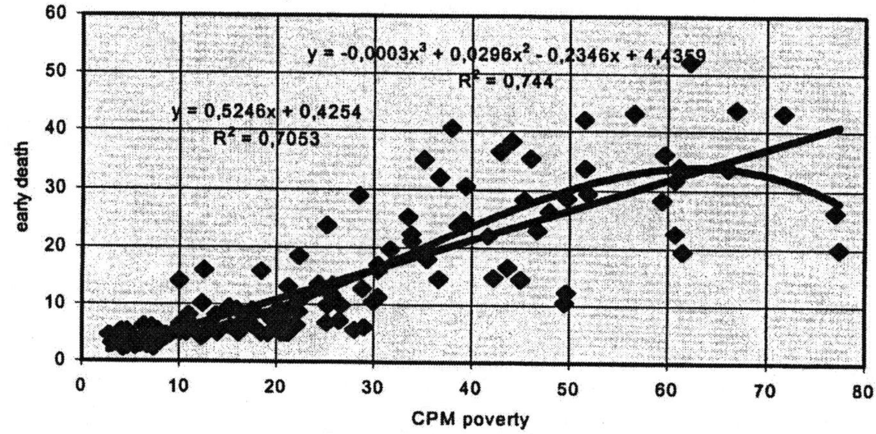

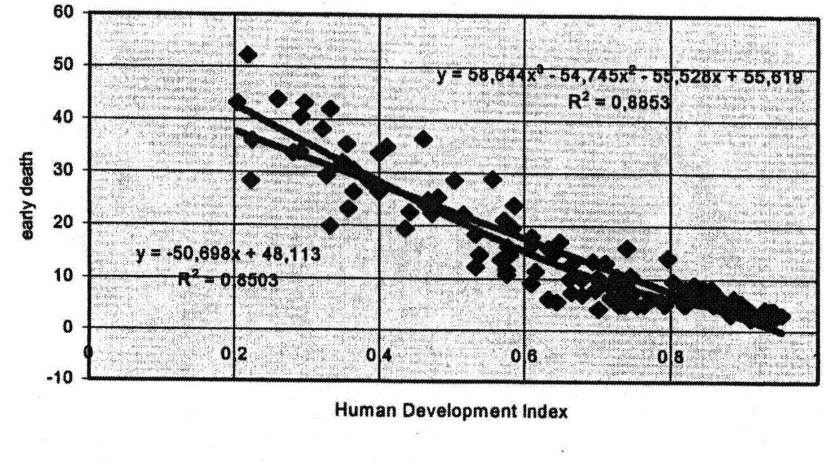

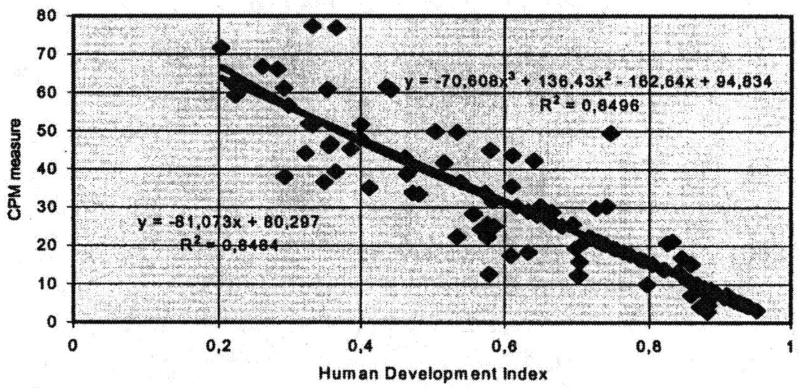
y = -70,808x³ + 136,43x² - 162,64x + 94,834
R² = 0,8496
y = -81,073x + 80,297
R² = 0,8484
CPM measure
Human Development Index

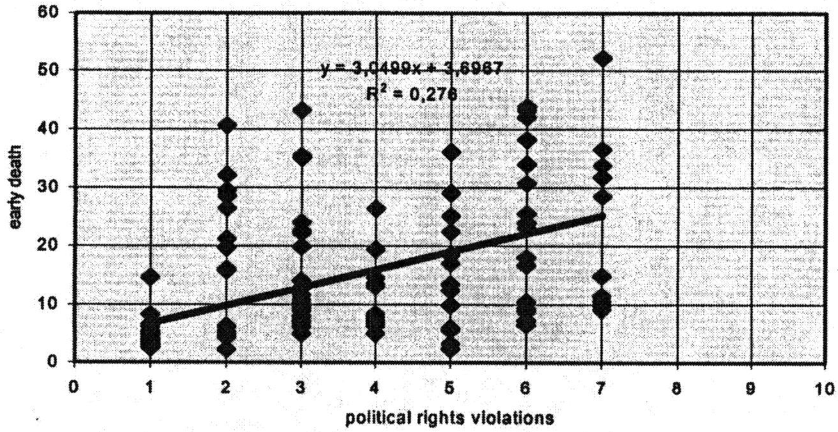
y = 3,0499x + 3,6967
R² = 0,276
early death
political rights violations

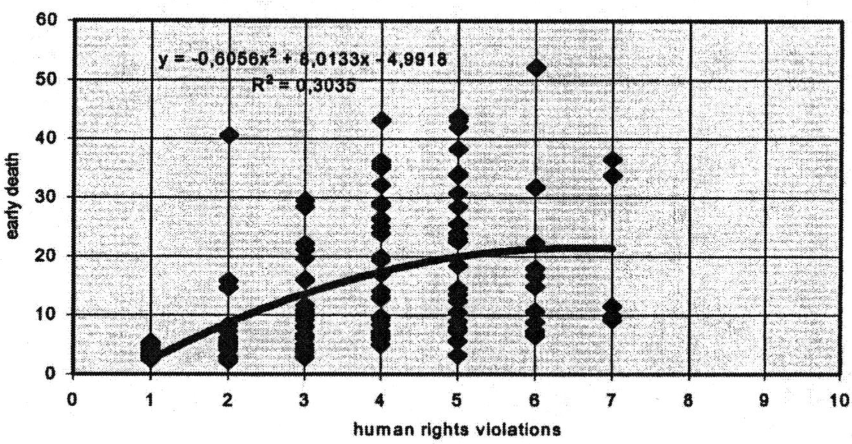
y = -0,6056x² + 8,0133x - 4,9918
R² = 0,3035
early death
human rights violations

Graph 13.8 now analyzes the trade-off between years of UN membership and economic growth. This trade-off is important, because it is central to the analysis of the recent increase in the number of nations and their growth chances in the capitalist world system. We have to distinguish the process of de-colonization (that itself greatly increased the number of member nations of the UN in the late 1940s, 1950s, 1960s, and early 1970s) from the process of decomposition of states. One might still argue, whether or not the break-away of the non-European republics of the former USSR can be classified under the first or the second heading, but certainly the disintegration of Pakistan into West Pakistan and Bangladesh in 1971 provided the turning point, to be followed by the ever faster shifting of international borders in the late 1980s and the 1990s. The serious and systematic analysis of the interrelationship between the number of states and the Kondratieff long economic cycles is as yet to be undertaken, but it can be argued that B - phases increase separatism, while A - phases increase national unity. The world capitalist system released a great number of states into independence - while their growth chances are the more miserable, the younger they are. Also, nations with a **very long history of communism** are practically marginalized in world society:

Graph 13.8: National Independence, Communist History and Economic Growth

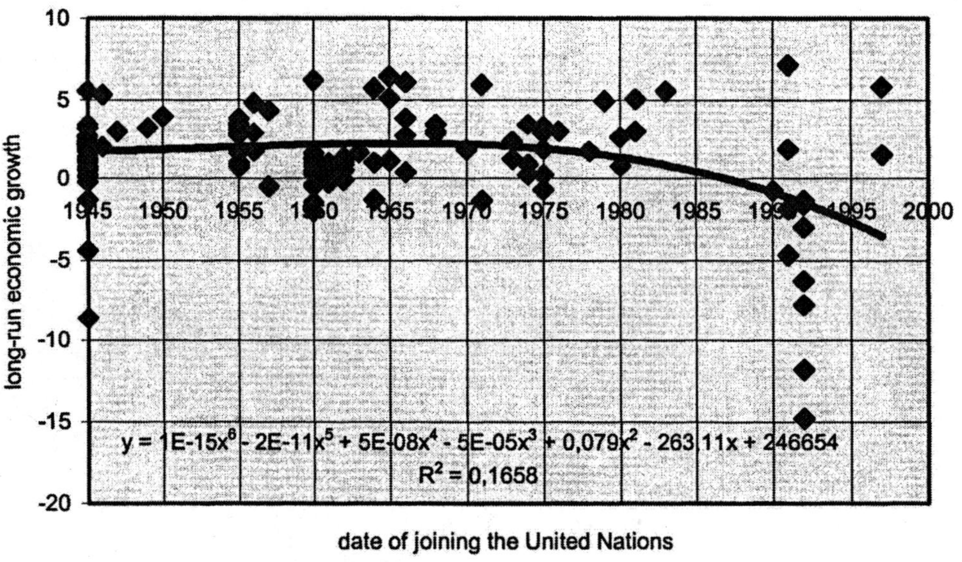

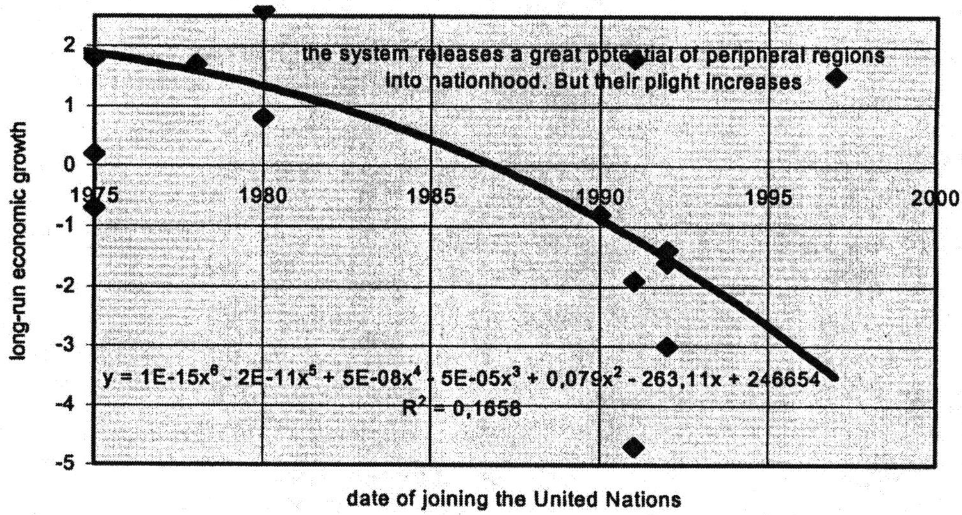

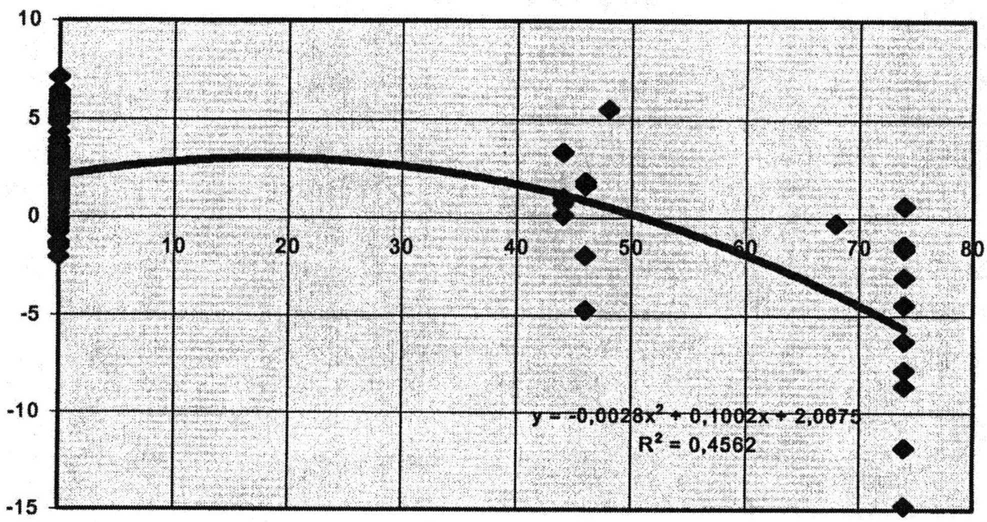

Legend for the last graph: Years of communism in power (x-axis) and economic growth (y-axis). Countries with a history of more than half a century of communism in power have the bleakest perspectives of economic growth

While in these nations a return to some kind of authoritarian models in between the drug cartels of Colombia, Getulio Vargas' or Juan Domingo Peron's *'populismo'* - or - for that matter - a slide into chaos and anarchy are real possibilities, we would like to share at least partially Wallerstein's qualified, recent optimism concerning **European development** in the capitalist world economy, perhaps against our own scholarly convictions. Is it just an empty hope, in view of all what we have said in our earlier publication (1998)? Asia learnt the bitter lessons of globalized capitalism in the turbulent months of 1997, 1998, and 1999; Russia and Latin America saw, how the system works in 1998, if not in the 500 years before that date, at the latest. In the long run, these regions will have had enough of the model, practiced in the 1990s. Perhaps more by good luck than by intention, the *Euro,* in the long run, will contribute to the fact that at last America realizes that it has current account balance deficit. Before long, the losers of globalization will realize, who at present disproportionately benefits from the system.

This is also true for the so-called *'new world information order'* (see especially, Gabriel Kolko, *Le Monde Diplomatique,* 15.5.1998; Philippe Queau, *LMD,* 12.2.1999). In the long run, Asia's recovery is inescapable, while America's hegemony will be more and more confronted - around the world - by the forces of de-legitimization. A European army, Wallerstein and Amin are again correct, is one of the imperatives of European integration in the 21st Century, and it is time to restore international law and the United Nations as guiding principles of the international system. Thus, we briefly discuss the external conditions for a successful enlargement policy.

Not before too long, the European Union can and must say good-bye to the present stage of the neo-liberal dogma, develop its own world political weight and its own European army, try to integrate the orthodox European East, and try to be a mediating force in the Middle-East conflict (Wallerstein, 1998; on the last point, see already Amin, 1994; see also Bornschier, as early as 1988; see also Samir Amin, 1999 in *Al Ahram Weekly,* issue 428, at *http://www.ahram.org.eg/weekly).* The current European backlash (aptly described in the April and May issue of *Le Monde Diplomatique, http://www.monde-diplomatique.fr/,* 1999) could still turn out to be a mere episode, which could soon be breaking up under the pressures this model creates. Such a renewed and true perspective of a European left position would also imply a certain critical distance towards the Southeastern expansion of the European Union under present conditions - implying all the dangers of human rights violations, and organized crime in Turkey, the key country for the present, American concept of European and Middle Eastern policy (for recent debates, see also *Mother Jones* at *http://www.mojones.com).*

The **pipeline from the Caspian Sea to the Turkish port of Ceyhan is indeed the key project of United States foreign and economic policy for the next Century,** and to achieve this aim, all other considerations threaten to be relegated to second or third place, including the concern for human rights. No one else than the US State Department, at its own official *website,* duly informs about the problems of human rights and justice and home affairs in that part of the world, especially Turkey. But good allies are never bombarded, to set a human rights record straight. Whether Europe has the power, the good luck and the resources to save Russia from the abyss, cannot be determined here, but at least the first wave of the 'eastward extension' of the European Union could become an *'extension with a human face'.* At present, we gain the impression, that **'Ceyhan' is much more on the minds of the transatlantic elites than the cohesion of the European model.**

In the end, the future decline of America has also important social and military aspects. Social, because with all the talk of the *'market economy superstar'* notwithstanding, 1 out of 5 children in America grow up in poverty, and African American young men, aged 18 - 25, are to be encountered more frequently in prison than in the educational system (IFRI, 1998: 66). Bill Clinton was elected for his second term in office by only 49% of those less than 50% of Americans, who bothered to vote - a sign how democracy is concentrated more and more in white, suburban America, composed by 89% white population (IFRI, 1988: 67). The 253 billion $ spent on defence in 1996 do not deliver the military power on the ground, that a real *world policeman* would need.

Therefore, also in military terms, there are absolute limits to US power. Military observers correctly remark, that these logistic and transport problems of the US Armed Forces were not significantly improved after the Gulf War (IFRI, 1998: 64).

Samir Amin proposed thoughts about a necessary European counter-project already in 1994, repeated in his *Al Ahram* piece in 1999, *http://www.ahram.org.eg/weekly.* These thoughts can be extended by analyzing the constellation of interests around the Caspian Sea oil fields and the Kosovo crisis with the help of such papers as the *Los Angeles Times* and the *Washington Post,* on file from *http://www.dialogselect.com.* Instead of concentrating on the details, let's just spell out here the general conclusions. America's geo-strategy - as we already mentioned above - for the entire region of Europe and the Middle East now rests on the following central assumptions:

- access of the US-multinationals to the oil fields of the Caspian Sea
- security for the pipelines from these oil-fields to Ceyhan in Southeastern Turkey
- early accession of Turkey into the EU *('we have the pipeline, but you Europeans carry the costs of Turkish membership')* as a strategy to appease the Turkish elites and to keep Turkey stable
- continued use of the US air force base at Incirlik in Turkey and an international policy power axis **Washington - London - Ankara - Tel Aviv,** that marginalizes other European interests, i.e. of extended cooperation and dialogue with the Orthodox and Islamic world in the 'backyard' of Europe
- retention of the Mediterranean command of NATO in US hands (because of its importance for US power projections into the Middle East)
- the further weakening of Russia as a kind of Latin American early 20th Century client state of international capitalism
- an *'Euro'* that does not de-throne the US $ from its central role in the world economy
- the further *Americanization* of European policies and institutions, i.e. their adaptation to the neo-liberal Anglo-American socio-political creed
- the blocking of further *'Gaullist'* attempts at European integration; i.e. the prevalence of NATO over European security and defense structures

There is a danger, that not the left, but the right will - in the end - realize such a *'Gaullist'* European project after the demise of *Blairism* in a few years or months time. The fate of the *multilateral agreement on investment*, that center piece of the US project for hegemony in the 21st Century, will tell us a lot on the future measure of control and power, that American influence still wields in the world system.

The monopoly of US world power could give way to a trilateral structure, dominated by the USA, Japan and East Asia, and Europe. Here, our analysis is totally in agreement with such diverse authors as Samir Amin, Giovanni Arrighi, Christopher Chase Dunn, Andre Gunder Frank, Joshua Goldstein, and Immanuel Wallerstein. The forces of contention, unleashed by unfettered globalization, meanwhile will be more than a motive for challengers of the existing power structure - and not only these odd half a dozen military dictatorships and old/new neo-stalinist regimes around the globe. The costs of continued, challenged hegemony will rise for the US, while Europe will be left to have a chance to re-center its integration process around democratization of the European structures and the human capital factor. The forces in Europe, opposed to the political project of unfettered globalization, would do well to concentrate their energies, then, on the following key areas

- a *Tobin tax* in international economic relations
- democratization of the structures of the European Union. There is a federalist variety (with a greatly strengthened European parliament) and a national parliamentary variety (with increased national parliamentary control powers against the Commission in Brussels) under debate here
- a long-term strategy for the *Euro* that sufficiently recognizes the interests of export industries in the South and East and not only wealth owners in the North
- a slowing down of the process of unfettered globalization, especially regarding financial markets, also in view of the threats posed by money laundering and by international criminal groups
- a harmonization of European tax policies, social dialogue and social policies
- the creation of a European foreign and defence policy
- a dialogue with democratic forces in the Islamic world and the non-violent opposition in Turkey
- the insistence on a true peace in the Middle East
- and active human rights policy and solidarity with the victims of regional conflicts and ethno-politically motivated denial of minority rights in the Sudan, in Turkey, in Central Asia, in Indonesia (East Timor), and in much of Africa and in parts of Latin America
- finally, a strengthening of the United Nations and the return of the observance of international law, with the aim of establishing democratic world government by around 2030 at the latest

ONCE AGAIN - THE ISSUE OF PENSION REFORM AND TRANSFORMATION

A classic European pension model of the *'Bismarck'* type presupposes that you work and/or are socially insured for a certain minimum number of years. Usually, a retiree needs to have accumulated a certain number of insurance years (say, 15 years contributory periods plus fictitious qualifying periods) within the last 30 years prior to the desired time of retirement. Persons, not meeting these criteria are nevertheless entitled to a pension, when they have accumulated 15 contributory years (without fictitious qualifying periods) or 25 insurance years in the course of their life. All recipients of incomes among the working population pay a certain percentage of their income, say 22.8%, into the social security fund. Upon reaching retirement age, say 65/60 years, the average income of your last 15 or so work years is being calculated as the basis of assessment, and after some algebraic operations with certain factors for the year 15, 14, 13 *et cetera,* the assessment base is multiplied by a certain factor (say 0.019) for each contributory year, to arrive at your monthly pension to be paid. There are maximum and minimum pensions, and special privileges for special groups. The pension in Europe is most often the basic result of a generation contract between those who are in retirement and those who work. Some countries, however, base their pension system entirely on their budget and finance it from taxes. This is also a solution, but it is not the Bismarck-type of solution.

Critics of the Bismarck system pointed out the weaknesses and exploding costs of the model. Generous early retirement provisions, an exploding demographic proportion between those who work and those who are out of work by 2005 (or even earlier) and after, special privileges for the police, for the armed forces *et cetera* were among the most glaring weaknesses of the system in many countries. In Poland, only employers, and not employees paid contributions to the ZUS, the social security institution, and the peasant retirement scheme, known as KRUS, was a huge single deficit-creating machine. But to be just, several weaknesses of the old system were tackled by the World Bank reform of pillar (1) (compulsory state run insurance), that was put in place recently. The only relevant question is, whether or not the system could survive with these reforms, without a *'second pillar'*. Many of the special privileges could be abolished, the necessary social insurance time was standardized, and the retirement age was pushed up.

The solution, worked out in Poland and other EU accession countries, that is in place from January 1st 1999 onward, combines generous reforms of the still existing 'pillar 1' (Bismarck) with compulsory payments of all workers and employees into 'pillar 2' (World-Bank-funds). Each employee receives an account number, a credit-card-format social security card, and has to choose between about a dozen private funds, having the possibility to switch from one to the other in the course of development.

In the end, about 50% of the mandatory retirement system will be financed by the classical *'Pay as You Go'* system, while the rest - 50% - eventually will be funded. Gora and Rutkowski mention the following rates to be paid from gross incomes, to be in force:

old age (employer + employee 50/50)	19.52%
second pillar (employees)	7.3%
buffer fund	1%
disability and survivor pensions (50/50)	13%
sickness (employee)	2.45%
injury (employer)	0.81%-8.12%

Old 'Bismarck' will receive a Swedish type of overhaul, basically derived from a 'devaluation' factor, calculated against too high pensions, when life expectancy is rising over time. The procedure boils down to the simple arithmetic, that, the higher the life expectancy is in a given year, when you reach retirement age, the lower will be the pension for the rest of your life.

Beside **pillar 1 ('Bismarck'**, the classical system) and **pillar 2 (the new pension funds**, that will receive 9% of the gross income of **all** workers and employees, which will invest the capital in the market but will have to pay pensions in exchange) there will be also a **pillar 3 - private and enterprise pensions**, that will correspond to the demands of the market (Gora and Rutkowski, 1998).

The arguments for and against this system are manifold. Suffice to mention here, that Gora and Rutkowski themselves calculate the rising losses to the state budget, caused by the new pension system during the first years of operation. Since the former 45% social security contribution paid in Poland, has to be - in a rising proportion - divided between 'Bismarck', the various other funds (like accident insurance etc.) and the new capitalized funds, money going to them will be lacking in the state coffins, until, well - until the moment that these funds start to dynamize economic growth (at least this is hoped). The losses will amount to 0.68% of GDP in 1999, rising to 1.68% in 2003, and only then they should be declining. We should emphasize, that these huge costs were also existing in Chile, the model country number 1 of the new system (often called *Cartagena declaration* countries). Real earnings per employee grew from 1970 to 1980 by +8.1%, although in this period we had the recession of the Allende experiment years, and the harsh neo-liberal economic recovery program of the IMF after 1973. During and after the introduction of the system, in the 1980s, real earnings declined by 0.3% per annum, however. Such a leveling of the burden on the shoulders of the wage earners was - at a time of 3.6% real growth during 1980-93, practically only possible in a military dictatorship (UNDP, Human Development Report, 1998). It should also be recalled, that, technically speaking, privatization in Chile was well advanced already at the beginning of the 1980s, with a full-fledged private banking and insurance sector in place, dating back to long years of 'normal' capitalist development in a country of the Southern cone of Latin America, where capitalism and democracy existed for decades in a framework of admittedly still existing social poverty of sections of society, interrupted by a very brief socialist experiment in the years 1970-73. In Poland, many of the funds, that form part and parcel of the very structure of the Second Pillar, still have to undergo privatization. Thus, let us be clear, there will be a redistribution of incomes away from wage earners to pension funds to the tune of several percentage points of GDP each year, until - in the end - a pay-off in favor of pensioners will take place:

Graph 13.10: The World Bank Model of Pension Reform in Poland Leads to Astronomical Economic Losses during the First Years of Operation

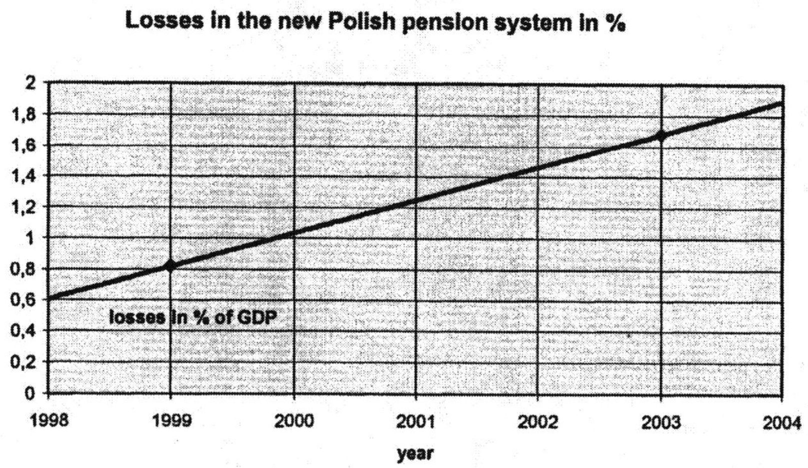

Source: our own compilation from Gora and Rutkowski, 1998

In terms of the budget, this will mean an additional annual deficit of, say, 1-2% that has to be coped with. The proceeds of privatization will be used to prop up that additional hole in the budget, that - *ceteris paribus* - would face up to all the existing difficulties of the second phase of the transformation process (steel, coal, agriculture, EU accession). An implicit additional deficit to the tune of almost the Maastricht criteria of up to two percent per annum is considerable. No funds for schools, human capital, research and development, rural regions, the fight against crime *etc.* are then available from the proceeds of privatization - the income from the privatization process have to be used to cover the deficits incurred in favor of a dozen privileged oligopolistic private firms, called private pension funds.

In view of the many perceived or real challenges to the present 'Bismarck' system, critics have maintained that a large part of the savings of society are being withdrawn. The costs of the old system will reflect the relative privilege or under-privilege of the pensioners in society. Defendants of the system will maintain, that mass demand, inter-generation re-distribution and solidarity in the family are enhanced by generous pensions, and that poverty among the aged works against a high life expectancy. The relationships between social security benefits expenditures and poverty reduction are startling indeed.

In line with the re-birth of a human-capital oriented Keynesian thinking, presented in this volume, we dare to say, that it would be the concentration on the reduction of poverty and on the formation of human capital by the East Central European governments, which, in the end, would yield the most long-lasting and thorough results for stable economic growth, which would transform their countries into a really successful new EU members. The decision makers should also re-consider the staggering rates of poverty, existing in the neo-liberal model country number 1, the United States of America, already discussed above.

The social performance of several EU member states suggests, that a thorough change in the European model could be necessary. Data provided by the Austrian Federal Ministry of Labor (1997, *Bericht ueber die soziale Lage)* show the following connection between social security expenditures and poverty in the countries of the European Union:

Graph 13.11: Social Security Benefits Expenditures and Poverty Reduction in Industrial Nations

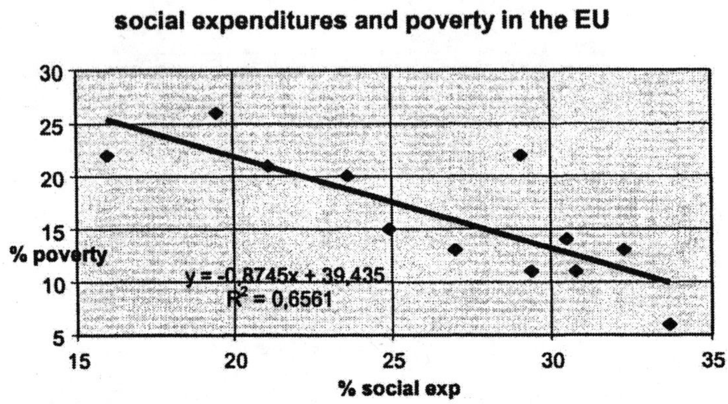

Legend: social expenditures per GDP, 1994; percent of the total population endangered by poverty, 1993. Compiled by the Austrian Federal Ministry of Labor.

Social security creates the mass demand that is necessary for mass consumption; decent pensions are an enormously successful instrument for the social cohesion of society, and enhance the savings rate as well as a kind of redistribution from the grandparents to their grandchildren. Pensioners from the First Pillar, are among the most stable and best consumers in Europe.

As the Austrian Karl Polanyi, in contrast to his fellow Austrian Friedrich A. Hayek so correctly foresaw, it is society, that somehow will defend itself against the unfettered mechanisms of the market, and - in the end - the social protection of the poor and the aged will determine the future stability of society.

The elimination of poverty among the aged, a clear and decent *'Pay as You Go'* pension system without too many loopholes and a clear policy of unemployment insurance, health insurance, and a tax and redistribution system in favor of the disabled remain thus the basic pillars of a world economically successful social welfare state.

While the monopoly position in the international system, as expressed by years of membership in the UN, together with the social security effort are a significant positive contribution to long-run growth, human rights violations and population density rates are significantly blocking long-run economic growth. The second equation listed below even more optimistically mentions social security expenditures, mean years of schooling and the Human Development Index as a precondition of absolute income growth. In between them, our predictor variables account for over 80% of the real, absolute income growth in the world system between 1960 and 1990:

Table 13.6: The Absolute Real Income Increase from 1960 To 1990 in the World System (N=123 Countries)

	Violations of Political Rights	Violation of Civil Rights	Population Density^0,5	Terms of Trade	MNC PEN73	Government Consumption
growth in the	-387,6044339	-335,5309726	-38,35553994	-159,3658871	-2,142065598	-38,08417293
sense of Arrighi's and Amin's theory	147,1946027	756,8905041	14,7393743	773,404945	18,01237032	28,8547924
	0,80679169					
	29,78709404	107				
t-Test	-2,633278848	-0,443301866	-2,602250215	-0,206057497	-0,118921916	-1,319856071

Trade Dependency	social security effort	UN membership years	% Women in Parliament	Women % Labor Force	ethno-linguistic fractionalization
3,383706329	353,0850466	14,16819598	58,90557906	-2,079932631	-8,378867087
16,17414266	42,82585478	6,800556167	44,53034007	1,379485421	14,31186935
0,209204679	8,244670153	2,083387833	1,322818981	-1,507759777	-0,585448825

public investment	ln(MPR+1)(military personnel)	Fertility Rate	constant
24,90210293	-166,5370259	137,2074945	3642,23847
7,916573906	280,3858807	209,1100071	2191,222144
3,145565649	-0,593956534	0,656149825	

Legend: first row: unstandardized regression coefficients, second row: standard errors, last row: t-Test. The values immediately below the standard errors are R^2 (third row, left side entry), *F*, and degrees of freedom (fourth row).

Alternatively, one might also express:

Table 13.7: The Social Preconditions of World Growth, 1960-90 In 123 Nations

	MNCP 85	Gov expenditures	Trade Dependency	social security	UN-member years	Women in Parliament	Women % LF	mean years of schooling	HDI	ln(MPR +1)	Fertility Rate	Constant
absolute	-0,1024	-313,04	1145,54	304,721	14,0635	-33,038	-15,546	336,965	28,15	-25,605	-6,937	-907,19
growth	195,851	697,948	1775,06	146,832	17,3298	27,872	15,0547	43,5687	5,40439	15,8157	12,008	1882,33
	0,80028											
	40,4342	111										
t-Test	-0,0005	-0,4485	0,64535	2,07531	0,81152	-1,1853	-1,0326	7,73411	5,20873	-1,6189	-0,5777	

Legend: As in all EXCEL 5.0 outprints in this work, first row: unstandardized regression coefficients, second row: standard errors, last row: t-Test. The values immediately below the standard errors are R^{2} (third row, left side entry), *F*, and degrees of freedom (fourth row). Absolute real income increase is understood to be the difference between PPP $ income in 1990 to PPP $ income in 1960

Time will show, that the three pillar system, adopted now, will prove to be costly and a highly risky approach:

- the **original model country of the system, Chile, today shows, that the funds are in deep crisis.** As people like professor Salvador Valdes Prieto from the Catholic University in Santiago have spelt out, only 2.5 million of the 5.6 million strong labor force are in the system at all, and difficulties of the system were mounting in recent months *(Economist,* October 24, 1998; *Quarterly Review of Economics and Finance,* 38, 3, 1998 (M. D. Ramirez); UNDP, Human Development Report, Chile, 1998 (the UNDP report ran a survey, according to which the majority of Chileans expressed dissatisfaction with the present day retirement system; see also: Chips, September 07, 1998); Jonathan Kendall in Institutional Investor, 31, 6, 1997: *'the funds are now ... underperforming or performing moderately'.)* Administrative costs of the system are rising enormously, 5 of the 15 AFP pension funds - as they are called in Chile - are currently making losses, the returns on assets under management have declined dramatically since 1994. Professor Carmelo Mesa-Lago from Pittsburgh University, one of the world's most famous Latin America specialists, says: *'the costs of transition (i.e. from the old system to the three pillar system) are enormous' (Nation's Business,* Volume 85, 5, May 1997). Carmelo Mesa-Lago also observes that low-income earners try to avoid payments for the 'Second Pillar', so that they depend entirely on Pillar number 1 - the poor man's social insurance. The poorest 20% have a real income of 1558 $ (PPP per capita GDP), while the richest 20% get away with 27145 $ (UNDP, *Human Development Report,* 1998, Table 7). Such trends have also led World Bank economists Robert Holzmann and Joseph Stiglitz to evaluate pension reforms differently today, as the following Chapters from an article in the *Financial Times* (03rd July 2001) shows:

A so-called pensions revolution in Latin America and elsewhere has done little to expand workforce coverage, and may in some countries have reduced the proportion of workers with pensions, according to a new World Bank publication (*Financial Times,* 3rd July 2001):

> *The book suggests that the widespread shift towards private, funded pensions that accelerated over the last decade has not yielded all that was expected of it.*
> *Of the world's 6bn people, only 15 per cent or fewer have access to a formal system of retirement income. The book suggests that strong efforts in poor countries to provide complete formal pension coverage may come at a heavy price.*
>
> *The book examines the experience of countries since the Bank set out its attitude to pensions reform in a 1994 publication, Averting the Old Age Crisis. It includes a chapter outlining what Joseph Stiglitz, the World Bank's former chief economist, and Peter Orszag, a former White House economics adviser, call 10 myths about social security reform.*

These "myths" include the idea that private pension plans increase national savings, that rates of return are higher under individual accounts than in pay-as-you-go systems and that competition ensures low administrative costs for private pensions.

Not all of these myths are generally accepted as such, but according to Robert Holzmann, a co-editor of the book with Mr Stiglitz, the experience of a number of countries and research has shaded understanding of the issue since 1994.

The Bank still supports a multi-pillar approach to pensions reform, including an unfunded pillar with mandatory contributions, a funded pillar with mandatory contributions and a voluntary private pillar.

But questions have been raised about whether a second, funded pillar is needed at all - because of high transaction costs, difficulties in regulation, a lack of financial sophistication and the existence in such countries as the US and Denmark of efficient public trust funds.

Some expected results of reform have not occurred, the book concludes. For example, though reforming the pension system has been expected to induce workers in the informal economy to join the formal sector, there is little evidence this has happened.

The book also reflects a debate about the high administrative costs of privately managed individual pensions accounts, and the related issue of how much it costs to convert pension assets into annuities.

Mr Holzmann says high administrative costs can have a significant impact on pension fund returns. A chapter in the book about the UK experience estimates administrative charges can reduce the value of an individual personal pension account by over 40 per cent.

Mr Holzmann says this and other examples suggest that more competition is not necessarily the answer to reducing high costs. Individuals often do not possess a sophisticated understanding of their investments, so there is a case for product standardisation. "There appears to be a trade-off between choice and cost," he says.

It has become clearer since 1994 that although funding pensions provides advantages at the margin, it is not a panacea. The reason is that with either funded or unfunded systems the burden is on the next generation, either to pay the ongoing costs of an unfunded pension system or to buy the private assets that the elderly are selling. "The benefits are always had out of the GDP of the current period," he says.

"Funding still provides advantages because at the margin, it's likely to be less sensitive to shifts in ageing," he says. It also provides opportunities for diversifying pension assets abroad.

The cost of the failure of Chilean and Malaysian pension funds to diversify adequately became evident after sharp currency depreciations in the two countries.

Although the book does not go much into the question, Mr Holzmann says it is now widely accepted that funded private pension funds do not help increase national savings.

However, such contractual saving - together with insurance savings - have an important impact on the depth and liquidity of financial markets, allowing, for example, the development of longer maturity financial instruments.

"The importance of moving towards funding pensions is not to do with the level of savings; it's to do with the composition of savings," he says.

- state guarantees for private funds, going bankrupt, could entice fund managers in a country like Chile to pack the 9% of gross earnings of working people received together, and fly out with full suitcases of money to Caribbean Islands
- compulsory payments to private dozen or so funds will increase the monopoly power of insurance institutions and banks in the economy; in fact, structurally, the system, thought to the end, very much works – an ill-meaning cynic could say - like *il pizzo* paid to the mafia in Sicily in the 1960s in return for their specific kind of *'protection'*. They also take away by compulsion money and invest it somewhere else. The system in Chile at any rate could become a powerful mechanism to discriminate between the *'ins'* (the dozen or so funds) and the *'outs'* (the rest of the banking and insurance market). It will create a privileged zone of a dozen firms, that can rely on the regular incomes of the working population, and will work against competition in the insurance and banking sector. Even for a neo-liberal, there are some question marks when looking at the new three pillar systems in East Central Europe - several of the banks and insurance companies that are already accepted parts of the Second Pillar still have to be privatized, and it is entirely possible, that the pension system will in fact block the process of privatization, since the state-class owned banks and insurance companies will now have ample compulsory funds at their disposal. Another scenario is possible and must be avoided: the huge costs of the introduction of the system in the first years - admitted even by Gora and Rutkowski - will be carried not by the proceeds of privatization, but by the weaker segments of society, which will be politically powerless in the struggle for the distribution of budget money, compared to the state-class-owned banks and insurance companies, with the very best of links to parliamentary deputies, ministries, and other structures of power.
- The system in Chile also fundamentally contradicts the principle of consumer sovereignty of those wage earners, that would like to invest, say, the 9% of their gross income in the Third Pension Pillar and not in the Second Pillar. One has also to doubt, whether the system as such - with it's element of compulsion and tying of parts of the funds to be invested in the home country (like in Poland) - is compatible at all with European Union law. It basically contradicts the mobility of capital in the Union and discriminates one country - the pension reform country - against the other members of the Union.
- the model in Chile is very much tied to the present-day logic of the liberalization of financial markets; in order to make profits, the funds will have to be engaging in the kind of speculative behavior that dealt a death-blow to the former real growth region in the world, East and Southeast-Asia. The Chilean type funds could greatly increase the kind of casino-capitalism, that pushes up real interest rates. It is estimated, that Latin American pension funds alone will have

accumulated by 2004 a wealth of $40 billion *(Latin American Law and Business Report,* February 28, 1998, Vol. 6).

- Henry Aaron, an economist from the Brookings Institutions, spelt out the entire logic that is behind the system in Chile: it can only work well, if the rate of interest is higher than the nominal increase in the wage bill, i>g, the so-called **Aaron condition** (see also, Laski, 1998). The consequence is, amongst others, **a pushing up of interest rates**, and thus a strangulation of full employment, that leaves ever larger and larger holes in the public budgets, to the detriment of 'Bismarck' pillar 1.

Although the issue will be dealt with in a forthcoming NOVA Science publication by the present author of this Chapter in great detail, it might be permitted to say here already that a decent solution to the old age crisis might be constituted by the new pension reform model in Sweden, that combines notional pension accounts and a moderate second pillar, and that is compatible with the principle of welfare society (not necessarily any more welfare state).

Chapter 14

THE CROSS-NATIONAL RELEVANCE OF THE DEBATE AND EU ENLARGEMENT

Gernot Köhler's particular contribution to the theory of periphery capitalism is

(a) to explain in measurable terms the concept of unequal exchange and
(b) to provide a practical answer to the processes of international currency fluctuations, that cause the stability of the three-layer structure of international exploitation under which the East European semi-periphery has suffered for the last 500 years

By and large, the theory not only enriches, but deepens our knowledge on the mechanisms of dependency. By relying on the relationship between the purchasing power parity rate $ incomes and the GDP at exchange rates, the 'exchange rate deviation index' (ERDI), we better understand human and social development on a world scale. Unequal exchange affects the chances of a nation for economic growth. 1/ERDI is simply called *'unequal exchange'*, operationalization (2), while *'unequal exchange'*, concept (1) is reflecting the trade-weighted measure of the share of the gains or losses from unequal exchange in total product, presented in Part A of this study. While one of the authors (Köhler) seems to prefer operationalization (1), Tausch prefers the formulation

unequal exchange = 1/ERDI

THE TWO MEASURES OF UNEQUAL EXCHANGE

The first results are:

Graph 14.1: Unequal Exchange and Development

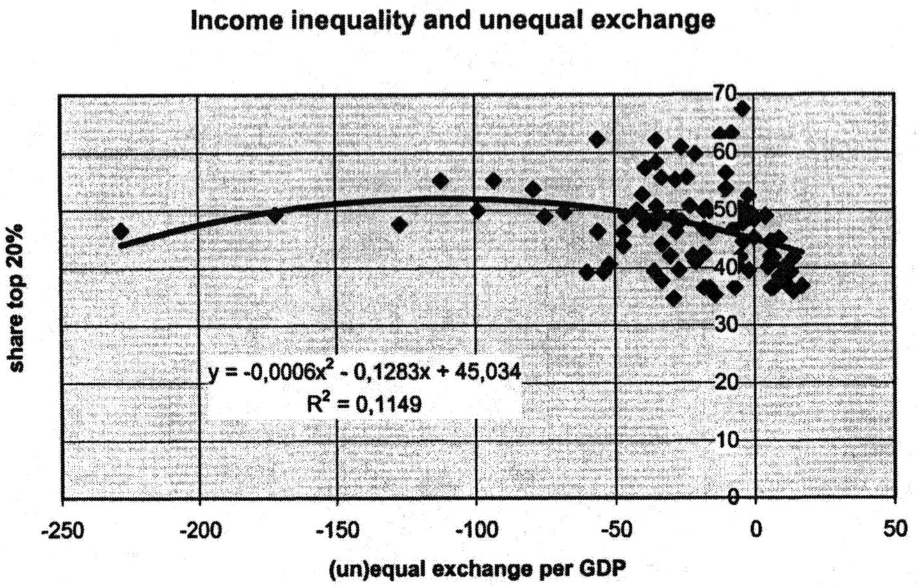

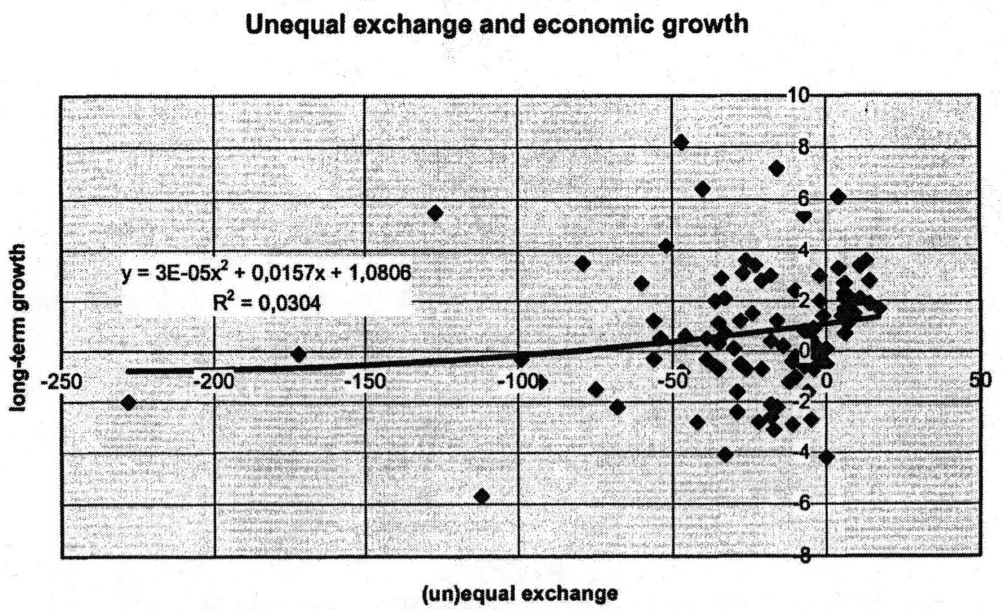

Operationalization (2) yields the following bi-variate results, which, in our opinion, are superior to the results achieved by the T-measure (proceeds from unequal exchange per GNP):

Graph 14.2: Unequal Exchange (1/ERDI) and Development

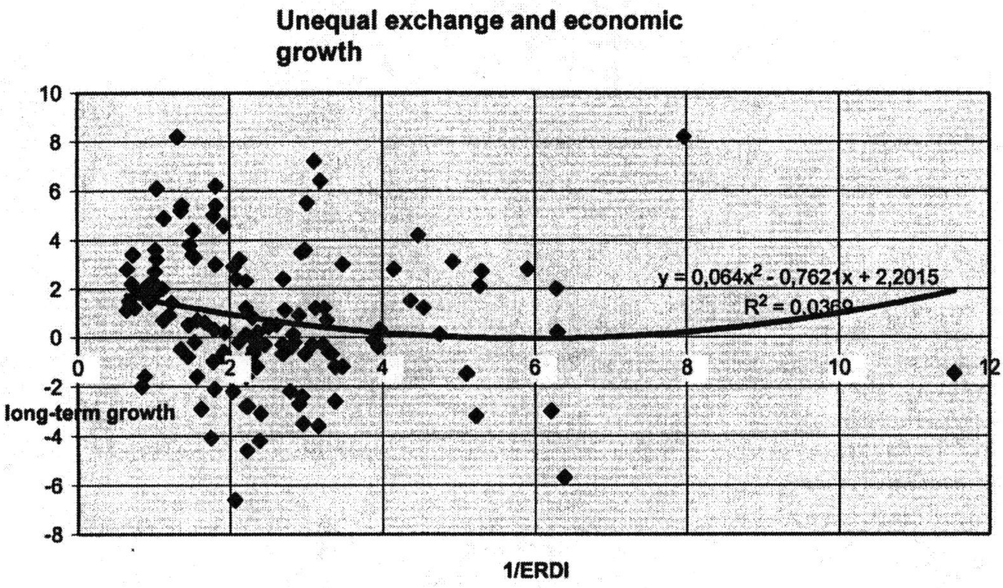

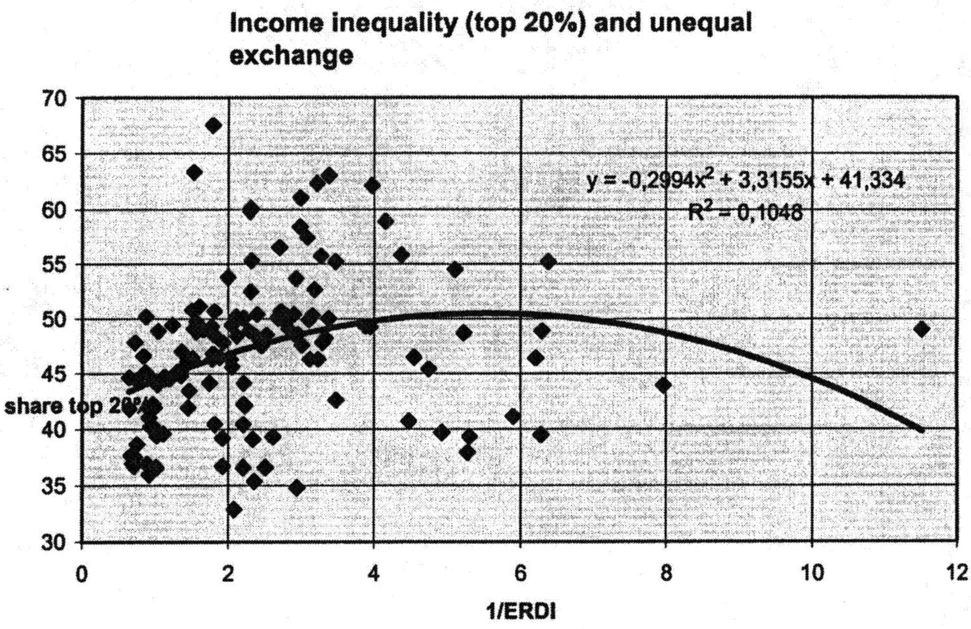

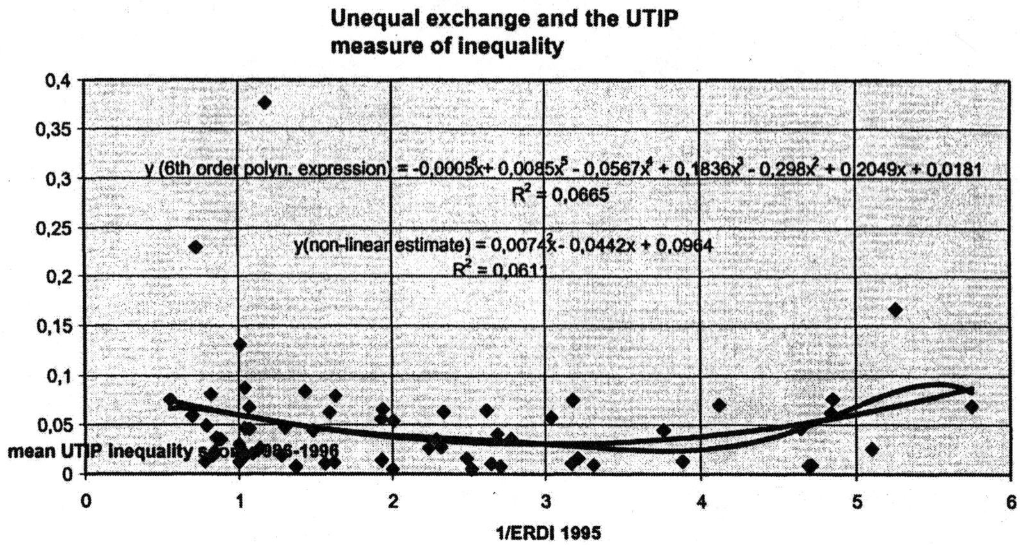
Unequal exchange and the UTIP measure of inequality
y (6th order polyn. expression) = -0,0005x6 + 0,0085x5 - 0,0567x4 + 0,1836x3 - 0,298x2 + 0,2049x + 0,0181
R2 = 0,0665
y(non-linear estimate) = 0,0074x2 - 0,0442x + 0,0964
R2 = 0,0611
mean UTIP inequality score 1986-1996
1/ERDI 1995

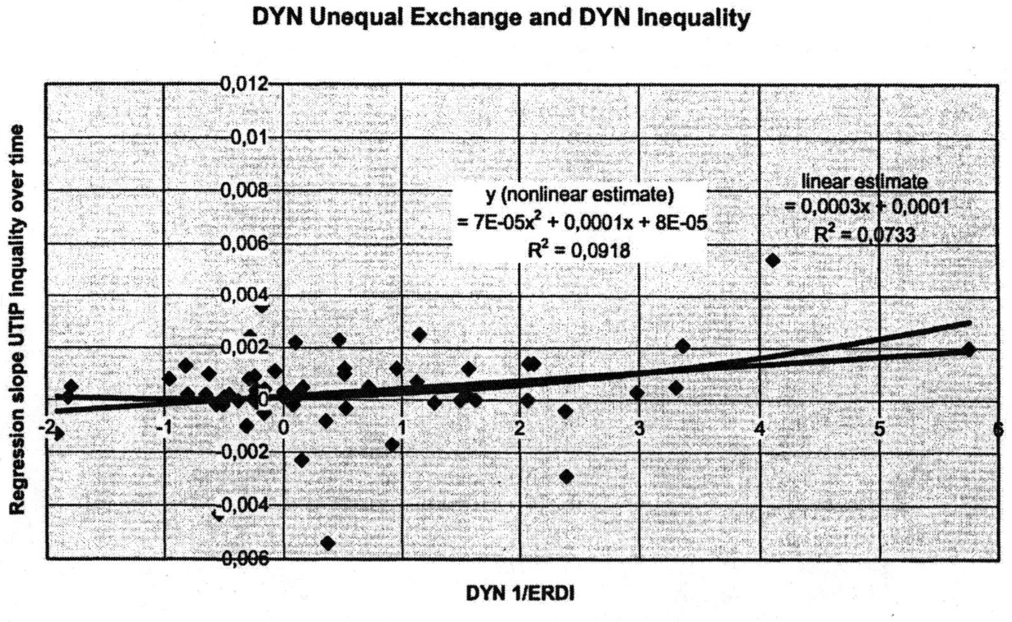
DYN Unequal Exchange and DYN Inequality
y (nonlinear estimate)
= 7E-05x2 + 0,0001x + 8E-05
R2 = 0,0918
linear estimate
= 0,0003x + 0,0001
R2 = 0,0733
Regression slope UTIP inquality over time
DYN 1/ERDI

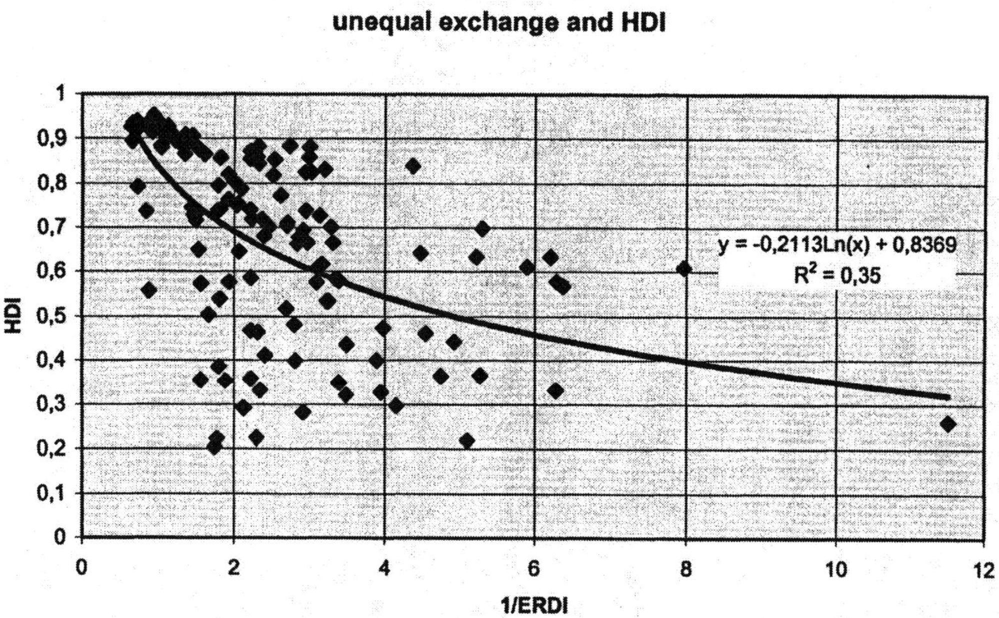

UNEQUAL EXCHANGE AND RISING INEQUALITY

Aghion and Williamson are very outspoken in their analysis of the polarizing effects of globalization in the 1980s and the 1990s, and produce extensive evidence in favor of their hypothesis, that this recent rise in inequality contradicts some optimistic assumptions, deduceable from a generalized, but not necessarily correct interpretation of Simon Kuznets' early writing on the subject of inequality. Bi-variate evidence does not reproduce this relationship very clearly, mainly because inequality in the 1960s and 1970s reflected the cumulative effects of peripherization over the past economic cycle since the early 1930s, but multivariate analysis shows, that if we take the existing initial tendencies for income polarization into account (initial long-run mean of inequality, as expressed in the UTIP data series 1963-1980), **the extent of unequal exchange** in the 1980s and 1990s (1/ERDI; 1995, as a **proxy** for the force of the **globalization** process in the late 1980s and early 1990s) **explains more than 57% of rising inequality scores** along the UTIP data series **over time** (regression slopes of inequality, 1960 - 1996):

Rising Inequality (Regression Slope Over Time - 1963 to 1996) =

1/ERDI	initial inequality	constant
1995		mean 1963-80
0,028057	-0,0001	-0,00076
0,003062	0,000125	0,000357
0,576167		
42,82169	63	
9,161564	-0,83663 T-Test	
1/ERDI	initial inequality	
	mean 1963-80	

As in all EXCEL 5.0 outprints in this work, first row: unstandardized regression coefficients, second row: standard errors, last row: t-Test. The values immediately below the standard errors are R^2 (third row, left side entry), *F,* and degrees of freedom (fourth row). Due to lacking data, for Costa Rica the initial inequality value for 1984 had to be used

UNEQUAL EXCHANGE AND DEVELOPMENT A CROSS-NATIONAL ANALYSIS

Unequal exchange (operationalization (2)) will be bad for growth and social development, thus supporting Gernot Köhler's assertions. In the re-run of the dependency-explanation of economic and social development in 123 countries, presented in Tausch, 1998, 1/ERDI achieves similar or even better results than MNC Penetration, with adjustment, dyn life expectancy and growth affected in an even more significant way than in the earlier study, modeled around the tradition of Bornschier and Chase Dunn. For the study of growth and social development in 134 countries, including many transformation countries with fairly complete data, it is social development, that is explained in a still more comprehensive way by the re-formulation of dependency theory.

Table 14.1: Gernot Köhler's Reformulation of Dependency and World System Theory: Its Relevance for Future Cross-National Development Studies

Dependency and world system theory in a Köhlerian formulation (dependency = 1/ERDI)
n = 123 countries

	1/ERDI	Govex	Trade Dep	social sec	UN-membery	Women Parl	Women %LF	ln PCI	ln PCI^2	ln(MPR+1)	**Fertility Rate**	Constant
Adjustment	-0,6964	-0,3993	0,22208	-4,89	0,02855	-0,0685	-0,0678	0,18341	0,00212	-0,0425	0,16995	28,6793
	0,18741	0,93336	0,34259	5,11057	0,02479	0,03947	0,02135	0,06132	0,00728	0,02208	0,17405	19,5255
	0,32846											
	4,93555	111										
t-Test	**-3,7162**	-0,4278	0,64824	-0,9568	1,15169	-1,7345	-3,1743	2,99096	0,29048	-1,9244	**0,97643**	

	1/ERDI	Govex	Trade Dep	social sec	UN-membery	**Women Parl**	**Women %LF**	**social sec**	ln PCI^2	**ln(MPR+1)**	**Fertility Rate**	Constant
growth	-0,9334	0,02624	0,2474	-5,3295	0,01277	-0,0936	-0,0513	0,17915	0,00898	-0,0512	0,20127	32,0922
	0,16359	0,81477	0,29906	4,46123	0,02164	0,03446	0,01864	0,05353	0,00636	0,01927	0,15194	17,0447
	0,43578											
	7,79383	111										
t-Test	**-5,7055**	0,0322	0,82723	-1,1946	0,59025	**-2,7173**	**-2,7508**	**3,34672**	1,4126	**-2,6538**	**1,3247**	

	LEX 1960	1 der e-funct	1 der pi-func	**1/ERDI**	Viol Civ Rits	Trade Dep	Terms Trade	UN-membery	Women Parl	**Women %LF**	**ln(MPR+1)**	Constant
DYN	1,00277	-0,0432	-0,0309	-0,0306	0,01411	-0,0005	0,1347	-0,3631	-0,4702	-29,328	-0,3145	29,0699
LEX	0,78723	0,02003	0,03019	0,01777	0,01576	0,00605	0,17425	0,14832	0,70341	6,72499	0,03583	2,60679
	0,75567											
	31,2093	111										
t-Test	1,2738	-2,1554	-1,0243	**-1,7203**	0,89581	-0,082	0,77301	-2,4483	-0,6684	**-4,361**	**-8,7765**	

	e-func Encon	pi-func Enc	**1/ERDI**	Viol Civ Rits	**Trade Dep**	Terms Trade	pub invest	Women Parl	Women %LF	**ln(MPR+1)**	Fertility Rate	Constant
green	0,01078	0,05969	0,00138	-0,0017	-0,0033	-0,0004	-1E-05	0,01049	0,00429	1,7E-05	0,01957	0,08837
house	0,01523	0,06781	0,00176	0,00251	0,00134	0,00132	0,00049	0,01325	0,01232	3,9E-06	0,08039	0,30405
index	**0,42025**											
	7,31458	111										
t-Test	0,70788	0,88032	*0,783*	-0,6725	**-2,447**	-0,2685	*-0,0216*	0,79159	0,348	**4,43626**	0,2435	

pol rights	**1/ERDI**	**Govex**	Trade Dep	social sec	UN-membery	**Women Parl**	**Women %LF**	ln PCI	ln PCI^2	ln(MPR+1)	Fertility Rate	Constant
violations	0,51475	1,355	0,12566	-2,2499	0,00349	0,0462	0,01573	-0,0985	0,00564	0,01458	0,18345	8,78801
	0,10869	0,54133	0,1987	2,96401	0,01438	0,02289	0,01238	0,03557	0,00422	0,01281	0,10095	11,3243
	0,58004											
	13,9373	111										
t-Test	**4,73587**	**2,5031**	0,63245	-0,7591	0,24294	**2,01822**	**1,27051**	-2,7694	1,33406	1,13868	1,81731	

	1/ERDI	Govex	Trade Dep	social sec	UN-membery	Women Parl	Women %LF	ln PCI	ln PCI^2	ln(MPR+1)	Fertility Rate	Constant
civil rights	0,32113	1,50312	0,03196	-0,9128	-0,0033	0,02921	0,02404	-0,0896	0,00184	-0,0068	0,13245	5,75519
violations	0,08442	0,42042	0,15432	2,30201	0,01117	0,01778	0,00962	0,02762	0,00328	0,00995	0,0784	8,7951
	0,61093											
	15,8451	111										
	3,80414	**3,57525**	0,20709	-0,3965	-0,2962	**1,64301**	**2,49991**	-3,2456	0,56178	-0,6816	1,68943	

HDI	1/ERDI	Govex	Trade Dep	social sec	UN-membery	Women Parl	Women %LF	ln PCI	ln PCI^2	ln(MPR+1)	Fertility Rate	Constant
	-0,0897	0,14667	-0,0009	0,1196	0,00016	-0,0015	9,9E-05	-0,0009	-0,0001	0,00058	-0,0252	0,13371
	0,00761	0,0379	0,01391	0,20753	0,00101	0,0016	0,00087	0,00249	0,0003	0,0009	0,00707	0,7929
	0,88243											
	75,7357	111										
	-11,788	**3,86963**	-0,0613	0,57628	0,15686	-0,952	0,11432	-0,3692	-0,3889	0,64536	-3,5716	

Gender Developme nt Index	1/ERDI	Govex	Trade Dep	social sec	UN-membery	Women Parl	Women %LF	ln PCI	ln PCI^2	ln(MPR+1)	Fertility Rate	Constant
	-0,0672	0,07364	-0,0125	0,25195	0,00118	-0,0013	0,00021	0,00057	-4E-05	0,00036	-0,0217	-0,3073
	0,0055	0,02738	0,01005	0,14992	0,00073	0,00116	0,00063	0,0018	0,00021	0,00065	0,00511	0,5728
	0,88692											
	79,1446	111										

Gender Development Index

	-12,214	**2,6894**	-1,2433	1,68051	1,62108	**-1,1345**	0,33238	0,31654	-0,1926	0,55902	-4,2493	
Gender Empowerment Index	**1/ERDI**	Govex	**Trade Dep**	social sec	**UN-membery**	**Women Parl**	Women %LF	ln PCI	ln PCI^2	ln(MPR+1)	Fertility Rate	Constant
	-0,0205	1,8E-06	0,01368	-0,1578	0,00154	0,00554	0,0007	0,00187	-7E-05	0,00011	-0,0046	0,7455
	0,00418	0,02084	0,00765	0,11409	0,00055	0,00088	0,00048	0,00137	0,00016	0,00049	0,00389	0,4359
	0,8195											
	45,8141	111										

Gender Empowerment Index

	1/ERDI	Govex	Trade Dep	social sec	UN-membery	Women Parl	Women %LF	ln PCI	ln PCI^2	ln(MPR+1)	Fertility Rate
	-4,9041	8,4E-05	**1,78916**	-1,383	**2,78919**	**6,28924**	1,45886	1,36827	-0,4424	0,22869	-1,1805
Life expectancy	e-func Encon	pi-func Enc	**1/ERDI**	Viol Civ Rits	**Trade Dep**	**Terms Trade**	Constant	**Life Expectancy**			
	0,03886	0,00925	-1,3254	-0,3777	-0,0004	16,8837	27,018				
	0,03546	0,01315	0,30996	0,33659	9,7E-05	1,60518	5,31598				
	0,77613										
	67,0262	116									
	1,09602	0,70357	**-4,276**	-1,1223	**-3,8432**	**10,5182**					

Life expectancy

Maternal Mortality	e-func Encon	pi-func Enc	**1/ERDI**	Viol Civ Rits	Trade Dep	Terms Trade	Constant	**Maternal Mortality**		
	-1,5702	-0,2718	18,9468	15,9548	0,01303	-534,63	1593,72			
	1,14748	0,42547	10,031	10,8925	0,00315	51,9463	172,034			
	0,72812									
	51,777	116								
	e-func Encon	pi-func Enc	**1/ERDI**	Viol Civ Rits	Trade Dep	Terms Trade				
	-1,3684	-0,6388	**1,88883**	1,46476	**4,13151**	**-10,292**				

n = 134 countries including transformation countries

LONG TERM GROWTH

UN memb.y	**mean y scho**	absolute GNP	1/ERDI	Years of Comm	**populati on gr**	state sector	**%labor force**	**ln PPP**	ln PPP^2	agr.share GP	**MILEX**	HDI	constant
3,781	0,1775	-0,016	-0,3593	6,4638	0,0863	-0,0025	-0,5778	-0,0948	0,247	4E-05	-0,2506	0,0078	-31,279
3,6692	0,1003	0,026	0,27	4,7743	0,0376	0,0177	0,2521	0,0126	0,1476	0,0003	0,1355	0,014	20,814
0,572	2,1197												
12,355	120												
1,0305	**1,771**	-0,6149	-1,3307	1,3539	**2,296**	-0,1394	**-2,292**	**-7,539**	1,6734	0,1187	**-1,85**	0,5545	

Dependency and world system theory in the Bornschier tradition (dependency = accumulated FDI/GNP, UNCTAD data series)
n = 123 countries

	MNCP85	Govex	Trade Dep	social sec	UN-membery	Women Parl	Women %LF	ln PCI	ln PCI^2	ln(MPR+1)	**Fertility Rate**	Constant
Adjustment	-0,6536	-0,4296	0,18737	-4,4018	0,02979	-0,0597	-0,0634	0,17243	0,00238	-0,0434	0,00138	26,9826
	0,18486	0,93968	0,34225	5,10895	0,02494	0,03895	0,02138	0,06059	0,00752	0,02227	0,0165	19,5313
	0,32273											
	4,80851	111										
t-Test	**-3,5359**	-0,4572	0,54748	-0,8616	1,1945	-1,5331	-2,9647	2,84593	0,31578	-1,9511	**0,08334**	

	MNCP85	Govex	Trade Dep	social sec	UN-membery	**Women Parl**	**Women %LF**	**social sec**	ln PCI^2	**ln(MPR+1)**	**Fertility Rate**	Constant
growth	-0,8651	0,04917	0,21394	-4,8786	0,01265	-0,0798	-0,0431	0,16897	0,00789	-0,054	0,01436	30,3598
	0,16123	0,81958	0,2985	4,45597	0,02175	0,03397	0,01865	0,05285	0,00656	0,01942	0,0144	17,035
	0,43195											
	7,67324	111										
t-Test	**-5,3655**	0,05999	0,71671	-1,0948	0,58151	**-2,3495**	**-2,3112**	**3,19734**	1,20292	**-2,7782**	**0,99729**	

	LEX 1960	1 der e-funct	1 der pi-func	**MNCP85**	Viol Civ Rits	Trade Dep	Terms Trade	UN-membery	Women Parl	**Women %LF**	**ln(MPR +1)**	Constant
DYN	1,34679	-0,0505	-0,0334	-0,0282	0,01475	-0,0056	0,05987	0,03476	-0,4974	-25,575	-0,2919	27,1079
LEX	0,78235	0,02011	0,02998	0,0179	0,01572	0,00624	0,17097	0,01375	0,70321	6,64776	0,03532	2,5246
	0,75649											
	31,3492	111										
t-Test	1,72147	-2,5087	-1,115	**-1,578**	0,93816	-0,9028	0,35016	2,52799	-0,7073	**-3,8472**	**-8,2649**	

	e-func Encon	pi-func Enc	**MNCP85**	Viol Civ Rits	**Trade Dep**	Terms Trade	pub invest	Women Parl	Women %LF	**ln(MPR+1)**	Fertility Rate	Constant
green	0,01068	0,05143	0,00156	-0,0018	-0,0032	-0,0003	0,00013	0,01159	-0,001	1,7E-05	0,02489	0,08234
house	0,01518	0,06812	0,00177	0,00249	0,00134	0,00132	0,00051	0,01286	0,00111	3,9E-06	0,07976	0,29977
index	**0,42383**											
	7,42272	111										
t-Test	0,70346	0,75494	*0,8822*	-0,7418	**-2,351**	-0,2596	*0,2535*	0,90095	-0,9008	**4,328**	0,31207	

pol rights	**MNCP85**	**Govex**	Trade Dep	social sec	UN-membery	**Women Parl**	**Women %LF**	ln PCI	ln PCI^2	ln(MPR+1)	Fertility Rate	Constant
violations	0,56333	1,33026	0,08924	-1,7402	0,00461	0,05611	0,02086	-0,11	0,00573	0,01333	0,00322	6,99429
	0,10828	0,55042	0,20047	2,9926	0,01461	0,02282	0,01253	0,03549	0,00441	0,01304	0,00967	11,4406
	0,56798											
	13,2663	111										
t-Test	**5,20236**	**2,41679**	0,44514	-0,5815	0,31583	**2,45943**	**1,66528**	-3,0982	1,29937	1,0218	0,33273	

	MNCP85	**Govex**	Trade Dep	social sec	UN-membery	**Women Parl**	**Women %LF**	ln PCI	ln PCI^2	ln(MPR+1)	Fertility Rate	Constant
civil rights	0,3549	1,4809	0,00509	-0,5354	-0,0024	0,03611	0,02752	-0,0981	0,00201	-0,0076	0,00138	4,43959
violations	0,08396	0,4268	0,15545	2,32045	0,01133	0,01769	0,00971	0,02752	0,00342	0,01011	0,0075	8,87101
	0,60105											
	15,2026	111										
	4,22687	**3,46979**	0,03275	-0,2307	-0,2101	**2,04125**	**2,83368**	-3,566	0,58883	-0,7477	0,18396	

Gender Empowerment Index

	MNCP85	Govex	Trade Dep	social sec	UN-membery	Women Parl	Women %LF	ln PCI	ln PCI^2	ln(MPR+1)	Fertility Rate
	-5,0887	0,18135	**1,98348**	-1,5705	**2,59536**	**6,36401**	1,53698	1,72517	-0,895	0,11117	1,64404
Life expectancy	e-func Encon	pi-func Enc	**MNCP85**	Viol Civ Rits	**Trade Dep**	**Terms Trade**	Constant	**Life Expectancy**			
	0,03872	0,0082	-1,4102	0,00462	-0,0004	17,2618	25,5606				
	0,03565	0,01383	0,30209	0,0303	9,9E-05	1,58004	5,18089				
	0,77374										
	66,1158	116									
	1,08625	0,59315	**-4,668**	0,15242	**-3,766**	**10,9249**					

Life expectancy

Maternal Mortality	e-func Encon	pi-func Enc	**MNCP85**	Viol Civ Rits	Trade Dep	Terms Trade	Constant	**Maternal Mortality**		
	-1,564	-0,2469	22,6058	-0,0505	0,01294	-551,29	1655,5			
	1,15803	0,44913	9,81394	0,9842	0,0032	51,33	168,31			
	0,7231									
	50,4872	116								
	e-func Encon	pi-func Enc	**MNCP85**	Viol Civ Rits	Trade Dep	Terms Trade				
	-1,3506	-0,5497	**2,30343**	-0,0513	**4,04127**	**-10,74**				

n = 134 countries, inlcuiding transformation countries

LONG TERM GROWTH

3,367	0,214	-0,01	-0,426	7,438	0,087	-0,008	-0,549	-0,094	9E-04	2E-05	-0,217	0,012	-34,3
3,705	0,099	0,027	0,272	4,816	0,038	0,018	0,255	0,013	0,011	3E-04	0,138	0,015	21,03
0,56	2,144												
11,86	120												
0,909	**2,15**	-0,365	-1,567	1,544	**2,27**	-0,43	**-2,2**	**-7,3**	0,077	0,054	**-1,6**	0,841	t-test
UN memb.y	**mean y scho**	absolute GNP	FDI per GDP	Years of Comm	**populati on gr**	state sector	**%labor force**	**ln PPP**	ln PPP^2	agr.share GP	**MILEX**	HDI	constant

INFANT MORTALITY

UN memb.y	mean y scho	absolute GNP	FDI per GDP	Years of Comm	populati on gr	state sector	%labor force	ln PPP	ln PPP^2	agr.share GP	MILEX	HDI	constant
-162,7	-0,37	-0,362	3,279	-56,28	0,134	0,032	0,554	-0,167	-0,063	2E-04	-1,415	0,122	398,7
21,48	0,576	0,157	1,575	27,93	0,222	0,103	1,476	0,075	0,065	0,002	0,8	0,084	122
0,91	12,43												
95,04	120												
-7,6	-0,642	**-2,3**	**2,082**	**-2,015**	0,606	0,307	0,375	**-2,2**	-0,975	0,112	**-1,767**	1,441	t-test
UN memb.y	mean y scho	**absolute GNP**	**FDI per GDP**	**Years of Comm**	populati on gr	state sector	%labor force	**ln PPP**	ln PPP^2	agr.share GP	**MILEX**	HDI	

EARLY DEATH

FDI per GDP	**Years of Comm**	population gr	state sector	%labor force	ln PPP	**ln PPP^2**	**agr.shareGP**	MILEX	**HDI**	violations pol rights	constant	
0,676	-53,4	-0,13	-0,053	0,497	-7,556	0,176	0,069	0,041	-0,078	0,006	67,67	
0,238	6,365	0,188	0,05	0,464	8,341	0,072	0,033	0,479	0,023	0,019	37,02	
0,89	4,023											
93,12	122											
2,84	**-8,4**	-0,69	-1,064	1,072	-0,906	**2,46**	**2,1**	0,085	**-3,4**	0,29	t-test	
FDI per GDP	**Years of Comm**	population gr	state sector	%labor force	ln PPP	**ln PPP^2**	**agr.shareGP**	MILEX	**HDI**	violations pol rights	violations hum rights	

UN memb.y	mean y scho	absolute GNP	FDI per GDP	Years of Comm	population gr	state sector	%labor force	ln PPP	ln PPP^2	agr.share GP	MILEX	HDI	
-0,815	0,153	0,024	0,085	-0,974	-0,02	-0,014	0,41	0,028	-0,002	8E-05	-0,287	0,005	6,762
2,568	0,069	0,019	0,188	3,338	0,026	0,012	0,176	0,009	0,008	2E-04	0,096	0,01	14,58
0,52	1,486												
9,932	120												

POLITICAL REPRESSION

-0,317	**2,23**	1,269	0,451	-0,292	-0,749	-1,169	**2,32**	**3,11**	-0,212	0,364	**-3**	0,459	t-test
UN memb.y	**mean y scho**	absolute GNP	FDI per GDP	Years of Comm	population gr	state sector	**%labor force**	**ln PPP**	ln PPP^2	agr.share GP	**MILEX**	HDI	

INCOME	ln PPP	(ln PPP)^2	mean y scho	absolute GNP	FDI per GDP	Years of Comm	population gr	state sector	%labor force	%lf agric.	%lf industry	agr.shareGP	MILEX	constant
INEQUAL	-0,233	-0,135	-0,085	-0,105	0,017	-0,005	3,23	-0,024	0,004	-6E-05	-0,373	-0,546	6,416	36,29
	0,251	0,07	0,097	0,052	0,103	0,044	0,649	0,036	0,028	8E-04	0,32	0,612	10,34	47,06
	0,41	5,41												
	6,502	120												
t-test	-0,929	**-1,9**	-0,876	**-2**	0,167	-0,111	**4,98**	-0,661	0,156	-0,081	-1,166	-0,891	0,621	
	ln PPP	**(ln PPP)^2**	mean y scho	**absoluteGNP**	FDI per GDP	Years of Comm	**population gr**	state sector	%labor force	%lf agric.	%lf industry	agr.shareGP	MILEX	constant
LEX	-2E-04	-9E-05	-4E-04	-7E-04	-0,001	-5E-04	-0,012	7E-04	2E-04	-9E-06	0,014	-0,03	0,644	-2,515
	0,002	7E-04	9E-04	5E-04	0,001	4E-04	0,006	3E-04	3E-04	8E-06	0,003	0,006	0,101	0,458
	0,95	0,053												
	161,3	120												
t-test	-0,091	-0,138	-0,426	**-1,4**	-1,162	-1,094	-1,911	**2,05**	0,678	-1,225	**4,42**	**-5**	**6,4**	
	ln PPP	(ln PPP)^2	mean years of schoolinging	**absoluteGNP**	FDI per GDP	Years of Comm	population gr	**state sector**	%labor force	%lf agric.	**%lf industry**	**agr.shareGP**	**MILEX**	

Legend: as in all EXCEL 5.0 outprints in this work, first row: unstandardized regression coefficients, second row: standard errors, last row: t-Test. The values immediately below the standard errors are R^2 (third row, left side entry), *F*, and degrees of freedom (fourth row).

HDI	**MNCP85**	**Govex**	Trade Dep	social sec	UN-membery	Women Parl	Women %LF	ln PCI	ln PCI^2	ln(MPR+1)	Fertility Rate	Constant
	-0,0951	0,15438	0,00472	0,04016	-0,0001	-0,0026	-0,0004	0,00086	-0,0002	0,00063	0,00049	0,4008
	0,00788	0,04003	0,01458	0,21766	0,00106	0,00166	0,00091	0,00258	0,00032	0,00095	0,0007	0,83212
	0,86948											
	67,2242	111										
	-12,076	**3,85622**	0,32366	0,18449	-0,1062	-1,5892	-0,4262	0,33478	-0,7165	0,66302	0,69494	

Gender Development Index	**MNCP85**	**Govex**	Trade Dep	social sec	UN-membery	**Women Parl**	Women %LF	ln PCI	ln PCI^2	ln(MPR+1)	Fertility Rate	Constant
	-0,0715	0,08139	-0,0076	0,18124	0,00092	-0,0022	-0,0002	0,00216	-0,0002	0,00037	0,00066	-0,0725
	0,00578	0,02938	0,0107	0,15974	0,00078	0,00122	0,00067	0,00189	0,00024	0,0007	0,00052	0,61068
	0,87045											
	67,8013	111										

Gender Development Index

	-12,362	**2,77028**	-0,7065	1,1346	1,17456	**-1,8088**	-0,2301	1,13821	-0,7071	0,53633	1,28497	
Gender Empowerment Index	**MNCP85**	Govex	**Trade Dep**	social sec	**UN-membery**	**Women Parl**	Women %LF	ln PCI	ln PCI^2	ln(MPR+1)	Fertility Rate	Constant
	-0,0208	0,00377	0,015	-0,1773	0,00143	0,00548	0,00073	0,00231	-0,0001	5,5E-05	0,0006	0,80515
	0,00409	0,02077	0,00756	0,11292	0,00055	0,00086	0,00047	0,00134	0,00017	0,00049	0,00036	0,43167
	0,82158											
	46,4654	111										

UN memb.y	mean y scho	absolute GNP	1/ERDI	Years of Comm	population gr	state sector	%labor force	ln PPP	ln PPP^2	agr.share GP	MILEX	HDI	
-0,6066	0,1345	0,0217	0,1272	-1,6038	-0,0209	-0,0118	0,3959	0,0281	0,136	9E-05	-0,3013	0,0029	8,738
2,5547	0,0698	0,0181	0,188	3,3241	0,0262	0,0123	0,1755	0,0088	0,1028	0,0002	0,0943	0,0098	14,492
0,525	1,4759												
10,205	120												
POLITICAL REPRESSION													
-0,2375	**1,927**	1,1943	0,6765	-0,4825	-0,7982	-0,9589	**2,256**	**3,211**	1,3238	0,423	**-3,195**	0,3014	
UN memb.y	**mean y scho**	absolute GNP	1/ERDI	Years of Comm	populati on gr	state sector	**%labor force**	**ln PPP**	ln PPP^2	agr.share GP	**MILEX**	HDI	

INCOME	ln PPP	(ln PPP)^2	mean y scho	absolute GNP	1/ERDI	Years of Comm	populati on gr	state sector	%labor force	%lf agric.	%lf industry	agr.shar eGP	MILEX	constant
INEQUAL	-0,256	-0,142	-0,092	-0,108	0,018	-0,002	3,187	-0,022	0,155	-6E-05	-0,413	-0,514	6,016	37,65
	0,256	0,067	0,095	0,053	0,103	0,045	0,645	0,036	0,372	8E-04	0,316	0,617	10,36	47,11
	0,41	5,407												
	6,522	120												
	-1,001	**-2,1**	-0,963	**-2**	0,177	-0,035	**4,94**	-0,62	0,417	-0,081	-1,308	-0,834	0,581	
	ln PPP	**(ln PPP)^2**	mean y scho	**absolute GNP**	1/ERDI	Years of Comm	**population gr**	state sector	%labor force	%lf agric.	%lf industry	agr.shar eGP	MILEX	constant
LEX	7E-05	-2E-04	-5E-04	-7E-04	-0,001	-5E-04	-0,012	7E-04	-0,003	-1E-05	0,014	-0,031	0,662	-2,574
	0,002	7E-04	9E-04	5E-04	0,001	4E-04	0,006	3E-04	0,004	8E-06	0,003	0,006	0,101	0,458
	0,95	0,053												
	161,5	120												
	0,028	-0,237	-0,506	-1,3	-1,141	-1,158	**-1,939**	**2,04**	-0,777	-1,28	**4,46**	**-5,2**	**6,57**	
	ln PPP	(ln PPP)^2	mean y scho	absolute GNP	1/ERDI	Years of Comm	populati on gr	state sector	%labor force	%lf agric.	%lf industry	agr.shar eGP	MILEX	

UN memb.y	mean y scho	absolute GNP	1/ERDI	Years of Comm	populati on gr	state sector	%labor force	ln PPP	ln PPP^2	agr.share GP	MILEX	HDI	constant
-160,91	-0,5424	-0,3566	3,8532	-64,992	0,1067	0,0523	0,4382	-0,1547	1,4447	0,0004	-1,4575	0,1205	426,46
21,357	0,5835	0,1516	1,5714	27,789	0,2187	0,1031	1,4674	0,0732	0,8591	0,0018	0,7884	0,0816	121,15
0,913	12,338												
96,659	120												
-7,534	-0,9296	**-2,352**	**2,452**	**-2,339**	0,4877	0,507	0,2986	**-2,114**	**1,682**	0,1978	**-1,849**	1,4763	
UN memb.y	mean y scho	**absolute GNP**	**1/ERDI**	**Years of Comm**	populati on gr	state sector	%labor force	**ln PPP**	**ln PPP^2**	agr.share GP	**MILEX**	HDI	

INFANT MORTALITY

EARLY DEATH

1/ERDI	**Years of Comm**	population gr	state sector	%labor force	ln PPP	**ln PPP^2**	**agr.share GP**	MILEX	**HDI**	violations pol rights	
0,6842	-53,475	-0,1211	-0,055	0,4553	-6,9204	0,1782	0,0681	0,0424	-0,0793	-0,0911	65,588
0,2385	6,3555	0,1902	0,0493	0,4585	8,2481	0,0714	0,033	0,4793	0,0223	0,2706	36,688
0,894	4,0221										
93,143	122										
2,869	**-8,414**	-0,6366	-1,1146	0,9931	-0,839	**2,498**	**2,064**	0,0885	**-3,556**	-0,3368	
1/ERDI	**Years of Comm**	population gr	state sector	%labor force	ln PPP	**ln PPP^2**	**agr.share GP**	MILEX	**HDI**	violations pol rights	

The comparison of the above models for n = 134 yields the following results and shows, that 1/ERDI is a legitimate indicator of dependency, possibly substituting or at least running parallel to the traditional MNC Penetration indicator in future quantitative studies:

Table 14.2: The Reformulated Theory of Dependency by Comparison

	Model based on:	R^2 for the 134 countries with fairly complete data	F for the entire equation	t-test for the dependency predictor and direction of the influence	further positive, significant predictors	further negative, significant predictors
Explanation of growth	reformulated world system theory	57,20%	12,35	-1,33	mean years of education, population growth	labor force participation rate, military expenditures
	Bornschier	**56%**	**11,86**	**-1,57**	mean years of education, population growth	labor force participation rate, military expenditures
Explanation of infant mortality	**reformulated world system theory**	**91,30%**	**96,7**	**2,45**		UN membership years, absolute GNP, years of Communism, military expenditures
	Bornschier	91,00%	95,04	2,08		UN membership years, absolute GNP, years of Communism, military expenditures
Explanation of early death	**reformulated world system theory**	**89,40%**	**93,14**	**2,87**	agrarian share per GDP	years of Communism, human development index
	Bornschier	89,00%	93,12	2,84	agrarian share per GDP	years of Communism, human development index
Explanation of political repression	**reformulated world system theory**	**52,50%**	**10,2**	**0,68**	educational level, labor force participation rate	military expenditures

	Bornschier	52,00%	9,9	0,45	educational level, labor force participation rate	military expenditures
Explanation of income concentration for the top 20%	**reformulated world system theory**	**41,00%**	**6,52**	**0,17**	population growth	absolute GNP
	Bornschier	41,00%	6,5	0,16	population growth	absolute GNP
Explanation of life expectancy	**reformulated world system theory**	**95%**	**161,5**	**-1,14**	state sector expenditures	population growth
	Bornschier	95%	161,3	-1,16	state sector expenditures, military expenditures	absolute GNP, agrarian share per GDP

Chapter 15

UNEQUAL EXCHANGE, UNEMPLOYMENT AND THE DESTRUCTION OF THE SOCIAL WELFARE STATE

UNEMPLOYMENT

Irrational and socially polarizing as it might be, unequal exchange contributes to the rental interests of the priviledged groups in the centers. One of the main consequences of this process will be rsing unemployment in the centers. Although multivariate evidence speaks in favor of such an interpretation, compatible with Köhler's theory, there could be another possible interpretation. We believe that Köhler's T-ratio could still be negatively linked to unemployment, i.e. the burden of rising unemployment is shifted on to the periphery, and not to the centers, when we take several other variables, that determine the unemployment rate, into account. Under certain conditions, an important qualification of Köhler's theory should be made: Köhler's T-ratio or 1/ERDI could become decisive in determining unemployment if and only of we consider the seperate positive effect of economic growth on the employment situation. Unequal exchange - by reaping the benefits of growth away from the peripheries to the centers, creates a rentier behavior, that pushes unemployment upward. The bi-variate analysis between Köhler's T-ratio and unemployment leads to the following Graph:

Graph 15.1: The Benefits or Losses from Unequal Exchange and Unemployment in the World System

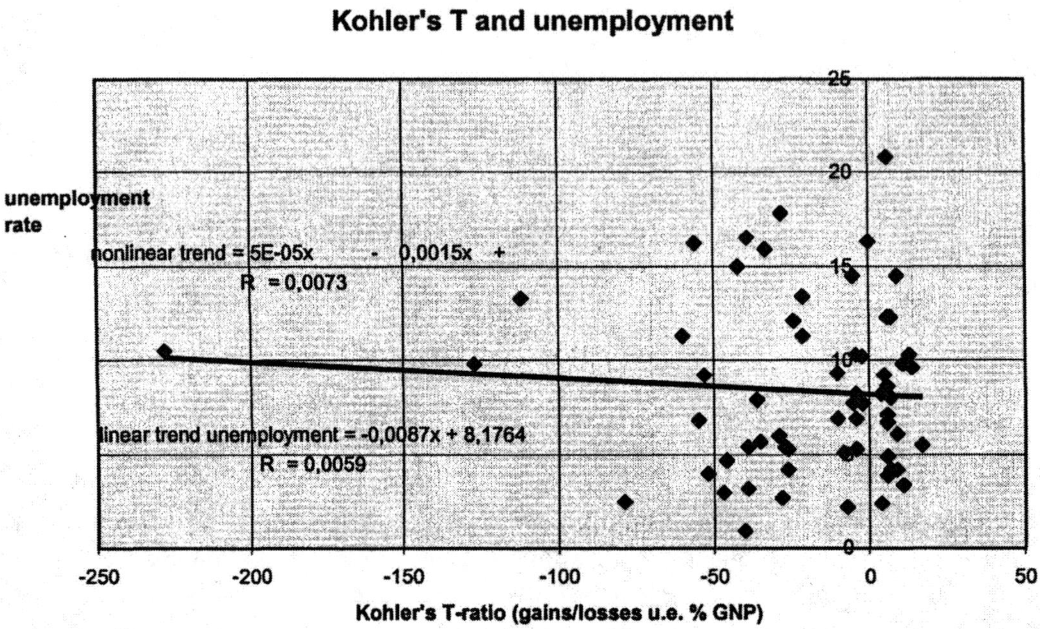

The multi-variate analysis shows the following results:

(15.1) Unemployment =

(un)equal exchange (Köhler's T-ratio)	economic growth 80-95	constant
-0,62484909	-0,01171626	8,98348558
0,26304966	0,01393264	
0,09135972		
3,01636604	60	
-2,37540351	-0,84092202	T-Test
(Köhler's T-ratio)	economic growth 80-95	constant

Note: As in all EXCEL 5.0 outprints, first rows are unstandardized regression coefficients, second rows are standard errors of the estimate, the third row shows the value for R^2 of the whole equation and the standard deviation of the estimate for y; the fourth row are the F-value and the degrees of freedom of the whole equation

In the periphery and semi-periphery, unequal growth takes place, whose benefits are reaped by the transnationals and their allied social strata. The acceptance of inequality *('wage flexibility')* and the dominance of transnational capital in the process become determining conditions for the integration of the reserve army into the employment process, with still rising levels of inequality as a result:

(15.2) Unemployment =

unequal exchange (Köhler's T-ratio)	economic growth 80-95	inequality	constant
-0,14628517	-0,76509924	-0,01931708	15,8104505
0,07709871	0,26795145	0,01422029	
0,1487789			
3,37913631	58		
unequal exchange (Köhler's T-ratio)	**economic growth 80-95**	inequality	unemployment
-1,89737502	**-2,85536515**	-1,35841673	T-Test

Note: as in all EXCEL 5.0 outprints, first rows are unstandardized regression coefficients, second rows are standard errors of the estimate, the third row shows the value for R^2 of the whole equation and the standard deviation of the estimate for y; the fourth row are the F-value and the degrees of freedom of the whole equation

(15.3) Unemployment =

unequal exchange (Köhler's T-ratio)	economic growth 80-95	inequality	Human Development Index	net foreign direct investment as % of GNP	constant
-0,13794483	1,14621461	-0,13383358	-0,76002019	-0,02392859	14,4034281
0,31296029	4,96053901	0,08203541	0,27754667	0,01715502	6,03180242
0,15268095					
2,01816141	56				
-0,44077423	0,23106655	*-1,63141241*	-2,73835092	-1,39484503	T-Test
unequal exchange (Köhler's T-ratio)	economic growth 80-95	*inequality*	Human Development Index	net foreign direct investment as % of GNP	

Note: as in all EXCEL 5.0 outprints, first rows are unstandardized regression coefficients, second rows are standard errors of the estimate, the third row shows the value for R^2 of the whole equation and the standard deviation of the estimate for y; the fourth row are the F-value and the degrees of freedom of the whole equation

Under another specification, the following results are achieved:

(15.4) Unemployment =

Viol Pol Rits	Viol Civ Rits	PopDens *0,5	Terms Trade	1/ERDI	Govex	Trade Dep	social sec	**UN-member years**	Fertility Rate	%agland	ln PCI	ln PCI^2	ln(MPR +1)	constant
-1,2788	-1,185	17,0995	-0,0078	0,99459	-0,0591	-0,1623	-0,0135	0,19489	-0,8063	0,01508	-0,0217	0,28365	-1,2778	-51,83
2,71872	1,2046	18,5641	0,04541	0,7362	0,06399	0,1404	0,02384	0,06666	0,97454	0,05551	0,0298	1,0866	0,75979	70,6909
0,36227														
2,27229	56													
-0,4704	-0,9837	0,92111	-0,1726	1,35098	-0,9233	-1,1561	-0,5674	**2,92357**	-0,8274	0,27161	-0,7276	0,26104	-1,6817	T-Test

econ growth	Viol Civ Rits	PopDens *0,5	Terms Trade	1/ERDI	Govex	Trade Dep	social sec	**UN-member years**	Fertility Rate	%agland	ln PCI	ln PCI^2	ln(MPR +1)	constant
-0,05	-0,911	11,863	-0,016	0,6468	-0,054	-0,131	-0,019	0,1661	-0,978	0,0167	-0,007	-0,945	-0,742	-24,88
2,8065	1,2458	19,38	0,0462	0,8188	0,0645	0,1437	0,0237	0,0656	0,984	0,0561	0,03	0,7653	0,5798	75,166
0,3491														
2,1455	56													
-0,018	-0,731	0,6122	-0,338	0,79	-0,837	-0,913	-0,791	**2,5297**	-0,994	0,2981	-0,24	-1,235	-1,28	T-Test

Legend: As in all EXCEL 5.0 outprints in this work, first row: unstandardized regression coefficients, second row: standard errors, last row: t-Test. The values immediately below the standard errors are $R^{\wedge 2}$ (third row, left side entry), *F*, and degrees of freedom (fourth row). The sample for this analysis is stated in Table 5.1. The other data are from the analysis (n = 123) contained in Tausch, 1998.

At present macro-quantitative knowledge, there is some evidence that speaks in favor of Köhler's employment theory, and there is evidence that would suggest another line of interpretation, already proposed in Tausch (1998) and in Part B above. The international system is functioning like a huge assembly of vested interests that resemble distribution coalitions at the national level. Just like at the national level, where political systems age is a decisive phenomenon, integration age into the system (years of membership at the United Nations) is an important variable. Being part of the vested coalitions, reaps benefits (rents), that increase the privledges of the elites, but block economic growth, redistribution, and full employment. Under these conditions, the significance of unequal exchange for the explanation of unemployment dwindels, and is taken up by *'years of membership at the United Nations'*.

1/ERDI - The Consequences of Unequal Exchange

The empirical evidence presented in this volume also allows us to project the consequences of non-enlargement of the European Union and the continuation of the mechanisms of unequal exchange on a global level. Non-enlargement, and non-membership of the East in the European Monetary Union would mean above all a constant artificial downward drift in the international value of the currencies of the East, allowing the elites in the European West to further benefit from unequal exchange.

1/ERDI, the guarantee, that wages in the East are low in terms of world market exchange rates, has very **profound negative effects on the social development** of the industrialized and transformation countries, as the following Table shows:

Table 15.1: The Effects of Unequal Exchange on the Social Systems of the 'First' and Former 'Second World'

	Unequal Exchange = 1/ERDI
functional illiteracy	0,85
dependence of the economy on agriculture	0,7
prison population rate	0,7
infant mortality	0,69
under five mortality	0,69
maternal mortality rate	0,64
births to young mothers	0,62
predominance of private consumption	0,61
single parent homes	0,61
population below income poverty level (EU standard)	0,57
inflation 1985-95	0,56
waste recycling paper	0,55
burdening of government expenditures by unemployment	0,53

expenditures	
people not expected to survive age 60	0,53
population below 14,40 $ income a day	0,51
SO2 emissions per capita	0,51
CO2 emissions per US $ GDP (energy intensity)	0,51
human poverty index HPI -2-UNDP	0,47
long-term unemployment	0,39
male adults who smoke	0,34
female 6 month long-term unemployment	0,26
female 12 month long-term unemployment	0,26
male heart attacks after 65	0,26
homicide rate	0,25
female heart attacks after 65	0,24
youth unemployment	0,23
imports per GDP	0,23
trees defoliated	0,23
male 12 month long-term unemployment	0,21
male 6 month long-term unemployment.	0,2
deforestation rate	0,16
female unpaid family workers	0,14
female youth unemployment	0,13
total unemployment	0,12
male unemployment	0,08
female unemployment	0,02
involuntary part-time workers	-0,01
exports per GDP	-0,02
gross domestic investment	-0,24
public expenditure on education	-0,25
growth of real earnings per employee	-0,26
government consumption	-0,32
full-time students	-0,33
public expenditure on health	-0,35
increase of labor union participation	-0,36
tax revenue	-0,38
contraceptive prevalence	-0,38
women in government	-0,42
female tertiary students	-0,43
tertiary students	-0,48
R&D scientists and technicians	-0,53
gross domestic savings	-0,54
women in government at ministerial level	-0,56
female net primary enrolment	-0,58
secondary net enrolment	-0,6

export growth rate	-0,62
total expenditure on health	-0,65
export growth 1980-94	-0,65
growth of female net primary enrolment	-0,66
development of the service economy	-0,72
GNP growth 1980-95	-0,73
real GDP per capita poorest 20%	-0,74
waste recycling glass	-0,777
female net secondary enrolment	-0,87

Racism

Small wonder, that - under the pressure of globalization - income polarization tends to widen in European countries such as Austria. Above (Chapter B 4), we already hinted at the fact, that income polarization is nothing but a consequence of the structures of unequal exchange. Our hypothesis now is, that it is this globalization crisis that is to blame for the radicalization of politics - especially in Europe. The latest Eurobarometer survey (October 2001) among the European Union member countries' populations shows that

- support for EU membership in the EU countries has fallen from 70 % in 1991 to 48 %
- only 45 % feel, that EU memberships benefits them (down from 60 % in 1990)
- 14 % of the population of the EU countries would be very relieved, and 45 % of the population would be indifferent, if the EU were scrapped all together. Only 28 % would feel very sorry
- Only 41 % of the population of the EU countries trust the EU, while 40 % distrust it.
- 89 % of the EU population want the fight against poverty and social exclusion as the top EU priority, while welcoming new member countries is a priority for only 29 %
- Only 43 % of the EU population are in favor of EU-enlargement, while 35 % of the population are against it. The worst results (% of the population for enlargement minus % of the population against enlargement) were recorded in Germany (minus 7), France (minus 12) and Austria (minus 16). Generally, only Europeans from the European periphery are favorable towards enlargement: the Greeks (70 % in favor), the Irish (59 %), the Spaniards (55 %), the Portuguese (51 %) and the Italians (51 %).

There will be heterogeneous protest movements around the globe, and in the centers, up to now winner of unequal exchange, income polarization increases:

Graph 15.1: Income polarization in Austria, 1976 - 1997

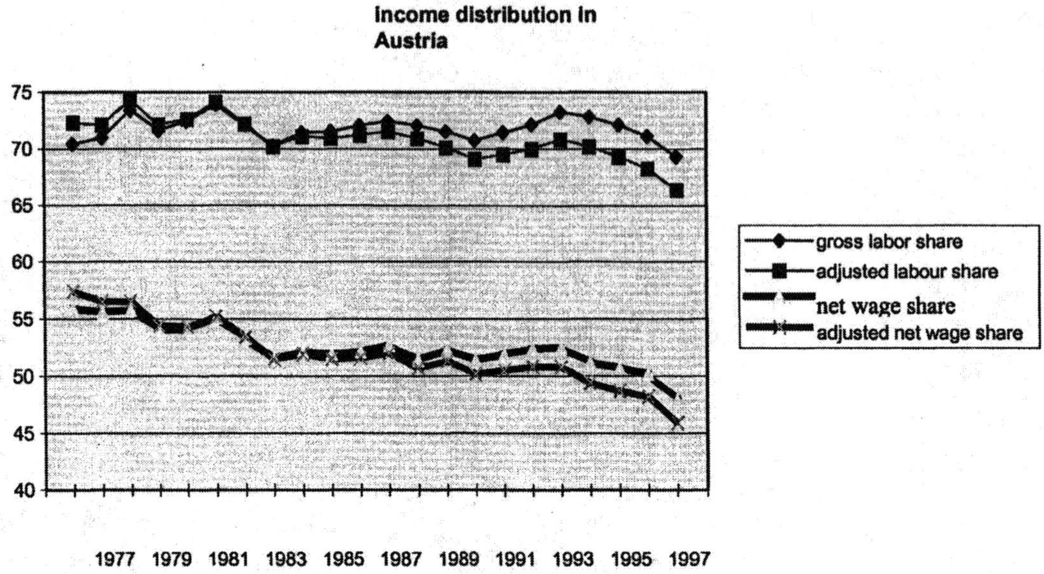

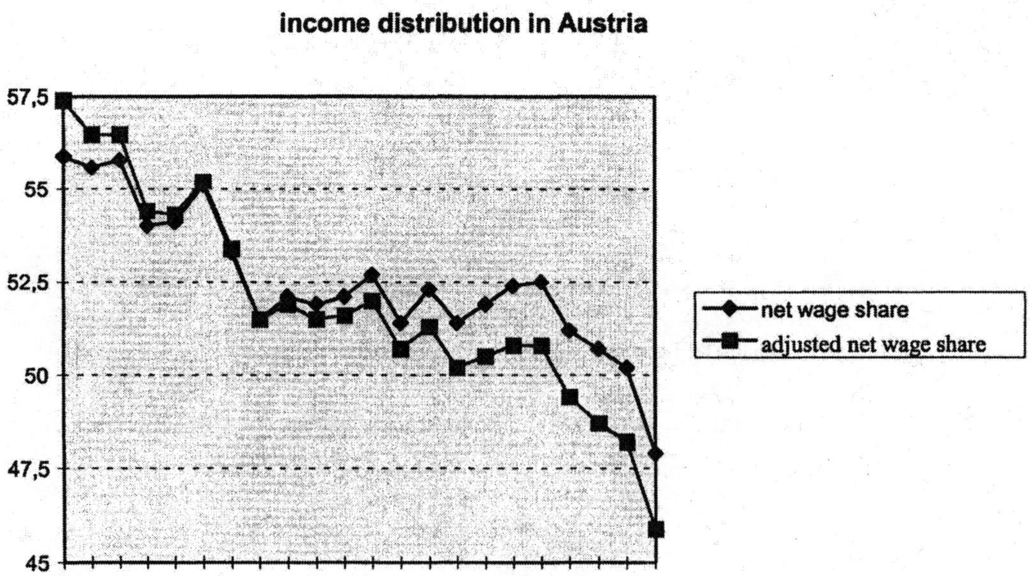

Source: Our own compilations from the data of BMAGS VII.3 and WIFO

Racism (in % of the total adult population, as expressed in EU-wide Eurobarometer research) and enlargement phobia (again in % of the total adult population) are not just an isolated Austrian phenomenon, but are to be strongly encountered in various other European countries:

Table 15.2: Racism and EU-enlargement Phobia in Europe

	racism in %	**rejection of EU enlargement** in %
F	48	35
DK	43	31
D	34	31
L	14	31
A	42	30
IRL	24	22
B	55	19
P	17	19
UK	32	19
NL	31	18
S	18	18
SF	35	17
I	30	13
E	20	12
GR	27	8

Graph 15.3: Racism and EU-enlargement Phobia in Europe - Combined Scales

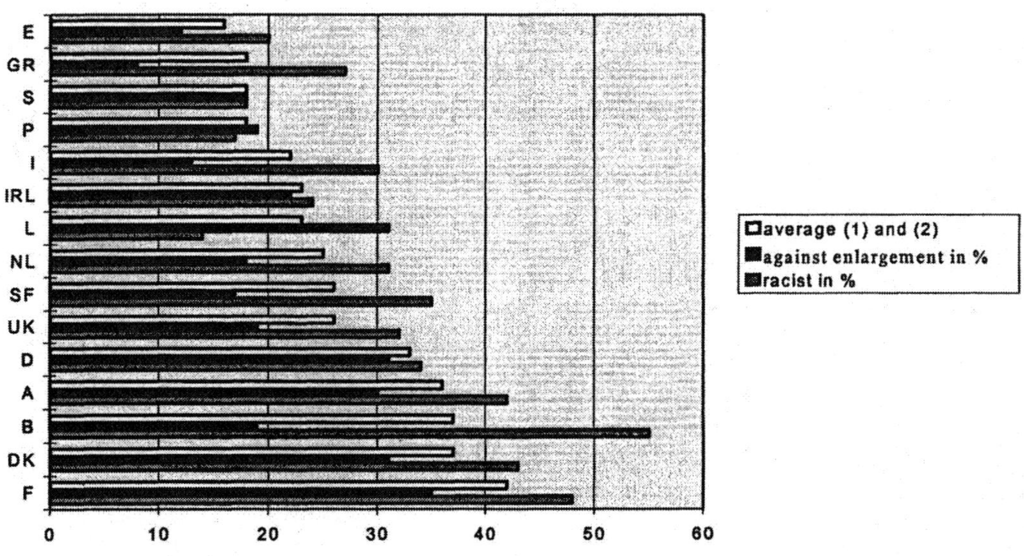

Source: Eurobarometer, 47.1, 1997, and DG X: *http://europa.eu.int/en/comm/dg10/infcom/epo/eo/eo9/tables9/tab05.html*

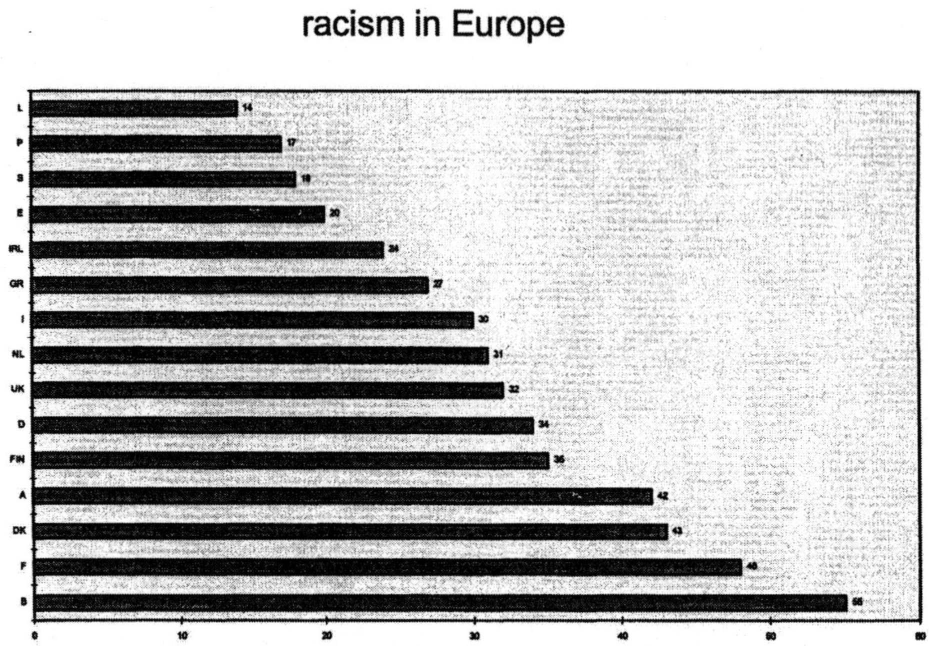

Legend: Eurobarometer 47.1, 1997 (very strong or strong racism in %)

Belgium, France, Denmark and Germany all have considerable potentials along the mentioned scales. Open racism above all is a phenomenon of the rich European North, and not such much the poorer European South:

Graph 15.4: Racism and Development Level in Europe

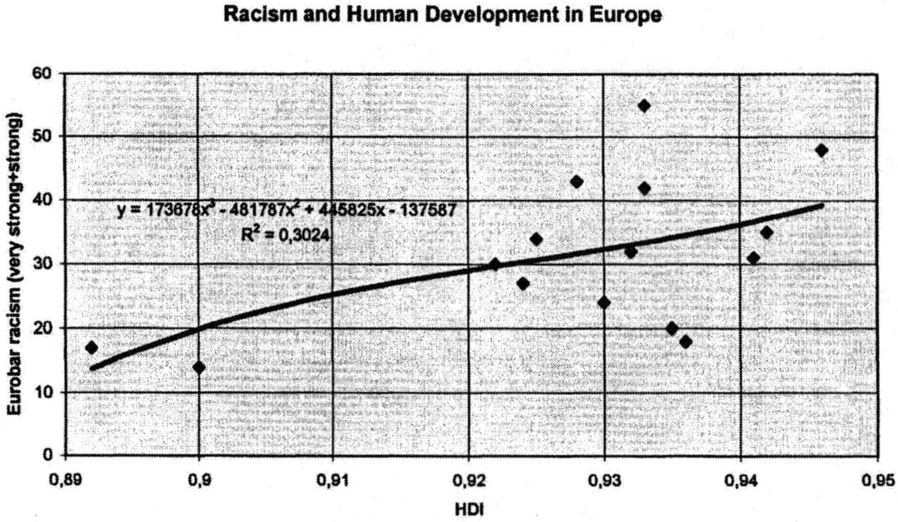

Legend: x-axis UNDP Human development Index; y-axis: Eurobarometer 47/1 1997 - racism and xenophobia (% population very racist or strongly racist)

Our analysis shows furthermore, that both racism and EU-enlargement phobia are fairly clear-cut bi-variate functions of unequal exchange. The victims of unequal exchange tend towards international solidarity, while the beneficiaries of unequal exchange tend towards EU-enlargement phobia. If our analysis is correct, **Europe threatens to be seperated** by a North-South-wall, with the North tending towards an exclusionist far right, and the South towards the Left:

Graph 15.5: Unequal Exchange and Racism/Enlargement Phobia

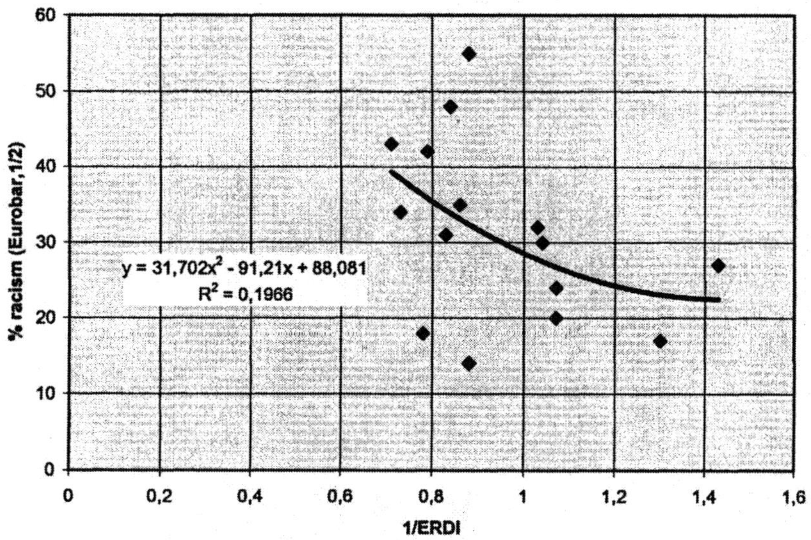

Legend: 1/ERDI (x-axis)measures unequal exchange

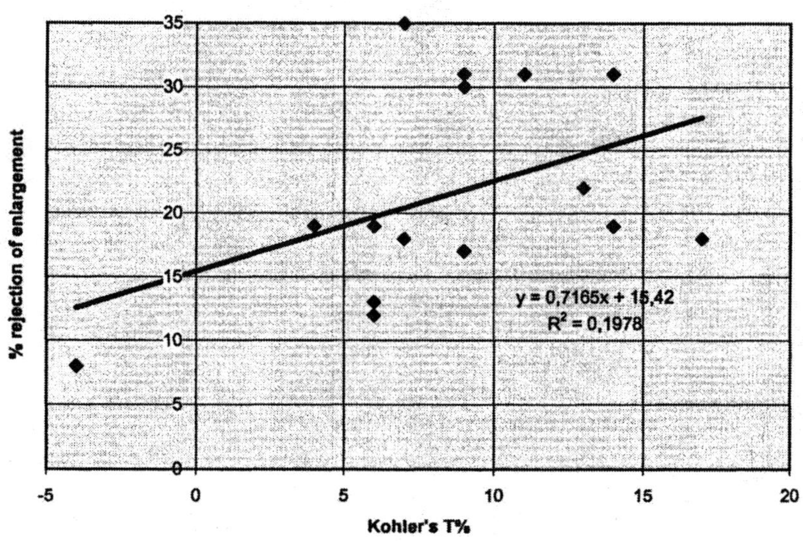

Legend: Köhler's T%-scale: gains from unequal exchange in % des GNP (x-axis); racism/xenophobia (y-axis)

The multivariate explanation of racism and EU-enlargement phobia is:

Racism in Europe =

430,849298 (Coefficient b)	0,26497935 (Coefficient b)	-370,727249 (Constant)
197,246654 (standard error)	0,57083956 (standard error)	182,388576
31,08 % (R^2 of the whole equation)		
2,70521537 (F)	12 (degrees of freedom)	
2,18431739	0,46419234	students t
gains from unequal exchange (Köhler's T-scale)	*human development*	

Note: As in all EXCEL 5.0 outprints, first rows are unstandardized regression coefficients, second rows are standard errors of the estimate, the third row shows the value for R^2 of the whole equation and the standard deviation of the estimate for y; the fourth row are the F-value and the degrees of freedom of the whole equation

Enlargement Phobia in Europe =

-30,4619154 (Coefficient b)	0,15151252 (Coefficient b)	-274,846932 (Coefficient b)	300,612772 (Constant)
8,71427479 (standard error)	0,15848744 (standard error)	136,701281 (standard error)	
58,92 % (R^2 of the whole equation)			
5,2608564 (F)	11 (DF)		
-3,49563402	0,95599074	**-2,01056588**	student's t
UNDP HDI	*racism*	***unequal exchange (1/ERDI)***	*constant*

Note: As in all EXCEL 5.0 outprints, first rows are unstandardized regression coefficients, second rows are standard errors of the estimate, the third row shows the value for R^2 of the whole equation and the standard deviation of the estimate for y; the fourth row are the F-value and the degrees of freedom of the whole equation

The aim of this Chapter was to show the political relevance of the phenomena of unequal exchange for the explanation of unemployment, social polarization and racism. Left to itself, unequal exchange will increase the dangers of authoritarian developments, especially in Europe.

APPENDIX TO PART B

1) NET MIGRATION

The following data were used:

	net migration (foreign population as % of total population or nearest concept minus nationals abroad working as % of total population or nearest concept)	unemployment
NL	4,6	5,5
Belgium	9,1	9,6
Ireland	2,5	10,3
Germany	7,9	9,8
Japan	1,1	3,4
Finland		14,5
Denmark		6,1
Austria	6,6	4,2
France	6,4	12,3
Sweden	5,7	8
Switzerland	17,9	4,2
Norway		4,1
Spain	-2,6	20,8
Italy	0	12,3
Australia	24,7	8,6
UK	3,3	7,1
New Zealand		6,7
USA	8,4	4,9
Iceland		3,9
Canada	15,1	9,2
Portugal	-6,9	8,2
Singapore	10	2,4
Argentina	5	16,3
Uruguay	-6,5	10,2

Israel		7,7
Greece	-3,2	10,3
Paraguay		8,2
Brazil		6,9
El Salvador		5,3
Barbados		14,5
Peru		7,7
Hong Kong	5,2	2,2
South Africa	4,9	5,1
Russia	-2,6	9,3
Turkey	-4,3	6,9
Panama		13,4
Egypt	-16,8	11,3
Colombia	-3,9	12,1
Chile		5,3
Bolivia		4,2
Pakistan	-3,8	5,4
Morocco	-6,4	17,8
Mexico		2,7
Romania		6
Dom Rep		15,9
Costa Rica		5,7
Philippines	-2	7,9
Jamaica		16,5
Fiji		5,4
Honduras		3,2
Thailand	-0,4	0,9
Trinidad & Tob		15
Czech R		4,7
China		3
Indonesia	-0,8	4
Ecuador		9,2
Suriname		10,5
Tunisia	-6,7	16,2
Sri Lanka	-4,1	11,3
Malaysia	5	2,5
Nicaragua		13,3
Mauritius		9,8

Source. Our own compilations from Stalker and Tausch (1998)

	dispersion measure of wages, 1870	adjusted labor force migration rate per 1000, 1870-1910	gains or losses in rel. wages, 1870-1910	dispersion measure of wages, 1910
Argentina	61	15,5	34	95
Australia	127	8,73	8	135
Belgium	60	2,2	27	87
Brazil	39	0,98	46	85
Canada	99	9,14	106	205
Denmark	36	-3,67	63	99
France	50	-0,13	21	71
Germany	58	-0,96	29	87
GB	67	-2,97	28	95
Ireland	49	-14,84	42	91
Italy	26	-12,21	24	50
NL	57	-0,78	20	77
Norway	32	-6,93	47	79
Portugal	18	-1,4	6	24
Spain	30	-1,53	6	36
Sweden	28	-5,55	72	100
USA	115	5,31	55	170

Source. our own compilation from Aghion and Williamson, 1998

2) UNEQUAL EXCHANGE AND UNEMPLOYMENT

Our analysis starts from the following data:

Table: Unequal Exchange and Unemployment - the Data for the Multivariate Model

	unequal exchange (Köhler's T-ratio - gains/losses from unequal exchange as % of GDP)	economic growth 80-95	unemployment
NL	17	1,6	5,5
Belgium	14	1,6	9,6
Ireland	13	3	10,3
Germany	11	1,5	9,8
Japan	11	2,7	3,4
Finland	9	1,2	14,5
Denmark	9	1,8	6,1
Austria	9	1,7	4,2
France	7	1,4	12,3
Sweden	7	0,7	8
Switzerland	7	0,7	4,2

Norway	7	2,5	4,1
Spain	6	2,1	20,8
Italy	6	1,7	12,3
Australia	6	1,5	8,6
UK	6	1,9	7,1
New Zealand	6	1	6,7
USA	6	1,5	4,9
Iceland	6	0,9	3,9
Canada	5	1,1	9,2
Portugal	4	2,4	8,2
Singapore	4	6	2,4
Argentina	0	-0,4	16,3
Uruguay	-2	-0,6	10,2
Israel	-2	2,3	7,7
Greece	-4	1,6	10,3
Paraguay	-4	0	8,2
Brazil	-4	-0,4	6,9
El Salvador	-4	0,5	5,3
Barbados	-5	1,2	14,5
Peru	-5	-0,8	7,7
Hong Kong	-7	4,8	2,2
South Africa	-8	-1	5,1
Russia	-10	-3,3	9,3
Turkey	-10	2,3	6,9
Panama	-21	0,1	13,4
Egypt	-21	1,9	11,3
Colombia	-24	1,6	12,1
Chile	-26	3,2	5,3
Bolivia	-26	-0,5	4,2
Pakistan	-27	2,7	5,4
Morocco	-28	0,7	17,8
Mexico	-28	-0,9	2,7
Romania	-29	-0,6	6
Dom Rep	-33	1,1	15,9
Costa Rica	-35	0,7	5,7
Philippines	-36	-0,3	7,9
Jamaica	-39	1,4	16,5
Fiji	-39	0,6	5,4
Honduras	-39	-0,5	3,2
Thailand	-40	6,3	0,9
Trinidad & Tob	-42	-1,5	15
Czech R	-46	-1	4,7
China	-47	8,6	3

Indonesia	-52	4,9	4
Ecuador	-53	-0,1	9,2
Syria	-55	0,1	6,8
Tunisia	-56	1,2	16,2
Sri Lanka	-60	3,2	11,3
Malaysia	-79	4	2,5
Nicaragua	-112	-3,7	13,3
Mauritius	-127	4,6	9,8
Suriname	-228	3,4	10,5

	unequal exchange (Köhler's T-ratio)	economic growth 80-95	inequality (share of top 20% in total incomes)	Human Development Index	net foreign direct investment as % of GNP	unemployment
NL	17	1,6	36,9	0,941	-1,4	5,5
Belgium	14	1,6	36	0,933	*-1,4*	9,6
Ireland	13	3	39,4	0,93	0,2	10,3
Germany	11	1,5	40,3	0,925	-0,8	9,8
Japan	11	2,7	37,5	0,94	-0,3	3,4
Finland	9	1,2	37,6	0,942	-1,3	14,5
Denmark	9	1,8	38,6	0,928	0,2	6,1
Austria	9	1,7	45,1	0,933	-0,3	4,2
France	7	1,4	41,9	0,946	0	12,3
Sweden	7	0,7	36,9	0,936	1,1	8
Switzerland	7	0,7	44,6	0,93	-2,3	4,2
Norway	7	2,5	36,7	0,943	1	4,1
Spain	6	2,1	36,6	0,935	0,8	20,8
Italy	6	1,7	41	0,922	-0,3	12,3
Australia	6	1,5	42,2	0,932	0,5	8,6
UK	6	1,9	44,3	0,932	-1,1	7,1
New Zealand	6	1	44,7	0,939	*0,5*	6,7
USA	6	1,5	41,9	0,943	-0,6	4,9
Iceland	6	0,9	44,4	0,942	0,1	3,9
Canada	5	1,1	40,2	0,96	-0,2	9,2
Portugal	4	2,4	49,1	0,892	1,3	8,2
Singapore	4	6	48,9	0,896	6	2,4
Argentina	0	-0,4	45,2	0,888	0,5	16,3
Uruguay	-2	-0,6	52,5	0,885	0,7	10,2
Israel	-2	2,3	39,6	0,913	-0,5	7,7
Greece	-4	1,6	44,5	0,924	1,2	10,3
Paraguay	-4	0	50,2	0,707	2,6	8,2
Brazil	-4	-0,4	67,5	0,809	0,7	6,9
El Salvador	-4	0,5	47,8	0,604	0,4	5,3
Barbados	-5	1,2	41,9	0,909	0,7	14,5
Peru	-5	-0,8	50,4	0,729	3,3	7,7
Hong Kong	-7	4,8	47	0,909	5,2	2,2

	unequal exchange (Köhler's T-ratio)	economic growth 80-95	inequality	Human Development Index	net foreign direct investment as % of GNP	unemployment
South Africa	-8	-1	63,3	0,717	0	5,1
Russia	-10	-3,3	53,8	0,769	0,6	9,3
Turkey	-10	2,3	56,5	0,782	0,5	6,9
Panama	-21	0,1	59,8	0,868	3,1	13,4
Egypt	-21	1,9	41,1	0,612	1,3	11,3
Colombia	-24	1,6	55,8	0,85	3,4	12,1
Chile	-26	3,2	61	0,893	2,6	5,3
Bolivia	-26	-0,5	48,2	0,593	2,6	4,2
Pakistan	-27	2,7	39,7	0,453	0,7	5,4
Morocco	-28	0,7	46,3	0,557	0,9	17,8
Mexico	-28	-0,9	55,3	0,855	2,9	2,7
Romania	-29	-0,6	34,8	0,767	1,2	6
Dom Rep	-33	1,1	39,2	0,72	2,3	15,9
Costa Rica	-35	0,7	50,7	0,889	4,3	5,7
Philippines	-36	-0,3	47,8	0,677	1,9	7,9
Jamaica	-39	1,4	47,5	0,735	5,3	16,5
Fiji	-39	0,6	48,5	0,869	3,5	5,4
Honduras	-39	-0,5	57,4	0,573	1,4	3,2
Thailand	-40	6,3	52,7	0,838	1,3	0,9
Trinidad & Tob	-42	-1,5	50	0,88	6,3	15
Czech R	-46	-1	32,6	0,884	5,7	4,7
China	-47	8,6	43,9	0,65	5,2	3
Indonesia	-52	4,9	40,7	0,679	2,3	4
Ecuador	-53	-0,1	50,3	0,767	2,8	9,2
Suriname	-228	3,4	46,6	0,796	4,2	10,5
Tunisia	-56	1,2	46,3	0,774	1,5	16,2
Sri Lanka	-60	3,2	39,3	0,716	0,5	11,3
Malaysia	-79	4	53,7	0,834	7,2	2,5
Nicaragua	-112	-3,7	55,2	0,547	4,4	13,3
Mauritius	-127	4,6	47,6	0,833	0,4	9,8

	unemployment	long-term growth
USA	4,9	1,9
Switzerland	4,2	1,5
Canada	9,2	2,3
Germany	9,8	2,3
Japan	3,4	4,8
France	12,3	2,7
Swe	8	2
DK	6,1	2,4
Aus	4,2	2,9
SF	14,5	2,7
Blg	9,6	2,7
Austral	8,6	2,1
Norw	4,1	3,4
Ital	12,3	3,1
Sing	2,4	6,4
UK	7,1	2
NL	5,5	2,3
Hong	2,2	5,8
NZ	6,7	1,4
Spa	20,8	3,4
Bangl	2,5	0,9
Israel	7,7	3,2
Ire	10,3	3,5
Port	7,2	3,8
Barb	14,5	2,7
Gree	10,3	3,4
Trinid	15	1,3
Ven	10,3	-0,2
Malay	2,5	4,3
Mex	2,7	1,8
Urug	10,2	1
Maurit	9,8	3,4
South A	5,1	0,5
Syria	6,8	2,2
Braz	6,9	2,6
TRK	6,9	2,6
Costa	5,7	1,7
Fiji	5,4	1,8
Arg	16,3	1
Colom	12,1	2,2
Guya	11,7	0,4

Thai	0,9	5,3
Sur	10,5	2,9
Tune	16,2	2,9
Botsw	21,5	6,1
Pan	13,4	2,4
Hond	3,2	0,8
Ecu	9,2	2,3
Alger	26,4	0,5
Jamai	16,5	0,9
Para	8,2	2,0
Peru	7,7	0,2
Boliv	4,2	0,7
Sri L	11,3	2,7
Domin	15,9	1,7
El Sal	8	0,8
Pak	5,4	3
Moroc	17,8	1,7
Egypt	11,3	3,2
Phil	7,9	1,2
Antig	6	5
Baham	9,8	1,2
Belize	12,7	3
Domi	23,1	1,7
Gren	17	3,4
Hun	8,7	3,3
Indonesia	4	3,9
Korea	2	7,1
China	3	5,5
Saint Lucia	20,5	4,9
Saint Vincent	19,8	2,6

Legend: our own compilation from Köhler, Unequal Exchange 1965 - 1995 (in this volume); UNDP HDR 1998 and Fischer Weltalmanach (economic growth; human development; net foreign direct investment); Tausch (1998; inequality; share of the top 20% in total incomes) and UN Statistics Divsion, *http://www.un.org/Depts/unsd/social/unempl.htm* (unemployment)

3) Eastern Europe in the World Economy

The Fall of the Berlin Wall makes it necessary to re-arrange existing data bases and research designs for the study of transnational capitalism. Data compiled by the author from recent issues of the *Economist* and *Business Central Europe* allow for a more detailed assessment of TNC dependence in East Central Europe and its effect on the economic well-being of countries, very recently integrated completely into the capitalist orbit:

Basic Data: Transformation Countries

Country	Capital	Population	GDP growth	Inflation	Unemployment	GDP per cap	FDI stock	Exports bn $	Imports bn $
Yugoslavia	Belgrade	10,5	6	70	26	777	1,1	2,4	4,8
Uzbekistan	Tashkent	23,6	2	40	0,6	611	0,423	3,7	3,8
Ukraine	Kiev	50,9	0	11	2,3	976	1,6	15,4	19,6
Turkmenistan	Dushanbe	6,1	3	46,3	2,9	179	0,087	0,746	0,81
Slovenia	Ljubljana	2	4	8,5	14,4	9101	2,5	8,4	9,2
Slovakia	Bratislava	5,4	5	7,5	11,6	3624	1,4	8,8	10,3
Russia	Moscow	147	-5	40	10,9	3056	10,3	88,8	72,2
Romania	Bucharest	22,5	-5	60	8,8	1,549	2,8	8,4	10,4
Poland	Warsaw	38,7	5,2	11	10,5	3512	26,6	27,2	38,5
Albania	Tirana	3,2	9	21,9		708	0,339	0,226	0,901
Armenia	Yerevan	3,7	6	11	10,7	435	0,265	0,233	0,793
Azerbaijan	Baku	7,6	6,7	0,9	19,3	509	3,2	1,6	1,2
Belarus	Minsk	10,2	5	50	2,8	1314	0,346	7,4	8,7
Bosnia H.	Sarajevo	4,1	30	3	40	1087		0,57	2,199
Bulgaria	Sofia	8,3	4	25	13,7	1227	1	4,9	4,5
Moldova	Chisinau	4,3	-2	13	1,6	504	0,342	0,823	1,142
Macedonia	Skopje	2	5	1,3	36	1663	0,124	1,2	1,6
Lithuania	Vilnius	3,7	3	5,5	5,9	2581	1	4,2	5,3
Croatia	Zagreb	4,5	2,5	5,8	17,5	4267	2,1	4,2	9,4
Czech R	Prague	10,3	-1,5	11	5,2	5050	7,6	22,5	27,1
Estonia	Tallinn	1,5	5	11	10,5	3230	1,4	2,3	3,4
Georgia	Tbilisi	5,4	9	4	5,2	968	0,512	0,463	0,947
Hungary	Budapest	10,1	4,6	15	10,4	4462	22,5	19,6	21,4
Kazakhstan	Astana	15,7	1	10	4,1	1434	5,7	6,8	7,2
Kyrgyzstan	Bishkek	4,6	4	12	3,2	366	0,309	0,631	0,646
Latvia	Riga	2,5	4	5,3	7	2211	1,9	1,8	2,7

Country	FDI penetration	Population	GDP in bn$	GDP growth	Inflation	Unemploy-ment	GDP per cap	FDI stock	Exports bn $	Imports bn $	(M-X)/GDP
Albania	14,963	3,2	2,2656	9	21,9		708	0,339	0,226	0,901	29,79
Armenia	16,465	3,7	1,6095	6	11	10,7	435	0,265	0,233	0,793	34,79
Azerbaijan	82,722	7,6	3,8684	6,7	0,9	19,3	509	3,2	1,6	1,2	-10,34
Belarus	2,582	10,2	13,4028	5	50	2,8	1314	0,346	7,4	8,7	9,7
Bosnia H.	0	4,1	4,4567	30	3	40	1087		0,57	2,199	36,55
Bulgaria	9,819	8,3	10,1841	4	25	13,7	1227	1	4,9	4,5	-3,93
Croatia	10,937	4,5	19,2015	2,5	5,8	17,5	4267	2,1	4,2	9,4	27,08
Czech R	14,611	10,3	52,015	-1,5	11	5,2	5050	7,6	22,5	27,1	8,84
Estonia	28,896	1,5	4,845	5	11	10,5	3230	1,4	2,3	3,4	22,7
Georgia	9,795	5,4	5,2272	9	4	5,2	968	0,512	0,463	0,947	9,26
Hungary	49,927	10,1	45,0662	4,6	15	10,4	4462	22,5	19,6	21,4	3,99
Kazakhstan	25,318	15,7	22,5138	1	10	4,1	1434	5,7	6,8	7,2	1,78
Kyrgyzstan	18,354	4,6	1,6836	4	12	3,2	366	0,309	0,631	0,646	0,89
Latvia	34,374	2,5	5,5275	4	5,3	7	2211	1,9	1,8	2,7	16,28
Lithuania	10,472	3,7	9,5497	3	5,5	5,9	2581	1	4,2	5,3	11,52
Macedonia	3,728	2	3,326	5	1,3	36	1663	0,124	1,2	1,6	12,03
Moldova	15,781	4,3	2,1672	-2	13	1,6	504	0,342	0,823	1,142	14,72
Poland	19,571	38,7	135,914	5,2	11	10,5	3512	26,6	27,2	38,5	8,31
Romania	8,034	22,5	34,8525	-5	60	8,8	1549	2,8	8,4	10,4	5,74
Russia	2,293	147	449,232	-5	40	10,9	3056	10,3	88,8	72,2	-3,7
Slovakia	7,154	5,4	19,5696	5	7,5	11,6	3624	1,4	8,8	10,3	7,66
Slovenia	13,735	2	18,202	4	8,5	14,4	9101	2,5	8,4	9,2	4,4
Turkmenistan	7,968	6,1	1,0919	3	46,3	2,9	179	0,087	0,746	0,81	5,86
Ukraine	3,221	50,9	49,6784	0	11	2,3	976	1,6	15,4	19,6	8,45
Uzbekistan	2,934	23,6	14,4196	2	40	0,6	611	0,423	3,7	3,8	0,69
Yugoslavia	13,483	10,5	8,1585	6	70	26	777	1,1	2,4	4,8	29,42

From these data, it is possible to draw some generalized conclusions. First, inflation is a clearly decreasing function of economic growth in the transformation region:

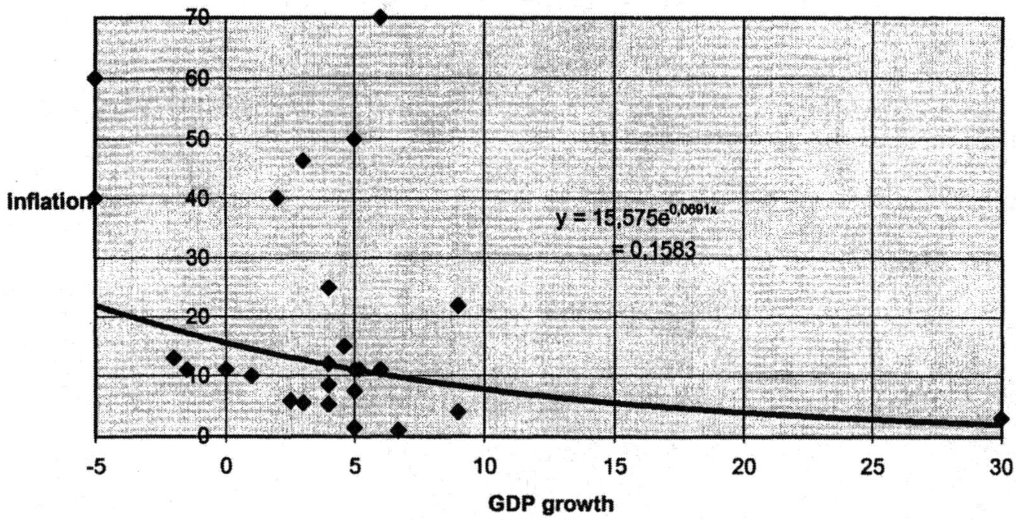

Secondly, FDI's flow into these regions, where GDP per capita is already higher. FDI stocks - in absolute terms - are a neat function of achieved GDP per capita:

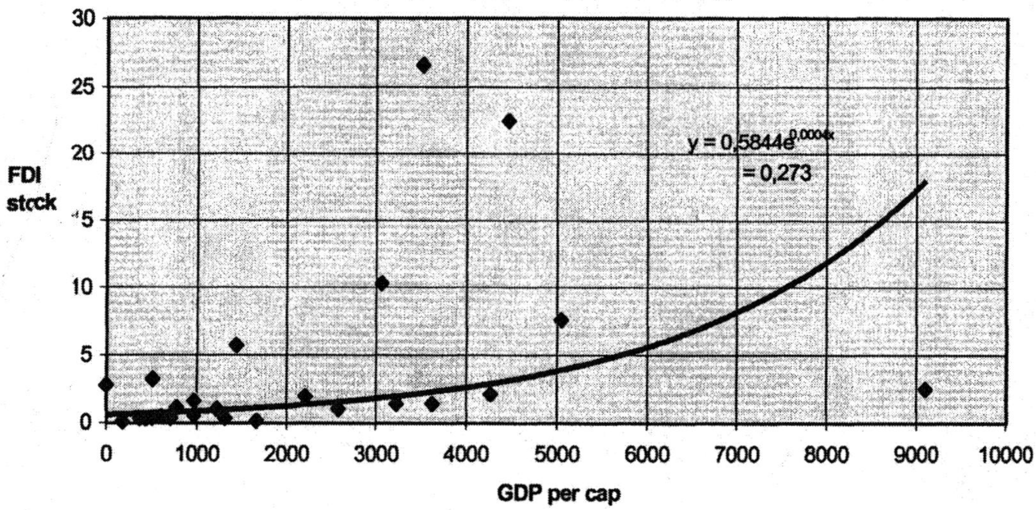

Thirdly, FDI stocks largely determine exports; in a world economy, structured by oligopolies, market access for the periphery largely depends on FDI stock:

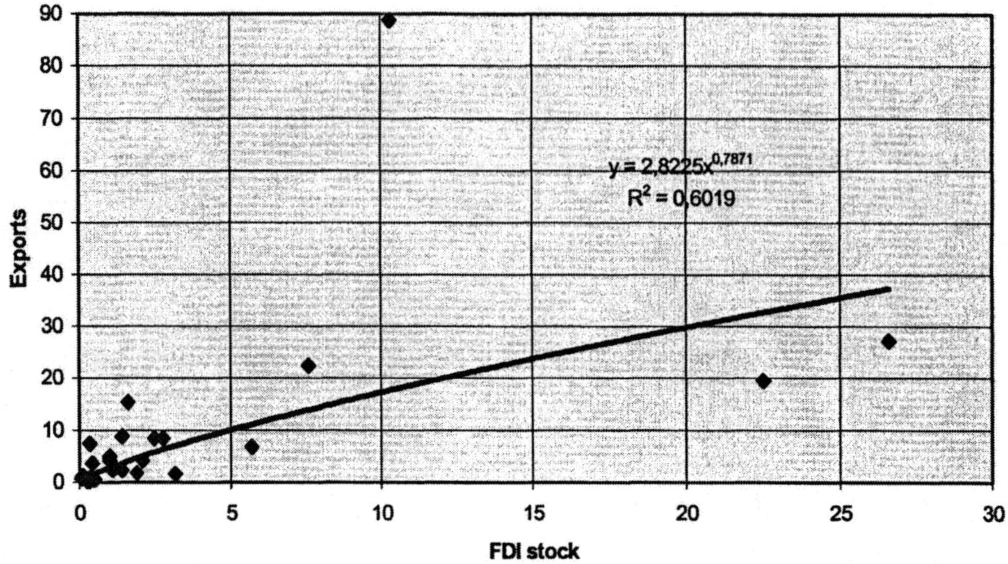

Fourthly, FDI stock per GDP, and thus MNC penetration, alleviates unemployment, but only to a certain degree:

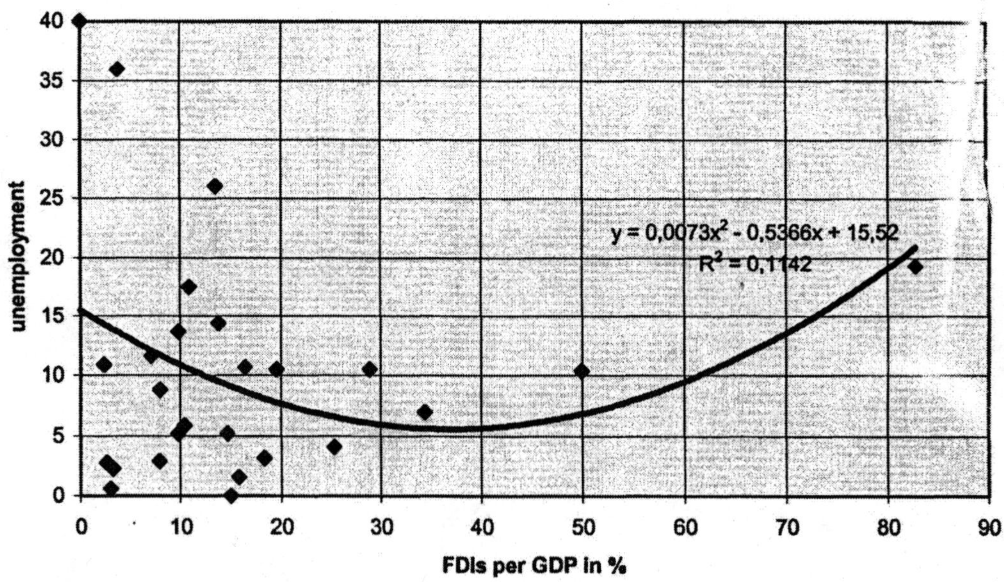

Fifthly, economic growth is not affected by MNC penetration in a positive direction, expected by modernization theories:

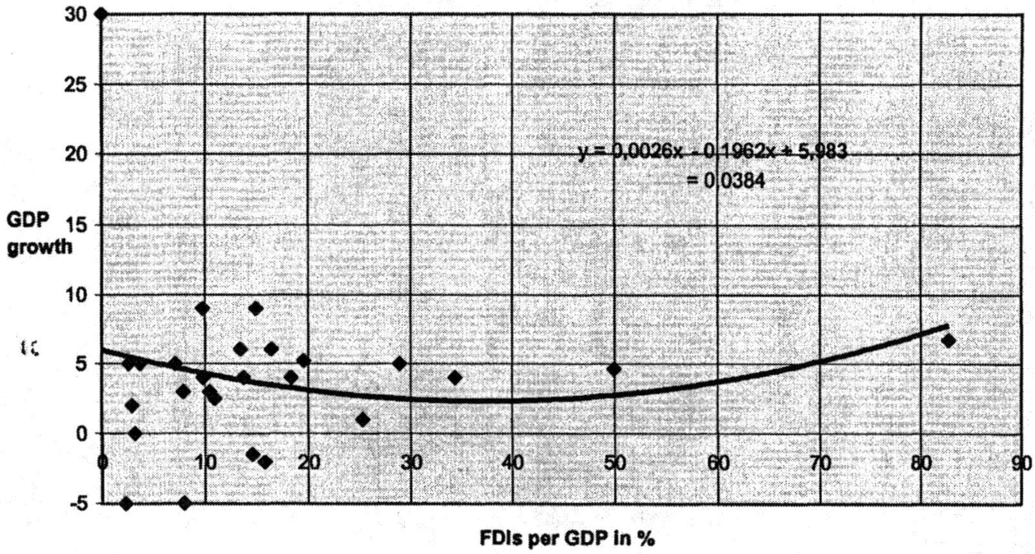

4) THE EU ACCESSION OF POLAND

The EU integration of Poland will become a critical test case for theories of peripheral capitalism. Ever since the reception of the original Polish debate by Wallerstein's classic (1976), the case of Poland - once the biggest state in Europe, that went into decline after the onset of the expansion of world capitalism after the re-discovery of America in 1492 - has a theoretical significance that goes far beyond the borders of this country. The European Union, that Poland is about to enter, is a Union, characterized by distribution coalitions and market interventions. The basic data about EU finance recently were published by *Le Monde* and *Bilan du Monde,* published by the same newspaper:

EU-country	GNP in $	contr budget Euros	Eur contribution, in explained GNP	paying by much or little in Euros	too net too contribution Mill	net contr in % gross contr.	GNP per capita	net contr in % of gross contr.
Germany	2319,5	21217,3	19976,9	1240,4	-10943,5	-51,6	28260	-51,6
France	1526	13185,9	13195,2	-9,3	-781,1	-5,9	26050	-5,9
UK	1220,2	8928,1	10581,7	-1653,6	-1798,8	-20,1	20710	-20,1
Italy	1165,4	8667,1	10113,4	-1446,3	-61,3	-0,7	20120	-0,7
Spain	570,1	5367,6	5025,7	341,9	5936	110,6	14510	110,6
NL	402,7	4837,6	3595	1242,6	-2276,2	-47,1	25820	-47,1
BLG	268,4	2971,4	2447,2	524,2	1079,5	36,3	26420	36,3
Sweden	232	2326	2136,1	189,9	-1129,5	-48,6	26220	-48,6
Austria	225,9	2110,4	2084	26,4	-723,6	-34,3	27980	-34,3
DK	171,4	1505,8	1618,2	-112,4	68,6	4,6	32500	4,6
Portugal	103,9	1077,8	1041,3	36,5	2721,8	252,5	10450	252,5
SF	123,8	1061,9	1211,4	-149,5	56,1	5,3	24080	5,3
Ireland	66,4	687	720,8	-33,8	2676,7	389,6	18280	389,6
Luxembourg	18,8	170,7	314	-143,3	725,5	425	45330	425
Greece	126,2	1178,4	1231,9	-53,5	4371,8	371	12010	371

A reasoning, symbolized by a line of perfect social justice would now show, that the poorer nations proportionately to their low per capita income receive back a greater share of their contributions to the common budget (the straight line); while in reality, the line corresponds to an 'U', with Luxembourg, Ireland, Greece, and Portugal disproportionately gaining from the Union budget, in a set-up that benefits the poor and the super-rich tax heaven at the expense of the 'EU middle class':

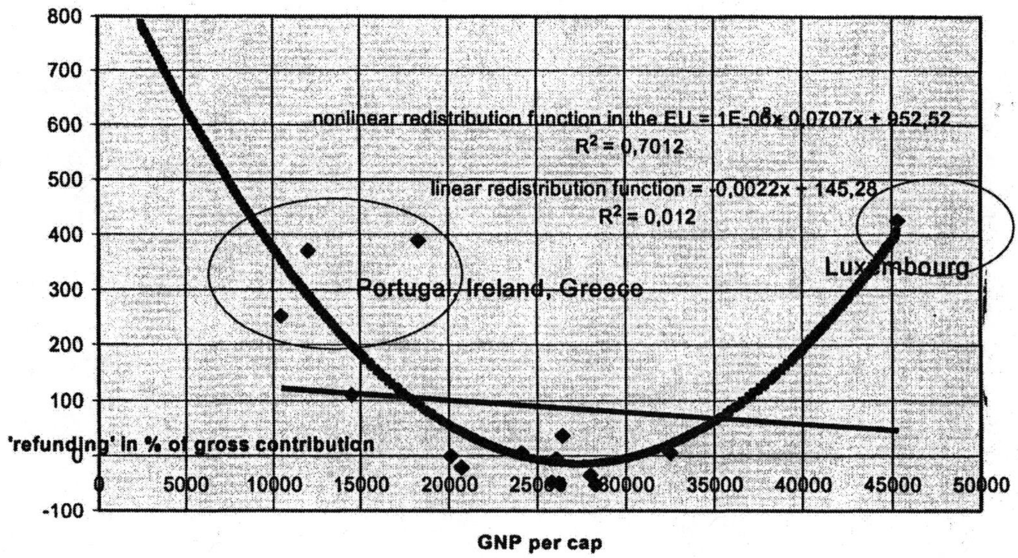

Based on the special issue of the *Austrian Political Science Journal (OeZP,* 4, 1998), and the UNDP data set (1998), it is also possible to draw conclusions about the most probable length of negotiations to be expected for the Polish case. The share of agriculture in total employment should provide, paradoxically enough, no major stumbling bloc, if the former negotiations are to be any guideline for the present enlargement process:

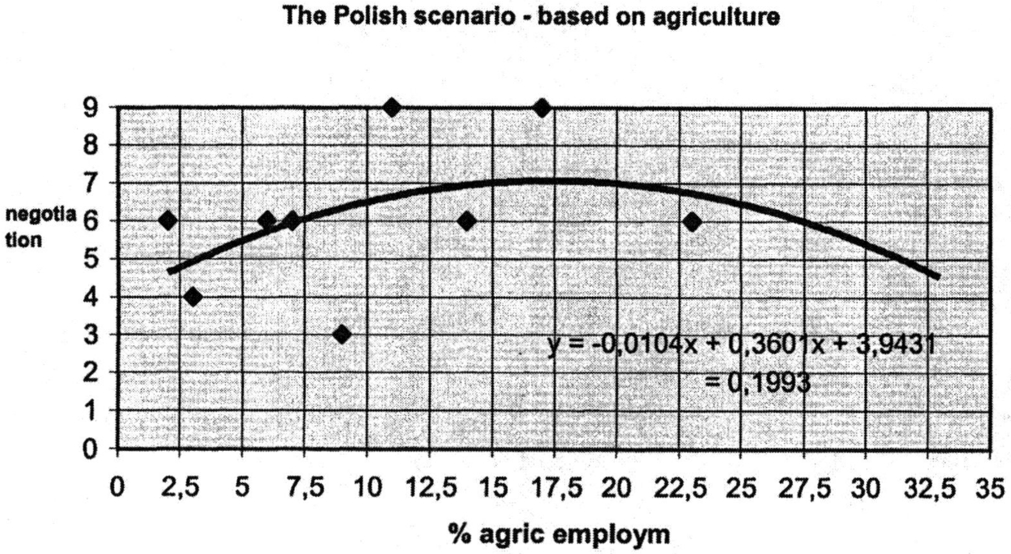

However, differences in real per capita incomes are a much more serious stumbling bloc, and would make us expect, that Poland will be able to finish its accession by 2005, 11 years after its bid for membership. Countries below the 5000 $ real purchasing power parity benchmark (in 1987 dollars) see their negotiation process increased dramatically in length, while only the very rich countries (> 15000 $) had a shorter negotiation process:

The Polish scenario - based on PCI

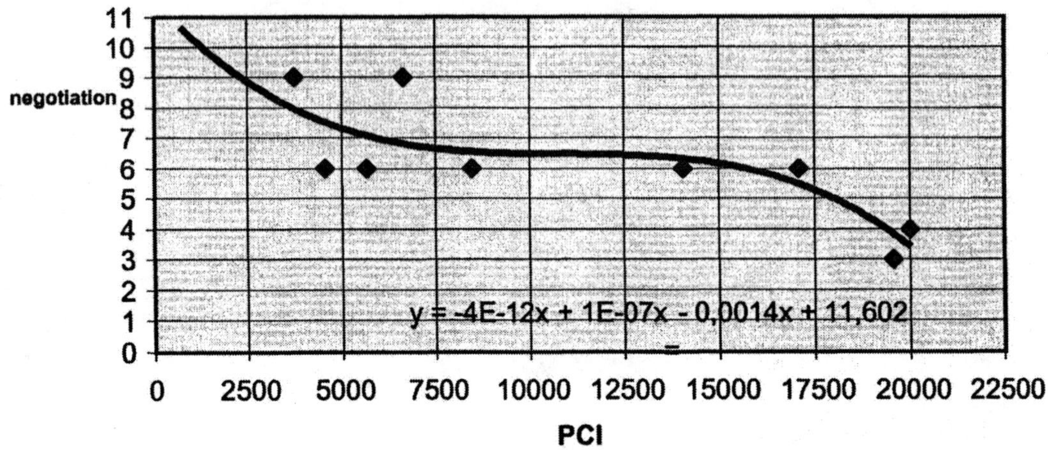

Quite a similar scenario emerges from a comparison of the length of negotiations and the Human Development Index at the time of accession:

Polish scenario based on HDI

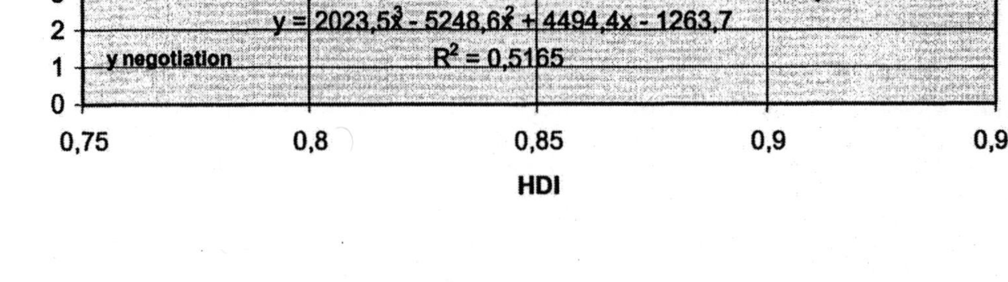

5) The Social Sector and Development

Country Code	top/bottom	social sec	educ exp	health exp	top 20%
Canada	7,1	21,7	7,6	7,4	40,2
USA	8,9	10,5	5,3	6,2	41,9
Japan	4,3	11,5	4,7	5,2	37,5
NL	4,5		5,9	6,8	36,9
NOR	5,9	19,6	8,4	7,6	36,7
SF	6	30,5	7,3	7	37,6
France	7,5		5,7	7,3	41,9
Iceland			5,8	6,9	44,4
Swed	4,6	38,3	8,3	6,2	36,9
Spain	4,4		4,6	5,7	36,6
Australia	9,6		5,5	5,8	42,2
Belgium	4,6		5,2	7,3	36
Austria		24,5	5,8	6	45,1
NZ	8,8	20,2	7,1	5,9	44,7
CH	8,6	14	5,2	6,8	44,6
UK	9,6		5,2	5,9	44,3
DK	7,1	29,5	7,4	5,5	38,6
GER	5,8	24,5	4,7	6	40,3
IRE		19,4	6,2	5,1	39,4
ITA	6		5,4	6,2	41
GRE			3,1	4,3	44,5
ISR	6,6	11,8	5,8	4,2	39,6
LUX			4,1	6,3	41,8
MAL			4,6	4,169	44
POR		9	5	4,1	49,1
HUNG	3,2	17,3	7	6	36,6
LATV		9,1	6,7	2,58	36,7
POL	3,9	17	5,6	5,1	36,6
RUS	11,4		4	3,9	53,8
BELR		12	6,6	3,2	32,9
BULG	4,7	19,8	5,9	5,4	39,3
EST			5,8	4,59	46,3
KAZ			7,7	4,4	40,4
ROM		16,9	3,6	3,9	34,8
UKR			7,8	3,3	35,4
LITH			5,5	3,6	42,1
ARM			7,3	4,2	48,4
UZB			9,5	5,9	50,1
AZER			7,7	4,3	48,6
KYR			6,9	5	49,1

Country Code	top/bottom	social sec	educ exp	health exp	top 20%
GEO			5,2	4,5	45,6
ALB			3,4	4	48,7
TAJ			8,6	6	50,3
Hong Kong	8,7		2,8	1,1	47
Cyprus			4	1,788	44,5
Barbados			7		41,9
Bahamas			3,6	3	49,4
S-Korea	5,7	2,3	4,2	2,7	45,2
Argentina		4,5	3,1	2,5	45,2
Costa Rica	12,7		4,4	5,67	50,7
Uruguay		14,8	2,8	2,5	52,5
Chile	18,3		2,9	3,4	61
Singapore	9,6	7,2	3	1,1	48,9
Trinidad			4		50
Bahrein			4,8	3,276	51,1
Antigua			2,7		44,8
Panama	29,9		5,5	5,76	59,8
Venezuela	10,3		5,3	2	58,4
Saint Kitts			3,3		40,4
Fiji			5,6	2,322	48,5
Mexico	13,6		4,9	1,6	55,3
Colombia	15,5	2,4	3,1	1,8	55,8
Thailand	8,3	0,1	4	1,1	52,7
Malaysia	11,7	2,3	5,5	1,3	53,7
Mauritius		3,6	3,7	1,98	47,6
Brazil	32,1		4,6	2,8	67,5
Seychelles			8,5	2	47,8
Dominica			5,8		39,2
Belize			5,7	3,809	49,4
Algeria	6,7		8,1	5,4	46,1
Botswana	16,4		8,3	2	50,7
Saint Vincent			6,7	3,25	46,3
Suriname			7,3		46,6
Saint Lucia			9,9		46,4
Grenada			6,7	2,5	43,4
Tunesia	7,8	4,1	6,1	3,3	46,3
Oman			3,8	3,84	50,8
Turkey		4,9	3,4	1,5	56,5
Paraguay			2,6	1,2	50,2
Jamaica	8,1		4,7	2,254	47,5
Dominican R	13,2		1,6	2,1	55,7
Sri Lanka	4,4	2,5	3,3	1,8	39,3

Country Code	top/bottom	social sec	educ exp	health exp	top 20%
Peru	10,5		3,8	1,9	50,4
Philippines	7,4	1,2	2,9	1	47,8
South Africa	19,2		7	3,2	63,3
Indonesia	4,9		2,2	0,7	40,7
Guyana			7,8		46,4
Egypt			5	1	41,1
Maldives			6,6	2	49,9
China	6,5		2	2,1	43,9
Swaziland			6		50,1
Bolivia	8,6	1,6	6,6	2,4	48,2
Guatemala	30		1,5	2,1	63
Mongolia			8,5	1	48,9
Honduras	23,5		4,1	2,9	57,4
El Salvador			1,6	2,6	47,8
Namibia			9,4	4	49,7
Nicaragua	13,2		6,8	6,7	55,2
Gabon			4,5		50,2
Cape Verde			4,2		48,5
Morocco	7	1,8	5,8	0,9	46,3
Zimbabwe	15,6		9,1	3,2	62,3
Congo			8,6		50
Papua NG			5,4	2,8	49
Cameroon			3,1	1	49,7
Kenya	18,2	0,7	5,4	2,7	62,1
Ghana	6,3	0,1	3,1	1,7	42,2
Lesotho	20,7		6	4,16	60,1
Equatorial G			1,8		46,5
Pakistan	4,7		2,7	1,8	39,7
India	4,7	0,3	3,7	1,3	42,6
Zambia	8,9		2,6	2,2	50,4
Nigeria	9,6		0,708	1,2	49,3
Comoros			4,1	3,3	50,3
Togo		1,1	6,7	2,5	46,8
Bangladesh	4,1		2,3	1,4	37,9
Tanzania	26,1		5	3,2	45,4
Cote d'Ivoire	6,5		6,636	1,7	44,1
C African R			2,8	2,6	48,8
Mauritania	13,2	0,9	5	1,336	46,5
Madagascar			2,9	1,3	50
Nepal	4,3		2,9	2,2	39,5
Rwanda	4		3,8	1,9	39,1
Benin			3,1	2,8	49,2

Country Code	top/bottom	social sec	educ exp	health exp	top 20%
Malawi			3,3	2,9	55,2
Guinea-Biss.	28		3,2	0,725	58,9
Gambia			2,7	2,142	50,2
Chad			2,3	4,7	48,4
Burundi		0,4	3,7	1,7	48,6
Mozambique			6,2	4,4	49
Burkina F.		0,6	2,7	7	48,9
Mali			2,8	2,8	49,3
Sierra L.			1,4	1,7	54,5
Niger		0,4	2,3004	3,4	44,1

6) Samples and Data on a World Level

List of Variables

The models based on 134 countries
The sample:

Canada
USA
Japan
NL
NOR
SF
France
Iceland
Swed
Spain
Australia
Belgium
Austria
NZ
CH
UK
DK
GER
IRE
ITA
GRE
ISR
LUX

MAL
POR
HUNG
LATV
POL
RUS
BELR
BULG
EST
KAZ
ROM
UKR
LITH
ARM
UZB
AZER
KYR
GEO
ALB
TAJ
Hong Kong
Cyprus
Barbados
Bahamas
S-Korea
Argentina
Costa Rica
Uruguay
Chile
Singapore
Trinidad
Bahrein
Antigua
Panama
Venezuela
Saint Kitts
Fiji
Mexico
Colombia
Thailand
Malaysia
Mauritius
Brazil

Seychelles
Dominica
Belize
Algeria
Botswana
Saint Vincent
Suriname
Saint Lucia
Grenada
Tunesia
Oman
Turkey
Paraguay
Jamaica
Dominican R
Sri Lanka
Peru
Philippines
South Africa
Indonesia
Guyana
Egypt
Maldives
China
Swaziland
Bolivia
Guatemala
Mongolia
Honduras
El Salvador
Namibia
Nicaragua
Gabon
Cape Verde
Morocco
Zimbabwe
Congo
Papua NG
Cameroon
Kenya
Ghana
Lesotho
Equatorial G

Pakistan
India
Zambia
Nigeria
Comoros
Togo
Bangladesh
Tanzania
Cote d'Ivoire
C African R
Mauritania
Madagascar
Nepal
Rwanda
Benin
Malawi
Guinea-Biss.
Gambia
Chad
Burundi
Mozambique
Burkina F.
Mali
Sierra L.
Niger

*% **labor force participation** ratio (UNDP, 1996)*
*% of the **labor force in agriculture** (UNDP, 1996; Fischer Weltalmanach, 1996)*
*% of the **labor force in industry** (see: labor force agriculture)*
***absolute GNP** (UNDP, 1996)*
***absolute income growth** (growth in the sense of Arrighi's and Amin's theory) 1960-1990.*
***agricultural share** in GDP (UNDP, 1996; Fischer Weltalmanach, 1996)*
***average population growth** (UNDP, 1996)*
***CPM poverty** (UNDP, 1996) (combines lack of access to health personnel during birth, underweight children, female illiteracy, and real per capita income in purchasing power parity rates) (for the substitution of missing values, see below)*
***early death** at age 40 in % of total population (UNDP, 1998)*
***economic growth 80 - 93**, pc. and year (UNDP, 1996)*
***EU membership years** (Fischer Weltalmanach, 1995, 1996)*
***FDI per GDP** (UNCTAD, 1996; Business Central Europe, 1996)*
***human development index** (UNDP)*
***income distribution: share of top 20% in total incomes** (World Bank WDR 1996; UNDP 1996; Moaddel 1994; the few missing cases were substituted with the means from*

linear trendline estimates, based on the countries with complete data, using mean years of schooling and population growth as predictor variables)(see below)

infant mortality rates, *1993 (UNDP, 1996)*

inflation ***93*** *(UNDP, 1996)*

main telephone lines *per 100 population (UNDP, 1996)*

mean ***years of schooling****, population aged >25y*

military expenditures per GDP *(UNDP, 1996)*

state sector size *(gov. expenditures per GDP; UNDP 1996; Weltalmanach, 1995, 1996; World Resources Institute)*

structural heterogeneity *(labor force share in agriculture divided by product share of agriculture; see labor force data)*

total fertility rate *(UNDP, 1996)*

UN membership years *(Weltalmanach, 1996, 1995)*

violation of political rights *(1, democracy, to 7, dictatorship) (Stiftung Entwicklung und Frieden, 1996, based on Freedom House)*

violations of civil rights *(see political rights)*

war years *(from D. Smith, 1997)*

years of Communist Rule *(Autorenkollektiv; Weltalmanach)*

The reduced sample of OECD and underdeveloped countries, excluding most of the former communist nations:

Barb
Hong
Urug
Trinid
Baham
Korea
Costa
Sing
Arg
Ven
Domi
Kuw
Mex
Maurit
Malay
Gren
Antig
Colom
Seych
Sur
UAE

Pan
Jamai
Braz
Fiji
Saint L
TRK
Thai
Saint V
Saint K
Syria
Belize
Saudi
South A
Sri L
Liby
Ecu
Para
Phil
Tune
Oman
Peru
Domin
Jord
China
Iran
Botsw
Guya
Alger
Indon
Gabon
El Sal
Mald
Guat
Hond
Swaz
Solom
Moroc
Lesoth
Zimbab
Boliv
Egypt
Sao T
Congo

Kenya
Madag
Papua
Zambia
Ghana
Pak
Camer
India
Cote
Haiti
Tanz
Comor
Zaire
Lao
Nigeria
Togo
Ugan
Bangl
Rwanda
Ethi
Malaw
Burun
CAfricR
Mozam
Bhut
Angol
Maure
Benin
GuiBis
Chad
Somal
Gamb
Mali
Niger
Burki
Sierr
Japan
Canada
Norw
Switzerland
Swe
USA
Austral

France
NL
UK
Germany
DK
SF
Aus
Blg
NZ
Israel
Ire
Ital
Spa
Gree
Hun
Port

The General Model of World Development, based on 123 Nations

Indicators of Globalisation:

- ***aid dependency*** *(UNDP, 1994) net per capita aid in $. Donor countries are listed according to their donations per capita and are recorded as (-)*
- ***export processing zones*** *(Bailey et al., 1993). The variable codes the number of export processing zones per country at the beginning of the 1990s*
- ***migration dependency*** *(UNDP, 1993) net worker remittances per GNP/GDP at the beginning of the 1990s*
- ***MNC penetration*** *index: penetration by transnational capital, weighted by population and capital stock, mid - 1970s (Bornschier/Heintz, 1979, based on OECD)*
- ***share of outward FDI stock in gross domestic product in 1985*** *(UNCTAD, 1996. For a very small number of countries, regional averages had to be taken to substitute for the few, missing values)*
- ***terms of trade index*** *1987 - 90 (UNDP, 1994, Weltalmanach, 1994, based on UN)*
- ***trade dependency*** *index: exports plus imports as % of GDP 1990 (UNDP, 1993/94)*
- *vulnerability of a nation in terms of the expansion of the new international division of labor, 1990* ***(share of women in the national labor force)*** *(UNDP, 1993/94)*

Indicators for the Institutional Environment:

- ***ethno - linguistic fractionalization** index, mid - 1960s (Bornschier/Heintz, 1979, based on Taylor/Hudson). Ethnic discrimination is thought to be the purest form of a 'distribution coalition'*
- ***government consumption** per GDP, 1990 (UNDP, 1993/94)*
- ***government expenditures** per GNP, 1991 (UNDP, 1993/94; UNICEF, Regional Monitoring Report, 1, 11, 1993, see Cornia, 1993; World Resources Research Institute)*
- ***public investment** in the preceding Kondratieff cycle (Bornschier/Heintz)*
- *total area in thousands of square kilometers (World Bank, WDR, 1994. This variable measures the role, that territory and resources could play for attracting foreign capital)*
- ***violation of civil rights**, 1991 (Stiftung, 1993/94, based on Freedom House, combining freedom of religion, the press, freedom of assembly and association, freedom of trade unions, the right to property and equality before the law)*
- ***violation of political rights** index, 1991 (Stiftung, 1993/94, based on Freedom House, combining free elections, role of the elected parliament in political decision making, party competition, protection of minorities)*
- *world political threats to a country, to be measured by the percentage of **armed forces per population**. Some neo - liberals maintain that world political threats increase the growth potential of a nation. Due to the skewness of the indicator, the natural logarithm ln (MPR+1) has to be taken (calculated from UNDP, 1993/94; see also: Weede, 1985)*
- ***years of membership in the United Nations** (coded from Weltalmanach, 1995)*

Indicators for the social policy approach:

- ***human development** index (UNDP, 1994) as an indicator for the quality of past social policy*
- ***increase/decrease of fertility rates** 1960 - 90 (UNDP, 1993/94)*
- ***life expectancy** at birth as an indicator for the quality of past social policy, 1990 (UNDP, 1993/94 and World Bank, WDR, 1994)*
- *share of **women in the membership of national legislature** (lower house) (UNDP, 1993/94)*
- ***social security** benefits expenditure as % of GDP in the era of the evolving contemporary Kondratieff cycle, 1985 - 90 (UNDP, 1994). Social security benefits expenditures include here the compensations for the loss of income for the sick and the temporarily disabled; payments to the elderly, the permanently disabled and the unemployed; they also include family, maternity and child allowances and the cost of welfare services. The UNDP data collection is based on ILO sources*
- ***total fertility** rate (most recent estimate) (UNDP, 1993/94)*

- *total number of inhabitants, divided by the surface area of a country* ***(population density)****. Due to the skewness of the indicator, the squared root (population density^.50) had to be taken (calculated from UNDP, 1993/94)*
- ***violation of civil rights****, 1991 (Stiftung, 1993/94, based on Freedom House)*
- ***violation of political rights*** *index, 1991 (Stiftung, 1993/94, based on Freedom House)*

The Dependent Variables of the General Models

- ***absolute income growth*** *(growth in the sense of Arrighi's and Amin's theory) 1960-1990. This measure is the simple difference between real purchasing power parity rate per capita incomes in US $ 1990 and 1960 (UNDP, 1993 ff.)*
- ***adjustment*** *1965/80 - 80/93(calculated from UNDP, 1993/94/96). Adjustment is calculated by a simple, standard linear regression model of growth 1965-80 predicting growth in the period 1980/93. The residuals from this regression are the 'adjustment scores'*
- ***capability poverty measure*** *(CPM - value) (UNDP, 1996. The measure weights unattended births, underweight children, and female illiteracy. It is regarded by the UNDP as a direct measure of absolute poverty)*
- ***deforestation rate*** *(UNDP, 1993 - 95; World Bank, 1995; World Resources Research Institute). The index measures annual rates of deforestation in the 1980s in %. Because of missing data, a number of countries had to be coded by the LDC average or the OECD average*
- ***destabilization index*** *(coded according to Weltalmanach, 1995. The indicator codes all those countries as '1' (destabilized), that have entries about serious armed internal or external conflict in 1994. The rest is coded as '0'*
- ***employment*** *(UNDP, 1994) labor force as % of total population*
- ***ethno - warfare*** *(Gurr, 1994) magnitude of ethno - political conflict. The scores are country sums of the squared roots of the deaths (in 10s of thousands) from ethno - political conflict 1993 - 94 plus refugees (in 100s of thousands). Countries with no entries according to Gurr's main research results, 1994, are coded as '0'*
- ***forest area per total land area*** *(UNDP, 1993 - 95). In contrast to the above indicator, that measures flows, this measure rather captures stocks of already existent forest destruction. Agricultural land per total land area has to be taken into consideration as an independent variable, because else the regression equations would be biased by a desert - factor*
- ***gender empowerment measure*** *(UNDP, 1995. The index weights seats held by women in parliament, the percentage share of women and managers, the share of women in the professional and technical workforce, and the share of women in total earned income*

- ***gender - related development index*** *(GDI) (UNDP, 1995) - dimension female life chances. This index was developed by the UNDP especially for the 1995 women's conference in Beijing. The index weights the share of earned income for females and males, the gender - specific life expectancies, the gender - specific adult literacy rates, and the gross primary, secondary and tertiary enrollment ratios. It ranges theoretically from 0.0 to 0.999, with Sweden (0.919) at the top of the international scale, and Afghanistan (0.169) at the bottom. Since there unfortunately no were no data for Dominica, Grenada, Antigua, Seychelles, Saint Lucia, Saint Vincent, Saint Kits, Belize, South Africa, Oman, Jordan, Gabon, Solomon Islands, Sao Tome, Congo, Rwanda, Bhutan, Angola, Mauritania, Somalia, Gambia, Germany and Israel, we had to substitute these missing values with averages for the socio - economic groups concerned: a) the industrialized democracies (gender development index average 0.87) b) developing countries with a Human Development Index above 0.6 (in our 123 nations analysis: Barbados to Tunisia, gender development index average 0.721) c) developing countries with a Human Development Index from 0.599 to 0.389 (Oman to Egypt, gender development index average 0,542) d) developing countries with a Human Development Index under 0.388 (except for the very least developed countries; Kenya to Sierra Leone; gender development index average 0.33) and e) the very least developed countries Benin, Guinea Bissau, Chad, Mali, Niger, Burkina Faso and Sierra Leone with a gender development index of 0.2. This procedure can be regarded only as a first approximation and should be substituted in future research*
- *GNP per capita* ***growth*** *(1965 - 1980 and 1980 - 90/1980 - 92, 1980 - 93) (UNDP, 1993/94/95/96; Fischer Weltalmanach) - dimension growth*
- ***greenhouse index****, 1989 (greenhouse index per 10 million people, UNDP, 1994. The greenhouse index measures the net emissions of three major greenhouse gases: carbon dioxide, methane and chlorofluorocarbons. The index weights each gas according to it's heattrapping quality in carbon dioxide equivalents and expresses them in metric tons of carbon per capita) - dimension environmental quality/degradation*
- ***human development index*** *(HDI) (UNDP, 1994)*
- ***income distribution*** *(Moaddel, 1994. The measure focuses on the share of the top 20% in total incomes in over 80 countries. Wherever possible, Moaddel's data were updated by World Bank WDR, 1994, 1995 and 1996). For the calculation of the relationship with income distribution, a reduced sample of the n = 123 world sample with complete data was taken*
- ***increase in life expectancy*** *1960 - 90 (calculated from UNDP, 1993/94 via a regression procedure, predicting 1990 life expectancy on 1960 life expectancy, and then taking the residuals as growth rates) - dimension redistribution and human development*
- ***mean years of schooling of the population aged 25 and > (UNDP, 1993 and 1994)***

- *mobility in the international system (calculated from UNDP, 1993 ff.) This indicator is the difference in relative positions of a country on the PPP $ per capita income scale in 1990 (USA = 100) vis-à-vis 1960 (USA = 100)*
- ***violation of civil rights**, 1991 (Stiftung, 1993/94, based on Freedom House) - dimension democracy*
- ***violation of political rights index**, 1991 (Stiftung, 1993/94, based on Freedom House) - dimension democracy*
- *mobility in the international system (calculated from UNDP, 1993 ff.) This indicator is the difference in relative positions of a country on the PPP $ per capita income scale in 1990 (USA = 100) vis-à-vis 1960 (USA = 100)*

The Models Based on 49 Polish Voivodships

Variables taken from the Polish Central Statistical Office and from the daily Polish Press:

- *big estates (> 25 ha) per total land*
- *percent employment in agriculture*
- *percent employment in foreign capital enterprises per total employment*
- *percent employment in mixed enterprises per total employment*
- *external migration per total population*
- *female excess infant mortality rates (based on regression residuals of male on female infant mortality rates in the different voivodships of the country). Voivodships are said to have an excess female infant mortality, when the regression residual is positive*
- *human development index*
- *industrial employment*
- *industrial waste*
- *private land per total land*
- *real GDP per capita*
- *religious practice*
- *urbanization*
- *voting data on a voivodship level for all the elections and referenda since 1993*
- *wage level*

The CPM Poverty Measure

This measure was developed by the United Nations UNDP in 1996. It is a composite measure of the basic-human needs oriented variety, and combines the percentages of people, not having access to such basic services as water, health etc. For the industrialized countries and for several developing countries, we had to estimate the measure:

Country	*CPM*	*CPM est.*	*CPM estimate (2)*	*HDI Human Development Index*
Canada		3,1966	3,7081	0,951
USA		4,0884	3,8742	0,94
Japan		4,2505	4,6991	0,938
NL		4,2505	4,5817	0,938
NOR		4,3316	4,1137	0,937
SF		4,4937	5,0614	0,935
France		4,4937	4,4803	0,935
Iceland		4,6559	5,0202	0,933
Swed		4,6559	4,5536	0,933
Spain		4,6559	7,405	0,933
Australia		4,9802	4,3397	0,929
Belgium		4,9802	4,7236	0,929
Austria		5,0613	4,747	0,928
NZ		5,1423	5,013	0,927
CH		5,2234	4,7909	0,926
UK		5,3855	4,7406	0,924
DK		5,3855	4,5233	0,924
GER		5,7098	5,1277	0,92
IRE		5,7909	6,2979	0,919
ITA		6,1963	6,8216	0,914
GRE		6,6016	8,4514	0,909
ISR		6,6827	6,4936	0,908
LUX		7,7367	4,8605	0,895
MAL		8,4663	9,3748	0,886
POR		9,1149	9,4562	0,878
HUNG		10,98	9,4282	0,855
LATV		13,817	12,502	0,82
POL		13,898	11,756	0,819
RUS		15,114	13,69	0,804
BELR		16,493	15,324	0,787
BULG		17,628	15,209	0,773
EST		19,573	14,928	0,749
KAZ		20,303	23,522	0,74
ROM		20,465	17,206	0,738
UKR		22,006	20,053	0,719
LITH		22,006	17,376	0,719
ARM		25,167	25,244	0,68
UZB		25,248	26,644	0,679
AZER		26,383	29,225	0,665
KYR		26,546	27,687	0,663
GEO		28,005	27,14	0,645
ALB		28,978	21,748	0,633
TAJ		30,356	27,943	0,616
Hong Kong	7,3	7,3	7,1448	0,909
Cyprus		6,6016	7,8503	0,909
Barbados	6,5	6,5	7,0111	0,906
Bahamas		7,7367	7,9895	0,895
S-Korea	8,6	8,6	8,8131	0,886
Argentina	6,3	6,3	8,0552	0,885
Costa Rica	6,1	6,1	9,6924	0,884
Uruguay	4,7	4,7	8,6287	0,883

Country	*CPM*	*CPM est.*	*CPM*	*HDI*
Chile	2,8	2,8	8,8302	0,882
Singapore	7,7	7,7	8,3455	0,881
Trinidad	4,1	4,1	8,7269	0,872
Bahrein		10,088	10,724	0,866
Antigua		10,088	11,529	0,866
Panama	7,2	7,2	10,105	0,859
Venezuela	15,2	15,2	10,372	0,859
Saint Kitts		10,736	11,362	0,858
Fiji		11,142	12,332	0,853
Mexico	16,9	16,9	12,08	0,845
Colombia	13,4	13,4	10,655	0,84
Thailand	21,1	21,1	12,956	0,832
Malaysia	20,6	20,6	12,274	0,826
Mauritius	20,6	20,6	13,384	0,825
Brazil	10	10	14,856	0,796
Seychelles		16,087	15,009	0,792
Dominica		18,357	19,182	0,764
Belize		19,168	19,495	0,754
Algeria	49,5	49,5	21,793	0,746
Botswana	30,4	30,4	19,385	0,741
Saint Vincent		20,465	20,07	0,738
Suriname		20,546	20,117	0,737
Saint Lucia		20,87	17,046	0,733
Grenada		21,195	19,921	0,729
Tunesia	29,9	29,9	22,378	0,727
Oman		22,249	29,365	0,716
Turkey	21,2	21,2	20,723	0,711
Paraguay	15,9	15,9	19,03	0,704
Jamaica	12,3	12,3	17,669	0,702
Dominican R	12,4	12,4	19,94	0,701
Sri Lanka	19,3	19,3	17,262	0,698
Peru	25,7	25,7	17,833	0,694
Philippines	28,8	28,8	16,952	0,665
South Africa	30,4	30,4	23,281	0,649
Indonesia	42,3	42,3	23,051	0,641
Guyana	18,4	18,4	22,464	0,633
Egypt	43,7	43,7	30,621	0,611
Maldives	35,5	35,5	25,969	0,61
China	17,5	17,5	26,665	0,609
Swaziland	25,1	25,1	28,872	0,586
Bolivia	31,6	31,6	27,204	0,584
Guatemala	45	45	30,719	0,58
Mongolia	12,6	12,6	26,838	0,578
Honduras	22,4	22,4	27,847	0,576
El Salvador	25,6	25,6	28,921	0,576
Namibia		33,842	28,537	0,573
Nicaragua	24,3	24,3	28,136	0,568
Gabon	28,4	28,4	34,113	0,557
Cape Verde		36,599	37,151	0,539
Morocco	49,7	49,7	39,607	0,534
Zimbabwe	22,3	22,3	30,894	0,534
Congo	41,7	41,7	39,614	0,517

Country	*CPM*	*CPM est.*	*CPM*	*HDI*
Papua NG	49,8	49,8	43,181	0,504
Cameroon	33,5	33,5	45,718	0,481
Kenya	33,8	33,8	37,191	0,473
Ghana	39,3	39,3	39,726	0,467
Lesotho	38,6	38,6	32,042	0,464
Equatorial G		42,922	50,647	0,461
Pakistan	60,8	60,8	53,794	0,442
India	61,5	61,5	40,727	0,436
Zambia	35,1	35,1	40,739	0,411
Nigeria	51,6	51,6	56,109	0,4
Comoros		47,949	50,953	0,399
Togo	45,4	45,4	44,502	0,385
Bangladesh	76,9	76,9	55,623	0,365
Tanzania	39,4	39,4	36,285	0,364
Cote d'Ivoire	46,7	46,7	59,75	0,357
C African R	46	46	52,278	0,355
Mauritania	60,8	60,8	67,819	0,353
Madagascar	36,7	36,7	39,654	0,349
Nepal	77,3	77,3	51,856	0,332
Rwanda	51,5	51,5	48,731	0,332
Benin	51,9	51,9	72,718	0,327
Malawi	44,1	44,1	44,769	0,321
Guinea-Biss.	56,6	56,6	62,385	0,297
Gambia	38	38	70,538	0,292
Chad	61,2	61,2	51,878	0,291
Burundi	66,1	66,1	55,192	0,282
Mozambique	66,9	66,9	57,975	0,261
Burkina F.	59,7	59,7	71,822	0,225
Mali	59,4	59,4	56,775	0,223
Sierra L.	62,3	62,3	82,333	0,219
Niger	71,7	71,7	74,866	0,204

CPM measure: UNDP, 1996
*CPM (1): = 80,29 - (81,073 * HDI)*
CPM (2): = combined EXCEL 7.0 variation estimate from the predictor variables:

- *% labor force participation rate*
- *absolute GNP*
- *agricultural share*
- *FDI per GDP*
- *human development index*
- *ln PPP (purchasing power)*
- *ln PPP^2*
- *mean years adult education*
- *military expenditures per GDP*
- *population growth*
- *state sector size per GDP*
- *UN accession*
- *UN member years*
- *years of Communism*

Income Inequality Benefiting the Top 20% of the Population

country code	(1) top 20%	Y^top20%	CPM-measure	estimate top20%	LFPR	original data		estimate = 0,7752*POPDYN^2+7,099*POPDYN+36,93	estimate=0,1424*MEANEDUC^2+0,9301*MEANEDUC+48,031
Canada	40,2	43,017	3,1966	42	53	40,2	Canada	45,834	38,183
USA	41,9	40,853	4,0884	40,7	50	41,9	USA	43,801	37,669
Japan	37,5	41,741	4,2505	42,1	52	37,5	Japan	42,691	41,467
NL	36,9	41,782	4,2505	41,8	46	36,9	NL	42,691	40,81
NOR	36,7	39,13	4,3316	39,7	50	36,7	NOR	40,91	38,436
SF	37,6	40,224	4,4937	40,4	52	37,6	SF	39,646	41,251
France	41,9	40,437	4,4937	40,1	44	41,9	France	41,519	38,687
Iceland	44,4	42,363	4,6559	44,4	56		Iceland	44,333	44,535
Swed	36,9	39,788	4,6559	40,2	54	36,9	Swed	40,286	40,128
Spain	36,6	45,512	4,6559	44,9	41	36,6	Spain	42,113	47,669
Australia	42,2	42,998	4,9802	42,5	50	42,2	Australia	46,304	38,687
Belgium	36	39,635	4,9802	39,8	41	36	Belgium	38,99	40,585
Austria	45,1	39,581	5,0613	39,6	46	45,1	Austria	38,99	40,128
NZ	44,7	42,676	5,1423	43	48	44,7	NZ	44,333	41,68
CH	44,6	39,561	5,2234	40,9	53	44,6	CH	42,113	39,659
UK	44,3	38,667	5,3855	39,2	50	44,3	UK	38,99	39,42
DK	38,6	38,617	5,3855	40,3	57	38,6	DK	39,646	41,032
GER	40,3	38,847	5,7098	39,3	50	40,3	GER	38,99	39,659
IRE	39,4	42,433	5,7909	43,3	37	39,4	IRE	41,519	45,029
ITA	41	41,473	6,1963	43,3	43	41	ITA	39,646	46,997
GRE	44,5	43,768	6,6016	44,5	42		GRE	41,519	47,564
ISR	39,6	46,718	6,6827	46,7	39	39,6	ISR	50,73	42,703
LUX	41,8	38,981	7,7367	41,8	43		LUX	41,519	42,097
MAL	44	44,056	8,4663	44	37		MAL	39,646	48,406
POR	49,1	42,591	9,1149	43,6	49	49,1	POR	38,99	48,151
HUNG	36,6	42,536	10,98	40,6	46	36,6	HUNG	37,632	43,47
LATV	36,7	42,235	13,817	42,9	55	36,7	LATV	40,91	44,868
POL	36,6	44,891	13,898	44,1	49	36,6	POL	42,113	46,083
RUS	53,8	40,892	15,114	42,9	52	53,8	RUS	40,91	44,868
BELR	32,9	42,352	16,493	44,5	52	32,9	BELR	41,519	47,564
BULG	39,3	42,135	17,628	43,6	51	39,3	BULG	39,646	47,564

EST	46,3	42,436	19,573	43,2	54	46,3	EST	41,519	44,868
KAZ	40,4	44,584	20,303	47,7	47	40,4	KAZ	46,304	49,122
ROM	34,8	41,905	20,465	44,5	46	34,8	ROM	41,519	47,456
UKR	35,4	39,413	22,006	44,7	50	35,4	UKR	40,91	48,485
LITH	42,1	41,177	22,006	43,8	52	42,1	LITH	42,691	44,868
ARM	48,4	44,297	25,167	48,4	48		ARM	47,62	49,122
UZB	50,1	50,69	25,248	50,1	39		UZB	50,998	49,122
AZER	48,6	45,762	26,383	48,6	42		AZER	48,027	49,122
KYR	49,1	46,102	26,546	49,1	41		KYR	49,157	49,122
GEO	45,6	38,659	28,005	45,6	49		GEO	42,113	49,122
ALB	48,7	44,097	28,978	48,7	48		ALB	49,157	48,324
TAJ	50,3	51,642	30,356	50,3	36		TAJ	51,487	49,122
Hong Kong	47	48,134	7,3	47,5	51	47	Hong Kong	47,62	47,346
Cyprus	44,5	42,198	6,6016	44,5	48		Cyprus	41,519	47,564
Barbados	41,9	42,718	6,5	41,9	51		Barbados	39,646	44,191
Bahamas	49,4	49,869	7,7367	49,4	50		Bahamas	50,446	48,324
S-Korea	45,2	46,366	8,6	45,6	46	45,2	S-Korea	46,758	44,365
Argentina	45,2	48,031	6,3	45,2	38		Argentina	45,834	44,535
Costa Rica	50,7	56,154	6,1	50	38	50,7	Costa Rica	51,25	48,706
Uruguay	52,5	46,392	4,7	43,9	44	52,5	Uruguay	41,519	46,222
Chile	61	48,223	2,8	46,9	38	61	Chile	47,197	46,622
Singapore	48,9	47,739	7,7	47,9	49	48,9	Singapore	46,304	49,473
Trinidad	50	47,09	4,1	45,3	39	50	Trinidad	44,849	45,796
Bahrein	51,1	53,355	10,088	51,1	45		Bahrein	52,712	49,397
Antigua	44,8	49,022	10,088	44,8	47		Antigua	40,286	49,296
Panama	59,8	53,499	7,2	48,8	39	59,8	Panama	49,833	47,771
Venezuela	58,4	53,927	15,2	49,8	37	58,4	Venezuela	51,487	48,06
Saint Kitts	40,4	39,889	10,736	40,4	43		Saint Kitts	32,392	48,485
Fiji	48,5	51,822	11,142	48,5	34		Fiji	48,027	49,071
Mexico	55,3	54,457	16,9	49,8	37	55,3	Mexico	50,446	49,169
Colombia	55,8	50,626	13,4	48,1	40	55,8	Colombia	49,157	46,997
Thailand	52,7	52,592	21,1	49,5	57	52,7	Thailand	49,502	49,492
Malaysia	53,7	49,597	20,6	49,5	39	53,7	Malaysia	50,147	48,774
Mauritius	47,6	45,419	20,6	47,6	41		Mauritius	45,834	49,451
Brazil	67,5	53,965	10	49,5	44	67,5	Brazil	49,502	49,473
Seychelles	47,8	49,778	16,087	47,8	40		Seychelles	46,304	49,296

Dominica	39,2	38,888	18,357	39,2	40		Dominica	29,056	49,257
Belize	49,4	50,258	19,168	49,4	31		Belize	49,502	49,296
Algeria	46,1	53,085	49,5	50,1	28	46,1	Algeria	50,73	49,519
Botswana	50,7	55,891	30,4	50,7	44		Botswana	51,915	49,466
Saint Vincent	46,3	46,004	20,465	46,3	40		Saint Vincent	43,254	49,296
Suriname	46,6	48,05	20,546	46,6	34		Suriname	43,801	49,425
Saint Lucia	46,4	46,057	20,87	46,4	40		Saint Lucia	43,254	49,492
Grenada	43,4	44,005	21,195	43,4	40		Grenada	37,632	49,257
Tunesia	46,3	50,712	29,9	49,1	35	46,3	Tunesia	48,796	49,356
Oman	50,8	49,863	22,249	50,8	26		Oman	52,825	48,753
Turkey	56,5	51,169	21,2	49,5	45	56,5	Turkey	49,502	49,534
Paraguay	50,2	52,186	15,9	50,2	37		Paraguay	51,25	49,169
Jamaica	47,5	46,827	12,3	46,6	49	47,5	Jamaica	44,333	48,961
Dominican R	55,7	51,957	12,4	49,8	40	55,7	Dominican R	50,147	49,397
Sri Lanka	39,3	46,122	19,3	47,3	40	39,3	Sri Lanka	47,197	47,346
Peru	50,4	52,509	25,7	49,1	35	50,4	Peru	50,147	48,06
Philippines	47,8	50,707	28,8	48,5	40	47,8	Philippines	50,147	46,875
South Africa	63,3	53,172	30,4	49,7	39	63,3	South Africa	49,833	49,492
Indonesia	40,7	48,848	42,3	48,9	44	40,7	Indonesia	48,419	49,451
Guyana	46,4	45,443	18,4	46,4	40		Guyana	43,801	49,071
Egypt	41,1	48,016	43,7	49,5	35	41,1	Egypt	49,502	49,54
Maldives	49,9	51,957	35,5	49,9	41		Maldives	50,446	49,333
China	43,9	43,84	17,5	48,2	59	43,9	China	47,197	49,122
Swaziland	50,1	52,566	25,1	50,1	34		Swaziland	50,73	49,509
Bolivia	48,2	50,823	31,6	49,3	40	48,2	Bolivia	49,157	49,473
Guatemala	63	48,296	45	50,2	35	63	Guatemala	50,998	49,451
Mongolia	48,9	47,02	12,6	48,9	47		Mongolia	50,446	47,346
Honduras	57,4	52,435	22,4	50,6	34	57,4	Honduras	51,709	49,473
El Salvador	47,8	49,871	25,6	49,3	36	47,8	El Salvador	49,157	49,425
Namibia	49,7	49,878	33,842	49,7	42		Namibia	50,147	49,201
Nicaragua	55,2	50,09	24,3	50,4	34	55,2	Nicaragua	51,487	49,333
Gabon	50,2	51,928	28,4	50,2	49		Gabon	50,998	49,487
Cape Verde	48,5	48,55	36,599	48,5	37		Cape Verde	47,62	49,388
Morocco	46,3	45,76	49,7	49,7	38	46,3	Morocco	49,833	49,54
Zimbabwe	62,3	52,146	22,3	50,6	46	62,3	Zimbabwe	51,709	49,546

Congo	50	50,986	41,7	50	42		Congo	50,73	49,356
Papua NG	49	49,424	49,8	49	49		Papua NG	49,157	48,819
Cameroon	49,7	49,261	33,5	49,7	40		Cameroon	50,147	49,155
Kenya	62,1	53,827	33,8	50,9	48	62,1	Kenya	52,44	49,417
Ghana	42,2	45,87	39,3	50	47	42,2	Ghana	50,446	49,542
Lesotho	60,1	54,46	38,6	49,7	40	60,1	Lesotho	49,833	49,542
Equatorial G	46,5	45,894	42,922	46,5	45		Equatorial G	44,333	48,684
Pakistan	39,7	47,617	60,8	50,3	35	39,7	Pakistan	51,25	49,284
India	42,6	47,435	61,5	49,1	43	42,6	India	48,796	49,443
Zambia	50,4	54,205	35,1	50,6	42	50,4	Zambia	51,709	49,504
Nigeria	49,3	50,226	51,6	49,8	40	49,3	Nigeria	50,73	48,942
Comoros	50,3	51,003	47,949	50,3	44		Comoros	51,709	48,819
Togo	46,8	49,051	45,4	50,1	42	46,8	Togo	50,998	49,155
Bangladesh	37,9	47,028	76,9	49,6	49	37,9	Bangladesh	49,833	49,322
Tanzania	45,4	50,616	39,4	50,4	52	45,4	Tanzania	51,487	49,322
Cote d'Ivoire	44,1	48,888	46,7	51,1	37	44,1	Cote d'Ivoire	52,825	49,284
C African R	48,8	47,019	46	48,8	49		C African R	48,796	48,882
Mauritania	46,5	47,027	60,8	48,9	46	46,5	Mauritania	49,502	48,38
Madagascar	50	52,65	36,7	50,2	48	50	Madagascar	50,998	49,388
Nepal	39,5	43,846	77,3	49,4	47	39,5	Nepal	49,502	49,356
Rwanda	39,1	52,465	51,5	50,2	52	39,1	Rwanda	51,487	48,882
Benin	49,2	44,568	51,9	49,2	46		Benin	49,833	48,612
Malawi	55,2	54,178	44,1	50,7	45	55,2	Malawi	52,105	49,201
Guinea-Biss.	58,9	47,857	56,6	48,2	48	58,9	Guinea-Biss.	48,027	48,38
Gambia	50,2	51,014	38	50,2	50		Gambia	51,915	48,538
Chad	48,4	47,11	61,2	48,4	49		Chad	48,419	48,297
Burundi	48,6	45,859	66,1	48,6	54		Burundi	48,796	48,38
Mozambique	49	48,447	66,9	49	53		Mozambique	48,796	49,155
Burkina F.	48,9	45,148	59,7	48,9	54		Burkina F.	49,502	48,211
Mali	49,3	46,03	59,4	49,3	50		Mali	50,147	48,38
Sierra L.	54,5	47,377	62,3	48,4	37	54,5	Sierra L.	48,027	48,753
Niger	44,1	49,569	71,7	50	49	44,1	Niger	51,709	48,211

The Rank Scale of Inequality in the World System

Brazil	67,5
South Africa	63,3
Guatemala	63
Zimbabwe	62,3
Kenya	62,1
Chile	61
Lesotho	60,1
Panama	59,8
Guinea-Biss.	58,9
Venezuela	58,4
Honduras	57,4
Turkey	56,5
Colombia	55,8
Dominican R	55,7
Mexico	55,3
Nicaragua	55,2
Malawi	55,2
Sierra L.	54,5
RUS	53,8
Malaysia	53,7
Thailand	52,7
Uruguay	52,5
Bahrein	51,1
Oman	50,8
Costa Rica	50,7
Botswana	50,7
Peru	50,4
Zambia	50,4
TAJ	50,3
Comoros	50,3
Paraguay	50,2
Gabon	50,2
Gambia	50,2
UZB	50,1
Swaziland	50,1
Trinidad	50
Congo	50
Madagascar	50
Maldives	49,9
Namibia	49,7
Cameroon	49,7
Bahamas	49,4

Belize	49,4
Nigeria	49,3
Mali	49,3
Benin	49,2
POR	49,1
KYR	49,1
Papua NG	49
Mozambique	49
Singapore	48,9
Mongolia	48,9
Burkina F.	48,9
C African R	48,8
ALB	48,7
AZER	48,6
Burundi	48,6
Fiji	48,5
Cape Verde	48,5
ARM	48,4
Chad	48,4
Bolivia	48,2
Seychelles	47,8
Philippines	47,8
El Salvador	47,8
Mauritius	47,6
Jamaica	47,5
Hong Kong	47
Togo	46,8
Suriname	46,6
Equatorial G	46,5
Mauritania	46,5
Saint Lucia	46,4
Guyana	46,4
EST	46,3
Saint Vincent	46,3
Tunesia	46,3
Morocco	46,3
Algeria	46,1
GEO	45,6
Tanzania	45,4
S-Korea	45,2
Argentina	45,2
Austria	45,1
Antigua	44,8

NZ	44,7
CH	44,6
GRE	44,5
Cyprus	44,5
Iceland	44,4
UK	44,3
Cote d'Ivoire	44,1
Niger	44,1
MAL	44
China	43,9
Grenada	43,4
India	42,6
Australia	42,2
Ghana	42,2
LITH	42,1
USA	41,9
France	41,9
Barbados	41,9
LUX	41,8
Egypt	41,1
ITA	41
Indonesia	40,7
KAZ	40,4
Saint Kitts	40,4
GER	40,3
Canada	40,2
Pakistan	39,7
ISR	39,6
Nepal	39,5
IRE	39,4
BULG	39,3
Sri Lanka	39,3
Dominica	39,2
Rwanda	39,1
DK	38,6
Bangladesh	37,9
SF	37,6
Japan	37,5
NL	36,9
Swed	36,9
NOR	36,7
LATV	36,7
Spain	36,6

HUNG	36,6
POL	36,6
Belgium	36
UKR	35,4
ROM	34,8
BELR	32,9

(^Y) is an EXCEL 5.0 variation trendline estimate of inequality, based on the following variables:

early death	e- function	pi- function	mean scho	y absolute GNP	FDI per GDP	Years of Comm	populati on gr	state sector	%labor force	ln PPP	ln PPP^2	agr.shar eGP	MILEX	HDI

estimate top 20% is based on the averages of the two far-right hand columns above. POPDYN is the population growth rate, MEAN EDU are the average years of education of the population above 25 years of age. The results are rounded at 1 decimal point.

7) KONDRATIEFF CYCLE DATA

For the calculations of Kondratieff cycles, I used J. Goldstein's classic (1988), plus the following data (estimates) for world (and or OECD) growth 1975 - 1997, based on IMF, IFRI, UN ECE, and Fischer Weltalmanach:

year	*growth rate*	*5-year aver.*	*9-year aver.*
1741	-4,8		
1742	10,1		
1743	-4,6	2,16	
1744	14,3	4	
1745	-4,2	2,8	1,81
1746	4,4	5,34	3,73
1747	4,1	0,26	2,61
1748	8,1	3,6	3,12
1749	-11,1	2,72	1,94
1750	12,5	1,9	2,02
1751	0	1,02	1,94
1752	0	2,54	0,3
1753	3,7	0,78	-0,16
1754	-3,5	-1,36	1,08
1755	3,7	-0,56	-0,74
1756	-10,7	-1,3	-0,74
1757	4	-1,38	-0,21
1758	0	-2,12	-0,62

1759	-3,9	0,98	-0,67
1760	0	0,18	-0,18
1761	4,8	-0,6	1,01
1762	0	1,8	2,21
1763	-3,9	1,8	2,21
1764	8,1	3,8	2,29
1765	0	3,8	3,02
1766	14,8	3,94	2,14
1767	0	3,64	2,14
1768	-3,2	3,02	3,66
1769	6,6	0,06	2,1
1770	-3,1	2	1,41
1771	0	1,46	0,13
1772	9,7	-1,1	0,5
1773	-5,9	0,18	1,2
1774	-6,2	0,84	0,81
1775	3,3	-0,48	0,5
1776	3,3	1,32	0,5
1777	3,1	1,38	-0,92
1778	3,1	0,72	1,89
1779	-5,9	-0,56	2,28
1780	0	2,7	2,22
1781	-3,1	1,54	3,96
1782	19,4	3,28	4,11
1783	-2,7	7,06	4,01
1784	2,8	8,58	4,43
1785	18,9	5,14	6,61
1786	4,5	5,26	6,76
1787	2,2	8,62	4,81
1788	-2,1	4,48	5,92
1789	19,6	3,96	4,1
1790	-1,8	4,98	2,43
1791	1,9	2,68	2,57
1792	7,3	-0,46	3,11
1793	-13,6	1,04	2,42
1794	3,9	2,08	1,26
1795	5,7	-1,04	3,49
1796	7,1	3,5	3,9
1797	-8,3	6,38	2,5
1798	9,1	6,36	4,63
1799	18,3	3,88	4,34
1800	5,6	6,66	4
1801	-5,3	5,1	3,5

1802	5,6	1,96	4,56
1803	1,3	1,36	3,96
1804	2,6	2,66	1,39
1805	2,6	2,28	1,04
1806	1,2	1,06	2,58
1807	3,7	1,04	2,58
1808	-4,8	2,22	1,72
1809	2,5	3,1	1,56
1810	8,5	1,08	1,39
1811	5,6	2,26	2,49
1812	-6,4	1,98	2,08
1813	1,1	2,5	2,61
1814	1,1	1,38	4,56
1815	11,1	2,66	2,69
1816	0	6,44	2,07
1817	0	4,56	2,78
1818	20	2,34	3,67
1819	-8,3	2,34	4,47
1820	0	4,16	3,23
1821	0	1,82	4,09
1822	9,1	3,48	3,29
1823	8,3	5,02	2,78
1824	0	3,58	4,44
1825	7,7	4,84	3,76
1826	-7,2	4,52	5,23
1827	15,4	3,28	4,22
1828	6,7	4,4	2,64
1829	-6,2	5,84	4,03
1830	13,3	1,58	3,8
1831	0	2,74	5,19
1832	-5,9	5,1	4,59
1833	12,5	3,5	2,83
1834	5,6	5,5	4,63
1835	5,3	4,86	4,17
1836	10	4,36	4,17
1837	-9,1	5,06	4,82
1838	10	4	2,97
1839	9,1	2	2,83
1840	0	2,98	3,63
1841	0	1,86	3,34
1842	-4,2	2,54	4,36
1843	4,4	4,02	2,86
1844	12,5	4,02	3,03

1845	7,4	4,16	3,03
1846	0	5,42	3,03
1847	-3,5	2,92	4,58
1848	10,7	1,44	5,07
1849	0	3,38	4,57
1850	0	5,84	4,3
1851	9,7	5,3	4,82
1852	8,8	6,3	6,22
1853	8	7,24	4,8
1854	5	7,12	4,8
1855	4,7	4,94	5,51
1856	9,1	3,34	5,1
1857	-2,1	3,62	4,12
1858	0	3,88	1,98
1859	6,4	2,06	2,37
1860	6	0,22	2,5
1861	0	1,92	1,69
1862	-11,3	1,82	3,53
1863	8,5	0,98	3,36
1864	5,9	3,88	3,54
1865	1,8	5,82	3,38
1866	14,5	5,74	3,07
1867	-1,6	5,46	5,3
1868	8,1	4,54	5,56
1869	4,5	3,4	4,77
1870	-2,8	5,88	4,57
1871	8,8	4,02	2,68
1872	10,8	3,12	3,28
1873	-1,2	3,18	2,51
1874	0	2,18	2,28
1875	-2,5	0,26	2,84
1876	3,8	0,98	2,77
1877	1,2	1,44	2,16
1878	2,4	3,56	3,07
1879	2,3	3,86	3,49
1880	8,1	5,02	3,47
1881	5,3	5,3	2,93
1882	7	4,3	3,43
1883	3,8	2,48	4,06
1884	-2,7	2,56	4,27
1885	-1	2,76	4,33
1886	5,7	2,84	4,31
1887	8	5,12	3,69

1888	4,2	6,34	3,42
1889	8,7	5,48	3,36
1890	5,1	4,16	3,86
1891	1,4	2,66	4,28
1892	1,4	1,62	3,67
1893	-3,3	2,5	3,73
1894	3,5	2,72	3,79
1895	9,5	3,4	4,04
1896	2,5	5,9	3,94
1897	4,8	6,68	4,22
1898	9,2	4,88	5,48
1899	7,4	5,16	5,33
1900	0,5	5,8	4,32
1901	3,9	4,4	5,18
1902	8	3	5,16
1903	2,2	4,94	4,46
1904	0,4	5,08	2,72
1905	10,2	4,06	3,74
1906	4,6	1,98	4,1
1907	2,9	3,84	3,4
1908	-8,2	3,22	4,13
1909	9,7	2,64	4,62
1910	7,1	3,82	2,5
1911	1,7	6,42	2,33
1912	8,8	2,7	2,86
1913	4,8	1,9	3,86
1914	-8,9	3,08	2,12
1915	3,1	1,48	0,41
1916	7,6	-0,66	0,87
1917	0,8	-0,54	-1,68
1918	-5,9	0	0,29
1919	-8,3	-4,34	1,86
1920	5,8	0	2,16
1921	-14,1	2,22	2,21
1922	22,5	5,04	2,49
1923	5,2	5,5	3,88
1924	5,8	8,98	5,31
1925	8,1	5,8	5,48
1926	3,3	5,68	5,68
1927	6,6	5,98	1,71
1928	4,6	1,9	-0,47
1929	7,3	-1,4	0,29
1930	-12,3	-5,6	0,63

1931	-13,2	-4	1,57
1932	-14,4	-3,22	2,24
1933	12,6	1,58	2,86
1934	11,2	6,76	0,89
1935	11,7	11,66	4,14
1936	12,7	7,06	6,43
1937	10,1	8,22	10,19
1938	-10,4	7,36	10,64
1939	17	8,7	10,94
1940	7,4	10,02	9,08
1941	19,4	14,88	4,26
1942	16,7	10,46	1,48
1943	13,9	2,84	4,03
1944	-5,1	-4,02	2,98
1945	-30,7	-4,84	2,38
1946	-14,9	-6,12	1,74
1947	12,6	-4,7	0,84
1948	7,5	4,18	-0,43
1949	2	8,88	0,96
1950	13,7	6,84	4,37
1951	8,6	6,82	7,34
1952	2,4	6,42	6,49
1953	7,4	6,06	6,02
1954	0	5,32	5,51
1955	11,9	5,5	5,24
1956	4,9	3,5	5,02
1957	3,3	5,76	5,16
1958	-2,6	4,7	5,07
1959	11,3	4,44	5,63
1960	6,6	5,1	5,22
1961	3,6	6,64	5,5
1962	6,6	6,02	6,01
1963	5,1	6,18	6,47
1964	8,2	7,04	5,91
1965	7,4	6,02	6
1966	7,9	6,26	5,83
1967	1,5	6,1	5,32
1968	6,3	5,04	5,62
1969	7,4	3,86	5,72
1970	2,1	5,12	4,99
1971	2	5,68	3,38
1972	7,8	4,36	3,74
1973	9,1	2,62	3,46

1974	0,8	3,18	3,09
1975	-6,6	2,36	3,19
1976	4,8	1,36	3,01
1977	3,7	1,8	2,31
1978	4,1	3,2	1,27
1979	3	2,54	1,49
1980	0,4	1,74	2,77
1981	1,5	1,48	2,61
1982	-0,3	1,86	2,49
1983	2,8	2,46	2,41
1984	4,9	2,68	2,56
1985	3,4	3,42	2,92
1986	2,6	3,72	3,06
1987	3,4	3,48	3,29
1988	4,3	3,34	3,29
1989	3,7	3,18	3,04
1990	2,7	3,06	3,12
1991	1,8	2,74	3,24
1992	2,8	2,82	3,31
1993	2,7	3,02	3,32
1994	4,1	3,46	
1995	3,7	3,78	
1996	4		
1997	4,4		

1975	*-6,6 (-0,7)*
1976	*4,8*
1977	*3,7*
1978	*4,1*
1979	*3*
1980	*0,4*
1981	*1,5*
1982	*-0,3*
1983	*2,8*
1984	*4,9*
1985	*3,4*
1986	*2,6*
1987	*3,4*
1988	*4,3*
1989	*3,7*
1990	*2,7*
1991	*1,8*
1992	*2,8*

1993	*2,7*
1994	*4,1*
1995	*3,7*
1996	*4*
1997	*4,4*
1998	
1999	

The graphical results for these data were already published in Tausch (1998) at: http://csf.colorado.edu/wsystems/archive Books -> Website documents

8) THE GEOGRAPHY OF THE DEVELOPMENT MARATHON

Some further details on the geography of the development marathon should be considered:

Map 1: Development Reversals. GDP per Capita Lowest Values, 1960-95

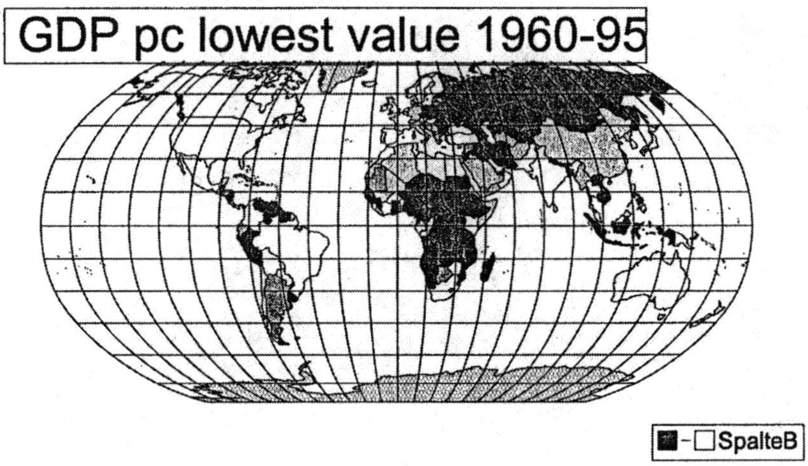

Legend: Lowest value for GDP per capita in 1987 constant real values, 1960-95 in the year ... The darker, the later that date. Only countries, marked by white color, had their lowest real income back in 1960. All the others suffered a setback since 1960; the darker, the later the date of that setback. The dark zones of our map are zones of late impoverishment in the world economy.

The UNDP data series also permits the analysis of the question, in which year a country achieved its highest per capita income in real terms. **A very fortunate and small number of countries achieved their highest GNP per capita in 1995, while others have to realize that they were better off ten, fifteen, or even twenty years from now.** Their racing along the last 10, 15, or even 20 last kilometers was totally in vain, and they have to start again by kilometer 10 or 20. Will they ever mile number 26? In terms of the marathon race, they stumbled on their way, while approaching the finish, or they even took a wrong direction:

Map 2: Development Stability. GDP per Capita Highest Values, 1960-95

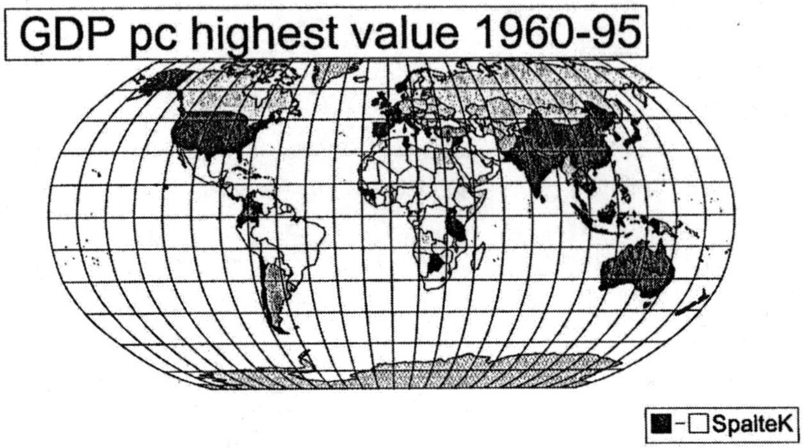

Legend: Highest value for GDP per capita in 1987 constant real values, 1960-95 in the year ... The darker, the later that date. Only countries, marked by dark color, had its highest real income in 1995. All the others suffered a setback; the lighter, the earlier the date of that severe setback, that could not be made good until 1995.

Map 3: The Stability and Strength of the Growth Engine. Development Stability and Avoidance of Development Reversals Combined

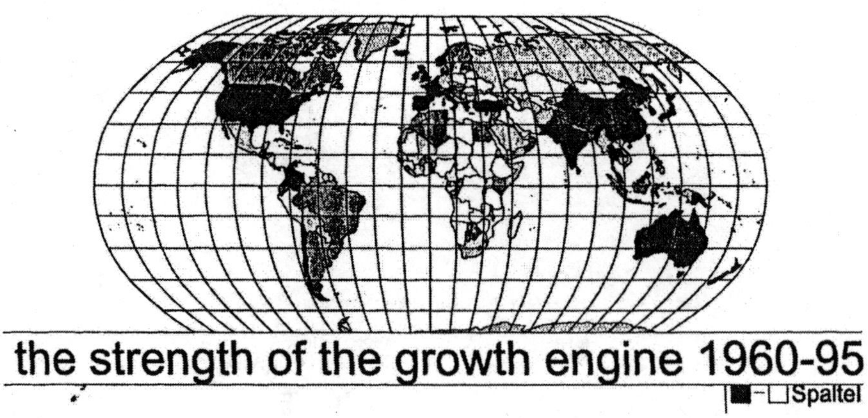

Legend: Highest value for GDP per capita in 1987 constant real values minus lowest value for GDP per capita in 1987 constant real values. The darker, the longer the period of uninterrupted ascending growth. Countries, marked by white or light colors, had their lowest real income often well in the 1980s and beyond and their highest real income often in the 1960s or early 1970s. The lighter the shade of the country, the greater the setback since 1960.

9) Data for the Operationalization of the Concept of Unequal Exchange

Country Code	ERDI	GDP pc PPP 1991 $	GNP per cap 1991	Country Code
Canada	1,06	19320	20510	Canada
USA	1,01	22130	22340	USA
Japan	1,38	19390	26840	Japan
NL	1,12	16820	18840	NL
NOR	1,4	17170	24090	NOR
SF	1,48	16130	23930	SF
France	1,11	18430	20460	France
Iceland	1,33	17480	23230	Iceland
Swed	1,44	17490	25180	Swed
Spain	0,99	12670	12480	Spain
Australia	1,03	16680	17120	Australia
Belgium	1,09	17510	19010	Belgium
Austria	1,14	17690	20200	Austria
NZ	0,88	13970	12360	NZ
CH	1,55	21780	33710	CH
UK	1,02	16340	16600	UK
DK	1,33	17880	23760	DK
GER	1,04	19770	20510	GER
IRE	0,98	11430	11150	IRE
ITA	1,09	17040	18580	ITA
GRE	0,84	7680	6420	GRE
ISR	0,9	13460	12110	ISR
LUX	1,53	20800	31860	LUX
MAL	0,96	7575	7300	MAL
POR	0,65	9450	6180	POR
HUNG	0,45	6080	2750	HUNG
LATV	0,52	7540	3920	LATV
POL	0,4	4500	1790	POL
RUS	0,5	6930	3470	RUS
BELR	0,48	6850	3280	BELR
BULG	0,38	4813	1840	BULG
EST	0,49	8090	3970	EST
KAZ	0,45	4490	2030	KAZ
ROM	0,34	4360	1480	ROM
UKR	0,42	5180	2190	UKR
LITH	0,45	5410	2420	LITH
ARM	0,42	4610	1930	ARM
UZB	0,35	2790	980	UZB
AZER	0,34	3670	1240	AZER

Country Code	ERDI	GDP pc PPP 1991 $	GNP per cap 1991	Country Code
KYR	0,35	3280	1160	KYR
GEO	0,49	3670	1780	GEO
ALB	0,19	3500	670	ALB
TAJ	0,32	2180	690	TAJ
Hong Kong	0,73	18520	13580	Hong Kong
Cyprus	0,88	9844	8670	Cyprus
Barbados	0,69	9667	6650	Barbados
Bahamas	0,81	14710	11940	Bahamas
S-Korea	0,76	8320	6350	S-Korea
Argentina	0,74	5120	3790	Argentina
Costa Rica	0,37	5100	1870	Costa Rica
Uruguay	0,43	6670	2880	Uruguay
Chile	0,33	7060	2360	Chile
Singapore	0,96	14734	14140	Singapore
Trinidad	0,45	8380	3790	Trinidad
Bahrein	0,62	11536	7150	Bahrein
Antigua	0,74			Antigua
Panama	0,43	4910	2130	Panama
Venezuela	0,33	8120	2720	Venezuela
Saint Kitts	0,55	9410	5170	Saint Kitts
Fiji	0,4	4858	1920	Fiji
Mexico	0,43	7170	3080	Mexico
Colombia	0,23	5460	1250	Colombia
Thailand	0,31	5270	1650	Thailand
Malaysia	0,34	7400	2520	Malaysia
Mauritius	0,33	7178	2380	Mauritius
Brazil	0,56	5240	2920	Brazil
Seychelles	1,38	3683	5070	Seychelles
Dominica	0,52			Dominica
Belize	0,49	5400	2630	Belize
Algeria	0,69	2870	1990	Algeria
Botswana	0,55	4690	2580	Botswana
Saint Vincent	0,56			Saint Vincent
Suriname	1,19	3072	3650	Suriname
Saint Lucia	0,66			Saint Lucia
Grenada	0,68	3374	2300	Grenada
Tunesia	0,32	4690	1500	Tunesia
Oman	0,67	9230	6140	Oman
Turkey	0,37	4840	1790	Turkey
Paraguay	0,37	3420	1270	Paraguay
Jamaica	0,41	3670	1490	Jamaica
Dominican R	0,31	3080	940	Dominican R

Country Code	ERDI	GDP pc PPP 1991 $	GNP per cap 1991	Country Code
Sri Lanka	0,19	2650	500	Sri Lanka
Peru	0,34	3110	1070	Peru
Philippines	0,3	2440	740	Philippines
South Africa	0,65	3885	2540	South Africa
Indonesia	0,22	2730	610	Indonesia
Guyana	0,16	1862	300	Guyana
Egypt	0,17	3600	610	Egypt
Maldives	0,32	3080	990	Maldives
China	0,13	2946	370	China
Swaziland	0,45	2506	1130	Swaziland
Bolivia	0,3	2170	650	Bolivia
Guatemala	0,3	3180	940	Guatemala
Mongolia	0,16	1950	310	Mongolia
Honduras	0,32	1820	590	Honduras
El Salvador	0,52	2110	1090	El Salvador
Namibia	0,64	2381	1520	Namibia
Nicaragua	0,16	2550	400	Nicaragua
Gabon	1,14	3498	3980	Gabon
Cape Verde	0,55	1360	750	Cape Verde
Morocco	0,31	3340	1030	Morocco
Zimbabwe	0,31	2160	670	Zimbabwe
Congo	0,37	2800	1040	Congo
Papua NG	0,6	1550	930	Papua NG
Cameroon	0,36	2400	860	Cameroon
Kenya	0,25	1350	340	Kenya
Ghana	0,45	930	420	Ghana
Lesotho	0,43	1780	770	Lesotho
Equatorial G	0,22			Equatorial G
Pakistan	0,2	1970	400	Pakistan
India	0,29	1150	330	India
Zambia	0,42	1010	420	Zambia
Nigeria	0,26	1360	350	Nigeria
Comoros	0,36	1320	470	Comoros
Togo	0,56	738	410	Togo
Bangladesh	0,19	1160	220	Bangladesh
Tanzania	0,21	570	120	Tanzania
Cote d'Ivoire	0,45	1510	680	Cote d'Ivoire
C African R	0,64	641	410	C African R
Mauritania	0,53	962	510	Mauritania
Madagascar	0,3	710	210	Madagascar
Nepal	0,16	1130	180	Nepal
Rwanda	0,43	680	290	Rwanda

Country Code	ERDI	GDP pc PPP 1991 $	GNP per cap 1991	Country Code
Benin	0,25	1500	380	Benin
Malawi	0,29	800	230	Malawi
Guinea-Biss.	0,24	747	180	Guinea-Biss.
Gambia	0,47	763	360	Gambia
Chad	0,47	447	210	Chad
Burundi	0,34	640	220	Burundi
Mozambique	0,09	921	80	Mozambique
Burkina F.	0,44	666	290	Burkina F.
Mali	0,56	480	270	Mali
Sierra L.	0,2	1020	200	Sierra L.
Niger	0,57	542	310	Niger

LITERATURE

Achen Ch. H. (1982), *'Interpreting and Using Regression'* Beverly Hills: Sage University Papers.

Adamczyk F *et al.* (1992), *'Rynek Oracy w Polsce'* Warsaw: Fundacja 'Promocja'.

Addo H. (1986), *Imperialism: the permanent stage of capitalism* Tokyo: United Nations University.

Afheldt H. (1994), *'Wohlstand fuer niemand? Die Marktwirtschaft entlaesst ihre Kinder'* Munich: Kunstmann.

Agence France Press English Wire, Dialog - online.

Aghion Ph. and Williamson J. G. (1998), *'Growth, Inequality and Globalization. Theory, History and Policy'* Cambridge: at the University Press

Ahluwalia M.S. (1974), 'Income Inequality: Some Dimensions of the Problem' in *'Redistribution with Growth'* (Chenery H.B. *et al.* (Eds.)), pp. 3 - 37, New York and Oxford: Oxford University Press.

Akerman J. (1936) *'Economic Progress and Economic Crises'* London and Basingstoke: Macmillan.

Alexander, T. (1996) Unravelling Global Apartheid: An Overview of World Politics. Cambridge, UK: Polity Press

Allen, C. and D. Vines (1993) "Should Clinton Cut the Deficit or is there a Global Paradox of Thrift?" *The World Economy*, no. 2, vol. 16 (March 1993), pp. 133-158

Almond G. (1991), 'Capitalism and Democracy' *PS. Political Science and Politics,* 24, 3, September: 467 - 474.

Althaler A. and Hohenwarter A. (Eds.)(1992), *'Torschluss. Wanderungsbewegungen und Politik in Europa'* Vienna: Verlag fuer Gesellschaftskritik.

Altzinger W., Beer E., Bellak Chr. (1998) 'Exportieren österreichische Unternehmen Arbeitsplätze nach Osteuropa?' in: *Wirtschaft und Gesellschaft*

Amankwaa A. A. (1995), 'The World Economic System and International Migration in Less Developed Countries: An Ecological Approach' *International Migration*, 33, 1: 93 - 114.

Amato G. and Batt J. (1999), *'Final Report of the Reflection Group on The Longterm Implications of EU Enlargement: The Nature of the New Border'* The Robert

Schuman Centre for Advanced Studies, European University Institute and The Forward Studies Unit, European Commission (mimeo)

Amin S. (1973), *'Le developpement inegal. Essai sur les formations sociales du capitalisme peripherique'* Paris: Editions de Minuit.

Amin S. (1976), *Unequal Development: An Essay on the Social Formations of Peripheral Capitalism.* New York: Monthly Review Press. [translated from the 1973 French original]

Amin S. (1984), 'Was kommt nach der Neuen Internationalen Wirtschaftsordnung? Die Zukunft der Weltwirtschaft' in *'Rote Markierungen International'* (Fischer H. and Jankowitsch P. (Eds.)), pp. 89 - 110, Vienna: Europaverlag.

Amin S. (1992), *'Empire of Chaos'* New York: Monthly Review Press.

Amin S. (1994), 'Die neue kapitalistische Globalisierung - die Herrschaft des Chaos' *Starnberger Forschungsberichte,* 3, 4, May: 7 - 26.

Amin S. (1997), *'Die Zukunft des Weltsystems. Herausforderungen der Globalisierung. Herausgegeben und aus dem Franzoesischen uebersetzt von Joachim Wilke'* Hamburg: VSA.

Amin, S. (1994) 'The Future of Global Polarization', *Review* (Fernand Braudel Center, USA), XVII, 3 (Summer), p. 337-347

Amin, S. (1997) *'Capitalism in the Age of Globalization'.* London, England: Zed Books

Amin, Samir (1980) "The Class Structure of the Contemporary Imperialist System", *Monthly Review* (USA), 31 (1980), 8: 9-26

Ammon G. (1994), *'Das Europa der Regionen'* Munich: Eberhard.

Ammon G. and Eberhard Th. (Ed.)(1993), *'Kultur, Identitaet, Kommunikation. 2. Versuch'* Munich: Eberhard.

Amnesty International (current issues), *'Jahresbericht'* Frankfurt a.M.: Fischer TB.

Amsden A.H. *et al.* (1994), 'From Pseudo - Socialism to Pseudo - Capitalism: Eastern Europe's First Five Years' *Internationale Politik und Gesellschaft. International Politics and Society (Friedrich Ebert Foundation)*, 2: 107 - 116.

Angresano J. (1994), 'Evolving Socio - economic Conditions in Central and Eastern Europe: A Myrdalian View' *Development Policy Review,* 12: 251 - 275.

Anonymous (1997) 'The Overcapacity Bomb', *Business Week* (USA), October 13, 1997, p. 138

Apter D. (1987), *'Rethinking Development: Modernization, Dependency and Post - Modern Politics'* Newbury Park, CA.: Sage.

Ardelt R. and Haas H. (1975), 'Die Westintegration Oesterreichs nach 1945' *Oesterreichische Zeitschrift fuer Politikwissenschaft,* 3: 379 - 399.

Arnold E. (1991), 'German foreign policy and unification' *International Affairs,* 67, 3: 453 - 471.

Arrighi G. (1989), *'The Developmentalist Illusion: A Reconceptualization of the Semiperiphery'* paper, presented at the Thirteenth Annual Political Economy of the World System Conference, University of Illinois at Urbana - Champaign, April 28 - 30.

Arrighi G. (1991), *'World Income Inequalities and the Future of Socialism'* Fernand Braudel Centre, State University of New York at Binghamton.

Arrighi G. (1995), *'The Long 20th Century. Money, Power, and the Origins of Our Times'* London, New York: Verso.

Arrighi G. and Silver, B. J. (1984), 'Labor Movements and Capital Migration: The United States and Western Europe in World - Historical Perspective' in *'Labor in the Capitalist World - Economy'* (Bergquist Ch. (Ed.)), pp. 183 - 216, Beverly Hills: Sage.

Arrighi G. *et al.* (1991), *'The Rise of East Asia. One Miracle or Many?'* State University of New York at Binghamton: Fernand Braudel Centre.

Arrighi G. *et al.* (1996a), *'Modelling Zones of the World-Economy: A Polynomial Regression Analysis (1964-1994)'* State University of New York at Binghamton: Fernand Braudel Center.

Arrighi G. *et al.* (1996b), *'The Rise of East Asia in World Historical Perspective'* State University of New York at Binghamton: Fernand Braudel Center.

Arrighi G. *et al.* (1996c), *'Beyond Western Hegemonies'* State University of New York at Binghamton: Fernand Braudel Center.

Asimakopulos, A. (1991) *'Keynes's General Theory and Accumulation'.* Cambridge, England: Cambridge University Press

Aslund, A. (1992), 'The Soviet Economy After the Coup', *Problems of Communism,* 40, Nov. - Dec.: 44 - 52.

Austrian Central Statistical Office (current issues), *'Statistische Nachrichten'.* Vienna: Austrian Central Statistical Office.

Austrian Federal Ministry for Foreign Affairs (current issues), *'Austrian Foreign Policy Yearbook'* Vienna: Manzsche Buchdruckerei.

Austrian Federal Ministry for Foreign Affairs (current issues), *'Jahrbuch der oesterreichischen Aussenpolitik. Aussenpolitischer Bericht'* Vienna: Manz'sche Buchdruckerei.

Austrian Federal Ministry of Labor and Social Affairs (1994), *'Austria's Labor Market Policy'* Vienna: Federal Ministry of Labor and Social Affairs.

Austrian Federal Ministry of Labor and Social Affairs (1997), *'Bericht ueber die soziale Lage. Analysen und Ressortaktivitaeten, 1996'* Vienna: Federal Ministry of Labor and Social Affairs.

Austrian Federal Ministry of Labor, Vienna (current issues), *'Arbeitsmarktdaten'* Vienna: Federal Ministry of Labor and Social Affairs.

Austrian Federal Ministry of Labor, Vienna (current issues), *'Statistik ueber die bewilligungspflichtig beschaeftigten Auslaender'* Vienna: Federal Ministry of Labor.

Autorenkollektiv (1981), *'Laender der Erde. Politisch - oekonomisches Handbuch'.* Koeln: Pahl Rugenstein Verlag.

Axtmann R. (1995) 'Kulturelle Globalisierung, kollektive Identitaet und demokratischer Nationalstaat' *Leviathan,* 1: 87 - 101.

Bablewski Z. (1995), 'Development studies and the changes in Eastern *Europe' Afryka, Azja, Ameryka Lacinska (Warsaw),* 73: 17 - 32.

Babones, S. (1998) *'A Credit-Market Theory of Surplus Value',* forthcoming. See, memorandum, wsn mail archive, 08 Dec 1997, online: http://csf.colorado.edu/mail/wsn/current/0331.html

Bailey P.; Parisotto A. and Renshaw G. (1993), *'Multinationals and Employment. The Global Economy of the 1990s'* Geneva: International Labor Office.

Baldwin R. E. *et al.* (1997), *'The Costs and Benefits of Eastern Enlargement: The Impact on the EU and Central Europe'* Economic Policy, April (quoted from the typescript).

Balibar E. (1991), 'Es gibt keinen Staat in Europa: Racism and Politics in Europe Today' *New Left Review,* March/April, 186: 5 - 19.

Bandt J. de *et al.* (Eds.)(1980), *'European Studies in Development. New Trends in European Development Studies'* Basingstoke and London: Macmillan.

Bank Austria East - West Report. Business Information for the Central European Investor (current issues), Vienna: Z - Laenderbank Bank Austria AG.

Bank Austria Report (current issues), Vienna: Z - Laenderbank Bank Austria AG.

Baran P. A. (1957), *'The Political Economy of Growth'* New York: Monthly Review Press.

Barnes S.H. *et al.* (1979), *'Political Action. Mass Participation in Five Western Democracies'* Beverly Hills: Sage.

Barro R. (1996), *'Getting It Right. Markets and Choices in a Free Society'* Cambridge, Mass.: MIT Press.

Barro R. and Grilli V. (1994) *'European Macroeconomics'* Basingstoke and London: Macmillan

Barro R. and X. Sala-i-Martin (1991) 'Convergence across States and Regions' *Brookings Papers on Economic Activity,* 1: 107-182

Barro R. and X. Sala-i-Martin (1995/98) *'Wirtschaftswachstum (Economic Growth)'* München: Oldenbourg (McGraw Hill, New York).

Barro R. J. and Sala-i-Martin X. (1991), 'Convergence across States and Regions' *Brookings Papers on Economic Activity,* 1: 107 - 179.

Barta V. and Richter S. (1996), *'Eastern Enlargement of the European Union from a Western and an Eastern Persepctive'* Research Reports, 227, Vienna Institute for Comparative Economic Studies.

Barwinek H. and Kirisits, M. (1998), *'EU-Osterweiterung. Regionalwirtschaftliche Auswirkungen der EU-Osterweiterung in grenznahen Regionen der Steiermark'* Graz: Arbeiterkammer Steiermark

Bauboeck, R. (1991a), 'Migration and citizenship', *New Community,* 18, 1: 27 - 48.

Bauboeck, R. (1991b), 'Einwanderungs - und Minderheitenpolitik. Ein Plaedoyer fuer neue Grundsaetze' *Oesterreichische Zeitschrift fuer Soziologie,* 16, 3: 42 - 56.

Bauer P. (1998), 'Die Union vor der Osterweiterung. Die Transformationsstaaten - Von der Startlinie ins Abseits?' *Oesterreichische Zeitschrift fuer Politikwissenschaft,* 27, 4: 363 - 376.

Bauer P. (1998), 'Die Union vor der Osterweiterung. Die Transformationsstaaten - Von der Startlinie ins Abseits?' *Oesterreichische Zeitschrift fuer Politikwissenschaft,* 27, 4: 363 - 376.

Bauer Th. and Zimmermann, K. F.(1999) *'Assessment of Possible Migration Pressure and It's Labour Market impact Following EU Enlargement to Central and Eastern Europe.'* A Study for the Department for Education and Employment, London, 1999

Bayer K. and Kreisky P. (1987), 'Die oesterreichische Gemeinwirtschaft nach dem Debakel bei VOEST - Alpine' *Das Argument,* 162: 200 - 209.

BBC World Service (current news broadcasts) short - wave, 31 - m - band.

Beaud M. (1990), *'Histoire du capitalisme de 1500 à nos jours'* 4e édition revue et corrigée en 1990, Paris: Éditions du Seuil.

Beck N. (1991), 'The Illusion of Cycles in International Relations' *International Studies Quarterly,* 35: 455 - 476.

Becker G. (1993), 'Europe Wastes Its Human Capital' *The Wall Street Journal Europe,* 18 - 19 June: 10.

Beckerman W. (1992), *'Economic Development and the Environment. Conflict or Complementarity?'* World Bank Policy Research Papers, WPS 961, Washington D.C.: The World Bank.

Behan T. (1996), *'The Camorra'* London: Routledge.

Beirat fuer Gesellschafts-, Wirtschafts- und Umweltpolitische Alternativen (Beigewum) (1996), *'Was hat der Euro mit den Arbeitslosen zu tun?'* Vienna: Department of Economics, Economics University, Vienna.

Bello W. (1989), 'Confronting the Brave New World Economic Order: Toward a Southern Agenda for the 1990s' *Alternatives,* XIV, 2: 135 - 168.

Bellofiore, R. (1997) memorandum, pkt mail archive, 13 Nov 1997, online: http://csf.colorado.edu/mail/pkt/nov97

Benard Ch. and Schlaffer E. (1985), *'Die Grenzen des Geschlechts. Anleitungen zum Sturz des Internationalen Patriarchats'* Reinbek: rororo Sachbuch.

Bergesen A. (1983a), '1914 Again? Another Cycle of Interstate Competition and War' in *'Foreign Policy and the Modern World - System'* (Mc Gowan P. and Kegley Ch.W. Jr. (Eds.)), pp. 255 - 273, Beverly Hills: Sage.

Bergesen A. (1983b), 'Modeling Long Waves of Crisis in the World - System' in *'Crisis in the World System'* (Bergesen A. (Ed.)), pp. 73 - 92, Beverly Hills: Sage.

Bergesen, Albert, and Laura Parisi (1997) "Discovering the Environment," *Journal of World-Systems Research* 3:364-368, online at: http://csf.colorado.edu/wsystems/jwsr/

Berman R.A. (1987), 'The Vienna Fascination' *Dialog,* 3, 8: 173 - 204.

Bernal - Restrepo S. *Societas Jesu* (1991), 'Katholische Soziallehre und Kapitalismus' in *'Veraendert der Glaube die Wirtschaft? Theologie und Oekonomie in Lateinamerika'* (Fornet - Betancourt R. (Ed.)), pp. 21 - 38, Freiburg im Breisgau: Herder.

Bernhard M. (1996), 'Civil Society After the First Transition. Dilemmas of Postcommunist Democratization in Poland and Beyond' *Communist and Post - Communist Studies,* 29, 3: 309 - 330.

Berry A. *et al.* (1981), *'The Level of World Inequality: How Much Canada One Say?'* Document 38, Laboratoire d'Economie Politique, CNRS, 45, rue d'Ulm, F - 75230 Paris Cedex 05.

Berry B. J. L. (1991), *'Long Wave Rhythms in Economic Development and Political Behavior'* Baltimore: John Hopkins University Press.

Berry W.D. and Feldman S. (1985), *'Multiple Regression in Practice'* Beverly Hills: Sage University Papers.

Berryman, Ph. (1987), *'Liberation Theology: The Essential Facts about the Revolutionary Movement in Latin America and Beyond'* New York: Pantheon Books.

Betz J. and Bruene St. (1995), *'Jahrbuch Dritte Welt 1995'* Munich: C.H. Beck.

Betz J. and Matthies V. (Eds.)(1992), *'Jahrbuch Dritte Welt 1992'* Munich: C.H. Beck.

Bhaduri A. and Laski K. (1996), *'Lessons to be drawn from main mistakes in the transition strategy'* Paper, presented at the 'Colloquium on Economic Transformation and Development of Central and Eastern Europe', OECD, Paris, 29/30 May 1996.

Bhagwati J.N. (1989), 'Nation States in an International Framework: An Economist's Perspective' *Alternatives,* XIV, 2: 231 - 244.

Biehl K. (1999) EU-Osterweiterung und Arbeitsmarkt, in: *Wirtschaftspolitische Blätter,* 1-2

Birdsall N. (1993), *'Social Development is Economic Development'* Policy Research Working Papers, WPS 1123, Washington D.C.: The World Bank.

Blaas W. (1984), *'Stabilisierungspolitik. Zur politischen Oekonomie marktwirtschaftlicher Instabilitaet'* habilitation thesis, Vienna Technical University.

Blank S. (1994), *'Russia and the Baltic States. Is There a Threat to European Security?'* Carlisle, Pennsylvania: Strategic Studies Institute, US Army War College.

Boehring W.R. and Schloeter - Paredes M.L. (1994*), 'Aid in place of migration?. A World Employment Programme Study'* Geneva: International Labor Office.

Boff C. and Boff L. (1984), *'Salvation and Liberation: In Search of a Balance between Faith and Politics'* Maryknoll, NY: Orbis Books.

Boff L. (1979), *'Liberating Grace'* Maryknoll, NY: Orbis Books.

Boff L. (1985), *'Kirche: Charisma und Macht. Studien zu einer streitbaren Ekklesiologie'* Duesseldorf: Patmos - Verlag.

Boff L. and Boff C. (1988*), 'Introducing Liberation Theology'* Trans. Paul Burns. Maryknoll, NY: Orbis Books.

Boli J. (1983), 'The Contradictions of Welfare Capitalism in the Core: The Role of Sweden in the World System' in *'Foreign Policy and the Modern World System'* (Mc Gowan P. and Kegley Ch.W.Jr. (Eds.)), pp. 187 - 221, Beverly Hills: Sage.

Bollen K. A. (1980), 'Issues in the Comparative Measurement of Political Democracy' *American Sociological Review,* 45: 370 - 390.

Bornschier V. (Ed.) (1994*), 'Conflicts and new departures in world society'* New Brunswick, N.J.: Transaction Publishers.

Bornschier V. (1976), *'Wachstum, Konzentration und Multinationalisierung von Industrieunternehmen'* Frauenfeld and Stuttgart: Huber.

Bornschier V. (1988), *'Westliche Gesellschaft im Wandel'* Frankfurt a.M./ New York: Campus.

Bornschier V. (1992), *'The Rise of the European Community. Grasping Towards Hegemony or Therapy against National Decline in the World Political Economy?'.* Vienna: paper, presented at the First European Conference of Sociology, August 26 - 29.

Bornschier V. (1996), *'Western society in transition'* New Brunswick, N.J.: Transaction Publishers.

Bornschier V. and Chase - Dunn Ch. K (1985), *'Transnational Corporations and Underdevelopment'* N.Y., N.Y.: Praeger.

Bornschier V. and Heintz P., reworked and enlarged by Th. H. Ballmer - Cao and J. Scheidegger (1979), *'Compendium of Data for World Systems Analysis'* Machine readable data file, Zurich: Department of Sociology, Zurich University.

Bornschier V. and Nollert M. (1994); 'Political Conflict and Labor Disputes at the Core: An Encompassing Review for the Post - War Era' in *'Conflicts and New Departures in World Society'* (Bornschier V. and Lengyel P. (Eds.)), pp. 377 - 403, New Brunswick (U.S.A.) and London: Transaction Publishers, World Society Studies, Volume 3.

Bornschier V. and Suter Chr. (1992), 'Long Waves in the World System' in *'Waves, Formations and Values in the World System'* (Bornschier V. and Lengyel P. (Eds.)), pp. 15 - 50, New Brunswick and London: Transaction Publishers.

Bornschier V. *et al.* (1980), *'Multinationale Konzerne, Wirtschaftspolitik und nationale Entwicklung im Weltsystem'* Frankfurt a.M.: Campus.

Boswell T. (1989), *'Revolutions in the World System'* Greenwich CT: Greenwood.

Boswell T. and Dixon W.J. (1990), 'Dependency and Rebellion: A Cross - National Analysis' *American Sociological Review,* 55, August: 540 - 559.

Boswell T. and Sweat M. (1991), 'Hegemony, Long Waves, and Major Wars: A Time Series Analysis of Systemic Dynamics, 1496 - 1967' *International Studies Quarterly,* 35, 2: 123 - 149.

Botz G. (1987), *'Krisenzonen einer Demokratie. Gewalt, Streik und Konfliktunterdrueckung in Oesterreich seit 1918'* Frankfurt a.M.: Campus.

Bourdieu, P. (1998) 'The essence of neoliberalism: Utopia of endless exploitation', *Le monde diplomatique,* December 18, 1998; online: http://www.monde-diplpmatique.fr/en/1998/12/08bourdieu.html

Boxberger G. and Klimenta H. (1998), *'Die 10 Globalisierungslügen. Alternativen zur Allmacht des Marktes'* Munich: dtv.

Boyer M. (1996), 'Seid vernuenftig, vertagt den Euro!' *Zeit-Punkte, (Hamburg),* 4: 60 - 62.

Brackley D. SJ (1996), *'Divine Revolution. Salvation and Liberation in Catholic Thought. Foreword by Jon Sobrino'*. Maryknoll, New York: Orbis.

Bradshaw Y. (1987), 'Urbanization and Underdevelopment: A Global Study of Modernization, Urban Bias, and Economic Dependency' *American Sociological Review,* 52: 224 - 239.

Bradshaw Y. and Huang J. (1991), 'Intensifying Global Dependency. Foreign Debt, Structural Adjustment, and Third - World Underdevelopment' *Sociological Quarterly,* 32, 3: 321 - 342.

Brandt Commission (1980) *'North-South: A programme for survival'* [Report of the Independent Commission on International Development Issues] Cambridge, USA: MIT Press

Braun G. and Topan A. (1998), *'Internationale Migration. Ihre Folgen fuer die Ursprungslaender und Ansaetze eines Migrationsregimes'*. Sankt Augustin: Interne Studien, 153, Konrad Adenauer-Stiftung.

Brecher, J. and T. Costello (1994) *'Global Village or Global Pillage'.* Boston, USA: Southend Press

Brenner R. (1977), 'The Origins of Capitalist Development: A Critique of Neo - Smithian Marxism' *New Left Review,* 104: 25 - 92.

Breuss F. (1996), 'Die Osterweiterung der EU: Oekonomische Auswirkungen auf Oesterreich' *Die Union. Oesterreichische Zeitschrift fuer Integrationsfragen,* 4: 17 - 26.

Breuss F. (1997), 'Macht die Agenda 2000 bisherige Kosten-Nutzen-Schaetzungen der EU-Osterweiterung obsolet?' *Europa-Institut der Universitaet des Saarlandes, Vortraege, Reden und Berichte,* 50, Dezember 1997.

Brill H. (1996); 'Dimensionen der Sicherheitspolitik aus geopolitischer Sicht nach dem Ende des Ost - West - Konfliktes.' *Oesterreichische Militaerische Zeitschrift,* 5: 519 - 528.

Brown J.F. (Ed.), (1994), 'The Politics of Intolerance' *RFE/RL Research Report,* 3, 16, 22 April 1994 (special issue).

Brown L.R. *et al.* (1992), *'Zur Lage der Welt - 1992. Worldwatch Institute Report'* Frankfurt a.M.: Fischer TB.

Brown, R.S. (1993) 'The IMF and the World Bank in the New World Order,' in: P. Bennis and M. Moushabeck, eds., *Altered States: A Reader in the New World Order.* New York, USA: Olive Branch Press

Brundtland Commission (1987). *Our Common Future.*

Bruno M. and Sachs J. D. (1985), *'Economics of Worldwide Stagflation'* Cambridge, MA.: Harvard University Press.

Buckley, K. D. and Wheelwright E. L. (1988) *'No paradise for workers: capitalism and the common people in Australia, 1788 - 1914'* Melbourne; New York: Oxford University Press.

Bulletin of Electoral Statistics and Public Opinion Research Data (1994), 'Parliamentary Elections in Poland' *East European Politics and Society,* 8, 2: 369 - 379.

Bullock B. and Firebaugh G. (1990), 'Guns and Butter. The Effect of Militarization on Economic and Social Development in the Third World' *Journal of Political and Military Sociology,* 18, 2: 231 - 266.

Bundeskanzleramt der Republik Oesterreich (1992), *'Bericht ueber Oesterreichs Massnahmen fuer die Zentral - und Osteuropaeischen Reformstaaten (ZOR)'.* Vienna: Bundeskanzleramt, IV/1.

Bundesministerium fuer Arbeit und Soziales (1993), *'Von Ausgrenzung bedroht. Struktur und Umfang der materiellen Armutsgefährdung im österreichischen Wohlfahrtsstaat der achtziger Jahre'* Vienna: BMAS.

Bundesministerium fuer Arbeit und Soziales (current issues), *'Auslaenderbeschaeftigung'* (monthly) Vienna: BMAS.

Bundesministerium fuer Arbeit und Soziales (current issues), *'Bericht ueber die soziale Lage'* Vienna: BMAS.

Bundesministerium fuer Arbeit und Soziales (current issues), *'Statistik ueber die bewilligungspflichtig beschaeftigten Auslaender'* Vienna: BMAS.

Bundesministerium fuer Finanzen (1987), *'Staatliche Verteilungspolitik in Oesterreich'* Vienna: Bericht des Bundesministers fuer Finanzen an den Nationalrat.

Bundesministerium fuer Landesverteidigung, Landesverteidigungs - akademie Wien (1993), *'Militaer - Strategisches Umwelt - und Konfliktbild (Synopse)'* Vienna: Bundesministerium fuer Landesverteidigung.

Bunzl J. and Marin B. (1983), *'Antisemitismus in Oesterreich. Sozialhistorische und soziologische Studien'* Innsbruck: Inn - Verlag.

Burant St.R. (1993), 'International Relations in a Regional Context: Poland and Its Eastern Neighbours - Lithuania, Belarus, Ukraine' *Europe - Asia Studies,* 45, 3: 395 - 418.

Bush K. (1992), 'The Disastrous Last Year of the USSR' *RFE/RL Research Report,* 12, 20 March: 39 - 41.

Business Central Europe (1996) *'Europe's Emerging Markets, 1997'* London: The Economist Group.

Business Central Europe (current issues).

Butterwege Ch. (1991), 'Rechtsruck in Ostdeutschland? Neofaschismus, Rassismus und Auslaenderfeindlichkeit nach der Wiedervereinigung' *Zukunft,* Oktober: 25 - 29.

Çakmak, A. (1998), *'living peoples',* memorandum to wsn mailing list, September 1998, online: http://csf.colorado.edu/mail/wsn

Caporaso J. A. (1978), 'Dependence, Dependency, and Power in the Global System: A Structural and Behavioral Analysis' *International Organization,* 32: 13 - 43.

Cardoso F.H. (1969), *'Mudancas sociais na América Latina'* Sao Paulo: DIFEL.

Cardoso F.H. (1972), *'O Modelo Politico Brasileiro, e outros ensaios'* Sao Paulo: DIFEL.

Cardoso F.H. (1973), 'Associated - Dependent Development. Theoretical and Practical Implications' in *'Authoritarian Brazil. Origins, Policies and Future'* (Stepan A. (Ed.)), New Haven and London: Yale University Press.

Cardoso F.H. (1977), 'El Consumo de la Teoria de la Dependencia en los Estados Unidos' *El Trimestre Economico,* 173, 44, 1, Enero: 33 - 52.

Cardoso F.H. (1979), *'Development under Fire'* Mexico D.F.: Instituto Latinoamericano de Estudios Transnacionales', DEE/D/24 i, Mayo (Mexico 20 D.F., Apartado 85 - 025).

Cardoso F.H. and Faletto E. (1971), *'Dependencia y desarrollo en América Latina'* Mexico D.F.: editorial siglo XXI.

Central European Quarterly (current issues). Vienna: Creditanstalt.

Central Statistical Office of the Polish Republic (1993a), *'Historia Polski w Liczbach. Ludnosc. Terytorium'* Warsaw: Glowny Urzad Statystyczny (CSO).

Central Statistical Office of the Polish Republic (1993b), *'Border Crossings'* Warsaw: CSO, unpublished data outprint.

Central Statistical Office of the Polish Republic (1994), *'Economic History of Poland in Numbers'* Warsaw: Glowny Urzad Statystyczny (CSO).

Central Statistical Office of the Polish Republic (current issues), *'Rocznik Statystyczny'* Warsaw: CSO.

Central Statistical Office of the Polish Republic (current issues), *'Maly Rocznik Statystyczny'* Warsaw: CSO.

Central Statistical Office of the Polish Republic (current issues), *'Research Bulletin'* Warsaw: CSO.

Central Statistical Office of the Polish Republic (current issues), *'Rocznik Statystyczny Wojewodztw'* Warsaw: CSO.

Central Statistical Office of the Polish Republic (current issues), *'Kosciol Katolicki w Polsce 1918 - 1990. Rocznik Statystyczny'* Warsaw: CSO.

Central Statistical Office of the Polish Republic (current issues), *'Statistical Bulletin'* Warsaw: CSO.

Central Statistical Office of the Polish Republic (current issues), *'Information on Social and Economic Situation in Poland'* Warsaw: CSO.

Central Statistical Office of the Polish Republic (current issues), *'Poland Quarterly Statistics'* Warsaw: CSO.

Central Statistical Office of the Polish Republic (current issues), *'Polen in Zahlen'* Warsaw: CSO.

Central Statistical Office of the Polish Republic (current issues), *'Quarterly Report on the Employment Situation'* Warsaw: CSO (in Polish).

Central Statistical Office of the Polish Republic (current issues), *'Aktywnosc Ekonomiczna Ludnosci Polski'* Warsaw: CSO.

Central Statistical Office of the Polish Republic (current issues), 'Unemployment in Poland' Warsaw: CSO.

Chaloupek G. (1977), 'Die Verteilung der persoenlichen Einkommen in Oesterreich' *Wirtschaft und Gesellschaft,* 3, 1: 9 - 21.

Chaloupek G. (1997), 'Arbeitsmigration - Komplementarität und Substitution' Beitrag zur Konferenz *Migration und Arbeitsmarkt*, veranstaltet vom Österreichisch-Französischen Zentrum für die wirtschaftliche Annäherung in Europa (3./4.10.1997), Paris, 1997.

Chaloupek G. (1999): Arbeitsmarktauswirkungen einer EU-Erweiterung, Unterlagen zum Vortrag bei der IDM Summerschool *Arbeitsmarkt und Beschäftigungspolitik in einer erweiterten EU*, Juli

Chaloupek G. and Swoboda H. (1975), 'Sozialpartnerschaft und Wirtschaftsentwicklung in den fuenfziger und sechziger Jahren' *Oesterreichische Zeitschrift fuer Politikwissenschaft,* 3: 333 - 343.

Chase-Dunn, Christopher (1975), 'The Effects of International Economic Dependence on Development and Inequality: a Cross - national Study' *American Sociological Review,* 40: 720 - 738.

Chase-Dunn, Christopher (Ed.), (1982), *'Socialist States in the World System'* Beverly Hills and London: Sage.

Chase-Dunn, Christopher (1983), 'The Kernel of the Capitalist World Economy: Three Approaches' in *'Contending Approaches to World System Analysis'* (Thompson W.R. (Ed.)), pp. 55 - 78, Beverly Hills: Sage.

Chase-Dunn, Christopher (1984), 'The World - System Since 1950: What Has Really Changed?' in *'Labor in the Capitalist World - Economy'* (Bergquist Ch. (Ed.)), pp. 75 - 104, Beverly Hills: Sage.

Chase-Dunn, Christopher (1989) *'Global Formation: Structures of the World-Economy.'* Cambridge, USA: Basil Blackwell

Chase-Dunn, Christopher (1991), *'Global Formation: Structures of the World Economy'* London, Oxford and New York: Basil Blackwell.

Chase-Dunn, Christopher (1992a), 'The National State as an Agent of Modernity' *Problems of Communism,* January - April: 29 - 37.

Chase-Dunn, Christopher (1992b), 'The Changing Role of Cities in World Systems' in *'Waves, Formations and Values in the World System'* (Bornschier V. and Lengyel P. (Eds.)), pp. 51 - 87, New Brunswick and London: Transaction Publishers.

Chase-Dunn, Christopher, and P. Grimes (1995), 'World-Systems Analysis', *Annual Review of Sociology* (USA), 21: 387-417

Chase-Dunn, Christopher, and Podobnik B. (1995), 'The Next World War: World - System Cycles and Trends' *Journal of World Systems Research* 1, 6 (unpaginated electronic journal at world - wide - web site of the World System Network: *http://csf.colorado.edu/wsystems/jwsr.html).*

Chase-Dunn, Christopher, and Hall, Th. D. (1997), *'Rise and Demise. Comparing World - Systems'* Boulder, Colorado: Westview Press.

Chase-Dunn, Christopher, and Thomas D. Hall (1998) "Paradigms Bridged: Institutional Materialism and World-Systemic Evolution," Paper presented at the XIV World Congress of Sociology of the International Sociological Association, July 26-August 1, 1998, Montreal, Canada; online: http://csf.colorado.edu/wsystems/archive/papers/c-d&hall/intsoc98.htm

Choucri N. and North R.C. (1989), 'Roots of War: The Master Variables' in *'The Quest for Peace'* (Vaerynen R. *et al.* (Eds.)), pp. 204 - 216, London, Beverly Hills: Sage.

Clad J.C. (1994), 'Slowing the Wave' *Foreign Policy,* 95: 139 - 150.

Clark R. (1992), 'Economic Dependency and Gender Differences in Labor - Force Sectoral Change in Non - Core Nations' *Sociological Quarterly,* 33, 1: 83 - 98.

Clark R. *et al.* (1991), 'Culture, Gender, and Labor - Force Participation. A Cross - National Study' *Gender and Society,* 5, 1: 47 - 66.

Clarke D.L. (1993), 'Europe's Changing Constellations' *RFE/RL Research Report,* 2, 37: 17 September: 13 - 15.

Clauss G. and Ebner H. (1978), *'Grundlagen der Statistik. Fuer Psychologen, Paedagogen und Soziologen'* Berlin: Volk and Wissen.

Cline M. (1992), 'Political Parties and Public Opinion in Poland' *RFE/RL Research Report,* 1, 43, 30 October: 66 - 69.

Cline M. (1993), 'The Demographics of Party Support in Poland' *RFE/RL Research Report,* 2, 36, 10 September: 17 - 21.

Clinton B. (1993), *'National Drug Control Strategy'* Washington D.C.: Report by the President of the United States of America to Congress.

Cohen R. (1991), 'East - West and European migration in a global context' *New Community,* 18, 1: 9 - 26.

Cohn - Bendit D. (1993), 'Europe and its borders: the case for a common immigration policy' in *'Towards a European Immigration Policy'* (Ogata S. *et al.*), pp. 22 - 31, London: Philip Morris Institute for Public Policy Research.

Coleman J. S. (1965), *'Education and Political Development'* Princeton: Princeton University Press

Commission of the European Communities (1995); *'White Paper. Preparation of the Associated Countries of Central and Eastern Europe for Integration into the Internal Market of the Union'* Brussels, 10.05.1995, Com (95) 163, final.

Commission of the European Communities (current issues), *'Employment Observatory Central and Eastern Europe'* Brussels: EU, DG Employment, Industrial Relations and Social Affairs.

Connolly B. (1995), *'The Rotten Heart of Europe. The Dirty War for Europe's Money'* London and Boston: Faber and Faber.

Corden, W.M. (1987) 'How Valid is International Keynesianism?' International Monetary Fund, Research Department: *IMF Working Paper* WP/87/56

Cordova A. (1973), *'Strukturelle Heterogenitaet und wirtschaftliches Wachstum'* Frankfurt a.M.: edition suhrkamp.

Cordova A. and Silva - Michelena H. (1972), *'Die wirtschaftliche Struktur Lateinamerikas. Drei Studien zur politischen Oekonomie der Unterentwicklung'* Frankfurt a.M.: edition suhrkamp.

Cornia G.A. (Ed.)(1993), *'Economies in Transition Studies, Regional Monitoring Report, 1'* Firenze: UNICEF.

Cornia G.A. (Ed.)(1994), *'Economies in Transition Studies, Regional Monitoring Report, 2'* Firenze: UNICEF.

Cox, R.W. (1994) 'Global Restructuring: Making Sense of the Changing International Political Economy,' in: G. Stubbs and Underhill (eds.), *Political Economy and the Changing Global Order.*

Crenshaw E. (1991), 'Foreign Investment as a Dependent Variable: Determinants of Foreign and Capital Penetration in Developing Nations, 1967 - 1978' *Social Forces,* 69, 4: 1169 - 1182.

Crenshaw E. (1992), 'Cross - National Determinants of Income Inequality: A Replication and Extension Using Ecological - Evolutionary Theory' *Social Forces,* 71: 339 - 363.

Crough, G. J. and Wheelwright E. L. (1982), *'Australia, a client state'* Ringwood, Vic., Australia: Penguin Books Australia; New York, N.Y.: Penguin Books.

Dadush U. and Brahmbhatt M. (1995), 'Anticipating Capital Flow Reversals' *Finance and Development,* December: 3 - 5.

Dalby, S. (1999) 'Globalization or Global Apartheid? Boundaries and Knowledge in Postmodern Times', *Geopolitics* 4/1

Dallinger A. *et al.* (1975), 'Auslaendische Arbeitnehmer in Oesterreich' Vienna: Bundesministerium fuer Arbeit und Soziales.

Daly M. (1973), *'Beyond God the Father: Toward a Philosophy of Women's Liberation'* Boston: Beacon Press.

Daly, Herman E. (1997) *Beyond Growth: The Economics of Sustainable Development.* Beacon Press, USA

Datta A. (1993), 'Warum fluechten Menschen aus ihrer Heimat?' in *'Die Neuen Mauern. Krisen der Nord - Sued - Beziehungen'* (Datta A. (Ed.)), pp. 31 - 46, Wuppertal: P. Hammer.

Dauderstaedt, M. and A.Pfaller (editors) (1983) '*Unfaehig zum Ueberleben? Reaktionen auf den Brandt-Report.*' Frankfurt, Germany: Ullstein Verlag

David A. and Wheelwright T. (1989), *'The Third Wave. Australia and Asian Capitalism'* Sutherland, New South Wales: Left Book Club Cooperative Ltd.

Davidson, P. (1994) *'Post Keynesian Macroeconomic Theory'*. Brookfield, USA: Elgar

Deacon B. (1992a),'East European Welfare: Past, Present and Future in Comparative Context' in *'The New Eastern Europe. Social Policy Past, Present and Future'* (Deacon B. (Ed.)), pp. 1 - 31, London and Newbury Park: Sage.

Deacon B. (1992b),'The Future of Social Policy in Eastern Europe' in *'The New Eastern Europe. Social Policy Past, Present and Future'* (Deacon B. (Ed.)), pp. 167 - 191, London and Newbury Park: Sage.

Delacroix J. and Ragin Ch. (1981), 'Structural Blockage: A Cross - National Study of Economic Dependency, State Efficacy, and Underdevelopment' *American Journal of Sociology,* 86, 6: 1311 - 1347.

Deshingkar G. (1989), 'Arms, Technology, Violence and the Global Military Order' in *'The Quest for Peace'* (Vaerynen R. *et al.* (Eds.)), pp. 260 - 274, London, Beverly Hills: Sage.

Deutsch K. W. (1960), 'Ansaetze zu einer Bestandsaufnahme von Tendenzen in der vergleichenden und internationalen Politik' in *'Political Science. Amerikanische Beitraege zur Politikwissenschaft'* (Krippendorff E. (Ed.)), Tuebingen: J.C.B. Mohr.

Deutsch K. W. (1966), *'Nationalism and Social Communication. An inquiry into the foundations of nationality'* Cambrigde, Massachusetts and London: M.I.T. Press.

Deutsch K. W. (1978), *'The Analysis of International Relations'* Englewood Cliffs, N.J.: Prentice Hall.

Deutsch K. W. (1979), *'Tides Among Nations'* New York: Free Press.

Deutsch K. W. (1982), 'Major Changes in Political Science' in *'International Handbook of Political Science'* (Andrews W.G. (Ed.)), pp. 9 - 33, Westport, Con.: Greenwood Press.

Dialog (current issues) (electronic archive, containing practically the entire English-language world press, the main international news agencies and newsletters and the Social Science Citation and Arts and Humanities Index, as well as the possibility to order on-line or fax copies from the international social science journals at *http://www.dialogselect.com)*

Die Presse (current issues) (free electronic archive at *http://www.diePresse.at)*

Dietz R. and Havlik P. (1995), *'Auswirkungen der EU-Ost-Integration auf den oesterreichischen und den EU-Osthandel'* Reprint Series, 161, Vienna Institute for Comparative Economic Studies.

Dixon W. J. (1984), 'Trade Concentration, Economic Growth and the Provision of Basic Human Needs' *Social Science Quarterly,* 65: 761 - 774.

Dixon W. J. and Boswell T. (1996), 'Dependency, Disarticulation, and Denominator Effects. Another Look at Foreign Capital Penetration' *American Journal of Sociology,* 102, 2: 543 - 562.

Doran Ch. F. (1983), 'Power Cycle Theory and the Contemporary State System' in *'Contending Approaches to World System Analysis'* (Thompson W.R. (Ed.)), pp. 165 - 182, Beverly Hills: Sage.

Douthwaite, R. (1998) *'Good Growth and Bad Growth'*, online: http://csf.colorado.edu/lists/ecol-econ/good_bad_growth.douthwaite.html

Dubiel I. (1983), *'Der klassische Kern der lateinamerikanischen Entwicklungstheorie. Ein metatheoretischer Versuch'* Munich: Eberhard.

Dubiel I. (1993), 'Andere Zeiten - Andere Wirtschaftstheorien. Elemente einer oekonomischen Theorie von morgen' in *'Kultur - Identitaet - Kommunikation. 2. Versuch'* (Ammon G. and Eberhard Th. (Eds.)), pp. 81 - 124, Munich: Eberhard - Verlag.

Dunn J. F. (1992), 'Hard Times in Russia Foster Conspiracy Theories' *RFE/RL Research Report,* 1, 46, 20 November: 24 - 29.

Dussel E. (1981), 'A History of the Church in Latin America, Colonialism to Liberation (1492 - 1972)' Grand Rapids, MI: Eerdmans.

Ebermann, W. (1998), interview entitled 'Links? Rechts? Oder was?' in: *taz mag* (the magazine of the newspaper die tageszeitung, Germany), No. 47, August 15-16, 1998, p. 3.

Eckhardt, W. (1992) *'Civilizations, Empires and Wars: A Quantitative History of War'*. Jefferson, USA: McFarland & Co. ISBN 0-89950-709-3

Economist (1994), 'Against the grain. A survey of Poland' *The Economist (London),* April 16 - 22: Survey 1 - 22.

Economist Intelligence Unit, Dialog - online.

Ehrlich S. (1981), 'The Rationality of Pluralism' *The Polish Sociological Bulletin,* 54, 2: 27 - 38.

Eklund K. (1980), 'Long Waves in the Development of Capitalism?' *Kyklos,* 33 (3): 383 - 419.

El Pais (Madrid) (current issues) (free electronic archive at *http://www.elpais.es)*

Ellacuria I. *Societas Iesu* (1989), 'Utopia y profetismo desde América Latina. Un ensayo concreto de soterología historica' *Revista Latinoamericana de Teología (San Salvador, El Salvador),* 6, 17: 141 - 84.

Ellacuria I. *Societas Iesu* (1990, posth.), *'Teólogo mártir por la liberación del pueblo'* Madrid: editorial nueva utopía.

Ellacuria I. *Societas Iesu* (1990b, posth.), *'Filosofía de la realidad historica'* San Salvador: Universidad Centroamericana Editores.

Ellacuria I. *Societas Iesu* (1991), *'Veinte anos de historia en El Salvador (1969 - 1989): escritos politicos'* 1. ed. San Salvador, El Salvador: UCA Editores.

Ellacuria I. *Societas Iesu* and Sobrino J. *Societas Iesu* (1993), *'Mysterium liberationis: Fundamental Concepts of Liberation Theology'* Maryknoll, NY: Orbis Books.

Elsenhans H. (1983), 'Rising mass incomes as a condition of capitalist growth: implications for the world economy' *International Organization,* 37, 1: 1 - 39.

Elsenhans H. (1992), *'Equality and development'* Dhaka, Bangladesh: Centre for Social Studies: Distributor, Dana Publishers.

Elsenhans H. (1996),' *State, class, and development'*. New Delhi: Radiant Publishers.

Elsenhans H. (Ed.), (1978), *'Migration und Wirtschaftsentwicklung'* Frankfurt a.M.: Campus.

Emmanuel, A. (1972) *Unequal Exchange: A Study of the Imperialism of Trade.* New York, USA: Monthly Review Press [translated from the 1969 French original] [his first article on "unequal exchange" in 1962, French]

Engelbrekt K. (1994), 'Sharp Rise in Drug Trafficking and Abuse in Former East Bloc' *RFE/RL Research Report,* 3, 9, 4 March: 48 - 51.

Ernst A. *et al.* (1987), *'Sozialstaat Oesterreich. Bei Bedarf geschlossen'* Vienna: Orac.

Ernst D. (1973), 'Wirtschaftliche Entwicklung durch importsubstituierende Industrialisierung?' *Das Argument,* 79, July, p. 332 ff.

Esping - Andersen G. (1985), *'Politics against markets. The social democratic road to power'* Princeton: Princeton University Press.

Evans P. B. and Timberlake M. (1980), 'Dependence, Inequality, and the Growth of the Tertiary: A Comparative Analysis of Less Developed Countries' *American Sociological Review,* 45: 531 - 552.

Eyal G. and Townley E. (1995), 'The social composition of the Communist nomenklatura: A comparison of Russia, Poland and Hungary' *Theory and Society,* 24: 723 - 750.

Falk, R. (1975) *'A Study of Future Worlds'.* New York, USA: Free Press

Farmer P. (1996), 'On Suffering and Structural Violence: A View from Below' Daedalus, 4: 261 - 283.

Fassmann H. and Hintermann Ch. (1997), 'Migrationspotential Osteuropa. Struktur und Motivation potentieller Migranten aus Polen, der Slowakei, Tschechien, und Ungarn' Vienna: Austrian Academy of Sciences

Fassmann H. and Muenz R. (1995), '*Einwanderungsland Oesterreich?* Vienna: Jugend und Volk.

Fassmann H. and Muenz R. (1992), *'Einwanderungsland Oesterreich? Gastarbeiter - Fluechtlinge - Immigranten'* Vienna: Oesterreichische Akademie der Wissenschaften und Bundesministerium fuer Unterricht und Kunst.

Fassmann H. and Muenz R. (1993), 'Oesterreich - Einwanderungsland wider Willen' *Migration. A European Journal of International Migration and Ethnic Relations,* 1, 17: 11 - 38.

Faßmann H./ Hintermann C.(1997) *'Migrationspotential Ostmitteleuropa'* - Institut für Stadt u. Regionalforschung, 1997.

Feder E. (1972), *'Violencia y despojo del campesino: el latifundismo en América Latina'* Mexico D.F.: siglo XXI.

Felipe, Jesus (1998) *'Singapore's Aggregate Production Function and its (Lack of) Policy Implications,'* Paper (forthcoming)

Felipe, Jesus, and JSL McCombie (1998) *'Methodological Problems with Recent Analyses of the East Asian Miracle,'* Paper (forthcoming)

Felix F. (1998), 'Pensionsreform - das 'Chilenische Modell'' *Soziale Sicherheit. Fachzeitschrift der oesterreichischen Sozialversicherung,* 11: 836 - 837.

Fiala R. (1992), 'The International System, Labor Force Structure, and the Growth and Distribution of National Income, 1950 - 1980' *Sociological Perspectives,* 35, 2: 249 - 282.

Financial Times, Dialog - online.

Fink G. (1989), 'Die verplante Planwirtschaft. *Perestroijka* und das Problem der Kapitalverwertung im 'Arbeiterstaat'' *Akzente (Vienna),* 9/10: 11 - 14.

Firebaugh G. (1992), 'Growth Effects of Foreign and Domestic Investment' *American Journal of Sociology,* 98: 105 - 130.

Firebaugh G. (1996), 'Does Foreign Capital Harm Poor Nations? New Estimates Based on Dixon and Boswells Measures of Capital Penetration' *American Journal of Sociology,* 2, 102: 563 - 575.

Fischer - Lexikon (1975), *'Das Grosse Fischer - Lexikon in Farbe'* 20 vols., Frankfurt a.M.: Fischer Taschenbuch Verlag.

Fischer - Welt - Almanach (current issues), *'Der Fischer Welt - Almanach. Zahlen, Daten, Fakten'* Frankfurt a.M.: Fischer Taschenbuch Verlag.

Flechsig St. (1987), 'Raul Prebisch - ein bedeutender Oekonom Lateinamerikas und der Entwicklungslaender' *Wirtschaftswissenschaft,* 35, 5: 721 - 741.

Flechsig St. (1994), 'Raúl Prebisch (1901 - 1986) - ein bedeutendes theoretisches Vermaechtnis oder kein alter Hut' *Utopie kreativ,* 45/46, Juli/August: 136 - 155.

Flechsig St. (2000) 'The Heritage of Raúl Prebisch for a Humane World' *in 'Globalization, Liberation Theology and the Social Sciences. An Analysis of the Contradictions of Modernity at the Turn of the Millennium'* (Andreas Müller OFM et al.) Commack, New York: Nova Science

Forrester J.W. (1978), 'A Great Depression Ahead?' *The Futurist,* December: 379 - 385.

Foxley A. (1982), 'Experimentos neoliberales en América Latina' *Estudios CIEPLAN (Santiago de Chile),* 7.

Foye St. (1994), 'The Armed Forces of the CIS: Legacies and Strategies' *RFE/RL Research Report,* 3, 1, 7 January: 18 - 21.

Frank A. G. (1978), *'Dependent accumulation and underdevelopment'* London: Macmillan.

Frank A. G. (1978), *'World accumulation, 1492 - 1789'* London: Macmillan.

Frank A. G. (1980) *'Crisis in the world economy'* New York: Holmes & Meier Publishers.

Frank A. G. (1981), *'Crisis in the Third World'* New York: Holmes & Meier Publishers.

Frank A. G. (1983), 'World System in Crisis' in *'Contending Approaches to World System Analysis'* (Thompson W.R. (Ed.)), pp. 27 - 42, Beverly Hills: Sage.

Frank A. G. (1990), 'Revolution in Eastern Europe: lessons for democratic social movements (and socialists?),' *Third World Quarterly,* 12, 2, April: 36 - 52.

Frank A. G. (1992), 'Economic ironies in Europe: a world economic interpretation of East - West European politics' *International Social Science Journal,* 131, February: 41 - 56.

Frank A. G. and Frank - Fuentes M. (1990), *'Widerstand im Weltsystem'* Vienna: Promedia.

Frank A. G. and Gills B. (Eds.)(1993), *'The World System: Five Hundred or Five Thousand Years?'* London and New York: Routledge, Kegan&Paul.

Frank, A.G. (1998) *'ReOrient: Global Economy in the Asian Age'.* Ewing, USA: University of California Press

Frank, Andre Gunder (1999 ?) "Transitional Ideological Modes: Feudalism, Capitalism, Socialism," online: ftp://csf.colorado.edu/psn/authors/Frank.Gunder/feudalism-capitalism-socialism

Franzmeyer F./Brücker H. (1997): 'Europäische Union - Osterweiterung u. Arbeitskräftemigration' - DIW Berlin, 1997 (DIW-Wochenbericht 5).

Friedman M. (1997), 'Monetary Unity, Political Disunity' *Transitions,* December: 32 - 33.

Froebel F. *et al.* (1977a), 'Internationalisierung von Kapital und Arbeitskraft' in *'Armut in Oesterreich'* (Junge Generation der SPOe Steiermark und Erklaerung von Graz fuer Solidarische Entwicklung (Eds.)), pp. 12 - 46, Graz: Leykam.

Froebel F. *et al.* (1977b), *'Die neue internationale Arbeitsteilung. Strukturelle Arbeitslosigkeit in den Industrielaendern und die Industrialisierung der Entwicklungslaender'* Reinbek: rororo aktuell (English translation: Cambridge University Press).

Froebel F. *et al.* (1984), 'The Current Development of the World Economy: Reproduction of Labor and Accumulation of Capital on a World Scale' in *'Transforming the World Economy? Nine Critical Essays on the New International Economic Order'* (Addo H. (Ed.)), pp. 51 - 118, London and Sydney: Hodder & Stoughton.

Froebel F. *et al.* (1986), *'Umbruch in der Weltwirtschaft'* Reinbek: rororo aktuell (English translation: Cambridge University Press).

Fuest C. (1996), 'Die finanzielle Last der EU - Ausgaben. Bleibt Europa noch finanzierbar?' *Die Neue Gesellschaft. Frankfurter Hefte,* 43, 7: 594 - 598.

Fukuyama F. (1991), 'Liberal Democracy as a Global Phenomenon' *PS: Political Science and Politics (Washington D.C.),* 24, 4: 659 - 664.

G - 24 (1992), *'G - 24 Assistance Poland'* Brussels: EU Commission and G - 24, Data discette.

Gabrisch H. *et al.* (1992), *'Depression and Inflation: Threats to Political and Social Stability. The Current Economic Situation of the former CMEA Countries and Yugoslavia'* Vienna: *Forschungsberichte,* 180, Vienna Institute for Comparative Economic Studies.

Gächter A. (1995), 'Auswirkungen einer allfälligen Osterweiterung der Europäischen Union auf die Zuwanderung nach Österreich und auf die Akzeptanz von Zuwanderern' in *'Europa 1996. Auswirkungen einer EU-Osterweiterung'* pp. 47-86, (WIFO/WIIW/IHS (Eds.)) Wien: Schriftenreihe des Bundeskanzleramts

Gaechter A. (1991), 'Illusionen einer Einwanderungspolitik' *Oesterreichische Zeitschrift fuer Politikwissenschaft,* 4: 351 - 366.

Galbraith, J.K. (1995) 'Global Keynesianism in the Wings,' *World Policy Journal* (USA)

Galganek A. (1992), *'Zmiana w globalnym systemie miedzynarodowym. Supercycle i wojna hegemoniczna'* Poznan: Uniwersytet im. Adama Mickiewicza w Poznanie, Seria Nauki Polityczne, 13 (entire).

Galtung J. (1971), 'A Structural Theory of Imperialism' *Journal of Peace Research,* 8, 2: 81 - 118.

Galtung, J. (1994) *'Human Rights in Another Key'*. Cambridge, UK: Polity Press

Gardawski J. (1992), *'Robotnicy 1991. Swiadomosc ekonomiczna w czasach prelomu'* Warsaw: *Polityka ekonomiczna i spoleczna,* 25, Fundacja im. Friedricha Eberta w Polsce.

Garson J. P. et al. (1997), 'Regional Integration and Outlook for Temporary and Permanent Migration in Central and Eastern Europe' in *'Migration, Free Trade and Regional Integration in Central and Eastern Europe'* pp. 299-333, Wien: Schriftenreihe des Bundeskanzleramts

Gartner R. (1990), 'The Victims of Homicide: A Temporal and Cross - National Comparison' *American Sociological Review,* 55, February: 92 - 106.

Gerlich P. *et al.* (1988), 'Corporatism in Crisis: Stability and Change of Social Partnership in Austria' *Political Studies,* 36: 209 - 223.

Geschwender J.A. (1982), 'The Hawaiian Transformation: Class, Submerged Nation, and National Minorities' in *'Ascent and Decline in the World - System'* (Friedman E. (Ed.)), pp. 189 - 226, Beverly Hills: Sage.

Gibellini R. (1987), *'The Liberation Theology Debate'* Trans. John Bowden. Maryknoll, NY: Orbis Books.

Giering C. (1998), 'Die Europaeische Union vor der Erweiterung - Reformbedarf der Institutionen und Verfahren nach Amsterdam' *Oesterreichische Zeitschrift fuer Politikwissenschaft,* 27, 4: 391 - 405.

Giering C. (1998), 'Die Europaeische Union vor der Erweiterung - Reformbedarf der Institutionen und Verfahren nach Amsterdam' *Oesterreichische Zeitschrift fuer Politikwissenschaft,* 27, 4: 391 - 405.

Gierus J. (1998), *'Russia's Road to Modernity'* Warsaw: Instytut Studiow Politycznych, Polskiej Akademii Nauk.

Gilpin R. (1989), 'International Politics in the Pacific Rim Era' *The Annals of the American Academy of Political and Social Science,* 505, September: 56 - 67.

Global Capitalism, Liberation Theology and the Social Sciences. An Analysis of the Contradictions of Modernity at the Turn of the Millennium (*Andreas Müller Director, Missionary Centre of the Order of Saint Francis, Bonn, Arno Tausch, Associate Visiting Professor, Department of Political Science, Innsbruck University, and Paul Michael Zulehner, Chairperson and Professor, Department of Pastoral Theology, Vienna University (Eds.) under collaboration of Henry Wickens, Strasbourg (forthcoming)*

Goble P. (1989), 'Ethnic Politics in the USSR' *Problems of Communism,* 38, 4: 1 - 14.

Goedings S. (1997), *'The Expected Effect of the Enlargement of the European Union with Central and Eastern European Countries in the Area of the Free Movement of Workers'* Study for the European Commission, DG V, Amsterdam: International Institute of Social History

Goedings S. (1999), *'EU Enlargement to the East and Labour Migration to the West'* International Institute of Social History Amsterdam, Research Paper 36

Goldfrank W.L. (1978), 'Fascism and the World Economy' in *'Social Change in the Capitalist World Economy'* (Kaplan B.H. (Ed.)), pp. 75 - 117, Beverly Hills: Sage.

Goldfrank W.L. (1982), 'The Soviet Trajectory' in *'Socialist States in the World - System'* (Chase - Dunn Ch. K. (Ed.)), pp. 147 - 156, Beverly Hills: Sage.

Goldfrank W.L. (1990), 'Fascism and the Great Transformation' in *'The Life and Work of Karl Polanyi'* (Polanyi - Levitt K. (Ed.)), Montreal: Black Rose (quoted from the author's typescript).

Goldstein J.S. (1985a), 'Kondratieff Waves as War Cycles' *International Studies Quarterly,* 29, 4: 411 - 444.

Goldstein J.S. (1985b), 'Basic Human Needs: The Plateau Curve' *World Development,* 13, 5: 595 - 609.

Goldstein J.S. (1988), *'Long Cycles. Prosperity and War in the Modern Age'* New Haven and London: Yale University Press.

Goldstein J.S. (1994), *'Introduction to the Japanese Edition of Long Cycles'* Tokyo: Tsuge Shobo (quoted from the author's manuscript).

Goldstein J.S. (1996), *'International Relations'* New York, N.Y.: Harper Collins, College Publishers, 2nd edition.

Golinowska S. *et al.* (1996), *'Children in Diffcult Circumstances in Poland'* UNICEF: Innocenti Occasional Papers, Economic Policy Series, Number 57, Spedale degli Innocenti, Firenze, Italia.

Golinowska St. (1995), 'Migration Processes in Poland' and 'Main problems of employment transfer in Central and Western Europe' in *'Migration processes in Central and Eastern Europe'*, pp. 66-79 and 165-182 (Wachowicz R. (Ed.)), Warsaw: Ministry of Labour and Social Policy

Gonzales Casanova P. (1973), *'Sociología de la explotación'* Mexico D.F.: Siglo XXI.

Gora M. and Rutkowski M. (1998), *'The Quest for Pension Reform. Poland's Security through Diversity'* Warsaw: Office of the Government Plenipotentiary for Social Security Reform.

Gore A. (1994), *'Wege zum Gleichgewicht. Ein Marshallplan fuer die Erde'* Frankfurt a.M.: Fischer *('Earth in the Balance. Ecology and Human Spirit'* Boston, New York: Houghton Mifflin Company).

Gourevitch P.A. (1989), 'The Pacific Rim: Current Debates' *The Annals of the American Academy of Political and Social Science,* 505, September: 8 - 23.

Gower J. (1996), 'EU Enlargement to Central and Eastern Europe: Issues for the 1996 IGC' *Die Union. Oesterreichische Zeitschrift fuer Integrationsfragen,* 4: 85 - 93.

Gray C.S. (1990), 'The Soviet Threat in the 1990s' *Global Affairs,* 5, 2: 25 - 44.

Greider, W. (1997) *'One World, Ready or Not: The Manic Logic of Global Capitalism'*. New York, USA: Simon & Schuster

Griffin K. (1987), *'World Hunger and the World Economy. And Other Essays in Development Economics'* London, Basingstoke and New York: Macmillan/Saint Martin's Press.

Griffin K. (1996), *'Studies in Globalization and Economic Transitons'* Basingstoke and New York: Macmillan/Saint Martin's Press.

Griffin K. and Gurley J. (1985), 'Radical Analyses of Imperialism, the Third World, and the Transition to Socialism: A Survey Article' *Journal of Economic Literature,* 23, September: 1089 - 1143.

Griffin K. and Knight J. (Eds.)(1990), *'Human Development and the International Development Strategy for the 1990s'* London and Basingstoke: Macmillan.

Grimes, Peter (1997) "The Horsemen and the Killing Fields: The Final Contradiction of Capitalism", Paper presented at the XXI. Annual Meeting of the Political Economy of the World-System, April 3-6, University of California at Santa Cruz 1997, online at: http://csf.colorado.edu/forums/wsn/99/msg01593 (see, 28 November 1999, Jones)

Grosser I. (1992), *'Szenarien des Uebergangs zur Marktwirtschaft in ehemaligen RGW - Laendern Europas'* Studie im Auftrag des Beirats fuer Wirtschafts - und Sozialfragen, Vienna: Vienna Institute for Comparative Economic Studies.

Gstoehl S. (1998), 'Vertiefung versus Erweiterung: Wie flexibel ist die Europaeische Union?' *Oesterreichische Zeitschrift fuer Politikwissenschaft,* 27, 4: 377 - 390.

Gstoehl S. (1998), 'Vertiefung versus Erweiterung: Wie flexibel ist die Europaeische Union?' *Oesterreichische Zeitschrift fuer Politikwissenschaft,* 27, 4: 377 - 390.

Gurr T. R. (1991), 'America as a Model for the World? A Skeptical View' *PS: Political Science and Politics (Washington D.C.),* 24, 4: 664 - 667.

Gurr T. R. (1994) *'Ethnic conflict in world politics'* Boulder: Westview Press.

Gurr T. R. (1994), 'Peoples Against States: Ethnopolitical Conflict and the Changing World System' *International Studies Quarterly,* 38: 347 - 377.

Gutierrez G. (1987), *'On Job: God - Talk and the Suffering of the Innocent'* Trans. Matthew J. O'Connell. Maryknoll, NY: Orbis Books.

Gutierrez G. (1988), *'A Theology of Liberation: History, Politics and Salvation'* Trans. and ed. Sister Caridad Inda and John Eagleson. Rev. edition, Maryknoll, NY: Orbis Books.

Gutierrez G. (1991), *'The God of Life'.* Trans. Matthew J.O'Connell. Maryknoll, NY: Orbis Books.

Gwynne, S.C. (1998), 'Just Hide Me the Money', *Time* (magazine, USA-Canada), December 14, 1998, p. 24

Haas E. B. (1989), 'War, Interdependence and Functionalism' in *'The Quest for Peace'* (Vaerynen R. *et al.* (Eds.)), pp. 108 - 126, London, Beverly Hills: Sage.

Hadden K. and London B. (1996), 'Educating Girls in the Third World. The Demographic, Basic Needs, and Economic Benefits' *International Journal of Comparative Sociology,* 37, 1 - 2: 31 - 46.

Haeusler W.. (1988) 'Wege zur Oesterreichischen Nation' *Roemische Mitteilungen,* Oesterreichische Akademie der Wissenschaften und Historisches Institut beim oesterreichischen Kulturinstitut in Rom), 30: 380 - 411.

Halevi, J., and P. Kriesler (1992), 'An Introduction to the Traverse in Economic Theory,' in: J. Halevi, D. Laibmann, E.J.Nell (eds.), *Beyond the Steady State: A Revival of Growth Theory.* London, UK: MacMillan Academic & Professional Ltd., 1992, pp. 225 -234

Halevi, Joseph (1994) 'Structure and Growth', Economie Appliquée, 1994, no. 2, 57-80

Haller M. *et al.* (1985), 'Patterns of careers: mobility and structural positions in advanced capitalist societies: a comparison of men in Austria, France and the United States' *American Sociological Review,* 50, 5: 579 - 603.

Hallett A.J.H. (1994), 'The Impact of EC - 92 on Trade in Developing Countries' *The World Bank Research Observer,* 9, 1, January: 121 - 146.

Handelman St. (1994), 'The Russian 'Mafiya'' *Foreign Affairs,* 73, 2: 83 - 95.

Hausner J. (1992), *'Populist Threat in Transformation of Socialist Society'* Warsaw: *Economic and Social Policy Series, 29,* Friedrich Ebert Foundation.

Hausner J. and Owsiak St. (1992), *'Financial crisis of a state in transformation: The Polish case'* Warsaw: *Economic and Social Policy Series,* 26, Friedrich Ebert Foundation, Poland.

Havlik P. (1996), *'Exchange Rates, Competitiveness and Labour Costs in Central and Eastern Europe'* Research Reports, 231, Vienna Institute for Comparative Economic Studies.

Havlik, P. (1996) 'Exchange Rates, Competitiveness and Labour Costs in Central and Eastern Europe,' *WIIW Research Report* No. 231 (October). Abstract available online: http://www.wiiw.at/summ231.html

Heilbroner, R.L. and L.C. Thurow (1978) *'Understanding Macroeconomics'*. 6th edition. Englewood Cliffs, USA: Prentice-Hall

Heilbroner, Robert L. (1986) *'The Worldly Philosophers'*. 6th ed. New York, USA: Simon & Schuster

Hertoghe A./Labrousse A. (1990), *'Die Koksguerilla'* Berlin: Rotbuch - Verlag.

Hesoun J. (Ed.), (1993), *'Bericht ueber die soziale Lage. Taetigkeitsbericht des Bundesministeriums fuer Arbeit und Soziale Lage'* Vienna: Federal Ministry of Labor.

Hettne B. (1983), 'The Development of Development Theory' *Acta Sociologica,* 26, 3 - 4: 247 - 266.

Hettne B. (1989), 'Three Worlds of Crisis for the Nation State' in *'Crisis in Development'* (Bablewski Z. and Hettne B. (Eds.)), pp. 45 - 77, Goeteborg: United Nations University: European Perspectives Project 1986 - 87, Peace and Development Research Institute, Gothenburg University, P.A.D.R.I.G.U Papers.

Hettne B. (1994), 'The Political Economy of Post - Communist Development' *The European Journal of Development Research,* 6, 1, June: 39 - 60.

Hettne B. (1995a), *'International political economy: understanding global disorder.'* Halifax, N.S.: Fernwood Pub.; Cape Town: SAPES SA ; Dhaka: University Press Ltd. ; London ; Atlantic Highlands, N.J.: Zed Books.

Hettne B. (1995b), *'Development theory and the three worlds: towards an international political economy of development'* 2nd ed. Essex, England: Longman Scientific & Technical ; New York, NY. Copublished in the United States by John Wiley.

Hickmann Th. (1994), 'Wenn Ost und West zusammenwachsen sollen...' *Osteuropa - Wirtschaft,* 39, 2, Juni: 115 - 127.

Hilferding R. (1915), 'Europaer, nicht Mitteleuropaer' *Der Kampf (Vienna),* 8, 11 - 12: 357 - 365.

Hillgenberg H. (1994), 'Fluechtlinge als Herausforderung fuer Europa. Ansaetze fuer eine Politik der Schutzgewaehrung an Kriegs - und Buergerkriegsfluechtlinge' *Europa - Archiv,* 18: 537 - 544.

Hinnells J. (Ed.), (1984), *'The Penguin Dictionary of Religions'* London: Penguin Books.

Hintjens H.M. (1992), 'Immigration and Citizenship Debates: Reflections on Ten Common Themes' *International Migration,* 30, 1: 5 - 16.

Hirschman A. O. (1980), *'National Power and the Structure of Foreign Trade'* Berkeley, CA: University of California Press.

Hoell O. (Ed.), (1983), *'Small States in Europe and Dependence'* Vienna/ Boulder CO.: W. Braumueller/Westview Press.

Hoell O. and Kramer H. (1986), 'Internationalization and the Position of Austria: Problems and Current Development Trends of a Small State' in *'Security for the Weak Nations. A Multiple Perspective'* (Farooq Hasnat S. and Pelinka A. (Eds.)), pp. 201 - 230, Lahore: Izharsons.

Hoensch J.K. (1990), *'Geschichte Polens'* Stuttgart: Ullmer, 2nd edition.

Holst J.J. (1993), *'A Changing Europe: Security Challenges of the 1990's'* Warsaw: *Occasional Papers,* 35, Polish Institute of International Affairs.

Holtbruecke D. (1996), 'Oekonomische Voraussetzungen und Folgen einer Osterweiterung der Europaeischen Union' *Osteuropa,* 46, 6: 537 - 547.

Holy Bible (1958 edition), King James Version. London and New York: Collins Clear Type Press.

Hopkins T.K. (1982), 'The Study of the Capitalist World - Economy. Some Introductory Considerations' in *'World Systems Analysis. Theory and Methodology'* (Hopkins T.K. and Wallerstein I. *et al.*), pp. 3 - 38, Beverly Hills: Sage.

Hopkins T.K. and Wallerstein I. *et al.* (1982), 'Patterns of Development of the Modern World System' in *'World Systems Analysis. Theory and Methodology'* (Hopkins T. K. and Wallerstein I. *et al.*), pp. 41 - 82, Beverly Hills: Sage.

http://www.economics.harvard.edu/faculty/jwilliam/papers/

Huang J. (1995), 'Structural Disarticulation and Third World Human Development' *International Journal of Comparative Sociology,* 36, 3 - 4: 164 - 183.

Huber P. (1999), *'Labour Market Adjustment in Central and Eastern Europe: How Different?'* Austrian Institute for Economic Research (WIFO).

Huber P. (1999a), *'Wirtschaftliche und soziale Folgen der Erweiterung der EU'* in *'Zukunft ohne Grenzen'* Wien: Institut für den Donauraum und Mitteleuropa

Huber P. (1999b), *'Labour Market Adjustment in Central and Eastern Europe: How Different?'* Vienna: WIFO

Huber Peter, Pichelmann K. (1998) 'Osterweiterung, struktureller Wandel und Arbeitsmärkte' in: *Wirtschaftspolitische Blätter* 4

Huebner K. (1994), 'Wege nach Nirgendwo: Oekonomische Theorie und osteuropaeische Transformation' *Berliner Journal fuer Soziologie,* 3: 345 - 364.

Huntington S.P. (1991), *'The Third Wave: Democratization in the Late Twentieth Century'* Norman, Oklahoma: University of Oklahoma Press.

Huntington S.P. (1993), 'The Clash of Civilizations?' *Foreign Affairs,* Summer: 22 - 49.

Huntington S.P. (1996) *'The clash of civilizations and the remaking of world order'* New York: Simon & Schuster.

IBnGR Gdansk (1998), *Regionalne rynki pracy w procesie integracji Unia Europejska,* 16/1998 Red. M. H. Grabowski

ICMPD (1998), *'Auswirkungen der EU-Osterweiterung auf die Zuwanderung in die Europäische Union unter besonderer Berücksichtigung Österreichs'* Studie im Auftrag des Bundeskanzleramtes, Sektion IV, Wien (3 Bände): ICMPD

IFO-Institut (1999) 'Auswirkungen der Arbeitnehmer-Frezügigkeit auf innereuropäische Migrationsbewegungen' Vorstudie im Auftrag des Bundesministeriums für Arbeit und Sozialordnung, München

IFRI (Institut Francais des relations internationales) (1998), *'Ramses 98. Rapport Annuel Mondial sur le Système Economique et les Stratégies'* Paris: Dunod

ILO (1999) online statistical database, entitled "LABORSTA on the WEB", at: http://laborsta.ilo.org (or can be found via the ILO home page at: http://www.ilo.org), Table 5A

ILO 'Key Indicators of the Labour Market' *http://www.ilo.org/public/english/60empfor /polemp/kilm/*

ILO World Labor Yearbook (current issues).

Inglehart R. and Carballo M. (1997), 'Does Latin America Exist? (And is there a Confucian Culture?): A Global Analysis of Cross - Cultural Differences' PS: Political Science & Politics, 30, 1, March: 47 - 52.

Inoguchi T. (1989), 'Shaping and Sharing Pacific Dynamism' *The Annals of the American Academy of Political and Social Science,* 505, September: 46 - 55.

Inotai A. (1993), 'Central and Eastern Europe' in *'Reviving the European Union'* (Austrian National Bank and IMF (Eds.)), pp. 139 - 176. Washington D.C. and Vienna: IMF and Austrian National Bank.

Institut fuer Fremdenverkehr, Warsaw *(current issues), 'Polen. Fremdenverkehr in Zahlen'* Warsaw: Amt fuer Koerperliche Kultur und Tourismus, ul. Merliniego 9, PL - 02511 Warsaw.

Institute of Labor and Social Studies (1995) 'Social Policy in 1993 - 1994: Main Problems in Transition Period' *Occasional Papers,* 6, 1995.

Institute of Labor and Social Studies (current issues), *'Occasional Papers'* Warsaw: Institute of Labor and Social Studies, Ministry of Labor and Social Policy.

International Labor Office and United Nations Centre on Transnational Corporations (1988), *'Economic and social effects of multinational enterprises in export processing zones'* Geneva: ILO.

International Labor Office Geneva (1995), *'World Labor Report'* Geneva: International Labor Office.

Internationale Politik (current issues).

IOM (1999), *'Migration Potential in Central and Eeastern Europe'* Geneva: IOM

IOM (International Organization for Migration) (1999), *'Migration Potential in Central and Eastern Europe'* Geneva: IOM

Jackman R.W. (1975), *'Politics and Social Equality: A Comparative Analysis'* New York: Wiley.

James E. (1995), 'Averting the Old - Age Crisis' *Finance and Development*, June: 4 - 7.

Janacek K. (1992), 'Poland: Survey of Major Trends in 1991' *RFE/RL Research Report*, 1, 12, 20 March: 31 - 32.

Janos A.C. (1994), 'Continuity and Change in Eastern Europe: Strategies of Post - Communist Politics' *East European Politics and Societies*, 8, 1: 1 - 31.

Janowska Z. *et al.* (1992), 'Female Unemployment in Poland' Warsaw: *Economic and Social Policy Series*, 18, Friedrich Ebert Foundation, Poland.

Jenkins R. (1987), *'Transnational Corporations and Uneven Development: The Internationalization of Capital and the Third World'* London and New York: Methuen.

Jodice D.H. *et al.* (1980), *'Cumulation in Social Science Data Archiving. A Study of the Impact of the two World Handbooks of Political and Social Indicators'* Koenigstein: Anton Hain.

John Paul II, Pope (1988), 'Sollicitudo Rei Socialis' *Origens*, 17, 38: 641 - 60.

John Paul II, Pope (1991a), *'Vor neuen Herausforderungen der Menschheit. Enzyklika 'Centesimus annus' Papst Johannes Pauls II. Kommentar von Walter Kerber'* Freiburg im Breisgau: Herder.

John Paul II, Pope (1991b), 'Redemptoris missio' *Catholic International*, 2, 6, March, 16 - 31.

Juchler J. (1992a), 'Zur Entwicklungsdynamik in den sozialistischen bzw. postsozialistischen Laendern' *Schweizerische Zeitschrift fuer Soziologie*, 17, 2: 273 - 307.

Juchler J. (1992b), 'The Socialist Societies: Rise and Fall of a Societal Formation' in *'Waves, Formations and Values in the World System'* (Bornschier V. and Lengyel P. (Eds.)), pp. 145 - 174, New Brunswick (USA),: Transaction Publishers.

Juchler J. (1995), 'Kontinuitaet oder Wende? Polen seit dem Wahlsieg der 'Postkommunisten'' *Osteuropa*, 45, 1: 65 - 76.

Kabashima T. (1984), 'Supportive Participation With Economic Growth: The Case of Japan' *World Politics*, 36, 3: 309 - 338.

Kaldor M. (1986), 'The Global Political Economy' *Alternatives*, 11, 4: 431 - 460.

Kaldor N. (1957), 'A model of economic growth' *The Economic Journal*, 67: 591 ff.

Kaldor N. (1974), 'Model of Distribition' in *'Growth Economics'* (Sen A. K. (Ed.)), Harmondsworth: Penguin Modern Economics Readings.

Kalecki M. (1972), *'The Last Phase in the Transformation of Capitalism'* New York: Monthly Review Press.

Kalecki M. (1979), *'Essays on Developing Economies. With an Introduction by Professor Joan Robinson'* Hassocks, Sussex: The Harvester Press.

Karatnycky A. (1994), 'Freedom in Retreat' *Freedom Review*, 25, 1: 4 - 9.

Kasarda J.D. and Crenshaw E.M. (1991), 'Third - World Urbanization. Dimensions, Theories and Determinants' *Annual Review of Sociology*, 17: 467 - 501.

Katzenstein P.J. (1984), *'Corporatism and Change. Austria, Switzerland and the Politics of Industry'* Ithaca and London: Cornell University Press.

Kausel A. (1998), *'Five Decades of Success. Austria's Economic Rise within the OECD since 1950'*. Vienna: Special Issue of *Finanznachrichten*, Economic policy weekly.

Kawato A. (1990), 'The Soviet Union: A Player in the World Economy?' in *'Perestroika: Soviet Domestic and Foreign Policies'* (Hasegawa T. and Pravda A. (Eds.)), pp. 122 - 140, London: Sage.

Kay C. (1989), *'Latin American Theories of Development and Underdevelopment'* London and New York: Routledge, Kegan and Paul.

Kay C. (1991), 'Reflections on the Latin American Contribution to Development Theory' *Development and Change,* 22, 1: 31 - 68.

Keman H. *et al.* (1987), *'Coping with the Economic Crisis'* London: Sage Publications.

Kennedy P. (1989), *'The Rise and Fall of the Great Powers. Economic Change and Military Conflict from 1500 to 2000'* New York: Vintage Books, paperback edition.

Kennedy P. (1993), *'In Vorbereitung auf das 21. Jahrhundert'* Frankfurt a.M.: S. Fischer TB.

Kent G. (1984) *'The political economy of hunger: the silent holocaust'* New York: Praeger.

Kent G. (1991) *'The politics of children's survival'* New York: Praeger. .

Kent G. (1995) *'Children in the international political economy'* Houndmills, Basingstoke, Hampshire: MacMillan Press LTD, New York, N.Y.: St. Martin's Press.

Kent N. J. (1990), 'The End of the American Dream: A Break in Political Economy' *Occasional Papers in Political Science, Manoa Campus: University of Hawaii, Department of Political Science,* 3, 3, Jan.: 93 - 107.

Kentor J. (1998), 'The Long-Term Effects of Foreign Investment Dependence on Economic Growth, 1940-1990' *American Journal of Sociology,* 103, 4, January: 1024 - 46.

Keuschnigg C. and Köhler W. (1999), *'Eastern Enlargement to the EU: Economic Costs and Benefits for the EU Present Member States?'* Study XIX/B1/9801, European Commission

Keynes J.M. (1936), *'The General Theory of Employment, Interest and Money'* London and Basingstoke: Macmillan.

Keynes, J.M. (1964) *'The General Theory of Employment, Interest, And Money'.* New York, USA: Harcourt Brace Jovanovich [reprint of the 1936 original]

Khoury A. Th. (1991), *'Was its los in der islamischen Welt? Die Konflikte verstehen'* Freiburg, Basel, Vienna: Herder.

Kidron M. and Segal R. (1996), *'Der Fischer Atlas zur Lage der Welt'* Frankfurt a.M.: Fischer Taschenbuch Verlag.

Kiljunen K. (1985), *'Towards a Theory of International Division of Labor'* Helsinki: Helsinki University, Department of Political Science Publications, Sarja A, 69.

Kiljunen K. (1992), *'Finland and the new international division of labor'* Houndmills, Basingstoke, Hampshire: Macmillan Press.

Kirkpatrick J. (1987), 'Ethnic Antagonism and Innovation in Hawaii' in *'Ethnic Conflict. International Perspectives'* (Boucher J. *et al.* (Eds.)), pp. 298 - 316, Newbury Park: Sage.

Klaus V. (1996), 'Europaeische Waehrungsunion - ihre ordnungspolitischen und fiskalpolitischen Konsequenzen' Alpbach, 28. August 1996: European Forum Alpbach (Tyrol)

Klecatsky H. and Morscher S. (1993), *'Die oesterreichische Bundesverfassung. Bundes - Verfassungsgesetz in der gegenwaertigen Fassung mit wichtigen Nebenverfassungsgesetzen'* Vienna: Manzsche Verlags - und Universitaetsbuchhandlung.

Kleinknecht A (1987) *'Innovation patterns in crisis and prosperity: Schumpeter's long cycle reconsidered'* New York: St. Martin's Press.

Kleinknecht A. (1987), *'Innovation Patterns in Crisis and Prosperity: Schumpeter's Long Cycle Reconsidered'* London and Basingstoke: Macmillan.

Kleinknecht A. *et al.* (Eds.) (1993), *'New Findings in Long - Wave Research'* New York: Saint Martin's Press.

Klitgaard R. and Fedderke J. (1995), 'Social Integration and Disintegration: An Exploratory Analysis of Cross - Country Data' *World Development,* 23, 3: 357 - 369.

Köhler, Gernot (1975) 'Imperialism as a Level of Analysis in Correlates of War Research', Journal of Conflict Resolution (USA), 10: 48-62. French version: 'L'imperialisme, dimension de l'analyse des aspects correlatifs de la guerre' (1976) *Impact: science et societe* (UNESCO), 28: 47-56

Köhler, Gernot (1976) 'An Empirical Table of Structural Violence' (with Norman Alcock) *Journal of Peace Research* (Norway), 13: 343-356 [includes 'plateau curve' of life expectancy with income]

Köhler, Gernot (1976)'The Global Contract: An Essay on International Economic Order and Foreign Policy Theory', Alternatives (World Policy Institute, USA), 2: 449-477

Köhler, Gernot (1978) 'Disarmament and Global Apartheid', Humanity Calls (New Delhi, India), (June): 9-14,47-50

Köhler, Gernot (1978) 'Global Apartheid', Alternatives (Institute for World Order/World Policy Institute, USA), vol. 4, no. 2 (October), pp. 263-275

Köhler, Gernot (1980) 'Structural and Armed Violence in the 20th Century: Magnitudes and Trends' (with William Eckhardt) International Interactions (USA), 8: 347-375

Köhler, Gernot (1980)'Determinants of the British Defense Burden, 1689 - 1977: From Imperialism to the Nuclear Age' (1980) Bulletin of Peace Proposals (Norway), 11: 79-85

Köhler, Gernot (1981) 'Approaches to the Study of the Causes of War', UNESCO Yearbook on Peace and Conflict Studies 1980. Paris, France: UNESCO, 1981: 115-127

Köhler, Gernot (1981) 'Soviet/Russian Defense Burden, 1862 - 1980: From Czarism to Socialism', Bulletin of Peace Proposals (Norway), 11: 131-140

Köhler, Gernot (1981) 'Toward Indicators of Detente: An Extension of the Zurich Content Analysis' in: Daniel Frei, ed., Definitions and Measurements of Detente: East and West Perspectives. Cambridge, USA: Oelschlager, Gunn & Hain, 1981: 39-55

Köhler, Gernot (1995) 'The Three Meanings of Global Apartheid: Empirical, Normative, Existential', Alternatives (World Policy Institute, USA), 20: 403-423

Köhler, Gernot (1998a), "The Structure of Global Money and World Tables of Unequal Exchange." *Journal of World-Systems Research* 4: 145-168, online: http://csf.colorado.edu/wsystems/jwsr.html

Köhler, Gernot (1998b), "Unequal Exchange 1965 - 1995: World Trend and World Tables", *World-Systems Archive, Working Papers,* http://csf.colorado.edu/wsystems/archive/papers/kohlertoc.htm

Köhler, Gernot (1999) 'A Theory of World Income', World-Systems Archive, Working Papers, online: http://csf.colorado.edu/wsystems/archive/papers/ kohlertoc.htm

Köhler, Gernot (1999) 'Global Keynesianism and Beyond', *Journal of World-Systems Research,* 5: 225-241, online: http://csf.colorado.edu/wsystems/jwsr.html

Komlosy A. and Hofbauer H. (1992), 'Gemeinsames Haus Europa' *Forum,* 39, 465 - 467, 10.11.1992: 34 - 39.

Kondratieff N.D. (1926), 'Die langen Wellen der Konjunktur' *Archiv fuer Sozialwissenschaft und Sozialpolitik,* 56, 3: 573 - 609.

Kondratieff N.D. (1928), 'Die Preisdynamik der industriellen und landwirtschaftlichen Waren (Zum Problem der relativen Dynamik und Konjunktur),' *Archiv fuer Sozialwissenschaft und Sozialpolitik,* 60, 1: 1 - 84.

Korbonski A. (1996), 'How Much Is Enough? Excessive Pluralism as the Cause of Poland's Socioeconomic Crisis' *International Political Science Review,* 17, 3: 297 - 306.

Korcelli P. (1992), 'International Migrations in Europe: Polish Perspectives for the 1990s' *International Migration Review,* 26, 2, Summer: 292 - 304.

Koronkiewicz A. (1996), *'The Polish Health Care Reform Programme. Description worked out for Members of the World Bank Mission'* Ministry of Health and Social Welfare, Warsaw, Republic of Poland, Ministry of Health and Social Welfare: 23 October 1996.

Korpi W. (1985), 'Economic growth and the welfare state: leaky bucket or irrigation system?' *European Sociological Review,* 1, 2: 97 - 118.

Korpi W. (1996), 'Eurosclerosis and the Sclerosis of Objectivity. On the Role of Values Among Economic - Policy Experts' *Economic Journal,* 106, 439: 1727 - 1746.

Kothari R. (1986), 'Masses, Classes and the State' *Alternatives,* XI, 2: 167 - 183.

Kothari, R. (1974) *Footsteps into the Future.* New York, USA: Free Press

Kovel, Joel (1999) "Beyond the World Trade Organization", online: http://www.greens.org/ny/tohtml.cgi?kovel (October 26, 1999)

Kowalewski A.T. (1994), *'We Are Doing Less Than Nothing'* Warsaw: Polish Institute of International Affairs.

Koydl W. (1994), 'Kehren die Kommunisten zurueck? Gefahren fuer Mittel - und Osteuropa' *Europa - Archiv,* 5: 141 - 148.

Kramer H. (1998), 'Politikwissenschaft und EU-Osterweiterung' *Oesterreichische Zeitschrift fuer Politikwissenschaft,* 27, 4: 473 - 480.

Kramer H. (1998), 'Politikwissenschaft und EU-Osterweiterung' *Oesterreichische Zeitschrift fuer Politikwissenschaft,* 27, 4: 473 - 480.

Kravis, I.B. and R.E. Lipsey (1983) 'Toward an Explanation of National Price Levels,' Princeton Studies in *International Finance,* No. 52, November 1983 (Princeton University, USA. Department of Economics.)

Kravis, I.B., A. Heston and R. Summers (1978) *International Comparisons of Real Product and Purchasing Power.* Baltimore, USA: Johns Hopkins University Press

Kreisky B. (posth., 1992), *'Stellungnahmen Bruno Kreiskys zum Asylproblem'* Vienna: Bruno - Kreisky Archive, August 18, 1992.

Kreissler F. (1980), *'La Prise de Conscience de la Nation Autrichienne 1938 - 1945 - 1978'* Paris: Presses Universitaires de France.

Kriz J. (1978), *'Statistik in den Sozialwissenschaften'* Reinbek: rororo studium.

Krzysztofiak M. and Luszniewicz A. (1979), *'Statystyka'* Warsaw: PWE.

Kueng H. (1968), *'The Church'* New York: Sheed and Ward.

Kurth J.R. (1989), 'The Pacific Basin versus the Atlantic Alliance: Two Paradigms of International Relations' *The Annals of the American Academy of Political and Social Sciences,* 505, September: 34 - 45.

Kurz R. (1991), 'Die Krise, die aus dem Osten kam. Wider die Illusion vom Sieg des Westens und seiner Marktwirtschaft' *Basler Magazin,* 44, 2, 11.6.1991: 6 - 7.

Kuttner, R. (1998) 'What sank Asia? Money sloshing around the world', *Business Week* (USA), July 27, 1998, p. 16

Kuznets S. (1940), 'Schumpeter's Business Cycles' *The American Economic Review,* 30, 2: 257 - 271.

Kuznets S. (1955), 'Economic Growth and Income Inequality' *The American Economic Review,* 45, 1: 1 - 28.

Lachmann, W. (1994) *Entwicklungspolitik.* Muenchen, Germany: Oldenbourg Verlag

Landesmann M. (1996), *'Emerging Patterns of European Industrial Specialization: Implications for Labour Market Dynamics in Eastern and Western Europe'* Research Reports, 230, Vienna Institute for Comparative Economic Studies.

Landesmann M. and Burgstaller J. (1997), *'Vertical Product Differentiation in EU Markets: the Relative Position of East European Producers'* Research Reports, 234a, Vienna Institute for Comparative Economic Studies.

Landesverteidigungsakademie Zentraldokumentation Informationshefte (current issues). Vienna: National Defense Academy, Federal Ministry for Defense of the Republic of Austria.

Lange O. (1970), *'Ensayos sobre planificación económica'* Esplugues de Llobregat, Barcelona: Ediciones Ariel.

Lapid Y. (1989), 'The Third Debate: On the Prospects of International Theory in a Post - Positivist Era' *International Studies Quarterly,* 33, 3: 235 - 254.

Launer E. (1992), *'Datenhandbuch Sued - Nord'* Goettingen: Lamuv.

Layard R. et al. (1994), *'East-West Migration: The Alternatives'*. Cambridge Ma.: MIT Press

Le Monde (1998), *'Le Bilan du Monde'* Paris: Le Monde.

Le Monde (current issues).

Le Monde Diplomatique (current issues). Free electronic archive at *Tageszeitung,* Berlin *http://www.taz.de*

Leggett J. (Ed.)(1991), *'Global Warming. Die Waermekatastrophe und wie wir sie verhindern koennen. Der Greenpeace - Report'* Munich and Zurich: Piper.

Lengauer R. et. al. (1999), *'Arbeitsmarkt und Osterweiterung'* IOS-Management, A-1010 Wien, Babenbergerstraße 1

Lepingwell J.W.R. (1994a), 'The Soviet Legacy and Russian Foreign Policy' *RFE/RL Research Report,* 3, 23, 10 June: 1 - 8.

Lepingwell J.W.R. *et al.* (1994b), 'Russia: A Troubled Future' *RFE/RL Research Report,* 3, 24, 17 June: 1 - 12.

Lernoux P. (1980), *'Cry of the People'* Garden City, NY: Doubleday.

Lernoux P. (1989), *'People of God: The Struggle for World Catholicism'* New York: Viking Press.

Levy - Pascal E. (1976), *'An Analysis of the Cyclical Dynamics of Industrialized Countries'* Washington D.C.: U.S. Central Intelligence Agency Staff Report PR 76 10009..

Levy J.S. (1983), 'World System Analysis: A Great Power Framework' in *'Contending Approaches to World System Analysis'* (Thompson W.R. (Ed.)), pp. 183 - 201, Beverly Hills: Sage.

Lewis - Beck M.S. (1980), *'Applied Regression. An Introduction'* Beverly Hills: Sage University Paper.

Lewis Sir W.A. (1978), *'The Evolution of the International Economic Order'* Princeton N.J.: Princeton University Press.

L'Express (1992), 'En Couverture. Elle Envahit la France et l'Europe' *L'Express,* 4/12: 24 - 35.

Liemt G. van (1992), *'Industry on the move. Causes and consequences of international relocation in the manufacturing industry'* Geneva: International Labor Office.

Linder S. B. (1986), *'The Pacific Century. Economic and Political Consequences of Asian - Pacific Dynamism'* Stanford, CA.: Stanford University Press.

Linnemann H. and Sarma A. (1991), 'Economic Transformation in Eastern Europe: Its Genesis, Adjustment Process, and Impact on Developing Countries' *Development and Change,* 22, 1: 69 - 92.

Lipset S.M. (1994), 'The Social Requisites of Democracy Revisited. 1993 Presidential Address' *American Sociological Review,* 59, February: 1 - 22.

Lipton M. (1977), *'Why Poor People Stay Poor: Urban Bias in World Development'* Cambrige, MA: Harvard University Press.

Lipton M. and Ravallion M. (1993), *'Poverty and Policy'* Policy Research Working Papers, WPS, 1130, Washington D.C.: The World Bank.

Lisiecki M. (1993), *'Obrona i ochrona granicy panstwowej Polski jako element bezpieczenstwa panstwa'* Warsaw: *Studia i Materialy,* 60, Polish Institute of International Affairs.

Loeffelholz H. D., und G. Köpp (1998), *'Ökonomische Auswirkungen der Zuwanderungen nach Deutschland'* Berlin: Duncker und Humblot

Loeschnak F. (1993), *'Menschen aus der Fremde. Fluechtlinge, Vertriebene, Gastarbeiter'* Vienna: Holzhausen.

London B. (1987), 'Structural Determinants of Third World Urban Change: An Ecological and Political Economic Analysis' *American Sociological Review,* 52: 28 - 43.

London B. and Robinson Th. D. (1989), 'The Effect of International Dependence on Income Inequality and Political Violence' *American Sociological Review,* 54: 305 - 308.

London B. and Ross R. J. S. (1995), 'The Political Sociology of Foreign Direct Investment: Global Capitalism and Capital Mobility, 1965 - 1980' *International Journal of Comparative Sociology,* 36, 3 - 4: 198 - 218.

London B. and Smith D. A. (1988), 'Urban Bias, Dependence, and Economic Stagnation in Noncore Nations' *American Sociological Review,* 53: 454 - 463.

London B. and Williams B. A. (1988), 'Multinational Corporate Penetration, Protest, and Basic Needs Provision in Non - Core Nations: A Cross - National Analysis' *Social Forces,* 66, 3: 747 - 773.

London B. and Williams B. A. (1990), 'National Politics, International Dependency, and Basic Needs Provision. A Cross - National Analysis' *Social Forces,* 69, 2: 565 - 584.

Longerich *et al.* (1993), *'Der neue alte Rechtsradikalismus'* Munich: Piper.

Luif P. (1988), *'Neutrale in die EG? Die westeuropaeische Integration und die neutralen Staaten'* Vienna: Oesterreichisches Institut fuer Internationale Politik, W. Braumueller.

Luxemburg R. (1905/without year) *'Kirche und Sozialismus. Kosciol a Socjalism.* Mit einer Einfuehrung von Dorothee Soelle und Klaus Schmidt' Frankfurt a.M.: Stimme-Verlag.

Luza R. (1984), *'The Resistance in Austria, 1938 - 1945'* Minneapolis: University of Minnesota Press.

Lynch A. (1994), Postcommunist Political Dynamics: Ex Uno Plura' *RFE/RL Research Report,* 3, 1, 7 January: 1 - 8.

Maerz E. (1983), *'Joseph Alois Schumpeter - Forscher, Lehrer und Politiker'* Vienna: Verlag fuer Geschichte und Politik.

Magenheimer H. (1994), 'Neue Bedrohungen und Konflikte. Herausforderungen und Konsequenzen' *Oesterreichische Militaerische Zeitschrift,* 4: 357 - 366.

Makhijani, A. (1993), 'Economic Apartheid in the New World Order', in: P. Bennis and M. Moushabeck (eds.), Altered States: A Reader in the New World Order. New York, USA: Olive Branch Press

Malcolm N. (1995) 'The Case Against 'Europe'' *Foreign Affairs,* March, April: 52 - 68.

Mandel E. (1973), *'Der Spaetkapitalismus'* Frankfurt a.M.: edition suhrkamp.

Mandel E. (1980), *'Long Waves of Capitalist Development'* Cambridge: at the University Press.

Mandel, E. (1978) *The Second Slump: A Marxist Analysis of Recession in the Seventies.* London, England: NLB, 1978 [revised and translated from the 1977 German edition]

Mankiw, N. Gregory (1994) *Macroeconomics.* 2nd edition. New York, USA: Worth Publishers

Marin B. (1983), 'Organizing Interests by Interest Organizations. Associational Prerequsites of Corporatism in Austria' *International Political Science Review,* 4, 2: 197 - 216.

Maritain J. (1936), *'Freedom in the Modern World'* Trans. Richard O'Sullivan. New York: Charles Scribner's Sons.

Maritain J. (1944), *'Christianity and Democracy'* Trans. Doris C. Anson. New York: Charles Scribner's Sons.

Maritain J. (1959), *'Distinguished to Unite: Or, The Degrees of Knowledge'* Trans. Gerald B. Phelan *et al.* London: Geoffrey Bles.

Maritain J. (1973), *'Integral Humanism: Temporal and Spiritual Problems of a New Christiandom'* Trans. Joseph W. Evans. Notre Dame, IN: University of Notre Dame Press.

Marshall D. D. (1996), 'Understanding Late 20th Century Capitalism. Reassessing the Globalization Theme' *Government and Opposition,* 31, 2: 193 - 215.

Martin K. (1994), 'Central Asia's Forgotten Tragedy' *RFE/RL Research Report,* 3, 30, 29 July: 35 - 48.

Martin P. (1992), 'Rising Unemployment in Czechoslovakia' *RFE/RL Research Report,* 1, 17 January: 38 - 42.

Marx K. and Engels F. (posth.), *'Werke'* Berlin: Dietz.

Marx, K. (1992) *Capital,* vol. 2. Penguin edition 1978 [reprinted 1992]

Mazrui, A. (1994) 'Global Apartheid: Structural and Overt', *Alternatives* (USA/India), vol.19, no. 2, p. 185-188

Mc Sweeny B. (1987), 'The Politics of Neutrality. Focus on Security for Smaller Nations' *Bulletin of Peace Proposals,* 18, 1: 33 - 46.

Mead, W.R. (1989) 'American Economic Policy in the Antemillenial Era,' *World Policy Journal* (USA), vol. 6, no. 3 (Summer 1989), p. 385-468

Meek, Ronald L. (1956) *Studies in the Labour Theory of Value.* London, England: Lawrence & Wishart

Meier G.M. and Seers D. (Eds.) (1984), *'Pioneers in Development'* New York and Oxford: Oxford University Press.

Mendlovitz, S. (ed.) (1975) *On the Creation of a Just World Order.* New York, USA: Free Press

Metz J.B. (1981), *'The Emergent Church: The Future of Christianity in a Postbourgeois World'* Trans. Peter Mann. New York: Crossroad.

Michelsen G. (Ed.)(current issues), *'Der Fischer Oeko - Almanach'* Frankfurt a.M.: Fischer TB.

Michna W. (1992), *'Poland's Food Security and Agricultural Policy at the Turn of the 20th and 21st Centuries'* Warsaw: *Economic and Social Policy Series,* 23, Friedrich Ebert Foundation, Poland.

Microsoft Excel (1992), *'Microsoft Excel. Verzeichnis der Funktionen'* Microsoft Corporation.

Mihalka M. (1994), 'German and Western Response to Immigration from the East' *RFE/RL Research Report,* 3, 23, 10 June: 36 - 48.

Millard F. (1992), 'Social Policy in Poland' in *'The New Eastern Europe. Social Policy Past, Present and Future'* (Deacon B. (Ed.)), pp. 118 - 143, London, Newbury Park: Sage.

Misik, R. (1997) 'Der Euro ist ein linkes Projekt', die *tageszeitung* (Germany), 25 August 1997, p. 10

Mittelman J. (1994); 'The Globalization of Social Conflict' in *'Conflicts and New Departures in World Society'* (Bornschier V. and Lengyel P. (Eds.)), pp. 317 - 337, New Brunswick (U.S.A.) and London: Transaction Publishers, World Society Studies, Volume 3.

Mizgala J.J. (1994), 'The Ecology of Transformation: The Impact of the Corporatist State on the Formation and Development of the Party System in Poland, 1989 - 93' *East European Politics and Societies,* 8, 2: 358 - 368.

Moaddel M. (1994), 'Political Conflict in the World Economy: A Cross - national Analysis of Modernization and World - System Theories' *American Sociological Review,* 59, April: 276 - 303.

Mock A. (1994), 'Religionsfriede durch Dialog' *Salzburger Nachrichten,* Neujahrsbeilage, 31. 12. 1994: X.

Modelski G. (1983), 'Long Cycles of World Leadership' in *'Contending Approaches to World System Analysis'* (Thompson W.R. (Ed.)), pp. 115 - 139, Beverly Hills: Sage.

Modelski G. (1987), *'Long Cycles in World Politics'* Basingstoke: Macmillan.

Moggridge, Donald (ed.) (1981) *The Collected Writings of John Maynard Keynes.* London, UK: MacMillan Press. Volume XX (1981)

Monatsberichte des Oesterreichischen Instituts fuer Wirtschaftsforschung (current issues).

Moon B.E. and Dixon W.J. (1992), 'Basic Needs and Growth Welfare - Trade Offs' *International Studies Quarterly,* 36, 2: 191 - 212.

Moore, B. (1988) *Horizontalists and Verticalists: The Macroeconomics of Credit Money.* Cambridge, USA: Cambridge University Press

Morawetz R. (1991), *'Recent foreign direct investment in Eastern Europe: Towards a possible role for the Tripartite Declaration of Principles concerning Multinational Enterprises and Social Policy'* Geneva: International Labor Office, Multinational Enterprises Programme, Working Paper 71.

Morawska E. (2000) *'International Migration and Consolidation of Democracy in East Central Europe: A Problematic Relationship in a Hostorical Perspective'* University of Pennsylvania, emorawsk@as.upenn.edu

Moreira A. F. (1997), *'Saint Francis and Modernity'* Universidade Sao Francisco, Avenida Sao Francisco de Assis, 218 CEP 12.900-000, Caixa Postal 163, Fax 011 404 1825 - Brazil, Braganca Paulista, Sao Paulo, Brazil (mimeo).

Moseley, Fred (1991) *The Falling Rate of Profit in the Postwar United States Economy.* New York, USA: St. Martin's Press

Mueller G.P. (1988, with Volker Bornschier) *'Comparative World Data. A Statistical Handbook for Social Science'* Frankfurt a.M., Baltimore and London: Campus/John Hopkins University Press.

Müller Andreas et al. (2000): *'Global Capitalism, Liberation Theology, and the Social Sciences: An Analysis of the Contradictions of Modernity at the Turn of the Millenium'* Nova Sciences: Huntington and Commack, New York

Muller E. N. (1988), 'Democracy, Economic Development, and Income Inequality' American Sociological Review, 53: 50 - 68.

Muller E. N. (1995), 'Economic Determinants of Democracy' *American Sociological Review,* 60, 6: 966 - 982.

Muller E. N. and Seligson M. (1987), 'Inequality and Insurgency' *American Political Science Review,* 81, 2: 425 - 452.

Munoz O. (1982), 'La economía mixta como camino al pleno empleo. Lecciones de un cuarto de siglo' *Estudios CIEPLAN (Santiago de Chile)*, 9: 107 - 138.

Myrdal G. (1956/1974), *'Oekonomische Theorie und unterentwickelte Regionen. Weltproblem Armut'* Frankfurt a.M.: Fischer TB.

Myrdal G. (1972), *'Politisches Manifest ueber die Armut in der Welt'* Frankfurt a.M.: suhrkamp TB.

Myrdal G. (1984), 'International Inequality and Foreign Aid in Retrospect' in *'Pioneers in Development. A World Bank Publication'* (Meier G.M. and Seers D. (Eds.)) pp. 151 - 165. New York and Oxford: Oxford University Press.

Nederveen-Pieterse J. (1997), 'Equity and Growth Revisited: A Supply-Side Approach to Social Development' *The European Journal of Development Research,* 9, 1, June: 128-149.

Nelson D.N. (1994), 'Waffen im Ueberfluss. Ruestungsgueter des Warschauer Paktes und ihre Verbreitung' *Europa - Archiv,* 6: 179 - 186.

Neue Zuercher Zeitung (current issues). Free electronic archive at *http://www.nzz.ch/*

Nikolinakos M. and Nikolaou, K. (1969), *'Die verhinderte Demokratie: Modell Griechenland'* Frankfurt a.M.: edition suhrkamp.

Nohlen D. (1991), *'Lexikon Dritte Welt'* Reinbek: rororo.

Nollert M. (1990), 'Social Inequality in the World System: An Assessment' in *'World Society Studies. Volume 1'* (Bornschier V. and Lengyel P. (Eds.)), pp. 17 - 54, Frankfurt and New York: Campus.

Nollert M. (1994a), 'Ressourcenmangel, Soziooekonomische Ungleichheit und Delinquenz: Ein internationaler Vergleich' *Schweizerische Zeitschrift fuer Soziologie,* 20, 1: 127 - 156.

Nollert M. (1994b), 'World Economic Integration and Political Conflict in Latin America' in *'Conflicts and New Departures in World Society'* (Bornschier V. and Lengyel P. (Eds.)), pp. 159 - 179, New Brunswick (U.S.A.) and London: Transaction Publishers, World Society Studies, Volume 3.

Nollert M. (1996), 'Verbandliche Interessenvertretung in der Europaeischen Union: Einflussressourcen und faktische Einflussnahme' *Zeitschrift fuer Politikwissenschaft (vormals Jahrbuch fuer Politik),* 6, 3: 647 - 667.

Nollert M. and Fielder N. (1997), *'Lobbying for a Europe of Big Business: the European Roundtable of Industrialists'* Department of Sociology, University of Zurich, Research paper (Raemistrasse 69, CH-8001, Zurich).

Nolte H.H. (1982), *'Die eine Welt. Abriss der Geschichte des internationalen Systems'* Hannover: Fackeltraeger.

Nolte H.H. (1989), *'Tradition des Rueckstands. West - Ost - Technologietransfer in der Geschichte'* Department of History, University of Hannover, FRG.

Nowotny I. (1991), 'Auslaenderbeschaeftigung in Oesterreich. Die Gesamtproblematik und aktuelle Situation' *WISO (Chamber of Workers and Employees, Linz),* 14, 1: 38 - 63.

Nowotny Th. (1985), *'Bleibende Werte - Verblichene Dogmen. Die Zukunft der Sozialdemokratie'* Koeln, Graz and Vienna: Hermann Boehlaus Nachfolger.

Nowotny Th. (1994), *'The Politics of Unemployment'* Vienna: paper, presented for the Bruno Kreisky Commission, 21 - 22 March.

Nuscheler F. (1993), 'Nach dem Fall von Mauern und Grenzen in Europa' in *'Die Neuen Mauern. Krisen der Nord - Sued - Beziehungen'* (Datta A. (Ed.)), pp. 13 - 30, Wuppertal: P. Hammer.

O'Leary Ch. J. (1995), 'Performance Indicators: A management tool for active labour programmes in Hungary and Poland' *International Labour Review,* 134, 6: 729 - 751.

O'Neill H. (1997), 'Globalisation, Competitiveness and Human Security: Challenges for Development Policy and Institutional Change' *The European Journal of Development Research,* 9, 1, June: 7-37.

Odom W. (1990), 'Only Ties to America Provide the Answer' *Orbis,* Fall: 483 - 504.

OECD (1995) *National Accounts 1960-93.* Vol. 1. Main Aggregates.

OECD (1999) *'The Future of the Global Economy. Towards a Long Boom?'* Paris: OECD

OECD (1999) *21st Century Technologies: Promises and Perils of a Dynamic Future.* OECD Publication: Code 031999021P1

Oesterreichischer Arbeiterkammertag (current issues), *'Wirtschafts - und Sozialstatistisches Taschenbuch'* Vienna: Verlag der Arbeiterkammer Vienna.

Okolski M. (1992) 'Anomalies in Demographic Transition in Poland' *Geographia Polonica (Warsaw),* 59: 41 - 53.

Olbrich E. (1993), 'Polityka Spoleczna w Austrii' *Polityka Spoleczna* (Institute for Labor and Social Affairs, Ministry of Labor and Social Policy, Republic of Poland), 11/12: 19 - 21.

Olson M. (1982), *'The Rise and Decline of Nations'* New Haven and London: Yale University Press.

Olson M. (1986), 'A Theory of the Incentives Facing Political Organizations. Neo - Corporatism and the Hegemonic State' *International Political Science Review,* 7, 2, April: 165 - 89.

Olson M. (1987), 'Ideology and Economic Growth' in *'The Legacy of Reaganomics. Prospects for Long - term Growth'* (Hulten Ch.R. and Sawhill I.V. (Eds.)), pp. 229 - 251, Washington D.C.: The Urban Institute Press.

OMRI Research Institute Prague, Daily digest (e - mail).

Opitz P. J. (1988), *'Das Weltfluechtlingsproblem. Ursachen und Folgen'* Munich: C.H. Beck.

Opp K.D. and Schmidt P. (1976), *'Einfuehrung in die Mehrvariablenanalyse. Grundlagen der Formulierung und Pruefung komplexer sozialwissenschaftlicher Aussagen'* Reinbek: rororo studium.

Orenstein M. (1996), 'The Failures of Neo - Liberal Social Policy in Central Europe' *Transition,* 28 June 1996.

Orlowski L. T. (1995), 'Preparations of the Visegrad Group countries for admission to the European Union: monetary policy aspects' *Economics of Transition,* 3, 3: 333-353.

Orlowski L. T. (1995), 'Social Safety Nets in Central Europe: Preparation for Accession to the European Union?' *Comparative Economic Studies,* 37, 2, Summer: 29-48.

Orlowski L. T. (1996*), 'Fiscal Consolidation in Central Europe in Preparation for Accession to the European Union'* Center for Social and Economic Research, Bagatela 14, PL-00-585 Warsaw, Studies and Analyses, 77.

Österreichische Gesellschaft für Europapolitik (1999), *'Die EU-Erweiterung aus der Sicht der Öszterreicher und seiner Nachbarn'* Wien: Österreichische Gesellschaft für Europapolitik

Papademetriou D.G. (1992), 'Contending Approaches to Reforming the U.S. Legal Immigration System' *Migration. A European Journal of International Migration and Ethnic Relations,* 4, 16: 5 - 54.

Parnreiter Ch. (1994), *'Migration und Arbeitsteilung. Auslaenderbeschaeftigung in der Weltwirtschaftskrise'* Vienna: promedia.

Pasinetti, Luigi L. (1993) *Structural Economic Dynamics: A Theory of the Economic Consequences of Human Learning.*

Passel J.S. and Fix M. (1994), 'Myths about Immigrants' *Foreign Policy,* 95: 151 - 160.

Patterson, W.A. (1997) *memorandum* to an internet forum, 05 Oct 1997

Pelinka A. (1985), *'Windstille. Klagen ueber Oesterreich'* Vienna: Medusa - Verlag.

Pelinka A. (1990), *'Zur oesterreichischen Identitaet. Zwischen deutscher Vereinigung und Mitteleuropa'* Vienna: Ueberreuter.

Pelinka A. (1993), *'Der Westen hat gesiegt - hat der Westen gesiegt?'* Vienna: Picus.

Pelinka A. (1995), *'Europa 1996: Mitbestimmen, Menschenrechte und mehr Demokratie'* Vienna: Verlag Osterreich: Osterreichische Staatsdruckerei.

Pelinka A. (1996) *'Austro - corporatism: past, present, future'* New Brunswick, NJ: Transaction Publishers.

Pelinka A. (1997), *'Austrian historical memory & national identity'* New Brunswick: Transaction Publishers.

Pelinka A. *et al.* (1994), *'Ausweg EG? Innenpolitische Motive einer aussenpolitischen Umorientierung'* Vienna, Koeln, Graz: Boehlau.

Penn World Table (Mark 5.6a) (1999); online: http://datacentre.chass.utoronto.ca:5680/pwt

Perroux F. (1961), *'L'économie du XXe siècle'* Paris: P.U.F.

Petrella R. (1995), 'Europe between competitive innovation and a new social contract' *International Social Science Journal,* 143: 11 - 23.

Petrella R. (1995), 'Europe between competitive innovation and a new social contract' *International Social Science Journal,* 143: 11 - 23.

Pfister U. and Suter Chr. (1991), 'Politische Regimes und Staatsentwicklung in der Dritten Welt: Peru seit den 1950er Jahren' *Schweizerische Zeitschrift fuer Soziologie,* 17, 2: 343 - 374.

Pilsudski J. (1936), *'Erinnerungen und Dokumente. Von Josef Pilsudski dem Ersten Marschall von Polen, persoenlich autorisierte deutsche Gesamtausgabe. Mit einem Geleitwort von Ministerpraesident Hermann Goering'* Essen: Essener Verlagsanstalt.

Piore M. (1990), 'Work, labor and action: Work experience in a system of flexible production' in *'Industrial Districts and Inter - Firm Cooperation in Italy'* (Pyke F. *et al.* (Eds.)), pp. 52 - 74, Geneva: International Institute for Labor Studies.

Podkaminer L. *et al.* (1996), *'Continuing Improvements in Central and Eastern Europe - Russia and Ukraine Have Not Yet Turned the Corner'*, Research Reports, 225, February 1996, Vienna Institute for Comparative Economic Studies.

Podolec B. (1992) *'Household Budgets in Poland 1979 - 1991'* Warsaw: *Economic and Social Policy Series*, 15, Friedrich Ebert Foundation, Poland.

Polanyi, K. (1944/1957), *'The Great Transformation'* Boston: Beacon.

Polanyi, K. (1979), *'Oekonomie und Gesellschaft'* Frankfurt a.M.: suhrkamp taschenbuch wissenschaft.

Polish Institute of International Affairs (1993), *'Report on the State of National Security - External Aspects'* Warsaw: Polish Institute of International Affairs.

Polish Labor Statistical Yearbook (1996), Central Statistical Office, Warsaw (in Polish).

Pollack M. (1991), 'Zurueck in die Vergangenheit. Der Nationalitaetenhader im verschwindenden Osteuropa' *Kursbuch*, 102, Dezember: 54 - 64.

Pollins B. M. (1996), 'Global Political Order, Economic Change, and Armed Conflict: Coevolving Systems and the Use of Force' *American Political Science Review*, 90, 1: 103 - 117.

Popper Sir K. (1991), 'The Best World We Have Yet Had. George Urban Interviews Sir Karl Popper' *Report on the USSR*, 3, 22, May 31: 20 - 22.

Poulantzas N. (1977), *'Die Krise der Diktaturen. Portugal, Griechenland, Spanien'* Frankfurt a.M.: suhrkamp.

Prader H. (1974), 'Ziele und Resultate kooperativer Gewerkschaftspolitik im Wiederaufbau nach 1945' *Oesterreichische Zeitschrift fuer Politikwissenschaft*, 3: 345 - 366.

Prader H. and Unterleitner M. (1976), 'Das 'Trade Union Recovery Program' der amerikanischen Gewerkschaften im Westeuropa und Oesterreich der Nachkriegszeit' *Oesterreichische Zeitschrift fuer Politikwissenschaft*, 1: 89 - 106.

Prader Th. (Ed.)(1992), *'Moderne Sklaven. Asyl - und Migrationspolitik in Oesterreich'* Vienna: Promedia.

Pradetto A. (1991a), 'Internationale Politik osteuropaeischer Staaten. Grundlegende Bedingungen und Tendenzen' *Oesterreichische Osthefte*, 33, 4: 663 - 678.

Pradetto A. (1991b); 'Politik und Oekonomie im postkommunistischen Polen' *Osteuropa*, 41, 10: 941 - 952.

Pradetto A. (1994), 'Europaeisierung oder Renationalisierung. Europa nach dem Ende des Ost - West - Konflikts' *SWS - Rundschau*, 33, 1: 5 - 21.

Prebisch R. (1983), 'The crisis of capitalism and international trade' *CEPAL Review*, 20, August: 51 - 74.

Prebisch R. (1984), 'Five Stages in My Thinking on Development' in *'Pioneers in Development. A World Bank Publication'* (Meier G.M. and Seers D. (Eds.)), pp. 175 - 191. New York and Oxford: Oxford University Press.

Prebisch, R. (1986), 'The Dynamic Role of the Periphery,' in: K. Ahooja-Patel, A.G. Drabek and M. Nerfin (eds.), *World Economy in Transition: Essays presented to Surendra Patel.* Oxford, UK: Pergamon Press, 1986, p. 3-9

Prebisch, R. (1988), 'Dependence, development, and interdependence,' in: G. Ranis and T.P. Schultz (eds.), *The State of Development Economics*. Oxford, UK: Basil Blackwell, 1988.

Preston P.W. (1987), *'Rethinking Development. Essays on development and Southeast Asia'* London and New York: Routledge & Kegan Paul.

Przeworski A. (1991), *'Democracy and the Market. Political and Economic Reforms in Eastern Europe and Latin America'* Cambridge: at the University Press.

Przeworski A. (1996), 'Public Support for Economic Reforms in Poland' *Comparative Political Studies,* 29, 5: 520 - 543.

Rabinbach A. (1985), *'Austrian Social Democracy 1918 - 1934: The Socialist Experiment and Its Collapse'* Boulder, CO: Westview.

Radio Free Europe and Radio Liberty Research Institute (current issues), *'RFE/RL Research Reports'* Munich: Radio Free Europe/Radio Liberty.

Radio Free Europe/Radio Liberty (current issues), *'News Briefs'* Munich: Radio Free Europe/Radio Liberty.

Radio Free Europe/Radio Liberty, electronic files (world - wide - web: *http://www.rferl.org)*.

Raffer K. & H.W. Singer (1996) *The Foreign Aid Business, Economic Assistance and Development Co-operation*, E.Elgar, Cheltenham [paperback: 1997].

Raffer K. (1987b), 'Tendencies Towards a 'Neo Listian' World Economy', *Journal für Entwicklungspolitik*, vol.3, n.3, pp.45ff.

Raffer K. (1993) 'International financial institutions and accountability: The need for drastic change', in: S.M. Murshed & K. Raffer (eds), *Trade, Transfers, and Development, Problems and Prospects for the Twenty First Century*, E.Elgar, Aldershot, pp.151ff.

Raffer K. (1995) 'The Impact of the Uruguay Round on Developing Countries', in: F. Breuss (ed), *The World Economy after the Uruguay Round*, Service Fachverlag, Vienna, pp.169ff.

Raffer K. (1997) 'Debt Management and Structural Adjustment: Neglected Issues', in: S.D. GUPTA (ed) *The Political Economy of Globalization*, Kluwer, Boston etc., pp.269ff.

Raffer K. (1987a), *'Unequal Exchange and the Evolution of the World System Reconsidering the Impact of Trade on North-South Relations'* London, Basingstoke and New York: Macmillan and Saint Martin's Press.

Raffer K. (1996) 'Exportorientierte Entwicklung und Weltmarkt - Das Beispiel der asiatischen 'Tiger'', in: E. Binderhofer, I. Getreuer-Kargl, H. Lukas (eds), *Das pazifische Jahrhundert?*, Brandes & Apsel/Südwind, Frankfurt aM/Wien, pp.41ff.

Raffer, K. (1987) *Unequal Exchange and the Evolution of the World System*. London, England: MacMillan Press

Ragin C.C. and Bradshaw Y.W. (1992), 'International Economic Dependence and Human Misery, 1938 - 1980. A Global Perspective' *Sociological Perspectives,* 35, 2: 217 - 247.

Rahr A. (1993), 'Russia: The Struggle for Power Continues' *RFE/RL Research Report*, 2, 6, 5 February: 1 - 5.

Rahr A. (1994), 'The Implications of Russia's Parliamentary Elections' *RFE/RL Research Report,* 3, 1, 7 January: 32 - 37.

Raith W. (1994a), *'Das neue Mafia - Kartel: wie die Syndikate den Osten erobern'* Berlin: Rowohlt.

Raith W. (1996a), *'The red mafia: the Eastern European mob'* New York: Four Walls Eight Windows.

Raith W. (1994b), 'Mafia als Lehrstueck. Die Behandlung als exotisches Fremdgewaechs lenkt vom Problem der organisierten Kriminalitaet ab' *Gewerkschaftliche Monatshefte,* 4: 240 - 247.

Raith W. (1996b) *'Organisierte Krminilatitaet'* Reinbek: rororo aktuell.

Ray J.L. (1983), 'The 'World System' and the Global Political System: A Crucial Relationship?' in *'Foreign Policy and the Modern World - System'* (Mc Gowan P. and Kegley Ch.W. Jr. (Eds.)), pp. 13 - 34, Beverly Hills: Sage.

Redmond, D. R. (1997) *'Re: Globalization and world systems (& EU)'*, memorandum to wsn mailing list, 17 Nov 1997, online: http://csf.colorado.edu/mail/wsn

Reich R. B. (1992), *'The Work of Nations. Preparing Ourselves for 21st - Century Capitalism'* New York: Random House, Vintage Books Edition.

Reports and Summaries (current issues). Vienna: Austrian National Bank.

Republic of Poland, Ministry of Health and Social Welfare (1996), *'Health Care System in Transition (HiT) Profile Poland'* Ljubljana: The World Health Organization Conference on European Health Care Reforms.

Research Centre for Economic and Statistical Studies of the Central Statistical Office and the Polish Academy of Sciences (current issues), *'Research Bulletin'* Warsaw: Central Statistical Office.

Reuters Textline, Dialog - online.

Riggs F. (1990), *'Presidentialism in the USA A Comparative Perspective'* Honolulu: Department of Political Science, University of Hawaii at Manoa.

Ringel E. (1987), *'Zur Gesundung der oesterreichischen Seele'* Vienna: Europaverlag.

Robinson J. (1947), *'An Essay on Marxian Economics'* London: Basil and Blackwell.

Robinson T.D. and London B. (1991), 'Dependency, Inequality, and Political Violence. A Cross - National Analysis' *Journal of Political and Military Sociology,* 19, 1: 119 - 156.

Rode R. (1991), 'Deutschland: Weltwirtschaftsmacht oder ueberforderter Euro - Hegemon?' *Leviathan,* 2: 229 - 246.

Roehrich W. (1979) 'Sozialgeschichte politischer Ideen. Die buergerliche Gesellschaft' Reinbek: rororo wissen.

Rogers R. (1992), 'The Politics of Migration in the Contemporary World' *International Migration,* 30, Special Issue: Migration and Health in the 1990s: 30 - 55.

Rosecrance R. (1987), 'Long cycle theory and international relations' *International Organization,* 41, 2: 283 - 301.

Ross R.J.S. and Trachte K.C. (1990), *'Global Capitalism: The New Leviathan'* Albany: State University of New York Press.

Rostow W.W. (1978), *'The World Economy: History and Prospects'* London and Basingstoke: Macmillan.

Roth J. (1995) *'Der Sumpf: Korruption in Deutschland'* Munchen: Piper.

Rothgeb, Jr. J. M. (1995), 'Investment Penetration, Agrarian Change, and Political Conflict in Developing Countries' Studies in Comparative International Development, 30, 4: 46 - 62.

Rothschild K. W. (1944), 'The Small Nation and World Trade' *The Economic Journal,* April: 26 - 40.

Rothschild K. W. (1963), 'Kleinstaat und Integration' *Weltwirtschaftliches Archiv,* 90, 2: 239 - 275.

Rothschild K. W. (1966), *'Marktform, Loehne, Aussenhandel'* Vienna: Europa - Verlag.

Rothschild K. W. (1984), *'Politische Oekonomie in Oesterreich seit 1945'* Roma: Instituto A. Gramsci, 10 - 11.5 (mimeo).

Rothschild K. W. (1985), 'Felix Austria? Zur Evaluierung der Oekonomie und Politik in der Wirtschaftskrise' *Oesterreichische Zeitschrift fuer Politikwissenschaft,* 3: 261 - 274.

Rothschild K. W. (1993a), *'Employment, wages, and income distribution: critical essays in economics'* London; New York: Routledge.

Rothschild K. W. (1993b), *'Ethics and economic theory: ideas, models, dilemmas'* Aldershot, Hants., England; Brookfield, Vt.: E. Elgar.

Rothschild K. W. (1997), *'Some Considerations on the Economics and Politics of the EU and the Maastricht Treaty'* Vienna: quoted from the author's typescript

Rozov, N.S. (1992) *Structure of Civilization and World Development Trends.* (In Russian; for a book note, see memorandum by Rozov, dated 16 Sept 1998, to wsn mailing list, online: http://csf.colorado.edu/mail/wsn/98.III)

Rubinson R. (1976), 'The World - Economy and the Distribution of Income within States: A Cross - National Study' American Sociological Review, 41: 638 - 659.

Rummel R. R. (1994), 'Power, Genocide and Mass Murder' *Journal of Peace Research,* 31, 1: 1 - 10.

Rummel R. R. (1995), 'Democracy, Power, Genocide, and Mass Murder' *The Journal of Conflict Resolution,* 39, 1, March: 3 - 26.

Russett B. (1967), *'International Regions and the International System. A Study in Political Ecology'* Westport, Con.: Greenwood Press.

Russett B. (1978), 'The marginal utility of income transfers to the Third World' *International Organization,* 32, 4: 913 - 928.

Russett B. (1983a), 'International Interactions and Processes: The Internal versus External Debate Revisited' in *'Political Science: The State of the Discipline'* (Finifter A. (Ed.)), pp. 541 - 68, Washington D.C.: American Political Science Association.

Russett B. (1983b), 'The Peripheral Economies. Penetration and Economic Distortion, 1970 - 75' in *'Contending Approaches to World System Analysis'* (Thompson W.R. (Ed.)), pp. 79 - 114, Beverly Hills: Sage.

Russett B. (1994), 'The Democratic Peace' in *'Conflicts and New Departures in World Society'* (Bornschier V. and Lengyel P. (Eds.)), pp. 21 - 43, New Brunswick (U.S.A.) and London: Transaction Publishers, World Society Studies, Volume 3.

Sabbat - Swidlicka A. (1994a), 'Local Elections Redress Political Imbalance in Poland' *RFE/RL Research Report,* 3, 27, 8 July: 1 - 8.

Sabbat - Swidlicka A. (1994b), 'Pawlak Builds Up Peasant Power' *RFE/RL Research Report,* 3, 24, 17 June: 13 - 20.

Sabbat - Swidlicka A. (1994c), 'Poland: The End of the Solidarity Era' *RFE/RL Research Report,* 3, 1, 7 January: 81 - 86.

Sachs J. (1993), *'Poland's Jump to the Market Economy'* Cambridge MA: MIT Press.

Saffioti H.B. (1978), *'Women in Class Society'* New York and London: Monthly Review Press.

Sakamoto, T. (1975) 'Toward Global Identity', in S. Mendlovitz (ed.), *On the Creation of a Just World Order.* New York, USA: Free Press, 1975, pp. 189-210

Salt J. (1996), *'Current trends in international migration in Europe'* Council of Europe, 6th Conference of European Ministers responsible for migration affairs, MMG - 6 (96) 3 E, Warsaw, 16 - 18 June 1996.

Salt J. et al. (1999): *'Assessment of Possible Migration Pressure and Its Labour Market Impact Following EU Enlargement to Central and Eastern Europe'.* Migration Research Unit, Department of Geography, University College, London

Salzburger Nachrichten (current issues).

Scandella L. (1998), *'Le Kondratieff. Essai de théorie des cycles longs économiques et politiques'* Paris: Economica, Economie poche

Scandella L. (1998), *'Le Kondratieff. Essai de théorie des cycles longs économiques et politiques'* Paris: Economica, Economie poche

Schade W. (1991), 'Das Parteienspektrum in der Republik Polen' *Osteuropa,* 41, 10: 953 - 962.

Scharpf F.W. (1987), *'Sozialdemokratische Krisenpolitik in Europa'* Frankfurt and New York: Campus.

Scharsach H.H. (1992), *'Haider's Kampf'* Munich: Wilhelm Heyne.

Schmidt M.G. (1983), 'The Welfare State and the Economy in Periods of Economic Crisis: A Comparative Study of Twenty - three OECD Nations' *European Journal of Political Research,* 11, 1: 1 - 26.

Schmidt M.G. (1986), 'Politische Bedingungen erfolgreicher Wirtschaftspolitik. Eine vergleichende Analyse westlicher Industrielaender (1960 - 1985),' *Journal fuer Sozialforschung,* 26, 3: 251 - 273.

Schmidt P.G. (1990), 'Soziale Marktwirtschaft als wirtschaftspolitisches Leitbild' *Wirtschaftswissenschaft,* 7: 961 - 997.

Schock K. (1996), 'A Conjunctural Model of Political Conflict. The Impact of Political Opportunities on the Relationship Between Economic Inequality and Violent Political Conflict' *Journal of Conflict Resolution,* 40, 1: 98 - 133.

Schoppa M. (1992), 'Der Wandel in Europa und die Sicherheit Polens' *Hamburger Beitraege zur Friedensforschung und Sicherheitspolitik,* 61 (January).

Schulz-Weidner (1998), 'Die Rentenversicherung in Chile - ein staatlicher Rahmen fuer private Vorsorge' *Soziale Sicherheit. Fachzeitschrift der oesterreichischen Sozialversicherung,* 11: 823 - 835.

Schumpeter J.A. (1942/50), *'Kapitalismus, Sozialismus und Demokratie'* Munich: A. Francke, 5th printing, 1980 ('Capitalism, Socialism and Democracy' New York: Harper and Brothers).

Schwartzmann, David (1996) on "solar communism" in: *Science & Society,* Special Issue "Marxism and Ecology", 60, No.3, p. 307-331.

Seager J. and Olson A. (1986), *'Der Frauenatlas'* Frankfurt a.M.: Fischer TB.

Seccareccia, M. (1991), 'Salaire minimum, emploi et productivité dans une perspective post-keynésienne', *L'Actualité économique. Revue d'analyse économique* (Canada), vol. 67, No. 2, juin 1991, p. 166-191

Seers D. (Ed.)(1978), *'Underdeveloped Europe'* Hassocks: Harvester Press.

SEF (Stiftung Entwicklung und Frieden) (1995) *Globale Trends* 1996: Fakten, Analysen, Prognosen (edited by I. Hauchler). Frankfurt, Germany: Fischer

Segbers K. (1991), 'Migration and Refugee Movements from the USSR: Causes and Prospects' *Report on the USSR,* 3, 46: 6 - 14.

Segundo Montes J. L. (1992), *'The Liberation of Dogma'* trans. Phillip Berryman, Maryknoll, N.Y.: Orbis Books.

Sell R. R. and Kunitz St.J. (1987), 'The Debt Crisis and the End of an Era in Mortality Declines' *Studies in Comparative International Development,* 21: 3 - 30.

Senghaas D. (1985), *'The European Experience: A Historical Critique of Development Theory'* Leamington Spa, Dover: Berg.

Senghaas D. (1989), 'Transcending Collective Violence, the Civilizing Process and the Peace Problem' in *'The Quest for Peace'* (Vaerynen R. *et al.* (Eds.)), pp. 3 - 18, London, Beverly Hills: Sage.

Senghaas D. (1994) *'Wohin driftet die Welt?: uber die Zukunft friedlicher Koexistenz'* Frankfurt am Main: Suhrkamp.

Senghaas D. (1994), *'Wohin driftet die Welt?'.* Frankfurt a.M.: edition suhrkamp.

Shafik N. and Bandyopadhyay S. (1992), *'Economic Growth and Environmental Quality. Time Series and Cross - Country Evidence'* Policy Research Working Papers, WPS, 904, Washington D.C.: The World Bank.

Shaikh, Anwar (1974) 'Laws of Production and Laws of Algebra: The Humbug Production Function.' *The Review of Economics and Statistics,* Vol. LVI, No. 61 (February): 115-20

Shaikh, Anwar (1987) "humbug production function", *The New Palgrave* (London, UK: MacMillan), Vol. 2, p. 690-692

Shaw T. M. (1984), 'The Non - Aligned Movement and the New International Economic Order' in *'Transforming the World - Economy? Nine Critical Essays on the New International Economic Order'* (Addo H. (Ed.)), pp. 138 - 162, London: Hodder and Stoughton.

Shaw T. M. (1994), *'The South at the end of the twentieth century: rethinking the political economy of foreign policy in Africa, Asia, the Caribbean, and Latin America'* New York: St. Martin's Press.

Shaw T. M. (1995), 'Globalisation, Regionalisms and the South in the 1990s: Towards a New Political Economy of Development' *The European Journal of Development Research*, 7, 2, Dec.: 257 - 275.

Sheahan M. D. (1995), *'Aspects of Health Policy in Poland'* Public Health Reports, May (available to the author only without pagination).

Shiva, V. (1994), 'Conflicts of Global Ecology: Environmental Activism in a Period of Global Reach', *Alternatives* (USA/India), 19: 185-188

Shlaes A. (1994), 'Germany's Chained Economy' *Foreign Affairs,* 73, 5: 109 - 124.

Sideri S. (1999), 'Globalisation's Dilemma: Economic Blocs or Global Economic Apartheid?' *The European Journal of Development Research,* 11, 2, December: 141 - 175

Siebert, H. (1997) *Weltwirtschaft.* Stuttgart, Germany: Lucius & Lucius

Sik E. (1998), *'Migration Potential in Contemporary Hungary'* Starsbourg: Strategic Task Force for European Integration, WG 10

Sikorski R. (1996), 'How We Lost Poland' *Foreign Affairs,* September/October, 75, 5: 15 - 22

Silver B. J. (1994); 'Cycles of Hegemony and Labor Unrest in the Contemporary World' in *'Conflicts and New Departures in World Society'* (Bornschier V. and Lengyel P. (Eds.)), pp. 339 - 359, New Brunswick (U.S.A.) and London: Transaction Publishers, World Society Studies, Volume 3.

Simatupang B. (1991), *'The Polish Economic Crisis of 1979 - 1982. Background, Circumstances and Causes'* Universiteit van Amsterdam: Academisch Proefschrift.

Singer P.I. (1971), *'Dinámica de la población y desarrollo'* Mexico D.F.: Ed. Siglo XXI.

Singer P.I. (1981), 'O feminino e o feminismo' in *'Sao Paulo: O povo em movimento'* (Singer P.I. *et al.* (Eds.)), pp. 109 - 142, Petropolis, Rio de Janeiro: Editora Vozes.

Singh, A. and A. Zammit (1995),'Employment and Unemployment, North and South', in: J. Mitchie and J.Grieve Smith, eds., *Managing the Global Economy.* New York, USA: Oxford University Press, p. 93-110

Singh, R.P., and S. Gatade (eds.) (1997), *Globalisation of Capital: An Outline of the Recent Changes in the Modus Operandi of Imperialism.* (Study commissioned by Lal Parcham and Lok Dasta). New Delhi, India: Lok Dasta and Lal Parcham Publisher

SIPRI (1993), *'SIPRI Report'* Goettingen: Lamuv.

Slater W. (1994), 'Russia: The Return of Authoritarian Government?' *RFE/RL Research Report,* 3, 1, 7 January: 22 - 31.

Slay B. (1992), 'Poland: The Rise and Fall of the Balcerowicz Plan' *RFE/RL Research Report,* 31 January: 40 - 57.

Slay B. (1993), 'Evolution of Industrial Policy in Poland since 1989' *RFE/RL Research Report,* 2, 2, Jan. 8: 21 - 28.

Slay B. (1994a), 'The Polish Economy under the Post - Communists' *RFE/RL Research Report,* 3, 33, 26 August: 66 - 76.

Slay B. (1994b), 'The Macroeconomics of Transition in Eastern Europe' *RFE/RL Research Report,* 3, 1, 7 January: 139 - 143.

Smith D. (1997), *'Der Fischer Atlas. Kriege und Konflikte'.* Frankfurt a.M.: Fischer Taschenbuch Verlag.

So A. Y. (1990), *'Social Change and Development. Modernization, Dependency, and World - System Theories'* Newbury Park, CA.: Sage Library of Social Research, 178.

Sobrino J. SJ and Ellacuria I. SJ (posth.) (1996), *'Systematic Theology. Perspectives from Liberation Theology'.* Maryknoll, New York: Orbis.

Socher K. (1996), 'Die Waehrungsunion - eine kritische Buerteilung politischer und oekonomischer Aspekte' *Finanznachrichten,* 24, 13. Juni 1996: 1 - 8.

Solow, Robert M. (1956) 'A Contribution to the Theory of Economic Growth,' *Quarterly Journal of Economics,* Vol. 70, p. 65-94

Spiesberger M. (1998), 'Uebergangsregime zur Abfederung von Differenzen bei EG/EU-Beitritten' *Oesterreichische Zeitschrift fuer Politikwissenschaft,* 27, 4: 407 - 423.

Spiesberger M. (1998), 'Uebergangsregime zur Abfederung von Differenzen bei EG/EU-Beitritten' *Oesterreichische Zeitschrift fuer Politikwissenschaft,* 27, 4: 407 - 423.

Srubar I. (1994), 'Variants of the Transformation Process in Central Europe. A Comparative Assessment' *Zeitschrift fuer Soziologie,* 23, 3, Juni: 198 - 221.

Stalker P. (1994), *'The Work of Strangers: A Survey of international labor migration'* Geneva: International Labor Office.

Staniszkis J. (1985), *'Poland: Self-Limiting Revolution'* Princeton: Princeton University Press.

Staniszkis J. (1991), *'The Dynamics of Breakthrough'* San Francisco: University of California Press.

Staniszkis J. (1992), *'The Ontology of Socialism'* Oxford: Oxford University Press.

Staniszkis J. (1994a), *'Ontology, Context and Change'* Cambridge, MA.: Minda de Ginzburg Center of European Studies, Working Paper, Harvard University.

Staniszkis J. (1998), *'Prolegomena to the theory of transition in Eastern Europe'* Warsaw: Instytut Studiow Politycznych, Polskiej Akademii Nauk (typescript)

Staniszkis J. (Ed.) (1994b), *'W Poszukiwania Paradygmatu Transformacji'* Warsaw: Instytut Studiow Politycznych, Polskiej Akademii Nauk.

Stankovsky J. (1992), 'Direktinvestitionen Oesterreichs in den Oststaaten' *Monatsberichte des oesterreichischen Instituts fuer Wirtschaftsforschung,* 8: 415 - 420.

Stankovsky J. (1993), 'Marktstellung in Ost - Mitteleuropa bedroht Oesterreichs Osthandel 1992' *Monatsberichte des oesterreichischen Instituts fuer Wirtschaftsforschung,* 6 (quoted from the author's typescript).

Stark O. and Taylor J.E. (1991), *'Relative Deprivation and Migration. Theory, Evidence and Policy Implications'* World Bank Policy, Research and External Affairs Working Papers, WPS 656, Washington D.C.: The World Bank.

Stauffer R. B. (1982) *'Losing hegemony: U.S. TNCs and the global capitalist crisis'* Sydney: Transnational Corporations Research Project, University of Sydney.

Stauffer R. B. (1983) *'The Manila - Washington connection: continuities in the transnational political economy of Philippine development'* Sydney: Transnational Corporations Research Project.

Stauffer R. B. (1985a) *'Transnational corporations and the state'* Sydney: Transnational Corporations Research Project, University of Sydney.

Stauffer R. B. (1985b), *'The Marcos Regime: Failure of Transnational Developmentalism and Hegemony - Building from Above and Outside'* Transnational Corporations Research Project, Faculty of Economics, The University of Sydney, Research Monograph no. 23.

Stauffer R. B. (1986) *'The Philippines under Marcos: failure of transnational developmentalism'* Sydney: Transnational Corporations Research Project, University of Sydney.

Stauffer R. B. (1990), 'Capitalism, 'Development', The Decline of the Socialist Option, and the Search for Critical Alternatives' *Occasional Papers in Political Science, Department of Political Science, University of Hawaii at Manoa,* 3, 3, Jan.: 29 - 43.

Steger H. A. (1989), *'Weltzivilisation und Regionalkultur. Wege zur Entschluesselung kultureller Identitaeten'* Munich: Eberhard.

Steger H. A. (1990), *'Europaeische Geschichte als kulturelle und politische Wirklichkeit. Hornruf von der anderen Seite des Limes.'* Munich: Eberhard.

Steger H. A. and Morell R. (1988), *'ein Gespenst geht um ....: MITTELEUROPA'* Munich: Eberhard.

Stephens J. D. (1989), 'Democratic Transition and Breakdown in Western Europe, 1870-1939: A Test of the Moore Thesis' *American Journal of Sociology,* 94, 5, March: 1019-77.

Stephens J. D. (1991), 'Industrial Concentration, Country Size, and Trade Union Membership' *American Political Science Review,* 85, 3, September: 941 - 949.

Stiftung Entwicklung und Frieden (1993), *'Globale Trends 93/94. Daten zur Weltentwicklung'* Frankfurt a.M.: Fischer Taschenbuch Verlag.

Stiftung Entwicklung und Frieden (1996), *'Globale Trends 1996. Fakten Analysen Prognosen'* Frankfurt a.M.: Fischer Taschenbuch Verlag.

Stokes R.G. and Andreson A. (1990), 'Disarticulation and Human Welfare in Less Developed Countries' *American Sociological Review,* 55, February: 63 - 74.

Stpiczynski T. (1992), *'Polacy w swecie'* Warsaw: Central Statistical Office.

Sunkel O. (1966), 'The Structural Background of Development Problems in Latin America' *Weltwirtschaftliches Archiv,* 97, 1: pp. 22 ff.

Sunkel O. (1972/3), 'Transnationale kapitalistische Integration und nationale Desintegration: der Fall Lateinamerika' in *'Imperialismus und strukturelle Gewalt. Analysen ueber abhaengige Reproduktion'* (Senghaas D. (Ed.)), pp. 258 - 315, Frankfurt a.M.: suhrkamp. English version: 'Transnational capitalism and national disintegration in Latin America' *Social and Economic Studies,* 22, 1, March: 132 - 76.

Sunkel O. (1973), *'El subdesarrollo latinoamericano y la teoria del desarrollo'* Mexico: Siglo Veintiuno Editores, 6a edicion.

Sunkel O. (1978a), 'The Development of Development Thinking' in *'Transnational Capitalism and National Development. New Perspectives on Dependence'* (Villamil J.J. (Ed.)), pp. 19 - 30, Hassocks, Sussex: Harvester Press.

Sunkel O. (1978b), 'Transnationalization and it's National Consequences' in *'Transnational Capitalism and National Development. New Perspectives on Dependence'* (Villamil J.J. (Ed.)), pp. 67 - 94, Hassocks, Sussex: Harvester Press.

Sunkel O. (1980), *'Transnacionalizacion y dependencia'* Madrid: Ediciones Cultura Hispanica del Instituto de Cooperacion Iberoamericana.

Sunkel O. (1984), *'Capitalismo transnacional y desintegracion nacional en America Latina'* Buenos Aires, Rep. Argentina: Ediciones Nueva Vision.

Sunkel O. (1990), *'Dimension ambiental en la planificacion del desarrollo.* English The environmental dimension in development planning ' 1st ed. Santiago, Chile: United Nations, Economic Commission for Latin America and the Caribbean.

Sunkel O. (1991), *'El Desarrollo desde dentro: un enfoque neoestructuralista para la America Latina'* 1. ed. Mexico: Fondo de Cultura Economica.

Sunkel O. (1994), *'Rebuilding capitalism: alternative roads after socialism and dirigisme'* Ann Arbor, Mich.: University of Michigan Press.

Suter Ch. (1994); 'Genesis and Dynamics of Populist Regimes at the Periphery' in *'Conflicts and New Departures in World Society'* (Bornschier V. and Lengyel P. (Eds.)), pp. 181 - 207, New Brunswick (U.S.A.) and London: Transaction Publishers, World Society Studies, Volume 3.

Suter Ch. *et al.* (1990), 'External public debt of the periphery. A recurrent problem of world society' in *'World Society Studies. Volume 1'* (Bornschier V. and Lengyel P. (Eds.)), pp. 237 - 271, Frankfurt and New York: Campus.

Sweezy P. M. (1971), *'Theorie der kapitalistischen Entwicklung'* Frankfurt a. M.: edition suhrkamp.

Swoboda H. (1973), 'Sozialstaat und kapitalistische Entwicklung' *Oesterreichische Zeitschrift fuer Politikwissenschaft,* 4: 333 - 353.

Szelenyi I. and Kostello E. (1996), 'The Market Transition Debate. Toward a Synthesis' *American Journal of Sociology,* 101, 4: 1082 - 1096.

Szlajfer H. (1977), 'Nachzuholende Entwicklung unter den Bedingungen des Weltmarktes: Das Beispiel der polnischen Entwicklung' *Probleme des Klassenkampfes,* 7, 27: 7ff.

Szlajfer H. (1979), *'Economic surplus and surplus - value: an attempt at comparison'* Dar es Salaam: Economic Research Bureau, University of Dar es Salaam.

Szlajfer H. (1984), *'The Faltering economy: the problem of accumulation under monopoly capitalism'* New York: Monthly Review Press.

Szlajfer H. (1985), *'Modernizacja zaleznosci: kapitalizm i rozwoj w Ameryce Lacinskiej'* Wroclaw: Zaklad Narodowy im. Ossolinskich.

Szlajfer H. (1990), *'Economic nationalism in East - Central Europe and South America: 1918 - 1939 = Le Nationalisme economique en Europe du Centre - Est et en Amerique du Sud'* Geneve: Librairie Droz.

Szlajfer H. (1993), 'Dezintegracja prestrzeni eurazjatyckiej a bezpieczenstwo Europy Srodkowej i Wschodniej' *Studia i Materialy,* 65, Polish Institute of International Affairs, Warsaw.

Szlajfer H. (1995), *'From the Polish underground: selections from Krytyka, 1978 - 1993'* University Park, Pa.: Pennsylvania State University.

Szylko - Skoczny M. (1992), *'Spoleczne skutki bezrobocia w wymiarze lokalnym. Raport z badan empirycznych'* Warsaw: Polityka ekonomiczne i spoleczna, Fundacja im. Friedrich Eberta w Polsce.

Tabatabai H. and Fouad M. (1993), *'The incidence of poverty in developingcountries. An ILO compendium of data'* Geneva: ILO.

Taggart P. (1995), 'New Populist Parties in Western Europe' *West European Politics,* 1: 34 - 51.

Talos E. (1981), *'Staatliche Sozialpolitik in Oesterreich. Rekonstruktion und Analyse'* Vienna: Verlag fuer Gesellschaftskritik.

Tandon, Y. (1994) 'Recolonization of Subject Peoples', *Alternatives* (USA/India), vol. 19, no. 2, pp. 173-184

Tatur M. (1994), ''Corporatism' as a paradigm of transformation' in *'W Poszukiwania Paradygmatu Transformacji'* (Staniszkis J. (Ed.)), pp. 93 - 130, Warsaw: Instytut Studiow Politycznych, Polskiej Akademii Nauk.

Tausch A. (1980a, together with O. Hoell), 'Austria and the European Periphery' in *'European Studies of Development'* (J. de Bandt J./Mandi P./Seers D. (Eds.)), pp. 28 - 37, London, Basingstoke and New York: Macmillan/Saint Martin's Press.

Tausch A. (1979), *'Armut und Abhaengigkeit. Politik und Oekonomie im peripheren Kapitalismus'* Vienna: W. Braumueller, Studien zur oesterreichischen und internationalen Politik, Band 2 (edited by P. Gerlich and A. Pelinka).

Tausch A. (1980b), 'Gierek - Dengisme' in *'Transfert de Technologie et Developpement: Un Debat'* (Masini J. (Ed.)), pp. 82 - 84, Paris: Institut d'Etude du Developpement Economique et Social - Universite de Paris I - Pantheon Sorbonne.

Tausch A. (1982), *'Aggregate Data Set Eastern Europe'* Cologne: Koelner Zentralarchiv fuer empirische Sozialforschung, MRDF + Codebook, ZA Study 1159.

Tausch A. (1985), *'Development, Social Justice, and Dependence in Poland'* Occasional Paper, 9, Transnational Corporations Research Project, Faculty of Economics, University of Sydney (N.S.W.).

Tausch A. (1986), 'Positions within the Global Order, Patterns of Defense Policies, and National Development: Austria and Pakistan Compared' in *'Security for the Weak Nations. A Multiple Perspective. A Joint Project of Pakistani and Austrian Scholars'* (S. Farooq Hasnat and Pelinka A. (Eds.)), pp. 245 - 55, Lahore: Izharsons.

Tausch A. (1987), 'Transnational Corporations and Underdevelopment' *Acta Sociologica,* 30, 1: 118 - 121.

Tausch A. (1989a), 'Stable Third World Democracy and the European Model. A Quantitative Essay' in *'Crisis in Development'* (Z. Bablewski and B. Hettne (Eds.), pp. 131 - 161, Goeteborg: The European Perspectives Project of the United Nations University, University of Gothenburg, P.A.D.R.I.G.U - Papers.

Tausch A. (1989b, appeared 1991), 'Armas socialistas, subdesarrollo y violencia estructural en el Tercer Mundo' *Revista Internacional de Sociologia, CSIC, Madrid,* 47, 4: 583 - 716.

Tausch A. (1990), 'Bundesheer abschaffen? Von der Destruktion oesterreichischer Neutralitaetspolitik durch die 'gruene' Programmatik' *Akzente - Der sozialistische Akademiker (Vienna),* 3, September: 24 - 25.

Tausch A. (1991a), *'Russlands Tretmuehle. Kapitalistisches Weltsystem, lange Zyklen und die neue Instabilitaet im Osten'* Eberhard, Munich.

Tausch A. (1991b), *'Jenseits der Weltgesellschaftstheorien. Sozialtransformationen und der Paradigmenwechsel in der Entwicklungsforschung'* Munich: Eberhard.

Tausch A. (1991c), 'Amerikanisiert die Universitaeten. Die Hochschulreform bleibt auf der politischen Tagesordnung' *Zukunft (Vienna),* 8: 5 - 9.

Tausch A. (1993a), *'Produktivkraft soziale Gerechtigkeit? Europa und die Lektionen des pazifischen Modells'* Munich. Eberhard.

Tausch A. (1993b, with Fred Prager as co-author), *'Towards a Socio - Liberal Theory of World Development'* Basingstoke and New York: Macmillan/St. Martin's Press.

Tausch A. (1993c), "Kanadisierung' der Einwanderungspolitik. Die Grundlage der oesterreichischen 'Auslaenderpolitik" *Zukunft (Vienna),* 12: 15 - 19.

Tausch A. (1997), *'Schwierige Heimkehr. Sozialpolitik, Migration, Transformation und die Osterweiterung der Europaeischen Union'* Munich: Eberhard.

Tausch A. (1998) *'Globalization and European Integration'* Electronic book publication at the World Systems Archive (Coordinator: Christopher K. Chase-Dunn, Johns Hopkins University), http://csf.colorado.edu/wsystems/archive/books/tausch/spartoc.htm

Tausch A. (2001) *'Sozial- und gesundheitspolitische Aspekte der EU-Erweiterung'* Band 48, Schriftenreihe des Zentrums für europäische Studien, Jean Monnet Lehrstuhl für europäische Studien, Universität Trier, available at http://www.uni-trier.de/zes/bd48.html

Tausch K. (1993), *'Frauen in Peru. Ihre literarische und kulturelle Praesenz'* Munich: Eberhard, Schriften zu Lateinamerika, Band 5.

Taylor Ch.L. and Jodice D.H. (1983), *'World Handbook of Political and Social Indicators III.'* Machine readable data file, University of Michigan: ICPSR.

Tazi-Breve et al. (1999), *'Bevölkerung in Österreich'* Hrsgb. vom Institut für Demographie der Österreichischen Akademie der Wissenschaften

Teague E. (1994), 'The CIS: An Inpredictable Future' *RFE/RL Research Report,* 3, 1, 7 January: 9 - 12.

Tedstrom J. (1989), 'Recent Trends in the Soviet Economy: A Balance Sheet on the Reforms' *Radio Liberty Report on the USSR,* 1, 5, February 3: 10 - 19.

The Economist (1999) *'The World in 1999'* London: The Economist

The Times, Dialog - online.

Thee M. (1993), *'Armament and Disarmament in the Post - Cold - War Period'* Warsaw: *Occasional Papers,* 36, Polish Institute of International Affairs.

Thee M. (1994), 'Armaments and Disarmament in the Post - Cold War Period: The Quest for a Demilitarized and Nuclear - Free World' in *'Conflicts and New Departures in World Society'* (Bornschier V. and Lengyel P. (Eds.)), pp. 61 - 91, New Brunswick (U.S.A.) and London: Transaction Publishers, World Society Studies, Volume 3.

Therborn G. (1985), *'Arbeitslosigkeit. Strategien und Politikansaetze in OECD - Laendern'* Hamburg: VSA.

Therborn G. (1986), 'Karl Marx Returning. The Welfare State and Neo - Marxist, Corporatist and Statist Theories' *International Political Science Review,* 7, 2, April: 131 - 164.

Thompson W.R. (1983a), 'The World - Economy, the Long Cycle, and the Question of World - System Time' in *'Foreign Policy and the Modern World System'* (Mc Gowan P. and Kegley Ch.W.Jr. (Eds.)), pp. 35 - 62, Beverly Hills: Sage.

Thompson W.R. (1983b), 'Cycles, Capabilities and War: An Ecumenical View' in *'Contending Approaches to World System Analysis'* (Thompson W.R. (Ed.)), pp. 141 - 163, Beverly Hills: Sage.

Thun-Hohenstein Ch. and Cede F. (1995), *'Europarecht'* Vienna: Manz.

Thygesen N. *et al.* (1991), *'Business Cycles: Theories, Evidence, and Analysis'* London and Basingstoke: Macmillan.

Tibi B. (1992), 'Kreuzzug oder Dialog? Der Westen und die arabo - islamische Welt nach dem Golfkrieg' in *'Kreuzzug oder Dialog. Die Zukunft der Nord - Sued - Beziehungen'* (Matthies V. (Ed.)), pp. 107 - 120, Bonn: J.H.W. Dietz Nachfolger.

Tilton T.A. (1979), 'A Swedish Road to Socialism: Ernst Wigforss and the Ideological Foundations of Swedish Social Democracy' *American Political Science Review, 73,* 2: 505 - 20.

Timberlake M. and Kantor J. (1983), 'Economic Growth: A Study of the Less Developed Countries' *Sociological Quarterly,* 24: 489 - 507.

Timberlake M. and Williams K.R. (1984), 'Dependence, Political Exclusion, and Government Repression: Some Cross - National Evidence' *American Sociological Review,* 49: 141 - 46.

Timberlake M. and Williams K.R. (1987), 'Structural Position in the World - System, Inequality and Political Violence' *Journal of Political and Military Sociology,* 15: 1 - 15.

Toekes R.L. (1992), 'From Visegrad to Krakow: Cooperation, Competition, and Coexistence in Central Europe' *Problems of Communism,* 40, Nov. - Dec.: 100 - 114.

Tolz V. (1992), 'Russia: Westernizers Continue to Challenge National Patriots' *RFE/RL Research Report,* 1, 49, 11 Dec.: 1 - 9.

Tomasson, G., and A.M. Daastol (1998), *'Letter to the Editor, Wall Street Journal Europe, Tuesday Nov. 17th 1998'* (here quoted from a memorandum by Arno Mong Daastol to the wsn mailing list, online: http://csf.colorado.edu/mail/wsn/98.III)

Tracy M. A. and Tracy M. B. (1996), 'The Impact of Market - Economy Transition on Social Security and Social Welfare in Poland' *Journal of Sociology and Social Welfare,* 23, 1: 23 - 39.

Transition (current issues) OMRI Prague.

Treiman D.J. and Roos P.A. (1983), 'Sex and earnings in industrial society: a nine - nation comparison' *American Journal of Sociology,* 89, 3: 612 - 650.

Tyson L.D'A. (1986), 'The debt crisis and adjustment responses in Eastern Europe: a comparative perspective' *International Organization,* 40, 2: 239 - 285.

Ulrich Ch.J. (1994), 'The Growth of Crime in Russia and the Baltic Region' *RFE/RL Research Report,* 3, 23, 10 June: 24 - 32.

UN ECE (1994) *'International Migration: Regional Processes and Responses'* Geneva: UN ECE Economic Studies, 7 (entire)

UN ECE (1996); *'International Migration in Central and Eastern Europe and the Commonwealth of Independent States'* Geneva: UN ECE Economic Studies, 8 (entire)

UN ECE (1998), *'In-Depth Studies on Migration in Central and Eastern Europe: The Case of Poland'* Geneva: UN ECE Economic Studies, 11 (entire)

UN Economic and Social Council (1993), *'International Migration Flows among ECE Countries'* New York: UN ECE CES 778, 27 May

UNDP (1998) *'Overcoming Human Poverty'*. UN New York, UNDP

UNDP (1998) *'The Shrinking State'* UN New York, UNDP

UNDP (United Nations Development Program) (1997) *Human Development Report 1997*

UNICEF (1999), online statistics, entitled "Statistical Data", at: http://www.unicef.org/statis

United Nations (1948) *Universal Declaration of Human Rights*

United Nations (1965) International Trade Statistics Yearbook 1965

United Nations (1995) *International Trade Statistics Yearbook* 1995, 2 Vols.

United Nations Centre on Transnational Corporations (1983), *'Transnational Corporations in World Development'* New York: United Nations.

United Nations Conference on Trade and Development (1996), 'World Investment Report 1996. Investment, Trade and International Policy Arrangements' New York and Geneva: United Nations.

United Nations Department of International Economic and Social Affairs, Statistical Office (current issues), *'Compendium of Social Statistics'* New York: United Nations.

United Nations Development Programme (current issues), *'Human Development Report'* New York and Oxford: Oxford University Press.

United Nations Development Programme Warsaw (current issues), *'Human Development Report Poland'* Warsaw: UNDP Poland: Split Trading Publishing House, and current subsequent issues.

United Nations Economic and Social Council (1978), *'Transnational Corporations in World Development: A Re - examination.'* New York: United Nations.

United Nations Economic and Social Council (1993), *'International Migration Flows Among ECE Countries, 1991'* New York: United Nations, CES/778, 27 May.

United Nations Economic Commission for Europe (current issues), *'Economic Survey of Europe'* New York: United Nations.

United Nations Economic Commission for Europe and United Nations Population Fund (1998), *'In-Depth Studies on Migration in Central and Eastern Europe: The Case of Poland'* Geneva: UN ECE, Economic Studies, 11 (entire).

United Nations High Comissioner for Refugees, Warsaw Liaison Office (1993), unpublished data on the refugee situation in Eastern Europe.

United States Arms Control and Disarmament Agency (current issues), *'World Military Expenditures and Arms Transfers'* Washington DC.: US Government Printing Office.

United States Central Intelligence Agency, National Foreign Assesment Center (1980), *'Developed Country Imports of Manufactured Products from LDC's. A Research Paper'* Washington D.C.: US - CIA, ER 80 - 10476.

United States Commission on Immigration Reform (1994), *'U.S. Immigration Policy: Restoring Credibility'* Washington D.C.: US Government Printing Office.

United States Department of State (curent issues), *'International Drug Control Strategy Report'* Washington D.C.: US Government Printing Office.

United States Department of State (current issues), *'Country Reports on Human Rights Practices'* Washington D.C.: US Government Printing Office.

Vaerynen R. (1987), 'Global Power Dynamics and Collective Violence' in *'The Quest for Peace. Transcending Collective Violence and War among Societies, Cultures and States'* (Vaerynen R. *et al.* (Eds.)), pp. 80 - 96, London: Sage.

Van Rossem R. (1996), 'The World System Paradigmas General Theory of Development: A Cross - National Test' *American Sociological Review,* 61, June: 508 - 527.

Vickrey W. (1996), 'Fifteen Fatal Fallacies of Financial Fundamentalism. A Disquisition on Demand Side Economics' New York: Columbia University, Web-Site: http://www.columbia.edu/dlc/wp/econ/vickrey.htm.

Vinton L. (1992a), 'Poland: Government Crisis Ends, Budget Crisis Begins' *RFE/RL Research Report,* 1, 3, 17 January: 14 - 21.

Vinton L. (1992b), 'Poland's Governing Coalition: Will the Truce Hold?' *RFE/RL Research Report,* 1, 31, 31 July: 34 - 40.

Vinton L. (1992c), 'Poland's Government Crisis: An End in Sight?' *RFE/RL Research Report,* 1, 30, 24 July: 15 - 25.

Vinton L. (1992d), 'Polish Government Proposes Pact on State Firms' *RFE/RL Research Report,* 1, 42, 23 October: 10 - 18.

Vinton L. (1992e), 'Sejm Approves New Law on Radio and Television' *RFE/RL Research Report,* 1, 43, 30 October: 32 - 34.

Vinton L. (1993a), 'Walesa Applies Political Shock Therapy' *RFE/RL Research Report,* 2, 24: 11 June: 1 - 11.

Vinton L. (1993b), 'Poland's New Election Law: Fewer Parties, Same Impasse?' *RFE/RL Research Report,* 2, 28, 9 July: 7 - 17.

Vinton L. (1993c), 'Dissonance: Poland on the Eve of New Elections' *RFE/RL Research Report,* 2, 33, 20 August: 1 - 7.

Vinton L. (1993d), 'Poland's Political Spectrum on the Eve of the Elections' *RFE/RL Research Report,* 2, 36, 10 September: 1 - 16.

Vinton L. (1994), 'Power Shifts in Poland's Ruling Coalition' *RFE/RL Research Report,* 3, 11, 18 March: 5 - 14.

Voggenhuber J. (1995), 'Die EU reformieren!' in *'Oesterreichisches Jahrbuch fuer Politik 1994'* (Khol A. *et al.* (Eds.)), pp. 379 - 412, Munich, Oldenbourg - Verlag.

Vogt W. (Ed.) (1973), *'Seminar: Politische Oekonomie. Zur Kritik der herrschenden Nationaloekonomie'* Frankfurt a. M.: suhrkamp taschenbuch wissenschaft.

Vranitzky F. (1992a), 'Aufbruch in das Europa der Zukunft' *Akzente,* 1, Februar: 5 - 10.

Vranitzky F. (1992b), *'Die russisch - oesterreichischen Beziehungen. Entwicklungen und Perspektiven in einem neuen Europa'* Moskau: Vortrag von Bundeskanzler Dr. Franz Vranitzky im Institut fuer Internationale Beziehungen, Moskau, 1. April 1992 (mimeo).

Wade L. L. *et al.* (1995), 'Searching for Voting Patterns in Postcommunist Poland Sejm Elections' *Communist and Post - Communist Studies,* 28, 4: 411 - 425.

Wagar, W.W. (1996) 'Toward a Praxis of World Integration'. *Journal of World-Systems Research,* vol. 2, no. 2

Walker, R.B.J. (1994), 'On the Possibility of World Order Discourse', *Alternatives* (USA/India), 19: 237:246

Wallace Cl. (1999): Economic Hardship, Migration and Survival Strategies in East Central Europe, *IHS-Reihe Soziologie* Nr. 35.

Wallerstein I. (1974), *'The Modern World System I. Capitalist Agriculture and the Origins of the European World - Economy in the Sixteenth Century'* New York: Academic Press.

Wallerstein I. (1976), 'Semi - Peripheral Countries and the Contemporary World Crisis' *Theory and Society,* 4: 461 - 483.

Wallerstein I. (1979a), *'The Capitalist World Economy'* Cambridge, England: Cambridge University Press.

Wallerstein I. (1979b), 'Underdevelopment and Phase B: Effect of the Seventeenth - Century Stagnation on Core and Periphery of the European World - Economy' in *'The World - System of Capitalism: Past and Present'* (Goldfrank W.L. (Ed.)), pp. 73 - 85, Beverly Hills: Sage.

Wallerstein I. (1982), 'Socialist States: Mercantilist Strategies and Revolutionary Objectives' in *'Ascent and Decline in the World - System'* (Friedman E. (Ed.)), pp. 289 - 300, Beverly Hills: Sage.

Wallerstein I. (1983a), 'Crises: The World Economy, the Movements, and the Ideologies' in *'Crises in the World - System'* (Bergesen A. (Ed.)), pp. 21 - 36, Beverly Hills: Sage.

Wallerstein I. (1983b), *'Historical Capitalism'* London: Verso.

Wallerstein I. (1984), *'Der historische Kapitalismus. Uebersetzt von Uta Lehmann - Grube mit einem Nachwort herausgegeben von Hans Heinrich Nolte'* Westberlin: Argument - Verlag.

Wallerstein I. (1986), ''Krise als Uebergang' in *'Dynamik der globalen Krise'* (Amin S. and associates), pp. 4 - 35, Opladen: Westdeutscher Verlag.

Wallerstein I. (1989), *'The National and the Universal: Canada There Be Such a Thing as World Culture?'.* Fernand Braudel Centre for the Study of Economies, Historical Systems, and Civilizations, Binghamton, New York: Suny Binghamton.

Wallerstein I. (1990), *'America and the World: Today, Yesterday, and Tomorrow'* Fernand Braudel Centre for the Study of Economies, Historical Systems, and Civilizations, Binghamton, New York: Suny Binghamton.

Wallerstein I. (1991a), *'Who Excludes Whom? or The Collapse of Liberalism and the Dilemmas of Antisystemic Strategy'* Fernand Braudel Centre for the Study of

Economies, Historical Systems, and Civilizations, Binghamton, New York: Suny Binghamton.

Wallerstein I. (1991b), *'The Concept of National Development, 1917 - 1989: Elegy and Requiem'* Fernand Braudel Centre for the Study of Economies, Historical Systems, and Civilizations, Binghamton, New York: Suny Binghamton.

Wallerstein I. (1998) 'Commentary 3: Is Japan Rsing or Declining?' *http://fbc.binghamton.edu/03!en.htm*

Wallerstein M. (1989), 'Union Organization in Advanced Industrial Democracies' *American Political Science Review,* 83, 2, June: 481 - 501.

Wallerstein, I. (1978) 'World-System Analysis: Theoretical and Interpretive Issues,' in: Kaplan, B.H. (ed.), *Social Change in the Capitalist World Economy.* Beverly Hills, USA: SAGE Publishing, p. 219-235

Walterskirchen E./Dietz R.(1998): *'Auswirkungen der EU-Osterweiterung auf den österr. Arbeitmarkt'* Studie im Auftrag der Bundesarbeiterkammer - WIFO, 1998.

Walton J. and Ragin Ch. (1990), 'Global and National Sources of Political Protest: Third World Responses to the Debt Crisis' *American Sociological Review,* 55: 876 - 890.

Ward K.B. (1985), 'The Social Consequences of the World Economic System. The Economic Status of Women and Fertility' *Review,* 8, 4, Spring: 561 - 93.

Washington J. M. (1986), *'A Testimony of Hope: The Essential Writings of Martin Luther King'* San Francisco: Harper and Row.

Watzal L. (1997), 'Die Europaeische Union vor der Einfuerhung des Euro' *Europaeische Rundschau,* 4: 15-25.

Weber R.Ph. (1983), 'Cyclical Theories of Crises in the World - System' in *'Crises in the World - System'* (Bergesen A. (Ed.)), pp. 37 - 55, Beverly Hills: Sage.

Weede E. (1985), *'Entwicklungslaender in der Weltgesellschaft'* Opladen: Westdeutscher Verlag.

Weede E. (1986a), 'Catch - up, distributional coalitions and government as determinants of economic growth or decline in industrialized democracies' *The British Journal of Sociology,* 37, 2: 194 - 220.

Weede E. (1986b), 'Verteilungskoalitionen, Staatstaetigkeit und Stagnation' *Politische Vierteljahresschrift,* 27, 2: 222 - 236.

Weede E. (1990), *'Wirtschaft, Staat und Gesellschaft'* Tübingen: J.C.B. Mohr

Weede E. (1990), *'Wirtschaft, Staat und Gesellschaft'* Tuebingen: J.C.B. Mohr.

Weede E. (1992), *'Mensch und Gesellschaft. Soziologie aus der Perspektive des methodoligischen Individualismus'* Tuebingen: J.C.B. Mohr.

Weede E. (1994), 'Determinanten der Kriegsverhuetung waehrend des Kalten Krieges und danach: Nukleare Abschreckung, Demokratie und Freihandel' *Politische Vierteljahresschrift,* 35, 1: 62 - 84.

Weggel O. (1994), 'Die Internationalisierung der chinesischen Mafia' *Europa - Archiv,* 11: 325 - 332.

Weidenfeld W. and Hillenbrand, O. (1994a), 'EG - Einwanderungspolitik: Herausforderungen - Optionen - Folgen' *Internationale Politik und Gesellschaft. International Politics and Society (Friedrich Ebert Foundation),* 1: 31 - 39.

Weidenfeld W. and Hillenbrand, O. (1994b), 'Wie kann Europa die Immigration bewaeltigen? Moeglichkeiten und Grenzen eines Einwanderungskonzepts' *Europa - Archiv,* 1: 1 - 10.

Weil F.D. (1985), 'The variable effect of education on liberal attitudes: a comparative - historical analysis of antisemitism using public opinion survey data' *American Sociological Review,* 50, 4: 458 - 474.

Weixner B. and Wimmer M. (1997), *'Stichwort EURO'* Munich: Wilhelm Heyne.

Weltgeschehen (current issues), Sankt Augustin: Siegler&Co. Verlag fuer Zeitarchive.

Weydenthal J.B. (1992), 'The Realignment of Polish Foreign and Military Policies' *RFE/RL Research Report,* 1, 30, 24 July: 40 - 42.

Weydenthal J.B. (1993a), 'Poland on Its Own: The Conduct of Foreign Policy' *RFE/RL Research Report,* 2, 2, 8 January: 1 - 4.

Weydenthal J.B. (1993b), 'Economic Issues Dominate Poland's Eastern Policy' *RFE/RL Research Report,* 2, 10, 5 March: 23 - 26.

Weydenthal J.B. (1994), 'Poland's Eastern Policy' *RFE/RL Research Report,* 3, 7, 18 February: 10 - 13.

Wheelwright E. L. (1974) *'Radical political economy: collected essays'* Sydney: Australia & New Zealand Book Co.

Wheelwright E. L. (1980) *'Australia and world capitalism'* Ringwood, Australia; New York: Penguin Books.

Wheelwright E. L. (1991) *'Oil & world politics: from Rockefeller to the Gulf War'* Sydney: Left Book Club.

Wheelwright E. L. (1994), 'Book Review: Richard Cocket *'Thinking the Unthinkable: Think - Tanks and the Economic Counter - Revolution',* London, 1994' *Journal of Australian Political Economy,* 34: 128 - 135.

Wickrama K. A. S. and Mulford Ch. L. (1996), 'Political Democracy, Economic Development, Disarticulation, and Social Well - Being in Developing Countries' *The Sociological Quarterly,* 37, 3: 375 - 390.

Wieczorek P. (1993), *'Polski przemysl obronny w kontekscie nowego modelu sil zbrojnych'* Warsaw: Polish Institute of International Affairs, *Studia i Materialy, 9.*

Wiehn E.R. (1993), *'Ghetto Warschau. Aufstand und Vernichtung 1943 fuenfzig Jahre danach zum Gedenken'* Konstanz: Hartung Gorre Verlag.

WIIW (1999): *'Potential size of migration from Poland after joining the EU'* WIIW monthly report, 2

WIIW and EcoGI (1999) 'Hungary's Accession to the EU. State and prospects of Hungarian Austrian relations. Bilateral Synthetic report. Vienna and Budapest: WIIW and Economic Growth Institute

Wilkiewicz Z. (1996) 'Arbeitslosigkeit und ihr Stellenwert in der polnischen Sozialpolitik' *Osteuropa,* 46, 1, 1996: 64 - 79.

Williamson J (1998), *'Real Wages and Relative Factor Prices in the Third World 1820 - 1940: The Mediterranean Basin'.* Discussion Paper 1842, Harvard Institute of Economic Research

Williamson J. (1996), 'Globalization, Convergence and History' *The Journal of Economic History,* 56, 2: 277 - 306.

Williamson J. (1997) 'Globalization and Inequalities, Past and Present' *The World Bank Research Observer,* 12, 2, August: 117-135.

Williamson J. A. (1998), Harvard Institute of Economic Research, Internet site (with link-up to the data base on wages in the world periphery 1820-1940): *http://www.economics.harvard.edu/~jwilliam/*

Wimberley D. W. (1990), 'Investment Dependence and Alternative Explanations of Third World Mortality: A Cross - National Study' *American Sociological Review,* 55: 75 - 91.

Wimberley D.W. and Bello R. (1992), 'Effects of Foreign Investment, Exports and Economic Growth on Third - World Food Consumption' *Social Forces,* 70, 4: 895 - 921.

Winckler G. (Ed.), (1992), *'Central and Eastern Europe. Roads to Growth'* Washington D.C.: International Monetary Fund and Austrian National Bank.

Winters A. (1993), 'The Europe Agreements: with a little help from our friends' in *'Trade, Transfers and Development. Problems and Prospects for the Twenty - First Century'* (Murshed S. M. and Raffer K. (Eds.)), pp. 196 - 209, Aldershot, UK: Edward Elgar.

Wippermann W. (1983), *'Europaeischer Faschismus im Vergleich (1922 - 1982)'.* Frakfurt a.M.: edition suhrkamp.

Wishnevsky J. (1992), 'Antidemocratic Tendencies in Russian Policy - Making' *RFE/RL Research Report,* 1, 45, 13 November: 21 - 25.

Wistrich R.S. (Ed.)(1992), *'Austrians and Jews in the Twentieth Century. From Franz Joseph to Waldheim'* Basingstoke and New York: Macmillan and Saint Martin's Press.

Wlodarczyk C. and Mierzewski P. (1991), 'From words to deeds: health service reform in Poland' *International Social Security Review,* 44, 4: 5 - 8.

Woehlcke M. (1987), *'Umweltzerstoerung in der Dritten Welt'* Munich: C.H. Beck.

Woehlke M. (1993), *'Der oekologische Nord - Sued - Konflikt'* Munich: C.H. Beck.

Wolf J. (1996), 'Pluralitaet statt Uniformitaet. Werthaltungen der polnischen Buerger' *Soziale Welt,* 47, 2: 202 - 222.

Wolf K.D. (1991), 'Das neue Deutschland - eine Weltmacht?' *Leviathan,* 2: 247 - 260.

Wolffsohn M. (1991), 'Deutschland: eine verwirrte und verwirrende Nation' *Europa - Archiv,* 7: 211 - 214.

Wolfgruber E. (1994), 'Parteipolitischer Diskurs und Strategien in der Auslaender/innen/politik in Oesterreich 1989 bis 1993' *Oesterreichische Zeitschrift fuer Politikwissenschaft,* 23, 3: 299 - 313.

Wollenberg J. and Friedrich J. (1987), *'Licht in den Schatten der Vergangenheit'* Stuttgart: Ullstein.

Wood A. (1994), *'Structural Unemployment in the North: Global Causes, Domestic Cures'* Vienna: Kreisky Commission Symposion, 21 - 22 March.

World Bank (1991a), *'Staff Appraisal Report Poland. Employment Promotion and Services Project'* Washington D.C.: World Bank, Country Department IV, Report 9408 - POL.

World Bank (1991b), *'Managing Development: The Governance Decision'* Washington D.C.: World Bank.

World Bank (1993), *'Social Indicators of Development 1993'* Baltimore and London: The John Hopkins University Press.

World Bank (1994) *World Tables* 1994

World Bank (1994), *'Poverty in Poland'* Washington D.C.: Country Operations, Central Europe Department, Europe and Central Asia Region (in two volumes).

World Bank (1995) *World Tables* 1995

World Bank (1995), *'Understanding Poverty in Poland'* Washington D.C.: The World Bank.

World Bank (1999) online statistical database, entitled "Global Development Network Growth Database", at: http://www.worldbank.org/html/prdmg/grthweb/GDNdata.htm

World Bank (current issues), *'World Development Report'* Washington D.C.: World Bank and Oxford University Press.

World Economy Research Institute Warsaw (current issues), *'Poland International Economic Report'* Warsaw: Warsaw School of Economics.

World Economy Research Institute Warsaw and International Centre for Economic Growth, San Francisco (current issues), *'Transforming the Polish Economy'* Warsaw: Warsaw School of Economics.

World Reporter (1997 ff.) *World Reporter,* in conjunction with Financial Times and Dow Jones & Co, at http://www.dialogselect.com

World Resources Institute in collaboration with The United Nations Environment Programme and The United Nations Development Programme (1992), *'World Resources 1992 - 93'* New York and Oxford: Oxford University Press.

Yasmann V.A. (1994), 'Imperiale Ideologie fuer die russische Aussenpolitik. Die Rolle von Militaer und Sicherheitsapparat' *Europa - Archiv,* 9: 248 - 256.

Yotopoulos, P.A. (1996) Exchange Rate Parity for Trade and Development: Theory, tests, and case studies. Cambridge, England: Cambridge University Press

Zeitpunkte (current issues) Hamburg: Die Zeit.

Zentner Chr. (1980), *'Geschichtsfuehrer in Farbe. Weltgeschichte in Bildern, Daten, Fakten'* Berlin and Darmstadt: Deutsche Buch - Gemeinschaft and Delphin - Verlag.

Zielonka J. (1991), 'East Central Europe: Democracy in Retreat?' *The Washington Quarterly,* 14, 3, Summer: 107 - 120.

Zienkowski L. (Ed.), (1993), *'Polish Economy in 1990 - 1992. Experience & Conclusions'* Warsaw: Research Centre for Economic and Statistical Studies of the Central Statistical Office and the Polish Academy of Sciences.

Zimmerman E. and Saalfeld Th. (1988), 'Economic and Political Reactions to the World Economic Crisis of the 1930s in Six European Countries' *International Studies Quarterly,* 32, 3: 305 - 334.

Zoethout T. (1993), 'Financing Eastern Europe's Capital Requirements' *RFE/RL Research Report,* 2, 7, 12 February: 38 - 43.

Zolberg A.R. (1983), "World' and 'System': A Misalliance' in *'Contending Approaches to World System Analysis'* (Thompson W.R. (Ed.)), pp. 269 - 290, Beverly Hills: Sage.

INDEX

S

T

U